OXFORD STUDIES ON THE ROMAN ECONOMY

General Editors

ALAN BOWMAN   ANDREW WILSON

OXFORD STUDIES ON THE ROMAN ECONOMY

This innovative monograph series reflects a vigorous revival of interest in the ancient economy, focusing on the Mediterranean world under Roman rule (c.100 BC to AD 350). Carefully quantified archaeological and documentary data are integrated to help ancient historians, economic historians, and archaeologists think about economic behaviour collectively rather than from separate perspectives. The volumes include a substantial comparative element and thus will be of interest to historians of other periods and places.

The Economy of Roman Religion

Edited by
ANDREW WILSON, NICK RAY,
AND ANGELA TRENTACOSTE

Great Clarendon Street, Oxford, OX2 6DP,
United Kingdom

Oxford University Press is a department of the University of Oxford.
It furthers the University's objective of excellence in research, scholarship,
and education by publishing worldwide. Oxford is a registered trade mark of
Oxford University Press in the UK and in certain other countries

© Oxford University Press 2023

The moral rights of the authors have been asserted

All rights reserved. No part of this publication may be reproduced, stored in
a retrieval system, or transmitted, in any form or by any means, without the
prior permission in writing of Oxford University Press, or as expressly permitted
by law, by licence or under terms agreed with the appropriate reprographics
rights organization. Enquiries concerning reproduction outside the scope of the
above should be sent to the Rights Department, Oxford University Press, at the
address above

You must not circulate this work in any other form
and you must impose this same condition on any acquirer

Published in the United States of America by Oxford University Press
198 Madison Avenue, New York, NY 10016, United States of America

British Library Cataloguing in Publication Data
Data available

Library of Congress Control Number: 2022947380

ISBN 978–0–19–288353–7

DOI: 10.1093/oso/9780192883537.001.0001

Printed and bound in the UK by
Clays Ltd, Elcograf S.p.A.

Links to third party websites are provided by Oxford in good faith and
for information only. Oxford disclaims any responsibility for the materials
contained in any third party website referenced in this work.

Preface

Most of the chapters in this volume derive from an OxREP (Oxford Roman Economy Project) conference on 'The Economics of Roman Religion', held in the Ioannou Centre for Classical and Byzantine Studies in Oxford on 22 and 23 September 2016. We regret that we were not able to include Rachel Hesse's paper on a holocaust sacrifice at Omrit (Israel) in the volume, but that loss is somewhat offset by the addition of a paper by Jörg Rüpke instead; the editors are grateful to Richard Gordon for suggesting and helping facilitate its inclusion. As always, we thank Baron Lorne Thyssen-Bornemisza and the Augustus Foundation for generously supporting OxREP over many years, and All Souls College, Oxford, for support in kind including the provision of accommodation for speakers.

Andrew Wilson

January 2023

Contents

List of Figures ix
List of Tables xiii
List of Abbreviations xv
List of Contributors xvii

1. Introduction: Religion and the Roman Economy 1
   Andrew Wilson

2. What Did Religion Cost in Ancient Rome? 30
   Jörg Rüpke

3. Investing in Religion: Religion and the Economy
   in Pre-Roman Central Italy 50
   Charlotte R. Potts

4. Cost Differences in Temple-Building between Rome
   and the Provinces 75
   Javier Domingo

5. Moneychangers in the Temple? Coins and Religion
   in the Roman World 130
   David Wigg-Wolf

6. Cult Economy in the Eastern Provinces of the Roman Empire 155
   Marietta Horster

7. Impact of the Roman Conquest on Temple Economies
   in Egypt: A Case Study of the Temple of Soknopaios in Dime 180
   Marie-Pierre Chaufray

8. Animals in Roman Religion: The Economics behind the Rituals 198
   Michael MacKinnon

9. Sacred Flocks and Herds? The Implications of Animal Sacrifice
   at Rural and Suburban Romano-Celtic Shrines 224
   Anthony C. King

10. Sacred Gifts, Profane Uses? Transfers and the Roman
    Religious Sphere 245
    Marta García Morcillo

11. Guilds and Gods: Religious Profiles of Occupational *collegia* and the Problem of the *dendrophori* 267
   Koenraad Verboven

12. Economic Implications of Roman Religious Systems 310
    Greg Woolf

Index 329

List of Figures

4.1. Reconstruction of the ground plan of the Temple of the Victories of Caracalla in Dougga (drawn by the author). 82

4.2. Axonometric views of reconstructions of the Arch of Caracalla in Theveste, crowned by a dome (left) or by a simple flat-roofed attic (right) (image created by J. Á. Domingo & J. R. Domingo). 84

4.3. Ground plan of the area of the Capitolium and Basilica of Volubilis (redrawn by the author, after Brouquier and Rebuffat 1998: 128, fig. 1). 85

4.4. Ground plan of the *temenos* of Temple C at Volubilis (redrawn by the author, after Euzennat 1957: 46, fig. 3a). 86

4.5. Ground plan of the upper terrace of the Tarraco Provincial Forum (top), the Claudianum (middle), and the Templum Pacis (bottom) (drawn by the author). 90

5.1. (*a*) *As*, 280–276 BC, *RRC* 14/1. Diameter 71 mm (scale 1:1.5). (*b*) *Semis*, 280–276 BC, *RRC* 14/2. Diameter 56 mm (scale 1:1.5).
Source: (a) American Numismatic Society, http://numismatics.org/collection/1944.100.745. Public Domain Mark; (b) American Numismatic Society, http://numismatics.org/collection/1944.100.746. Public Domain Mark. 133

5.2. (*a*) *Denarius*, 211 BC, *RRC* 44/5. (*b*) *Victoriatus*, 211 BC, *RRC* 44/1. Scale 1:1.
Source: (a) American Numismatic Society, http://numismatics.org/collection/1994.25.2. Public Domain Mark; (b) gallica.bnf.fr/BnF: ark:/12148/btv1b104223777. 134

5.3. *Denarius*, Marcius Censorinus, 88 BC, *RRC* 346/1a. Scale 1:1.
Source: gallica.bnf.fr/BnF: ark:/12148/btv1b10436914c. 134

5.4. *Denarius*, Julius Caesar, 47–46 BC, *RRC* 458/1. Scale 1:1.
Source: American Numismatic Society, http://numismatics.org/collection/1937.158.262. Public Domain Mark. 134

5.5. *Sestertius*, Vespasian, *RIC*² 245, AD 71. Scale 1:1.
Source: American Numismatic Society, http://numismatics.org/collection/1980.187.1. Public Domain Mark. 135

5.6. *Aureus*, Marcus Aurelius for Faustina II, *RIC* 693, AD 161–76. Scale 1:1.
Source: British Museum: https://www.britishmuseum.org/collection/object/C_1867-0101-725. CC BY-NC-SA 4.0. 136

List of Figures

5.7. *Antoninianus*, Aurelian, *RIC* 225, AD 270–5. Scale 1:1.
Source: Kunsthistorisches Museum, Vienna, http://www.ikmk.at/object.php?id=ID206987. CC BY-NC-SA. 136

5.8. *Solidus*, Marcian, *RIC* 502, AD 450–7. Diameter 22 mm (scale 2:1).
Source: © The Hunterian, University of Glasgow, GLAHM:32543, http://collections.gla.ac.uk/#/details/ecatalogue/92124. 137

5.9. *Aes*, Heliopolis, AD 244–9; obv.: bust of Philip I; rev.: temple of Jupiter Heliopolitanus. Scale 1:1.
Source: http://numismatics.org/collection/1944.100.83839. Public Domain Mark. 138

5.10. *Aes*, Abydos, AD 222–35; obv.: bust of Severus Alexander; rev.: Leander swimming across the Hellespont to Hero. Scale 1:1.
Source: gallica.bnf.fr/BnF: ark:/12148/btv1b10323660w. 138

9.1. Tripole (ternary) graph of cattle, sheep/goat, and pig in temple assemblages from Roman Britain. Data from King (2005) with additions. 225

9.2. Tripole (ternary) graph of cattle, sheep/goat, and pig in non-temple assemblages from Roman Britain. Data from King (1999: table 3). 226

9.3. Harlow: mammal species by phase. Data from King (2005: fig. 7). 227

9.4. Harlow: age-at-death for sheep (n = 221, all phases), based on mandibular tooth wear, using Payne's method. A, 0–2 months; B, 2–6 months; C, 6–12 months; D, 1–2 years; E, 2–3 years; F, 3–4 years; G, 4–6 years; H, 6–8 years; I, 8–10 years. Data from King (2005: fig. 8). 227

9.5. Uley: mammal species by phase. Data from King (2005: fig. 4). 228

9.6. Ashwell: incidence of burnt bone by phase. Phases 2–6 represent the main period of use of the temple, late 1st–2nd century AD. From Jones and King (2018). 230

9.7. Ashwell: mammal species by phase. From Jones and King (2018). 230

9.8. Springhead sanctuary site: mammal species, numbers of fragments (NISP) by phase. Data from Grimm (2011). 231

9.9. Tabard Square, Southwark: reconstruction of an offering at the temple.
Source: From Killock (2015). Illustrated by Chris Mitchell (c.mitchell02@btinternet.com), reproduced by kind permission of Pre-Construct Archaeology (www.pre-construct.com). 232

9.10. Tabard Square, Southwark: mammal species, numbers of fragments (NISP), by phase. Phases 6–9 are the main period of use and abandonment of the temple sites, late 2nd century to late 4th century or later. Data from Rielly (2015). 233

9.11. Fesques: mammal species, numbers of fragments (NISP), in the boundary ditch and the inner enclosure. US 1, Late Iron Age outer boundary ditch; US 60, Roman-period outer boundary ditch; US 250, Late Iron Age inner enclosure ditch. Data from Méniel (1997). 234

List of Figures

9.12. Ribemont-sur-Ancre: mammal species, numbers of fragments (NISP), from well/shaft 34, lowest contexts. Data from Fercoq du Leslay and Lepetz (2008: fig. 3). 235

9.13. Maiden Castle, Dorset: LiDAR image of the Iron Age hillfort, with the Romano-Celtic temple marked at A. Digital terrain model, resolution 1.0 m, 3D view.
Source: Raw data from the Environment Agency: https://data.gov.uk/. Image created by Rouven Meidlinger—own work, CC BY-SA 4.0, https://commons.wikimedia.org/w/index.php?curid=111,073,754 with additions by A. C. King. 236

11.1. Distribution of associations of *Mercuriales*.
Source: Ghent Database of Roman Guilds and Occupation-Based Communities; basemap from Natural Earth. 283

11.2. Religious profiles of the *fabri*, *centonarii*, and *nautae*: number of inscriptions in different categories. 286

11.3. Religious profile of the *nautae* excluding the *nautae Parisiaci*: number of inscriptions in different categories. 287

11.4. So-called relief of the *dendrophori*.
Source: Bordeaux, Musée d'Aquitaine. 297

11.5. Geographical distribution of the *tria collegia principalia*.
Source: Ghent Database of Roman Guilds and Occupation-Based Communities; basemap from Natural Earth. 299

11.6. Religious profile of the *dendrophori*: number of inscriptions in different categories. 301

List of Tables

2.1.	Expenditures and revenues of a Roman priesthood (in HS).	34
4.1.	Dimensions of the columns of the main temples in Rome.	76
4.2.	Dimensions of the columns of the main temples of Hispania and Gallia Narbonensis.	77
4.3.	Quantification of each of the variables involved in the cost of the temple of the Victories of Caracalla.	83
4.4.	Quantification of each of the variables involved in the cost of the Arch of Caracalla in Theveste.	84
4.5.	Building costs of some African temples in the second and third centuries AD (based on data from Duncan-Jones 1974: 90–1).	88
4.6.	Quantification of each of the variables involved in the cost of the Capitolium of Volubilis.	88
4.7.	Quantification of each of the variables involved in the cost of Temple C at Volubilis.	89
4.8.	Cost of the Templum Pacis: Hall of Worship.	95
4.9.	Cost of the Templum Pacis: portico (Luna marble).	99
4.10.	Cost of the Templum Pacis: portico (*marmo africano*).	103
4.11.	Cost of the upper terrace of the Tarraco Provincial Forum: Hall of Worship.	108
4.12.	Cost of the upper terrace of the Tarraco Provincial Forum: portico.	112
4.13.	Cost of the upper terrace of the Tarraco Provincial Forum: propylaeum.	116
11.1.	Names of associations combining religious and professional references.	280
11.2.	Epigraphic evidence for religious dedications by the *fabri, centonarii, nautae,* and *dendrophori*.	288
11.3.	Ratio of strong deity-links to numbers of inscriptions.	289
11.4.	Types of epigraphic evidence for *centonarii, fabri, nautae,* and *dendrophori*, by numbers of inscriptions.	290

List of Abbreviations

Abbreviations for ancient literary texts follow the system used in the third edition of the *Oxford Classical Dictionary*.

Abbreviations for editions of papyrological texts follow the Web edition of the *Checklist of Greek, Latin, Demotic and Coptic Papyri, Ostraca and Tablets* (J. F. Oates et al., https://library.duke.edu/rubenstein/scriptorium/papyrus/texts/clist_papyri.html (accessed 10 January 2023)).

Journal abbreviations follow the style in *L'Année Philologique*. For epigraphic corpora and other major reference works, the abbreviations used are listed below.

AE	*L'Année Épigraphique* (1888–). Paris.
BGU	*Berliner Griechische Urkunden (Ägyptische Urkunden aus den Königlichen (later Staatlichen) Museen zu Berlin, Griechische Urkunden)* (1895–). Berlin.
Chr.Wilck.	Mitteis, L. and Wilcken, U. (1912). *Grundzüge und Chrestomathie der Papyruskunde*, I Bd. *Historischer Teil*, II Hälfte *Chrestomathie*. Leipzig-Berlin. Nos. 1–382.
CIE	*Corpus Inscriptionum Etruscarum* (1907–). Leipzig/Rome.
CIL	Mommsen, T., et al. (1862–). *Corpus Inscriptionum Latinarum*. Berlin.
CPR	*Corpus Papyrorum Raineri* (1895–). Vienna.
FIRA	Riccobono, S. (1941). *Fontes Iuris Romani AnteIustiniani*. Florence.
FIRA III	Arango-Ruiz, V. (1943) (ed.). *Fontes Iuris Romani Antejustiniani, pars tertia, Negotia*, 2nd edn. Reprint 1969 with an appendix of material prepared by Arango-Ruiz before his death. Florence.
IAM	Euzennat, M., Gascou, J., and Marion, J. (1982). *Inscriptions antiques du Maroc*, vol. 2: *Inscriptions latines*. Paris.
IAph2007	Reynolds, J., Roueché, C., and Bodard, G. (2007). *Inscriptions of Aphrodisias*, online at: http://insaph.kcl.ac.uk/iaph2007.
IDélos	Dürrbach, F. (1929). *Inscriptions de Délos. Nos. 372–509, Comptes des hiéropes: Lois et règlements, contrats d'entrepris et devis*. Paris.
IEleusis	Clinton, K. (2005). *Eleusis: The Inscriptions on Stone*, 2 vols. Athens.
IEphesos	Wankel, H., et al. (eds) (1979–1984). *Die Inschriften von Ephesos* (9 vols; *IK* vols 11–17.4). Bonn.
IG	*Inscriptiones Graecae* (1873–). Berlin.
IGBulg	Mihailov, G. (1958–70). *Inscriptiones Graecae in Bulgaria repertae*. Sofia.
IGRom	*Inscriptiones Graecae ad res Romanas pertinentes* (1906–). Paris and Chicago.
IK	*Die Inschriften griechischer Städte aus Kleinasien* (1972–). Bonn.

IKyme	Engelmann, H. (ed.) (1976). *Die Inschriften von Kyme* (*IK*, vol. 5). Bonn.
ILabraunda	Crampa, J. (1969–1972). *Labraunda. Swedish Excavations and Researches*, vol. III 1–2, *The Greek Inscriptions*. Lund, and Stockholm.
ILAf	Cagnat, R. and Merlin, A. (1923). *Inscriptions Latines d'Afrique (Tripolitaine, Tunisie, Maroc)*. Paris.
ILAlg	*Inscriptions Latines de l'Algérie*, vol. 1, ed. S. Gsell (1922); vol. 2, ed. H.-G. Pflaum (1957). Paris/Algiers.
ILM	Chatelain, L. (1942). *Inscriptions latines du Maroc*, vol. 1. Paris.
ILS	Dessau, H. (1892–1916). *Inscriptiones Latinae Selectae*, 3 vols. Berlin.
IMylasa	Blümel, W. (ed.) (1987–1988). *Die Inschriften von Mylasa* (*IK* vols 34–35). Bonn.
InscrIt	*Inscriptiones Italiae* (1931/2–). Rome.
IPerinthos	Sayar, M. H. (ed.) (1998). *Perinthos-Herakleia (Marmara Ereğlisi) und Umgebung. Geschichte, Testimonien, griechische und lateinische Inschriften* (Österreichische Akademie der Wissenschaften. Philosophisch-historische Klasse. Denkschriften, 269 = Veröffentlichungen der kleinasiatischen Kommission 9). Vienna.
IProse	Bernand, A. (1992). *La prose sur pierre dans l'Égypte hellénistique et romaine*. Paris.
IScM	Pippidi, D. M. and Stoian, I. (1980–). *Inscripțiile din Scythia Minor grecești și latine*. București.
ISmyrna	Petzl, G. (ed.) (1982–1990). *Die Inschriften von Smyrna*, 3 vols. (*IK* vols. 23, 24.1, 24.2). Bonn.
OGIS	Dittenberger, W. (1903). *Orientis Graeci Inscriptiones Selectae. Supplementum sylloges inscriptionum Graecarum*, 2 vols. Leipzig, repr. Hildesheim 1960.
PSI	*Papiri greci e latini* (1912–) (Pubblicazioni della Società Italiana per la ricerca dei papiri greci e latini in Egitto). Florence.
RIB	Collingwood, R. G., Wright, R. P., et al. (1965–). *The Roman Inscriptions of Britain*. Oxford.
RIC	Mattingly, H., Sydenham, E. A., et al. (1923–). *Roman Imperial Coinage*. London.
RRC	Crawford, M. H. (1974). *Roman Republican Coinage*, 2 vols. London.
SB	*Sammelbuch griechischer Urkunden aus Aegypten* (1915–). Strasbourg.
SEG	*Supplementum Epigraphicum Graecum* (1923–). Leiden and Amsterdam.
Stud. Pal.	Wessely, C. (ed.) (1901–1924). *Studien zur Palaeographie und Papyruskunde*. Leipzig.
Syll.[3]	Dittenberger, W. (1915–24). *Sylloge Inscriptionum Graecarum*, 3rd edn. Leipzig.
TPSulp	Camodeca, G. (1999). *Tabulae Pompeianae Sulpiciorum (TPSulp). Edizione critica dell'archivio puteolano dei Sulpicii*, 2 vols. (Vetera: richerche di storia epigrafia e antichità). Roma.

List of Contributors

Marie-Pierre Chaufray, Researcher in Papyrology, CNRS, Ausonius, University of Bordeaux-Montaigne. Her research focuses on Greek and demotic papyrology, and in particular on the study of texts of everyday life (accounts, contracts, letters), and how they illuminate the economic and social history of Egypt in the Hellenistic and Roman periods. She is currently leading two research projects: an ERC Starting Grant project (GESHAEM) on bilingual administrative archives from the Ptolemaic period, and an ANR/DFG project (DimeData) on the accounting rolls of the temple of Soknopaios in Roman Dime. She has been a member of the French archaeological mission in the eastern desert of Egypt (MAFDO) since 2014.

Javier Domingo, Adjunct Professor in Christian Archaeology, Pontifical University of the Holy Cross. His research focuses on Roman architectural decoration, the phenomenon of the reuse and preservation of classical decorative motifs in early medieval architecture, and finally on the development of a methodology for calculating the economic cost of building construction in the Roman and late Roman world. He is the author of *Capiteles tardo-romanos y visigodos en la península Ibérica* (Tarragona, 2011), and other studies on Roman architecture and its costs, published in the journals *Archeologia dell'Architettura*, *Boreas*, *Archeologia Classica*, and *Marmora*.

Marta García Morcillo, Ancient Historian and Research Fellow at Durham University. She specializes in Roman economic and financial history, and has a particular interest in markets, auctions, price formation and value, as well as in ancient economic mentality and decision-making, and Roman law. She is UK PI of the AHRC-DFG project Twisted Transfers: Discursive Constructions of Corruption in Ancient Greece and Rome. Recent publications include *Managing Information in the Roman Economy* (ed. with Cristina Rosillo-López, Cham, 2021) and *The Real Estate Market in the Roman World* (ed. with Cristina Rosillo-López, London–New York, 2023).

Marietta Horster, Professor of Ancient History, Johannes Gutenberg-Universität Mainz. Her research focus is on forms of knowledge transfer in antiquity, on inscriptions and the materiality of written evidence, on the organizational structures and political discourses of the Roman imperial period, and on Greek and Roman cult and religious history. Recent publications include 'Sacred Personnel as Role Models in the Post-Classical Period' (in T. Scheer (ed.), *Religion and Education in the Ancient Greek World*, Tübingen 2021, 78–98), and *The Impact of Empire on Landscapes* (ed. with Nikolas Hächler, Leiden 2021).

Anthony C. King, Emeritus Professor of Roman Archaeology at the University of Winchester. He has been closely involved with temple and villa excavation projects throughout his career, including Hayling Island and Meonstoke in Hampshire, and Monte Gelato in Lazio. He also has a long-standing research interest in ancient diet through the study of animal bones. Recent publications include *Celtic Religions in the Roman Period* (ed. with R. Haeussler, Aberystwyth, 2017), *Villas, Sanctuaries and Settlement in the Romano-British Countryside* (ed. with M. Henig, G. Soffe, and K. Adcock, Oxford, 2022), and *Religious Individualisation: Archaeological, Iconographic and Epigraphic Case Studies from the Roman World* (ed. with R. Haeussler, Oxford, 2023). Tony is President of the Association for Roman Archaeology.

Michael MacKinnon, Professor of Classics, University of Winnipeg. As an archaeologist he has worked at more than sixty sites throughout the Mediterranean, including projects in an array of countries and regions—Albania, Egypt, Greece, Italy, Macedonia, Portugal, Romania, Sicily, Spain, Tunisia, and Turkey. His research interests focus on the role of animals within ancient Greek and Roman societies, as drawn from interdisciplinary exploration of zooarchaeological, ancient textual, and iconographical evidence. He is the author of *Production and Consumption of Animals in Roman Italy: Integrating the Zooarchaeological and Textual Evidence* (Journal of Roman Archaeology, Supplementary series 54, 2004).

Charlotte R. Potts, Sybille Haynes Associate Professor in Etruscan and Italic Archaeology and Art, University of Oxford, and Katharine and Leonard Woolley Fellow in Archaeology at Somerville College. Her research interests include the social aspects of architecture and continuities between Etruscan and Roman material culture, as well as the use of ancient material in museums. She is the author of *Religious Architecture in Latium and Etruria, c.900–500 BC* (Oxford, 2015), and numerous articles and chapters on Etruscan and Roman archaeology.

Nick Ray, Assistant Director of the Oxford Roman Economy Project, 2014–18, and now with the Maritime Endangered Archaeology (MarEA) project. His research focuses on consumption practices in the Roman world, particularly relating to durable commodities, North African funerary archaeology, and post-conflict/contested heritage. He is co-editor of *Burials, Migration and Identity in the Ancient Sahara and Beyond* (Cambridge, 2019), which contains several co-authored articles. He also co-edited *De Africa Romaque: Merging Cultures across North Africa* (London, 2016) and has published on consumer behaviour at Pompeii and fieldwork in Libya and Morocco.

Jörg Rüpke, Fellow in Religious Studies and Vice-Director of the Max Weber Centre for Advanced Cultural and Social Studies of the University of Erfurt, Germany. His research interests focus on ritual, religion, and urbanity. Recent publications include *Religious Deviance in the Roman World: Superstition or Individuality?* (Cambridge, 2016); *On Roman Religion: Lived Religion and the Individual in Ancient Rome* (Ithaca, 2016); *Pantheon: A New History of Roman Religion* (Princeton, 2018); *Urban Religion: A Historical Approach to Urban Growth and Religious Change* (Berlin, 2020); *Religion and its History: A Critical Inquiry* (London, 2021).

List of Contributors

Angela Trentacoste, Humboldt Fellow, University of Kiel. Her research interests include environmental archaeology, bioarchaeology, ancient farming, mobility, and the economic role of religious activity. Recent publications on Roman themes include contributions to *Theoretical Roman Archaeology Journal* (2020), *Archaeological and Anthropological Sciences* (2021), and *Roman Animals in Ritual and Funerary Contexts* (Wiesbaden, 2021).

Koenraad Verboven, Professor of Ancient History at Ghent University. He specializes in ancient social and economic history, particularly of the Roman world, and has a special interest in monetary history and numismatics, friendship- and patronage-based networks, guilds (*collegia*), (neo-)institutional analysis, and complexity economics. Recent publications include *Ownership and Exploitation of Land and Natural Resources in the Roman World* (ed. with Paul Erdkamp and Arjan Zuiderhoek, Oxford, 2015), *Work, Labour, and Professions in the Roman World* (ed. with Paul Erdkamp and Arjan Zuiderhoek, Leiden, 2016), *Capital, Investment, and Innovation in the Roman World* (ed. with Paul Erdkamp and Arjan Zuiderhoek, Oxford, 2020), and *Complexity Economics: Building a New Approach to Ancient Economic History* (ed., Cham, 2021).

David Wigg-Wolf, senior researcher at the Römisch-Germanische Kommission des Deutschen Archäologischen Instituts. His research interests include the production, circulation, and use of coinage in Western and Central Europe from the late pre-Roman Iron Age to the early medieval period, and digital numismatics. He is a member of the steering committee of nomisma.org, co-chair of the DARIAH-EU Digital Numismatics Working Group, and convenor of the European Coin Find Network (https://orcid.org/0000-0002-8604-544X).

Andrew Wilson, Professor of the Archaeology of the Roman Empire, University of Oxford. His research interests include the economy of the Roman empire, ancient technology, ancient water supply and usage, Roman North Africa, and archaeological field survey. Recent publications include *The Economy of Pompeii* (ed. with Miko Flohr, Oxford, 2017); *Trade, Commerce, and the State in the Roman World* (ed. with Alan Bowman, Oxford, 2018); *Recycling and Reuse in the Roman Economy* (ed. with Chloë Duckworth, Oxford, 2020); *Coin Hoards and Hoarding in the Roman World* (ed. with Jerome Mairat and Chris Howgego, Oxford, 2022); and *Simulating Roman Economies: Theories, Methods, and Computational Models* (ed. with Tom Brughmans, Oxford, 2022).

Greg Woolf, Ronald J. Mellor Professor of Ancient History at the University of California, Los Angeles. He has published on various aspects of Roman imperialism and cultural history and is currently working on mobility and migration in antiquity. Recent publications include *The Life and Death of Ancient Cities: A Natural History* (Oxford, 2020); *Sensorium: The Senses in Roman Polytheism* (ed. with Anton Alvar Nuño and Jaime Alvar Ezquerra, Leiden 2021); *Rome: An Empire's Story*, 2nd edition (Oxford, 2021); and *Religion in the Roman Empire* (ed. with Jörg Rüpke, Stuttgart, 2021).

1

Introduction

Religion and the Roman Economy

Andrew Wilson

It is a commonplace to say that religion pervaded ancient life: people consulted oracles, referred to soothsayers, and made sacrifices before embarking on undertakings both large and small, whether setting out for war or simply laying a mosaic floor. Temples and shrines abounded in ancient cities and rural sanctuaries; a polytheistic religious landscape populated all niches of the world with deities major and minor. Even the sewers at Rome had their own goddess, Venus Cloacina. No aspect of ancient life was untouched by the divine.

And yet religion has been almost totally absent from most discussions of the Roman economy, and certainly from any sustained analysis of it. For example, and this is wholly typical, there is no entry for 'religion' in the index of the *Cambridge Economic History of the Graeco-Roman World*; 'sacrifice' is mentioned on 4 out of the book's 768 pages, and 'sanctuaries' on 2 pages, but these are no more than incidental bit players in the discussion—and, in all cases, they occur in the parts of the book dealing with Archaic, Classical, and Hellenistic Greece.[1] There is rather more on temples, but, again, all Greek: nothing after page 457—Rome starts on page 487. There is nothing, *nothing*, in the book on Roman religion.

This is an area where Roman history is notably out of step with its chronological neighbours. While in general I would argue that research agendas on the ancient Greek economy have lagged some thirty years behind the study of the Roman economy,[2] in this particular area Greek economic history is far in advance of its Roman counterpart. Landmark studies include Catherine Morgan's work on *Athletes and Oracles* (1990), Lisa Bendall's study *Economics of Religion in the Mycenaean World: Resources Dedicated to Religion in the*

---

[1] Scheidel, Morris, and Saller (2007).   [2] See, e.g., my remarks in Wilson (2013: 126–7).

Andrew Wilson, *Introduction: Religion and the Roman Economy* In: *The Economy of Roman Religion*. Edited by: Andrew Wilson, Nick Ray, and Angela Trentacoste, Oxford University Press. © Oxford University Press 2023. DOI: 10.1093/oso/9780192883537.003.0001

Mycenaean Palace Economy (2007), and Véronique Chankowski on 'Divine Financiers: Cults as Consumers and Generators of Value' (2011).[3] Jumping past the Roman period, scholarship on late antiquity and the early Middle Ages of course has no shortage of focus on the growing economic role of the Church, as landowner and economic agent;[4] monastic economies,[5] and the donations of food, money, and children to monasteries (and the use of hagiography and sermons to encourage such donations);[6] and the economies of pilgrimage, pilgrim flasks, and sacred mementoes.[7]

Yet curiously the Roman period before Christianity took hold has been largely passed over by such interests. Five exceptions are worth mentioning. The first is Beate Dignas's book on the *Economy of the Sacred in Hellenistic and Roman Asia Minor* (2002), which argues that temple economies were not simply subsumed into civic funds but were separate and sometimes at odds with civic aims and funding, finding themselves in conflict with city councils over revenues and resources.[8] But the book did not really generate a follow-up debate.[9] The second exception is Jörg Rüpke, who has been thinking about this subject for a while, and gave a lecture at Lancaster University in 1995 on the cost of religion;[10] we are most grateful to him for permission to publish as Chapter 2 in this volume a modified and updated version of that lecture.[11] Thirdly, some particularly useful work has been done since 2017 on the economy of the Jewish Temple in Jerusalem, about which we are relatively well informed through Jewish religious laws, rabbinical literature, and the writings of Josephus; Hayim Lapin has constructed an economic model of consumption demand for the Jerusalem Temple, and, despite the considerable religious differences between Judaism and Roman paganism, the close similarities in the financing and economic function of the Jerusalem Temple and large pagan temples such as the Temple of Artemis at Ephesos or the Temple of Bel at Palmyra have been well explored by Anthony Keddie.[12] Fourthly, a special issue of the journal *Religion in the Roman Empire* published in 2019, and edited by Claudia Moser and Christopher Smith, has an introduction and five articles (one of which deals with pre-Roman Italy, and two with Christian late antiquity)

---

[3] Chankowski (2011).   [4] Wipszycka (1972).   [5] Blanke (2019).
[6] Déroche (1995); Papaconstantinou (2002b, 2002a); Déroche (2006); Papaconstantinou (2012); Blanke (2020).
[7] Caner (2006); Bell and Dale (2011); Foskolou (2012); Collar and Kristensen (2020).
[8] Dignas (2002).
[9] For reviews, see, e.g., Erskine (2004); Kindt (2004); Pirenne-Delforge (2004); Kramer (2005); Corsten (2006).
[10] Rüpke (1995).
[11] and to Richard Gordon for bringing this paper to our attention in the first place.
[12] Lapin (2017a, 2017b).

devoted to the theme of 'Transformations of Value: Lived Religion and the Economy'.[13] Lastly, Dan-el Padilla Peralta published in 2020 a book called *Divine Institutions: Religions and Community in the Middle Roman Republic*, which draws on aspects of New Institutional Economics, the economics of religion, and a quantified study of temple-building, to explore some connections between religion and the economy of mid-Republican Rome.[14]

There have indeed been studies on some of the obvious individual dimensions: the role of temples as banks,[15] festivals and pilgrimage,[16] and so on; but none of this has been synthesized into any kind of analysis of the overall economic significance and role of religious institutions, or of the costs of religion to the economy—or, conversely, the potentially productive and economically beneficial aspects of religion (on which more later). Why, with the exceptions of Dignas, Rüpke, and Padilla Peralta, and the recent issue of the *Journal of Roman Religions*, is there this blind spot? Perhaps in part because of a lingering, and certainly erroneous, view that the Romans did not believe, could not really have believed, in their crazy pagan religion, and therefore it could not have had a significant impact on their mentality or their economic behaviour.[17]

Ancient Religion and Economic Mentality

Roman religion was transactional, as exemplified by the idea *do ut des*, 'I give so that you may give'.[18] You sacrificed to a god and promised to dedicate an altar if the god ensured that some matter turned out favourably for you— a harvest; a business venture; success in love; and so on. The innumerable votive altars set up across the Roman world testify to this, the practice being so common that the key formula *votum solvit libens merito* ('discharged his vow willingly to [the god who] deserved it') was often simply abbreviated to *VSLM*. In many cases the nature of the vow is unclear, but the groups of altars dedicated to the goddess Nehalennia at Colijnsplaat and Domburg on the Dutch coast offer clear examples of dedications by traders made for the success of a cross-Channel trading voyage and safe landfall on their return from Britain.[19]

---

[13] Introduction: Moser and Smith (2019); articles: Biella (2019); Digeser (2019); Moser (2019); Rives (2019); Salzman (2019).
[14] Padilla Peralta (2020a). [15] Bromberg (1940).
[16] Collar and Kristensen (2020); Kowalzig (2020).
[17] Ando (2008: pp. x–xv), noting that a model of elite maintenance of ritual or orthopraxy was accepted by scholars for much of the twentieth century.
[18] Rüpke (2007: 149). [19] Raepsaet-Charlier (2003); Stuart (2003).

Around 160 BC, Cato in his treatise on farming sandwiched in between his recommendations for standard terms for leasing land and vineyards to share-cropping tenants, and instructions to the overseer of a farm, a set of prayers and sacrifices to be performed when thinning a grove, tilling the ground, or purifying a farm and its land (*De Agricultura* 139–41).[20] For Cato and his readership these religious rituals were just as much a part of the necessary economic running of a farm as dealing with tenants or one's *vilicus*. Festivals were concentrated at key points of the agricultural year:[21] Ten Harkel, Franconi, and Gosden note that 'it is an important detail that until the fourth century AD, the Roman senate did not meet during the autumnal months so that the necessary harvest rituals could be observed.'[22] Economic failure could be a punishment from the gods, especially when impiety had clearly occurred. When Verres stole the cult statue of Ceres from the temple at Enna, the town's inhabitants believed the failure of the grain harvest that followed was a result of his sacrilege (Cicero, *In Verrem* IV.14).

Funding Religion

The burgeoning field of study called 'the economics of religion' is more about applying the approaches of economics (rational self-interest, supply, demand) to questions of religion than it is about understanding the economic basis of religion.[23] 'Strange as it may seem, the economics of religion has yet to pay much attention to financial matters';[24] and it is for this reason that we have called this book *The Economy of Roman Religion* and not *The Economics of Roman Religion*. But some recent work in that field is beginning to examine how religions are financed, and Laurence Iannaccone and Feler Bose suggest that '"private" religions will depend heavily on fees for services, whereas "collective" religions will emphasize contributions and membership fees'.[25] They observe that Greco-Roman pagan cults tended to be more akin to the 'private' style of religion than the congregational or 'collective' religions such as Christianity or Judaism. Their dichotomy works well to predict the funding of religion in the modern world (Christianity, Judaism, Islam, as examples of collective religions,

---

[20] Cf. Ten Harkel, Franconi, and Gosden (2017: 426–7). [21] Scullard (1981).
[22] Quotation from Ten Harkel, Franconi, and Gosden (2017: 427); cf. Rüpke (2011: 148).
[23] e.g. Anderson (1988); Iannaccone (1991, 1992, 1994); Stark, Iannaccone, and Finke (1996); Iannaccone (1998); Iannaccone et al. (2005); Stonebraker (2005); Stark (2006); Iannaccone (2010); Witham (2010); McCleary (2011); Iyer (2016).
[24] Iannaccone and Bose (2011). [25] Iannaccone and Bose (2011: 336).

versus Japanese Shinto and Buddhism, or American 'New Age' religion, as 'private' styles), but the situation with Greco-Roman paganism is more complex than they allow. It is probably true that most temple cults lacked a regular congregational, collective community aspect for much of the year, and that some of their income was doubtless on a fee-for-service model, such as payment to the priest for conducting a sacrifice. The bargains with the gods struck through vows and dedications fall within this framework. Yet, actually, civic priesthoods at least were held on payment of membership fees. And donations or contributions accrued to temple cults throughout: some temples were built by private euergetism (discussed later), while temple sanctuaries received donations of statues, plate, and precious objects. It may be hard to draw the line between seeing these as 'contributions', or as fees-for-service, dedications to the god in return for services rendered. To complicate the economics of ancient religion further, one should note that at times of festivals these cults did become collective. Moreover, in contrast to most temple cults, ancient mystery cults operated normally on a 'collective' basis, as closed membership clubs; one should therefore expect, on Iannaccone and Bose's model, to find that they were funded from dues and contributions by members.

Some of these different modes of funding are illustrated by Tertullian, who around the turn of the second to third centuries AD made the nakedly financial aspects of pagan religion one of the targets of his attack on paganism while defending Christianity (*Apology* 13). First, he points out that cult images of small-scale domestic figurines are sold or recycled:

> The family deities you call Lares, you exercise a domestic authority over, pledging them, selling them, changing them—making sometimes a cooking-pot of a Saturn, a firepan of a Minerva, as one or other happens to be worn down, or broken in its long sacred use, or as the family head feels the pressure of some more sacred home necessity.

Then he ridicules the fees paid to hold the major municipal priesthoods, which are auctioned off:

> In like manner, by public law you disgrace your state gods, putting them in the auction-catalogue, and making them a source of revenue. Men seek to get the Capitol, as they seek to get the vegetable market, under the voice of the crier, under the auction spear, under the registration of the quæstor. Deity is struck off and farmed out to the highest bidder. But indeed lands burdened with tribute are of less value; men under the assessment of a poll-tax are less

noble; for these things are the marks of servitude. In the case of the gods, on the other hand, the sacredness is great in proportion to the tribute which they yield; nay, the more sacred is a god, the larger is the tax he pays. Majesty is made a source of gain. Religion goes about the taverns begging.

And, finally, he attacks the overt fee-for-service model of Roman religion (apparently suggesting that some temples charged fees for entrance to the precinct):

You demand a price for the privilege of standing on temple ground, for access to the sacred services; there is no gratuitous knowledge of your divinities permitted—you must buy their favours with a price.[26]

Clearly Tertullian is far from a neutral witness; but if one looks past the rhetorical flourishes, it appears that there is an essential validity in the basic points he is making about the financial aspects of pagan religion, and indeed his attack would lose its force if there were not.

Temple Construction

For the mid-Republican period, Dan-el Padilla Peralta has analysed the labour and capital inputs implied by the construction of some thirty-seven temples at Rome in the fourth and third centuries BC, pointing out that they were of fairly modest size and that mid-Republican Rome did not engage in the spectacular monumentality seen in Periclean Athens, or even in Archaic Rome. Many of these Republican temples were built in fulfilment of battlefield vows, and Padilla Peralta argues that 'translating wealth into a multitude of small temples was a more efficacious way of setting up and perpetuating the "shell game" through which the middle Republic ensured the continuing

---

[26] Tertullian, *Apologia* 13.4–5, translated by S. Thelwall in Roberts, Donaldson, and Coxe (1887), with adaptations: *Domesticos deos, quos Lares dicitis, domestica potestate tractatis pignerando venditando demutando aliquando in caccabulum de Saturno, aliquando in trullam de Minerva, ut quisque contritus atque contusus est, dum diu colitur, ut quisque dominus sanctiorem expertus est domesticam necessitatem. Publicos aeque publico iure foedatis, quos in hastario vectigales habetis. Sic Capitolium, sic olitorium forum petitur; sub eadem voce praeconis, sub eadem hasta, sub eadem adnotatione quaestoris divinitas addicta conducitur. Sed enim agri tributo onusti viliores, hominum capita stipendio censa ignobiliora (nam hae sunt notae captivitatis), dei vero, qui magis tributarii, magis sancti; immo qui magis sancti, magis tributarii. Maiestas quaestuaria efficitur: Circuit cauponas religio mendicans; exigitis mercedem pro solo templi, pro aditu sacri. Non licet deos gratis nosse; venales sunt.*

commitment of its population to the one enterprise that did consume bodies and time: nearly ceaseless belligerence'.[27]

By the imperial period the impetus for temple-building had shifted somewhat; while a few temples were still built in fulfilment of battlefield or campaign vows (Mars Ultor), many were built as part of a process of local elite competition in provincial towns in an empire much of which was at peace. There is a considerable body of evidence for the funding of temple construction, mostly from building inscriptions, which often give information on the donor(s), their social status, and sometimes the amount spent, or the reasons for construction (fulfilment of a vow, competition for municipal office or priesthoods). Archaeological/architectural approaches may also shed light on the approximate costs involved—as, for example, Javier Domingo does in Chapter 4 of this book. But to what extent was temple-building any different from other kinds of euergetism in terms either of the status or roles of the donors, or of their motives? Were such donations on a par with donating a theatre, or a baths building; or was there, over and above the kudos, political prestige, and statue honours expected from one's fellow citizens, an anticipation of divine favour? Did the donor expect to assume the first priesthood in the newly constructed temple? Monica Hellström has shown that temples and shrines are far and away the most common type of building to have been funded by private euergetism in the small towns within the territory or *pertica* of Carthage, and has suggested that holding the flaminate in one of these towns was both a necessary prerequisite and a stepping stone to a political career in Carthage itself.[28]

The Economics of the Priesthood

The economics of the priesthood deserve further exploration, beyond the question of payment to priests for officiating at sacrifices—not merely what did one pay to hold a priesthood, but what exactly did one get in return? Priesthoods could be expensive—in North Africa, the flaminate of the imperial cult was the most expensive civic office, because also the most prestigious. As Tertullian says, 'the more sacred is a god, the larger is the tax he pays'—at Thubursicu Numidarum in North Africa, the office of *flamen* of the imperial cult cost 6,000 *sestertii*, as against 4,000 for membership of the town council,

---

[27] Padilla Peralta (2020a); quotation from p. 76.   [28] Hellström (2020).

or for being a duumvir.²⁹ Presumably such sums were expended for more than just the pleasure of strutting around in a big fancy priest's hat: the Roman system of local government included an imbrication of civic and religious offices, and priesthoods meant power.³⁰ The flaminate was also the most powerful post in local politics, and, as just mentioned with towns in the *pertica* of Carthage, could be a step towards political office-holding in the provincial capital. But in what exactly did that power consist? More precisely, was there an *economic* return from holding such posts, either financial or in terms of social capital; and how did that work?

In a series of studies on the Roman priesthood, Richard Gordon has argued that one of the chief functions of Roman religion under the principate, and of priesthoods in general, was the accumulation of symbolic capital by the elite, underpinning and reinforcing the deep inequality in the social order.³¹ Acquiring (purchasing) a priesthood was a means of parlaying wealth into symbolic capital. Euergetism was part of the role of the priesthood (whether by the giving of banquets, by sacrifices,³² or by the construction of temples); the generosity of the elites 'serves a social purpose none the less in displaying as spectacularly as possible the social inequality which enabled them to give so generously and forced the recipients gratefully to receive'.³³ On this reading, then, the holding of priesthoods by civic elites was a financial expense undertaken in return for status, prestige, and local power. This was viable so long as the elites were and continued to be extremely wealthy—as seen most obviously in North Africa or Asia Minor; but was unsustainable if they were not, as, for example, in post-conquest Britain, when the costs of holding the priesthoods to honour Claudius at Camoludunum were said to be one of the factors behind the Boudiccan revolt.³⁴

There could, however, be more direct benefits. The charter of Urso stipulates that priests and augurs are exempt from military duties and public *munera*.³⁵ In Egypt, priests benefited from tax exemptions, as illustrated from the evidence from the village of Dime presented in Chapter 7 of this volume by Marie-Pierre Chaufray.

So priesthoods might not necessarily always be a financial drain on the priest. But could temple revenues ever actually be a source of *profit* for the priest (rather than the temple), whether legitimately or by corruption? Certainly,

---

[29] ILAlg 1.1236; 1.1223; Duncan-Jones (1974: 85–6, 109–10).
[30] Gordon (1990c), on the blurring of distinctions between magistracy and priesthood.
[31] Gordon (1990c, 1990a, 1990b). [32] Cf. Rives (2019). [33] Gordon (1990c: 224).
[34] Tacitus, *Annals* XIV.31.
[35] *Lex Julia Coloniae Genetivae* 66: *CIL* II.5439; Crawford (1996: no. 25); Gordon (1990c: 224–5).

this was true (legitimately) of Jewish priests, who received the tithes paid to the Temple in Jerusalem. The economic activities of the Jerusalem Temple, and of its priests, are relatively well documented by comparison with pagan temples. The Jewish priestly elite benefited both from tithes, which went directly to the priests, and from the particular institution of the Temple tax, levied annually on Jews in both Judaea and in diaspora communities for the upkeep of the Temple at Jerusalem, and for sacrifices there—but the surplus, after expenditure on these purposes, was at the disposal of the priests.[36] The 'Testament of Moses' (AD 6–30) includes a diatribe against the Temple priests who use the contributions of the poor for gluttonous banquets and their own self-glorification. The Temple tax was, of course, a peculiarly Jewish institution, which was exceptional in the large tax base supporting a single temple. Most pagan temples would have had far smaller resources, although large temples such as the temple of Artemis at Ephesos or of Bel at Palmyra might have provided substantial opportunities for enrichment of their priests; in both cases their priests were also, under the principate, holders of other powerful civic offices.[37] Temples run on the older, Classical and Hellenistic model of temple guardianship, as opposed to the 'euergetic' model of priesthood, would, of course, need to provide an income for their priests, met largely (one imagines) from fees for service.[38] Some of these questions (and others) about the financing of priesthoods and temple cults are explored in Chapter 2 (for Rome), Chapter 6 (for the Greek east), and Chapter 7 (for Egypt).

Costs of Sacrifices

Sacrifices were originally about giving up something dear to oneself, dedicating a piece of property to the god. Pastoral herdsmen naturally offered an animal from the herd. But, of course, by the Classical and Roman periods most animal sacrifices were dedicated by people who did not themselves raise animals and therefore had to buy them; an element of market exchange was introduced.[39] But market exchange was not always the case: some villages were taxed on the costs of ritual and sacrifice in the cities on which they were

---

[36] Keddie (2019: 176–95).   [37] Keddie (2019: 156–61).
[38] On this distinction, see in passing Gordon (1990b: 247), with references to instances of temple guardianship mentioned by Pausanias.
[39] On the monetization of sacrifice in the Classical and Hellenistic world, see Naiden (2020).

dependent and in whose territory they lay; this could involve tribute in kind.[40] In the case of temples that kept their own sacred herds, was selling the animals to dedicants who then sacrificed them in the temple a source of profitable income? It is clear that, in addition to the cost of the animal(s) sacrificed, one had to pay the priest for offering a sacrifice.[41] Chapters 8 and 9 consider the economics of animal sacrifice.

Sacrifice did not only involve animals, of course; offerings of grain, cakes, or flowers, and libations of wine, milk, honey, and so on also involved some form of expenditure, though usually on a much smaller monetary scale, allowing even the poorer members of society to offer sacrifices to the gods.[42] Incense, however, was very costly, and the religious demand for it, coupled with the limited geographical area of its production, led to a long-distance trade,[43] which, in turn, gave rise to tax revenues for the state, sufficiently appreciable to make it worth auctioning the concession for the tax on frankincense in the city of Oxyrhynchus as a concession in its own right.[44] Although the cost of frankincense was very high in terms of price per pound, such small quantities might be burned, almost symbolically, that it became affordable for offerings made by those below the level of the elite. Molecular analysis of resins has detected the use of frankincense in mortuary ritual and the embalming process in the catacombs of St Peter and Marcellinus at Rome, and in Britain.[45]

Donations and Offerings to Temples

The commutation of sacrifices into monetary offerings had already begun in the Classical period, and collection boxes—stone receptacles for coins—were a Greek innovation; they stood by the altars at the Asklepeion at Corinth, the shrine of Artemis at Messene, the Serapeion on Delos, and the temple of the Egyptian gods on Thera.[46] Although less research appears to have been done pulling together the evidence for collection boxes in the Roman world than it has for ancient Greece, we might expect that perhaps they were common in the Roman world; Sophia Zoumbaki has catalogued some from the Roman period in Greece,[47] and David Wigg-Wolf's chapter in this volume explores

---

[40] Ando (2017).
[41] e.g. (for the Hellenistic period) *ILabraunda* 1, no. 1, 11. 2–6; Dignas (2002: 60); cf. Tertullian, *Apologia* 13, already quoted.
[42] Cf. Rives (2019: 86). [43] Peacock and Williams (2007); Purcell (2016).
[44] Benaissa (2016). [45] Brettell et al. (2015); Devièse et al. (2017).
[46] Kaminski (1991); Zoumbaki (2019); Naiden (2020: 178–83). [47] Zoumbaki (2019).

the effect of their introduction into the sanctuaries of north-west Europe in the Roman period. Such offerings of coins, of course, being fungible in a way that animal sacrifice was not, gave much greater scope for the priests of the temple or shrine to decide how that money was spent.

In addition to monetary offerings, sanctuaries amassed considerable wealth in the form of offerings and dedications in precious metals. Much of this might sit immobile for centuries, locked up and taken out of circulation. But, from time to time, offerings might be sold off to generate income. Periodically this precious metal might be de-thesaurised and injected back into circulation, as when the Phocians plundered the treasures of Delphi to pay their mercenaries in the Third Sacred War (355 BC), or during Sulla's looting of Delphi in 86/85 BC, or the closure(s) of the pagan temples in the fourth century AD. The short-term impact of such events could be considerable. The sack of Jerusalem and the consequent injection into the money supply of the booty from the Temple there halved the price of gold in Syria,[48] while the anonymous author of the *De rebus bellicis* commented on the inflationary effects resulting from the de-thesaurisation of pagan temple treasures (gold, silver, and precious gems) in the reign of Constantine I.[49] But the advent of Christianity certainly did not put an end to the practice of religious accumulation of precious metal offerings; some of the wealth thus released in the fourth century was taken out of circulation again as it was turned into church plate.[50] Indeed, Christianity provided conditions that enabled even greater institutional concentration of wealth, since the Church could be a legal heir. By contrast, before Christianity became the state religion, a special *Senatus Consultum* or *constitutio* of the princeps was necessary in order to designate a god as one's heir in a will,[51] raising barriers to testamentary benefaction in favour of temples and preventing the kind of institutional accumulation of wealth by temples that we see in the Christian Church. Gifts to temples were, therefore, usually made during the benefactor's lifetime, in the hope of divine

---

[48] Howgego (1992: 5).   [49] *De Rebus Bellicis* 2.
[50] And again in the fifth century, when bishops had to re-equip with liturgical silver plate churches that were looted in the sacks of Rome in AD 410, 455, and 472: Salzman (2019).
[51] Ulpian, *apud* Riccobono, Baviera, and Arangio-Ruiz (1909), *FIRA* 2, 285: *deos heredes instituere non possumus praeter eos, quos senatus consulto constitutionibusve principum instituere concessum est, sicuti Iovem Tarpeium, Apollinem Didymaeum Mileti, Martem in Gallia, Minervam Iliensem, Herculem Gaditanum, Dianam Ephesiam, Materem Deorum Sipylenen, Nemesim, quae Smyrnae colitur, et Caelestem Salinensem Carthagini* ('We cannot designate the gods as heirs, except for those whom it has been allowed so to designate by a decree of the senate or constitutions of the emperor, such as Tarpeian Jove, Apollo Didymaeus of Miletus, Mars in Gaul, Trojan Minerva, Hercules of Cadiz, Diana of Ephesos, the Mother of the Gods of Mt Sipylos, Nemesis who is worshipped at Smyrna, and Caelestis Salinensis at Carthage.'); cf. Dignas (2002: 145–6). Ulpian's list is not exclusive, and we can add the Temple of Aphrodite at Aphrodisias to it (see n. 71).

favour. Again this perhaps fits Iannaccone and Bose's model of private religion with fee-for-service favour during life, not donations made in the expectation of salvation or reward in the next life.

Temple Revenues

Apart from donations, temples clearly received income as fees for sacrifices and various services.[52] Oracular shrines charged for their oracles; and the question of the economics of healing sanctuaries, where some patients might remain for a considerable time, deserves investigation. The social role of religion as a means of regulating public behaviour might also translate into forms of income for temples—the *collegium pontificum* at Rome, and at Aphrodisias, the board of *neopoioi* who administered the finances of the temple of Aphrodite, received fines levied on anyone who was found to have violated a grave.[53]

Some temple precincts evidently included shops selling offerings or animals for sacrifice. Although it refers to the Jewish Temple rather than to pagan religion, the story of Jesus chasing the merchants out of the Temple in Jerusalem well illustrates the commercial opportunities afforded by the practice of ritual sacrifice, especially at the time of major festivals, when temples were crowded (see Chapter 5). On arriving in Jerusalem for the Passover festival, Jesus overturned the tables of the moneychangers and the seats of the sellers of doves in the courtyard of the Temple, and chased out those buying and selling cattle and sheep.[54] The moneychangers were presumably there to change coins into the particular shekels with which the Jerusalem Temple tax had to be paid. More generally, merchants in Roman pagan temples might include sellers of sacrificial animals, and also sellers of votive offerings—whether of pottery or metal. Some temples may have supported not merely sellers of votives, but artisans who made them;[55] such artisans might have been either formally dependent on the sanctuary, or independent but still reliant on the sanctuary as their main market, like the silversmiths at Ephesos.[56] Temples, or rather the priests who ran them, will surely have charged shopkeepers or stallholders rent on their shops or stalls, or a fee for a licence to trade there.

---

[52] See n. 36.
[53] Rome: see Chapter 2, p. 37. Aphrodisias: *IAph2007* 15.245 and 15.247. For the board of *neopoioi*: *IAph2007* 1.161 and 5.204 (early third century AD). I owe these references to Angelos Chaniotis.
[54] Matthew 21:12–17; Mark 11:15–19; Luke 19:45–8; John 2:13–16.
[55] Cf., for pre-Roman Italy, Biella (2019: 36–40).
[56] Silversmiths at Ephesos: *Acts* 19:24–41; *IEphesos* II 425 + III 636; Keddie (2019: 156 n. 19).

The larger temples might also have owned considerable lands, which provided an income through rent or the sale of their produce. Most famously, the Temple of Artemis at Ephesos owned vineyards, pastureland and sacred herds, quarries and salt pans.[57]

Religion and the Roman Economy

We have already seen something of the economic character of Roman religious practice, in terms of how it was often expressed as transactions with the gods. But religion and the ancient economy were imbricated in other ways too, and it is worth considering what were the effects—even perhaps the benefits—of religion on the Roman economy at large. Religion was evidently a factor in people's economic choices and actions, and belief in its efficacy doubtless had some positive economic effects. Most obvious here is the role of the gods as guarantors of markets, overseeing transactions and, to an extent, dissuading traders from cheating each other; here religion worked with the market to establish trust. Standards for weights and measures of volume were kept in the Capitoline Temple at Rome; duplicates were provided in the temples of Castor and Pollux, Mars Ultor, and Ops at Rome, and issued to the provinces.[58] Oaths by the gods might be necessary, over and above the force of the law, to guarantee repayment by a debtor whose standing was in doubt. On 18 June AD 37, C. Novius Eunus borrowed HS 10,000 from one Hesychus, the slave of an imperial freedman, and a further HS 3,000 on 2 July 37; two years later, he was evidently having difficulty repaying and still owed HS 1,250. The final contract to secure repayment of the outstanding amount not only stipulated a punitive rate of interest but also made Eunus swear an oath by Jupiter Optimus Maximus, the *numen* of the deified Augustus, and the *genius* of the current emperor, Gaius (Caligula)—a triad of the most powerful deities, living, dead, and Olympian.[59] Such an oath had no force in Roman law, but that was not the point: for the parties concerned, it did serve to guarantee the transaction; breaking it would render Eunus guilty of perjury, ruin his credibility and reputation, and no doubt call down divine wrath upon him.

On a larger scale, gods oversaw markets. Vitruvius, expounding a set of theological ideas not necessarily followed in practice, suggests that temples of Mercury should be located in the forum, or in port (*emporium*) districts

---

[57] Keddie (2019: 156). [58] Lanciani (1892: 39–41).
[59] *TPSulp* 45, 51, 52, 67, and 68 (the oath); Broekaert (2017: 396–7); Barron (2019).

along with temples of Isis and Serapis.[60] An example of the latter is the Temple of Serapis at Puteoli, which looms over the *macellum* there.[61] Indeed, the temples of Serapis along the North African coastline at the port cities of Lepcis Magna, Sabratha, Carthage, and probably also Gigthis, do not merely reflect the presence of Alexandrian traders there,[62] but were no doubt also necessary to enable those traders to give thanks for a successful voyage, or make dedications to ensure the safety of the next leg of their trip. Pausanias says that, before the troops of Mithridates VI of Pontus sacked it (in 87 BC), Delos had been thought to be a safe emporium for traders because it had been protected by a wooden statue of Apollo.[63] The theme of how sacred statues might influence economic behaviour, and how religion could serve to lower transaction costs by promoting trust between traders, is well explored by Dan-el Padilla Peralta in an essay on the gods of Delos.[64]

Lisa Fentress has made the attractive argument that, in North Africa, periodic markets or *nundinae* were held at extramural shrines on the outskirts of cities, and particularly at shrines of Mercury, the patron of trade.[65] 'The divine element is essential for the sanctity of the transaction', and the practice lives on in North Africa in the Berber custom of holding markets at the shrine of a marabout or saint.[66] Charlotte Potts's contribution in this volume (Chapter 3) traces this kind of practice in Italy back to the Etruscan period, with monumental sanctuaries constructed at points of contact and exchange, helping to facilitate the creation of markets at those places, whose transactions they sanctified and guaranteed.

Festivals no doubt served as an economic stimulus, as they attracted people from the city's territory and well beyond, and they naturally went hand-in-hand with periodic markets—as later, in medieval Europe, fairs and religious festivals were held in conjunction.[67] They created a particular demand for flowers for garlands, which had to be grown close to cities because they could not survive long-distance transport.[68] Routine ritual needs, increased at times of festivals, sustained the incense trade from the Arabian peninsula.[69] The

---

[60] Vitr. *De Architectura*, I.7.1–2: *Mercurio autem in foro aut etiam, ut Isidi et Serapi, in emporio*; Stambaugh (1978: 561).
[61] Fentress (2020: 188–9).   [62] Wilson, Schörle, and Rice (2012: 373).
[63] Pausanias 3.23.3; for discussion, see Padilla Peralta (2020b).   [64] Padilla Peralta (2020b).
[65] Fentress (2007); cf. Fentress (2020: 188–94).   [66] Fentress (2007: 128).
[67] Broughton (1938: 870, 899); see de Ligt (1993: 225–34, 243–59), who emphasizes civic prestige as the prime motive for holding festivals, but concedes the importance of their economic function. See also Fentress (2020: 188–94).
[68] Fentress (2020: 180–3); cf. Wilson (2009) on irrigated flower gardens in the *suburbium* of Rome.
[69] Peacock and Williams (2007); Purcell (2016); cf. Seland (2012) for continued gifts of incense to the Church at Rome by estates in Egypt.

larger and more famous temple sanctuaries, including oracular shrines and healing sanctuaries, attracted visitors and pilgrims on a year-round basis,[70] and their continual importance to the local economies of their host cities is well exemplified by the scene at Ephesos in *Acts* (19:24–41), where the silversmiths, led by one Demetrios, protested in the theatre against Paul and his companions, whose preaching of Christianity they felt threatened their business of making statuettes of Artemis for dedication in her sanctuary.

Temples were also economic actors in their own right—most obviously as landowners if they owned estates from which they drew revenues. Somewhat less obviously, they might on occasion even act as civic benefactors: at Aphrodisias, 'Aphrodite' dedicated the marble entablature of the eastern forecourt of the Hadrianic baths from her own resources and from the bequest given to her by Epigonos son of Dioscourides—in other words, the goddess, or rather her temple, was acting on a par with other civic donors drawn largely from the ranks of the town council.[71] The Temple of Soknopaios at Dime in Egypt appears also to have acted as a tax collector for certain licence taxes for the state (Chapter 7).

Some temples played an institutional role as deposit banks (see Chapter 5). Temples tended to have strong rooms, often vaulted chambers within the temple podium, which served to store votive offerings; and the physical security of these arrangements as well as the divine protection afforded by the god encouraged the development of their role as depositories for private valuables, and thus as deposit banks.[72] At Rome, the Temple of Castor, the Temple of Mars in the Forum of Augustus, the Temple of Peace in the Forum of Peace, and the Temple of Ops Consiva served this function; but Juvenal suggests that, when thieves stole the helmet of the cult statue of Mars, confidence in his temple was shattered and people deposited their valuables in the Temple of Castor instead.[73] Herodian records that the destruction of the Temple of Peace in an accidental fire in AD 191 reduced many of those who had deposited their valuables there to poverty.[74] The state treasury, or *aerarium Saturni*, was located in the Temple of Saturn, but there is no evidence that private

---

[70] On festivals and pilgrimage, see now various contributions in Collar and Kristensen (2020); and Keddie (2019: 173–4) for the pilgrimage role of the Jewish Temple in Jerusalem.
[71] *IAph2007* 5.5 (where the title in the modern edition misconstrues the inscription as a dedication *to* Aphrodite; Aphrodite is in fact in the nominative and is the donor); Wilson (2016: 185). The inscriptions recording this dedication imply that the Temple of Aphrodite at Aphrodisias should be added to the brief list of temples that could receive testamentary bequests (see p. 11 n. 51 above).
[72] Bromberg (1940) collects the literary references to Roman temple deposit banking.
[73] Juvenal, *Satires* XIV, 261–3; Stambaugh (1978: 556, 586).
[74] Herodian, *History of the Empire from the Death of Marcus* I.14.

individuals deposited their wealth there.[75] The state also stored certain goods in temples; from the reign of Aurelian, wine was stored in the Temple of Sol, and sold by the state at a subsidized price.[76] There is limited evidence that some temples loaned money at interest, especially in the eastern provinces (see Chapter 5)—but most credit-lending was done by non-temple bankers.[77] Debate about temple-banking turns also on the question of whether temples provided deposit-banking as a public service (a perhaps anachronistic view), or charged for storage of valuables.[78] There is no evidence either way; but the idea of charging a fee would fit unproblematically with a fee-for-service model of other aspects of Roman religion. One might envisage either a set percentage of the value of the goods deposited, or the expectation of a donation to the god, left unspecified in an environment where social pressure and divine expectations might lead depositors to err on the side of not displeasing the god.

The Structure of This Book

As with other volumes in this series, this book does not pretend to be a comprehensive handbook to the subject, but rather offers a series of essays showcasing a range of perspectives—historical, epigraphic, papyrological, archaeological, zooarchaeological—sketching possible approaches to different economic facets of ancient religion. It aims to serve as a stimulus opening up further lines of enquiry both into the economic aspects of Roman religious practice, and into the religious component of the economy as a whole.

In the following chapter, Jörg Rüpke focuses on the cost of priesthoods, using the pontifical college at Rome as an example. Much is unknown on both sides of the balance sheet, but the exercise in quantification highlights the amount of expenditure on priestly meals that accompanied sacrifices (and exceeded the cost of the sacrifices themselves), and on *ludi scaenici* given by the priests; in addition, major costs were incurred for wages for the priests' assistants, and the costs of public slaves. The priests themselves did not draw a wage, but probably received fees or handouts (*sportulae*) for participating in rituals; they also benefited, of course, from the fairly frequent banquets and ritual meals—perhaps once every three or four days on average. However, the

---

[75] Bromberg (1940: 130).
[76] *Historia Augusta, Aurelian* 48.1–4; *CIL* VI.1785 = 31,931; Rougé (1957); cf. Watson (1999: 140).
[77] See, e.g., Keddie (2019: 156) for the Temple of Artemis at Ephesos making interest-bearing loans.
[78] Bromberg (1940: 131).

extent of this benefit depends greatly on whether we think the priests paid for many of these meals in rotation, as a form of elite competition, or if the costs of the meals were met from the priestly college's funds. As far as revenue is concerned, fees for sacrifices and other rituals must have formed part of the income, but probably not the major part, which seems to have come from leased land. The costs of inaugural meals when a new priest took up his priesthood (this seems to have been the equivalent in the colleges at Rome of the *summae honorariae* or entrance fees for priestly office in *municipia* and *coloniae* outside Rome) were also considerable, but these would not have passed through the college's accounts.

Chapter 3, 'Investing in Religion: Religion and the Economy in Pre-Roman Central Italy' by Charlotte Potts, argues that many economic features of Roman religion can be traced back to the Archaic period (*c.*580–480 BC). Increasing Mediterranean trade and contact coincided with the construction of temples at ports and other points of exchange. The existence of kilns and metalworking activity at several cult sites in Archaic Italy suggests that the demand for votives, ritual equipment, and even construction elements for the temple buildings generated artisanal activity that required local production infrastructure. Traders are linked with religious festivals; and already in the seventh century BC the sanctuary at Satricum appears to have housed weight standards. The transactional nature of bargains with the gods is already present at this early date; and the role of religion in overseeing and guaranteeing markets and trading transactions is apparent at temples not only in Egypt and the Archaic Greek world, but also in Archaic Latium and Etruria. At Pyrgi and Satricum in the late sixth century BC the arrangement of temple and surrounding colonnaded space adumbrates the design of Roman fora, while at Rome the earliest known podium temple was built at the Forum Boarium *c.*580 BC. If the scale and complexity of the religious economy may have been greater in the Republican and imperial periods, many of its basic elements are already found in Archaic Italy.

In Chapter 4, Javier Domingo examines the cost of temple-building, using a calculation methodology pioneered by Janet DeLaine,[79] based on relative prices from Diocletian's *Edict on Maximum Prices* and labour rates for pre-industrial building construction taken from mid-nineteenth-century Italian building manuals. Provided that sufficient detail is available on the building's plan and architectural elements, approximate construction costs can be estimated that can in some cases be compared with costs known from building

---

[79] DeLaine (1997).

inscriptions. Four North African examples of the early third century are considered, all dedicated between AD 214 and AD 217. For two of these, the Temple of the Victories of Caracalla in Dougga (Tunisia), and the Arch of Caracalla in Theveste (Tébessa, Algeria), the calculated costs are very close to the costs recorded on their building inscriptions—HS 104,633 versus HS 100,000, and HS 241,000 or 243,000 versus HS 250,000, respectively. But for the Capitolium and Temple C at Volubilis, the calculated costs fall far short of the costs recorded, suggesting that the calculation has not accounted for some elements—additional decoration? statuary? endowment? A comparison of the costs of the marble for the Vespasianic Temple of Peace in Rome with the contemporary upper terrace of the Provincial Forum at Tarraco suggests that costs in Rome may have been approximately double those in Spain. Yet, although construction costs in the provinces were very much lower than costs at Rome, elite competition in the practice of civic euergetism led to considerable expenditure on temples even of modest size, which, if decorated in marble, could cost between HS 100,000 and HS 400,000.

Chapter 5, by David Wigg-Wolf, considers the relationship between money and religion, taking as its point of departure two stories from the New Testament: Jesus overturning the moneychangers' tables in the Temple at Jerusalem, and the story of the widow's mite. It looks at religious iconography on Roman coinage, the roles that temples played as financial institutions, and the role of coinage in religious ritual. The purpose of religious iconography on coinage changed over time: on Republican coinage, the representation of deities often served to distinguish different denominations; Julius Caesar paired Venus on the obverse of his *denarii* with Aeneas carrying Anchises out of Troy on the reverse, alluding to the Julii's claim of divine descent from Venus and Anchises. Under the empire, representations of deities on the imperial coinage served to illustrate qualities or achievements of the emperor or imperial family, while the civic coinages of the Greek east used deities to allude either to major sanctuaries or to the foundation myths of the cities for which they were struck. The role of temples as financial institutions was chiefly as treasuries and safe deposit houses, although the mint of Rome was originally located in the Temple of Juno Moneta. But there is evidence for temples acting also as lending banks, more so in the east than in the west, and much of it from Egypt; it is not clear whether this is a function of the nature and survival of the evidence or a genuine regional distinction. In the western provinces of the empire one can trace a change in the use of money at sanctuaries and temples; in pre-Roman Iron Age times, precious metal and coinage was deposited in open areas within sanctuaries. With the shift to masonry structures and paved or gravelled courtyards, coins deposited on them would be much more easily collected for re-deposition, or reuse. Instead, we find the appearance of offering or collecting boxes; rather than the coinage being ritually buried and put beyond use as an offering to the god, the offerings could now be used as temple funds, spent on the maintenance or operation of the sanctuary, or on the priests.

Marietta Horster's contribution, on 'Cult Economy in the Eastern Provinces of the Roman Empire' (Chapter 6), focuses on the effects of the introduction of new cults of Roma and the imperial cult in cities of the Greek east. It reviews key areas of expenditure—the cost of sacrifices was probably relatively small compared to temple construction and expenses on festivals (especially dramatic festivals), both often financed by private euergetism from civic elites. Roman rule saw a shift of emphasis from dramatic festivals to gladiatorial games in connection with festivals associated with the imperial cult. Revenues might come from leases of sacred land or property, civic contributions, entry fees for office, liturgies and obligations by priests, and private benefactions, testamentary or otherwise, and in some cases fines (for the violation of tombs, or the misuse of endowments), which were hypothecated to particular temples. Horster questions the idea that these new Roman or imperial cults necessarily outranked the traditional (civic) cults in status locally, although it would surely have been advantageous for cities to be able to include priests of the imperial cult in any embassies sent to the emperor.

Chapter 7, by Marie-Pierre Chaufray, considers the effect of the Roman Conquest on temple economies in Egypt. Roman reforms of traditional temple religion in Egypt included the transformation under Augustus of some temple land into public land, the registration of priestly status (which carried exemption from the poll tax), and the abolition of the hereditary notarial functions of some families whose function was taken over by the village record offices (*grapheia*). The mid-second-century *Gnomon of the Idios Logos* contains a number of regulations to do with priests, mostly concerned with state revenues linked to the acquisition of priestly offices, and fines for violations of ritual. We learn from the *Gnomon of the Idios Logos* that a temple prophet was entitled to one-fifth of temple revenues, and that the public auction of such posts was prohibited at some point around the middle of the second century.

The bilingual archives of papyri from the temple of the crocodile god Soknopaios in the village of Dime (ancient Soknopaiou Nesos) in the Fayyum, in Greek and demotic Egyptian, give a remarkable amount of detail on that temple's role in the local economy after the Roman reforms. The state's acquisition of temple property affected some aspects of the temple's operation—for example, rather than benefiting from rents from a laundry in the nearby village of Nicopolis, as it had done under the Ptolemies, in the Roman period its role *vis-à-vis* the laundry was relegated to that of a tax collector, passing on those rents to the state. Yet Roman rule did not destroy the temple's economic activity. Annual temple declarations give inventories of temple furniture, and both revenues and expenditure in money and in kind (wheat, oil, and wine). The temple owned an oil mill, which was rented out. The archives give some idea of the size of the temple economy and the importance of the tax exemption it provided—in the second century, 100 priests in the village of Dime are recorded as being exempt from the *laographia*, from among a headcount of up to 169 priests in AD 179. Priests were also exempt from the *corvée* cultivation of public land, and from the liturgy of distributing seed corn to public farmers. On the other hand, priests had to pay an entrance fee on assuming office, and the temple, or priests, was subject to certain other taxes.

The next two chapters consider animal sacrifice. Michael MacKinnon (Chapter 8) focuses on the costs of animal sacrifice in the Mediterranean region, especially Italy. He notes the surprising lack of clearly sacrificial animal deposits from public sacrifices; private sacrifice is better represented. Private sacrifice tended to involve smaller pigs or domestic fowl; chickens in particular were a convenient size for familial funerary meals at the burial or commemoration of a loved one, which may explain why their bones are sometimes found in burials. There is some evidence for sacred herds, but it was probably also possible simply to buy an animal and then sacrifice it. Conversely, sacrificial meat may have ended up on the open market via *macella*, although the evidence is not definitive on this point. Livestock are far more common in sacrificial deposits than are hunted game.

In Chapter 9, Tony King examines the question of sacred flocks and herds in the north-western provinces by looking at the implications of animal sacrifice at Romano-Celtic shrines. Faunal analysis indicating seasonal slaughter patterns may point to festivals held at certain times of year. Bone assemblages from temples in Roman Britain have a larger emphasis on sheep/goat and pig than non-temple assemblages, possibly a continuation of Iron Age practice. At Uley, particular characteristics of many of the very numerous goat bones may suggest the evolution of a local breed, and hay and sheep/goat coprolites indicate the feeding and keeping of animals very close to the temple—all this points to the goats sacrificed at Uley being from a temple herd. King makes a strong case that the temple's relative isolation in the Roman period implies that the animals were purchased from the temple herd for sacrifice by worshippers who came from considerable distances to deposit curse tablets or attend festivals. In Gaul, enclosures around temples may have served as spaces for raising and keeping livestock; in Britain, abandoned Iron Age hillforts may have served as stock enclosures for the Romano-Celtic temples built within them, as at Maiden Castle and perhaps Chanctonbury Ring, and enclosures or boundaries around the temples at Brean Down and Hayling Island also suggest landed estates around them that could have maintained sacred flocks or herds. Temples in more urban areas, however, on major road networks, seem to have been more integrated into urban networks of livestock supply. The chapter develops a suggestive argument for how careful work correlating temples with rich faunal remains and earthwork enclosures around them may be used to infer patterns of keeping temple livestock that resonate with better-attested epigraphic data from the Greek east.

Gifts and donations for religious purposes are considered in Chapter 10, by Marta García Morcillo. Religious gifts could include monetary donations or property given to funerary foundations for purposes such as maintaining a tomb, celebrating the birthday of the deceased, or reserving/protecting burial places within a family group; professional *collegia* might assume the function of administering the endowment. Tombs could not be sold off, but the right to bury people in them could. Gifts to temples might be consecrated and made sacred but were not necessarily permanently inalienable; the decision whether to consecrate such gifts seems to have rested with the authority administering the temple, who could also desacralize and sell such gifts, turning them into commodities that could be used for the profit of the sanctuary. Clearly gifts of money were most easily fungible, but written and archaeological evidence combine to demonstrate the fact that melting down and recycling metal *ex votos* was not uncommon.

In Chapter 11, Koen Verboven examines the religious functions of several guilds with primarily occupational identities, through the lens of epigraphic evidence collected in the Ghent Database of Roman Guilds. He distinguishes between *collegia* whose identity was professional or occupational, and other associations whose identity was primarily religious (for example, the *Augustales*)—although he notes that, since they all worked as trust networks, even purely religious associations may have had an impact on the economic choices and actions of their members. It is clear that guild buildings might serve both religious and non-religious functions; for example, guild temples might be used for meetings to conduct business as well as for worship, and the divide between religious and non-religious purposes was often blurred—an illustration of the interweaving of religious activity and thought throughout all facets of ancient life. Verboven also considers the vexed question of whether the *dendrophori* were primarily a religious or a professional organization; the evidence is ultimately inconclusive, but he is inclined towards thinking they were primarily religious, although their constant connection with the occupational guilds of the *fabri* and *centonarii* gives one pause for thought. He concludes that religion was not 'the reason why professional *collegia* were formed, nor did it define their identity', but rather that *collegia* served a triple purpose—binding together their members in a nexus of guild institutions (regulations and procedures, overseen and guaranteed by the gods); and then structuring the *collegium* within the civic order, and also within the imperial order, through regulations and procedures guaranteed by the gods.

Finally, in Chapter 12, Greg Woolf provides a concluding discussion assessing the state of the field and offers some thoughts and future questions to be addressed about the interrelationship of Roman religion and the economy.

Future Directions

The foregoing discussion, and the various chapters in this book, do not of course encompass all the questions that could be asked of the economic aspects of Roman religion. Rather, they sketch a range of possible approaches, which we hope may stimulate others to pursue some of these topics further, or spark considerations of still other aspects of the interrelationship between religion and the Roman economy. There is still much research to be done into the ways in which religion affected and even shaped economic mentalities. How important were the functions of religion as serving to guarantee transactions and build trust, lowering transaction costs? Did these outweigh the diversion of resources into temples, statues, and offerings? To what extent did the expenditure of wealth on temple-building and votive offerings support an economy of builders and artisans? Was the introduction of new cults, such as Eastern cults in Rome, viewed with suspicion or resented, not merely because they were new, foreign, untraditional, but because they represented additional competition for a finite pool of money that worshippers might give to temples? How important were the functions of temples as economic actors—as landowners, banks, civic benefactors, and perhaps other roles too? How financially profitable were priesthoods, or did their attractions lie more in status and political power than in the money one might make from them?

These and many other questions are still waiting to be explored; but we can no longer treat Roman religion and the economy as separate, non-overlapping spheres. We need to work economic angles into our treatment of religion, and, importantly, consider the role that religion played in shaping the Roman economy, through *mentalités*, institutions, and lived experience.

References

Anderson, G. M. (1988). 'Mr Smith and the Preachers: The Economics of Religion in the Wealth of Nations', *Journal of Political Economy* 96/5: 1066–88.

Ando, C. (2008). *The Matter of the Gods: Religion and the Roman Empire* (Transformation of the Classical Heritage 44). Berkeley and Los Angeles, and London.

Ando, C. (2017). 'City, Village, Sacrifice: The Political Economy of Religion in the Early Roman Empire', in R. Evans (ed.), *Mass and Elite in the Greek and Roman Worlds: From Sparta to Late Antiquity*. New York, 118–36.

Barron, C. (2019). 'An Oath Sworn to Jupiter (TPSulp 68)', *Judaism and Rome: Re-Thinking Judaism's Encounter with the Roman Empire* (blog post), http://www.judaism-and-rome.org/oath-sworn-jupiter-tpsulp-68.

Bell, A. R., and Dale, R. S. (2011). 'The Medieval Pilgrimage Business', *Enterprise & Society* 12/3: 601–27.

Benaissa, A. (2016). 'Perfume, Frankincense, and Papyrus: Collecting the State Revenues', *ZPE* 200: 379–88.

Bendall, L. M. (2007). *Economics of Religion in the Mycenaean World: Resources Dedicated to Religion in the Mycenaean Palace Economy* (Oxford University School of Archaeology monograph 67). Oxford.

Biella, M. C. (2019). 'Gods of Value: Preliminary Remarks on Religion and Economy in Pre-Roman Italy', *Religion in the Roman Empire* 1: 23–45, doi: 10.1628/rre-2019-0004.

Blanke, L. (2019). *An Archaeology of Egyptian Monasticism: Settlement, Economy and Daily Life at the White Monastery Federation* (Yale Egyptological Publications 2). New Haven, CT.

Blanke, L. (2020). 'Pricing Salvation: Visitation, Donation and the Monastic Economies in Late Antique and Early Islamic Egypt', in A. Collar and T. M. Kristensen (eds), *Pilgrimage and Economy in the Ancient Mediterranean*. Leiden, 228–53.

Brettell, R. C., Schotsmans, E. M. J., Walton Rogers, P., Reifarth, N., Redfern, R. C., Stern, B., and Heron, C. P. (2015). '"Choicest Unguents": Molecular

Evidence for the Use of Resinous Plant Exudates in Late Roman Mortuary Rites in Britain', *JAS* 53: 639–48, doi: http://dx.doi.org/10.1016/j.jas.2014.11.006.

Broekaert, W. (2017). 'Conflicts, Contract Enforcement, and Business Communities in the Archive of the Sulpicii', in M. Flohr and A. I. Wilson (eds), *The Economy of Pompeii* (Oxford Studies on the Roman Economy). Oxford, 387–414.

Bromberg, B. (1940). 'Temple Banking in Rome', *Economic History Review* 10/2: 128–31.

Broughton, T. R. S. (1938). 'Roman Asia Minor', in T. Frank (ed.), *An Economic Survey of Ancient Rome*, vol. 4. Baltimore, 499–918.

Caner, D. (2006). 'Towards a Miraculous Economy: Christian Gifts and Material "Blessings" in Late Antiquity', *The Second Century: A Journal of Early Christian Studies* 14/3: 329–77.

Chankowski, V. (2011). 'Divine Financiers: Cults as Consumers and Generators of Value', in Z. Archibald, J. K. Davies, and V. Gabrielsen (eds), *The Economies of Hellenistic Societies, Third to First Centuries* BC. Oxford, 142–65.

Collar, A., and Kristensen, T. M. (2020) (eds). *Pilgrimage and Economy in the Ancient Mediterranean* (Religions in the Greco-Roman World 192). Leiden.

Corsten, T. (2006). 'Review of *Economy of the Sacred in Hellenistic and Roman Asia Minor*, Beate Dignas', *Classical World* 99/2: 189–90, doi: 10.2307/4353041.

Crawford, M. H. (1996). *Roman Statutes* (Bulletin of the Institute of Classical Studies: Supplement 64). London.

de Ligt, L. (1993). *Fairs and Markets in the Roman Empire: Economic and Social Aspects of Periodic Trade in a Pre-Industrial Society*: Dutch Monographs on Ancient History and Archaeology. Amsterdam.

DeLaine, J. (1997). *The Baths of Caracalla. A Study in the Design, Construction and Economics of Large-Scale Building Projects in Imperial Rome* (JRA Supplementary Series 25). Portsmouth, Rhode Island.

Déroche, V. (1995). *Études sur Léontios de Néapolis* (Acta Universitatis Upsaliensis. Studia Byzantina Upsaliensia 3). Uppsala.

Déroche, V. (2006). 'Vraiment anargyres? Don et contredon dans les recueils de miracles protobyzantins', in B. Caseau, J.-C. Cheynet, and V. Déroche (eds), *Pèlerinages et lieux saints dans l'antiquité et le moyen âge: Mélanges offerts à Pierre Maraval* (Monographies du Centre de Recherche d'Histoire et Civilisation de Byzance 23). Paris, 153–8.

Devièse, T., Ribechini, E., Castex, D., Stuart, B., Regert, M., and Colombini, M. P. (2017). 'A Multi-Analytical Approach Using FTIR, GC/MS and Py-GC/MS Revealed Early Evidence of Embalming Practices in Roman Catacombs', *Microchemical Journal* 133: 49–59, doi: http://dx.doi.org/10.1016/j.microc.2017.03.012.

Digeser, E. D. (2019). 'Crisis as Opportunity: Urban Renewal and Christianisation in Constantine's Gaul', *Religion in the Roman Empire* 1: 103–24, doi: 10.1628/rre-2019-0007.

Dignas, B. (2002). *Economy of the Sacred in Hellenistic and Roman Asia Minor*. Oxford.

Duncan-Jones, R. (1974). *The Economy of the Roman Empire. Quantitative Studies*. Cambridge.

Erskine, A. (2004). 'Review of *Economy of the Sacred in Hellenistic and Roman Asia Minor*, Beate Dignas', *JRS* 94: 263–4, doi: 10.2307/4135084.

Fentress, E. W. B. (2007). 'Where Were North African *Nundinae* Held?', in C. Gosden, H. Hamerow, P. de Jersey, and G. Lock (eds), *Communities and Connections: Essays in Honour of Barry Cunliffe*. Oxford, 125–41.

Fentress, E. W. B. (2020). 'Sacred Transactions: Religion and Markets in Roman Urbanism', in M. Flohr (ed.), *Urban Space and Urban History in the Roman World* (Studies in Roman Space and Urbanism). London, 179–97.

Foskolou, V. (2012). 'Blessing for Sale? On the Production and Distribution of Pilgrim Mementoes in Byzantium', *ByzZeit* 105/1: 53–84, doi: https://doi.org/10.1515/bz-2012-0004.

Gordon, R. L. (1990a). 'From Republic to Principate: Priesthood, Religion and Ideology', in M. Beard and J. North (eds), *Pagan Priests: Religion and Power in the Ancient World*. London, 179–98.

Gordon, R. L. (1990b). 'Religion in the Roman Empire: The Civic Compromise and its Limits', in M. Beard and J. North (eds), *Pagan Priests: Religion and Power in the Ancient World*. London, 235–55.

Gordon, R. L. (1990c). 'The Veil of Power: Emperors, Sacrificers and Benefactors', in M. Beard and J. North (eds), *Pagan Priests: Religion and Power in the Ancient World*. London, 201–31.

Hellström, M. (2020). 'Epigraphy and Ambition: Building Inscriptions in the Hinterland of Carthage', *JRS* 110: 57–90.

Howgego, C. J. (1992). 'The Supply and Use of Money in the Roman World 200 BC to AD 300', *JRS* 82: 1–31.

Iannaccone, L. R. (1991). 'The Consequences of Religious Market Structure: Adam Smith and the Economics of Religion', *Rationality and Society* 3/2: 156–77.

Iannaccone, L. R. (1992). 'Religious Markets and the Economics of Religion', *Social Compass* 39/1: 123–31.

Iannaccone, L. R. (1994). 'Progress in the Economics of Religion', *Journal of Institutional and Theoretical Economics (JITE)/Zeitschrift für die gesamte Staatswissenschaft* 150/4: 737–44.

Iannaccone, L. R. (1998). 'Introduction to the Economics of Religion', *Journal of Economic Literature* 36/3: 1465–95.

Iannaccone, L. R. (2010). 'The Economics of Religion: Invest Now, Repent Later', *Faith & Economics* 55: 1–10.

Iannaccone, L. R., and Bose, F. (2011). 'Funding the Faiths: Toward a Theory of Religious Finance', in R. M. McCleary (ed.), *The Oxford Handbook of the Economics of Religion*. Oxford, 323–39.

Iannaccone, L. R., Neal, D., Boettke, P., and McCloskey, D. (2005). 'The Economics of Religion: A Symposium', *Faith and Economics* 46/3: 2005.

Iyer, S. (2016). 'The New Economics of Religion', *Journal of Economic Literature* 54/2: 395–441, doi: 10.1257/jel.54.2.395.

Kaminski, G. M. (1991). '*Thesauros*: Untersuchungen zum antiken Opferstock', *Jahrbuch des deutschen archölogischen Instituts* 106: 63–181.

Keddie, A. (2019). *Class and Power in Roman Palestine: The Socioeconomic Setting of Judaism and Christian Origins*. Cambridge.

Kindt, J. (2004). 'Review of *Economy of the Sacred in Hellenistic and Roman Asia Minor*, Beate Dignas', *CP* 99/3: 272–5. doi: 10.1086/429201.

Kowalzig, B. (2020). 'Festivals, Fairs and Foreigners: Towards an Economics of Religion in the Mediterranean *longue durée*', in A. Collar and T. M. Kristensen (eds), *Pilgrimage and Economy in the Ancient Mediterranean* (Religions in the Greco-Roman World). Leiden, 287–328.

Kramer, N. (2005). 'Review of *Economy of the Sacred in Hellenistic and Roman Asia Minor*, Beate Dignas', *Gnomon* 77/5: 424–7.

Lanciani, R. A. (1892). *Pagan and Christian Rome*. London.

Lapin, H. (2017a). 'Feeding the Jerusalem Temple: Cult, Hinterland, and Economy in First-Century Palestine', *Journal of Ancient Judaism* 8/3: 410–53.

Lapin, H. (2017b). 'Temple, Cult, and Consumption in Second Temple Jerusalem', in O. Tal and Z. Weiss (eds), *Expressions of Cult in the Southern Levant in the Greco-Roman Period: Manifestations in Text and Material Culture* (Contextualising the Sacred 6). Turnhout, 241–53.

McCleary, R. M. (2011). *The Oxford Handbook of the Economics of Religion*. Oxford.

Morgan, C. (1990). *Athletes and Oracles: The Transformation of Olympia and Delphi in the Eighth Century BC*. Cambridge.

Moser, C. (2019). 'Sacred Outreach: The Infrastructure of Port Sanctuaries in Republican Latium', *Religion in the Roman Empire* 1: 46–82, doi: 10.1628/rre-2019-0005.

Moser, C., and Smith, C. (2019). 'Transformations of Value: Lived Religion and the Economy', *Religion in the Roman Empire* 5: 3–22, doi: 10.1628/rre-2019-0003.

Naiden, F. S. (2020). 'The Monetisation of Sacrifice', in A. Collar and T. M. Kristensen (eds), *Pilgrimage and Economy in the Ancient Mediterranean* (Religions in the Greco-Roman World). Leiden, 163–86.

Padilla Peralta, D.-e. (2020a). *Divine Institutions: Religions and Community in the Middle Roman Republic*. Princeton and Oxford.

Padilla Peralta, D.-e. (2020b). 'Gods of Trust: Ancient Delos and the Modern Economics of Religion', in A. Collar and T. M. Kristensen (eds), *Pilgrimage and Economy in the Ancient Mediterranean* (Religions in the Greco-Roman World). Leiden, 329–56.

Papaconstantinou, A. (2002a). 'Notes sur les actes de donation d'enfant au monastère thébain de Saint-Phoibammon', *JJurP* 32: 83–105.

Papaconstantinou, A. (2002b). 'Theia Oikonomia: Les Actes thébains de donation d'enfants ou la gestion monastique de la pénurie', in *Mélanges Gilbert Dagron* (Travaux et mémoires du Centre d'histoire et civilisation de Byzance 14). Paris, 511–26.

Papaconstantinou, A. (2012). 'Donation and Negotiation: Formal Gifts to Religious Institutions in Late Antiquity', in J.-M. Spieser and É. Yota (eds), *Donations et donateurs dans la société et l'art byzantins* (Réalités Byzantines). Paris, 75–95.

Peacock, D. P. S., and Williams, D. (2007) (eds). *Food for the Gods: New Light on the Ancient Incense Trade*. Oxford.

Pirenne-Delforge, V. (2004). 'Review of Beate Dignas, *Economy of the Sacred in Hellenistic and Roman Asia Minor*', *Kernos* 17: 326–7.

Purcell, N. (2016). 'Unnecessary Dependences: Illustrating Circulation in Pre-Modern Large-Scale History', in J. Belich, J. Darwin, M. Frenz, and C. Wickham (eds), *The Prospect of Global History*. Oxford, 65–79.

Raepsaet-Charlier, M. T. (2003). 'Nouveaux cultores de Nehalennia', *AntCl* 72: 291–302.

Riccobono, S., Baviera, G., and Arangio-Ruiz, V. (1909). *Fontes iuris Romani anteiustiniani*, vol. 2. Florence.

Rives, J. B. (2019). 'Animal Sacrifice and Euergetism in the Hellenistic and Roman Polis', *Religion in the Roman Empire* 1: 83–102, doi: 10.1628/rre-2019-0003.

Roberts, A., Donaldson, J., and Coxe, A. C. (1887). *The Ante-Nicene Fathers*, vol. 3, trans. S. Thelwall. Buffalo, NY.

Rougé, J. (1957). 'Ad ciconias nixas', *RÉA* 59: 320–8.

Rüpke, J. (1995). 'Was kostet Religion? Quantifizierungsversuche für die Stadt Rom', in H. G. Kippenberg and B. Luchesi (eds), *Lokale Religionsgeschichte*. Marburg, 273–8.

Rüpke, J. (2007). *The Religion of the Romans*, trans. R. L. Gordon. Cambridge.

Rüpke, J. (2011). *The Roman Calendar from Numa to Constantine: Time, History, and the Fasti*, trans. D. M. B. Richardson. Chichester.

Salzman, M. R. (2019). 'The Religious Economics of Crisis: The Papal Use of Liturgical Vessels as Symbolic Capital in Late Antiquity', *Religion in the Roman Empire* 1: 125–41, doi: 10.1628/rre-2019-0008.

Scheidel, W., Morris, I., and Saller, R. P. (2007) (eds). *The Cambridge Economic History of the Greco-Roman World.* Cambridge.

Scullard, H. H. (1981). *Festivals and Ceremonies of the Roman Republic.* London.

Seland, E. H. (2012). 'The *Liber Pontificalis* and Red Sea Trade of the Early to Mid 4th Century AD', in D. A. Agius, J. P. Cooper, A. Trakadas, and C. Zazzaro (eds), *Navigated Spaces, Connected Places. Proceedings of Red Sea Project V Held at the University of Exeter, 16–19 September 2010* (BAR International Series 2346). Oxford, 117–26.

Stambaugh, J. E. (1978). 'The Functions of Roman Temples', in W. Haase (ed.), *Aufstieg und Niedergang der römischen Welt,* vol. II.16.1: *Teilband Religion (Heidentum: Römische Religion, Allgemeines).* Berlin and New York, 554–608.

Stark, R. (2006). 'Economics of Religion', in R. A. Segal (ed.), *The Blackwell Companion to the Study of Religion* (Blackwell Companions to Religion). Malden, Oxford, and Victoria, 47–67.

Stark, R., Iannaccone, L. R., and Finke, R. (1996). 'Linkages between Economics and Religion', *American Economic Review* 86/2: 433–7.

Stonebraker, R. J. (2005). 'Economics of Religion', in S .W. Bowmaker (ed.), *Economics Uncut: A Complete Guide to Life, Death and Misadventure.* Cheltenham, 264–88.

Stuart, P. (2003). *Nehalennia: Documenten in steen.* Goes.

Ten Harkel, L., Franconi, T. V., and Gosden, C. (2017). 'Fields, Ritual and Religion: Holistic Approaches to the Rural Landscape in Long-Term Perspective (*c.*1500 BC–AD 1086)', *OJA* 36/4: 413–37.

Watson, A. (1999). *Aurelian and the Third Century* (Roman Imperial Biographies Series). London.

Wilson, A. I. (2009). 'Villas, Horticulture and Irrigation Infrastructure in the Tiber Valley', in F. Coarelli and H. Patterson (eds), *Mercator Placidissimus: The Tiber Valley in Antiquity. New Research in the Upper and Middle River Valley.* Rome, 731–68.

Wilson, A. I. (2013). 'Trading across the Syrtes: Euesperides and the Punic World', in J. Quinn and J. Prag (eds), *The Hellenistic West: Rethinking the Ancient Mediterranean.* Cambridge, 120–56.

Wilson, A. I. (2016). 'The Olympian (Hadrianic) Baths: Layout, Operation, and Financing', in R. R. R. Smith, J. Lenaghan, A. Sokolicek, and K. Welch (eds), *Aphrodisias Papers 5: Excavation and Research at Aphrodisias, 2006–2012* (JRA Supplementary Series 103). Portsmouth, Rhode Island, 168–94.

Wilson, A. I., Schörle, K., and Rice, C. M. (2012). 'Roman Ports and Mediterranean Connectivity', in S. Keay (ed.), *Rome, Portus and the Mediterranean* (Archaeological Monographs of the British School at Rome). London, 367–91.

Wipszycka, E. (1972). *Les ressources et les activités économiques des églises en Égypte du IVe au VIIIe siècle*. Brussels.

Witham, L. (2010). *Marketplace of the Gods: How Economics Explains Religion*. New York and Oxford.

Zoumbaki, S. (2019). 'Monetization of Piety and Personalization of Religious Role of *thesauroi* in the Greek Mainland and the Cyclades', in S. Krmnicek and J. Chameroy (eds), *Money Matters: Coin Finds and Ancient Coin Use*. Bonn, 189–208.

2

What Did Religion Cost in Ancient Rome?

Jörg Rüpke

Introduction

Scholarship on the ancient world has paid little attention to problems of financing religion.[1] The relationship between money and religion has been discussed mainly in the light of two theses that are increasingly seen as discredited. These are Max Weber's thesis that the western capitalist economy is an offspring of Protestantism, and especially of Calvin's teaching on predestination; and the thesis that the state is an offspring of the centralizing redistributive function of Mesopotamian temple economies.[2] To give a hint of the fundamental critique: Weber analyses only a few letters and theological treatises and combines the results with a statement of some general correlations between economic development and confessional history in some European regions.[3] Detailed analysis of the social and economic history is missing. Criticism of the second thesis is even more radical: here, owing to a generalization from fragmentary sources, all the inhabitants of the Mesopotamian city state of Lagaš have been turned into employees of the temple.[4] How much money (or goods) religions owned, how they raised the money, or how they were forced to spend it have not been seen to be of importance.

But these questions are important.[5] Ritual is expensive. Sacrificial animals must be bought or raised,[6] buildings have to be erected and maintained,[7] religious specialists, from butchers and musicians to the transmitter and producer of liturgical texts, have to be supported, either temporarily or permanently.[8] Where do the resources come from? Is there anything like an intra-religious economy, religious cattle, or quarries? Does an accumulation

---

[1] For an overview of the concept of 'the economy of religion', see Koch (2014); briefly Rüpke (2008a). For antiquity, see Gordon, Raja, and Rieger (2021).
[2] Max Weber (1905/2014); Mesopotamia: e.g. Diakonoff (1969). [3] Schluchter (1988, 1989).
[4] Gelb (1969); Renger (1984, 1989); Postgate (1994/2009). [5] See, in general, Bruce (1992).
[6] Méniel (2015: 158–9). [7] e.g. Burford (1965). [8] Horster (2007).

Jörg Rüpke, *What Did Religion Cost in Ancient Rome?* In: *The Economy of Roman Religion.* Edited by: Andrew Wilson, Nick Ray, and Angela Trentacoste, Oxford University Press. © Oxford University Press 2023. DOI: 10.1093/oso/9780192883537.003.0002

of capital in the form of land or valuable dedications exist? Is it open to use when needed? Will costs be borne by users, participants, or members?[9] How much does religion cost for the individual? Are there cheap and expensive religions?[10]

These are not the kinds of question that define the self-image of a religion, but the answers do shape the appearance of religion in marble temples, magnificent processions, and a multitude of religious specialists, on the one hand, and terracotta votives, candles, and sacrificial cakes, on the other. The degree of financial autonomy, the possibility to use one's own funds, the dependency on short-term surplus or on the wealth of others could define the relationship to individuals, groups in society, and institutions of the state, and qualify these relationships in a manner not visible in the standard sources of the history of religion. Instead, the analytical instruments of economics might further our understanding; and this is what I shall try to demonstrate on the basis of an example from ancient Rome.

It needs to be made explicit that my focus is on so-called public religion—that is, on highly visible religious performances and infrastructure, religion on display that claims to be correct and exemplary, 'expensive religion' of the political elite that does not exclude, but dwarfs, the 'cheap religion' of the masses. These in turn appropriated such performances or locations by actually participating, cheering, or keeping silent, by dedicating votives or carving graffiti into the walls. Easily popular spaces and time slots were probably scarce, and continuous attraction entailed a matter of continuous expenses, in the upkeep of gardens, the dedication of new works of 'art', or the distribution of free meat or wine. All this is beyond quantification. What is on offer in this chapter is just an educated guess for a small segment of such spending, resulting in some—in details surprising—insights into factors and preferences.

What Did Religion Cost at Rome?

Within the empire, cultural and economic conditions varied widely, and any attempt at quantification must therefore limit itself to a small area. I have chosen the central locality, Rome, at least as a surface on which to project data gathered elsewhere. At Rome, the annual expenditure for public games and temples must have been in the order of thirty million to fifty million *sestertii* (HS).[11] The large games, lasting several days, cost from one million to three

---

[9] cf., for Greece, Sokolowski (1954).   [10] Rüpke (2018: 84, 320–1).
[11] Freyberg (1988: 118) gives the lower number, but cf. Knapowski (1967).

million *sestertii* without any special extravagance; a new temple in the city would have cost roughly the same.[12] It is not known how much the public treasury actually paid. The building or restoration of temples and certain rituals or games could be paid for by individuals, usually magistrates.[13] Largesse was expected, and was one of the most important means of preparing for the election of a magistrate during the Republic. In 58 BC, the aedile M. Aemilius Scaurus is said to have spent thirty million *sestertii* just for the scenery of his games.[14]

As it was necessary to secure the financing of rituals on a long-term and reliable basis, apart from liturgies, the institutionalization of a cult involved the allocation of certain revenues, usually derived from the lease of land. In Roman imagination King Numa's rituals already included such provisions.[15] To this form of security no real alternative existed until modern times.[16] As the usufructuaries usually had no adequate administrative organization, the normal procedure was to rent the land out to tenants. When Pliny donated property to his local town in order to secure the financing of orphans, he immediately rented the property back for an annual sum of HS 300,000, thus sparing the community any direct administrative costs.[17]

Which religious institutions coordinated this financing? Generally speaking, as in the ancient Orient, Egypt, Greece, and India, temples and their priesthoods normally fulfilled this function.[18] In these societies, temples owned large plots of land, which sometimes even included entire villages. This was not usually the case with temples in the city of Rome. In Roman sources, plots of sacred land belong to priesthoods;[19] as a rule, temples were not even entitled to inherit.[20] The large state-priesthoods, for their part, did

---

[12] Knapowski (1967: 55–6 for temples and 57–62 for games), supported by Cavallaro (1984: 132–3). Knapowski assumes a long-term average of HS 11,000,000 for the upkeep of the public Roman temples.

[13] See Orlin (1997) for the Republican period.

[14] Plin. *HN* 36.115; Aemilius Scaurus' expenditure was imitated and surpassed by Pompey (Cic. *off.* 2.57). Further extravagances are well attested: e.g. HS 2,000,000 for a driver or HS 9,000,000 for thirteen gladiators (Suet. *Calig.* 55.7 and 18.5). For lavish municipal games, Petronius' Trimalchio invests HS 400,000 (45.6, on which, see 84 n. 157).

[15] Livy 1.20.5.

[16] For a few exceptional Greek cases in the form of dedicated taxes, see Schlaifer (1940).

[17] Plin. *Ep.* 7.18; see, for the many details regulated in such contracts, Wörrle (1988: 141–64).

[18] See, e.g., Janssen (1979); Lipiński (1979); Renger (1979); India: Appadurai and Appadurai Breckenridge (1976); Fuller (1984); for Greece and the Roman Near East, see, e.g., Linders (1988); Lozano (2015).

[19] The sources are documented in Bodei Giglioni (1977): Oros. 5.18.27; App. *Mith.* 84; see also Dio 43.47.4; Suet. *Iul.* 20.3; *Liber coloniarum* p. 235.6–7; 239.9–10. See Wissowa (1912: 407 n. 3); Fest. p. 204.32–25 Lindsay; Sic. Flacc. *grom.* p. 162.28–163.4 Lachmann; Hyg. *grom.* p. 117.5–11 Lachmann; *Grom.* p. 283.18–20 Lachmann.

[20] Exceptional cases like the temple of Diana Tifatina clearly have Greek models or date to exceptional decisions of the imperial period. Cf. Introduction, pp. 11–12 and 15, n. 71.

not have economic relations with specific temples; exceptions concern temples that were not widely accessed by the general populace, as in the case of the sanctuary of Dea Dia of the Arval Brethren.

If we intend to apply an economic analysis to ancient Roman religion, then we need to focus on priesthoods.[21] I here examine the pontifical core of the pontifical college at Rome, which consisted of about twenty priests; thus, I exclude the minor pontiffs, the *flamines*, and the Vestal Virgins.[22] Of course, for the following calculations most of the figures stem from anecdotal sources and are not very reliable. Thus, in the absence of a proper balance sheet, rough magnitudes are given in Table 2.1.

Expenditure

We do not have precise figures for individual items of the ritual; the prices of draught animals as given in Diocletian's *Edict on Maximum Prices* cannot be used for sacrificial animals.[23] However, in the sources, there are several sums for complex rituals, sometimes in the form of a statement, more frequently as a definition of the necessary revenue of an endowment. These are the magnitudes for smaller towns that might be applicable for our priesthood, as we are considering small routine rituals without any or at least any larger audience: a simple sacrifice, HS 60–100;[24] a sacrifice with a meal for a smaller group, about HS 250;[25] for a good meal, HS 20–30 *per capita*.[26] The colleges of *Augustales*, who were responsible for the local emperor worship, spent HS 400–600 for their sacrificial meals called *epula*.[27] Small games, the *ludi scaenici*, theatrical games, cost about HS 2,000 a day.[28] In Rome, however, the ritual kernel of the small games of Equirria and Consualia, which were organized by urban priests, would have cost about HS 30,000 each.[29]

The monthly and weekly routine rituals of the pontifical college amount to about eighty a year (Table 2.1 (i): 1(*a*)); together with some twenty larger festivals and the four priestly games (1(*b*)), the costs would come to about HS

---

[21] See, for Greece, A. Weber (1924).
[22] For the composition of the pontifical college Rüpke (2008b): 43–6).
[23] *Edict. imp. Diocl.*. 30: for cattle 10,000 *denarii*, a cow 2,000, sheep 400 (14. 16. 18 Giacchero). Festus (p. 220.22–30 L; 270.2–5 L) refers to fines on the basis of conventional prices for animals, namely 100 *asses* for cattle and 10 *asses* for a sheep. Taking inflation into account, Knapowski (1967) calculates HS 1,000 for male cattle at the end of the Republic.
[24] Duncan-Jones (1982: 204–5).
[25] Duncan-Jones (1982: 204–5). Sometimes unspecified sums around HS 200 are given *ad sacra*.
[26] Duncan-Jones (1982: 140).   [27] Toller (1889: 97).   [28] Toller (1889: 97).
[29] Numbers taken from Knapowski (1961: 33–5; 1967: 58 and xxix).

Table 2.1 Expenditures and revenues of a Roman priesthood (in HS)

(i) Expenditures		HS
1. Material		
(a) Monthly routine rituals	36 + 45 × HS 100	
(b) Annual rituals:	15 small × 250	
	5 larger × 2,500	
	ludi (2 Equirria,	8,100
	2 Consualia) × 30,000	136,500
(c) Meals (*cenae*)	—	?
(d) Instruments	—	100
(e) Building activities	—	1,200
2. Personnel		
(a) (Calculated) salaries for *publici*	20 × 500	10,000
(b) Salaries for *kalatores*	23 × 8,750	201,250
(c) Salaries for other *apparitores*	10 × 7,000	70,000
(d) *sportulae* on average	15 × 12 + 5 × 100	25,500
3. Deductions/depreciations		
(a) Temples or *scholae*	—	1,200
(b) Instruments	—	10
(c) Slaves	—	5,000
4. Losses		
(a) Loss in land property (illegal, war, dispossession)	—	?
(b) Loss of instruments	—	?
(c) Loss/destruction of votive offerings	—	—
5. Interests		
6. Deductions on financial investments		
7. Fees/taxes		
Summary of expenditures		458,860 minimum

145,000. Once a month the college met. We do not know whether they had the same lavish meals as the augurs—the luxury of the *cenae sacerdotum*, the priestly meals, was proverbial (1(*c*)). However, again it is not known whether such *cenae* were paid for by the hosts in rotation or out of the college's treasury. The former is more probable, if we think in terms of members of an elite competing also in dining.[30]

---

[30] See Rüpke (1998) and later in this chapter.

(ii) Revenues	HS
1. Proceeds of turnover	
(a) Entrance fees	—
(b) *stips* (small monetary gifts)	—
(c) Votive offerings	—
(d) Participation in public fines	50,000
(e) Payments for assistance in third-party rituals	—
2. Increase in stock	50
3. Other direct revenues	
(a) From sales of property	—
(b) From *emancipationes*	—
(c) Direct public subsidies	296,250
(d) *summae honorariae*	—
4. Rents (on property)	200,000 minimum
5. Interest, etc.	—
6. Extraordinary revenues	
(a) Inheritances, legacies	—
(b) New foundations, newly allocated property	—
Summary of revenues	546,300 minimum
Annual difference in quantifiable positions	**+87,440**

If iron knives used in rituals could be easily replaced by a lead copy,[31] luxury in instruments must have been fairly restricted (1(d)). The maintenance of buildings (1(e)) amounts to 1–2 per cent a year. For the small communal halls (*scholae*) of the priesthoods, the sum of a few thousand *sestertii* would not have been surpassed.[32]

We have now to address the wages (Table 2.1 (i): 2).[33] Here, several groups of functionaries have to be differentiated. A more precise figure might be calculated only for the *kalatores*, a sort of personal companion and assistant, one for each priest. Their annual wages would total around HS 200,000.

---

[31] Suetonius refers to such an incident, a measure to avoid assassination attempts (*Tib.* 25.3).

[32] The number given here is taken from the expenditures of a municipal temple (Duncan-Jones 1982: 206). Late antique ecclesiastical norms demanded to set aside a third of a dedication for the building of a new church for the costs of upkeep, and a second third for the necessary clerics, who could not be joined by the dedicator (Pietri 1978).

[33] The numbers are calculated on the basis of Knapowski (1967: 13–14). As occasional attestations show that salaries could be five times higher in the imperial period, I have multiplied the numbers by 2.5.

The number of the official slaves employed (*publici*) and of the minor civil servants (*apparitores*) cannot be reconstructed. Judging by the many tasks in ritual as well as administration, a larger number of servants is to be expected. Yet some of the more specialized functionaries formed autonomous colleges that would serve all Roman magistrates and priests—for instance, the flute players (*tibicines*) or the *victimarii*, the butchers proper. It is certain that public slaves who were employed in tasks like those in the priestly colleges were given a sort of wage.[34] We cannot exclude that it was paid for directly by the state.[35] Taken all together, the figures would amount to a magnitude of HS 300,000.

No wages were paid to the priests themselves. The Vestal Virgins, unmarried and hence unprovided for, were an exception and were given a stipend. The minor priesthood of *curiones*, not even knights, were given an *aes curionum*, 'Curiones' money', of unknown value.[36] We cannot exclude, however, that fees (*sportulae*) were given to the priests participating in a ritual. It is known for the Arval Brethren and municipal colleges that such fees were given after sacrificial meals.[37] Already in Tertullian's work at the beginning of the third century we can observe that such fees formed the basis of the regular income of Christian clerics.[38] If such a fee of, often, HS 100 were given to the pontiffs, the expenditure would have increased by some HS 25,000.

The following positions (Table 2.1 (i): 3–6) are not known at all; they repeat earlier sums (for example, 1(*e*)) or are estimated on the basis of an average price of HS 2,000 for a well-trained slave, usable for a period of twenty years (a period approaching average durations of service of upper-class priests). They are given to illustrate the extent of the unknown as well as the differences from modern enterprises, the balance sheets of which are employed as a heuristic tool here. Investment credits in this field were not totally unthinkable; Tertullian at least imagines a priest in need of a creditor for a Salian meal.[39]

At Rome, temples and colleges had nearly no tax obligations (Table 2.1 (i): 7). In other places, however (for example, in Egypt), such taxes could be decisive for the affluence of a temple and its priesthood. It is not without profit that today's religious communities fight for their non-profit status.

---

[34] Mommsen (1887a: 322); Bömer (1981: 18).
[35] Thus the assumption of Mommsen (1887b: 64).
[36] See Mommsen (1887b: 65); Livy 1.20.3; Tac. *Ann.* 4.16 on payments to these priesthoods.
[37] Pasqualini (1969).   [38] Schöllgen (1990).   [39] Tert. *Apol.* 39.15.

Revenue

I turn now to the revenues (Table 2.1 (ii)). As far as we know, the pontiffs had only one source of income, directly connected with their activity: as the supervising authority on the inviolability of graves, the fines sanctioning offences against graves and tombs had to be paid to the college. According to the prescriptive texts on tombstones, these fines were very large, often several tens of thousands of *sestertii*.[40] Yet it is very questionable whether in the case of an offence these fines could really be materialized into actual payment.[41]

The sources do not reveal anything about fees for the pontiffs' cooperation in sacrifices or other rituals such as dedications of temples or patrician marriages (*confarreationes*) (1(e)).[42] Such fees were charged by private offerers of religious services, divinators male or female, producers of curses or the many producers of ritual cakes.[43] A single and very fragmentary inscription proves that private individuals had to pay fees when using state temples.[44] The fees for sacrifices varied according to the kind of animal and went up to HS 40; a holocaust was more expensive than a sacrifice from which the animal skin could go to the temple. Even the smallest items were charged for: a wreath cost four *asses*, hot water two, which is one *sestertius* and half a *sestertius* respectively. And, yet, the unqualified entrance fees, polemically presupposed by the Christian apologetic Tertullian, lack any further evidence (1(a)).[45] Probably the practice of monetary offerings (*stips*) is polemically reinterpreted as an entrance fee (1(b)).[46] Revenues from begging were restricted to the annual processions of the *Galli*, the priests of the Mater Magna.[47]

Of course, priestly colleges might have small stocks of material used in rituals that might increase (2) or decrease over the course of a year. Unlike temples, priesthoods would not profit from the acceptance of dedications (1(c)), a class of objects that might form an enormous financial asset, mobilized in exceptional situations.[48] For the sake of a more complex balance sheet, I accept the thesis of Theodor Mommsen that the salaries for public servants were directly paid from the *fiscus* (3(c)). Sometimes 'secular' colleges and even

---

[40] e.g. *CIL* VI.10219, 13152.
[41] Fines are dedicated to the financing of rituals at Urso (*lex Urson.* 65).
[42] See Wissowa (1912: 118–19).
[43] Wendt (2016); Rüpke (2018: 302–3); e.g. Plaut. *Mil.* 691–3; Cato, *Agr.* 4.3.   [44] *CIL* VI.820.
[45] See Tert. *Ad nat.* 1.10.24 (similar *Apol.* 13.6).
[46] See *Apol.* 42.8. Cic. *Leg.* 2.25 refers to the necessary expenses involved in approaching the gods, Sen. *Ep.* 41.1 talks of the bribing of an *aedituus* in order to get closer to an image of a god.
[47] This practice is taken up normatively in Cic. *Leg.* 2.22.
[48] See Bodei Giglioni (1977: 35–7) and the value of dedications offered by Augustus to five Roman temples, amounting to HS 100 million (August. *Res gest.* 21).

local administrations benefited from endowments that enabled the regular performance of rituals and banquets. Again, there is no proof that the urban priesthoods were beneficiaries of such endowments (6(*a*)).

I now turn to one of the most difficult points of the calculation (3(*d*)). On entering the municipal college of the *seviri Augustales*, new members had to pay a kind of entrance fee called *summa honoraria*, 'honorary sum'. It often amounted to HS 2,000. Such a fee had to be paid for nearly all local magistrates in colonies or *municipia* administrated on Roman lines. The sales of priesthoods in Greece or compulsory taxes due on any advancement in Egyptian temples are equivalents. With regard to the multitude of local positions and the annual recruiting of the magistrates, these entrance fees could be the most important type of revenue for communities or colleges that did not possess any land.[49] Such *summae* are not attested for the urban priesthoods of Rome; the two literary references to such payments concern priesthoods instituted by Caligula.[50] Instead of paying a fixed sum, Roman priests and magistrates seem to have been obliged to organize and pay for games, the *processus consularis*, the *sparsio*—that is, the sprinkling of audiences in places like an amphitheatre with perfumed water or presents,[51] or the like. Newly co-opted priests invited their older colleagues to come to an extremely luxurious 'inauguration banquet', the *cena aditialis*. Seneca, the philosopher, laments that, on the one hand, it was thought to be shameful to consume a knight's fortune—that is HS 400,000—in a sumptuous meal, yet, on the other hand, even extremely modest persons are obliged to organize 'inauguration banquets' costing a million *sestertii*.[52] These sums did not appear in the bookkeeping of the *arca pontificum*, the pontifical budget, but they have to be reckoned in the total balance of the individual members of the college. Allowing for exaggeration, on the basis of a college of twenty persons each holding such a banquet each year over, we might reach a sum of half a million *sestertii* each year—not showing up in the institutional balance.

Without doubt, the revenue from leased land would form the major position on the positive side of the balance sheet. Roman expectation of a net capital revenue of this type amounted to 4–6 per cent.[53] For the permanent minimum costs of HS 400,000 to 500,000 (including wages), the priesthood would have needed a minimum capital of about ten million *sestertii*. One *iugerum*, that is two-thirds of an acre, of good Italian land would have cost

---

[49] See Duncan-Jones (1990: 174–84) on the long-term financing of local building programmes.
[50] See Wissowa (1912: 491); Suet. *Calig.* 22; *Claud.* 9; Dio 59.28.5.
[51] Sen. *Contr.* 10, pr. 9.; Stat. *Silv.* 1.6.66. [52] Sen. *Ep.* 95.41.
[53] Shatzman (1975: 50); Wesch-Klein (1990: 22); see in detail Duncan-Jones (1982: 33 ff., 348 ff).

about HS 1,000. The minimum capital, then, represents some 7,000 acres of land. To finance the war against Mithridates, the late Republican general Sulla sold land belonging to the priesthoods for some thirty-six million *sestertii*.[54] At contemporary prices, this would have represented more than 50,000 acres, thus illustrating the margin of security inherent in this system of financing.

Consequences

I do not have to repeat the general remarks on the reliability of the figures in the sources and the hypothetical character of my whole calculation. Nevertheless, the attempt at quantification is a necessary step in an evaluation of the relative position of the religious institutions. Controlling only 1–2 per cent of the public spending on religion, the most important Roman priesthood was only minimally involved in the production of religious goods. This statement would not be seriously modified if we include all other major priesthoods. A sum of perhaps four million *sestertii*—that is, less than 10 per cent—would not be exceeded. The priesthoods were responsible for the routine rituals, but they were neither the financiers nor the consumers of the enormous costs caused by the large rituals intended for public display.

As a consequence, the economic importance of the public priesthoods for the economy and those areas deeply involved in religion is small: the production and selling of devotional objects, the meat industry, the international trade in exotic animals for the amphitheatres or in incense, and, last but not least, the building industry, did not depend on the *sacerdotes publici*.

The structure of the expenses, in particular the enormous share of the banquets, which would amount to 50 per cent of all costs if integrated into the balance sheet, shows the pontifical college mainly interacting among themselves. Status and personal interrelations were defined and maintained, not at the expense of religion, but through the medium of religion, and more precisely by a culinary potlatch. The religious activities of the priesthood—their jurisdiction, the routine rituals—were above all, from Cicero and the Tiberian period onwards, claimed to be important for the coherence of the religious practices as a whole,[55] but unimportant for the financing of religion and those economic sectors most intimately related to religious practices,[56] the

---

[54] App. *Mith*. 84.   [55] Thus Rüpke (2016).
[56] cf. already Felsmann (1937) for Delphi, and Castritius (1969: 52–62) for the late ancient Eastern Mediterranean.

production and distribution of votives, the production of meat, for trading exotic animals or incense.[57]

The lion's share of the costs of 'public', 'expensive' religion at Rome was accounted for by temples and games. They were financed by victorious generals, magistrates, or emperors. It was their willingness to contribute on a—statistically—regular basis that was responsible for the functioning of this part of the religious field. No fees for the private use of temples could replace these contributions. This is not to say, though, that religion was free of charge for the mass of the population. Instead, the structures of financing seem to repeat themselves. Monthly contributions of all members enabled the colleges to organize a minimum of cult and sociability, but only irregular endowments by patrons (or matrons) facilitated more frequent and more festive congregations.

The economic analysis enables us to test a frequently formulated hypothesis: did the public expropriations of the priesthoods' land possessions at the end of the fourth century by Valentinian and Gratian[58] cause the rapid end of the traditional cults now classified as 'pagan'?[59]

From an analysis of the structure of the priests' expenses, fixed costs are very limited. There are large possibilities to economize on expenditure. Parallel to the fiscal dispossessions, the state's demand of ritual and other services would be largely reduced. The ban on animal sacrifice rendered the purchase of sacrificial animals and the wages for the relevant specialists unnecessary. Other personnel could be replaced by each priest's own servants. The priests themselves belonged to the uppermost layer of society. Even the exorbitant costs of a *cena aditialis* would appear to be small in relation to their possessions; the share of the current costs of routine ritual would appear ridiculous. Thus, it was not the state dispossession of the priesthoods, but the general atmosphere in politics and society—of course furthered by such measures—that discouraged priests to continue their specifically ritual commitment and that led to the dissolution of the colleges within a few years, even if the pontiffs, for instance, continued the hunting-down of 'incestuous' Vestals.[60] This corroborates the interpretation of Alan Cameron that the lack

---

[57] See also Drexhage (1981); Montgomery (1991); Tert. *Idol*. 11.
[58] *Cod. Theod.* 5.13.3; 10.1.8; Symm. *Relat.* 3.11 ff.; Ambr. *Epist.* 72.14 and 73, *extr. coll.* 10.2. 6. 10 (all *CSEL* 82.3).
[59] As suggested by Cancik (1986: 72), and Chuvin (1990: 57).
[60] See the correspondence of Symmachus (O'Donnell 1979: 71–2). Cf., for local case studies in the decline of traditional religious investment, Leone (2013). See Rüpke and Glock (2008) for the prosopographical data; Salzman (1992) for the career perspectives. Cf. the case of the loss of state financing of Christian churches in the GDR (Hoffmann and Kehrer 1995).

of any evidence for the actual replacement of the easily replaceable public funding points to an unwillingness individually to associate with anything close to sacrificial ritual.[61]

Economics of Religion: Methodological Options

At the end of the historical analysis it should not be necessary to differentiate my approach from a theological reflection on the legitimacy of certain methods of financing in view of certain religious ends. It may, however, be useful to compare my approach and its stress on financing with those economics of religion that have been proffered in previous decades.

Theories of economics of religion have been propounded by Stark and Bainbridge, and by Iannaccone.[62] In a rather micro-economic approach, they concentrate on the individual as the subject of demand within a religious market. This market is occupied by different religions and cults, including the extreme of highly deviant sects. This is the market situation: what goods that are highly valued by the potential consumer are offered by the religions? Eternal bliss? And before that: integration within a community? Emotional support? Social security? How will the quality of the product be guaranteed (a central problem of all religious goods)? What will the acquisition of adequate information cost? What costs will be incurred after the choice, in terms of money, time, obligations to do without something, or obligations to behave in an unusual manner, let us say in the realm of food, sexual behaviour, or dress?

The economic theory of rational choice can explain the voluntary acceptance of such obligations. On the one hand, the religious group or organization erects high barriers to entrance in order to prevent free-riders—that is, people who take part in the evening orgy without having signed a standing order for their membership fee. The member who has accepted and passed the high barriers and is obliged to pay a high contribution in whatever form will intensify his deviant commitment in order to maximize his own benefits: once shorn, he will prefer participation in the morning prayer to secular activities.

My criticism of this approach may start from some general observations. The authors named take their test material and proofs from the US American middle classes only. This *is* a large segment of society, and probably some of

---

[61] Cameron (2011: 42–51). [62] e.g. Stark and Bainbridge (1987); Iannaccone (1998).

the results are transferable to western and central European societies. Yet, the specific conditions implied would have to have been reflected in the past. Thanks mostly to the electronic mass media, even in small localities a large spectrum of undogmatically differentiated denominations is present; charity plays an important role for the definition of social status; there is a large layer of society that controls freely allocatable money—all this is very important for the suitability of the concept of an ideal 'market'. For many religions of antiquity, and for the widespread forms of diffused, only minimally organized religiosity, 'membership' is a problematic concept. The 'resource mobilization theory' has demonstrated for the social and religious movements of the present that distant supporters or even benevolent spectators may be of high value.[63] Public support by the state might be more important than an additional number of members; in modern industrial societies, tax laws and the classification of an organization as non-profit are often a decisive criterion for the financial well-being and development of a religion.

The 'economics of religion' just criticized makes the far-reaching claim of explaining religious behaviour in general within the model of neoclassical economics. This attempt at an economic theory of religion is part of a neoclassical type of economics that defines economic behaviour, not substantially—that is, by limiting its subject to activities such as trade and production—but formally—namely, by conceptualizing every type of allocation of scarce resources as economic behaviour. The human actor is conceptualized as a rational human actor, rationally making his or her choices on the basis of quantifiable and comparable expectations.[64]

This theoretical enterprise, however, is neither left without criticism from within economics and the anthropology of economics, nor is it completed by using the market metaphor. To name just one example: Peter Berger, who—by the way—is the protagonist of the metaphor of a religious market, stresses the importance of a uniform horizon of plausibility for the functioning of religions.[65] If this claim is taken seriously, the market situation of religions has to be discussed within an alternative conceptual framework. Religion would then be a natural monopoly—that is, with a growing number of believers the marginal costs *per capita* would decrease instead of increase, as is the case

---

[63] McCarthy and Zald (1977); Richardson (1988: 3–7).

[64] Defence and critique of the rational choice theory is abundant: e.g. Young (1997); Spickard (1998); Zafirovski (1998) for an intensive debate. For a critique from a history-of-religion point of view, see, e.g., Brubaker (1984/2006); Chaves (1995); Kippenberg (1997); Bruce (1999); Mellor (2000); Boudon (2001); Heesterman (2001); Bankston (2002); Rüpke (2007).

[65] Fundamental: Berger (1967).

with usual goods. To put it less theoretically: the more persons believe in a specific god, the more easily others will join them. Another theoretical deficit of the rational-choice type of economics of religion is the lack of attention paid to external benefits. These external benefits are clearly demonstrated by the Roman example. The cost-intensive behaviour of individual benefactors—giving money for games or building temples—largely increases the utility for other users of the religious system, but does not improve the religion's utility for the donating individual and hence does not exert control over any market-adapted behaviour.

In contrast, the economics of religion as employed here has a much more limited object. It refers to a substantially defined, common-sense concept of economy. Its aim is to analyse economic relationships and interdependencies between religion and other systems of society, relations, and dependencies that might inform the conscious or subconscious behaviour of religious organizations. Of course, financial contributions by individuals are part of this analysis. However, it would be too hasty to interpret them as the outcome of market behaviour and use them as a scale of religious commitment. There are other economic models that might be more fruitful—for example, mechanisms such as redistribution and the different types of reciprocity that have been illustrated by the history of economics following Karl Polanyi.[66]

Such an enterprise renders the cooperation with the historical branch of economics necessary. If historians of religion analyse religious practices within the larger framework of culture and society, it is important to define the economic interaction of such practices and other fields not only in terms of quality, but—as far as possible—in terms of quantity, too. Here, methods and results would be the same as the ones of historical economics. Yet the primary object of interest is not the place of religion within a society's economic system, but the place of economic activities within the larger framework of religious agents and institutions' activities. Economics of religion, defined in this way, is not a new paradigm for the interpretation of religion, but just a field of historical research.

Conclusion

In this chapter I have tried to demonstrate the possibilities, or even the necessity, of 'economics of religion'. The answer to the question 'how much did

---

[66] Polanyi (1968).

religion cost at Rome?' appeared to be quite hypothetical, but the questions 'who paid?' and 'for what?' turned out to be quite fruitful. Finally, I have also tried to show the limits of an economic approach towards religion: this is not a plea for a new theory of religion, but for a fresh look at religious practices, agents, and institutions.

Acknowledgements

I am grateful to the editors and to Andrew Wilson in particular for the invitation to revise a paper published in a German version as 'Was kostet Religion? Quantifizierungsversuche für die Stadt Rom', in Hans G. Kippenberg and Brigitte Luchesi (eds), *Lokale Religionsgeschichte* (Marburg, 1995), 273–87. I am also grateful to Richard Gordon for more recent discussion of the topic, some of which is reflected here. I dedicate this chapter to Burkhard Gladigow, who first made me think about *Religionsökonomie*.

References

Appadurai, A., and Appadurai Breckenridge, C. (1976). 'The South Indian Temple: Authority, Honour and Redistribution', *Contributions to Indian Sociology* n.s. 10: 187–211.

Bankston, C. L. (2002). 'Rationality, Choice and the Religious Economy: The Problem of Belief', *Review of Religious Research* 43/4: 311–25.

Berger, P. L. (1967). *The Sacred Canopy: Elements of a Sociological Theory of Religion*. New York.

Bodei Giglioni, G. (1977). 'Pecunia fanatica: L'incidenza economica dei templi laziali', *Rivista storica italiana* 89: 33–76.

Bömer, F. (1981). *Untersuchungen über die Religion der Sklaven in Griechenland und Rom 1: Die wichtigsten Kulte und Religionen in Rom und im lateinischen Westen* (Forschungen zur antiken Sklaverei 14/1). Wiesbaden.

Boudon, R. (2001). 'Which Rational Action Theory for Future Mainstream Sociology: Methodological Individualism or Rational Choice Theory?', *European Sociological Review* 17/4: 451–7.

Brubaker, R. (1984/2006). *The Limits of Rationality: An Essay on the Social and Moral Thought of Max Weber*. Repr. edn. London.

Bruce, S. (1992). 'Funding the Lord's Work: A Typology of Religious Resourcing', *Social Compass* 39: 93–101.

Bruce, S. (1999). *Choice and Religion: A Critique of Rational Choice Theory.* Oxford.

Burford, A. (1965). 'The Economics of Greek Temple Building', *Proceedings of the Cambridge Philological Society* 191: 21–34.

Cameron, A. (2011). *The Last Pagans of Rome.* Oxford.

Cancik, H. (1986). 'Nutzen, Schmuck und Aberglaube: Ende und Wandlungen der römischen Religion im 4. und 5. Jahrhundert', in H. Zinser (ed.), *Der Untergang von Religionen.* Berlin, 65–90.

Castritius, H. (1969). *Studien zu Maximinus Daia* (Frankfurter Althistorische Studien 2). Kallmünz.

Cavallaro, M. A. (1984). *Spese e spettacoli: Aspetti economici-strutturali degli spettacoli nella roma giulio-claudia* (Antiquitas R. 1, 34). Bonn.

Chaves, M. (1995). 'On the Rational Choice Approach to Religion', *Journal for the Scientific Study of Religion* 34/1: 98–104.

Chuvin, P. (1990). *A Chronicle of the Last Pagans,* trans. B. A. Archer (Revealing Antiquity 4). Cambridge, MA.

Diakonoff, I. M. (1969) (ed.). *Ancient Mesopotamia: Socio-Economic History. A Collection of Studies by Soviet Scholars.* Moscow.

Drexhage, H.-J. (1981). 'Wirtschaft und Handel in den frühchristlichen Gemeinden (1.-3. Jh. n. Chr.)', *Römische Quartalschrift* 76: 1–72.

Duncan-Jones, R. (1982). *The Economy of the Roman Empire: Quantitative Studies.* Cambridge.

Duncan-Jones, R. (1990). *Structure and Scale in the Roman Economy.* Cambridge.

Felsmann, H. (1937). *Beiträge zur Wirtschaftsgeschichte von Delphi.* Hamburg.

Freyberg, H.-U. v. (1988). *Kapitalverkehr und Handel im römischen Kaiserreich (27 v. Chr.-235 n. Chr.)* (Schriftenreihe des Instituts für Allgemeine Wirtschaftsforschung der Albert-Ludwigs-Universität Freiburg 32). Freiburg.

Fuller, C. J. (1984). *Servants of the Goddess: The Priests of a South Indian Temple.* Cambridge.

Gelb, I. J. (1969). 'On the Alleged Temple and State Economies in Ancient Mesopotamia', in *Studi in onore di Eduardo Volterra,* vol. 6 (Pubblicazioni della Facoltà di giurisprudenza dell'Università di Roma). Rome, 137–54.

Gordon, R., Raja, R., and Rieger, A.-K. (2021). 'Economy and Religion', in J. Rüpke and G. Woolf (eds), *Religion in the Roman Empire* (Die Religionen der Menschheit 16.2). Stuttgart, 262–305.

Heesterman, J. C. (2001). 'Rituel et rationalité', in J. Bronkhorst (ed.), *La Rationalité en Asie/Rationality in Asia.* Lausanne, 153–64.

Hoffmann, T., and Kehrer, G. (1995). 'Finanzierung von Religion: Beispiel: DDR — Der Verlust von Staatsunterstützung', in H. G. Kippenberg and B. Luchesi (eds), *Lokale Religionsgeschichte.* Marburg, 289–93.

Horster, M. (2007). 'Living on Religion: Professionals and Personnel', in J. Rüpke (ed.), *A Companion to Roman Religion*. Oxford, 331–41.

Iannaccone, L. R. (1998). 'Introduction to the Economics of Religion', *Journal of Economic Literature* 36/3: 1465–95.

Janssen, J. J. (1979). 'The Role of the Temple in the Egyptian Economy during the New Kingdom', in E. Lipinński (ed.), *State and Temple Economy in the Ancient Near East*, vol. 2. Leuven, 505–15.

Kippenberg, H. G. (1997). 'Rationality in Studying Historical Religions', in J. S. Jensen (ed.), *Rationality and the Study of Religion*. Aarhus, 157–66.

Knapowski, R. (1961). *Der Staatshaushalt der römischen Republik* (Untersuchungen zur römischen Geschichte 2). Frankfurt a. M.

Knapowski, R. (1967). *Die Staatsrechnungen der römischen Republik in den Jahren 49–45 v. Chr* (Untersuchungen zur römischen Geschichte 4). Frankfurt a. M.

Koch, A. (2014). *Religionsökonomie eine Einführung*. 1. Aufl. edn. (Religionswissenschaft heute 10). Stuttgart.

Leone, A. (2013). *The End of the Pagan City: Religion, Economy, and Urbanism in Late Antique North Africa*. Oxford.

Linders, T. (1988). 'Continuity in Change: The Evidence of the Temple Accounts of Delos (Prolegomena to a Study of the Economic and Social Life of Greek Sanctuaries)', in R. Hägg, N. Marinatos, and G. C. Nordquist (eds), *Early Greek Cult Practice: Proceedings of the Fifth International Symposium at the Swedish Institute at Athens, 26–29 June, 1986*. Stockholm, 267–70.

Lipinński, E. (1979) (ed.). *State and Temple Economy in the Ancient Near East. Proceedings of the International Conference Organized by the Katholieke Universiteit Leuven from the 10th to the 14th of April 1978*, 2 vols (Orientalia Lovaniensia Analecta 5–6). Leuven.

Lozano, A. (2015). 'Imperium Romanum and the Religious Centres of Asia Minor: The Intervention of Roman Political Power on the Temples of Asia Minor', in J. M. Cortés Copete, E. Muñiz Grijalvo, and F. Lozano Gómez (eds), *Ruling the Greek World: Approaches to the Roman Empire in the East* (Potsdamer altertumswissenschaftliche Beiträge 52). Stuttgart, 67–90.

McCarthy, J. D., and Zald, M. N. (1977). 'Resource Mobilization and Social Movements: A Partial Theory', *American Journal of Sociology* 82/6: 1212–41, doi: 10.1086/226464.

Mellor, P. A. (2000). 'Rational Choice or Sacred Contagion? "Rationality", "Non-Rationality" and Religion', *Social Compass* 47/2: 273–92.

Méniel, P. (2015). 'Killing and Preparing Animals', in R. Raja and J. Rüpke (eds), *A Companion to the Archaeology of Religion in the Ancient World*. Malden, 155–66.

Mommsen, T. (1887a). *Römisches Staatsrecht*, vol. 1 (Handbuch der römischen Alterthümer). Leipzig.

Mommsen, T. (1887b). *Römisches Staatsrecht*, vol. 2.1 (Handbuch der römischen Alterthümer). Leipzig.

Montgomery, H. (1991). 'Old Wine in New Bottles? Some Views of the Economy of the Early Church', *Symbolae Osloenses* 66: 187–201.

O'Donnell, J. J. (1979). 'The Demise of Paganism', *Traditio*, 35: 45–88.

Orlin, E. M. (1997). *Temples, Religion and Politics in the Roman Republic* (Mnemosyne Suppl. 164). Leiden.

Pasqualini, A. (1969). 'Note su alcuni aspetti "politici" di un costume di epoca imperiale: Le sportulae municipali', *Helikon* 9–10: 265–312.

Pietri, C. (1978). 'Evergétisme et richesses ecclésiastique dans l'Italie du IVe à la fin du Ve s.: L'Exemple romain', *Ktèma* 3: 317–37.

Polanyi, K. (1968). *Primitive, Archaic and Modern Economies: Essays of Karl Polanyi*. Garden City, NY.

Postgate, N. (1994/2009). *Early Mesopotamia: Society and Economy at the Dawn of History*. Rev. edn. London.

Renger, J. (1979). 'Interaction of Temple, Palace, and "Private Enterprise" in the Old Babylonian Economy', in E. Lipinński (ed.), *State and Temple Economy in the Ancient Near East*, vol. 1. Leuven, 249–56.

Renger, J. (1984). 'Patterns of Non-Institutional Trade and Non-Commercial Exchange in Ancient Mesopotamia at the Beginning of the Second Millennium BC', in A. Archi (ed.), *Circulation of Goods in Non-Palatial Context in the Ancient Near East*. Rome, 31–123.

Renger, J. (1989). 'Probleme und Perspektiven einer Wirtschaftsgeschichte Mesopotamiens', *Saeculum* 40: 166–77.

Richardson, J. T. (1988). 'An Introduction', in J. T. Richardson (ed.), *Money and Power in the New Religions*. Lewiston, 1–20.

Rüpke, J. (1998). 'Kommensalität und Gesellschaftsstruktur: Tafelfreu(n)de im alten Rom', *Saeculum* 49: 193–215.

Rüpke, J. (2007). 'Der "Rational Choice Approach towards Religion": Theoriegeschichte als Religionsgeschichte', in W. Reinhard and J. Stagl (eds), *Menschen und Märkte: Studien zur historischen Wirtschaftsanthropologie* (Veröffentlichungen des Instituts für historische Anthropologie E.V.). Vienna, 435–49.

Rüpke, J. (2008a). 'Economy III. Economy and Religion 1. General', *RPP* 4: 278.

Rüpke, J. (2008b). *Fasti Sacerdotum: A Prosopography of Pagan, Jewish, and Christian Religious Officials in the City of Rome, 300 BC to AD 499*, trans. D. M. B. Richardson. Oxford.

Rüpke, J. (2016). 'Knowledge of Religion in Valerius Maximus' Exempla: Roman Historiography and Tiberian Memory Culture', in K. Galinsky (ed.), *Memory in Ancient Rome and Early Christianity*. Oxford, 89–111.

Rüpke, J. (2018). *Pantheon: A New History of Roman Religion*, trans. D. M. B. Richardson. Princeton.

Rüpke, J., and Glock, A. (2008). *Fasti sacerdotum: A Prosopography of Pagan, Jewish, and Christian Religious Officials in the City of Rome, 300 BC to AD 499*, trans. D. M. B. Richardson. Oxford.

Salzman, M. R. (1992). 'How the West Was Won: The Christianization of the Roman Aristocracy in the West in the Years after Constantine', in C. Deroux (ed.), *Studies in Latin Literature and Roman History*, vol. 6. Brussels, 451–79.

Schlaifer, R. (1940). 'Notes on Athenian Public Cults', *HSCP* 51: 233–60.

Schluchter, W. (1988) (ed.). *Max Webers Sicht des okzidentalen Christentums: Interpretation und Kritik*. Frankfurt a. M.

Schluchter, W. (1989). *Rationalism, Religion, and Domination: A Weberian Perspective*, trans. Neil Solomon. Berkeley and Los Angeles.

Schöllgen, G. (1990). 'Sportulae: Zur Frühgeschichte des Unterhaltsanspruchs der Kleriker', *ZKG* 101: 1–20.

Shatzman, I. (1975). *Senatorial Wealth and Roman Politics* (Collection Latomus 142). Brussels.

Sokolowski, F. (1954). 'Fees and Taxes in the Greek Cults', *HThR* 47: 153–64.

Spickard, J. V. (1998). 'Rethinking Religious Social Action: What is "Rational" about Rational Choice Theory?', *Sociology of Religion* 59/2: 99–115.

Stark, R., and Bainbridge, W. S. (1987). *A Theory of Religion*. New Brunswick, NJ.

Toller, O. (1889). *De spectaculis, cenis, distributionibus in municipiis romanis occidentis imperatorum aetate exhibitis* (Diss. Leipzig (Wachsmuth, Gardthausen)). Altenburg.

Weber, A. (1924). *De sacerdotum apud Graecos reditibus* (Diss. masch. Halle).

Weber, M. (1905/2014). *Gesamtausgabe I,9: Asketischer Protestantismus und Kapitalismus: Schriften und Reden 1904–1911*. Tübingen.

Wendt, H. (2016). *At the Temple Gates: The Religion of Freelance Experts in the Roman Empire*. New York.

Wesch-Klein, G. (1990). *Liberalitas in rem publicam: Private Aufwendungen zugunsten von Gemeinden im römischen Afrika bis 284 n. Chr* (Antiquitas, R. 1 (Abhandlungen zur Alten Geschichte), 40). Bonn.

Wissowa, G. (1912). *Religion und Kultus der Römer* (Handbuch der Altertumswissenschaft 5.4). Munich.

Wörrle, M. (1988). *Stadt und Fest im kaiserzeitlichen Kleinasien: Studien zu einer agonistischen Stiftung aus Oinoanda* (Vestigia 39). Munich.

Young, L. A. (1997). *Rational Choice Theory and Religion: Summary and Assessment.* New York.

Zafirovski, M. (1998). 'Socio-Economics and Rational Choice Theory: Specification of their Relations', *The Journal of Socio-Economics* 27/2: 165–205.

3

Investing in Religion

Religion and the Economy in Pre-Roman Central Italy

Charlotte R. Potts

Studies of the role of religion in a range of pre-industrial economies make it possible, and helpful, to assess the distinctive elements of this subject in ancient Rome by comparison with practice elsewhere. This chapter accordingly surveys the economic significance of Etrusco-Italic sanctuaries in the period preceding the Roman Republic. Beyond providing an analogy for later centuries, however, it suggests that many of the economic aspects of Roman religion were actually shaped by developments in the Archaic period (*c*.580–480 BC). The characteristic features of Archaic sanctuaries developed in response to a combination of Mediterranean-wide and local circumstances, and arguably met the needs of their communities so successfully that they had a lasting influence on the form and function of their Roman counterparts. This review furthermore indicates that the city of Rome may have had a precocious ability to capitalize on piety. As a result, this chapter contributes to discussions of Roman religious economics by reconstructing their broader historical and theoretical contexts, with 'Roman' referring to both a place and a period.

The range of evidence now available for early sanctuaries makes them a useful case study for exploring the economic force of religion in pre-Roman Italy. In the years since the 1960s, excavations have provided new information about religious sites and rituals at Rome, Pyrgi, Graviscae, Satricum, and Tarquinia, among others, and publications of finds and collections continue to permit further study. Yet the limits of this evidence are considerable. Although Etruria was once a highly literate culture, scant textual evidence has survived and the onus falls on archaeology to yield information about religion, the economy, and society. Greek and Roman authors can be mined for relevant material, but their accounts are often biased or anachronistic. It is also necessary to balance the fact that Etruscan cities had their own rituals, institutions, and aesthetics with evidence of shared social and political elements to avoid giving a misleading impression of coherence in data drawn from different times and places. The result is often a model informed by both classical and anthropological archaeology rather than a set of quantifiable data, and economic studies are no exception.[1]

With these cautions in mind, this chapter will analyse the economic role of sanctuaries in Archaic Etruria and Latium. The Archaic period saw unprecedented investment in sanctuaries after a long history of religious activity that saw cult sites marked and augmented over the course of many centuries. During the sixth century BC, temples were built in Rome, Satricum, Tarquinia, Pyrgi, and Veii, and rituals were enhanced with buildings in places such as Lavinium and Gravisca. Sanctuaries increased in size and prominence and became some of the most significant features of settlements and landscapes. The monumentalization of Archaic cult sites thus marks the sixth century BC as a turning point in the history of religious activity in early Italy and the resources accorded to it. The first two sections of this chapter will survey the consumption, production, and exchange of commodities at these flagship sanctuaries. The following two sections consider what conditions may have prompted new investment in cult sites at this time. Finally, it will be suggested that the results set the stage—almost literally—for the conduct of sanctified Roman business.

Tangible Commodities

Excavations and new analyses are continually informing reconstructions of the nature of Archaic sanctuaries and the resources committed to their creation, maintenance, and activities. It has long been clear that one of the largest categories of expenditure, and hence a logical starting point to assess consumption, is construction. Temples differed architecturally from other structures and the shrines that preceded them through distinctive combinations of high substructures, columns, and exuberant terracotta roofs. Although details of walls often remain unclear owing to the use of perishable building materials, even the bases and roofs of these buildings represent considerable expense. For example, reconstructions of the Archaic Capitoline Temple in Rome estimate that between 28,000 and 32,000 m³ of dressed stone were used in the foundations alone; the labour and skills required for the quarrying, transport, and interlocking placement of the stones establish that the

---

[1] cf. Perkins (2014: 64).

substructure itself was an immense architectural project.² The timbers and woodwork that supported the roofs of Archaic temples required mature trees and skilled carpenters, and tiles were another outlay. The roof tiles for the Temple of Castor in Rome, for example, required an estimated minimum of 25 tons of clay, while the Temple at Satricum would have used approximately 17 tons, and the decorative elements at the edges of most temple roofs would have increased such totals further.³ The mud bricks and *pisé* of temple walls, stucco on walls and columns, and the paint that coloured them all should also be added to tallies of the resources invested in Archaic temples. Cult buildings were an expense, but as offerings to secure favour and a means of gaining renown they may also have been seen as investments.

The objects that were ritually deposited in sanctuaries represent ongoing consumption. Etrusco-Italic votive items include vases, tableware, *aes rude*, weapons, jewellery, figurines, weaving implements, musical instruments, anatomical votives, and architectural models, sometimes inscribed with words referencing giving (in Etruscan, *mulvani-* and *tur-*), divinities (*ais-*, *flere*, and specific names of gods and goddesses), and the name of the donor. The quantity and quality of these dedications are significant. The so-called Archaic deposit at Satricum contained approximately twenty thousand artefacts,[4] and more than thirty thousand miniature vessels have been found at the northeast cult site at Pratica di Mare (Lavinium).[5] Expensive bronzes are also attested. More than forty-six bronzes with imagery referencing aristocratic activities including war, hunting, and banqueting were immersed in a swamp shrine at Brolio,[6] and fourth-century BC dedications of free-standing statues such as the Mars of Todi and the Chimera of Arezzo probably had earlier correlates. Such dedications mark sanctuaries as substantial consumers of art and repurposed goods.

Sacrifices are another form of religious consumption, the conduct of which is indicated by archaeological remains and artistic depictions. Some Etruscan altars had vertical channels suitable for carrying liquid offerings to chthonic deities, while rites of fire are suggested by images such as a relief on a Chiusine cippus and a painted panel from Caere.[7] Wine, blood, plants, and incense may all have been offered to the gods as well as meat. The Ricci hydria, thought to

---

[2] Hopkins (2016: 99).   [3] Rendeli (1990: 139).   [4] Waarsenburg and Maas (2001: 45).
[5] Fenelli and Guaitoli (1990: 185).   [6] Romualdi (1981).
[7] For an overview of altars in Etruria between the seventh and fourth centuries BC, see Menichelli (2009). Cippus from Chiusi: Perugia, Museo Archeologico Nazionale, inv. no. 634, pre-520 BC. Panel from Caere: The 'Campana Panel' from the Banditaccia necropolis at Caere, *c*.550–525 BC. 1.24 m high. Paris, Musée du Louvre, Collection Campana 1863. For other sacrificial images in Etruscan art, see Cristofani (1995b: plates XIX–XX).

have been made by a Greek or Greek-trained artist living in Etruria and working for a wealthy Etruscan client in Caere,[8] shows part of an animal being cooked on an altar, and zooarchaeological analyses at sanctuaries including Tarquinia, Pyrgi, and Poggio Colla have so far identified offerings of tortoises, molluscs, fish, birds, foxes, badgers, dogs, sheep or goats, pigs, horses, and cattle.[9] The level of meat in Etruscan diets has yet to be clarified, but the use of animal sacrifice to redistribute protein to the community should not be overlooked. Another resource that may have been removed from circulation at sanctuaries, albeit in small numbers, is people. While many of the literary sources cited in discussions of human sacrifice in early Italy were written by Greek and Roman authors later than the events they describe,[10] some burials in sanctuaries suggest ritual killing. At the Pian di Civita sanctuary at Tarquinia, Individuals 5 and 9 were buried next to and partially under new structures, possibly as 'construction sacrifices', and Individual 10, whose bones identify him as a male in his thirties and probably a foreign sailor, may have been a prisoner of war who was ritually killed and buried.[11] The scale of such activities is likely to have been small and disproportional to their significance.

If we turn from consumption to production, evidence of kilns and metallurgy in some sanctuaries suggests that cult sites could have dedicated artisans and workshops. Kilns have been found at the Archaic sanctuaries of Montetosto, Monte Li Santi, the Sanctuary of the Thirteen Altars at Lavinium, and the Pian di Civita plateau at Tarquinia, and wasters suggest there were once kilns at Pyrgi.[12] Ceramic production could have included roof tiles, architectural terracottas, and votives. The double kiln at Lavinium may have been used to make the hundreds of loom weights present in the building north-east of the altar complex, presumably a venue for weaving that may in turn have provided textiles for the matrimonial rites observed at the sanctuary.[13] Excavations at Gravisca have uncovered the remains of at least fifteen furnaces, wells, a number of small metal objects, and iron, copper, and lead slags that together indicate a long sequence of metallurgy,[14] presumably for

---

[8] Warden (2008: 121, 125). The vase was found in the Banditaccia necropolis at Caere, dates to c.540–530 BC, and is in the Museo Nazionale Etrusco di Villa Giulia.

[9] Rafanelli (2013: 571).

[10] e.g. Livy 22.57.1–6; Plutarch, *Marc.* 3.4; Macrobius, *Saturnalia* 1.7.35.

[11] Bonghi Jovino, Mallegni, and Usai (1997); Bonghi Jovino and Chiaramonte Treré (1997: 41, 100–2, 58–60); Bonghi Jovino (2008: 33–7; 2010: 165–6, with fig. 4 showing the location of the burials); De Grummond (2016: 146–9, 159–65).

[12] Sassatelli, Melis, and Ciaghi (1985); Edlund-Berry (2011: 355); Potts (2015: 138–9, 143) with references.

[13] Gleba (2008: 187).

[14] Fiorini (2001: 136–7); Fiorini and Torelli (2007: 79–88; 2010: 30–1).

offerings, trade, or the cult buildings. Similarly, iron slags have been found on the *arx* at Satricum, near the Temple of Mater Matuta, in multiple stratigraphic layers with a concentration in the seventh and sixth centuries BC.[15] The possible products can be gauged by the iron objects found close by in Votive Deposit I: an exceptional range and number of tools, weapons, shafts, rods, spits, nails, rings, and ornaments signal the high status of the sanctuary, and there is also evidence of copper working.[16] In Etruria, hundreds of pieces of worked antler have been found at the Pian di Civita sanctuary in Tarquinia with geometric shapes and consistent 4-mm-thick cross sections that could identify them as *sortes* for a divination rite.[17] If they were produced at the sanctuary for ritual use, then this is another example of a sanctuary capable of contributing to its own material needs.

It does not automatically follow, however, that these were closed cycles of production and consumption. Literary and archaeological evidence suggests that some sanctuaries hosted fairs and markets and as such played a role in local, regional, and even international trade. As part of an account of conflict between the Romans and Sabines in the time of the Roman king Servius Tullius (traditionally 578–534 BC), Dionysius of Halicarnassus offers this description of the sanctuary of Feronia:

> To this sanctuary people used to resort from the neighbouring cities on the appointed days of festival, many of them performing vows and offering sacrifice to the goddess and many with the purpose of trafficking during the festive gathering as merchants, artisans and husbandmen; and here were held fairs more celebrated than in any other places in Italy.[18]

The arrest of Roman traders at the festival became a rationale for war.[19] Merchants have also been connected with the celebrated Etruscan sanctuary of the Fanum Voltumnae. During his account of campaigns against the Volsci and the Aequi, Livy reports that the Romans received intelligence from traders that a hostile league of Etruscan *principes* was assembling at the sanctuary;[20] for this to be plausible, the traders must have been at the shrine or in contact with colleagues who had been. These historical asides are tantalizing but far from definitive. Archaeology offers more circumstantial evidence for exchange, although it is worth noting that attempts to distinguish

---

[15] Nijboer (1998: 259).   [16] Nijboer (1998: 263).   [17] De Grummond (2016: 149–51).
[18] *Ant. Rom.* 3.32.1. English translation by E. Cary (Loeb text, 1937).
[19] See also Livy 1.30.5.   [20] Livy 6.2.2.

between evidence of contact, gift-giving, trade, and exchange in pre-monetary economies are not straightforward and such distinctions may be anomalous.

In Latium, the first monumental temple was built at Rome in the space known as the Forum Boarium. The sanctuary arose on a low, riverside site next to the Tiber River that provided a natural landing area for ships coming from the coast and pausing at Rome or travelling upriver to Veii, Antemnae, Fidenae, and Crustumerium.[21] Connections with major roads are likely to have increased the appeal to travellers: here ended the Via Salaria, bringing salt and transhumant herds to local exchanges, while one of the principal roads between Etruria and Campania passed close by and may have motivated the construction of Rome's first bridge, the Pons Sublicius.[22] The significance of this area as a point of contact with outsiders may also be reflected in a range of myths and legends about the area that feature heroes, kings, and Greeks or other figures from the east. Aeneas, Evander, and Hercules were all linked with the locale in stories such as that of the battle between Hercules and Cacus over cattle that in turn evoke the use of the land as a general crossing point for people, goods, and animals.[23] International imports are evident from the eighth century BC onwards in sherds of late Geometric, Euboean, Cycladic, and Corinthian ceramics, as well as Ischian and Cumaean imitations of Corinthian styles.[24] Finds of carved amber, bone pendants, sheet-bronze figurines, a range of Greek ceramics, alabaster vases, and sherds inscribed with Latin and Greek names indicate that the site had become an international sanctuary by the Archaic period. A *tessera hospitalis* from the mid-sixth century gives more personal insight. On the back is the name *araz silqetenas spurianus*,[25] suggesting either visits by Etruscan aristocrats, as the Spurinna were a significant family at Tarquinia, or wider commercial contacts if the dedication was a trading token left by Araz of Sulcis in Sardinia.[26] There are thus clear indications that the site received goods and worshippers from outside Rome.

Like the Forum Boarium, Satricum was a highly accessible site situated at the intersection of important trade routes, including pathways running north and south between Caere and Campania and also east into the interior of Latium.[27] The Astura River, arguably the most important river in Latium

---

[21] Similarities with ceramics from Veii also suggest that travellers used the river as a route into Etruria, rather than viewing Latial ports as final destinations: Beijer (1995: 61). The existence of a sixth-century BC port at the Forum Boarium is the subject of scholarly debate: while Coarelli (1988: 113–27) argues in favour, Säflund (1932: 175) and Smith (1996: 180–1) offer another view.
[22] On the topography of the Archaic Forum Boarium, see Coarelli (1988); Pisani Sartorio (1989); Smith (1996: 179–80); Coarelli (2007: 307–8). On roads in the area, see Coarelli (1988: fig. 22).
[23] Livy 1.7.4–7; Virgil, *Aeneid* 8.193–270.
[24] La Rocca (1982: 47–8); Holloway (1994: 165–7).   [25] *CIE* II.2.8602.
[26] Cristofani (1990: 21); Glinister (2003: 138).   [27] Pellegrini (2002: 91).

south of the Tiber,[28] connected the settlement to the sea. Finds in tombs and the Archaic votive deposit include imports from Greece, Egypt, Rhodes, and the Levantine–Cypriot and Baltic regions as well as Corinthian and Proto-Corinthian wares, along with a wealth of artefacts in gold, silver, gilt silver, faience, ivory, and amber.[29] The Temple itself also provides evidence of contacts beyond Latium, as petrographic and stylistic analyses of the tiles placed on it in *c.*535 BC reveal that the roof was imported from Caere, presumably by sea.[30] Exchange, as opposed to contact, may be indicated by the discovery of two metallic weight standards at the site. The first weight roughly corresponds to a Roman–Oscan pound and dates to the second half of the seventh century BC.[31] The second is one gram short of an Italian or Campanian pound and was found in the Archaic votive deposit along with a small balance.[32] Weight standards could have been used in reciprocal or redistributive exchanges and do not necessarily signify a market system, but it has been suggested that the unusual quantity of metal artefacts and evidence for manufacturing at Satricum 'may indicate an Italian exchange mechanism based on commercial exchange with fixed correlations for the value of different metals'.[33] Finds of weights in other sanctuaries—for example, at Olympia in Greece and Francavilla Marittima in southern Italy—have been interpreted as a sign that certain sanctuaries could have guaranteed the value and content of fixed measures. Such practices potentially foreshadow the storage of weight standards in the Temple of Castor and Pollux at Rome.[34]

The Etruscan sanctuary of Pyrgi also clearly had contacts beyond Etruria. The cult site lay on the Tyrrhenian coast and was connected to the city of Caere further inland by a monumental road.[35] In 1964 excavations in the Monumental Sanctuary uncovered three gold tablets inscribed in Etruscan and Phoenician/Punic. The texts record the dedication of a structure to Uni/Astarte by the Caeretan leader Thefarie Velianas.[36] The tablets date to *c.*500 BC, roughly contemporary with Temple B, and nail holes around their sides suggest

---

[28] Nijboer et al. (1999–2000: 170). See also Attema, de Haas, and Tol (2011: 53).
[29] Beijer (1995: 58–9); Bouma (1996: i. 185–6).
[30] Lulof (2000: 211 with n. 13; 2006); Winter (2009: 537).
[31] Nijboer (1994; 1998: 303–4). It weighs *c.*267 g and has lost weight owing to corrosion and scratching. The Roman–Oscan pound weighs *c.*273 g.
[32] Nijboer (1998: 303–6). The weight is corroded and weighs *c.*340 g. The Italian or Roman–Attic/Campanian pound weighs *c.*341 g.
[33] Nijboer (1998: 306–7).
[34] Nijboer (1998: 306); see also Maggiani (2012) and Biella (2019) for other examples of weights from Etrusco-Italic sanctuaries (including Caere, Graviscae, Chianciano Terme, and Tarquinia) and discussion.
[35] The site has an enormous bibliography; for general reference, see Colonna (1970).
[36] *CIE* II.I.4.6312–16.

that they may have been attached directly to the cult building.[37] The bilingual inscriptions are often linked with Aristotle's later description of commercial treaties between the Tyrrhenians and the Carthaginians,[38] and the tablets anticipate a Phoenician audience and imply that a Phoenician scribe was present in the sanctuary or its vicinity. The strongest sign of trade, rather than contact, is a collection of nine silver *tetradrachms* excavated at the rear of Temple A. The coins date to approximately the mid-fifth century BC and were issued by Attica, Leontini, Messana, and Syracuse. The fact that these types of coins did not circulate in Etruria has given rise to proposals that Greek coins were hoarded at the sanctuary as a form of bullion.[39] In this scenario the sanctuary and its environs had separate exchange mechanisms, and the cult site assumes a significant role in long-distance trade. The coins have also been viewed as remnants of the legendary wealth of the sanctuary looted by Dionysius I of Syracuse in 384 BC.[40] Such riches have led the excavators to suggest that the sanctuary served as one of Caere's treasuries from *c.*460 BC onwards,[41] a situation with closer parallels in Greece than currently known in Etruria.

These select examples indicate that Etrusco-Italic sanctuaries probably had significant economic functions. Some would have focused on local needs and others been part of regional or international networks. Their most important functions, however, may have been even less quantifiable, as will now be shown.

Intangible Commodities

Etrusco-Italic sanctuaries were also centres for the production, consumption, and exchange of less tangible commodities. The seafaring and astronomical information that enabled maritime exploration, the myths and rituals that directed religious action, and the writing transmitted by scribal schools may all be regarded as sanctuary assets.[42] As venues for elite display, sanctuaries played a vital role in the creation and maintenance of status. These spaces thus functioned as repositories of knowledge and power.

---

[37] Heurgon (1966); Colonna (1970: 597–604); Pallottino (1970).
[38] Aristotle, *Politics* 3.5.10–11.
[39] Baglione (1985); Colonna (2005: 2194); Nijboer (1998: 60, 63).
[40] Diodorus Siculus 15.14.3–4.   [41] Baglione et al. (2015: 227).
[42] Pappa (2015: 55). On scribal schools, see Wallace (2008: 26).

The practice of giving an item to a god removed it from circulation and established sanctuaries as places for conspicuous consumption. By dedicating only items that they could afford to be without, worshippers turned lavish offerings such as statues and buildings into public statements of wealth. Inscribed objects could continue to advertise their generosity long after the fact. At the Campo della Fiera Sanctuary near Orvieto, an inscribed statue base records the religiosity and disposable income of a freedwoman named Kanuta from the *gens* Laracena.[43] The Pyrgi plaques, nailed to a doorjamb or wall, kept the magnanimity of Thefarie Velianas on permanent display. Piety could thus proclaim fortune and reinforce status.

Status was inherently relative. Gifts to the gods can be interpreted within a wider context of ancient gift-giving, as evident in Etruria and Latium as it was in contemporary Greece. Select artefacts in funerary and domestic contexts carried inscriptions that identify them as gifts between aristocrats and memorialize the names of their donors. Studies of gift exchange in premonetary cultures and the literary evidence from Archaic Greece suggest that the objects given derived prestige from both their intrinsic worth and their value as a marker of social ties.[44] Such exchanges were often viewed as social contracts creating debts to be discharged in future, functioning as stored capital. The Roman model of votive activity encapsulated in the formula *do ut des* ('I give so that you may give')—if applicable in Etruria—appears to have extended relationships between people to relationships with the gods. Votives asked the deity to reciprocate or showed that they had discharged their obligation, and thereby made relationships with the gods palpable.[45] It has been argued that human, noble, and divine were not distinct categories as much as a spectrum of existence in Etruria,[46] and votives that fostered expensive obligations could signal a privileged position on it.

Status may also have been displayed at sanctuaries in the conflation of religious and political leadership. Much of the evidence that priests and priestesses were elite members of Etrusco-Italic society postdates the Archaic period, but there are indications of continuity with earlier practice. In Etruria, epitaphs identify individuals who were both priests (most often *cepen* in Etruscan, attested from the seventh century BC) and magistrates (often titled *zilath*).[47] The inscribed sarcophagus of Laris Pulenas at Tarquinia, dating to the third century BC, identifies him as a priest of the cults of Catha, Hermes,

---

[43] Stopponi (2011: 42).
[44] Morris (1986); Mauersberg (2015); and Moser and Smith (2019: 5, 8–9) for central Italy.
[45] Becker (2009: 88–9).   [46] Warden (2009: 209).
[47] For overviews, see Lambrechts (1959); Haack (2003); De Grummond (2006: 34–9).

and Pacha, the author of a work on haruspicy, and holder of magisterial offices,[48] while the cinerary urn of Arnth Remzna of Chiusi, also dated to the third century BC, names the occupant as a *zilath* and depicts him wearing the hat of a haruspex.[49] The wall paintings of the Tomb of the Funerary Bed in Tarquinia, dating to *c.*460 BC, offer earlier evidence with the pointed hats worn by haruspices lying on a couch;[50] as painted tombs at Tarquinia probably belonged to an elite minority, this may show that religious offices were held by those with high social status during the fifth century BC. In Latin sources, Cicero describes religious duties being handed down between noble families and records a second-century BC decree of the Roman Senate ordering elite families to perpetuate the body of Etruscan religious lore known as the *etrusca disciplina*.[51] If a theocratic elite led activities at sanctuaries, then the exercise of religious power would have further reinforced their status.

Other activities can be entertained in reconstructions of sanctuary affairs. Spectacles are thought to have been as important in Etrusco-Italic religion as its Greek and Roman counterparts, and Livy's description of a festival with actors that took place in 403 BC has been interpreted as a reference to federated games at the Fanum Voltumnae.[52] Livy also writes that leaders from all over Etruria came to the sanctuary to discuss military campaigns and arrange civic affairs.[53] These activities are likely to have facilitated the exercise of power and the displays of status entwined with it. The more tangible elements of sanctuary business no doubt fed into this arrangement as well. It has been suggested that the rulers of Satricum used their control over both the cult and local industry to conduct ritualized exchanges and amass prestigious goods,[54] with the sanctuary's wealth representing both personal and institutionalized hoarding. It has also been proposed that Greek coins were found at Pyrgi but not in its hinterland, because economic regulation was instituted there by those who benefited from the protection of local agricultural production, the trading of its surplus, and the possession of imported items that could be purchased with that surplus—namely, landowning elites.[55] Such reconstructions posit that sanctuaries traded metals, crops, animals, pottery, and textiles, along with economic, social, and religious power. The system that may have facilitated this range will now be explored.

---

[48] *CIE* II.I.5430; Jannot (2005: 7). [49] *CIE* I.1192. Turfa (2005: 263–5).
[50] Steingräber (2006: 139–40). [51] Cicero, *Ad fam.* 6.6; *De div.* 1.92.
[52] Livy 5.1.5; Camporeale (2010: 158); Warden (2012: 95). [53] Livy 4.23.5; 4.25.6–7; 6.2.2.
[54] Waarsenburg and Maas (2001: 52–3). [55] Nijboer (1998: 60–3).

Archaic Rationales

A symbiotic relationship between religion and trade has been recognized in contexts well beyond pre-Roman central Italy. In ancient Asia Minor, Greece, and Egypt, there is evidence that religious sites benefited from, and may have actively exploited, a tendency for exchange to happen in their vicinity. Similar situations have also been found in societies far from the Classical world. This has led anthropologists, ethnographers, and sociologists to assert that religion can play a useful role in regulating market systems in the absence, or limited presence, of governmental oversight in pre-industrial societies.[56] The conduct of trade in such contexts is integral to this model. Studies have argued that, when fewer pre-existing social relationships exist between trading partners, there is a risk that one side will take advantage, and exchanges will be unequal or unfair. Encounters with unfamiliar trading partners furthermore have an inherent risk of misunderstandings and volatility. This higher risk of fraud, inequality, and danger is fertile ground for actions that promote trust. Here widely recognized rituals can create a standardized set of expectations and behaviour that function as a *lingua franca* for interaction. Exchanges that occur under divine oversight could use the gods as witnesses and guarantors: the possibility that fraudulent transactions may be punished with divine retribution meant that ritual observance could generate a degree of trust that is valuable, and even marketable, in an uncertain world.[57] Religion can thus serve as a mechanism for facilitating productive exchange, and sanctuaries can become desirable commercial spaces.

The fact that scholars have recognized a connection between religion and trade in chronologically and geographically disparate settings raises the question of why Etrusco-Italic communities seem to have invested so much in this relationship during the Archaic period. Changes affecting communities around the Mediterranean undoubtedly provided a spur. While contact between different Mediterranean cultures had long occurred through warfare, intermarriage, travel, and trade, archaeological evidence suggests that the movement of goods and peoples across long distances sharply intensified between the second half of the eighth and the end of the sixth centuries BC. The increasing circulation of luxury objects from the Levant, Anatolia, Egypt,

---

[56] Torelli (1986: 47); Smith (1996: 147); Garraty (2010: 24–5); Demetriou (2012: 233–5). Horden and Purcell (2000: 432–3) note the relationship but doubt whether it was deliberately cultivated. For particular case studies beyond the ancient Mediterranean, see Bohannan and Bohannan (1968), Nigeria; Hudson and Van de Mieroop (2002), ancient Near East; Abbott (2010), Arizona.

[57] Smith (2001: 21); Glinister (2003: 143–4); Garraty (2010: 24–5).

and western Asia through parts of Italy, Greece, Phoenicia, and Iberia around the seventh century BC is reflected in the common description of the period as 'Orientalizing', and there is also evidence that people travelled more extensively: the correspondence between names on pots dedicated at Gravisca and names recorded at Naukratis indicates the movement of sailors and traders, as does the discovery of an Etruscan text on lead at Pech Maho on the Languedoc coast, and pilgrims such as the Etruscan king Arimnestus appear to have travelled to wealthy Greek sanctuaries to make dedications.[58] Artisans are likely to have travelled between workshops, and the westward spread of new technical skills in bronze work, goldsmithing, ivory-carving, and gem-cutting, as well as the use of moulds, particularly during the period of the Assyrian conquests of Syria–Palestine, also indicate the movement of craftsmen and technology.[59] Permanent migrations are suggested by the considerable number of Greek, Carthaginian, Phoenician, and Etruscan colonies. The mobility of the seventh and sixth centuries BC is thus likely to have seen knowledge, languages, and stories circulating alongside objects.[60]

Sociological models would suggest that this increased contact between members of different cultures resulted in systems for managing, and benefiting from, such encounters. Many Hellenic communities seem to have capitalized on the opportunities offered by a religious framework. For example, it has been suggested that the exceptional wealth of the Heraion on Samos in the late eighth and early seventh centuries BC stemmed from dedications by emissaries of high-ranking individuals from Egypt, Cyprus, and the Near East.[61] These offerings could have been prompted by a wish to acknowledge the hosts' customs, signal good intentions, and build confidence that was subsequently used in the conduct of additional, often commercial, interactions.[62] The topography of the sanctuary also seems to have been significant. Rather than being placed in a settlement, the sanctuary stood 6 km to the east on the coast, near the

---

[58] Pausanias 5.12.5; Gran-Aymerich (2009); cf. Smith (1999: 189); Horden and Purcell (2000: 438–60). Names at Gravisca and Naukratis: Moretti (1984); Torelli (1982); Smith (1996: 145); Möller (2000: 166–81). Pech Maho: Lejeune, Pouilloux, and Solier (1988); Cristofani (1995a: 132–3); Gras (1995: 159–61); Malkin (2011: 166).

[59] Burkert (1992: 21–5); Ciafaloni (2006); cf. Smith (1996: 73). The story of the Veientine sculptor Vulca who undertook commissions in Rome (Pliny, *HN* 35.157) may recall similar movements, but is not direct evidence for them, nor is the tale of Demaratus, a Corinthian trader and nobleman who left Corinth to settle in Etruscan Tarquinia (Livy 1.34): Ridgway (2012).

[60] On horizontal social mobility, see Ampolo (1976–7). On mobility more generally, see Cristofani (1996) and Riva (2006: 111).

[61] Kyrieleis (2006; 2009: 140–1) with references.

[62] Kyrieleis (2009); cf. Gregory (1980: 644) on how some votives are 'manifestly a vehicle for the expression of relations between men', and Osborne (2004: 2) arguing that votives 'establish a particular model of reciprocity which has a profound effect on all exchange'.

marshy mouth of the Imbrasos River, where there was an area suitable for landing flat-bottomed Greek ships.[63] In c.560 BC a dipteral temple (the so-called Temple III) replaced an eighth-century building and a seventh-century shrine.[64] Within a decade the temple had been destroyed. Its replacement (Temple IV), begun in c.530 BC and located 40 m to the east, became renowned for having the largest known floor plan of any Archaic Greek temple.[65] Contact, wealth, and investment in religious infrastructure seem closely linked.

Further up the Ionian coast, the Artemision at Ephesos also offered favourable commercial conditions. The Archaic Temple of Artemis, completed in c.550 BC, drew pilgrims, royalty, sightseers, and merchants who traded and made votive offerings. 'Ephesian ware', found only in Ephesos and Sardis, indicates a special relationship with the Lydian empire, and gifts such as Corinthian aryballoi and Phoenician leg plates decorated with symbols of the Egyptian gods Bastet and Hathor can be traced back to mainland Greece and the Levantine coast.[66] Many of these visitors made use of the nearby harbour and 'holy port'.[67] The harbour was central to Ephesos' role as a gateway between the Aegean Sea and important land routes across Anatolia, including the east–west Laodicea road, the northern road to Smyrna, and the road to Sardis and Galatea in the north-east.[68] Its topography conferred sufficient wealth and influence for the city to be relocated more than once in response to the silting-up of a useful landing site. Again, a sanctuary and port underpinned a renowned Archaic centre of trade and religious tourism.

Archaic Egypt offered traders another sacred environment for conducting business. Naukratis was one of the earliest ports in the region. Excavations indicate that a mixed population of Greeks, Egyptians, and possibly Phoenicians resided in the settlement on the Canopic branch of the Nile prior to its transfer to Greek control shortly after 570 BC.[69] Its charter specified that non-Greek merchants were required to pass through Naukratis to carry out trade with Egypt and thus gave the settlement a pivotal role in Archaic maritime commerce.[70] Pottery demonstrates connections to Cyprus, Phoenicia, Cyrene, and Etruria as well as Greece and Egypt.[71] At least twelve Greek city

---

[63] Kyrieleis (1981: 9); see also Strabo 14.1.14.   [64] Barletta (2001: 108, 121).
[65] Young (1980: 72–6); Sacks (1995: 210); Barletta (2001: 121).   [66] Scherrer (2000: 44, 212).
[67] Ramsay (1901: 167); Zabehlicky (1995: 201–2); Stanley (2007: 143); Murphy-O'Connor (2008: 10, 18).
[68] Treblico (1994: 308).   [69] Villing and Schlotzhauer (2006b), with bibliography.
[70] Herodotus 2.179. Note that the traditional view of Naukratis as the first and only port in Egypt has recently been overturned by exploration of the harbour town of Herakleion-Thonis, also located on the Canopic branch of the Nile (Villing and Schlotzhauer 2006a: 5).
[71] Naso (2006); Villing and Schlotzhauer (2006a: 7).

states subsequently contributed to the architectural enrichment of the town and its port by financing a number of sanctuaries and temples.[72] Sanctuaries known from either remains or dedicatory inscriptions include those of Aphrodite, Hera, Apollo, and the Dioscuri, as well as the Hellenion, common to all the colonizing *poleis*.[73] These religious structures appear to have dominated the Archaic settlement, as no clear traces of contemporary houses, streets, and public architecture have yet been found;[74] sanctuaries were clearly a priority for traders and those financing building activity.

These Aegean and Egyptian examples have comparanda at Corinth, Corfu, on Sicily, and in Magna Graecia.[75] Monumental temples and divinely protected marketplaces thus appear to form a network in the Archaic period, one that people in central Italy may not just have been aware of but actively have tried to join through the construction of sanctuaries with temples, imagery, and deities that were remarkably congruent to those being built further afield.[76] Temples of Mater Matuta at Rome and Satricum, Uni/Astarte at Pyrgi, Artemis at Ephesos, and Hera at Corfu and Samos may have offered visitors a religious environment that was both recognizable and flexible. Similarly, the popularity of Herakles–Melqart at these sites may also have been more than coincidental. Hercules was worshipped at sanctuaries in the Roman Forum Boarium, at Pyrgi, Caere, Praeneste, through southern Italy, and along the Adriatic coast in his polyvalent capacity as a companion of female goddesses, a traveller to distant lands, and a protector of sailors, herders, and merchants wherever they encountered wilderness, thieves, monsters, and generic danger.[77] Herakles–Melqart and Athena–Artemis–Astarte are, moreover, thought to have been the quintessential deities of early Mediterranean religion.[78] People approaching a monumental sanctuary, marked out by relatively familiar architecture, were thus also likely to find it associated with the worship of a familiar, or at least translatable, figure. The great sanctuaries of Archaic Latium and Etruria can thus be viewed as participants in a system where cult facilitated contact.

---

[72] Herodotus 2.178.
[73] Möller (2000: 94–113, 200–2).
[74] House and streets are present but may date from the Ptolemaic period or later (Möller 2000: 118–19).
[75] Potts (2015: 107–11).   [76] Potts (2015: 112), with references.
[77] Glinister (2003: 143); Schwarz (2009: 245–6, 259); Malkin (2011: 119–41). In Italy, statues and acroterial figures of Herakles and Athena decorated temples at Rome, Caere, Veii, and Satricum: Lulof (2000).
[78] Bonnet (2005).

Privileged Space

Yet, while peer-polity interaction undoubtedly played a role in the prominence accorded to sanctuaries during the sixth century BC, local economic and social conditions must also account for the particularities of this phenomenon in central Italy. It is now well established that Etruria and Latium were not passive imitators of others' activities and changes, and developments must partly stem from local circumstances. The role of Etrusco-Italic sanctuaries within their communities should, therefore, also be considered.

Cult sites functioned within much broader systems of trade and exchange. The economies of Etruria and Latium were based on contrasting natural resources and political systems, and individual cities had their own economic ties with other communities in Italy and abroad that reflected geography, personal aristocratic connections, and specialist industries. Sites of production and exchange developed near harbours, natural resources, and elite residences.[79] Gravisca and Pithekoussai were ports now conventionally described as *emporia*; Lago dell'Accesa and Acquarossa processed nearby ores and metals; and Poggio Civitate hosted a range of craft activities near lavish accommodation. Sanctuaries accordingly appear to have been one, but not the only, type of economic centre in the seventh and sixth centuries BC.

The prominence of sanctuaries in the archaeological record nonetheless indicates that they were privileged spaces. In the Orientalizing period, economic surpluses were displayed at funerals and then interred. In contrast, Archaic wealth was often invested in temples and sanctuary infrastructure. Scholars have offered two contrasting explanations for this shift. The first holds that monumental sanctuaries were a tactical redeployment of elite resources, transferring wealth from the world of the dead to the community of the living via conspicuous religious euergetism.[80] The second sees monumental sanctuaries as signs of the decline, rather than the maintenance, of elite authority. Here the new cult sites represent community appropriation of cult following the loss of power of a figure or group that had formerly amalgamated religious, political, and social leadership.[81] There is insufficient evidence to prove either scenario, but, regardless of whether the change

---

[79] Nijboer (1998: 340–1).
[80] e.g. Bietti Sestieri and De Santis (2000: 29); Riva (2005: 213); Izzet (2007: 227).
[81] e.g. Coarelli (1983–5: i. 56–65); Colonna (1985: 53); Damgaard Andersen (1993: 85–6); Smith (1996: 19, 86–7); Marini Calvani (2001: 567); Camporeale (2004: 132). On the discrepancy between these two hypotheses, note Pollock (1999: 181) in the context of Mesopotamian architecture: 'Ideologically, monuments embody *at one and the same time* an expression of control over the labor of the people who constructed them and a sense of working together for the community.'

represents investment by a few or by a wider section of the population, the result is a prioritization of religious space.

Justification must have stemmed in part from the benefits conferred. Although workshops can be identified at some economic centres along with weights and measures that suggest market exchange,[82] to date there are no Archaic versions of later Roman fora or *macella*, of ordered spaces set aside for commercial or civic activities. Marzabotto offers alternatives in the form of wide, covered pavements suitable for stalls, and parts of houses that accommodated workshops and businesses. Some cities, such as Veii and Caere, had open spaces that presumably could be used for a range of activities including markets.[83] If cities did not have dedicated spaces for public business, then sanctuaries may have fulfilled a civic need. Festivals would provide merchants with large clienteles. Sanctuaries may, moreover, have offered elites an opportunity to justify their privilege at a time when a growing middle class might have been challenging traditional social dynamics.[84] If those with power could offer temples and dedications that would foster divine goodwill and promote cities, serve the public by mediating with the gods as priests, and also provide a framework for facilitating business, then sanctuaries could benefit more than one part of the population.

Spaces that combined religious, economic, and ceremonial functions may have proved so useful in western central Italy that they developed into a distinctive and lasting urban feature. In an overlooked passage, Albert Nijboer has suggested that the form and function of sanctuaries such as Pyrgi and Satricum mark them as 'incipient fora'.[85] The architectural elements of these sanctuaries formed a set that was repeated in the centuries that followed. At Pyrgi, the north sanctuary was monumentalized in *c.*510 BC with the construction of Temple B and an enclosure with a large arcaded entrance. On the south side of the temple stood the 'Building of the 20 Cells', a long row of rooms with a function that remains unclear.[86] A similar arrangement combining a temple and colonnaded space can also be seen in the late sixth century BC at Satricum, where the courtyard buildings surrounding Temple II were replaced with a number of rectangular columned buildings described as *stoai*.[87] Both of these examples may foreshadow the classic temple and portico elements of later Roman fora. The ability of a temple and buildings to provide a consecrated space where ritual, political, and commercial activities could occur arguably had long-lasting appeal.

[82] Nijboer (1998: 297–338).   [83] Steingräber (2001: 26).
[84] Proposed for Greece by Morris (1986: 13).   [85] Nijboer (1998: 333, 49–50).
[86] For an overview and reconstruction of the remains, see Colonna (1984–5).
[87] Maaskant-Kleibrink (1991: 105–8; 1992: 139–42).

The precocious development of the Forum Boarium and the Forum Romanum at Rome may signal that the city played an important role in the development of monumental, sanctified space. The Archaic Forum Boarium was a flood-prone valley and port with temporary industrial buildings.[88] It was also, from *c.*580 BC, the site of the first known podium temple in central Italy.[89] Monumental sanctuaries and meeting places under the protection of the gods appear to have been a concomitant development in central Italy, Sicily, and Magna Graecia during the first half of the sixth century BC, and the date of Rome's first temple places it at the forefront of this change in Rome, Latium, and further afield.[90] Later historians gave the Forum Boarium a colourful history that included the eponymous cattle trade and even the first Roman gladiatorial games.[91] In contrast to this outward-looking and dynamic space, the Forum Romanum appears to have remained architecturally conservative between the land reclamation project that created it at the end of the seventh century BC and the construction of the first monumental temples there at the start of the fifth. The Temple of Saturn was dedicated in 497 BC and the Temple of Castor in 484 BC, closely followed in the Forum Boarium by the twin temples at S. Omobono.[92] But, whereas the temples in the Forum Boarium faced the approaching world, those in the Forum Romanum turned their backs on it. This change may mark a transition in such spaces that began after the sixth century BC and produced archetypal urban fora.

The urbanization and reorientation of landmark sanctuaries away from coastlines and harbours at this time may reflect changes in trade and politics. During the fifth century BC, international exchange continued to decline, in some places, in favour of interregional trade, and settlements became increasingly occupied with domestic concerns. Satricum was subject to Volscian incursions,[93] and in 384 BC Dionysius I of Syracuse sacked Pyrgi.[94] Conflict with the Gauls and Sabines may have further encouraged reform of sacred communal spaces at Rome. By the early fourth century BC the Forum Romanum hosted temples, shops, and judicial and commemorative activities, and had become a stage for elite participation in politics, religion, and law: the difference with monumental sanctuaries in the preceding centuries consequently may be one of location rather than of form or function.

---

[88] Hopkins (2014: 36–7).
[89] Potts (2015: 90–1, 144–5), with references.   [90] Potts (2015: 107–17).
[91] Valerius Maximus 2.4.7.   [92] Livy 2.21.2, 2.42.5; Hopkins (2016: 146–52).
[93] Gnade (2002).   [94] Diodorus Siculus 15.14.

Conclusion

This overview of the economic significance of sanctuaries in Archaic central Italy has set out a model rather than a set of quantitative data. It suggests that, although the consumption and production of resources may have been a long-standing part of religious activities in pre-Roman Italy, the economic significance of sanctuaries changed during the Archaic period. It posits that changes in the form and function of cult sites at this time can be attributed to three intersecting factors: increasing volumes of trade and ways of managing resultant risk; the construction of temples at places of contact and exchange elsewhere around the Mediterranean; and adjustments in the actions and attitudes of those with economic power during a period of social and political change. Together these factors turned religion, and particularly cult sites, into a significant economic force. Sanctuaries became privileged places for the exchange of tangible and intangible commodities, and may have established a template for the site and conduct of similar activities in fora and other spaces in the centuries that followed. As such this model may go beyond providing a point of comparison for Republican and imperial practices by actually outlining their background and rationale: while the scale and complexity of the religious economy may have changed in the Roman period, the social, cultural, and theological elements of the underlying model may have not.

References

Abbott, D. R. (2010). 'The Rise and Demise of Marketplace Exchange among the Prehistoric Hohokam of Arizona', in Garraty and Stark (2010), 61–83.

Ampolo, C. (1976-7). 'Demarato. Osservazioni sulla mobilità sociale arcaica', *Dialoghi di archeologia* 9–10: 333–45.

Attema, P., de Haas, T., and Tol, G. (2011). 'Archaic Period (6th Century BC)', in P. Attema, T. de Haas, and G. Tol (eds), *Between Satricum and Antium: Settlement Dynamics in a Coastal Landscape in Latium Vetus*. Leuven, 53–6.

Baglione, M. P. (1985). 'Gruppo di tetradrammi', in Colonna (1985), 139–41.

Baglione, M. P., Belelli Marchesini, B., Carlucci, C., Gentili, M. D., and Michetti, L. M. (2015). 'Pyrgi: A Sanctuary in the Middle of the Mediterranean Sea', in Kistler et al. (2015), 221–37.

Barletta, B. (2001). *The Origins of the Greek Architectural Orders*. Cambridge.

Becker, H. (2009). 'The Economic Agency of the Etruscan Temple: Elites, Dedications and Display', in Turfa, Gleba, and Becker (2009), 87–99.

Beijer, A. J. (1995). 'Greek and Local Pottery in Ancient Latium: The Question of Greek Influence in Latium in the Iron Age', in M. Maaskant-Kleibrink (ed.), *The Landscape of the Goddess* (Caeculus, Papers on Mediterranean Archaeology and Greek & Roman Studies, 2). Leuven, 55–64.

Biella, M. C. (2019). 'Gods of Value: Preliminary Remarks on Religion and Economy in Pre-Roman Italy', in Moser and Smith (2019), 23–45.

Bietti Sestieri, A. M., and De Santis, A. (2000). *The Protohistory of the Latin Peoples: Museo nazionale romano, Terme di Diocleziano*. Milan.

Bohannan, P., and Bohannan, L. (1968). *Tiv Economy*. Evanston, IL.

Bonghi Jovino, M. (2008). *Tarquinia etrusca: Tarconte e il primato della città*. Rome.

Bonghi Jovino, M. (2010). 'The Tarquinia Project: A Summary of 25 Years of Excavation', *AJA* 114/1: 161–80.

Bonghi Jovino, M., and Chiaramonte Treré, C. (1997). *Tarquinia: Testimonianze archeologiche e ricostruzione storica: Scavi sistematici nell'abitato, campagne 1982–1988 (Tarchna I)*. Rome.

Bonghi Jovino, M., Mallegni, F., and Usai, L. (1997). 'Una morte violenta. Sul rinvenimento di uno scheletro nell'area del "complesso sacro-istituzionale" della Civita di Tarquinia', in G. Maetzke and L. T. Perna (eds), *Aspetti della cultura di Volterra etrusca fra l'età del ferro e l'età ellenistica e contributi della ricerca antropologica alla conoscenza del popolo etrusco. Atti del XIX Convegno di studi etruschi ed italici, Volterra, 15–19 ottobre 1995*. Volterra, 489–98.

Bonnet, C. (2005). 'Melqart in Occidente. Percorsi di appropriazione e di acculturazione', in P. Bernardini and R. Zucca (eds), *Il Mediterraneo di Herakles: Studi e ricerche*. Rome, 17–28.

Bouma, J. (1996). *Religio Votiva: The Archaeology of Latial Votive Religion. The 5th–3rd Century BC Votive Deposit South West of the Main Temple at 'Satricum' Borgo Le Ferriere*. 3 vols. Doctoral thesis. Rijksuniversiteit Groningen.

Burkert, W. (1992). *The Orientalizing Revolution: Near Eastern Influence on Greek Culture in the Early Archaic Age*. Cambridge, MA.

Camporeale, G. (2004). *Gli Etruschi: Storia e civiltà*. Turin.

Camporeale, G. (2010). 'Il teatro etrusco secondo le fonti scritte: Spettacolo, ritualità, religione', in van der Meer (2010), 155–64.

Cary, E. (1937). *Dionysius of Halicarnassus, Roman Antiquities*, vol. 1: *Books 1–2* (The Loeb Classical Library 319). Cambridge, MA.

Ciafaloni, D. (2006). 'Nota sulle tipologie architettoniche e murarie tarquiniesi: Ulteriori corrispondenze con il vicino oriente antico', in M. Bonghi Jovino (ed.), *Tarquinia e le civiltà del Mediterraneo: Convegno internazionale, Milano, 22–24 giugno 2004*. Milan, 145–61.

Coarelli, F. (1983–5). *Il Foro Romano*. 2 vols. Rome.

Coarelli, F. (1988). *Il Foro Boario: Dalle origini alla fine della Repubblica*. Rome.

Coarelli, F. (2007). *Rome and Environs: An Archaeological Guide*. Berkeley and Los Angeles.

Colonna, G. (1970) (ed.). *Pyrgi: Scavi del santuario etrusco (1959-1967)* (Notizie degli Scavi di Antichità Supplement 2). Rome.

Colonna, G. (1984-5). 'Novità sui culti di Pyrgi', *Atti della Pontificia Accademia romana di archeologia: Rendiconti* 57: 57-88.

Colonna, G. (1985) (ed.). *Santuari d'Etruria*. Milan.

Colonna, G. (2005). 'The Sanctuary at Pyrgi in Etruria', in G. Colonna, *Italia ante romanum imperium: Scritti di antichità etrusche, italiche e romane (1958-1998)*, vol. IV: *Pyrgi e storia della ricerca*. Pisa, 2187-214.

Cristofani, M. (1990) (ed.). *La grande Roma dei Tarquini: Catalogo della mostra, Roma, Palazzo delle Esposizioni, 12 giugno-30 settembre 1990*. Rome.

Cristofani, M. (1995a). 'Novità sul commercio etrusco arcaico: Dal relitto del Giglio al contratto di Pech Maho', in J. Swaddling, S. Walker, and P. Roberts (eds), *Italy in Europe: Economic Relations 700 BC-AD 50*. London, 131-7.

Cristofani, M. (1995b). *Tabula capuana: Un calendario festivo di età arcaica*. Florence.

Cristofani, M. (1996). *Etruschi e altre genti nell'Italia preromana: Mobilità in età arcaica*. Rome.

Damgaard Andersen, H. (1993). 'Archaic Architectural Terracottas and their Relation to Building Identification', in E. Rystedt (ed.), *Deliciae Fictiles I*. Stockholm, 71-86.

De Grummond, N. T. (2006). 'Prophets and Priests', in N. T. De Grummond and E. Simon (eds), *The Religion of the Etruscans*. Austin, 27-44.

De Grummond, N. T. (2016). 'Etruscan Human Sacrifice: The Case of Tarquinia', in C. A. Murray (ed.), *Diversity of Sacrifice: Form and Function of Sacrificial Practices in the Ancient World and Beyond*. New York, 145-68.

Demetriou, D. A. (2012). *Negotiating Identity in the Ancient Mediterranean: The Archaic and Classical Greek Multiethnic Emporia*. Cambridge.

Edlund-Berry, I. E. M. (2011). 'Artisans and Trade in the Etruscan World', *Thesaurus Cultus et Rituum Antiquorum* 6: 353-5.

Fenelli, M., and Guaitoli, M. (1990). 'Nuovi dati degli scavi di Lavinium', *ArchLaz* 10/2: 182-93.

Fiorini, L. (2001). 'Le officine metallurgiche scoperte presso il santuario di Gravisca', in A. M. Sgubini Moretti (ed.), *Tarquinia etrusca: Una nuova storia*. Rome, 136-40.

Fiorini, L., and Torelli, M. (2007). 'La fusione, Afrodite e l'*emporion*', *Facta: A Journal of Roman Material Culture Studies* 1: 75-106.

Fiorini, L., and Torelli, M. (2010). 'Quarant'anni di ricerche a Gravisca', in van der Meer (2010), 29–49.

Garraty, C. P. (2010). 'Investigating Market Exchange in Ancient Societies: A Theoretical Review', in Garraty and Stark (2010), 3–32.

Garraty, C. P., and Stark, B. L. (2010) (eds). *Archaeological Approaches to Market Exchange in Ancient Societies*. Boulder.

Gleba, M. (2008). *Textile Production in Pre-Roman Italy* (Ancient Textiles Series 4). Oxford.

Glinister, F. (2003). 'Gifts of the Gods: Sanctuary and Society in Archaic Tyrrhenian Italy', in J. Wilkins and E. Herring (eds), *Inhabiting Symbols: Symbol and Image in the Ancient Mediterranean*. London, 137–47.

Gnade, M. (2002). *Satricum in the Post-Archaic Period: A Case Study of the Interpretation of Archaeological Remains as Indicators of Ethno-Cultural Identity*. Leuven.

Gran-Aymerich, J. (2009). 'Gli Etruschi fuori d'Etruria: Dons et offrandes étrusques en Méditeranée Occidental et dans l'Ouest de l'Europe', in Turfa, Gleba, and Becker (2009), 15–41.

Gras, M. (1995). *La Méditerranée archaïque*. Paris.

Gregory, C. A. (1980). 'Gifts to Men and Gifts to Gods: Gift Exchange and Capital Accumulation in Contemporary Papua', *Man* 15/4: 626–52.

Haack, M.-L. (2003). *Les Haruspices dans le monde romain*. Pessac.

Heurgon, J. (1966). 'The Inscriptions of Pyrgi', *JRS* 56: 1–15.

Holloway, R. R. (1994). *The Archaeology of Early Rome and Latium*. London.

Hopkins, J. N. (2014). 'The Creation of the Forum and the Making of Monumental Rome', in Robinson (2014), 29–61.

Hopkins, J. N. (2016). *The Genesis of Roman Architecture*. New Haven; London.

Horden, P., and Purcell, N. (2000). *The Corrupting Sea: A Study of Mediterranean History*. Oxford.

Hudson, M., and Van de Mieroop, M. (2002) (eds). *Debt and Economic Renewal in the Ancient Near East* (International Scholars Conference on Ancient Near Eastern Economies 3). Bethesda, MD.

Izzet, V. (2007). *The Archaeology of Etruscan Society*. Cambridge.

Jannot, J.-R. (2005). *Religion in Ancient Etruria*, trans. J. Whitehead (Wisconsin Studies in Classics). Madison.

Kistler, E., Öhlinger, B., Mohr, M., and Hoernes, M. (2015) (eds). *Sanctuaries and the Power of Consumption: Networking and the Formation of Elites in the Archaic Western Mediterranean World*. Wiesbaden.

Kyrieleis, H. (1981). *Führer durch das Heraion von Samos*. Athens.

Kyrieleis, H. (2006). 'Archäologische Einführung', in A. Naso (ed.), *Stranieri e non cittadini nei santuari greci: Atti del convegno internazionale*. Grassina, 129–39.

Kyrieleis, H. (2009). 'Intercultural Commerce and Diplomacy: Near Eastern, Egyptian and Cypriote Artefacts from the Heraion of Samos', in V. Karageorghis and O. Kouka (eds), *Cyprus and the East Aegean: Intercultural Contacts from 3000 to 500 BC: An International Archaeological Symposium Held at Pythagoreion, Samos, October 17th–18th 2008*. Nicosia, 139–43.

La Rocca, E. (1982). 'Ceramica d'importazione greca dell'VIII secolo a.C. a Sant'Omobono: Un aspetto delle origini di Roma', in *La céramique grecque ou de tradition grecque au VIIIe siècle en Italie centrale et méridionale* (Cahiers du Centre Jean Bérard 3). Naples, 45–53.

Lambrechts, R. (1959). *Essai sur les magistratures des républiques étrusques*. Brussels.

Lejeune, M., Pouilloux, J., and Solier, Y. (1988). 'Etrusque et ionen archaïques sur un plomb de Pech Maho (Aude)', *Revue archéologique de Narbonnaise*, 21: 19–59.

Lulof, P. S. (2000). 'Archaic Terracotta Acroteria Representing Athena and Heracles: Manifestations of Power in Central Italy', *JRA* 13: 207–19.

Lulof, P. S. (2006). 'Roofs from the South: Campanian Architectural Terracottas in Satricum', in I. Edlund-Berry, G. Greco, and J. Kenfield (eds), *Deliciae Fictiles III: Architectural Terracottas in Ancient Italy: New Discoveries and Interpretations, Proceedings of the International Conference Held at the American Academy in Rome (November 7–8, 2002)*. Oxford, 235–42.

Maaskant-Kleibrink, M. (1991). 'Early Latin Settlement Plans at Borgo Le Ferriere (*Satricum*): Reading Mengarelli's Maps', *BABESCH* 66: 51–114.

Maaskant-Kleibrink, M. (1992). *Settlement Excavations at Borgo Le Ferriere 'Satricum'*, vol. 2: *The Campaigns 1983, 1985 and 1987*. Groningen.

Maggiani, A. (2012) 'Ancora sui sistemi ponderali in Etruria: Pesi di pietra dal territorio fiesolano', *MEFRA* 124/2: 393–405.

Malkin, I. (2011). *A Small Greek World: Networks in the Ancient Mediterranean*. Oxford.

Marini Calvani, M. (2001). 'The Ideal Forms', in M. Torelli (ed.), *The Etruscans*. London, 565–7.

Mauersberg, M. (2015). 'Obsolete Perceptions? Frameworks of Intercultural Exchange in Ancient Narrative', in Kistler et al. (2015), 3–19.

Menichelli, S. (2009). 'Etruscan Altars from the 7th to the 4th Centuries BC: Typology, Function, Cult', *Etruscan Studies* 12: 99–129.

Möller, A. (2000). *Naukratis: Trade in Archaic Greece*. Oxford.

Moretti, L. (1984). 'Epigraphia 26: Sulle iscrizioni greche di Gravisca', *Rivista di filologia e di istruzione classica* 112: 314–27.

Morris, I. (1986). 'Gift and Commodity in Archaic Greece', *Man* 21/1: 1–17.

Moser, C., and Smith, C. (2019) (eds). *Transformations of Value: Lived Religion and the Economy* (Religion in the Roman Empire 5.1). Tübingen.

Murphy-O'Connor, J. (2008). *St Paul's Ephesus: Texts and Archaeology*. Collegeville, MN.

Naso, A. (2006). 'Etruscan and Italic Finds in North Africa, 7th–2nd Century B.C.', in Villing and Schlotzhauer (2006b), 187–98.

Nijboer, A. J. (1994). 'A Pair of Early Fixed Metallic Monetary Units from Borgo Le Ferriere (Satricum)', *NC* 154: 1–16.

Nijboer, A. J. (1998). *From Household Production to Workshops: Archaeological Evidence for Economic Transformation, Pre-Monetary Exchange and Urbanisation in Central Italy from 800 to 400 BC*. Groningen.

Nijboer, A. J., ven der Plicht, J., Bietti Sestieri, A. M., and De Santis, A. (1999–2000). 'A High Chronology for the Early Iron Age in Central Italy', *Palaeohistoria* 41–2: 163–76.

Osborne, R. (2004). 'Hoards, Votives, Offerings: The Archaeology of the Dedicated Object', *World Archaeology* 36/1: 1–10.

Pallottino, M. (1970). 'Ragguaglio bibliografico e critico degli studi sui testi delle lamine', in *Pyrgi: Scavi del santuario etrusco (1959–1967)* (Notizie degli Scavi di Antichità Supplement 2, 1970). Rome, 732–43.

Pappa, E. (2015). 'Oriental Gods but Domestic Elites? Religous Symbolism and Economic Function of Phoenician-Period Cult Loci in South Iberia', in Kistler et al. (2015), 43–62.

Pellegrini, E. (2002). 'Satricum (Roma)', in E. Pellegrini and R. Macellari (eds), *I lingotti con il segno del ramo secco: Considerazioni su alcuni aspetti socio-economici nell'area etrusco-italica durante il periodo tardo arcaico* (Biblioteca di studi etruschi/Istituto nazionale di studi etruschi ed italici 38). Pisa, 91–2.

Perkins, P. (2014). 'Processes of Urban Development in Northern and Central Etruria in the Orientalizing and Archaic Periods', in Robinson (2014), 62–80.

Pisani Sartorio, G. (1989). 'L'Area Sacra dei Templi della Fortuna e della Mater Matuta, il Portus Tiberinus e il quadro storico della Roma dei Tarquini', in G. Pisani Sartorio (ed.), *Il viver quotidiano in Roma arcaica: Materiali dagli scavi del tempio arcaico nell'area sacra di S. Omobono*. Rome, 16–17.

Pollock, S. (1999). *Ancient Mesopotamia: The Eden that Never Was*. Cambridge.

Potts, C. R. (2015). *Religious Architecture in Latium and Etruria, c.900–500 BC* (Oxford Monographs on Classical Archaeology). Oxford.

Rafanelli, S. (2013). 'Etruscan Religious Rituals: The Archaeological Evidence', in J. M. Turfa (ed.), *The Etruscan World*. London, 566–93.

Ramsay, W. M. (1901). 'Ephesus', *Biblical World* 17/3: 167–77.

Rendeli, M. (1990). 'Materie prime, tecniche e tipi edilizi', in Cristofani (1990), 138–9.

Ridgway, D. (2012). 'Demaratus of Corinth and the Hellenisation of Etruria', in A. Hermary and G. R. Tsetskhladze (eds), *From the Pillars of Hercules to the Footsteps of the Argonauts* (Colloquia Antiqua 4). Leuven, 207–22.

Riva, C. (2005). 'The Culture of Urbanization in the Mediterranean *c*.800–600 BC', in R. Osborne and B. W. Cunliffe (eds), *Mediterranean Urbanization 800–600 BC*. Oxford, 203–32.

Riva, C. (2006). 'The Orientalizing Period in Etruria: Sophisticated Communities', in C. Riva and N. C. Vella (eds), *Debating Orientalization* (Monographs in Mediterranean Archaeology 10). London, 110–34.

Robinson, E. C. (2014) (ed.). *Papers on Italian Urbanism in the First Millennium BC.* (JRA Supplementary Series 97). Portsmouth, RI.

Romualdi, A. (1981). *Catalogo del deposito di Brolio in val di Chiana.* Rome.

Sacks, D. (1995). *Encyclopedia of the Ancient Greek World.* New York.

Säflund, G. (1932). *Le mura di Roma repubblicana* (Acta Instituti Romani Regni Sueciae I). Lund.

Sassatelli, G., Melis, F., and Ciaghi, S. (1985). 'Fornaci per terrecotte', in Colonna (1985), 46–8.

Scherrer, P. (2000) (ed.). *Ephesus: The New Guide*, trans. L. Bier and G. M. Luxon. Rev. edn. Turkey.

Schwarz, S. J. (2009). 'Herakles/Hercle', in *Lexicon Iconographicum Mythologiae Classicae, Supplementum 2009*, vol. 1. Düsseldorf, 244–59.

Smith, C. J. (1996). *Early Rome and Latium: Economy and Society c.1000 to 500 BC.* Oxford.

Smith, C. J. (1999). 'Medea in Italy: Trade and Contact between Greece and Italy in the Archaic Period', in G. R. Tsetskhladze (ed.), *Ancient Greeks West and East*. Leiden, 179–206.

Smith, C. J. (2001). 'Ritualising the Economy', *Caeculus IV: Interpreting Deposits*, 17–23.

Stanley, B. E. (2007). 'Ephesus', in M. Dumper and B. E. Stanley (eds), *Cities of the Middle East and North Africa: A Historical Encyclopedia*. Santa Barbara, 142–6.

Steingräber, S. (2001). 'The Process of Urbanization of Etruscan Settlements from the Late Villanovan to the Late Archaic Period (End of the Eighth to the Beginning of the Fifth Century BC): Presentation of a Project and Preliminary Results', *Etruscan Studies* 8: 7–33.

Steingräber, S. (2006). *Abundance of Life: Etruscan Wall Painting*, trans. R. Stockman. Los Angeles.

Stopponi, S. (2011). 'Campo della Fiera: New Discoveries', in N. T. De Grummond and I. Edlund-Berry (eds), *The Archaeology of Sanctuaries and Ritual in Etruria* (Journal of Roman Archaeology Supplement 81). Rhode Island, 16–43.

Torelli, M. (1982). 'Per la definizione del commercio greco-orientale: Il caso di Gravisca', *La parola del passato* 37: 304–25.

Torelli, M. (1986). 'La Storia', in G. Pugliese Carratelli (ed.), *Rasenna: Storia e civiltà degli Etruschi*. Milan, 15–76.

Treblico, P. (1994). 'Asia', in D. W. J. Gill and C. H. Gempf (eds), *The Book of Acts in its First Century Setting*, vol. 2: *The Book of Acts in its Graeco-Roman Setting*. Grand Rapids, 291–362.

Turfa, J. M. (2005). *Catalogue of the Etruscan Gallery of the University of Pennsylvania Museum of Archaeology and Anthropology*. Philadelphia.

Turfa, J. M., Gleba, M., and Becker, H. (2009) (eds). *Votives, Places, and Rituals in Etruscan Religion: Studies in Honor of Jean MacIntosh Turfa*. Leiden.

van der Meer, L. B. (2010) (ed.). *Material Aspects of Etruscan Religion: Proceedings of the International Colloquium in Leiden, May 29 and 30, 2008* (BABesch Supplement 16). Leuven.

Villing, A., and Schlotzhauer, U. (2006a). 'Naukratis and the Eastern Mediterranean: Past, Present and Future', in Villing and Schlotzhauer (2006b), 1–10.

Villing, A., and Schlotzhauer, U. (2006b) (eds). *Naukratis: Greek Diversity in Egypt: Studies on East Greek Pottery and Exchange in the Eastern Mediterranean*. London.

Waarsenburg, D. D. J., and Maas, H. (2001). 'Gods, Men and Money: Reflections on a Protohistoric Bronze Hoard from the Temple of Mater Matuta at *Satricum* (Latium)', in A. J. Niboer (ed.), *Interpreting Deposits: Linking Ritual with Economy* (Caeculus: Papers on Mediterranean Archaeology 4). Groningen, 45–56.

Wallace, R. E. (2008). *Zikh Rasna: A Manual of the Etruscan Language and Inscriptions*. Ann Arbor.

Warden, P. G. (2008). 'Ritual and Representation on a Campana Dinos in Boston', *Etruscan Studies* 11: 121–33.

Warden, P. G. (2009). 'The Blood of Animals: Predation and Transformation in Etruscan Funerary Representation', in S. Bell and H. Nagy (eds), *New Perspectives on Etruria and Early Rome: In Honor of Richard Daniel De Puma*. Madison, 198–219.

Warden, P. G. (2012). 'Monumental Embodiment: Somatic Symbolism and the Tuscan Temple', in M. Thomas and G. E. Meyers (eds), *Monumentality in Etruscan and Early Roman Architecture: Ideology and Innovation*. Austin, 82–110.

Winter, N. (2009). *Symbols of Wealth and Power: Architectural Terracotta Decoration in Etruria and Central Italy, 640–510 BC* (Memoirs of the American Academy in Rome Supplementary Volume 9). Ann Arbor.

Young, P. H. (1980). *Building Projects and Archaic Greek Tyrants*. Philadelphia.

Zabehlicky, H. (1995). 'Preliminary Views of the Ephesian Harbour', in H. Koester (ed.), *Ephesos: Metropolis of Asia. An Interdisciplinary Approach to its Archaeology, Religion and Culture*. Valley Forge, 201–15.

4

Cost Differences in Temple-Building between Rome and the Provinces

Javier Domingo

In this chapter I aim to demonstrate the possibilities offered for the study and analysis of architecture by a methodology of calculation that allows us to reconstruct the financial cost of the building process. Specifically, I focus my attention on the possibilities this method offers for reconstructing the cost differences there would have been between the grand building projects undertaken in Rome and their respective provincial imitations. The majority of the grand buildings in Rome that were imitated in the provinces were temples, generally those dedicated to imperial worship or a divinity linked to the emperor or his family. The dimensions of most of these buildings were colossal, with column shafts more than 12–14 m tall, and they were located inside porticoed squares. We have only to think of the Temple of Mars Ultor (Table 4.1),[1] whose gigantic columns were imitated in other buildings in the city of Rome; the Temple of Claudius, which has recently been reconstructed based on its capitals, a base, an architrave, and some fragments of the *Forma Urbis Romae*;[2] the Hall of Worship of the Templum Pacis;[3] and the immense columns found in the vicinity of Trajan's Forum that almost certainly came from a huge temple that would have formed the northern side of this forum.[4]

Indeed, examples of this monumental architecture are also found in some provincial cities, where the elites went to great lengths to imitate the decorative and architectural models of the *Urbs* and the use of marble, a practice often hitherto unknown in those provincial towns. Examples include:[5] the Temple of Augustus in Tarraco (Tarragona), built in A D 15;[6] the Hall of Worship, built in the Flavian period in the rear portico of the temple and with the same

---

[1] Wilson Jones (2000: 224). [2] Domingo, Mar, and Pensabene (2011, 2013).
[3] Facchin (2014); Montella (2014); Meneghini (2014).   [4] Baldassarri (2013).
[5] A list of some of the most outstanding examples of gigantic architecture in Rome and the provinces can be found in Barresi, Domingo, and Pensabene (2014).
[6] Pensabene and Mar (2010: 266–72).

Javier Domingo, *Cost Differences in Temple-Building between Rome and the Provinces* In: *The Economy of Roman Religion*. Edited by: Andrew Wilson, Nick Ray, and Angela Trentacoste, Oxford University Press. © Oxford University Press 2023.
DOI: 10.1093/oso/9780192883537.003.0004

Table 4.1 Dimensions of the columns of the main temples in Rome

Temples	Column height (m)	Shaft height (m)	Capital height (m)	Base height (m)	Shaft material
Templum Pacis Hall of Worship	17.82	14.85	1.98	0.99	Giallo antico
Temple of Divus Traianus[a]	18.00	15.00	2.08	—	Granite
Temple of Mars Ultor[b]	17.74	14.76	2.00	0.98	Carrara
Temple of Divus Claudius[c]	15.00	14.76	2.00	0.98	Carrara
Temple of Bellona (Augustan phase)	14.85	12.30	1.80	0.75	Carrara
Temple of Apollo in Circo (Augustan phase)[d]	14.83	12.50	1.65	0.68	Carrara
Temple of Hadrian[e]	14.83	12.35	1.66	0.81	Proconnesus
Temple of Castor and Pollux (Augustan phase)[f]	14.76	12.40	1.61	0.74	Carrara
Temple of Antoninus and Faustina[g]	14.19	11.80	1.65	0.73	Cipollino
Pantheon Pronaos	14.16	11.80	1.63	0.73	Granite
Temple of Vespasian[h]	14.13	11.79	1.64	0.70	Carrara

[a] Pensabene (1984: 73), Meneghini and Santangeli (2007: 112).
[b] Ventura (2007).
[c] Domingo, Mar, and Pensabene (2011, 2013).
[d] Wilson Jones (1989).
[e] Cozza (1982).
[f] Wilson Jones (1989: 67).
[g] Pensabene (1996: 240).
[h] De Angeli (1999).

dimensions;[7] the Temple of the Forum Adiectum in Cordoba;[8] the Capitolium of Narbonne;[9] the column shafts found in a shipwreck off Saint-Tropez in southern Gaul,[10] and so on (Table 4.2).

Many of these buildings were the first in which marble was used in provincial architecture, and the first to introduce the new decorative models created for the Forum of Augustus in Rome.[11] For example, the Temple of Augustus in Tarraco was the town's first marble building, and the decorative style of its capitals, derived from the Forum of Augustus,[12] led to the modification and updating of the methods used in the local workshops.[13] Another interesting

[7] Mar and Pensabene (2010: 535, fig. 18); Pensabene and Mar (2010: 272–7).
[8] Márquez (2004a); Ventura (2007).   [9] Sabrie and Sabrie (2004).
[10] Sabrie and Sabrie (2004); Pensabene (2006: 114).
[11] Pensabene (2013: 464–5, 493–7, 504–10).   [12] Pensabene (1993).
[13] Domingo, Garrido, and Mar (2011: 854–8).

Table 4.2 Dimensions of the columns of the main temples of Hispania and Gallia Narbonensis

Temples	Column height (m)	Shaft height (m)	Capital height (m)	Base height (m)	Shaft material
Capitolium of Narbonne[a]	—	15.00	2.10		Carrara
Saint-Tropez shipwreck[b]	—	15.00	—	1.00	Carrara
Temple of the Forum Adiectum in Cordoba[c]	15.90	13.30	1.82	0.89	Carrara
Temple of Augustus in Tarraco[d]	15.36	12.80	1.68	0.88	Carrara
Hall of Worship of the Provincial Forum of Tarraco[e]	15.36	12.80	1.68	0.88	Carrara
Temple of Claudius Marcellus in Cordoba[f]	>15.00	—	1.01	—	Carrara
Temple of the Provincial Forum of Merida[g]	14.25	—	2.00	—	Estremoz marble
Temple of Écija (first half of the first c. AD)[h]	12.96	10.80	1.62	0.54	Granite
Temple of Carmona[i]	12.26	10.40	1.70	0.66	Carrara
Traianeum of Itálica[j]	11.00	9.20	1.30	0.40	Granite
Mármoles Street in Seville[k]	—	8.68	1.30	0.56	Granite

[a] Sabrie and Sabrie (2004).
[b] Sabrie and Sabrie (2004); Pensabene (2006: 114).
[c] Márquez (2004a); Ventura (2007).
[d] Pensabene and Mar (2010: 266–72).
[e] Mar and Pensabene (2010: 535, fig. 18); Pensabene and Mar (2010: 272–7).
[f] Jiménez Salvador (1991); Márquez (1993: nn. 213–14; 1998).
[g] Mateos Cruz (2006, 2007).
[h] Buzón (2009).
[i] Márquez (2001).
[j] Montero (1988); Rodero (2002).
[k] Márquez (2003).

example is the Tiberian Forum Adiectum at Cordoba, whose shape, decorative elements (only fragments of which have been preserved), and reconstructed dimensions were very similar to those of the Temple of Mars Ultor; it has even been suggested that the same workshops that built the Forum of Augustus in Rome participated in its construction.[14]

However, they did not only imitate the dimensions, building materials, and decorative elements, but also sometimes the architectural form. Once again,

[14] Márquez (2004b: 112–14).

we refer to the upper terrace of the Provincial Forum at Tarraco. It was built in the time of Vespasian around the earlier Temple of Augustus with a monumental hall of worship at the back. It was a model that imitated the dimensions and structure of the Templum Pacis in Rome:[15] presided over by a large hall of worship at the rear of the portico, and of a type we also find, for example, in the shrine of Cigognier in Avenches.[16]

These examples, a small sample of all those that could be mentioned, demonstrate that such imitations, although they present certain variations or innovations, were a widely disseminated phenomenon in provincial architecture dedicated mainly to emperor worship. Therefore, the analysis of the costs of these architectural complexes, paying special attention to the differences that may have existed between Rome and the provinces, can help improve our understanding of the development and dissemination of these provincial imitations of Rome's imperial architecture. In fact, one of the first questions to analyse is whether the elites —local, civic, or provincial— needed to mobilize the same economic resources to build these provincial imitations as those needed to build the 'originals' in Rome. This question is directly relevant to understanding the presence of enormous marble temples in towns that had fewer financial resources than Rome.

The Cost of the Architecture

To undertake this analysis, we first need to know the cost of these building complexes—information we rarely have. However, since the late twentieth century a calculation methodology has been developed that allows us to reconstruct, albeit approximately, the cost of this architecture. It is a method based mainly on three sources of information.[17] First, the *Edictum Diocletiani et Collegarum de pretiis rerum venalium* (*Edict on Maximum Prices*), dating to AD 301, gives us the cost of more than a thousand items, including transportation, certain varieties of marble, and the daily salary paid to different tradesmen and craftsmen.[18] These prices are extrapolated to other historical periods on the basis of the evolution of the price of grain expressed in *modii castrenses*.[19] Secondly, nineteenth-century architecture and engineering manuals, one of

---

[15] Mar (1993: 120–8); Domingo and Pensabene (2017).   [16] Bögli (1989: 22–4).
[17] With regard to this calculation methodology, see especially DeLaine (1997); Barresi (2003); Pensabene (2003: 353–62); Mar and Pensabene (2010); Barresi (2010: 337–50); Soler (2012: 193–228); Domingo (2012b, 2012c).
[18] Giacchero (1974).   [19] DeLaine (1997: 209).

the most important of which was written by G. Pegoretti,[20] allow us to estimate the time needed for each of the building processes in a pre-industrial context, taking into account the type of construction and the materials used.[21] Thirdly, a large number of literary and papyrological sources allow us to add to and compare the values provided by the other sources.

In any case, some of the information in Diocletian's *Edict on Maximum Prices* poses problems of interpretation. For example, the costs given for building materials in Diocletian's *Edict* do not specify which phases of stone preparation are included: raw marble extracted from the quarry, a squared block, or a semi-prepared block? However, some indications suggest that the price given in the *Edict* was only for the material, without any kind of preparation.[22] Moreover, Diocletian's *Edict* does not quote the cost of Luna marble, although we have been able to reconstruct it based on certain indications.[23]

It is also necessary to take into account the fact that a large number of variables were involved in any construction process, and we are not always able to quantify them precisely. For example, using this methodology, Barresi calculates that the theatre of Nicaea would have cost some HS 2.5 million.[24] However, he also points out that a letter written by Pliny the Younger to the Emperor Trajan states that some HS 10 million had already been spent on that building.[25] The letter, which asks the emperor whether it was desirable to continue with such a costly project, explains the reasons for the high cost. They include different problems caused by damp and the softness of the ground, which meant that the plans had had to be changed several times. We cannot always verify these changes archaeologically and are therefore unable to quantify them. Finally, there were also cases of corruption, although these are also difficult to quantify economically.[26]

With these problems in mind, it is also necessary to consider two important issues:

The first is that the calculation of the building cost allows us to work out the theoretical total for the construction, perhaps the amount that was budgeted before the work began. This total, although it does not necessarily correspond

---

[20] Pegoretti (1863).
[21] In this way, it is possible to ascertain the time needed to quarry and rough out the stone blocks and partially prepare or cut them into the desired size and shape, as well as for their partial preparation, or to mark them with the basic lines for their placement, laying, and finishing.
[22] Domingo (2012a: 83–4).
[23] Pensabene (1978–9). A revision of the Luna marble cost calculation is in Domingo (2012a: 80–3).
[24] Barresi (2010: 339–48).
[25] Plin., *Ep.* 10.39–40.
[26] One of the best-known cases was the construction of a bridge in Rome in AD 383 (Marcone 1987: 103–4; Vera 1978).

to the actual final amount paid, allows us to calibrate the financial capacity of a town or its elites to undertake a specific building project. In fact, unexpected cost increases were probably not uncommon, as shown, for example, by a law passed in Ephesos that penalized architects of public works who exceeded their initial budgets, forcing them to pay the difference out of their own pockets. Vitruvius, however, lamented the fact that there was no such law among the Romans.[27]

The second observation refers to the fact that it is necessary to verify the reliability of this calculation methodology, as it has generally been applied to buildings for which we do not know the true cost.[28] This means we do not know if the value obtained approximates to the actual cost or how much it varies from it. Therefore, it is initially necessary to apply this methodology to buildings for which we know the actual cost.

Application of the Calculation Methodology to Buildings for which we Know the True Cost

The application of the calculation methodology to buildings and/or parts of buildings whose true cost is known has frequently yielded satisfactory results, if we are prepared to accept a certain—and logical—margin of error. For example, calculations for the four 30-foot-high columns mentioned by Cicero, with a known cost of 5,000 *denarii*, give us a cost of 4,844 *denarii*;[29] the nine, approximately 20-foot-tall, Antonine-period, local limestone columns made for a palaestra at a cost of 66 *denarii* each,[30] work out at an estimated cost of 65.5 *denarii*;[31] and, finally, the Arch of Marcus Aurelius in Lepcis Magna, built with a bequest of HS 120,000 to which an unknown amount from the municipal treasury was added, but which has been estimated at around HS 60,000,[32] is calculated at a cost of HS 201,470.[33]

---

[27] Vitr., *De arch.* 10.1.
[28] For example, the portico *in summa cavea* of the Flavian amphitheatre in Pozzuoli, with a calculated cost of HS 79,992 (Barresi 2004); the upper terrace of the Provincial Forum of Tarraco, with a calculated cost of HS 2,162,580 (Mar and Pensabene 2010); the architectural decoration of the *frons scaenae* in the theatre of Cartagena, with a calculated cost of HS 20,238 (Soler 2012); the Augustan forum of Segóbriga, with a calculated cost of HS 243,464 (Pensabene, Mar, and Cebrián 2012); the Baths of Caracalla, with a calculated cost equivalent to some two million *modii castrenses* of grain (DeLaine 1997: 220).
[29] Cic., *II Verr.* I.147; Barresi (2000: 366).   [30] P.Hib. II 217; Lukaszewicz (1986: 100).
[31] Barresi (2000: 338–9, 366).   [32] Di Vita-Evrard (1963: 389).
[33] Pensabene (2003: 353–62).

In other cases, however, the result obtained was far from the true cost. We can quote the aforementioned example of the theatre in Nicaea, or the study of the columns of the Temple of Apollo at Didyma, completed in the Roman period at a cost, according to the inscription, of 39,000 drachmae; the calculation methodology gives us a cost of only 24,500 drachmae.[34]

These examples show the need to undertake an empirical verification of the validity of this calculation methodology, applying it not to specific parts of buildings but to whole constructions for which we can reconstruct with great precision all the variables involved in the building process and for which we have accurate knowledge of their true cost. For this purpose, four buildings that meet these requirements have been selected: the Temple of the Victories of Caracalla in Dougga (Tunisia), the Arch of Caracalla in Theveste (present-day Tébessa, Algeria), and both the Capitolium and Temple C in Volubilis (Morocco). The four buildings are from the same chronological period—the time of Caracalla—and geographical context—North Africa—and built with local materials and a similar building technique. This means the variables involved in their construction would have been broadly similar. The following factors have been taken into account in calculating the cost of these buildings: the type and volume of stone used; the distance from the quarries; the cost of labour based on their chronology, the geographical area; the specialization of the workers; the execution time of each of the building phases, and so on.

The first building, the Temple of the Victories of Caracalla in Dougga[35] (Fig. 4.1), has a dedicatory inscription that informs us it was built in AD 214 thanks to a bequest of HS 100,000 in the will of one Gabinia Hermiona, who also ceded the land for its construction.[36] The temple is built on a 41.5 × 14 m plot. It is tetrastyle *in antis* and has a row of half columns abutting the exterior of the western wall of the cella. It was built with small blocks of local limestone that had been slightly squared and bonded with lime mortar. Inside the

---

[34] Barresi (2015).
[35] Khanoussi (2003); Brouquier-Reddé (2005); Brouquier-Reddé et al. (2005); Saint-Amans (2005).
[36] *CIL* VIII.26546, a–h; *CIL* VIII.26639; *CIL* VIII.26650; *ILAf* 527: *Pro salute Imp(eratoris) Caes(aris) Di[ui Septimi(i) S]eueri Pii, Arabici, Adiabenici, Pa[r]thici maximi, Britannici m[ax(imi) filii, D]i[u]i M(arci) Antonini Germ(anici), Sarm(atici) nepotis, Di[ui A]ntonini Pii pronepotis, Di[u]i Hadriani abne[potis, Diui] Traia[ni Parthici et Diui Ner]uae adnepotis, | M(arci) Aureli(i) Antonini Pii Felicis A[ug(usti), Parth(ici)] max(imi), Brit(annici) max(imi), Germ(anici) max(imi), pont(ificis) max(imi), [t]rib(unicia) potes(tate) XVII, imp(eratoris) III, co(n)s(ulis) IIII, p(atris) p(atriae), pro[co(n)] s(ulis), et Iu]liae Domnae Piae Felicis Aug(ustae), matris Aug(usti) et castr[o]rum et senatus et patriae, totiusque diuinae domus [eorum] templum Victoriae [Germ(anicae) Aug(ustae) D]omini nostri | quod G[a]binia Hermiona testamen[to suo ex] HS (=sestertium) C m(ilibus) n(ummum) fieri iussit, perfectum et dedicatum es[t s]uo testamento, die dedicationis, et dei[nceps] quodannis, epul[u]m decurionibus ab her[e]dibus suis dari praecepit, item agrum qui appellatur circus ad uo[l]uptatem po[p]uli reipubl(icae) remisit* (Kallala 2000: 117).

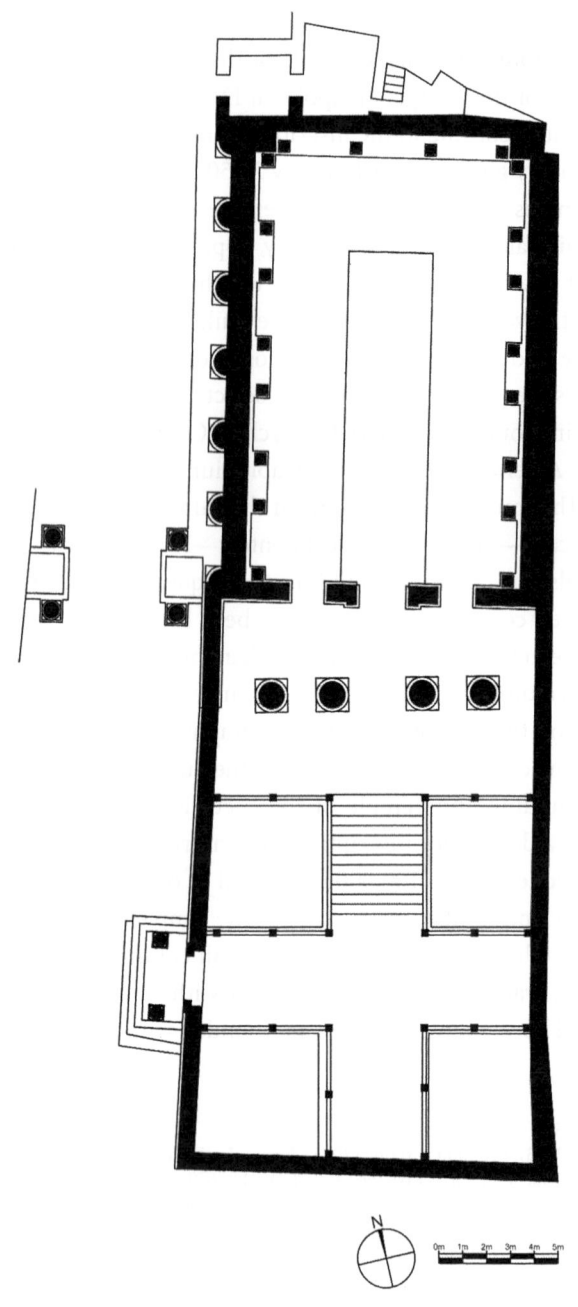

Fig. 4.1 Reconstruction of the ground plan of the Temple of the Victories of Caracalla in Dougga (drawn by the author).

Table 4.3 Quantification of each of the variables involved in the cost of the temple of the Victories of Caracalla

Construction variable	Cost (HS)
Construction material	44,224
Rough-out and semi-prepared material	13,969
Transport	13,382
Laying	15,842
Finishing	17,216
Total	104,633

cella there are two orders of superimposed columns, and some sectors were lined with marble. If we apply the calculation methodology to this building,[37] we obtain a cost of HS 104,633—reassuringly close to the true cost of the temple (Table 4.3).

The second building is the Arch of Caracalla in Theveste (Fig. 4.2).[38] It was dedicated in AD 214[39] and built in the town forum, according to a testamentary inscription carved on one of its pillars, recording that C. Cornelius Egrilianus bequeathed his fortune to his two brothers along with a series of conditions. One of them was that the sum of HS 250,000 be spent on building an arch in the forum.[40] The arch has survived in good condition, although there is some doubt as to the type of roof it would have had: a cupola similar to that of the Arch of Marcus Aurelius in Tripoli, built some forty years earlier, or a flat-roofed attic. The calculation methodology was applied to the two possible types of roof,[41] obtaining a cost for the arch without a cupola of HS 241,697 and a cost with a cupola of HS 243,661 (Table 4.4). With a margin for error, these amounts are close to the sum mentioned in the will.

---

[37] Domingo (2012c: 150–9, 166–7).
[38] Meunier (1938); Accame (1941); Ciotti (1946–8); De Roch (1952: 33–8); Bacchielli (1987); Blas de Roblès and Sintes (2003: 225).
[39] Bacchielli (1987: 296, 299, 303–4).
[40] *[Ex test]amento C. Corneli Egriliani*
praef. leg. XIIII Geminae; quo testamen-
to ex HS CCL mil. N arcum cum statuis
[Augg. NN., it]em tetrastylis duobus cum statuis
……[e]t Minervae, quae in foro fieri prae-
[cepit; prae]ter alia HS CCL mil. N, quae rei p., ita ut
[certis diebus gy]mnasia populo publice in thermis prae-
[berentur, legavit, et a]d Kapitol, arg. lib. CLXX, id est lances IIII,
……a]uri lib. XIIII, id est p[hi]al. III, scyphos II;
[haec]e omnia secundum voluntatem eius in con-
[tione populi] Corneli Fortunatus et Quinta fratres et
[heredes eius a]dsignaverunt et opus perfecerunt.
Inscription published in Bacchielli (1987: 301), with a slight variation in Accame (1941: 239).
[41] Domingo and Domingo (2017).

Fig. 4.2 Axonometric views of reconstructions of the Arch of Caracalla in Theveste, crowned by a dome (left) or by a simple flat-roofed attic (right) (image created by J. Á. Domingo & J. R. Domingo).

Table 4.4 Quantification of each of the variables involved in the cost of the Arch of Caracalla in Theveste

Construction variable	Cost (HS) (without cupola)	Cost (HS) (with cupola)
Construction material	40,331	40,870
Rough-out	59,631	60,443
Semi-prepared material	4,628	4,628
Transport	21,347	21,495
Laying	41,989	42,454
Finishing	53,771	53,771
Sculptures	20,000	20,000
Total	241,697	243,661

We do not find close agreement, however, between the true cost and that obtained using the calculation methodology for the other two buildings selected: the Capitolium and Temple C at Volubilis. In any case, as we shall see, it is highly likely that in these cases the cost differences are due not to a deficiency in the calculation methodology, but to an incorrect interpretation of the significance of the amount quoted in the inscriptions.

The first building, the Capitolium of Volubilis (Fig. 4.3),[42] was built abutting the back wall of a small 38 × 33 m plaza. The temple, dedicated in AD 217, was hexastyle, peripteral *sine postico*, and measured only 11 × 8.5 m. It was

---

[42] Chatelain (1944: 201–2); Luquet (1964); Thouvenot (1968–72).

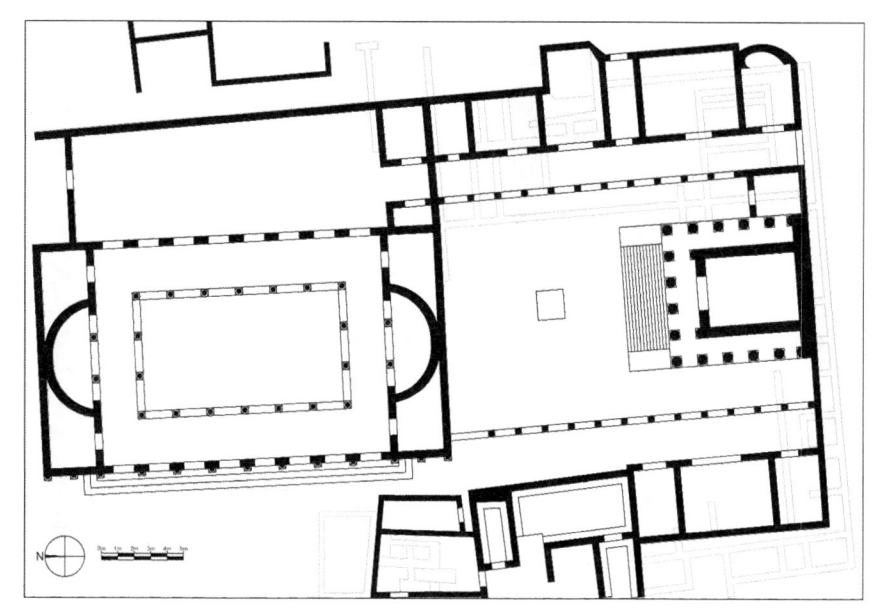

Fig. 4.3 Ground plan of the area of the Capitolium and Basilica of Volubilis (redrawn by the author, after Brouquier and Rebuffat 1998: 128, fig. 1).

built with small, irregular blocks of local stone from the quarries of Zerhoun. The dedicatory inscription, which has a lacuna exactly where the amount invested should be (*ex (sestertium) C[...] milib(us) [n(ummum)]*), allows us to reconstruct its cost only approximately.[43] At first it was thought to be *ex (sestertium) C[CC?] mil(ibus) [n(ummum)]*,[44] equivalent to HS 300,000, although now, owing to the fact that there is room to add three numerals, the more recent publication (in 1982) restores the missing figure as *ex (sestertium) C[CCC] mil(ibus) [n(ummum)]*,[45] HS 400,000. Yet in fact other reconstructions, like *C[XXX]*, *C[XXV]* (for HS 130,000 and 125,000 respectively), are equally possible. The same inscription also tells us that another allocation of funds, the amount of which we do not know, was used to finance the temple decorations.[46]

The second building, the so-called Temple C (Fig. 4.4),[47] was built abutting the rear wall of a 28 × 21 m plaza with porticoes on three sides. Dedicated in

---

[43] *[I(oui) O(ptimo)] M(aximo), Iunoni Reg[inae, Mine]ru[ae, pro] sal(ute) [et incol(umitate)/ I]mp(eratoris) Caes(aris) M(acri) Opelli S[eueri M]acrini, Pii, Felicis, [Aug(usti)],/trib(unicia) pot(estate), procos(ulis) et/M(arci) Opelli Ma[crini f(ilii) An]tonin[i, nob]ilissimi Cae[sar(is)],/Aug(usti), kap[itoliu]m ex (sestertium) C[...] milib(us) [n(ummum)] qua[e]/in hoc [opus decre]uerat coeptum, res[pu]blic(a) V[ol(ubilitanorum)]/add[itis signis? cete]risqué ornament[tis pe]rf[ecit,/dedicante M(arco) Aurelli]o Sebasten[o, proc(uratore) Aug(usti)]* (Chatelain 1942: n. 45; IAM 355).
[44] Chatelain (1925). [45] IAM 355. [46] Camporeale, Papi, and Passalacqua (2008: 290).
[47] Euzennat (1957); Jodin (1987: 168–9); Panetier (2002: 79).

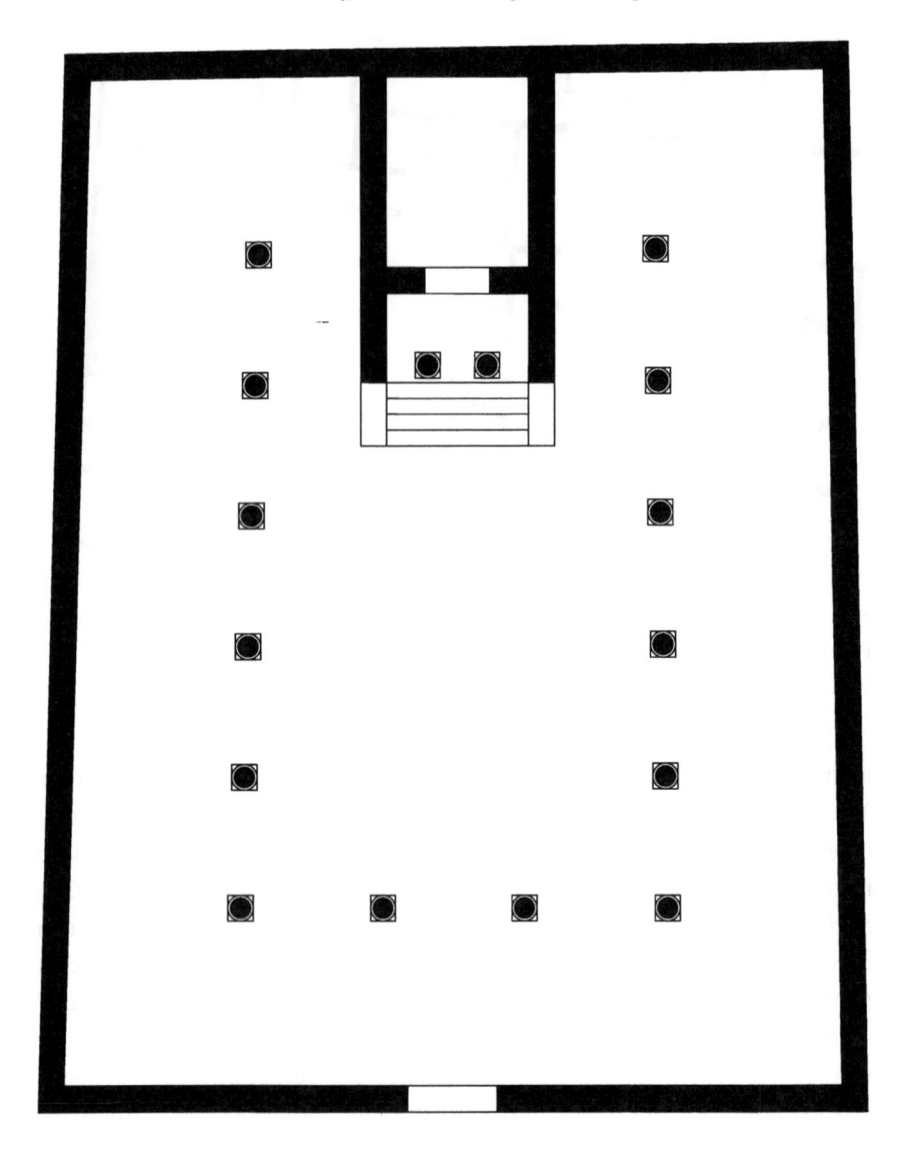

Fig. 4.4 Ground plan of the *temenos* of Temple C at Volubilis (redrawn by the author, after Euzennat 1957: 46, fig. 3a).

AD 216–17, it is distyle *in antis* and measures only 7.5 × 4.5 m. It was built using the same technique and stone type as the Capitolium, although the interior of the cella was lined with marble. The dedicatory inscription tells us it cost HS 400,000.[48]

Despite their different sizes, the inscriptions on both these temples give the same cost, HS 400,000 (if the reconstruction of the cost of the Capitolium, a building that is larger than Temple C, is correct), a very high price considering their small size and the costs quoted in the inscriptions of other North African temples. The vast majority were built at a much lower cost than these examples from Volubilis (Table 4.5).

In fact, if the calculation methodology is applied to these temples, for the Capitolium a result of only HS 47,817 is obtained, or HS 111,120 if the cost of the plaza around the temple is included (Table 4.6);[49] this is a long way from the HS 400,000 commonly restored as the cost, but not too far off the other possible restorations noted above, HS 125,000 or 130,000, if we include the surrounding precinct. For Temple C, though, the cost is calculated to be only HS 16,664 (Table 4.7).[50]

However, the following factors suggest that the amounts given in the inscriptions do not correspond solely to the cost of the temple construction, but must include other items that we cannot reconstruct (for example, costs of decoration, or cult statues, or gold and silver plate donated to the temple at its foundation):[51] the excessive difference between the amount obtained by applying the calculation methodology and the cost shown in the dedicatory inscriptions; the fact that both temples, despite their notable size differences, present the same cost; the fact that the amount mentioned in both cases, despite the small size of the temples, is very high in relation to the cost of other North African temples of a similar chronology.

---

[48] *[Pro sa]lut[e…imp(eratoris) Caesaris/M(acri) Aur]ell(i) An[tonini Pii Felicis Aug(usti) Parth(ici) Max(imi) Brit(annici)/Max(imi) G]erm(anici) [Max(imi) Pontificis Max(imi) trib(unicia) pot(estate) X]X, Imp(eratoris) [IV]…[ex] s(estertium) CCCCM…*(Euzennat 1957: 47).

[49] In a previous study, in which some variables were given an erroneous value (cost of the local stone of 20 HS/ft³ and cost of labour of 90 HS/day for an unqualified worker), a cost of HS 782,247 was obtained (Domingo 2012b: 381–418). This quantification of the variables was corrected in a subsequent study and the cost of the temple was recalculated (Domingo 2012c: 165–6).

[50] After correcting the erroneous reconstruction of the cost of some of the variables in an earlier study (Domingo 2012b), the cost for this temple was recalculated: HS 385,978 (Domingo 2012c).

[51] Domingo (2012c: 167–8).

Table 4.5 Building costs of some African temples in the second and third centuries AD (based on data from Duncan-Jones 1974: 90–1)

City	Building	Period	Cost (HS)	Bibliography
Lambaesis	Capitolium	AD 190–235	600,000	*CIL* VIII.18226–7
Volubilis	Temple C	AD 216–17	400,000	Euzennat (1957: 47)
Volubilis	Capitolium	AD 217	>400,000	*ILM* 45
Calama	Temple of Apollo	AD 286–305	>350,000	*CIL* VIII.5333
Thugga	Temple of Mercury	AD 185–92	>120,000	*CIL* VIII.26482, 1–7
Thugga	Temple of Saturn	AD 194–5	>100,000	*CIL* VIII.26498
Mustis	Temple of Fortuna	AD 164–5	70,000	*CIL* VIII.15576
Thugga	Temple of Fortuna	Second century AD	70,000	*CIL* VIII.26471
Macomades	Temple of Pluto	AD 265	67,500	*AE* 1905, 35
Theveste	Temple of Saturn	AD 163–5	63,000	*AE* 1933, 233
Thugga	Temple of Concordia	Second century AD	50,000	*CIL* VIII.26467, a–e
Madauros	Temple of Concordia	After AD 180	40,000	*ILAlg* I.2035
Numluli	Capitolium	AD 170	>24,000	*CIL* VIII.26121
Thibursicum Bure	Temple	After AD 200	20,000	*CIL* VIII.1463
Verecunda	Temple of Genius Patriae	AD 193–5	>20,000	*CIL* VIII.4192
Muzuc	Temple of Apollo	After AD 200	12,000	*CIL* VIII.12058
Thugga	Temple of Minerva I	Second century AD	10,000	*AE* 1997, 1655
Magifa	Temple of Dii Magifae	AD 198–211	8,000	*CIL* VIII.16749
Mustis	Temple of Mercury	AD 217–18	>5,000	*AE* 1968, 591
Vazi Sarra	Temple of Mercury Sobrius	AD 211–12	>3,000	*CIL* VIII.12006–7

Table 4.6 Quantification of each of the variables involved in the cost of the Capitolium of Volubilis

Construction variable	Cost (HS) (temple)	Cost (HS) (plaza)
Construction material	17,164	27,180
Rough-out and semi-prepared material	5,493	3,908
Transport	6,194	8,471
Laying	8,413	9,601
Finishing	10,553	14,143
Total	47,817	63,303
Total (temple + plaza)	111,120	

Table 4.7 Quantification of each of the variables involved in the cost of Temple C at Volubilis

Construction variable	Cost (HS)
Construction material	4,626
Rough-out	1,660
Semi-prepared material	227
Transport	1,552
Laying	3,695
Finishing	4,905
Total	16,664

Cost Comparison between the Templum Pacis and the Upper Terrace of the Tarraco Provincial Forum

From the examples just mentioned it is apparent that the calculation methodology developed since the end of the twentieth century does often allow us to ascertain approximate building costs. Perhaps the result of the calculation corresponds only to the initial budget or to the cost of the normal building process, without any complications that could increase the final price. I now return to the question posed at the beginning of this study, of whether there were cost differences between the major building projects dedicated to imperial worship in Rome and their provincial imitations.

For this experiment, I will use as an example two very similar complexes, both built in the time of Vespasian and with similar building techniques and materials: the Templum Pacis in Rome and the upper terrace of the Provincial Forum in Tarraco. Both complexes are based on a common preceding model, the Claudianum, built in Rome in AD 54 by Nero (Fig. 4.5).[52] The Claudianum was a hexastyle temple with columns identical to those of the Temple of Mars Ultor and was built within a porticoed plaza. Nero had it destroyed in AD 59, and Vespasian rebuilt it, successively increasing the size of the plaza and adding a huge hall on one of its sides. This hall was probably built for the worship of the new dynasty, judging by the remains of imperial portraits found in the area, including one of Titus found beneath the nearby church of San Gregorio Magno.[53]

---

[52] Domingo, Mar, and Pensabene (2011; 2013). On the similarities between the upper terrace of the provincial forum of Tarraco, the Forum Pacis, and the Claudianum, see Domingo and Pensabene (2017).

[53] Rosso (2007: 131).

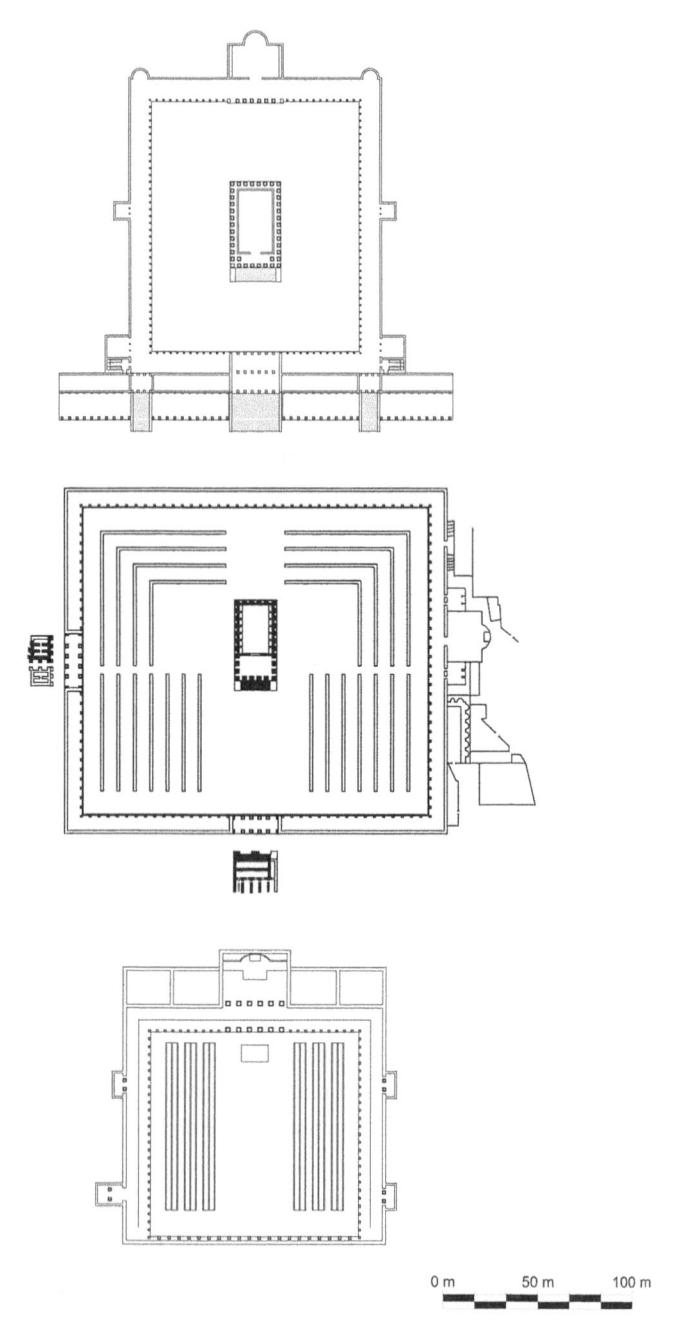

Fig. 4.5 Ground plan of the upper terrace of the Tarraco Provincial Forum (top), the Claudianum (middle), and the Templum Pacis (bottom) (drawn by the author).

We can observe a similar evolution on the upper terrace of the Tarraco Provincial Forum: the porticoed plaza that surrounded the Julio-Claudian temple dedicated to Augustus was expanded by Vespasian, who also built a massive Hall of Worship at the rear.[54] In this way, this terrace imitated the size and shape of the contemporary Templum Pacis, in which there was obviously no pre-existing temple in the middle of the plaza. Moreover, whereas in the Claudianum the Hall is hidden behind the portico, as it appears to be depicted in the preserved fragments of the *Forma Urbis Romae* where no monumental façade is shown, in the Tarraco complex and the Forum Pacis the Hall is situated at the rear of the plaza and is preceded by a monumental façade.

We cannot, therefore, consider the Tarraco Forum to be simply a provincial imitation of a model developed in Rome; rather it can be seen as another stage in the evolution that led from the Claudianum model to the Templum Pacis. This means that it would clearly have been built as a result of a particular political situation that saw the ascension to power of a new dynasty, thanks in part to the alliance with personages from Tarraconensis. In fact, at the beginning of the revolt against Nero, an important role was played by C. Iulius Vindex (governor of Gallia Lugdunensis), who brought to the venture Galba (governor of Tarraconensis), who then obtained the support of Vinius (governor of Gallia Narbonensis), Otho (governor of Lusitania), Aulus Caecina Alienus (quaestor of Baetica), and Vespasian, who at that time was in command of the three legions sent to put down the Jewish revolt in AD 66. Vespasian's accession to power, together with the granting of Latin rights to the whole of Hispania, must have been one of the reasons behind the construction of the Tarraco Provincial Forum, adopting architectural models from Rome: the Claudianum and the Templum Pacis.[55]

To compare the costs of the upper terrace of the Tarraco Provincial Forum and the Templum Pacis, I will calculate solely the cost of the columns and the entablatures of the porticos of each building, as we are as yet unable to reconstruct the rest of their constituent parts with any great accuracy.[56] Indeed, as

---

[54] Mar (1993: 113–28); Pensabene and Mar (2004: 83).
[55] Domingo and Pensabene (2017).
[56] Certain premises must be taken into account when calculating the costs of these buildings. In the Templum Pacis, the portico had 94 columns (22 of them made of African marble) with Corinthian capitals, whereas the façade of the Hall of Worship had 6 columns with Corinthian capitals. The portico of the upper terrace of the Forum of Tarraco had 120 columns with composite capitals, whereas the façade of the Hall of Worship had 6 columns with Corinthian capitals and the Propylaeum had 6 columns and 2 pilaster strips in the angles with composite capitals. The extraction of a block of marble of 1 m³ took 12 working days. The roughing-out of elements made with moulds and fine-grained marble took 157.5 hours/m³ (Pegoretti 1863: i. 402). The partial preparation of bases, capitals, and

the objective of this study is to carry out a methodological experiment, it is preferable to focus our attention only on those elements that can be reconstructed with great precision, thus avoiding the introduction of hypothetical variables that could falsify the results.

The Templum Pacis

The Templum Pacis[57] was built between AD 71 and 75 with war booty (*ex manubiis*)[58] from the victory over the Jews in AD 71. The preserved part of this complex is from the Severan period, built following the fire of AD 192 that destroyed it almost completely,[59] although we have some evidence that allows us to reconstruct the Flavian phase. For example, we know that the Severan temple did not substantially modify the preceding phase; the foundations were reused and thus the original perimeter of 110 × 105 m was maintained.[60] The northern portico, with shafts in *Africano* marble, appears not to have been damaged by the fire, and its columns are therefore the original ones from the first phase.[61] And, finally, the finds of fragments of enormous *giallo antico* shafts—some 2 m in diameter—allow us hypothetically to reconstruct the original façade of the Hall of Worship with that type of marble, although it has recently been suggested that these shafts may have belonged to the

---

shafts in fine-grained marble cost $a(1+0.25/x)$, in the case of monolithic shafts the cost was $a(2+0.25/x)$, where a = 4.33 hours of work and x represents the diameter, with the figure obtained equalling the number of working hours/m² of surface worked (Pegoretti 1863: i. 403). The semi-preparation of rectilinear pieces in fine-grained marble—architraves, friezes, and cornices—took 4.33 hours/m² of surface worked (Pegoretti 1863: i. 403). The cost of the overland transport was calculated using the formula 0.85 *denarii* per m³ per mile (DeLaine 1997: 210–11; Barresi 2003: 175; Mar and Pensabene 2010: 527, 531), the distance from the Carrara quarries to the port of embarkation being some 20 miles. For calculating the cost of sea transport we have various data: the cost of the transport between Italy and Tarraconensis was 10 *denarii* per m³ (Arnaud 2007: 334, 336), a value that also allows us to calculate the approximate cost of transport between Carrara and Rome at around 4 *denarii* per m³; as the cost of the transport between Sicily and Rome was 6 *denarii* per m³ (Arnaud 2007: 336), we can assume that the approximate cost of transport between Simitthus (*giallo antico* marble) and Rome was 8 *denarii* per m³; using a cost for transport between Asia and Rome of 16 *denarii* per m³ and between Alexandria and Rome also 16 *denarii* per m³ (Arnaud 2007: 336), we can assume that the cost between Siğacik (Turkey, *Africano* marble) and Rome was 16 *denarii* per m³. The setting in place of the elements weighing more than one ton took 35.3 hours/ton (Barresi 2000: 363; Mar and Pensabene 2010: 527).

[57] Fogagnolo and Mocchegiani (2009); Meneghini, Corsaro, and Pinna (2009); Tucci (2009, 2017); Fogagnolo and Rossi (2010); Coletta and Maisto (2014); Facchin (2014); Meneghini (2014); Montella (2014); Pinna (2014).
[58] Cass. Dio, 65.15. [59] Cass. Dio, 72.24.
[60] Meneghini, Corsaro, and Pinna (2009: 199); Fogagnolo and Rossi (2010: 96).
[61] Rizzo (2001: 241).

interior columns of the Severan-phase pronaos.⁶² Finally, in the rest of the portico the shafts would have been of Carrara marble.⁶³

One of the variables with the greatest impact on the price of a building is the cost of labour.⁶⁴ A labourer of the first to second century AD has traditionally been assigned an average salary of HS 2 a day.⁶⁵ However, the cost of living was not the same in Rome as in the provinces. Pliny tells us that Rome was a particularly expensive city, while Martial recalls with a certain nostalgia how life in Hispania was much cheaper than in Rome.⁶⁶ This means that salaries would also have been subject to regional variations.⁶⁷ Indeed, other sources give different amounts for workers: the sum of HS 4 is given in a work contract from Oxyrhynchus in the second century AD;⁶⁸ in an inscription in Pompeii;⁶⁹ and in a verse from the Gospel of St Matthew.⁷⁰

In addition to the cash salary, Diocletian's *Edict* indicates a daily ration of food, the cost of which in Italy we can reconstruct from various sources. For example, from Pompeii we have a list of nine days of shopping with the prices for each of the items purchased to feed three people; from that we can work out an average cost for a food ration of HS 2 per person per day.⁷¹ Other sources give us similar values.⁷² Therefore, the total wage received by a building worker would have been equivalent to HS 4 per day in Italy for an unqualified labourer and HS 5 a day for a marble mason.⁷³ Other sources, as we will

---

⁶² Coletta and Maisto (2014: 308).

⁶³ The dimensions of the Flavian phase architectural elements were reconstructed in cooperation with P. Pensabene and F. Caprioli, to whom I am very grateful for allowing me access to their research data, much of them still unpublished.

⁶⁴ Regarding the cost of construction labour and the probable differences between Rome and the provinces, see Domingo (2013). Slave labour may have been used in some of the building projects; maintaining a slave cost between HS 0.5–1 per day (Duncan-Jones 1974: 208), or HS 2–3 per day (Mrozek 1975: 73; West 1916: 304). Despite this, the archaeological evidence appears to suggest slaves were not common in the main quarries of the empire; in the majority—Carrara, Thasos, and Dokimeion—there do not appear to be any buildings that would suggest that slaves or prisoners worked there. In addition, the *ostraka* of the quarries of Mons Claudianus never mention the presence of *damnati*. Only one building from the third century AD in the quarries of Simitthus, walled and with controlled access, has been interpreted as possible accommodation for slaves or prisoners, although there are doubts as to its function, as it may also have been a military camp (Fant 2008; Marano 2014: 416–17). We do, on the other hand, have evidence of condemned labour in the Mons Porphyrites quarries in Egypt during the reign of Diocletian (Peacock 1995).

⁶⁵ DeLaine (1997: 119–21); Barresi (2000: 345).   ⁶⁶ Plin., *HN* 18.90; Mart., 12.31 and 10.96.

⁶⁷ Domingo (2013).   ⁶⁸ *P.Oxy* 488.   ⁶⁹ *CIL* IV.8566; Mrozek (1975: 70–5).

⁷⁰ Matthew 20.1–2.   ⁷¹ *CIL* IV.5380.

⁷² For example, other inscriptions from Pompeii (*CIL* IV, suppl. II.4428) suggest a cost of HS 1.25–2 per person per day (Kahrstedt 1958: 211).

⁷³ Domingo (2013: 132). The figures given in the *Edict* of Diocletian and their extrapolation to the first century AD based on the evolution of the price of the *modius castrensis* of grain gives us a fifty-fold increase in salaries between the first century AD (1 *denarius*/day) and Diocletian's era (50 *denarii*/day). This proportion is the same as that deduced from other sources that tell us of legionaries' salaries in different periods: the increase between the first century AD (225 *denarii*/year) and Diocletian's time (10,000–12,000 *denarii*/year) is indeed fifty-fold (Levrero 2014: 58–9).

see, give lower amounts for the provinces, around HS 2 in Egypt and Dacia, and probably also in Spain.

Finally, the cost of labour in the imperial quarries probably did not vary from one geographical area to another. It is quite plausible that the salaries were the same. For example, the *stipendium* paid to soldiers billeted in both Numidia and Antioch was identical, despite the very different geographical and economic contexts.[74] A similar situation can be seen with workers in two imperial mining and quarrying districts a considerable distance apart: the gold mines at Alburnus Maior in Dacia and the quarries at Mons Claudianus in Egypt. In the first case the workers received a salary of between HS 1.5 per day, plus a food ration,[75] and HS 2.3 per day,[76] whereas in the second case their salary was somewhat more than HS 2 per day.[77] Therefore, we can assume that unqualified workers in the imperial quarries earned around 2 HS per day, while the marble-cutters working in those quarries would have earned some 2.5 HS per day.

Taking these circumstances into account, the cost of the building's columns and entablatures is *c.* HS 1,500,000 (175,000 days of work) (Tables 4.8–4.10).

The Upper Terrace of the Provincial Forum at Tarraco

The upper terrace of the Provincial Forum at Tarraco is a plaza 133 × 152 m long, with a large Hall of Worship at the rear that reproduced the dimensions of the Julio-Claudian temple. Both the columns and the entablatures of the portico and the Hall of Worship were of Luna marble.[78]

As already stated, salaries in the provinces would have been lower than those of Rome;[79] additionally, the price of the *modius castrensis* of grain that has been used to extrapolate the values of Diocletian's *Edict* to other periods varied from one province to another.[80] Based on this information, I have been able to calculate an average salary of HS 2 a day for an unqualified labourer in Hispania.[81] Nevertheless, we must not lose sight of the fact that some of the

---

[74] De la Hoz (2011: 155).   [75] Carcopino (1937: 97–102).   [76] Mrozek (1975: 71).
[77] Serafino (2009: 47–9).
[78] Mar (1993); Pensabene and Mar (2004); Mar and Pensabene (2010); Macias et al. (2011). The dimensions of the architectural elements have been reconstructed in cooperation with P. Pensabene within the framework of a new study on the Provincial Forum of Tarraco that we are carrying out, still unpublished.
[79] Domingo (2013).
[80] For a compilation of the prices of grain in different periods and areas of the empire, see Domingo (2013: tables 2a, 2b).
[81] Domingo (2013: 132).

Table 4.8 Cost of the Templum Pacis: Hall of Worship

(i) Material

Type	Height (m)	Max. length (m)	Diameter (m)	Width (m)	Volume (m³)	Volume (ft³)	Weight (kg)	Price of marble (HS/ft³)	Cost (1 column) (HS)	Total cost (6 columns) (HS)
Capital (Luna)	2.00	2.83	1.55	—	16.02	616.77	43,254	5	3,084	18,504
Shaft (giallo antico)	14.76	—	2.00	—	65.09	2,505.96	175,743	8	15,560	93,360
Base (Luna)	0.98	2.55	—	—	6.37	245.25	17,199	5	1,226	7,356
Subtotal	17.74	—	—	—	87.48	3,367.98	236,196	—	19,870	119,220
Architrave (Luna)	1.18	34.00	—	2.50	100.30	3,861.55	270,810	5	—	19,308
Frieze (Luna)	1.09	34.00	—	2.50	92.65	3,567.02	250,155	5	—	17,835
Cornice (Luna)	1.79	34.00	—	2.80	170.41	6,560.78	460,107	5	—	32,804
Subtotal	4.06	—	—	—	363.36	13,989.35	981,072	—	—	89,817
Total										209,037

(ii) Extraction

Type	Labour	Salary/day (HS)	Time (days/m³)	Volume (m³)	Days (1 column)	Volume (m³)	Days (6 columns)	Cost (1 column) (HS)	Total cost (6 columns) (HS)
Capital	Worker	2	12	16.02	192.2	16.02	1,153.2	384	2,304
Shaft	Worker	2	12	65.09	781.1	65.09	4,686.6	1,562	9,372
Base	Worker	2	12	6.37	76.4	6.37	458.4	153	918
Subtotal				87.48	1,049.7	87.48	6,298.2	2,099	12,594
Architrave	Worker	2	12		—	100.30	1,203.6	—	2,407
Frieze	Worker	2	12		—	92.65	1,111.8	—	2,224
Cornice	Worker	2	12		—	170.41	2,044.9	—	4,090
Subtotal						363.36	4,360.3	—	8,721
Total							10,658.5		21,315

Continued

Table 4.8 *Continued*

(iii) Rough-out

Type	Labour	Salary/day (HS)	Time (hours/m³)	Volume (m³)	Days (1 column)	Days (6 columns)	Cost (1 column) (HS)	Total cost (6 columns) (HS)
Capital	Marble-cutter	2.5	157.5	16.02	252.3	1,513.8	631	3,786
Shaft	Marble-cutter	2.5	157.5	65.09	1,025.2	6,151.2	2,563	15,378
Base	Marble-cutter	2.5	157.5	6.37	100.3	601.8	251	1,506
Subtotal				87.48	1,377.8	8,266.8	3,445	20,670
Architrave	Marble-cutter	2.5	157.5	100.30	—	1,579.7	—	3,949
Frieze	Marble-cutter	2.5	157.5	92.65	—	1,459.2	—	3,648
Cornice	Marble-cutter	2.5	157.5	170.41	—	2,683.9	—	6,710
Subtotal				363.36		5,722.8	—	14,307
Total						13,989.6		34,977

(iv) Semi-Preparation

Type	Labour	Salary/day (HS)	Time	Area (m²)	Days (1 column)	Days (6 columns)	Cost (1 column) (HS)	Total cost (6 columns) (HS)
Capital	Marble-cutter	2.5	$a(1 + 0.25/x)$	22.64	11.3	67.8	28	168
Shaft (monolithic)	Marble-cutter	2.5	$a(2 + 0.25/x)$	92.74	83.5	501.0	209	1,254
Base	Marble-cutter	2.5	$a(1 + 0.25/x)$	10.00	5.0	30.0	12	72
Subtotal					99.8	598.8	249	1,494
Architrave	Marble-cutter	2.5	4.33 hours/m²	80.24	—	34.7	—	87
Frieze	Marble-cutter	2.5	4.33 hours/m²	74.12	—	32.1	—	80
Cornice	Marble-cutter	2.5	4.33 hours/m²	121.72	—	52.7	—	132
Subtotal						119.5	—	299
Total						718.3		1,793

(v) Transport

Type	Method	Formula	Volume (m³)	Cost (1 column) (HS)	Total cost (6 columns) (HS)
Capital + Base (Luna)	Land	0.85 *den.* × m³ × mile	22.39	1,524	9,144
	Maritime	4 *den.* × m³	22.39	360	2,160
Shaft (*giallo antico*)	Maritime	8 *den.* × m³	65.09	2,084	12,808
Subtotal				3,968	23,808
Entablature (Luna)	Land	0.85 *den.* × m³ × mile	363.36	—	24,708
	Maritime	4 *den.* × m³	363.36	—	5,812
Subtotal					30,520
Total					54,328

(vi) Installation

Type	Labour	Salary/day (HS)	Time (hours/tonne)	Volume (m³)	Weight (kg)	Days (1 column)	Days (6 columns)	Cost (1 column) (HS)	Total cost (6 columns) (HS)
Capital	Worker	4	35.3	16.02	43,254	152.7	916.2	611	3,666
Shaft	Worker	4	35.3	65.09	175,743	620.4	3,722.4	2,482	14,892
Base	Worker	4	35.3	6.37	17,199	60.7	364.2	243	1,458
Subtotal				87.48	236,196	833.8	5,002.8	3,336	20,016
Architrave	Worker	4	35.3	100.30	270,810	—	956.0	—	3,824
Frieze	Worker	4	35.3	92.65	250,155	—	883.0	—	3,532
Cornice	Worker	4	35.3	170.41	460,107	—	1,624.2	—	6,497
Subtotal				363.36	981,072	—	3,463.2	—	13,853
Total							8,466.0		33,869

Continued

Table 4.8 *Continued*

(vii) Finishing

Type	Labour	Salary/day (HS)	Time	Area (m²)	Days (1 column)	Days (6 columns)	Cost (1 column) (HS)	Total cost (6 columns) (HS)
Capital	Marble-cutter	5	1,800 hours[a]	—	180.0	1,080.0	900	5,400
Shaft	Marble-cutter	5	10 hours/m²[b]	92.74	92.7	556.2	463	2,778
Base	Marble-cutter	5	720 hours[c]	—	72.0	432.0	360	2,160
Subtotal					344.7	2,068.2	1,723	10,338
Architrave	Marble-cutter	5	5.6 hours/m²[d]	80.24	—	44.9	—	224
Frieze	Marble-cutter	5	277.5 hours/m²[e]	74.12	—	2,057.0	—	10,285
Cornice	Marble-cutter	5	250.0 hours/m²[f]	121.72	—	3,043.0	—	15,215
Subtotal						5,144.9		25,724
Total						7,213.1		36,062

OVERALL TOTAL FOR THE TEMPLUM PACIS HALL OF WORSHIP   41,045.5   391,381

[a] Pegoretti (1863: i. 408).
[b] Pegoretti (1863: i. 404).
[c] Barresi (2000: 362).
[d] Pegoretti (1863: i. 406).
[e] Pegoretti (1863: i. 407).
[f] Pegoretti (1863: i. 407).

Table 4.9 Cost of the Templum Pacis: portico (Luna marble)

(i) Material

Type	Height (m)	Max. length (m)	Diameter (m)	Width (m)	Volume (m³)	Volume (ft³)	Weight (kg)	Price of marble (HS/ft³)	Cost (1 column) (HS)	Total cost (72 columns) (HS)
Capital (Luna)	1.03	1.46	0.86	—	2.19	84.31	5,913	5	383	27,576
Shaft (Luna)	6.96	—	1.00	—	8.42	324.17	22,734	5	1,313	94,536
Base (Luna)	0.52	0.82	—	—	0.35	13.47	945	5	67	4,824
Subtotal	8.51	—	—	—	10.96	421.95	29,592	—	1,763	126,936
Entablature (Luna)	2.00	291.00	—	1.30	756.60	29,129.10	2,042,820	5	—	145,645
Total										272,581

(ii) Extraction

Type	Labour	Salary/day (HS)	Time (days/m³)	Volume (m³)	Days (1 column)	Days (72 columns)	Cost (1 column) (HS)	Total cost (72 columns) (HS)
Capital	Worker	2	12	2.19	26.3	1,893.6	53	3,816
Shaft	Worker	2	12	8.42	101.0	7,272.0	202	14,544
Base	Worker	2	12	0.35	4.2	302.4	8	576
Subtotal				10.96	131.5	9,468.0	263	18,936
Entablature	Worker	2	12	756.60	—	9,079.2	—	18,158
Total						18,547.2		37,094

Continued

Table 4.9 Continued

(iii) Rough-out

Type	Labour	Salary/day (HS)	Time (hours/m³)	Volume (m³)	Days (1 column)	Days (72 columns)	Cost (1 column) (HS)	Total cost (72 columns) (HS)
Capital	Marble-cutter	2.5	157.5	2.19	34.5	2,484.0	86	6,192
Shaft	Marble-cutter	2.5	157.5	8.42	132.6	9,547.2	331	23,832
Base	Marble-cutter	2.5	157.5	0.35	5.5	396.2	14	1,008
Subtotal				10.96	172.6	12,427.2	431	31,032
Entablature	Marble-cutter	2.5	157.5	756.60	—	11,916.4	—	29,791
Total						24,343.6		60,823

(iv) Semi-Preparation

Type	Labour	Salary/day (HS)	Time	Area (m²)	Days (1 column)	Days (72 columns)	Cost (1 column) (HS)	Total cost (72 columns) (HS)
Capital	Marble-cutter	2.5	$a(1 + 0.25/x)$	6.01	3.6	259.2	9	648
Shaft	Marble-cutter	2.5	$a(1 + 0.25/x)$	19.46	10.9	784.8	27	1,944
Base	Marble-cutter	2.5	$a(1 + 0.25/x)$	1.70	1.0	72.0	2	144
Subtotal					15.5	1,116.0	38	2,736
Entablature	Marble-cutter	2.5	4.33 hours/m²	1,164.00	—	504.0	—	1,260
Total						1,620.0		3,996

(v) Transport

Type	Method	Formula	Volume (m³)	Cost (1 column) (HS)	Total cost (72 columns) (HS)
Column (Luna)	Land	0.85 *den.* × mile × m³	10.96	744	53,568
	Maritime	4 *den.* × m³	10.96	176	12,672
Subtotal				920	66,240
Entablature (Luna)	Land	0.85 *den.* × mile × m³	756.60	—	51,448
	Maritime	4 *den.* × m³	756.60	—	12,104
Subtotal				—	63,552
Total					129,792

(vi) Installation

Type	Labour	Salary/day (HS)	Time (hours/tonne)	Volume (m³)	Weight (kg)	Days (1 column)	Days (72 columns)	Cost (1 column) (HS)	Total cost (72 columns) (HS)
Capital	Worker	4	35.3	2.19	5,913	20.9	1,504.8	84	6,048
Shaft	Worker	4	35.3	8.42	22,734	80.2	5,774.4	321	23,112
Base	Worker	4	35.3	0.35	945	3.3	237.6	13	936
Subtotal					29,592	104.4	7,516.8	418	30,096
Entablature	Worker	4	35.3	756.60	2,042,820	—	7,211.1	—	28,844
Total							14,727.9		58,940

Continued

Table 4.9 Continued

(vii) Finishing

Type	Labour	Salary/day (HS)	Time	Area (m²)	Days (1 column)	Days (72 columns)	Cost (1 column) (HS)	Total cost (72 columns) (HS)
Capital	Marble-cutter	5	800 hours[a]	6.01	80.0	5,760.0	400	28,800
Shaft	Marble-cutter	5	10 hours/m²[b]	19.46	19.5	1,404.0	97	6,984
Base	Marble-cutter	5	360 hours[c]	1.70	36.0	2,592.0	180	12,960
Subtotal					135.5	9,756.0	677	48,744
Entablature	Marble-cutter	5	177 hours/m²[d]	1,164.00	—	20,602.8	—	103,014
Total						30,358.8		151,758

OVERALL TOTAL FOR THE TEMPLUM PACIS PORTICO (LUNA MARBLE)   89,597.5   714,984

[a] Pegoretti (1863: i. 408).
[b] Pegoretti (1863: i. 404).
[c] Barresi (2000: 362).
[d] As we do not know the measurements of the architrave, the frieze, and the cornice, I take an average value based on the execution times for the pieces of the Hall of Worship: 5.6 hours/m² + 277.5 hours/m² + 250 hours/m² / 3 = 177 hours/m².

Table 4.10 Cost of the Templum Pacis: portico (*marmo africano*)

(i) Material

Type	Height (m)	Max. length (m)	Diameter (m)	Width (m)	Volume (m³)	Volume (ft³)	Weight (kg)	Price of marble (HS/ft³)	Cost (1 column) (HS)	Total cost (22 columns) (HS)
Capital (Luna)	1.36	1.92	1.05	—	5.01	192.88	13,527	5	964	21,208
Shaft (*africano*)	9.66	—	1.28	—	18.40	708.40	49,680	6	4,250	93,500
Base (Luna)	0.68	1.50	—	—	1.53	58.90	4,131	5	295	6,490
Subtotal	11.70	—	—	—	24.94	960.18	67,338	—	5,509	121,198
Entablature (Luna)	1.75	105.00	—	1.70	312.37	12,026.25	843,399	5	—	60,131
Total										181,329

(ii) Extraction

Type	Labour	Salary/day (HS)	Time (days/m³)	Volume (m³)	Days (1 column)	Days (22 columns)	Cost (1 column) (HS)	Total cost (22 columns) (HS)
Capital	Worker	2	12	5.01	60.1	1,322.2	120	2,640
Shaft	Worker	2	12	18.40	220.8	4,857.6	442	9,724
Base	Worker	2	12	1.53	18.4	404.8	37	814
Subtotal				29.94	299.3	6,584.6	599	13,178
Entablature	Worker	2	12	312.37	—	3,748.4	—	7,497
Total						10,333		20,675

Continued

Table 4.10 *Continued*

(iii) Rough-out

Type	Labour	Salary/day (HS)	Time (hours/m³)	Volume (m³)	Days (1 column)	Days (22 columns)	Cost (1 column) (HS)	Total cost (22 columns) (HS)
Capital	Marble-cutter	2.5	157.5	5.01	78.9	1,735.8	197	4,334
Shaft	Marble-cutter	2.5	157.5	18.40	289.8	6,375.6	724	15,928
Base	Marble-cutter	2.5	157.5	1.53	24.1	530.2	60	1,320
Subtotal				24.94	392.8	8,641.6	981	21,582
Entablature	Marble-cutter	2.5	157.5	312.37	—	4,919.8	—	12,300
Total						13,561.4		33,882

(iv) Semi-Preparation

Type	Labour	Salary/day (HS)	Time	Area (m²)	Days (1 column)	Days (22 columns)	Cost (1 column) (HS)	Total cost (22 columns) (HS)
Capital	Marble-cutter	2.5	$a(1 + 0.25/x)$	10.44	5.2	114.4	13	286
Shaft (monolithic)	Marble-cutter	2.5	$a(2 + 0.25/x)$	38.84	41.9	921.8	105	2,310
Base	Marble-cutter	2.5	$a(1 + 0.25/x)$	4.08	2.0	44.0	5	110
Subtotal					49.1	1,080.2	123	2,706
Entablature	Marble-cutter	2.5	4.33 hours/m²	367.50	—	159.1	—	398
Total						1,239.3		3,104

(v) Transport

Type	Method	Formula	Volume (m³)	Cost (1 column) (HS)	Total cost (22 columns) (HS)
Capital + Base (Luna)	Land	0.85 *den.* × m³ × mile	6.54	444	9,768
	Maritime	4 *den.* × m³	6.54	104	2,288
Shaft (africano)	Maritime	16 *den.* × m³	18.40	1,176	25,872
Subtotal				1,724	37,928
Entablature (Luna)	Land	0.85 *den.* × m³ × mile	312.37	—	21,240
	Maritime	4 *den.* × m³	312.37	—	4,996
Subtotal				—	26,236
Total					64,164

(vi) Installation

Type	Labour	Salary/day (HS)	Time (hours/tonne)	Volume (m³)	Weight (kg)	Days (1 column)	Days (22 columns)	Cost (1 column) (HS)	Total cost (22 columns) (HS)
Capital	Worker	4	35.3	5.01	13,527	47.7	1,049.4	191	4,202
Shaft	Worker	4	35.3	18.40	49,680	175.4	3,858.8	702	15,444
Base	Worker	4	35.3	1.53	4,131	14.6	321.2	58	1,276
Subtotal				24.94	67,338	237.7	5,229.4	951	20,922
Entablature	Worker	4	35.3	312.37	843,399	—	2,977.2	—	11,909
Total							8,206.6		32,831

Continued

Table 4.10 Continued

(vii) Finishing

Type	Labour	Salary/day (HS)	Time	Area (m²)	Days (1 column)	Days (22 columns)	Cost (1 column) (HS)	Total cost (22 columns) (HS)
Capital	Marble-cutter	5	1,100 hours[a]	38.84	110.0	2,420.0	550	12,100
Shaft	Marble-cutter	5	5.6 hours/m²[b]		21.7	477.4	108	2,376
Base	Marble-cutter	5	480 hours[c]		48.0	1,056.0	240	5,280
Subtotal					179.7	3,953.4	898	19,756
Entablature	Marble-cutter	5	177 hours/m²[d]	367.50	—	6,504.7	—	32,523
Subtotal					—	10,458.1	—	52,279
OVERALL TOTAL FOR THE TEMPLUM PACIS PORTICO (MARMO AFRICANO)						43,798.4		388,264

[a] Pegoretti (1863: i. 407).
[b] Pegoretti (1863: i. 406).
[c] Barresi (2000: 362).
[d] As we do not know the measurements of the architrave, the frieze, and the cornice, I take an average value based on the execution times for the pieces of the Hall of Worship: 5.6 hours/m² + 277.5 hours/m² + 250 hours/m² / 3 = 177 hours/m².

cutting of the marble used in Tarraco was carried out in the Carrara quarries, while the finishing of some of the decorative elements, which are very similar to those documented in the Templum Pacis, was carried out *in situ* by imperial workshops,[82] whose workers would have been paid a higher salary. For example, numerous remnants of marble-cutting were found in the fill strata just below the floor level of the Flavian phase, thus proving that the pieces were carved on site.[83] Taking these circumstances into account, the cost of the building's columns and entablatures was *c.* HS 780,000 (*c.* 105,000 man-days of work) (Tables 4.11–4.13).

Analysis of the Cost Differences

Based on these calculations, we see that the marble used in the upper terrace of the Provincial Forum at Tarraco cost approximately half the cost of that used for the Templum Pacis at Rome. These differences are partially due to the variations in wages paid to the workers, the difference in the distances from the quarries that supplied the marble, the fact that only Luna marble was used for the elevations in Tarraco (thus avoiding the costlier coloured varieties), and the use of marble plaques in the entablatures of the Tarraco portico instead of the large blocks found in the Templum Pacis. Marble blocks were, however, used in Tarraco in the temple and the Hall of Worship, which were the most prestigious areas.

A further variable that has a greater impact on the final cost of a building is the price of the marble used. It was sourced from imperial quarries,[84] but for imperial architecture it is not easy to determine through what channels it would have been obtained, as we do not yet know how the sale of marble was administered in these cases. Thanks to a mark on a block of marble in the Forum of Augustus (N XX [...] / CAES A [...]), and another in the Temple of Apollo Sosianus (-↓ XII ER-), we know that an imperial freedman oversaw the quarries at that time, at least as far as the pieces destined for public monuments or imperial residences were concerned.[85] We also know that, in the time of Vespasian, two imperial freedmen (Titus Flavius Celadus and Titus Flavius Successus) were working in Rome as *tabularii marmorum lunensium*. They were the clerks who administered the arrival of Carrara marble in Rome

---

[82] Pensabene (1993).   [83] Balil (1969: 21–7); Aquilué (2004: 48).
[84] Regarding the ownership of the quarries, see Russell (2013: 37–94) and Pensabene (2013: 197–212; 2016).
[85] Pensabene (2016: 452–4).

Table 4.11 Cost of the upper terrace of the Tarraco Provincial Forum: Hall of Worship

(i) Material

Type	Height (m)	Max. length (m)	Diameter (m)	Width (m)	Volume (m³)	Volume (ft³)	Weight (kg)	Price of marble (HS/ft³)	Cost (1 column) (HS)	Total cost (6 columns) (HS)
Capital (Luna)	1.50	2.10	1.42	—	6.61	254.48	17,847	5	1,272	7,632
Shaft (Luna)	11.50	—	1.50	—	25.87	995.99	69,849	5	4,980	29,880
Base (Luna)	0.80	2.10	—	—	3.52	135.52	9,504	5	678	4,068
Subtotal	13.80	—	—	—	36.00	1,385.99	97,200	—	6,930	41,580
Architrave (Luna)	0.70	27.50	—	0.60	11.55	444.67	—	5	—	2,223
Frieze (Luna)	0.89	27.50	—	0.60	14.68	565.18	—	5	—	2,826
Cornice (Luna)	1.60	27.50	—	0.70	30.80	1,185.80	—	5	—	5,929
Subtotal	3.19	—	—	—	57.03	2,195.65	—	—	—	10,978
Total										52,558

(ii) Extraction

Type	Labour	Salary/day (HS)	Time (days/m³)	Volume (m³)	Days (1 column)	Days (6 columns)	Cost (1 column) (HS)	Total cost (6 columns) (HS)
Capital	Worker	2	12	6.61	79.3	475.8	159	952
Shaft	Worker	2	12	25.87	310.4	1,862.6	621	3,725
Base	Worker	2	12	3.52	42.2	253.4	84	506
Subtotal				36.00	431.9	2,591.4	864	5,183
Architrave	Worker	2	12	11.55	—	138.6	—	277
Frieze	Worker	2	12	14.68	—	176.2	—	352
Cornice	Worker	2	12	30.80	—	369.6	—	739
Subtotal				57.03	—	684.4	—	1,369
Total						3,275,8		6,552

(iii) Rough-out

Type	Labour	Salary/day (HS)	Time (hours/m³)	Volume (m³)	Days (1 column)	Days (6 columns)	Cost (1 column) (HS)	Total cost (6 columns) (HS)
Capital	Marble-cutter	2.5	157.5	6.61	104.1	624.6	260	1,561
Shaft	Marble-cutter	2.5	157.5	25.87	407.4	2,444.7	1,018	6,108
Base	Marble-cutter	2.5	157.5	3.52	55.4	332.6	138	828
Subtotal				36.00	566.9	3,401.4	1,416	8,496
Entablature	Marble-cutter	2.5	157.5	57.03	—	898.2	—	2,245
Total						4,299.6		10,741

(iv) Semi-Preparation

Type	Labour	Salary/day (HS)	Time	Area (m²)	Days (1 column)	Days (6 columns)	Cost (1 column) (HS)	Total cost (6 columns) (HS)
Capital	Marble-cutter	2.5	$a(1 + 0.25/x)$	12.60	6.4	38.5	16	96
Shaft	Marble-cutter	2.5	$a(1 + 0.25/x)$	57.70	29.1	174.9	73	436
Base	Marble-cutter	2.5	$a(1 + 0.25/x)$	6.72	3.4	20.4	8	50
Subtotal					38.8	232.8	97	582
Entablature	Marble-cutter	2.5	4.33 hours/m²	175.45	—	76.6	—	190
Total						308.8		772

Continued

Table 4.11 Continued

(v) Transport

Type	Method	Formula	Volume (m³)	Cost (1 column) (HS)	Total cost (6 columns) (HS)
Column (Luna)	Land	0.85 *den.* × m³ × mile	36.00	2,448	14,688
	Maritime	10 *den.* × m³	36.00	1,440	8,640
Subtotal				3,888	23,328
Entablature (Luna)	Land	0.85 *den.* × m³ × mile	57.03	—	3,878
	Maritime	10 *den.* × m³	57.03	—	2,281
Subtotal				—	6,159
Total					29,487

(vi) Installation

Type	Labour	Salary/day (HS)	Time (hours/tonne)	Volume (m³)	Weight (kg)	Days (1 column)	Days (6 columns)	Cost (1 column) (HS)	Total cost (6 columns) (HS)
Capital	Worker	2	35.3	6.61	17,847	63.0	378.0	126	756
Shaft	Worker	2	35.3	25.87	69,849	246.6	1,479.4	493	2,958
Base	Worker	2	35.3	3.52	9,504	33.5	201.3	67	402
Subtotal				36.00	97,200	343.1	2,058.6	686	4,116
Entablature	Worker	2	35.3	57.03	153,981	—	543.5	—	1,087
Total							2,602.1		5,203

(vii) Finishing

Type	Labour	Salary/day (HS)	Time	Area (m²)	Days (1 column)	Days (6 columns)	Cost (1 column) (HS)	Total cost (6 columns) (HS)
Capital	Marble-cutter	5	1,500 hours[a]	—	150.0	900.0	750	4,500
Shaft	Marble-cutter	5	10 hours/m²[b]	57.7	57.7	346.2	288	1,728
Base	Marble-cutter	5	600 hours[c]	—	60.0	360.0	300	1,800
Subtotal					267.7	1,606.2	1,338	8,028
Architrave	Marble-cutter	5	5.6 hours/m²[d]	38.5	—	21.6	—	108
Frieze	Marble-cutter	5	400 hours/m²[e]	48.9	—	1,958.0	—	9,790
Cornice	Marble-cutter	5	250 hours/m²[f]	88.0	—	2,200.0	—	11,000
Subtotal						4,179.6		20,898
Total						5,785.8		28,926

OVERALL TOTAL FOR THE TARRACO PROVINCIAL FORUM (HALL OF WORSHIP)   16,272.1   134,239

[a] Pegoretti (1863: i. 408).
[b] Pegoretti (1863: i. 404).
[c] Barresi (2000: 362).
[d] Pegoretti (1863: i. 406).
[e] Pegoretti (1863: i. 407).
[f] Pegoretti (1863: i. 407).

Table 4.12 Cost of the upper terrace of the Tàrraco Provincial Forum: portico

(i) Material

Type	Height (m)	Max. length (m)	Diameter (m)	Width (m)	Volume (m³)	Volume (ft³)	Weight (kg)	Price of marble (HS/ft³)	Cost (1 column) (HS)	Total cost (120 columns) (HS)
Capital (Luna)	0.83	1.17	0.68	—	1.14	43.89	3,078	5	219	25,404
Shaft (Luna)	5.92	—	0.71	—	3.88	149.38	10,476	5	747	86,652
Base (Luna)	0.52	0.82	—	—	0.35	13.47	945	5	67	7,772
Subtotal	7.27				5.37	206.74	14,499	—	1,033	119,828
Architrave (Luna)	0.51	523.00	—	0.30	80.02	3,080.73	—	5	—	15,354
Frieze (Luna)	0.45	523.00	—	0.30	70.60	2,718.29	—	5	—	13,591
Cornice (Luna)	0.75	523.00	—	0.40	156.90	6,040.65	—	5	—	30,203
Subtotal	1.71				307.52	11,839.67	—	—	—	59,148
Total										178,976

(ii) Extraction

Type	Labour	Salary/day (HS)	Time (days/m³)	Volume (m³)	Days (1 column)	Days (120 columns)	Cost (1 column) (HS)	Total cost (120 columns) (HS)
Capital	Worker	2	12	1.14	13.7	1,644.0	27	3,240
Shaft	Worker	2	12	3.88	46.6	5,592.0	93	11,160
Base	Worker	2	12	0.35	4.2	504.0	8	960
Subtotal				5.37	64.5	7,740.0	128	15,360
Entablature	Worker	2	12	307.52		3,690.2		7,380
Total						11,430.2		22,740

(iii) Rough-out

Type	Labour	Salary/day (HS)	Time (hours/m³)	Volume (m³)	Days (1 column)	Days (120 columns)	Cost (1 column) (HS)	Total cost (120 columns) (HS)
Capital	Marble-cutter	2.5	157.5	1.14	18.0	2,160.0	45	5,400
Shaft	Marble-cutter	2.5	157.5	3.88	61.1	7,332.0	153	18,360
Base	Marble-cutter	2.5	157.5	0.35	5.5	660.0	14	1,680
Subtotal				5.37	84.6	10,152.0	212	25,440
Entablature	Marble-cutter	2.5	157.5	307.52		4,843.4		12,107
Total						14,995.4		37,547

(iv) Semi-Preparation

Type	Labour	Salary/day (HS)	Time	Area (m²)	Days (1 column)	Days (120 columns)	Cost (1 column) (HS)	Total cost (120 columns) (HS)
Capital	Marble-cutter	2.5	$a(1 + 0.25/x)$	—	2.3	276.0	6	720
Shaft (monolithic)	Marble-cutter	2.5	$a(2 + 0.25/x)$	—	13.6	1,632.0	34	4,080
Base	Marble-cutter	2.5	$a(1 + 0.25/x)$	—	1.0	120.0	2	240
Subtotal					16.9	2,028.0	42	5,040
Entablature	Marble-cutter	2.5	4.33 hours/m²	1,788.66	—	774.5	—	1,936
Total						2,802.5		6,976

Continued

Table 4.12 Continued

(v) Transport

Type	Method	Formula	Volume (m³)	Cost (1 column) (HS)	Total cost (120 columns) (HS)
Column (Luna)	Land	0.85 *den.* × m³ × mile	5.37	365	43,800
	Maritime	10 *den.* × m³	5.37	216	25,920
Subtotal				581	69,720
Entablature	Land	0.85 *den.* × m³ × mile	307.52	—	20,911
	Maritime	10 *den.* × m³	307.52	—	12,301
Subtotal					33,212
Total					102,932

(vi) Installation

Type	Labour	Salary/day (HS)	Time (hours/tonne)	Volume (m³)	Weight (kg)	Days (1 column)	Days (120 columns)	Cost (1 column) (HS)	Total cost (120 columns) (HS)
Capital	Worker	2	35.3	1.14	3,078	10.9	1,308.0	22	2,640
Shaft	Worker	2	35.3	3.88	10,476	37.0	4,440.0	74	8,880
Base	Worker	2	35.3	0.35	945	3.3	396.0	7	840
Subtotal				5.37	14,499	51.2	6,144.0	103	12,360
Entablature	Worker	2	35.3	307.52	830,304		2,931.0		5,862
Total							9,075.0		18,222

(vii) Finishing

Type	Labour	Salary/day (HS)	Time	Area (m²)	Days (1 column)	Days (120 columns)	Cost (1 column) (HS)	Total cost (120 columns) (HS)
Capital	Marble-cutter	5	600 hours[a]	—	60.0	7,200.0	300	36,000
Shaft	Marble-cutter	5	10 hours/m²[b]	13.20	13.2	1,584.0	66	7,920
Base	Marble-cutter	5	300 hours[c]	—	30.0	3,600.0	150	18,000
Subtotal					103.2	12,384.0	516	61,920
Architrave	Marble-cutter	5	5.6 hours/m²[d]	533.46	—	298.7	—	1,493
Frieze	Marble-cutter	5	166.5 hours/m²[e]	470.70	—	7,837.1	—	39,185
Cornice	Marble-cutter	5	250 hours/m²[f]	784.50	—	19,612.5	—	98,062
Subtotal						27,748.3	—	138,741
Total						40,132.3		200,661

OVERALL TOTAL FOR THE TARRACO PROVINCIAL FORUM (PORTICO)   78,435.4   568,054

[a] Pegoretti (1863: i. 408).
[b] Pegoretti (1863: i. 404).
[c] Barresi (2000: 362).
[d] Pegoretti (1863: i. 406).
[e] Pegoretti (1863: i. 407) (frieze decorated with a very simple wave motif).
[f] Pegoretti (1863: i. 407).

Table 4.13 Cost of the upper terrace of the Tarraco Provincial Forum: propylaeum

(i) Material

Type	Height (m)	Max. length (m)	Diameter (m)	Width (m)	Volume (m³)	Volume (ft³)	Weight (kg)	Price of marble (HS/ft³)	Cost (1 column) (HS)	Total cost (6 columns) (HS)
Capital (Luna)	1.18	1.67	0.90	—	3.29	126.66	8,883	5	633	3,798
Shaft (Luna)	8.87	—	1.06	—	9.96	383.46	26,892	5	1,917	11,502
Base (Luna)	0.59	1.99	—	—	2.33	89.70	6,291	5	448	2,688
Subtotal	10.64	—	—	—	15.58	599.83	42,066	—	2,998	17,988
Architrave (Luna)	0.70	27.50	—	0.47	9.05	348.42	—	5	—	1,742
Frieze (Luna)	0.70	27.50	—	0.47	9.05	348.42	—	5	—	1,742
Cornice (Luna)	1.10	27.50	—	0.70	21.17	815.04	—	5	—	4,075
Subtotal	2.50	—	—	—	39.27	1,511.88	—	—	—	7,559
Total										25,547

(ii) Extraction

Type	Labour	Salary/day (HS)	Time (days/m³)	Volume (m³)	Days (1 column)	Days (6 columns)	Cost (1 column) (HS)	Total cost (6 columns) (HS)
Capital	Worker	2	12	3.29	39.5	237.0	79	474
Shaft	Worker	2	12	9.96	119.5	717.1	239	1,434
Base	Worker	2	12	2.33	28.0	168.0	56	336
Subtotal				15.58	187.0	1,122.0	374	2,244
Architrave	Worker	2	12	9.05	—	108.6	—	217
Frieze	Worker	2	12	9.05	—	108.6	—	217
Cornice	Worker	2	12	21.17	—	254.0	—	508
Subtotal				39.27	—	471.2	—	942
Total						1,593.2		3,186

(iii) Rough-out

Type	Labour	Salary/day (HS)	Time (hours/m³)	Volume (m³)	Days (1 column)	Days (6 columns)	Cost (1 column) (HS)	Total cost (6 columns) (HS)
Capital	Marble-cutter	2.5	157.5	3.29	51.8	310.8	129	774
Shaft	Marble-cutter	2.5	157.5	9.96	156.9	941.4	392	2,353
Base	Marble-cutter	2.5	157.5	2.33	36.7	220.2	92	552
Subtotal				15.58	245.4	1,472.4	613	3,678
Architrave	Marble-cutter	2.5	157.5	9.05	—	142.5	—	356
Frieze	Marble-cutter	2.5	157.5	9.05	—	142.5	—	356
Cornice	Marble-cutter	2.5	157.5	21.17	—	333.4	—	833
Subtotal				39.27	—	618.5	—	1,545
Total						2,090.9		5,223

(iv) Semi-Preparation

Type	Labour	Salary/day (HS)	Time	Area (m²)	Days (1 column)	Days (6 columns)	Cost (1 column) (HS)	Total cost (6 columns) (HS)
Capital	Marble-cutter	2.5	$a(1 + 0.25/x)$	7.88	4.3	25.8	11	66
Shaft	Marble-cutter	2.5	$a(1 + 0.25/x)$	31.30	16.7	100.2	42	252
Base	Marble-cutter	2.5	$a(1 + 0.25/x)$	4.70	2.5	15.0	6	36
Subtotal					23.5	141.0	59	354
Entablature	Marble-cutter	2.5	4.33 hours/m²	137.50	—	59.5	—	149
Total						200.5		503

Continued

Table 4.13 Continued

(v) Transport

Type	Method	Formula	Volume (m³)	Cost (1 column) (HS)	Total cost (6 columns) (HS)
Column (Luna)	Land	0.85 *den.* × m³ × mile	15.58	1,059	6,354
	Maritime	10 *den.* × m³	15.58	623	3,738
Subtotal				1,682	10,092
Entablature (Luna)	Land	0.85 *den.* × m³ × mile	39.27	—	2,670
	Maritime	10 *den.* × m³	39.27	—	1,571
Subtotal					4,241
Total					14,333

(vi) Installation

Type	Labour	Salary/day (HS)	Time (hours/tonne)	Volume (m³)	Weight (kg)	Days (1 column)	Days (6 columns)	Cost (1 column) (HS)	Total cost (6 columns) (HS)
Capital	Worker	2	35.3	3.29	8,883	31.4	188.4	63	378
Shaft	Worker	2	35.3	9.96	26,892	94.9	569.4	190	1,140
Base	Worker	2	35.3	2.33	6,291	22.2	133.2	44	264
Subtotal				15.58	42,066	148.5	891.0	297	1,782
Entablature	Worker	2	35.3	39.27	106,029	—	374.3	—	749
Total							1,265.3		2,531

(vii) Finishing

Type	Labour	Salary/day (HS)	Time	Area (m²)	Days (1 column)	Days (6 columns)	Cost (1 column) (HS)	Total cost (6 columns) (HS)
Capital	Marble-cutter	5	1,100 hours[a]	—	110.0	660.0	550	3,300
Shaft	Marble-cutter	5	10 hours/m²[b]	31.30	31.3	187.8	156	936
Base	Marble-cutter	5	453 hours[c]	—	45.3	271.8	226	1,356
Subtotal					186.6	1,119.6	933	5,598
Architrave	Marble-cutter	5	5.6 hours/m²[d]	38.50	—	21.6	—	108
Frieze	Marble-cutter	5	400 hours/m²[e]	38.50	—	1,540.0	—	9,240
Cornice	Marble-cutter	5	250 hours/m²[f]	60.50	—	1,512.5	—	9,075
Subtotal						3,076.6		18,423
Total						4,196.2		24,021
OVERALL TOTAL FOR THE TARRACO PROVINCIAL FORUM (PROPYLAEUM)						9,346.1		75,344

[a] Pegoretti (1863: i. 408).
[b] Pegoretti (1863: i. 404).
[c] Barresi (2000: 362).
[d] Pegoretti (1863: i. 406).
[e] Pegoretti (1863: i. 407).
[f] Pegoretti (1863: i. 407).

and who came under the *procurator marmorum*, who was in turn overseen by the *procurator patrimonii*. Therefore, it seems that control of the quarries had already been transferred from the *fiscus* to the *patrimonium Caesaris*.[86]

It is, therefore, possible that the marble was supplied free of charge to the Templum Pacis, which was financed directly by the imperial household.[87] In this case, the calculated cost would be reduced to HS 831,682, a cost similar to that of the forum at Tarraco. Nevertheless, some experts suggest that the marble used in a project financed directly by the imperial household would not have been free, but would have had a cost a sum equivalent to half the figure quoted in Diocletian's *Edict*.[88] If this was the case, the cost of the Templum Pacis would have been HS 1,163,155.5, approximately 25 per cent higher than the Tarraco complex. These are scenarios to which we currently do not have the answers.

However, for the Tarraco forum, a provincial imitation, we cannot assume a donation of the marble by the imperial household, for the following reasons:

(1) The fact that the Carrara quarries were under imperial ownership did not necessarily mean the marble was ceded by the emperor, as we know that some sectors of those quarries were in private hands under the *locatio-conductio* system. Under this, the emperor authorized the *conductores* to extract a certain volume of marble, part of which was destined for the private market that supplied material for buildings financed by the provincial elites.[89]

(2) We know there was private enterprise in the Luna quarries until at least the second century AD from the dedication of a votive altar to Jupiter and Trajan by one *vilicus* Aithales, a *servus* of Florus, who made the dedication in the name of the entire *officina* with which he was associated.[90]

(3) Various inscriptions are preserved in Tarraco, one of them huge and reused in the interior of the cathedral; they are dedicated to L. Caecina Severus, who may have been related to the Volterran Caecina Severi family. We know that this family had important interests in the Carrara marble quarries and the presence of this person in Tarraco could mean that he was acting as an intermediary in the acquisition on the private

---

[86] Dolci (2003: 70); Segenni (2016). [87] Pensabene (2016: 452, 457).
[88] Barresi (2000: 352). [89] Pensabene (2013: 540–8; 2016: 452). [90] Dolci (2003: 68–9).

market of the enormous amounts of Carrara marble that were used in the Provincial Forum.[91]

Another aspect to consider is the ownership of the means of transport used to carry the stone blocks to the imperial building sites. Although there is the possibility that the state requisitioned animals and carts for the transport of stone blocks,[92] the general opinion is that this type of transport was not managed by the state but directly by private individuals.[93]

Thus we can see cost differences between the two complexes that vary—between approximately 25 per cent and 50 per cent—according to whether the marble used in the imperial complexes in Rome belonged to the emperor or not. In any case, it is necessary to point out that this question affects only the parts built with marble, the only ones we have taken into consideration when carrying out this calculation experiment. Nonetheless, we have to remember that large parts of these buildings were constructed with local stone. For example, in Trajan's Forum marble represented only 12 per cent of the total volume of building materials used.[94] Therefore, if we incorporate the other materials in the calculation process, the difference in cost between Rome and the provinces once again increases.

Conclusions

The examples in this chapter demonstrate that there were cost differences between the grand imperial architecture of Rome and its provincial imitations. It is now possible to quantify these differences, albeit approximately, by identifying the most important variables that determined the final cost: labour and building materials. We have to keep in mind that in my comparison of the costs of the Forum Pacis and the upper terrace of the Provincial Forum of Tarraco I have taken only the marble into account. This is a material whose cost, at least in the imperial architecture of Rome, could vary depending on the channels through which it was obtained—information that is unfortunately not always available to us. It is also important to remember that marble was only a small part of the volume of building material used—as we have seen, for example, in Trajan's Forum.

---

[91] Pensabene and Mar (2010: 296–7).   [92] Mitchell (1976); Adam (2001: 186).
[93] Russell (2013: 190–1); Pensabene (2016: 474). In fact, the transport of grain to Rome was also in private hands (Casson 1980: 24–9).
[94] Bianchi and Meneghini (2002: 403).

Although the examples in this chapter demonstrate the validity of the calculation methodology, the results must be considered as approximate values. For example, the results for the Temple of the Victories of Caracalla in Dougga (*c.* HS 105,000) and the Arch of Caracalla in Theveste (HS 241,000–243,000) are more likely to reflect the true values when we have accurate information on the characteristics of the building: its shape, the building techniques and materials that were used, the type of labour that worked on it, and so on. Thanks to this, in the first case, the difference between the real cost and the calculated cost is only HS 5,000 (5 per cent error), and in the second case about HS 8,000 (3 per cent error).

We can, however, now cautiously introduce building costs into the analysis of architecture. This variable allows us to compare different constructions and better to calibrate the effort made by specific towns or local elites in undertaking certain building projects. It also allows us to observe and quantify the approximate cost differences between different areas of the empire. Provincial building costs were substantially lower than costs at Rome, but the competitive nature of civic euergetism led local elites to spend considerable sums—often between HS 100,000 and HS 400,000—on temples of modest size, embellished with expensive marble decoration. Nevertheless, it is necessary to remember that the cost cannot be considered to be the principal key to interpreting the extent of the dissemination of grand monumental architecture. Indeed, the greater or lesser availability of economic resources would not necessarily have acted as a brake on a specific project with a strong symbolic or ideological significance, as is the case of the complexes dedicated to imperial worship; it would in fact have been a stimulus to seek out new sources of finance, as it was unlikely that the most important towns would have renounced the possibility of imitating the grand building projects of Rome.

References

Abbreviation

IAM Euzennat, M., Marion, J., and Gascou, J. (1982). *Inscriptions antiques du Maroc*, vol. 2: *Inscriptions latines*. Paris.

Accame, S. (1941). 'Il testamento di C. Cornelio Egriliano e l'arco di Caracalla in Tebessa', *Epigraphica* 3: 237–43.

Adam, C. E. P. (2001). 'Who Bore the Burden? The Organization of Stone Transport in Roman Egypt', in D. J. Mattingly and J. Salmon (eds), *Economies beyond Agriculture in the Classical World*. London, 171–92.

Aquilué, X. (2004). 'Arquitectura oficial', in X. Dupré (ed.), *Las capitales provinciales de Hispania. 3. Tarragona, Colonia Iulia Urbs Triumphalis Tarraco.* Rome, 41–53.

Arnaud, P. (2007). 'Diocletian's Prices Edict: The Prices of Seaborne Transport and the Average Duration of Maritime Travel', *JRA* 20: 321–36.

Bacchielli, L. (1987). 'Il testamento di C. Cornelio Egriliano e il coronamento dell'arco di Caracalla a Tebessa', in A. Mastino (ed.), *L'Africa Romana: Atti del IV Convegno di Studio, Sassari 1986.* Sassari, 295–321.

Baldassarri, P. (2013). 'Alla ricerca del tempio perduto: indagini archeologiche a Palazzo Valentini e il *Templum Divi Traiani et Divae Plotinae*', *ArchClass* 64: 371–481.

Balil, A. (1969). *Excavaciones en la Torre de Pilatos (Tarragona): Campañas de excavaciones de 1962* (Excavaciones arqueológicas en España 65). Madrid.

Barresi, P. (2000). 'Architettura pubblica e munificenza in Asia Minore: Ricchezza, costruzioni e marmi nelle provincie anatoliche dell'Impero', *Mediterraneo Antico* 3/1: 309–68.

Barresi, P. (2003). *Provincie dell'Asia Minore: Costo dei marmi, architettura pubblica e committenza.* Rome.

Barresi, P. (2004). 'Anfiteatro flavio di Pozzuoli, portico *in summa cavea*: una stima dei costi', in E. De Sena and H. Dessales (eds), *Metodi e approci archeologici: L'industria e il commercio nell'Italia antica* (British Archaeological Reports 1262). Oxford, 262–7.

Barresi, P. (2010). 'I teatri di *Aphrodisias* e di Nicea: Marmi e committenza nell'Asia Minore di età imperiale', in Camporeale, Dessales, and Pizzo (2010), 337–50.

Barresi, P. (2015). 'Calculating the Cost of Columns: The Case of the Temple of Apollo at Didyma', in P. Pensabene and E. Gasparini (eds), *ASMOSIA X: Proceedings of the Tenth International Conference. Interdisciplinary Studies on Ancient Stone.* Rome, 933–9.

Barresi, P., Domingo, J. Á., and Pensabene, P. (2014). 'Gigantismo nell'architettura templare delle provincie romane e le sue implicazioni nell'approvvigionamento e nella messa in opera delle componenti marmoree', in I. Koncani Uhač (ed.), *Akti XII. Međunarodnog kolokvija o rimskoj provincijalnoj umjetnosti: Datiranje kamenih spomenika i kriteriji za određivanje kronologijei; Proceedings of the 12th International Colloquium on Roman Provincial Art.* Pula, 159–65.

Bianchi, E., and Meneghini, R. (2002). 'Il cantiere costruttivo del foro di Traiano', *MDAI(R)* 109: 395–417.

Blas de Roblès, J.-M., and Sintes, C. (2003). *Sites et monuments antiques de l'Algérie.* Aix-en-Provence.

Bögli, H. (1989). *Aventicum: La ville romaine et le musée* (Guides archéologiques de la Suisse 19). Avenches.

Brouquier-Reddé, V. (2005). 'La place du sanctuaire de la Victoire Germanique de Caracalla à Dougga dans la typologie de l'architecture religieuse païenne de l'Afrique romaine', in Golvin and Khanoussi (2005), 457–70.

Brouquier-Reddé, V., Golvin, J.-Cl., Maurin, L., Saint-Amas, S., Haj Saïd, R., and Karoui, Kh. (2005). 'Le sanctuaire des Victoires de Caracalla', in Golvin and Khanoussi (2005), 33–77.

Brouquier, V., and Rebuffat, R. (1998). 'Recherches sur le bassin du Sebou. IV — Temple de Venus à Volubilis', *BAM* 18: 127–39.

Buzón, M. (2009). 'El templo astigitano de la calle Galindo: Análisis e interpretación de un puzle arqueológico', *Romula* 8: 65–123.

Camporeale, S., Dessales, H., and Pizzo, A. (2010) (eds). *Arqueología de la Construcción II: Los procesos constructivos en el mundo romano: Italia y provincias occidentales; Certosa di Pontignano, Siena, 13–15 de Noviembre de 2008* (Anejos de Archivo Español de Arqueología 57). Madrid and Mérida.

Camporeale, S., Papi, E., and Passalacqua, L. (2008). 'L'organizzazione dei cantieri a *Volubilis* (*Mauretania Tingitana*): Iscrizioni e opere pubbliche, la *Maison aux deux Pressoirs* e l'arco di Caracalla', in S. Camporeale, H. Dessales, and A. Pizzo (eds), *Arqueología de la Construcción I: Los procesos constructivos en el mundo romano: Italia y provincias occidentales* (Anejos de Archivo Español de Arqueología 50). Mérida, 285–308.

Carcopino, J. (1937). 'Note sur la Tablette de Cluj. C.I.L., III, n° X, p. 948', *RPh* 63/11: 97–104.

Casson, L. (1980). 'The role of the state in Rome's grain trade', in J. H. D'Arms and E. C. Kopff (eds), *The Seaborne Commerce of Ancient Rome: Studies in Archaeology and History* (MAAR 36). Rome, 21–33.

Chatelain, L. (1926). 'Note', *BCTH* 1925: ccxxviii–ccxxix.

Chatelain, L. (1942). *Inscriptions latines du Maroc*. Paris.

Chatelain, L. (1944). *Le Maroc des Romains: Étude sur les centres antiques de la Maurétanie occidentale*. Paris.

Ciotti, U. (1946–8). 'Del coronamento degli archi quadrifronti: Gli archi di Tebessa e di Tripoli', *Bullettino della commissione archeologica comunale di Roma* 72/15: 21–42.

Coarelli, F. (2009) (ed.). *Divus Vespasianus: Il bimillenario dei Flavi*. Rome.

Coletta, A., and Maisto, P. (2014). 'Il settore meridionale del templum Pacis', in R. Meneghini and R. Rea (eds), *La Biblioteca Infinita: I luoghi del sapere nel mondo antico*. Milan, 307–12.

Cozza, L. (1982) (ed.). *Tempio di Adriano* (Lavori e studi di archeologia 1). Roma.

De Angeli, S. (1999). 'Vespasianus, Divus, Templum', in M. Steinby (ed.), *Lexicon Topographicum Urbis Romae* V. Rome, 124–5.

De la Hoz, J. (2011). 'Circulación monetaria romana en la cuenca minera de Ríotinto', in J. A. Pérez Macías, A. Delgado, J. M. Pérez, and F. J. García (eds), *Río Tinto: Historia, Patrimonio Minero y Turismo Cultural*. Huelva, 143–70.

DeLaine J. (1997). *The Baths of Caracalla. A Study in the Designs, Construction and Economics of Large-Scale Building Projects in Imperial Rome*. Portsmouth, RI.

De Roch, S. (1952). *Tébessa. Antique Theveste*. Algiers.

Di Vita-Evrard G. (1963). 'Un nouveau proconsul d'Afrique parent de Septime Séverè: Caius Septimius Severus', *MEFRA* 75: 389–414.

Dolci, E. (2003). *Archeologia Apuana. Iscrizioni, lavorazioni, cave antiche a Carrara*. Carrara.

Domingo, J. Á. (2012a). 'El coste del mármol. Problemas e incertidumbres de una metodología de cálculo', *Marmora* 8: 75–91.

Domingo, J. Á. (2012b). 'Los costes de la arquitectura romana: El capitolio de Volúbilis (Mauretania Tingitana)', *ArchClass* 63: 381–418.

Domingo, J. Á. (2012c). 'El coste de la arquitectura: Avances, problemas e incertidumbres de una metodología de cálculo: Volúbilis y Dougga', *Archeologia dell'architettura* 17: 144–70.

Domingo, J. Á. (2013). 'The Differences in Roman Construction Costs: The Workers' Salary', *Boreas* 36: 119–43.

Domingo, J. Á., and Domingo, J. R. (2017). 'El coste del Arco de Caracalla en Theveste (Tébessa, Argelia): Verificación empírica de una metodología de cálculo', *Archeologia dell'architettura* 22: 35–53.

Domingo, J. Á., Garrido, A., and Mar, R. (2011). 'Talleres y modelos decorativos en la arquitectura pública del noreste de la Tarraconense en torno al cambio de era: el caso de *Barcino, Tarraco y Auso*', in Nogales and Rodà (2011), ii, 851–62.

Domingo, J. Á., Mar, R., and Pensabene, P. (2011). 'El Templum Divi Claudii. Decoración y elementos arquitectónicos para su reconstrucción', *Archivo Español de Arqueología* 84: 207–30.

Domingo, J. Á., Mar, R., and Pensabene, P. (2013). 'El complejo arquitectónico del templo del Divo Claudio en el monte Celio de Roma', *ArchClass* 64: 295–347.

Domingo, J. Á., and Pensabene, P. (2017). 'Il Claudianum: Elementi per un nuovo inquadramento topografico e architettonico', in A. Acconci, F. Astolfi, and A. Englen (eds), *Caelius II: Pars Superior. La Basilica dei santi Giovanni e Paolo* (Collana Palinsesti Romani 2, II). Rome.

Duncan-Jones, R. (1974). *The Economy of the Roman Empire. Quantitative Studies*. Cambridge.

Euzennat, M. (1957). 'Le Temple C de Volubilis et les origines de la cité', *BAM* 2: 41–64.

Facchin, G. (2014). 'L'aula di culto della Pace: Il periodo Flavio', in R. Meneghini and R. Rea (eds), *La Biblioteca Infinita. I luoghi del sapere nel mondo antico*. Milan, 270–5.

Fant, J. C. (2008). 'Marble Workshops at Simitthus', *JRA* 21: 577–80.

Fogagnolo, S., and Mocchegiani, C. (2009). 'Nuove acquisizioni e ritrovamenti nell'aula di culto del Templum Pacis', in Coarelli (2009), 184–9.

Fogagnolo, S., and Rossi, F. M. (2010). 'Settore meridionale del Foro della Pace: L'impatto del cantiere di restauro Severiano, corrispondenze e differenze rispetto al progetto originario', in Camporeale, Dessales, and Pizzo (2010), 93–104.

Giacchero, M. (1974). *Edictum Diocletiani et Collegarum de pretiis rerum venalium*. Genova.

Golvin, J.-C., and Khanoussi, M. (2005) (eds). *Dougga: Études d'architecture religieuse: Les sanctuaries des Victoires de Caracalla, de 'Pluton' et de Caelestis*. Bordeaux.

Jiménez Salvador, J. L. (1991). 'El templo romano de la calle Claudio Marcelo en Córdoba', *Templos romanos de Hispania* (Cuadernos de Arquitectura Romana 1). Murcia, 119–32.

Jodin, A. (1987). *Volvbilis Regia Ivbae: Contribution à l'étude des civilisations du Maroc antique préclaudien*. Paris.

Kahrstedt, U. (1958). *Kulturgeschichte der römischen Kaiserzeit*. Bern.

Kallala, N. (2000). 'Dédicace du temple de la Victoire Germanique de Caracalla par Gabinia Hermiona', in M. Khanoussi and L. Maurin (eds), *Mourir à Dougga. Recueil des inscriptions funéraires*. Bordeaux and Tunis, 114–17.

Khanoussi, M. (2003). 'Le temple de la Victoire Germanique de Caracalla à Dougga', in M. Khanoussi (ed.), *Afrique du Nord antique et médiévale: Protohistoire, cités de l'Afrique du nord, fouilles et prospections récentes; Actes du VIIIe colloque international sur l'histoire et l'archéologie de l'Afrique du Nord (Tabarka, 8–13 mai 2000)*. Tunis, 447–56.

Levrero, R. (2014). *Mercanti, prezzi e legislazione: Il commercio internazionale dei Romani*. Rome.

Lukaszewicz, A. (1986). *Les Édifices publics dans les villes de l'Égypte romaine: Problèmes administratifs et financiers*. Warsaw.

Luquet, A. (1964). 'Volubilis: Restauration du Capitole', *BAM* 5: 351–6.

Macías, J. M., Muñoz, A., Teixell, I., and Menchón, J. (2011). 'Nuevos elementos escultóricos del recinto de culto del Concilium Provinciae Hispaniae Citerioris (Tarraco, Hispania Citerior)', in Nogales and Rodà (2011), 873–86.

Mar, R. (1993). 'El recinto de Culto Imperial de Tárraco y la arquitectura Flavia', in R. Mar (ed.), *Els monuments provincials de Tàrraco: Noves aportacions al seu coneixement*. Tarragona, 107–56.

Mar, R., and Pensabene, P. (2010). 'Finanziamento dell'edilizia pubblica e calcolo dei costi dei materiali lapidei: il caso del Foro Superiore di Tarraco', in Camporeale, Dessales, and Pizzo (2010), 509–37.

Marano, Y. A. (2014). 'Le cave di marmo nella tarda antichità: Aspetti organizzativi e produttivi', in J. Bonetto, S. Camporeale, and A. Pizzo (eds), *Arqueología de la Construcción IV: Las canteras en el mundo antiguo: sistemas de explotación y procesos productivos; Actas del congreso de Padova, 22-24 de noviembre de 2012* (Anejos de Archivo español de arqueología 69). Mérida, 413-27.

Marcone, A. (1987). *Commento storico al Libro IV dell'epistolario di Q. Aurelio Simmaco* (Biblioteca di Studi Antichi 55). Pisa.

Márquez, C. (1993). *Capiteles Romanos de Corduba Colonia Patricia*. Cordoba.

Márquez, C. (1998). 'Acerca de la función e inserción urbanística de las plazas en Colonia Patricia', *Empúries* 51: 63-76.

Márquez, C. (2001). 'La ornamentación arquitectónica de la Carmona romana', in A. Caballos (ed.), *Carmona Romana*. Carmona, 251-62.

Márquez, C. (2003). 'Los restos romanos de la Calle Mármoles en Sevilla', *Romula* 2: 127-48.

Márquez, C. (2004a). 'La decoración arquitectónica en la Colonia Patricia en el periodo julioclaudio', in S. F. Ramallo (ed.), *La decoración arquitectónica en las ciudades romanas de Occidente; Actas del congreso internacional celebrado en Cartagena entre los días 8 y 10 de octubre de 2003*. Murcia, 337-53.

Márquez, C. (2004b). 'Baetica Templa', in Ruiz de Arbulo (2004), 109-27.

Mateos Cruz, P. (2006). 'El templo: La traslación de los modelos metropolitanos a la capital de la provincia lusitana', in P. Mateos Cruz (ed.), *El Foro Provincial de Augusta Emerita: Un conjunto monumental de culto imperial* (Anejos de AEspA XLII). Mérida, 251-76.

Mateos Cruz, P. (2007). 'El conjunto provincial de Culto Imperial de Augusta Emerita', in Nogales and González (2007), 369-93.

Meneghini, R. (2014). 'L'architettura del *templum Pacis*', in R. Meneghini and R. Rea (eds), *La Biblioteca Infinita. I luoghi del sapere nel mondo antico*. Milan, 284-99.

Meneghini, R., Corsaro, A., and Pinna, B. (2009). 'Il Templum Pacis alla luce dei recenti scavi', in Coarelli (2009), 190-201.

Meneghini, R., and Santangeli, R. (2007). *I Fori Imperiali: Gli scavi del Comune di Roma (1991-2007)*. Rome.

Meunier, J. (1938). 'L'Arc de Caracalla à Théveste', *Revue africaine* 82: 84-106.

Mitchell, S. (1976). 'Requisitioned Transport in the Roman Empire: A New Inscription from Pisidia', *JRS* 66: 106-31.

Montella, F. (2014). 'L'aula di culto della Pace: Il periodo severiano', in R. Meneghini and R. Rea (eds), *La Biblioteca Infinita. I luoghi del sapere nel mondo antico*. Milan, 276-83.

Montero, F. J. (1988). 'Arquitectura', in P. León (ed.), *Traianeum de Italica*. Seville, 89-101.

Mrozek, S. (1975). *Prix et rémunération dans l'occident romain (31 av. n.è.-250 de n.è.)*. Gdańsk.

Nogales, T., and González, J. (2007) (eds). *Culto Imperial: Política y poder; Actas del Congreso Internacional Culto Imperial: Política y poder, Mérida, Museo Nacional de Arte Romano, 18-20 de mayo, 2006* (Hispania Antigua, Serie Arqueológica, 1). Rome.

Nogales, T., and Rodà, I. (2011) (eds). *Roma y las provincias: modelo y difusión* (Hispania Antigua, Serie Arqueológica 3). Rome.

Panetier, J.-L. (2002). *Volubilis: Une cité du Maroc antique*. Paris.

Peacock, D. P. S. (1995). 'The Passio Sanctorum Quattuor Coronatorum: a petrological approach', *Antiquity* 69/263: 362–8.

Pegoretti, G. (1863). *Manuale pratico per l'estimazione dei lavori architettonici, stradali, idraulici e di fortificazione per uso degli ingegneri ed architetti*. Milan.

Pensabene, P. (1978–9). 'Stele funeraria a doppia edicola dalla via Latina', *BCom* 86: 17–38.

Pensabene, P. (1984). *Tempio di Saturno. Architettura e decorazione*. Rome.

Pensabene, P. (1993). 'La decorazione architettonica dei monumenti provinciali di Tarraco', in R. Mar (ed.), *Els monuments provincials de Tarraco: Noves aportacions al seu coneixement*. Tarragona, 33–105.

Pensabene, P. (1996). 'Programmi decorativi e architettura del tempio di Antonino e Faustina al Foro Romano', *Studi Miscellanei* 29: 239–69.

Pensabene, P. (2003). 'La Porta Oea e l'Arco di Marco Aurelio a Leptis Magna: Contributo alla definizione dei marmi e del loro costo, delle officine e delle committenze', *QAL* 18: 341–67.

Pensabene, P. (2006). 'Mármoles y talleres en la Bética y otras áreas de la Hispania Romana', in D. Vaquerizo and J. F. Murillo (eds), *El concepto de lo provincial en el mundo antiguo. Homenaje a la profesora Pilar León Alonso*, vol. 2. Cordoba, 103–42.

Pensabene, P. (2013). *I marmi nella Roma antica*. Rome.

Pensabene, P. (2016). 'I marmi bianchi di Luni (Carrara)', in E. Paribeni and S. Segenni (eds), *Notae Lapicidinarum dalle Cave di Carrara*. Pisa, 451–520.

Pensabene, P., and Mar, R. (2004). 'Dos frisos marmóreos en la Acrópolis de Tarraco, el Templo de Augusto y el complejo provincial de culto imperial', in Ruiz de Arbulo (2004), 73–88.

Pensabene, P., and Mar, R. (2010). 'Il Tempio di Augusto a Tarraco: Gigantismo e marmo lunense nei luoghi di culto imperiale in Hispania e Gallia', *ArchClass* 61: 243–307.

Pensabene, P., Mar, R., and Cebrián, R. (2012). 'Funding of Public Buildings and Calculation of the Costs of the Stone Materials: The Case of the Forum of Segóbriga (Cuenca, Spain)', in A. Gutiérrez, P. Lapuente, and I. Rodà (eds), *Interdisciplinary Studies on Ancient Stone: Proceedings of the IX ASMOSIA Conference (Tarragona 2009)*. Tarragona, 161–75.

Pinna, B. C. (2014). 'I portici e il muro di delimitazione settentrionale', in R. Meneghini and R. Rea (eds), *La Biblioteca Infinita. I luoghi del sapere nel mondo antico*. Milan, 300–6.

Rizzo, S. (2001). 'Indagini nei fori Imperiali: Oroidrografia, foro di Cesare, foro di Augusto, templum Pacis', *MDAI(R)* 108: 215–44.

Rodero, S. (2002). 'Algunos aspectos de la decoración arquitectónica del Traianeum de Itálica', *Romula* 1: 75–106.

Rosso, E. (2007). 'Culte imperial et image dynastique: les *divi* et *divae* de la Gens Flavia', in Nogales and González (2007), 125–51.

Ruiz de Arbulo, J. (2004) (ed.). *Simulacra Romae, Roma y las capitales provinciales del Occidente Europeo. Estudios Arqueológicos; Reunión celebrada en Tarragona, los días 12, 13 y 14 de diciembre del 2002*. Tarragona.

Russell, B. (2013). *The Economics of the Roman Stone Trade*. Oxford.

Sabrié, M., and Sabrié, R. (2004). 'Narbonne', in Ruiz de Arbulo (2004), 273–93.

Saint-Amans, S. (2005). 'Les Temples de Dougga', in Golvin and Khanoussi (2005), 17–24.

Segenni, S. (2016). 'Proprietà, amministrazione e organizzazione del lavoro nelle cave lunensi in età romana', in E. Paribeni and S. Segenni (eds), *Notae Lapicidinarum dalle Cave di Carrara*. Pisa, 441–50.

Serafino, C. (2009). 'Cave, miniere, salari: Il caso del Mons Claudianus', in A. Storchi Marino and G. D. Merola (eds), *Interventi imperiali in campo economico e sociale. Da Augusto al Tardoantico*. Bari, 43–53.

Soler, B. (2012). 'Planificación, producción y costo del programa arquitectónico del teatro romano de Cartagena', in V. García-Entero (ed.), *Marmora romanos en Hispania*. Carranque, 193–228.

Thouvenot, R. (1968–72). 'L'area et les thermes du Capitole de Volubilis', *BAM* 8: 179–95.

Tucci, P. L. (2009). 'Nuove osservazioni sull'architettura del Templum Pacis', in Coarelli (2009), 158–67.

Tucci, P. L. (2017). *The Temple of Peace in Rome*. Cambridge.

Ventura, A. (2007). 'Reflexiones sobre la arquitectura y advocación del templo de la Calle Morería en el Forum Adiectum de Colonia Patricia Corduba', in Nogales and González (2007), 215–37.

Vera, D. (1978). 'Lo scandalo edilizio di Cyriades e Auxentius e i titolari della Praefectura urbis dal 383 al 387. Oppere pubbliche in Roma alla fine del IV secolo d.C.', *Studia et Documenta Historiae et Iuris* 44: 45–94.

West, L. C. (1916). 'The Cost of Living in Roman Egypt', *CPh* 11: 293–314.

Wilson Jones, M. (1989). 'Designing the Roman Corinthian Order', *JRA* 2: 35–69.

Wilson Jones, M. (2000). *Principles of Roman Architecture*. London.

5

Moneychangers in the Temple? Coins and Religion in the Roman World

David Wigg-Wolf

Introduction

In contrast to the classic Roman authors, who were predominantly drawn from the senatorial and other elites, and whose literary intentions and interests lay elsewhere in the spheres of politics and intellectual pursuits, the New Testament is a rich source of information on everyday aspects of life in antiquity. This is well illustrated by two episodes in the life of Jesus that are to be found in the canonical gospels, and that illuminate the different ways in which in the ancient world coins were intricately interwoven with religious practices and institutions.

The first episode demonstrates the very close relationship between financial institutions and temples. It is the story of Jesus cleansing the Temple in Jerusalem, which had become the location not just for the sale of articles associated with temple ritual, but also for financial transactions:

> And the Jews' passover was at hand, and Jesus went up to Jerusalem, And found in the temple those that sold oxen and sheep and doves, and the changers of money sitting: And when he had made a scourge of small cords, he drove them all out of the temple, and the sheep, and the oxen; and poured out the changers' money, and overthrew the tables; And said unto them that sold doves, Take these things hence; make not my Father's house an house of merchandise.[1]

The second is the story of the widow's mite, which illustrates the role that coins could play in religious ritual:

---

[1] John 2:13–16. See also Matthew 21:12–17, Mark 11:15–19, and Luke 19:45–8. (All translations in this chapter are from the King James Bible.)

David Wigg-Wolf, *Moneychangers in the Temple? Coins and Religion in the Roman World* In: *The Economy of Roman Religion*. Edited by: Andrew Wilson, Nick Ray, and Angela Trentacoste, Oxford University Press.
© Oxford University Press 2023. DOI: 10.1093/oso/9780192883537.003.0005

And Jesus sat over against the treasury, and beheld how the people cast money into the treasury: and many that were rich cast in much. And there came a certain poor widow, and she threw in two mites, which make a farthing. And he called unto him his disciples, and saith unto them, Verily I say unto you, That this poor widow hath cast more in, than all they which have cast into the treasury: For all they did cast in of their abundance; but she of her want did cast in all that she had, even all her living.[2]

It is these two different aspects of the close link between religion and coinage that are to be addressed in this chapter. On the one hand, the role of temples as financial institutions, or as the site of financial activity; on the other, the role of coinage and money in ritual and religious practices in the Roman world.

That coins are a source of such rich and varied information, and are so closely interwoven with a wide range of social practices, is to a great extent due to their very nature as a combination of material, text, and image. Beyond this, coins operate at different levels, being struck and issued as an official medium, before then entering the more everyday environment of circulation (even if this could be officially regulated). It is important to bear this multifaceted character in mind when considering the relationship between coins and religion.

Religion and the Origins of Coinage

Before we consider the role of coins and money at religious institutions and in ritual or religious practices, it is worth very briefly considering the role of religion in the production of coinage, as well as its iconography. Although the outline presented here can do no more than draw attention to a few salient points, it nevertheless highlights another important aspect of the relationship between the medium of coinage in its various functions, religion, and religious institutions.

---

[2] Mark 12:41–4. See also Luke 21:1–4. Of relevance here is the question of what exactly is to be understood by 'treasury'. The word used in the *Novum Testamentum Graece* is γαζοφυλάκιον, which on the evidence of John 8:20 is clearly a building, as Jesus teaches there: 'These words spake Jesus in the treasury, as he taught in the temple: and no man laid hands on him; for his hour was not yet come.' Joseph. *BJ* 6.282 uses the same word to describe the treasuries that were destroyed when the Temple Mount was stormed by the Romans during the First Jewish War. That the word generally denoted a substantial institution is clear from Strabo 7.6.1: 'On this coast-line is Cape Tirizis, a stronghold, which Lysimachus once used as a treasury.' (trans. Jones 1924).

In 1869, the German archaeologist and historian Ernst Curtius, followed by Bernhard Laum, placed the origin of money in the temples.[3] They concluded this from the fact that coins were found in numbers at many temples, that they displayed religious symbols and figures, and that during the Republic the Roman mint was situated in the temple of Juno Moneta. Their proposal then received support when many of the very earliest Greek coins were found in the Temple of Artemis in Ephesos.

While this view is no longer generally accepted, and other factors are today accepted as being involved in the creation of coinage,[4] there is still some debate as to whether religious institutions and temples could have been responsible for particular coinages. For example, it is still a matter of debate as to whether the coinage of Elis was produced by the city itself, or by the temple authorities at Olympia.[5] In north-western Gaul certain Iron Age coinages are found only at religious sites, and it has been suggested that they were produced by the sanctuary authorities primarily for use in practices of ritual deposition at the respective sanctuaries.[6] However, there were no large central settlements in the region where such temples are found, and it is more likely that the sanctuaries were issuing coinages not as religious institutions for a religious purpose, but in their role as local centres acting as substitutes for central settlements.

The Role of Religion on coins

The Roman Republic

But, if it is uncertain whether temples could be involved in the production of coinage, one area where religion did indeed play an important role is in the iconography of coins, for religious content was widespread in ancient coinages.

From its very beginnings, the Roman coinage, like the coinage of Classical and Hellenistic Greece before it, often displayed religious content. Initially this generally came in the simple form of the use on the obverse of the coins of busts of various gods, which were frequently—though not exclusively—used to differentiate individual denominations. For example, on the early *aes* issues of 280–276 BC, the *as* was distinguished by the head of Mercury, the *semis* by the head of Minerva (Fig. 5.1). Similarly, the earliest Roman silver coins, the didrachms of 275–270 BC, featured the head of Apollo on the obverse. When

---

[3] Curtius (1869); Laum (1924).
[4] See, e.g., Price (1983), de Callataÿ (2001), and Reden (2015: 154) for a summary of more recent work.
[5] Proposed by Seltman (1921); *contra* Nollé (2004). [6] Delestrée (1991, 1996).

Fig. 5.1 (*a*) *As*, 280–276 BC, *RRC* 14/1. Diameter 71 mm (scale 1:1.5). (*b*) *Semis*, 280–276 BC, *RRC* 14/2. Diameter 56 mm (scale 1:1.5).

Source: (a) American Numismatic Society, http://numismatics.org/collection/1944.100.745. Public Domain Mark; (b) American Numismatic Society, http://numismatics.org/collection/1944.100.746. Public Domain Mark.

the *denarius* was introduced in 211 BC, it was the head of Roma that was placed on the obverse—although Roma should perhaps be regarded more as a personification than as a deity—while the *victoriatus* featured the head of Jupiter, a tradition that was continued when the silver *quinarius*, as the successor to the *victoriatus*, was reintroduced in 101 BC (Fig. 5.2). Although it would be misleading to see the delivery of a religious message as the primary purpose of these busts, it is nevertheless significant that religious motifs were chosen to guarantee the coinage—much as a temple, that of Juno Moneta, was chosen as the site of the Roman mint.

It was only in the late second and the first centuries BC that religious content and connotations on the Roman coinage changed, when the *tresviri monetales* from the aristocratic Republican families who were responsible for producing the coinage began to use coin designs as a means of presenting the past achievements of their families in order to promote their own status. Thus in 88 BC Marcius Censorinus struck *denarii* that had no direct religious

Fig. 5.2 (a) *Denarius*, 211 BC, *RRC* 44/5. (b) *Victoriatus*, 211 BC, *RRC* 44/1. Scale 1:1.
Source: (a) American Numismatic Society, http://numismatics.org/collection/1994.25.2. Public Domain Mark; (b) gallica.bnf.fr/BnF: ark:/12148/btv1b104223777.

Fig. 5.3 *Denarius*, Marcius Censorinus, 88 BC, *RRC* 346/1a. Scale 1:1.
Source: gallica.bnf.fr/BnF: ark:/12148/btv1b10436914c.

Fig. 5.4 *Denarius*, Julius Caesar, 47–46 BC, *RRC* 458/1. Scale 1:1.
Source: American Numismatic Society, http://numismatics.org/collection/1937.158.262. Public Domain Mark.

connotations, but on the obverse the busts of Ancus Marcius, the fourth King of Rome and founder of the *gens* Marcia, and his grandfather, Numa Pompilius, the second King of Rome (Fig. 5.3). In 47–46 BC, during his campaign in North Africa against the remaining supporters of Pompey, C. Julius Caesar had *denarii* issued that illustrated on the reverse Aeneas, the mythical ancestor of the Julii, carrying his father Anchises from the burning city of Troy following its fall to the Greeks. Although the goddess Venus appears on the obverse of Caesar's coin, she does this in part in her role as the mother of Aeneas, and so as an ancestor of Caesar (Fig. 5.4).

The Empire

This was the coinage that was then inherited by Augustus, who used the medium in very much the same way as his Republican predecessors, as part of the mechanisms designed to maintain the power base of himself and his family.

Again, we can use a biblical episode to illustrate this: the story of the tax coin that is recounted in the Gospels. Jesus was asked by some Pharisees and Herodians whether or not it is right for Jews to pay the taxes demanded by Caesar. In the Gospel of Mark[7] the additional, provocative question is asked, 'Shall we give or shall we not give?' Jesus first called them hypocrites, but then asked them to produce a Roman coin that would be suitable for paying Caesar's tax.[8] One of them showed him a Roman coin, and he asked them whose head and inscription were on it. They answered, 'Caesar's', and he responded: 'Render therefore unto Caesar the things which are Caesar's; and unto God the things that are God's.'[9]

This tale is a remarkably potent statement about how the Roman imperial coinage was perceived in the ancient world. It was very clearly the emperor's coinage, and it was in this function that religious content was employed on it. This is very much reflected in the coinage of the empire, for, generally speaking, when a deity is introduced on the coinage, then it is most often employed in some kind of relationship to or as an attribute of the emperor.

For example, on a brass *sestertius* of Vespasian (Fig. 5.5), Salus, who is seated on the reverse, is characterized as Salus Augusta, the Salvation of the Emperor, while on an *aureus* struck by Marcus Aurelius for his wife, Faustina II (Fig. 5.6), Juno Lucina, as the goddess of childbirth, appears as a reference

Fig. 5.5 *Sestertius*, Vespasian, *RIC*² 245, AD 71. Scale 1:1.
Source: American Numismatic Society, http://numismatics.org/collection/1980.187.1. Public Domain Mark.

---

[7] Mark 12:15. [8] The word used in the *Novum Testamentum Graece* is δηνάριον.
[9] Mark 12:17.

Fig. 5.6 *Aureus*, Marcus Aurelius for Faustina II, *RIC* 693, AD 161–76. Scale 1:1.
Source: British Museum: https://www.britishmuseum.org/collection/object/C_1867-0101-725.
CC BY-NC-SA 4.0.

Fig. 5.7 *Antoninianus*, Aurelian, *RIC* 225, AD 270–5. Scale 1:1.
Source: Kunsthistorisches Museum, Vienna, http://www.ikmk.at/object.php?id=ID206987.
CC BY-NC-SA.

to Faustina's role as the mother of Marcus' children, and to the future of the Antonine dynasty. In the late third century, Aurelian is receiving a globe as a symbol for the world and his dominion over it from Jupiter as the guarantor and source of Aurelian's power (Fig. 5.7), and this use of references to a deity continued after the introduction of Christian symbolism.

Initially Christian content generally appeared only in a subsidiary role, either replacing pagan or classical symbols and elements, or in a role emphasizing the divine nature of the emperor. The most famous example is perhaps the wedding *solidus* for Marcian: on the reverse Christ stands between Marcian and the Empress Pulcheria (Fig. 5.8), and the symbolism is particularly significant. The marriage between the new emperor and the sister of his predecessor secured Marcian's succession to Theodosius II, who had died without issue. However, Pulcheria agreed to marry Marcian only on condition that he did not violate her long-standing vow of virginity, and so, in order for the marriage not to seem scandalous, the Church proclaimed that 'Christ himself sponsored the union and it therefore should not provoke shock or unjustified suspicions'.[10] This is the first representation of Christ on a Roman

---

[10] Holum (1982: 209).

Fig. 5.8 *Solidus*, Marcian, *RIC* 502, AD 450–7. Diameter 22 mm (scale 2:1).
Source: © The Hunterian, University of Glasgow, GLAHM:32543, http://collections.gla.ac.uk/#/details/ecatalogue/92124.

coin, and a particularly potent example of how religious content could be used on the coinage to promote imperial identity.

The Greek East

If religious content was used on the Roman imperial coinage to present a particular image of the emperor, the coinage of the cities of the Greek east was very different, providing as it does at the same time both a contrast and a parallel to imperial coinage. It is a parallel in that, as a rule, the bust of the emperor, or a member of the imperial family, is to be found on the obverse, and the coins were struck in the emperor's name.[11] However, it is a contrast, since it is no longer the emperor and his virtues that we find at the centre of the programme of the reverses of the coins, and religious aspects play a very different role. Instead of references to imperial deeds and virtues, we find references to elements of the self-representation of the cities—for example, to local deities and their temples, or myths related to the cities. For example, at Heliopolis in Syria the temple of Jupiter Heliopolitanus features prominently on the reverse of the city's coinage (Fig. 5.9), while the reverse of coins of Abydos display the legend of Leander swimming across the Hellespont to his lover, Hero (Fig. 5.10). Here too religious content was one of the tools used to present a particular identity, but it is the identity of the issuing cities rather than that of the emperor in whose name the cities struck the coins.

---

[11] There are a number of exceptions to the rule: for example, the coinage of Athens generally displayed not the emperor's bust but the head of Athena on the obverse.

Fig. 5.9 *Aes*, Heliopolis, AD 244–9; obv.: bust of Philip I; rev.: temple of Jupiter Heliopolitanus. Scale 1:1.
Source: http://numismatics.org/collection/1944.100.83839. Public Domain Mark.

Fig. 5.10 *Aes*, Abydos, AD 222–35; obv.: bust of Severus Alexander; rev.: Leander swimming across the Hellespont to Hero. Scale 1:1.
Source: gallica.bnf.fr/BnF: ark:/12148/btv1b10323660w.

Competition and the Cosmic Order

When considering the role that religious content played on the Roman coinage, it is perhaps useful to turn to an ethnological model of money and its social functions. Jonathan Parry and Maurice Bloch differentiate between 'two related but separate transactional orders: on the one hand transactions concerned with the reproduction of the long-term social or cosmic order; on the other a "sphere" of short-term transactions concerned with the arena of individual competition…this long-term order is concerned with the attempt to maintain a static and timeless order'.[12] The model is illustrated by the Malay fishermen of the Lankawi: the men can use money only in (short-term) commercial transactions with comparative strangers, as the activity is contrary to the (long-term) sphere of kinship. Only when the money so gained is transferred to the women can it be used to support the (long-term) household and

---

[12] Parry and Bloch (1996: 24).

community. While Parry and Bloch apply the concept to the social framework of the economic function of money, by analogy it also provides insight on the social and political functions of the iconography and how religion was being instrumentalized on the coinage.

In the latter decades of the Republic, the choice of motifs for the coinage was intricately interwoven with the competition between the various aristocratic families and factions, and thus the level of individual competition, analogous to the sphere of short-term transactions as defined by Parry and Bloch. The coinages of the cities of the Greek east during the Early and Middle Empire display a similar element in that the cities used religious references on their coinage to present their own identities as part of the competition between *poleis*.

This contrasts starkly with the role of religious content on the imperial coinage. Although the religious content of the coinage of Augustus effectively followed in the tradition of the late Republic, in the context of the sole rule of an emperor it was now clearly intended to underpin his power and thus the existing cosmic order. In this respect, the provincial coinages of the Greek east present an interesting hybrid, for, while the reverses are generally located in the realm of inter-*polis* competition, the obverses parallel the imperial coinage in presenting the emperor and the reproduction of the long-term order.

Temples as Financial Institutions

The close link between religious institutions and coinage in the Roman world is perhaps no better expressed than in the English words 'money' and 'mint', derived as they are from 'Moneta', one of the names of the Roman goddess Juno. The temple of Juno Moneta, which stood on the Arx, the northern spur of the Capitoline Hill overlooking the Forum in the centre of Rome, was the site of the Roman mint in the last two and a half centuries of the Republic and the first century of the Roman Empire, before the second century AD, by which time it had been moved to a new location near the Colosseum.[13]

But this close relationship was not an isolated case. Not only in Jerusalem, but in many parts of the Mediterranean world, temples were intimately linked to finance. They not only housed rich offerings made to the gods—one

---

[13] '...his [sc. Manlius] house had stood where the temple and mint [*officina*] of Moneta now are' (Livy 6.20.13; trans. Forster 1924). On the location of the mint, see Burnett (1987: 28–9); for the evidence on the location of the new imperial mint, see Richardson (1992: 259).

need only think of the treasuries at sanctuaries such as Delphi and Olympia; they were also storehouses for valuable objects from a variety of sources, their sacrosanctity making them, at least normally, safe. This factor is emphasized by Dio Chrysostom in his *Rhodian Oration*, written in the second half of the first century AD. He notes the attitude of the Ephesians to the wealth stored in the temple of Artemis, and also tells us a great deal about where the wealth so stored comes from, as well as that deposits were officially documented:

> You know about the Ephesians, of course, and that large sums of money are in their hands, some of it belonging to private citizens and deposited in the temple of Artemis, not alone money of the Ephesians but also of aliens and of persons from all parts of the world, and in some cases of commonwealths and kings, money which all deposit there in order that it may be safe, since no one has ever yet dared to violate that place, although countless wars have occurred in the past and the city has often been captured. Well, that the money is deposited on state property is indeed evident, but it also is evident, as the lists show, that it is the custom of the Ephesians to have these deposits officially recorded.[14]

Similarly, the satirist Lucian of Samosata, writing about the temple of Atagartis in Hierapolis in Syria one century later, notes the amounts of wealth that flowed into it, although in this case he seems to be referring more to offerings that then belonged to the temple, rather than to private deposits:

> Of all these temples, and they are numerous indeed, none seems to me greater than those found in the sacred city; no shrine seems to me more holy, no region more hallowed. They possess some splendid masterpieces, some venerable offerings...And more: this temple is the principal source of their wealth, as I can vouch. For much money comes to them from Arabia, and from the Phœnicians and the Babylonians: the Cilicians, too, and the Assyrians bring their tribute. And I saw with my own eyes treasures stored away *secretly* [λάθρῃ ἀποκέαται] in the temple; many garments, and other valuables, which are exchanged for silver or gold.[15]

---

[14] Dio Chrys. *Or.* 31,54; trans. Cohoon and Crosby (1940).
[15] Luc. *Syr. D.* 10f.; trans. Strong and Garstang (1913). A revision by the current author is marked in italics.

Temples likewise enjoyed an important role as safe repositories in Rome itself, where the state treasury, the *Aerarium populi Romani*, was housed in the Temple of Saturn at the foot of the Capitoline Hill overlooking the Forum Romanum.[16] Funds involved in official transactions could also be placed in temples for safe-keeping. In a letter to Rufus, Cicero states that, acting on the orders of Pompey, he had deposited a sum of money in a temple, and that the arrangement was officially recorded. In the same letter he goes on to refer to a sum deposited by Rufus that Cicero had authorized to be paid out to Sestius, and for which a careful record had been kept:

> I should have been sorry to have omitted to record your having deposited the money in the temple on my order, had not that sum been attested by records of the most solemn and precise nature—stating to whom it was paid, by what decree of the senate, and in virtue of what written order from you and from myself it had been handed over to P. Sestius.[17]

From Juvenal we learn that in Rome during the second century AD many private citizens stored their wealth in the Temple of Castor, which had a military guard. There was a series of chambers in the intercolumniations of the podium that may have been used as strongrooms.[18] However, the same passage tells us that not all temples were safe; the Temple of Mars Ultor had apparently been the object of a robbery:

> Just think at what hazard to life men's fortunes are increased, what
> Risks they'll run to fill up their brassbound coffers
> And boost their deposit accounts! (They bank with Castor these days,
> Ever since Mars the Avenger was robbed of his helmet, and failed
> To safeguard the goods in his keeping.)[19]

Nor does the robbing of temples seem to have been such a rare occurrence, as is indicated by another passage in Juvenal, even allowing for the exaggeration typical of a satirist:

---

[16] Corbier (1974: 631–2); Richardson (1992: 344); Claridge (1998: 80–1). The strongrooms were probably situated in the vaulting still partly visible beneath the steps. In Pompeii, before the earthquake of AD 62, the *aerarium* was situated in vaulted chambers beneath the Capitolium: see Coarelli, La Rocca, and Allroggen-Bedel (1990: 173–6).
[17] Cic. *ad Fam.* 5.20.5; trans. Williams (1958).   [18] Richardson (1992: 75); Claridge (1998: 9).
[19] Juv. 14.258–62; trans. Green (1967).

> Think of the temple-robbers, who filch big chalices
> (The gifts of nations, so holy their very rust should be worshipped)
> From some ancient shrine, or the crowns that a long-dead monarch
> Left there in dedication. If no such prizes are going,
> Your small-time desecrator will scrape off the gold leaf
> From Hercules' thigh, or the very face of Neptune, will strip
> Castor of all his gilding, So why not go the whole hog, and
> Melt down the Thunderer's statue, what's solid gold right through?[20]

It is from Marcian, the early third-century AD jurist, that we learn of the lengths to which robbers might go. He recounts the ingenious attempt by a thief of good birth to steal deposits from one temple:

> The Divine Severus and Antoninus, having ascertained that a young man of very illustrious lineage had a small chest placed in a temple, and, after the temple was closed, emerged out of the chest and stole many things belonging to the temple, and afterwards again shut himself up in the chest, deported him to an island, after his conviction.[21]

Elsewhere we learn from Marcian that stealing goods or money deposited in temples was treated as normal theft, rather than as sacrilege, itself an indication that, although the location of the deposit was a sacred place, the temple as a depository was felt to be acting very much in a secular context:

> The Divine Severus and Antoninus stated in a rescript addressed to Cassius Festus that if the property of private individuals deposited in a temple should be stolen, an action for theft, and not one for sacrilege should be brought.[22]

However, it was just not common thieves who plundered temples. In his account of the life of Anthony, Plutarch tells us that the Triumvirs stole valuables and money that had been deposited for safe-keeping in the Temple of Vesta in Rome:

> For the triumvirate not only sold the properties of those whom they slew, bringing false charges against their wives and kindred, while they set on foot

---

[20] Juv. 13.150–2; trans. Green (1967). [21] *Dig.* 48.13.10.1; trans. Scott (1932).
[22] *Dig.* 48.13.5; trans. Scott (1932).

every kind of taxation, but learning that there were deposits with the Vestal Virgins made by both strangers and citizens, they went and took them.[23]

And, although, as we have seen, Dio Chrysostom tells us that the deposits in the Temple of Artemis at Ephesos had not been robbed in spite of 'countless wars', the temple's wealth had been in danger. Scipio was on the verge of plundering it when Pompey ordered him to Macedonia after Caesar had crossed the Adriatic,[24] while Caesar saved the temple when he forced T. Amfius Balbus to flee the city before he could lay his hands on the temple treasures.[25]

That such acts were not well regarded, even when committed against an enemy during the course of a war of conquest, is emphasized by the fact that Caesar himself was criticized for plundering the Gallic sanctuaries:

> In Gaul he pillaged shrines and temples of the gods filled with offerings, and oftener sacked towns for the sake of plunder than for any fault…while later on he met the heavy expenses of the civil wars and of his triumphs and entertainments by the most bare-faced pillage and sacrilege.[26]

Disapproval also marks Dio Cassius' account of the actions of Cleopatra, who had 'removed almost all the offerings from even the holiest of the shrines', thus, as Dio ironically adds, enabling the Romans 'to amass their spoils without committing any act of sacrilege'.[27]

But apparently, in times of need, recourse to such deposits could be officially sanctioned: the Peloponnesians had proposed to use the temple treasures in Delphi in order to finance the first Peloponnesian War against Athens in the fifth century BC, although the fact that the measure was not adopted indicates the very high hurdles that such a practice would have to overcome.

Finally, it should be noted that it was not just the malice and dishonesty of humans that endangered deposits held in temples. They were not immune from natural catastrophes either, as Herodian's description of the effects of a disastrous fire in Rome during the reign of Commodus indicates:

> Although no massing of dark clouds and no thunderstorm preceded it, and only a slight earthquake occurred beforehand, either as a result of a lightning bolt at night or a fire which broke out after the earthquake, the

---

[23] Plut. *Vit. Ant.* 21.3; trans. Perrin (1914).   [24] Caes. *BCiv.* 3.33.   [25] Caes. *BCiv.* 3.105.
[26] Suet. *Iul.* 54; trans. Rolfe (1913).   [27] Dio Cass. 51.17.6; trans. Scott-Kilvert (1987).

temple of Peace, the largest and most beautiful building in the city, was totally destroyed by fire. It was the richest of all the temples, and, because it was a safe place, was adorned with offerings of gold and silver; every man deposited his possessions there. But this fire, in a single night, made paupers of many rich men. All Rome joined in mourning the public loss, and each man lamented his own personal loss.[28]

A similar fate, though under very different circumstances, befell the treasuries at the Temple in Jerusalem when the Romans stormed the Temple Mount during the First Jewish War:

They further burnt the treasury chambers, in which lay vast sums of money, vast piles of raiment, and other valuables; for this, in short, was the general repository of Jewish wealth, to which the rich had consigned the contents of their dismantled houses.[29]

Temples as Lending Houses?

From the above it is clear that, not just in Rome, but in the ancient world generally, temples were not only furnished with rich offerings that had been dedicated to the gods and were thus temple property; they were also used widely as state treasuries and repositories for the safe-keeping of private valuables. We saw that Cicero deposited a sum of money to secure it for an official transaction, and it was by virtue of their security that temples were used to deposit official documents such as wills.[30] Stealing private possessions deposited in temples was regarded as theft, rather than as sacrilege, and thus places this function of temples clearly in the secular rather than the sacred sphere—even if it was their sacrosanctity that, at least in theory, ensured the security of valuables and documents deposited in them. This confirms that there was a clear differentiation between offerings made to the gods, which were temple property, and private deposits, which could later be withdrawn and recovered.

But, if temples could act as deposit houses, the question arises as to whether they also fulfilled another banking function—that is, as lending houses—and if so what funds they drew on when lending. Did they make use of money deposited in them in this way? At Delos, in the Hellenistic period, we know

---

[28] Hdn. 1.14.2–3; trans. Echols (1961).   [29] Joseph. *BJ* 6.282; trans. Thackeray (1928).
[30] Vidal (1965: 548).

that private deposits were sealed, thus ensuring that they remained intact, and so could not be used by the temple authorities.[31] Marcian's story of the would-be thief suggests that the practice in imperial Rome was similar. Furthermore, deposits will often have consisted of particular, individual objects rather than just sums of money: while, in theory, any money could have been removed and later replaced in a different form from that originally deposited, and thus have been used for money-lending, individual objects obviously could not. Lending money deposited in temples would thus have involved opening sealed deposits and treating coins differently from other individual objects they contained, an unlikely situation.[32] If temples were to act as lending houses, then they would be able to use only funds that belonged to the temple, not money deposited there.

In the Greek world and Egypt we have clear evidence that temples did indeed lend money. Raymond Bogaert, in his study on banks and bankers in Greek cities, records no less than twenty temples that did so, dating from the fifth century BC to the second century AD.[33] A stele at the sanctuary of Apollo, Athena, and Parthenos at Halicarnassus even records the sale of goods belonging to debtors who had defaulted: some debtors were apparently sold into slavery. Bogaert suggests that persons who could not provide security for a loan in the form of property ran the risk of being enslaved in order for the loan to be recovered in the case of default.[34]

Most of the loans that are recorded were made to state organizations or cities, and in many cases there was a direct relationship between the temple and the creditor. Thus, the temple of Athena at Ilion loaned money to seven of the cities in the *koinon* of Athena Ilias. Apparently, they had difficulties repaying the debts, and at the instigation of L. Julius Caesar in 77 BC new interest rates were agreed: for ten years the rate was reduced to just 1.67 per cent, before reverting to the original rate of 6.67 per cent.[35] Delos, for which we have the most evidence, seems to have been something of an exception, and to have lent money more widely than other temples. A large number of inscriptions from the period 432–145 BC record a wide range of loans to other cites, as well as to both Delians and foreigners. The sums involved generally did not exceed a few talents.[36] The temple of Artemis at Ephesos had a widespread reputation as a safe repository and was used as such as early as 394 BC, when Xenophon deposited part of the booty of the Ten Thousand,

---

[31] Bogaert (1968: 287).   [32] Cf. Debord (1982: 226), referring to Bogaert (1968).
[33] Bogaert (1968: 288–94).   [34] *Syll.*³ 46; Bogaert (1968: 271–2); Debord (1982: 227).
[35] Bogaert (1968: 239–40); Debord (1982: 229).   [36] Bogaert (1968: 125–90, 288).

which was to be returned to him on demand. However, it is not recorded as lending money before the first century BC; a decree of 85 BC records the remission of certain debts to the temple, while poor administration of lending by the temple led to intervention by the Proconsul of Asia, Paullus Fabius Persicus, in the first century AD.[37]

However, not all temples that acted as lending houses loaned to private persons. When they did, it was often in times of need or on a humanitarian basis, and then only for small amounts. The interest rates offered by temples seem to have been low in comparison with those offered by private persons. At Delos the rate was fixed at 10 per cent, while a rate of only 1.2 per cent is recorded for Athens.[38] Clearly such loans were not regarded by temples as investment opportunities, and they were not operating an extensive profit-generating business as lending houses.

Evidence for temples lending money during the Roman Empire is scarcer, and we know nothing of the situation in the west. Significantly, the economic survey of the Roman Empire in the series edited by Tenney Frank includes no references to banking of any kind in the Hispanic, Gallic, or Britannic provinces.[39] To what extent this is due to differences in epigraphic habits in the west in comparison to the long-standing epigraphic tradition in the Greek world is hard to determine, but it may well have played a role. Similarly, environmental conditions in the west are less favourable for the survival of papyri and other forms of written documents than, for example, in Egypt, from where we have extensive records for the wealth and transactions of temples.

Egypt in fact provides a well-documented case of a temple acting as a lending house during the imperial period: the Temple of Jupiter at Arsinoe, which was evidently run on Roman rather than Egyptian lines.[40] Although it owned property, its main source of income came from loans it made: the accounts for AD 215, fragments of which have survived, record a number of such loans.[41] For example, Demetrius, a former exegete of Alexandria, had long ago borrowed 2 talents and 2,000 drachmae for a mortgage, and had repaid 1 talent on the loan and 210 drachmae interest.[42] That Arsinoe was not just an isolated case in Egypt, even if it is the only well-documented one, is indicated by the code of regulations of the *idiologus*, the chief financial official in Roman

---

[37] *Syll.*³ 742; Bogaert (1968: 247–8). [38] Bogaert (1968: 290).
[39] Collingwood et al. (1937). Temple banks were in fact restricted to the east (Drexhage, Konen, and Ruffing 2002: 155).
[40] Johnson (1936: 635). [41] Johnson (1936: 662–8, no. 404) = BGU 362.
[42] Johnson (1936: 665).

Egypt, issued in AD 150–61. One of the provisions of the section dealing with priests and temples states: 'It is forbidden to lend temple revenues on second mortgages.'[43] Presumably this was due to the risk involved in such loans, in turn suggesting that other forms of loans were allowed.

Evidence from outside Egypt for the Roman period is scarce, even in the Greek world, where, as already shown, a number of temples had been lending money during the Hellenistic period. Jean Andreau even doubts whether in the Roman world temples were actually operating as such when they lent money. He suggests that, since they belonged to cities they were in fact operating on behalf of cities when they lent money, and temples play no role in his extensive monograph on banking in the Roman world.[44]

The Western Provinces

Beyond these few examples, evidence for Roman temples acting as lending houses is scarce. For the western provinces evidence for banks and banking institutions all told is almost completely lacking, but that similar practices did exist, if only at a private level, is confirmed by events in Britain in the mid-first century AD. One of the complaints that led to Boudicca's revolt was that Seneca, who was clearly turning the conquest of Britain into a profitable business, called in loans to the tune of 40 million *sestertii* that he had forced on important Britons at a heavy interest rate.[45] Presumably this was not an isolated practice. We must assume that one reason for our poor knowledge of banking and lending practices in the west is the nature of the evidence, or rather its lack, owing to poor survival conditions.

But other factors will also have been involved: the nature of pre-Roman religious practices and institutions in areas such as Gaul or Britain were very different to those in the east, and in the north-west there was a much shorter history of the use of money in the form of coins. Coins were first struck in the late fourth/early third century BC in the areas north of the Alps, and it was only in the second half of the second century that they were produced in any significant numbers and in small enough denominations or units to enjoy

---

[43] Johnson (1936: 648). Provisions 71–97 dealing 'with the priests of Egyptian temples' are excluded in the translation in Johnson et al. (1961: 210–13).

[44] Andreau (1999: 120). The blurring of the borders between temples and the civil authorities responsible for them parallels the question as to whether city or temple was responsible for striking coins (cf. Andreau 1999: n. 4).

[45] Dio Cass. 62. 2.

anything like 'everyday' use. Only with the production of large issues of small struck bronze denominations from the mid-first century BC can we begin to talk of 'monetization', and even then only on a limited level at the major settlements and oppida. Although coins are found in many temples in the western provinces under Roman rule, they were not a regular feature among the objects deposited at sanctuaries during the pre-Roman period, and the custom had only developed late in the Iron Age. As a result, there can have been no long-standing relationship between temples and finance comparable to that found in the Greek east.

What is more, actual temple buildings were a late development in pre-Roman sanctuaries. The numerous hoards of gold coins, often with torques and other objects, found in the pre-Roman north-west, many of which have been interpreted as ritual deposits, were generally deposited in open spaces, in many cases at natural features that today can no longer be recognized.[46] At the Martberg, a hilltop sanctuary and oppidum on the Lower Mosel in south-west Germany, it was only in the mid-first BC century that the first temple buildings were constructed in what, until then, had been an open-air sanctuary. The main temple was built within an existing central ditched enclosure that had been the site of extensive coin deposition, but with the temple's erection the focus for coin offerings moved to an open area between two other temples. We get the impression that, at least on the Martberg, actual temple structures and coin offerings were mutually exclusive.

An additional factor will have been that until the mid-first century AD the temples of northern Gaul, as indeed most structures in the region, were timber-built. These were not buildings that might have provided the secure storage that we know from the monumental temples of the Mediterranean world; indeed, no such facilities are known from sanctuaries in the north-western provinces in the Roman period. If we want to find anything of the kind, then, significantly, we have to look in the non-native environment of Roman military architecture: Roman forts often have underground strongrooms situated beneath the *aedes*, the shrine in the *principia* where the standards were kept. Here, too, a religious feature was employed as a secure store.

From the written sources we know that in pre-Roman Gaul there was in fact probably no need for such secure structures. Ancient authors comment on the huge quantities of precious metal and other valuable objects that were

---

[46] Fitzpatrick (2005); Nick (2005, 2006). Exceptions are the hoards from Snettisham (Stead 1995), which were all found within a ditched enclosure, and Niederzier (Göbel et al. 1991), which was buried in a pit adjacent to a posthole (for a wooden cult figure or idol?) within a small fortified settlement.

openly displayed in Gallic sanctuaries, but that their security was guaranteed by the imposition of the death penalty for stealing them[47]—although, as we have seen, this was not to prevent Julius Caesar from plundering them.

An important distinction that must be made in the context of the pre-Roman Gallic sanctuaries is that the objects that were deposited will have been offerings to the gods, rather than private wealth deposited for safe keeping. However, in a recent study on a series of coin hoards from the Belgica that he associates with the upheavals of the Gallic Wars, Nico Roymans has suggested that, under certain circumstances, religious protection may well have been invoked in order temporarily to store private wealth in a secure location.[48] There has been much discussion in Iron Age numismatics and archaeology as to whether the numerous hoards of gold coins and other precious metal objects such as torques were ritual deposits that had been permanently offered to the gods, or normal secular hoards placed in the ground for safe-keeping with the intention of later recovery (though not actually recovered, for whatever reason). In recent years the *communis opinio* is very much that these are ritual hoards destined for the gods. Roymans, on the other hand, asks whether we need to draw such a stark distinction between secular and sacred, and suggests that some hoards were not ritual at all, but may have been deliberately buried at sites with a religious context, and thus protected by the sacrosanctity of the site, but with the intention of recovering them later. In the case of the hoards in the Belgica that he studied, he suggests that they were buried under the protection of sacred sites at times when Caesar's army was threatening the region, but that their owners were unable to retrieve them subsequently. If this were indeed the case, then we would, after all, have evidence for the use of sacred sites as secure repositories in the pre-Roman period, much as was the case with temples in the Mediterranean world, albeit in a very different physical form.

Changing Practices in the North-West

A distinction that is of relevance here is that between offerings to the gods, which were untouchable and taboo, and temple property. In contrast to the eastern Mediterranean, for which there is ample evidence for the nature and extent of temple estates and property, evidence is lacking in the Roman

---

[47] e.g. Diod. Sic. 5.27; Strabo 4.1.13 C; cf. Nick (2006: 96–104).
[48] Roymans and Scheers (2012: 19–20).

north-west. We can, however, note a change in how monetary offerings were treated, indicating that contact with the Mediterranean world led to changes in practices, and thus to a change in the attitude towards monetary religious offerings.

From the mid-first century AD at the Martberg and a number of other sanctuaries in the region, there is a radical drop in the number of coins found minted after the mid-first century AD. But this does not necessarily mean that from the later first century coins were now no longer the object of ritual activity; it is more probably the result of a change in the architecture of the sanctuaries, from timber to masonry.[49] Previously, during the late Iron Age and early Roman periods, coins had been deposited at these sanctuaries in ditches or in open areas on 'natural' surfaces, where small articles such as coins, although initially visible and accessible, would after a while have become inaccessible, washed into the ditches or swallowed by the vegetation. But the advent of masonry architecture will have brought with it gravelled, paved, or even cemented surfaces. Coins or other votive objects no longer disappeared into the mud or grass, and instead the nature of the new surfaces made objects deposited on them more accessible; the surfaces could also be kept clean and swept. This will have required new practices and behaviour with regard to such objects. Any objects deposited could now be collected for redeposition elsewhere, or even reused.

In this connection, it is significant that from the late first/early second century AD we encounter evidence in north Gaul for a new practice with regard to coin offerings: collection boxes (German: *Opferstöcke*). One example in the form of an altar to Lenus Mars, who was also worshipped at the Martberg, was found in the Irminenwingert sanctuary at Trier, and dates to the mid-second century AD.[50] The coins placed in such containers could have been recycled, perhaps to pay for the upkeep of the sanctuary, or even for sacrificial offerings. A much-quoted text by Arrian written at about this time gives an indication of how this may have worked.[51] He tells of money being pledged for successful hunting, the amount collected then being used to buy a sacrificial animal to give thanks to the goddess Artemis. Coin offerings placed in temples could have been treated similarly, whether they were placed in collection boxes or were swept up from paved or gravelled floors.

---

[49] Wigg-Wolf (2005: 378–9); Wigg-Wolf (2017: 24).
[50] Religio Romana (1996: 188, no. 33c); cf. Kaminski (1991).
[51] Arr. *Cyn.* 13.

This would mark a significant departure from pre-Roman practices, when offerings were absolutely sacrosanct. But whether this meant that temples in the north-west now assumed some of the roles that they enjoyed elsewhere in the empire and were acting as storehouses for valuables, or even as lending houses, we can neither confirm nor disprove, owing to the lack of evidence. Overall, however, there appears to have been a significant difference in practices between the east and the west that can be traced back to pre-Roman practices and traditions.

References

Andreau, J. (1999). *Banking and Business in the Roman World*. Cambridge.

Bogaert, R. (1968). *Banques et banquiers dans les cités grecques*. Leiden.

Burnett, A. (1987). *Coinage in the Roman World*. London.

Callataÿ, F. de (2001). 'Sur les origines de la monnaie stricto sensu (nomisma): À propos de deux livres récents (S. von Reden et L. Kurke)', *Revue numismatique* 6/157: 83–93.

Claridge, A. (1998). *Rome: An Oxford Archaeological Guide*. Oxford and New York.

Coarelli, F., La Rocca, E., and Allroggen-Bedel, A. (1990) (eds). *Pompeji: archäologischer Führer*. Bergisch Gladbach.

Cohoon, J. W., and Crosby, H. L. (1940). *Dio Chrysostom. Discourses 31–36* (Loeb Classical Library 358). Cambridge, MA, and London.

Collingwood, R. G., Scramuzza, V. M., Frank, T., and Nostrand, J. J. van (1937). *An Economic Survey of Ancient Rome*, vol. 3: *Roman Britain, Spain, Sicily, Gaul*. Baltimore.

Corbier, M. (1974). *L'aerarium Saturni et l'aerarium militare: Administration et prosopographie sénatoriale* (Collection de l'École française de Rome 24). Rome.

Curtius, E. (1869). *Ueber den religioesen Charakter der griechischen Muenzen* (Monatsberichte der Berliner Akademie 1869). Berlin.

Debord, P. (1982). *Aspects sociaux et économiques de la vie religieuse dans l'Anatolie gréco-romaine* (Études préliminaires aux religions orientales dans l'Empire romain 88). Leiden.

Delestrée, L. P. (1991). 'Monnaies celtique, sanctuaires et territoire dans l'ouest de la Gaule Belgique', in J.-L. Brunaux (ed.), *Les sanctuaires celtiques et leurs rapports avec le monde méditerranéen. Actes du Colloque de St-Riquier (8 au 11 novembre 1990)*. Paris, 221–9.

Delestrée, L.-P. (1996). *Monnayages et peuples du Nord-Ouest*. Paris.

Drexhage, H.-J., Konen, H., and Ruffing, K. (2002). *Die Wirtschaft des Römischen Reiches (1.-3. Jahrhundert): Eine Einführung* (Studienbücher Geschichte und Kultur der Alten Welt). Berlin.

Echols, E. C. (1961). *Herodian of Antioch's History of the Roman Empire: From the Death of Marcus Aurelius to the Accession of Gordian III*. Berkeley and Los Angeles.

Fitzpatrick, A. P. (2005). 'Gifts for the Golden Gods: Iron Age hoards of Torques and Coins', in Haselgrove and Wigg-Wolf (2005), 157–82.

Forster, B. O. (1924). *Livy with an English Translation*. London; Cambridge, MA.

Göbel, J., Hartmann, A., Joachim, H. E., and Zedelius, V. (1991). 'Der spätkeltische Goldschatz von Niederzier', *Bonner Jahrbücher* 191: 27–84.

Green, P. (1967). *Juvenal: Sixteen Satires*. London; New York.

Haselgrove, C., and Wigg-Wolf, D. (2005) (eds). *Iron Age Coinage and Ritual Practices*. Mainz.

Holum, K. G. (1982). *Theodosian Empresses: Women and Imperial Dominion in Late Antiquity* (Transformation of the Classical Heritage 3). Berkeley and Los Angeles, and London.

Johnson, A. C. (1936). *An Economic Survey of Ancient Rome*, vol. 2: *Roman Egypt to the Reign of Diocletian*. Baltimore.

Johnson, A. C., Coleman-Norton, P. R., and Bourne, F. C. (1961). *Ancient Roman Statutes: A Translation, with Introduction, Commentary, Glossary, and Index* (Corpus of Roman law 2). Austin.

Jones, H. L. (1924). *The Geography of Strabo*. London and Cambridge, MA.

Kaminski, G. (1991). 'Untersuchungen zum antiken Opferstock', *Jahrbuch des Deutschen Archäologischen Instituts* 106: 63–181.

Laum, B. (1924). *Heiliges Geld: Eine historische Untersuchung über den sakralen Ursprung des Geldes*. Tübingen.

Nick, M. (2005). 'Am Ende des Regenbogens…Ein Interpretationsversuch von Hortfunden mit Keltischen Goldmünzen', in Haselgrove and Wigg-Wolf (2005), 115–55.

Nick, M. (2006). *Gabe, Opfer, Zahlungsmittel: Strukturen Keltischen Münzgebrauchs im Westlichen Mitteleuropa* (Freiburger Beiträge zur Archäologie und Geschichte des ersten Jahrtausends 12). Rahden, Westf.

Nollé, J. (2004). 'Die Münzen von Elis', in A. V. Seibert (ed.), *Olympia: Geld und Sport in der Antike* (Museum Kestnerianum 7). Hanover, 18.

Parry, J., and Bloch, M. (1996). 'Introduction: Money and the Morality of Exchange', in J. Parry and M. Bloch (eds), *Money and the Morality of Exchange*. Cambridge, 1–32.

Perrin, B. (1914). *Plutarch's Lives: With an English Translation by Bernadotte Perrin* (Loeb Classical Library). London and Cambridge, MA.

Price, M. (1983). 'Thoughts on the Beginnings of Coinage', in C. Brooke, B. Stewart, and J. G. Pollard (eds), *Studies in Numismatic Method Presented to Philip Grierson*. Cambridge, New York, and Melbourne, 1–10.

Reden, S. von (2015). *Antike Wirtschaft* (Enzyklopädie der griechisch-römischen Antike 10). Berlin.

Religio Romana (1996). *Wege zu den Göttern im antiken Trier* (exhibition catalogue, Rheinisches Landesmuseum Trier). Trier.

Richardson, L. (1992). *A New Topographical Dictionary of Ancient Rome*. Baltimore and London.

Rolfe, J. C. (1913). *Suetonius: Lives of the Caesars*, vol. 1 (Loeb Classical Library 31). London and Cambridge, MA.

Roymans, N. G. A. M., and Scheers, S. (2012). 'Eight Gold Hoards from the Low Countries: A Synthesis', in N. G. A. M. Roymans, G. Creemers, and S. Scheers (eds), *Late Iron Age Gold Hoards in the Low Countries and the Caesarian Conquest of Northern Gaul* (Amsterdam Archaeological studies 18). Amsterdam, 1–46.

Scott, S. P. (1932). *The Civil Law: Including the Twelve Tables, the Institutes of Gaius, the Rules of Ulpian, the Opinions of Paulus, the Enactments of Justinian, and the Constitutions*. Cincinnati.

Scott-Kilvert, I. (1987). *Cassius Dio: The Roman History, The Reign of Augustus*. Harmondsworth.

Seltman, C. T. (1921). *The Temple Coins of Olympia*. Cambridge.

Stead, I. (1995). 'Die Schatzfunde von Snettisham', in A. Haffner (ed.), *Heiligtümer und Opferkulte der Kelten* (Arch. Deutschland Sonderheft 1995). Stuttgart, 100–10.

Strong, H. A., and Garstang, J. (1913). *The Syrian Goddess: Being a Translation of Lucian's De dea Syria, with a Life of Lucian by Herbert A. Strong. Edited with Notes and an Introduction by John Garstang*. London.

Thackeray, H. St. J. (1928). *Josephus, The Jewish War*, vol. 3: Books 5–7 (Loeb Classical Library 210). London and Cambridge, MA.

Vidal, H. (1965). 'Le dépôt in "aede"', *Revue historique de droit français et étranger* 43: 545–87.

Wigg-Wolf, D. (2005). 'Coins and Ritual in Late Iron Age and Early Roman Sanctuaries in the Territory of the Treveri', in Haselgrove and Wigg-Wolf (2005), 361–79.

Wigg-Wolf, D. (2017). 'Death by Deposition? Coins and Ritual in the Late Iron Age and Early Roman Transition in Northern Gaul', in N. M. Burström and G. Ingvardson (eds), *Divina Moneta: Coins in Religion and Ritual* (Religion and Money in the Middle Ages). Farnham, 13–29.

Williams, W. G. (1958). *Cicero, Letters to his Friends*, vol. 1, rev. and repr. (Loeb Classical Library 205). London and Cambridge, MA.

6

Cult Economy in the Eastern Provinces of the Roman Empire

Marietta Horster

Introduction

The religious landscape of communities was dynamic. It was defined by communal and individual preferences influenced in particular by internal and external political factors, economic potency, demographic change, possible disasters, or the choice and number of cults that were to be funded. The economy of cults for traditional gods, foreign or newly created deities, Hellenistic kings, and Roman emperors was more or less the same. Differences did not correlate with the religious quality and character of the divinity *per se*, but with the importance of the cult for a specific community and with the economic basis of the municipality and its elites if it was a civic cult. Transformations in the cult 'map' of a community are made obvious, for example, by the new combination of deities in a sanctuary as *syntheoi*, the shift in the specific character or competence of a deity made explicit by a new epithet, the introduction of a new cult, a festival or an additional ritual element, the novel design of the décor of a temple or the elaborate extension of a sanctuary, the rearrangement or melting of valuable offerings in a cult place, the alteration of the number or kind of sacrifices, or the renaming of cult officials. Accordingly, cult economy had an impact in and on all fields of religious expression. In this chapter, however, only the aspects of cult economy are addressed that had a direct connection to the monetary economy and are or could be quantifiable, at least to some extent, if we had the necessary information.

For new cults, space had to be found in a city with already existing cults and funding had to be provided, if the rent from the land and the estates leased out and owned by the community had until then been used for other purposes. New cults and additional festivals, contests, and sacrifices were costly and required new, creative forms of funding or the reallocation of existing funds at the expense of other recipients.

In the post-classical period, political changes that had an impact on the sacred landscape of the cities included the military and political integration of cities via *synoikismos*[1] or their incorporation into a Hellenistic kingdom or a Roman province. Such cities lost political independence and financial autonomy by losing taxes and customs as sources of income as well as by incurring expenses in the form of tribute payment and additional taxes. Membership in a Hellenistic league and in the organized Roman provincial *koina* had less of a direct impact, as these organizations had little political scope and needed only small amounts of funding. However, the leagues and provincial assemblies reallocated the resources of the cities' elites—resources of time and money, as, for example, in the case of the assembly of Roman Lycia. The Lycian cities provided the *koinon* with a flat sum from the import taxes, part of which was then paid to the Romans.[2] The rest was left to the *koinon* as a budget, probably to fund the sacrifices of the imperial cult and other rituals at their meetings.

From archaic times, the cities' elites had always invested part of their social capital, time, and financial resources in the relationship with rulers, cities, and leagues outside their civic community. The issues negotiated and the addressees varied, but the means for such diplomatic activities remained similar. This personal aspect of diplomacy on behalf of a sanctuary and a city is exemplified by a decree of the Pergamene *demos* in honour of Mithridates, son of Menodotos. He was a hereditary high priest and a priest of Dionysos Kathegemon, who managed to gain support from the Romans for restoring the city and the lands to the gods.[3] A text matching this decree is a fragmentary letter of Julius Caesar (to the Pergamenes) that starts with praise of Mithridates' visit to Caesar and his great commitment to solving territorial disputes and other problems.[4]

In the imperial period, the advocacy of Greek members of the imperial elite for their province or home town, and the many embassies to the Roman governors and the emperors, often with distinguished orators presenting the issue in question, gave all such decisions a personal, arbitrary touch—as was adequate for the functioning of the socio-political structure of the

---

[1] Cf. Badoud (2015) for the Rhodian *synoikismos* with its consequences for the other cities and the traditional cults in the Hellenistic period.
[2] Marek (2006).   [3] *IGRom* 4. 1682.
[4] Sherk (1969: no. 54) = *ISmyrna* 590a, an inscribed letter of Julius Caesar found in Smyrna, in which he wrote that he was informed by Mithridates, son of Menodotos, about territorial disputes. A likely restoration of the fragment suggests that the letter was addressed to the *archontes*, *boule*, and *demos* of Pergamon in 48/44 BC.

Greco-Roman world, irrespective of the form of government.[5] A second Pergamene example for the later developments is the Roman senator and local notable C. Antius A. Iulius Quadratus (*cos. ord.* II, AD 105): he was a priest of Dionysos Kathegemon and financed (at least parts of) the games in honour of the emperor Trajan as *agonothetes* in his home town. He took over the priesthood of the temple of the imperial cult at Pergamon and invested in buildings for the local cults and a new Traianeum.[6] The elite's personal and financial engagement in cults of new gods and in the imperial cult was only one means of actively participating in the transformation of Greek culture within the Roman commonwealth. The perceived distance to the ruling authorities could be diminished by various media of interaction and influence.[7] In this context, the ruler cult may have signalled the respectful recognition and integration of the new political partner into the very heart of the civic body on the initiative of the citizens.[8] This *soi-disant* voluntariness *vis-à-vis* the ruling power affected all levels of cultural identity and civic economy.[9]

It is anything but certain which specific factors influenced communal and individual behaviour, benefaction patterns, and budget management within cities. Did Roman interventions have more than a temporary effect for a given city or sanctuary? Most imperial letters or those written by governors were directed to the institutions of just one city and dealt with just one problem, one privilege, one detail of behaviour, finance, or organization (not only in the context of religion and cult). Even the harsh letter of AD 44 from the proconsul of Asia Paullus Fabius Persicus, in which he characterized the Ephesians as corruptible and selfish at the expense of their main goddess Artemis and her

---

[5] Diplomacy and ambassadors of Greek cities in the imperial period: Millar (1977: 363–463); Rizakis (2007: 321–5).

[6] Halfmann (1979: 112–15) with references; see Burrell (2004: 22–4), Kantiréa (2011: 527–8), and Schowalter (2011) for the second neokorate temple but with different assessments of Quadratus' influence.

[7] For integrative functions of imperial iconography, see Bergmann (1998: 3–12) for Roman imperial and Horster (2013) for provincial coinage; the aspect of *syntheoi* of local gods and emperors as a religious phenomenon is discussed by Steuernagel (2010) and Camia (2012). A. S. Chankowski (2011) and Lozano (2011) downplay the religious aspect of the ruler cult that is supposed to be just one, though a very important, part of political and cultural exchange patterns; more nuanced are Galinsky (2011) and the 'response' of Friesen (2011) in the same volume.

[8] Before the Smyrnaeans became part of the Empire, in 195 BC they decided to be the first in the Greek world to build a temple to Dea Roma (Tac., *Ann.* 4.56.1). In a few cities, the Hellenistic ruler cult survived into the second century AD; in others names of months and other reminders of the Hellenistic kings and their families are attested well into the imperial period; cf. A. S. Chankowski (2010).

[9] See, for example, the following interpretations and evaluations of the effects: Alcock (1993) on the embeddedness of agricultural and economic changes in cultural transformations in Roman Greece; Veyne (1999) for 'collaboration'; Lafond (2006) for the many changes in the cultural, economic, and religious landscape of the Peloponnese in the Roman period; Melfi (2016) for the religious identity of a Roman colony (Corinth) that seems as 'individual' (plus Roman) as the respective religious landscapes of the Roman colonies in Italy (Bertrand 2015).

famous sanctuary, does not seem to have had a long-lasting effect:[10] some forty years later, boundary stones had to be set up again to restore Artemis' landed property.[11]

Persicus had, it seems, decided to cut down the expenses for a festival, the *megala Epheseia,* and hence forbade the expensive *hymnodes* from performing, except to honour Augustus and Julia Augusta; for the hymns to all the other deities, the amateurs of the sanctuary should do their best. We do not know if civic attitude or just details in organization changed thereafter.[12] It has been debated whether the notable turn in the Ephesian elite's benefactions towards building activities had something to do with the Romans,[13] but it would be arbitrary to see a connection to Persicus' letter, and/or to presumed changes in the management of the public budget and the sanctuary's economy.

Cult Economy

Sanctuaries accumulated and immobilized wealth by receiving and storing offerings of value and protecting deposits of money.[14] They were economic actors as well as generators of value: they needed raw materials and manpower for construction works, reconstruction, and maintenance of sanctuaries with shrines and impressive cult statues. The deities of the sanctuary were landowners, and their managers and priests leased land and other properties, while a few of them even provided loans at interest to individuals, the city, or its subdivisions. Apart from deposits, the banking operations seem to have been only occasional activities.[15] All in all, the impact of a sanctuary on the economy and infrastructure of a region depended on a large number of factors. The two most important ones were (*a*) the steady income through leasing and/or a regular budget and (*b*) its financial management.[16]

---

[10] *IEphesos* 17–19 Greek text with a German translation (pp. 119–21); Braund (1985: 213–15) with an English translation.

[11] Landed property of Artemis: *IEphesos* 459 (Augustus), 3501 (Augustus), 3506–10 (Domitian); cf. *SEG* 32.1129, *IEphesos* 3511–12 (Trajan).

[12] The letter of Persicus is the only evidence for a standard procedure of sales of priesthoods in Ephesos. If it did exist, it seems likely that it was short-lived. Some of the ways of accounting as well as managing the sacred finances may have changed as well, but the evidence would be *e silentio*.

[13] Halfmann (2001); but see Kokkina (2012).

[14] There is no way of calculating the ratio of, for example, precious metal offerings and money deposits in sanctuaries, as, even for sanctuaries with a rich epigraphic and literary record like Delphi or Delos, the evidence focuses on precious offerings and spectacular looting; cf. V. Chankowski (2011: 146) with further references.

[15] With a focus on the Hellenistic period: V. Chankowski (2005; 2011: 149–58). For the Roman period: Debord (1982: 225–30) and Dignas (2002: 146–9).

[16] V. Chankowski (2011: 143).

Expenditure

Building work was probably the most expensive (irregular) activity, but it was only one part of the turnover that had a significant effect on the economy in the region and community in which the cult centres were based.[17] The Hellenistic documents of the Delian sanctuary mention craftsmen and construction materials as permanent expenditures for the maintenance of the site.[18] Impressive cult-related buildings and, even more so, the religious festivals were instances of conspicuous consumption—important in quantity of expenditure as well as in quality to attract visitors.[19] Quantity and quality of festival expenditures defined the rank of a cult in relation to other cults in a *polis*. This standing depended, *inter alia*, on the number and choice of sacrifices and on the duration and character of the festivities related to the cult.[20]

Without question, the sacrifices were the religious heavyweights, but they represented only a small fraction of cult expenditure, at least for cults with priests and temples, compared to festivals including processions, performances of various kinds, and competitions. Larger sanctuaries even incorporated theatres for the dramatic festivals as well as stadia and hippodromes, several smaller temples for *syntheoi*, treasuries, larger and smaller porticoes, guest houses, and a supply of water for ritual bathing. Part of the expenditures on religious festivals with competitions and games was connected with specific buildings. Around seventy items of literary and epigraphic evidence from the Roman imperial period attest to the financing of theatres in Greece, the islands, and Asia Minor, with several attestations from Athens, Corinth, Messene, Sparta, Kourion, Gortyn, Salamis on Cyprus, Thasos, Aphrodisias, Ephesos, Hierapolis, Ilion, Miletos, Myra, and Patara.[21] The amounts expended are mentioned in only a few of these texts. They range from more than

---

[17] An overview of the various aspects of cults as consumers and generators of value is provided by V. Chankowski (2011) with a focus on the Hellenistic period.

[18] Feyel (2006).

[19] Cult-expenditures: Debord (1982: 185–93) and Dignas (2002: 13–35) for Hellenistic and Roman Asia Minor, Davies (2001) and Horster (2004: 194–5, 208–12) for Classical Greece. Building expenses are documented, for example, in the building accounts from Epidauros—cf. Burford (1969) and Prignitz (2014)—and Didyma in the third and second centuries BC—cf. Debord (1982: 187–91); for artisans and builders in sanctuaries, see Feyel (2006). Cult calendars of the late fifth and the fourth centuries BC like that of Thorikos (*SEG* 33.147) specify the expenditures for sacrifices; cf. Lupu (2005: 116–49); for a focus on the cults and festivals of Dionysos, see Horster (2011).

[20] Anthesteria and other Dionysiac rituals and festivals in Athens and Attica: Henrichs (1990); Parker (2005: 290–326).

[21] Moretti (2010) for theatres; Mathé (2010) for hippodromes and stadia, obviously less attractive for individual benefactions, as the small and sparsely built structures did not offer much space for self-advertisement via inscriptions and statues.

10 million *sestertii* in Nicaea and 250,000 *denarii* in Patara to 1,000 *denarii* in some cities for one or more tiers of seating. Such numbers give an idea of the amount needed, at least when the inscription either was found *in situ* or is written directly on the built structure, but most inscriptions and literary attestations do not mention any amount of money.

The problems of interpretating the few known amounts are obvious and have been debated, *inter alia*, as reactions to the gathering of costs and expenditures of all kinds by Richard Duncan-Jones and in Hélène Jouffroy's collection of building expenditures in the Roman west.[22] Nevertheless, these collections of evidence for sums expended on a large variety of building activities in sanctuaries and sacred precincts remind us not to restrict modern ideas of cult expenses to altars and temples, sacrifices and festivals, or the remuneration of priests.

Festivals were an important part of expenditure and income. Fairs and markets were often, though not always, connected to such events, and some even guaranteed tax exemption for buyers and sellers.[23] Although the accounts of Delos and Delphi with their detailed lists of expenditures for the upkeep and cleaning of the sanctuary as part of the preparation for the festivals are limited to the Classical and Hellenistic period, they give an idea of the different kinds of work that had to be done and paid for, even in less prominent cults and smaller sanctuaries. Festival expenditures also included professional artists. An attractive drama contest needed several choruses, tragic and comic groups, *didaskaloi*, and musicians. They received daily pay, sometimes with an addition for extraordinary expenses; victors won prizes, sometimes paid for by an *agonothetes*. William Slater has argued that the high costs for some of the professional artists at dramatic contests led to a decline of the Dionysia-type festivals in the Roman imperial period. The Dionysia festivals, with their choruses and especially their *khoraulai*, were perhaps too expensive when the Greek cities were under economic pressure owing to the Roman civil wars that took place in Greece and had a strong impact on the cities in Asia Minor. After the civil wars, 'the demands of imperial cult consumed public and euergetic money for festivals'.[24] Religious activities were competitive, as they

---

[22] Duncan-Jones (1982) and Jouffroy (1986); cf. Bowman and Wilson (2009) and Morley (2014) on the limits of quantification in the ancient economy. For a different approach to the assessment of expenditure based solely on the few known quantities, see, e.g., Domingo, Chapter 4, this volume.

[23] For markets and fairs connected to festivals in the Greek east, cf. De Ligt (1993: 225–34). For his lists of cities, festivals, taxes and their exemptions, and *agoranomoi* as responsible officials in that context, see De Ligt (1993: 253–9, with appendices I B 4 to I D).

[24] Slater (2010: 276). Moser and Smith (2019: 6) speak of a 'marketplace of religions', obviously having in mind competing religious groups such as Christians and non-Christians.

affected the handling of and the access to limited resources—financial resources of the community, but also those of individuals through the assumption of priestly offices and benefactions. 'Traditional' cults, such as the cult of Dionysos, could be replaced by, for example, the imperial cult as beneficiaries of these private donations or offerings.

However difficult the interpretation may be, except at Athens and few other places, the Dionysia disappeared from the epigraphic record, as, for example, in Ephesos. The cost may have been one factor, changes in taste another. The imperial cult festivals that were sometimes connected with gladiatorial games as competitions *à la romaine* were one such change in supply and demand; the sophistic performances with battles of erudite talk were another.[25] In any event, the cult of Dionysos continued to be attractive in civic organized forms as well as in private cult associations, but some of the former Dionysiac drama competitions were reorganized and integrated into other festivals. This observation seems to reflect a 'real' impact of Roman culture, but there were shifts and changes in the evidence as well, which restricts our knowledge of Greek cult economy in the Roman Empire.

Sources

From the Classical to the Roman period, inscriptions are the main sources for cult organization and priesthoods. Pausanias' second-century description of the sacred topography of Greece, which is nourished by many local stories, is one of the few literary texts to put flesh on these bones.[26] The inscribed evidence changed over time: whereas cult calendars, so-called *leges sacrae*, accounts, and inventories are well known from the Classical and Hellenistic periods, the inscribed honorific decrees of the cities are the common features from the Hellenistic period and dominate our record in the imperial period. Individual benefactions, known through building inscriptions and inscribed decrees, are therefore over-represented as a source of income of cities and

---

[25] Arnold (1972) discusses the Ephesian festivals of Hellenic appearance but with a Roman 'spirit'; cf. Spawforth (1997: 184) for the gladiatorial spectacles in the Theatre of Dionysos in Athens at the end of the first century AD (at the latest); imperial games (*Sebastoi agones*) were held in AD 41 for the emperor Claudius, on the initiative and funding of Ti. Claudius Novius (Spawforth 1997: 190), perhaps not for the first time; cf. Follet (2004: 148) and Schmalz (2009: 115–16, no. 145). The traditional athletic contests continued to be of economic and cultural importance for the hosting provinces, cities, and sanctuaries, and athletic success had social relevance for the local elites in the Roman east; cf. Spawforth (1989) and van Nijf (2001: 321–34).

[26] For Pausanias, see Pirenne-Delforge (2008).

sanctuaries in the Roman period.²⁷ Epitaphs that name a priesthood held by a deceased man are rare compared to such mentions of other offices of the imperial period. This is markedly different from the Roman west, where the function of *flamen*, a priest of the imperial cult, is often mentioned in the epitaphs. Votives sometimes preserve the name of the priest or priestess responsible, but most of the votives give no clue to cult organization, financial obligations, or cult attendants' responsibilities. The inscribed texts attached to large offerings and donations, such as built structures within a *temenos*, focused on the benefactor's name. However, at least in the imperial period, building inscriptions and those about large votives may present the donor's current status and office.²⁸

From the second century AD, inscribed details such as the sums spent or particular measures involved increase in number.²⁹ Building inscriptions are conspicuous demonstrations of changing epigraphic habits that reflect transformations in social values and behaviour in the second century AD.³⁰ This apparent affluence seems to indicate a new (or, until then, less vocal?), rather formalistic attitude behind the euergetic rhetoric, as if services for the community now could be calculated, and degrees of benevolence could be measured in volume and money.

The information provided by honorific decrees, as well as personal statements attached to small votives and large monuments, is meagre regarding cult economy compared to the earlier evidence.³¹ Classical and Hellenistic cult calendars, inventories, archives, leases of sacred land, and buildings give an insight into the workings of a sanctuary, the expenditures for a cult, the more or less costly preparations for a festival, the craftsmen and merchants involved, and so on. Such a detailed documentation provides plenty of

---

²⁷ Pont (2010: 24–32) has collected 101 inscriptions with building measures connected to sanctuaries of Greek local divinities in Roman Asia Minor, of which only 4 (or 5?) present the city as initiator and financier; for the distorted picture produced by the inscribed evidence of the proportion of individual benefactions with regard to other means of financing, cf. Horster (2014: 530–2).

²⁸ See, e.g., Oliver (1950: 109–14), who discusses the preferences and specific local contexts of inscriptions set up by Herodes Atticus (Roman consul, local priest, and rich benefactor of Athens and other Greek cities) to indicate one of his many offices in a text.

²⁹ Moretti (2010) presents 139 building measures in Greek theatres from Classical to Roman times, most often connected to religious festivals with agonistic features. Pont (2010: 253–6) presents a collection of the sums mentioned for building expenditure in cities of Asia Minor in the second and third centuries.

³⁰ A different change is noted by Rizakis (2007: 319): he points to a third-century transformation of eastern euergetic behaviour to support festivals rather than building activities.

³¹ Feyel (2006) discusses the work of artisans as attested in the accounts of the sanctuaries of Erechtheus at Athens (since 409/408 BC), Demeter and Kore at Eleusis and Athens (in 330 BC and some later ones), Apollo at Delphi (several decades of the fourth century), Asklepios at Epidauros (fourth century BC), and Apollo on Delos (between 314 and 166 BC). See also n. 19 with further literature.

specifics for a given year, such as the lead delivered to the Delian sanctuary by a certain Diophantos (in 177 BC) or the sum of 444 drachmae paid to a certain Eutychides for the extraction and removal of blocks of stone in 169 BC.[32] Such minutiae may give an impression of the variety of transactions in goods and services, of costs and prices, and of the origin and specialization of artisans and merchants in a handful of Greek sanctuaries in a given period. However, the information often remains anecdotal, as most inventories were neither coherent nor explicit concerning the amount, weight, size, and quality of the goods or the days or hours of work involved. Well into the Roman imperial period, large sanctuaries such as those of Apollo at Delphi, of Asclepius at Pergamon, and of Artemis at Ephesos continued to be such centres of employment, production, and movement of goods. For centuries it seemed a safe bet to invest in the long-term attractiveness of the Artemis cult, the stable economy of the Ephesian temple, and the steady flow of pilgrims. New Hellenistic 'Greek' settlements in western Anatolia and the hinterland in the east had increased the demand for Greek 'cultural products' and of Greek 'cultural symbols', which cities like Ephesos could and would meet.[33] After Mithridates VI of Pontus had finally been defeated by Pompey in 63 BC, it took some time to restore property rights and prosperity. However, even later, in the Roman imperial period, there is little written evidence for commercial activities in such sanctuaries and for markets and fairs held under the auspices of a religious festival. Details—such as the incident in Ephesos when the silversmiths producing offerings for the Temple of Diana protested in the theatre against Paul,[34] or the customs law of Asia granting immunity from taxes and customs for the penteteric festival of *Romaia Sebaste* at Pergamon—do not present a coherent picture of the commercial activities connected with sanctuaries and festivals.[35] The analysis of the material evidence, of buildings, kilns, ceramics, votives, bones, and coins, is therefore vital to understanding the volume and kind of economic activities at the sanctuaries in the different regions in the late Hellenistic and imperial periods. The written information is limited not only by purpose but also by scope, as cult organization and its

---

[32] *IDélos* 444 B, l. 104; cf. Feyel (2006: 221). *IDélos* 461 Ab, l. 32; cf. Feyel (2006: 227).
[33] Davies (2011: 198); V. Chankowski (2011: 163) goes even further and claims that sanctuaries were interfaces between cities and markets, and acted as a kind of 'hinterland of a market for the smaller cities', which seemed 'better tailored to their needs and their ambitions' than the global and uncontrollable economy of the Hellenistic (and Roman) age.
[34] *Acts* 19:24–41.
[35] Cottier et al. (2008: 77–8) with a translation of the customs law, ll. 128–33; cf. the commentary 153–4. The law was translated and published in AD 62, but the core of it was already part of a customs law of Republican times with modifications in Augustan times (19 and 12 BC). For a broader appraisal of Roman markets and fairs, see De Ligt (1993).

documentation practices differed, even within the same city. These differences include the funding of cults. There was no standard practice in a given city regarding what was paid for with the sacred money, the communal budget, or liturgical obligation, for example.

Although there was no standard, it seems that a rather common feature for a cult was that the sanctuaries' officials received payment from leases of land, fees for sacrifices, and other sources of revenues from the responsible institution (city, league, association, family)—a sufficient income to manage regular cult activities and to pay for the maintenance of the sanctuary.[36] Some of the civic regulations included obligations for priests and priestesses, liturgists and magistrates, such as the *agonothetes,* to provide oil for the competitions and animals for the sacrifices, to pay for specific services, or to make sure that there was enough grain available at a reasonable price during a festival.

New buildings, major reconstruction work, new festivals, and so on required financial resources. For these and all other budget gaps, the city had to find solutions, at least if this was a so-called civic cult (a cult organized mainly by the city and not by an individual person, a private group, or an association). Many, if not most, festivals of the Hellenistic and Roman periods were paid for by private foundations—the majority of which are known from inscriptions.[37]

Mismanagement and fraud of such private or public funding provoked documentation of accounting procedures and of cult expenditure in the imperial period. Attested are decrees and letters of Roman authorities, decrees of the council and the people of the respective cities, a few loan agreements and boundary stones, and even fewer hints in literary sources.[38]

Revenues

The main aspects of expenditure connected to the rituals in Greek cults just discussed had to be met out of revenues. A large variety of sources of income existed, which included: rents from leases of sacred land, buildings, and so on; fees for regular services like sacrifices; more or less regular and fixed budgets

---

[36] Landed property of gods belonging to sanctuaries: Horster (2004) for Archaic and Classical Greece; Papazarkadas (2011) for Classical Athens; Chandezon (2011) for a few modifications in the Hellenistic period with a trend towards larger units and professional management of estates; Debord (1982) and Dignas (2002) for Hellenistic and Roman Asia Minor.

[37] 'Most' is the assumption of van Nijf (2001: 312–14), but see n. 27 for the quantitative distortion of the inscribed information concerning individual euergetism.

[38] e.g. Aelius Aristides' *Sacred Tales,* Strabo's *Geography,* or Pausanias' *Travels.*

from the civic (or federal) institutions; special payments with a specific appropriation to, for example, construction works or cash distributions; entry fees for an office; liturgies; obligations of priests and officials; private benefactions and foundations that secured the cult a regular income; one-time private benefactions; and, finally, irregular payments such as fines.

Revenues from Lease Rentals and Rentals of Sacred Property

The aforementioned rich documentation for the Delian sanctuary of Apollo with its huge estates on Delos and Rheneia had stopped by 167 BC, when its independence ended and the Athenians took control again. The sanctuary and the inhabited part prospered until the raid by Mithridates' troops in 88 BC. In the imperial period, the sanctuary declined further. There was a short-lived revival in the second century AD supported by Hadrian, and the Athenians resumed sending offerings to the island for some years, but ultimately it seems that the Roman period brought about an economic collapse. The reasons are manifold, but a sanctuary with large estates for rent that nobody was interested in leasing deteriorated. The sanctuaries needed a strong partner, as they were unable to restore their fortunes by themselves. In the Greco-Roman world such partners were cities and their elites, but it seems that the Athenians, as the owners of the island, focused on their own affairs and were not particularly interested in financial investments or personal commitment to Delos.[39] Whenever institutions were committed to ensuring the solid financial basis of cults in their respective communities, the traditional leasing of land and other property as income for a cult continued to exist. The leases with an incoming rent to finance the cult in Carian Mylasa and for the temple at Olymos, are well documented.[40] Another kind of evidence for land leases is a decision by Hadrian and a letter of the proconsul of Asia from AD 125/6. After years of dispute about the revenues of Zeus' land in Aezanoi, the governor T. Avidius Quietus put an end to it by sending external land surveyors to measure the size of all the land lots and set up boundary stones: an unknown number of citizens had held plots of sacred land without paying rent. The city's council and assembly had addressed the Roman authorities

---

[39] However, Philostr., *VS* 527 (1.23), cannot be taken as serious information on Roman Athens. In fact, he praises a sophist for the brilliant idea (within an *oratio*) to let Delos make an escape by sea when the Athenians tried to sell the island; cf. Anderson (1986: 30).
[40] *IMylasa* 201–32 (lease contracts) and more inscriptions with e.g. boundary markers. The land was sold to the sanctuary and then leased back to its former owners, cf. Williamson (2021: 221–6).

more than once and had received verbal support but had not been able to enforce its claims.[41] Finally, the governor decided that the *kleroi* should be measured again, and, for these newly assigned plots of equal size, rents had to be paid to Zeus, the owner of the land.

This specific solution is in accordance with the general rule to be found in the Latin *Corpus Agrimensorum*: whenever disputes over land occur, sacred land has to be protected.[42] It is precisely in this sense that Augustus was praised in cities like Kyme, as he had restored sacred property (*IKyme* 17). Some boundary stones in Ephesos and the aforementioned letter of the proconsul Persicus refer to Augustus' provisions.[43] As a rule, the Roman administration respected the property of the gods, and the sacred land was looked after. At least in some cases, after republican tax collectors had violated the immunities of temples, the temples' property and rights were restored by the Roman senate.[44]

However, it seems that, in cases of the development of new urban centres, like Nicopolis and Patrae in Greece and the colony of Antioch in Pisidia, land had to be taken away from other cities' territories, including land that funded a cult and a sanctuary.[45] In addition, the emperors had no interest in creating administrative and economic structures parallel to the cities and civic communities in the eastern provinces in the form of large temple territories and powerful priests. The temple estate of Men Askaenus was stripped of parts of its land and income, seemingly to the profit of the new colony of Antioch in Pisidia, which installed a *curator arcae sanctuarii* for Men's remaining riches.[46] More frequent than confiscations by the Romans, rarely attested in the epigraphic record, are the praiseworthy and therefore documented restitutions of sacred land to the gods, so that the incoming rents would finance the cults.[47]

---

[41] Cf. Dignas (2002: 179–86). The cult of Zeus at Aezanoi continued to be an important point of reference and identification for the local elite of the imperial period; cf. Wörrle (1995: 71–2).

[42] Agennius Urbicus 48.4–12, focused on North Africa; cf. Campbell (2000: 44–5, with commentary p. 351).

[43] Augustus' restoration of sacred property in Ephesos: cf. n. 11 and Dignas (2002: 170–7); in Athens, cf. Schmalz (2007–8).

[44] Lozano (2015: 69).

[45] Colonies and land in Greece: Rizakis (1997); in Asia Minor: Levick (1967). For a short period in the first century AD, the Nicopolitans dominated the Amphictyonic league, with ten councillors representing the west of Greece; cf. Lefévre (1998: 127–8); Lozano and Gordillo (2015: 130–1). According to Spawforth (2012: 161), Nicopolis was presented as a kind of regenerated, 'true' Greece. By the time of Nero, the Thessalians had twelve councillors, it seems, and the number of the Nicopolitans at that time had dropped; cf. Sánchez (2001: 426–36); Lozano and Gordillo (2015: 140 f.). On newly acquired imperial landownership in the second century in Galatia and Pisidia (of *ager publicus* and private property), see Mitchell (1993: 156–7); in Phrygia, Mitchell (1993: 158).

[46] Lozano (2015: 80–2).   [47] Debord (1982: 148–51).

More or Less Regular and Fixed Budgets Given to Some Sanctuaries by the Civic (or Federal) Institutions

For the imperial period, part of our knowledge of economic issues like fixed budgets is based on disorder and malfunction, as the example of Sardis shows. In AD 188, Hermogenes, the priest of Men, wrote a letter of complaint to the saviour of the province (*eparchia*) of Asia, as he addressed the proconsul Arrius Antoninus:

> the god has the right of being given annually by the magistrates of the city the customarily determined and decided sum of 600 *denarii* to be spent on sacrifices and libations for the god and for the victory and eternal presence of the emperor and a rich harvest...this year they have not been given by the year's archon Aurelius Ctesippus.[48]

Hermogenes then asks the governor to order the archon to consign this money, obviously a successful undertaking.

Special Payments with a Specific Appropriation

Collecting money, as in Lindos in AD 22 for the sacrifices and festival of Athena Lindia, was a rather simple way to provide money in case of need.[49] In the first century AD, the Pamboiotia festival in Koroneia with musical and equestrian contests, by contrast, had a complicated financial background. The income of a specific plot of land, a tithe of wheat and barley, as well as two special taxes, one for wine and one for the *skenai*, which were probably the wooden sales booths used by the merchants during the event, were especially designated to fund the festival.[50] All in all, both these examples added up to only a small amount of money, some 1,000 *denarii*, but that was probably enough to guarantee the basic needs of the festival infrastructure and the sacrifices.

Private Benefactions to Secure a Regular Income from A Foundation

In the Roman period, many foundations were set up across Greece, the islands, and Asia Minor. Benefactors gave money or real estate, so that rent or

---

[48] Translation by Dignas (2002: 140).   [49] Migeotte (2010: 143).
[50] Migeotte (2010: 139).

interest of a given percentage would provide an annual income for the foundation. For example, in AD 104, C. Vibius Salutaris made the one-time gift of thirty-one gold and silver statuettes and images of Artemis, of a few other gods, and of Trajan and Plotina for processions from the Artemision to Ephesos and back again. He combined this one-time donation with the endowment of a foundation with 20,000 *denarii*. The revenue from the fixed interest rate (of 9 per cent) was supposed to guarantee the cash distributions, lotteries, and everything else that was needed for the celebration of the goddess's birthday in May and a few other occasions.[51]

From the late first to the early third centuries AD, some twenty foundations are attested from Aphrodisias that focused on festivals and cults.[52] One example is found in an inscription of the AD 180s. A former *curator* and designated high priest of the imperial cult of the province of Asia reports the results of his review of the financial basis of some contests and recommends starting the festival with a limited programme (based on Lysimachus' foundation):

> So far the competitions have not taken place because the provision of money needed to be increased in accordance both with the directions of the deceased (founders) and with the reckoning of the funds from which the contests are due to be carried out. However, the contest from the will of Flavius Lysimachus has reached a total endowment of 120,000 *denarii*, so that it is possible…for the musical contest to be held every four years, as the testator wished. The funds over and above the 120,000 *denarii*, which are a loan, and the interest accruing to this up to the beginning of the year, make a total of 31,839 *denarii*. You can therefore…carry out this contest…for prizes amounting to a talent, and with competitions according to the prizes [available].[53]

As in this case, the epigraphic record favours the survival of evidence for individual, one-time private benefactions over long-term foundations by individuals and over any kind of funding by public or sacred funds. It is, therefore, impossible to get an idea of the ratio of foundations, liturgical obligations, standard budgets, and non-recurring benefactions for the cult economy of a sanctuary in a given city.

---

[51] Rogers (1991: 39–79) for the lotteries and distributions.
[52] Cf. Laum (1914: no. 100–16); cf. Reynolds (1982: 185–9) = Rouché (1993: 164) for the example above.
[53] Translation by Rouché (1993: 165, document no. 50).

One-Time Private Benefactions

The building activities of Roman emperors in the east were not focused on sanctuaries, as there was no specific religious building policy.[54] Financial assistance, building materials, and manpower after earthquakes were positive imperial reactions to specific demands. For example, Claudius rebuilt the temple of Dionysos in Samos, *terrae motu conlapsam*,[55] and Hadrian invested in Athenian sanctuaries and rebuilt the temple of Dionysos at Teos. The members of the local elites were far more reliable partners. They contributed to the city's income and supported the civic cults through the communal budget by taking over magistracies, liturgies, and priesthoods and by individual benefactions. This commitment included investments by members of the senatorial families of Greece, Asia Minor, and the Aegean islands. The greater part of their landed property lay in or near the territory of their home town and in the province,[56] and a major part of their family lived in the region. They supported their respective home towns and provinces in various ways. Building activities were but one means and seemingly not very prominent among the senators. However, many of them had taken over offices and priesthoods before entering imperial service. Some returned home between offices and some financed a replacement for offices and priesthoods. One example of investment in a specific town, Peloponnesian Messene, illustrates that, for benefactors and cities, construction costs and building expenditure for cult-related structures were not specific or different from those of other edifices—although cult and religion were of primordial importance to civic identity. This list of reconstructions in the early first century AD mentions the temple of Demeter, then a certain *porticus* of Nicaios, followed by a temple of Herakles and Hermes near the gymnasium, and finally a long list of non-religious buildings.[57]

---

[54] Horster (2001: 248–50) and Pont (2010: 351–3) contra Dignas's claim (2002: 131–2) that 'cults and sanctuaries [were] one of the central objects of their [the emperor's] euergetism'.

[55] *CIL* III.7096: *Ti. Claudius Caesar Aug(ustus) / Germanicus, pontifex / maximus, tribuniciae / potestatis VII, imp(erator) XV, co(n)sul IIII, / pater patriae, censor / aedem Liberi Patris / vetustate et terrae motu / [conlapsam restituit]*; cf. Horster (2001: 240): Claudius' building investment had no specific religious focus.

[56] Bowersock (1982); Halfmann (1982); Oliver (1982). The following examples follow Halfmann (1982: 616). Parts of the family of Flavius Mar(cius?) Scribonianus, a senator of the mid-third century of Paros, lived in Samos. A female relative was priestess of Hera, the main deity of the island, whereas her brother was *basileus* of the thirteen Ionian cities, an office his family held for several generations, as the inscription states (*IEphesos* 3065). The priest of Athena Lindia of Lindos on Rhodes, M. Aelius Hellanicus, married a daughter of a consular. Their daughter then married another Lindian senator, Ti. Claudius Hermias Theopropus, who had property in Ephesos and elsewhere.

[57] *SEG* 23.307; cf. Lafond (2006: 233).

Irregular Income such as Fines

In pre-Roman times, the fines and penalties for misuse of endowments and for *sacrilegia* against the deities and their possessions were to be paid either to the public funds or to the sacred fund of a deity of a specific sanctuary.

Social control and clear-cut responsibilities of the officials or priests involved were to ensure that such transgressions were reported. From the late first century AD the Roman *fiscus* is mentioned, perhaps as a kind of empty threat to grave robbers, in funerary inscriptions in some remote parts of Asia Minor.[58] By the mid-second century, however, the Roman *fiscus* was the beneficiary of the fines collected for misuse of endowments. In this case, the civic and priestly authority was undermined, and the income was lost to the sanctuary or the civic institutions. One such example concerns the Eleusinian mystery cult. Around AD 169/170,[59] the *synhedrion*[60] passed a decree on the use of the income of an endowment that was supposed to be managed by the two Eleusinian priesthoods, the hierophant and the *daduchus*. The income was intended for cult purposes but had not been used for years, and a clarification about its use seemed necessary. In the future, the income of at least 6,000 drachmae was to be distributed as *sportulae* during the festival (probably the Mysteries) to all priests, priestesses, and cult officials of the Eleusinian sanctuary and the Eleusinian deme, a few dignitaries, and a certain Xenion, who may have been a relative of a hearth initiate. In case of a surplus income, the purchase of incense burners was recommended. This decree is followed by a governor's *apophasis* (decision) about this endowment, which was a validation of the original endowment and therefore had become part of the dossier.[61]

> Severus said: 'I too approve the act of generosity [*philoteim[ían]*] which he has displayed in respect to the gods. If anyone should dare to alter any of the consecrated arrangements, property of twice the value shall be vindicated to the *fiscus* from the person who has so dared, a penalty being levied as for *sacrilegium*. It is especially understood that the hierophant and the *daduchus* shall have complete charge in order that this capital investment be never

---

[58] But see Dignas (2002: 136), who reckons with Roman efficiency and protection.
[59] For the date, with good arguments, see Oliver (1952).
[60] Clinton (1999: 99) suggests that the *synhedrion* of the Panhellenion may have been responsible for the financial administration of the Eleusinian sanctuary. Oliver (1952: 384) argues in favour of the *synhedrion* of the Areopagus council, which used to manage the Athenian resources in the imperial period.
[61] *IG* II² 1092 = *IEleusis* 489a; English translation by Oliver (1952: 387–8).

endangered and in order that the amount of the consecrated interest be never reduced by a single *denarius*. For it is clear that for them [the two priests] nothing remains safe if they overlook any alteration of the terms.

The best guarantee for a steady income from foundations in the form of rents from leases and loans were people able and willing to invest money. In addition, social control and, if needed, efficient enforcement measures, as well as strict sanctions, helped raise funds on a local level (and a smaller scale).

Demography

Neither the many 'middle-class' people nor the elites of the cities in the Roman east were a homogeneous group. Differences in the demography of inland cities and harbour cities, between former royal residences like Pergamon and trading towns like Ephesos, between remote villages, Roman colonies with veterans in Greece, and those municipalities with the status of a free city make it difficult if not impossible to give a nuanced description of those responsible for the cults inside the cities and outside their walls in their *chora*. However, there were some general trends regarding priesthoods.[62]

Roman senators from the eastern provinces often came from a family background that held, *inter alia*, traditional and important civic priesthoods, some of them hereditary.[63] The family of M. Antonius Flamma, a senator in Trajanic times, held the priesthood of Apollo in Cyrene for generations; the ancestors of Herodes Atticus were priests of Apollo and *archiereus*, priests of the imperial cult at Athens. In the second century AD, six senators from Lycia, Crete, Achaia, and Asia are known to have had familial ties to provincial priests of the imperial cult. However, even in the second century, the number of those family members and senators who held traditional priesthoods still outnumbered those connected to the imperial cult.[64]

Prosopographical studies of the priests of the imperial cult in the cities in Achaia, the Peloponnese, Lycia, and Asia Minor have demonstrated that the

---

[62] For example, for changes in the epigraphic record and new options in office-holding by female priests in Greek cities of the Roman period, see van Bremen (1996: 41–81) and Horster (2006).

[63] The following arguments concerning senatorial engagement are based on Halfmann (1979, 1982), Eck (1980), and Oliver (1982).

[64] The evidence is too small to state that in the second century AD priesthoods of the imperial cult and especially those of provincial status gained ground in the families of the senators. See n. 24 for the competitive aspect of religious activities linked to the access to restricted human and economic resources.

question of whether other priesthoods and offices are mentioned for these imperial priests depends on the kind of inscription and its context. This also applies vice versa to civic offices and liturgies and to priesthoods of traditional gods. Because of gendered differences in life and documentation, the study of female priests in Asia Minor and the islands is more revealing about the continuity of traditional cults and the attractiveness of their respective priesthoods for members of the local elites. These offices were not a first step for a Rome-oriented career, and the imperial cult was just one of several cult offices a promising young man would accept.

The argument for an adaptation of an alleged Roman ideal of traditional priesthoods, being aristocratic and of long-term (even lifelong) duration, as another indicator of a Romanizing feature in Greek cult, is difficult to prove. This is because the unquestionable increase in the number of attested lifelong or heritable priesthoods all over the Greek world may in some cases indicate a rise in the standing of a specific priesthood, with or without the influence of the Romans; in other cases, however, it may have been an emergency solution for a lack of candidates or economic shortages.[65] In some cities, the lifetime priesthood may be an indicator for prestige and may even reflect Roman aristocratic ideas, but this was not a general feature of the Greek religion in the imperial period.

Concluding Remarks

Greek religion was not a success story during the imperial period, at least not for all cities, all cults, and all sanctuaries. But what went wrong? Probably nothing, as far as notions of religion and expressions and rituals of cult are concerned. However, the overall management of the civic cults (and likewise of private cult associations) was a mirror of the rather inflexible and static elite structure and of a civic organization narrowly bound to the Roman imperial system. Pausanias' description of the desolate situation of many Greek sanctuaries in the second century AD was not a consequence of religious shortcomings or Roman misbehaviour but rather reflected shifts in agricultural land use, migration and changing settlement patterns, and perhaps ecological problems.

Roman emperors and governors focused on cities and their elites, not only for tax collection and revenue but also for an efficient administrative and

---

[65] Dignas (2002: 188), with reference to Zeus of Aezanoi.

judicial structure with as few staff as possible. The cities' elites had their own interest in the workings of the system and were focused on their home towns and their own religious traditions. Without question, Greek religion mattered to the Romans. However, religion was secondary to the Roman goal of an overall peaceful, politically stable, and economically healthy situation in the cities and provinces in the imperial period. The Roman imperial administrative and social hierarchy allowed Roman law and political notions to adapt to provincial requests but was neither dynamic nor flexible. The imperial strategy of installing *curatores rei publicae* or *correctores* according to requirements may have nurtured the individual elite member's lack of initiative and sense of responsibility.[66] Similar to modern discussions about the negative consequences of a bailout of debt-ridden European countries, interventions by a governor like Pliny in Pontus and Bithynia to save civic finances and solve problems with unfinished buildings and ruins may have been one of the many factors that had a long-term negative impact on the investment culture of the cities' elites.

As long as the cities had a sound economy, their traditional and the new imperial cults maintained their income, and sustainable development was ensured for all cults. Beate Dignas has claimed that interventions in the funding of cult and sacred finances by the Roman government aimed 'at the healthy functioning of the cults even though this benevolent concern indirectly guaranteed Roman revenues as well'.[67] But, ultimately, the system of civic financing with benefactions, fees, and taxes adapted to and, at least partly, became dependent on the rules and regulations of Roman administration.

The imperial system created winners and losers, since all cities in the provinces were supposed to perform well to meet Roman needs and all cities had to compete for status, for donations in kind and money, and for various benefactions such as grants of rights and exemptions. Personal involvement of the members of the local elites was the only way to stay on the 'right side' as long as possible—with the help of the gods, the Roman governor, and the emperor. Some provinces and remote regions, however, had few such advocates. These less-advantaged areas included the two *Germaniae*, Roman Britain, parts of Greece, the hinterland of Asia Minor, and many other regions in the huge Roman Empire.

---

[66] But see Dmitriev (2005: 189–216) for the rather modest role of *logistai* (*curatores*) and other new offices in the Greek cities.
[67] Dignas (2002: 219).

References

Alcock, S. (1993). *Graecia Capta: The Landscapes of Roman Greece*. Cambridge.

Anderson, G. (1986). *Philostratus: Biography and Belles Lettres in the Third Century AD*. London.

Archibald, Z. H., Davies, J. K., and Gabrielsen, V. (2011) (eds). *The Economies of Hellenistic Societies, Third to First Centuries BC*. Oxford.

Arnold, I. R. (1972). 'Festivals of Ephesus', *AJA* 76: 17–22.

Badoud, N. (2015). *Le temps de Rhodes: Une chronologie des inscriptions de la cité fondée sur l'étude de ses institutions*. Munich.

Bergmann, M. (1998). *Die Strahlen der Herrscher: theomorphes Herrscherbild und politische Symbolik im Hellenismus und in der römischen Kaiserzeit*. Mainz.

Bertrand, A. (2015). *La religion publique des colonies dans l'Italie républicaine et impériale (IIIe s. av. n. è.-IIe s. de n. é.)*. Rome.

Bowersock, G. W. (1982). 'Roman Senators from the Near East: Syria, Judaea, Arabia, Mesopotamia', in Panciera (1982), 651–68.

Bowman, A., and Wilson, A. (2009). 'Quantifying the Roman Economy: Integration, Growth, Decline?', in A. K. Bowman and A. I. Wilson (eds), *Quantifying the Roman Economy: Methods and Problems* (Oxford Studies on the Roman Economy). Oxford, 3–84.

Braund, D. (1985). *Augustus to Nero: A Sourcebook on Roman History, 31 BC–AD 68*. London.

Brodd, J., and Reed, J. L. (2011) (eds). *Rome and Religion: A Cross-Disciplinary Dialogue on the Imperial Cult*. Atlanta.

Burford, A. (1969). *The Greek Temple-Builders at Epidaurus: A Social and Economic Study of Building in the Asclepian Sanctuary during the Fourth and Early Third Centuries BC*. Liverpool.

Burrell, B. (2004). *Neokoroi: Greek Cities and Roman Emperors*. Leiden.

Camia, F. (2012). 'Theoi Olympioi e Theoi Sebastoi: Alcune considerazioni sull'associazione tra culto imperiale e culti tradizionali in Grecia', in E. Franchi and G. Proietti (eds), *Forme delle memoria e dinamiche identiarie nell'antichità greco-romana*. Trento, 93–110.

Campbell, B. (2000). *The Writings of the Roman Land Surveyors: Introduction, Text, Translation and Commentary*. London.

Chandezon, Ch. (2011). 'Some Aspects of Large Estate Management in the Greek World during Classical and Hellenistic Times', in Archibald, Davies, and Gabrielsen (2011), 96–121.

Chankowski, A. S. (2010). 'Les cultes des souverains hellénistiques après des dynasties: formes de survie et d'extinction d'une institution dans un contexte civique', in I. Savalli-Lestrade and I. Cogitore (eds), *Des rois au prince: Pratiques du pouvoir monarchique dans l'Orient hellénistique et romain (IVe siècle avant J.-C.—IIe siècle après J.-C.)*. Grenoble, 271–90.

Chankowski, A. S. (2011). 'Le culte des souverains aux époques hellénistique et impériale dans la partie orientale du monde méditerranéen: question actuelles', in Iossif, Chankoswki, and Lorber (2011), 1–14.

Chankowski, V. (2005). 'Techniques financières, influence, performances dans les activités bancaires des sanctuaires grecs', *Topoi* 12/13: 69–93.

Chankowski, V. (2011). 'Divine Financiers: Cults of Consumers and Generators of Value', in Archibald, Davies, and Gabrielsen (2011), 142–65.

Clinton, K. (1999). 'Eleusis from Augustus to the Antonines: Progress and Problems', in S. Panciera (ed.), *Atti XI Congresso Internazionale di Epigrafia Greca e Latina*, vol. 2. Rome, 93–102.

Cortés Copete, J. M., Muñiz Grijalvo, E., and Lozano Gómez, F. (2015) (eds). *Ruling the Greek World: Approaches to the Roman Empire in the East.* Stuttgart.

Cottier, M., Crawford, M. H., Crowther, C. V., Ferrary, J.-L., Levick, B. M., Salomies, O., and Wörrle, M. (2008) (eds). *The Customs Law of Asia*. Oxford.

Davies, J. K. (2001). 'Rebuilding a Temple: The Economic Effects of Piety', in D. J. Mattingly and J. Salmon (eds), *Economies beyond Agriculture in the Classical World*. London, 209–29.

Davies, J. K. (2011). 'The Well-Balanced *Polis*: *Ephesos*', in Archibald, Davies, and Gabrielsen (2011), 177–206.

Debord, P. (1982). *Aspects sociaux et économiques de la vie religieuse dans l'Anatolie gréco-romaine*. Leiden.

De Ligt, L. (1993). *Fairs and Markets in the Roman Empire*. Amsterdam.

Dignas, B. (2002). *Economy of the Sacred in Hellenistic and Roman Asia Minor*. Oxford.

Dmitriev, S. (2005). *City Government in Hellenistic and Roman Asia Minor*. Oxford.

Duncan-Jones, R. (1982). *The Economy of the Roman Empire. Quantitative Studies*. 2nd edn. Cambridge.

Eck, W. (1980). 'Die Präsenz senatorischer Familien in den Städten des Imperium Romanum bis zum späten 3. Jahrhundert', in W. Eck (ed.), *Studien zur antiken Sozialgeschichte: Festschrift Friedrich Vittinghoff*. Cologne, 283–322.

Feyel, C. (2006). *Les artisans dans les sanctuaires grecs aux époques classique et hellénistique à travers la documentation financière de Grèce*. Athens.

Follet, S. (2004). 'Julius Nicanor et le statut de Salamine (Agora XVI, 337)', in S. Follet (ed.), *L'Hellénisme d'époque romaine: nouveaux documents, nouvelles approches (Ier s. a. C.-IIIe s. p. C.)*. Paris, 139–70.

Friesen, S. J. (2011). 'Normal Religion, or, Words Fail us: A Response to Karl Galinsky's "The Cult of the Roman Emperor: Uniter or Divider?"', in Brodd and Reed (2011), 23–6.

Galinsky, K. (2011). 'The Cult of the Roman Emperor: Uniter or Divider?', in Brodd and Reed (2011), 1–22.

Gauthier, Ph. (1985). *Les cités grecques et leurs bienfaiteurs (IVe-Ie siècle avant J.-C.), contribution à l'histoire des institutions.* Paris.

Halfmann, H. (1979). *Die Senatoren aus dem östlichen Teil des Imperium Romanum bis zum Ende des 2. Jahrhunderts n.Chr.* Göttingen.

Halfmann, H. (1982). 'Die Senatoren aus den kleinasiatischen Provinzen', in Panciera (1982), 603–50.

Halfmann, H. (2001). *Städtebau und Bauherren im römischen Kleinasien: Ein Vergleich zwischen Pergamon und Ephesos.* Tübingen.

Henrichs, A. (1990). 'Between Country and City. Cultic Dimensions of Dionysos in Athens and Attica', in M. Griffin and D. J. Mastronarde (eds), *Cabinet of the Muses: Essays on Classical and Comparative Literature in Honor of Thomas G. Rosenmeyer.* Atlanta, 257–77.

Horster, M. (2001). *Bauinschriften römischer Kaiser: Untersuchungen zu Inschriftenpraxis und Bautätigkeit in Städten des westlichen Imperium Romanum in der Zeit des Prinzipats.* Stuttgart.

Horster, M. (2004). *Landbesitz griechischer Heiligtümer in archaischer und klassischer Zeit* (Religionsgeschichtliche Versuche und Vorarbeiten 53). Berlin.

Horster, M. (2006). '(Weibliche) Priesterämter in griechischen Städten— Bemerkungen zum Wandel in der Überlieferung', in L. de Blois, P. Funke, and J. Hahn (eds), *The Impact of Imperial Rome on Religions, Ritual, and Religious Life in the Roman Empire.* Leiden, 194–207.

Horster, M. (2011). 'Cults of Dionysos: Economic Aspects', in R. Schlesier (ed.), *A Different God? Dionysos and Ancient Polytheism.* Berlin, 61–85.

Horster, M. (2013). 'Coinage and Images of the Imperial Family: Local Identity and Roman Rule', *JRA* 26: 243–62.

Horster, M. (2014). 'Urban Infrastructure and Euergetism outside the City of Rome', in C. Bruun and J. Edmondson (eds), *The Oxford Handbook of Roman Epigraphy.* Oxford, 515–36.

Iossif, P. P., Chankoswki, A. S., and Lorber, C. C. (2011) (eds). *More than Men, Less than Gods: Studies on Royal Cult and Imperial Worship.* Leuven.

Jouffroy, H. (1986). *La Construction publique en Italie et dans l'Afrique romaine.* Strasbourg.

Kantiréa, M. (2011). 'Étude comparative de l'introduction du culte impérial à Pergame, à Athènes et à Éphèse', in Iossif, Chankoswki, and Lorber (2011), 521–51.

Kokkina, C. (2012). 'Games vs Buildings as Euergetic Choices', in K. M. Coleman (ed.), *L'organisation des spectacles dans le monde romain: huit exposés suivis de discussions, Vandoeuvres—Genève, 22–26 août 2011*. Geneva, 97–124.

Lafond, Y. (2006). *La mémoire des cités dans le Péloponnèse d'époque romaine (IIe siècle avant J.-C.—IIIe siècle après J.-C.)*. Rennes.

Laum, B. (1914). *Stiftungen in der griechischen und römischen Antike*. Leipzig.

Lefévre, F. (1998). *L'amphictionie pyléo-delphique: histoire et institutions*. Athens.

Le Guen, B. (2010) (ed.). *L'argent dans les concours du monde grec: Actes du colloque international Saint-Denis et Paris, 5–6 décembre 2008*. Saint-Denis.

Levick, B. (1967). *Roman Colonies in Southern Asia Minor*. Oxford.

Lozano, F. (2011). 'The Creation of Imperial Gods: Not only Imposition versus Spontaneity', in Iossif, Chankoswki, and Lorber (2011), 475–519.

Lozano, A. (2015). 'Imperium Romanum and the Religious Centres of Asia Minor. The Intervention of Roman Political Power on the Temples of Asia Minor', in Cortés Copete, Muñiz Grijalvo, and Lozano Gómez (2015), 67–90.

Lozano, F., and Gordillo, R. (2015). 'A Dialogue of Power: Emperor Worship in the Delphic Amphictyony', in Cortés Copete, Muñiz Grijalvo, and Lozano Gómez (2015), 127–45.

Lupu, E. (2005). *Greek Sacred Law: A Collection of New Documents (NGSL)*. Leiden.

Marek, C. (2006). 'Stadt, Bund und Reich in der Zollorganisation des kaiserzeitlichen Lykien: Eine neue Interpretation der Zollinschrift von Kaunos', in U. Wiemer (ed.), *Staatlichkeit und politisches Handeln in der römischen Kaiserzeit*. Berlin, 107–21.

Mathé, V. (2010). 'Coût et financement des stades et des hippodromes', in Le Guen (2010), 189–223.

Melfi, M. (2016). 'The Making of a Colonial Pantheon in the Colonies of Caesar in Greece', in M. Melfi and O. Bobou (eds), *Hellenistic Sanctuaries: Between Greece and Rome*. Oxford, 228–53.

Migeotte, F. (2010). 'Le financement des concours dans les cités hellénistique: essai de typologie', in Le Guen (2010), 127–43.

Millar, F. (1977). *The Emperor in the Roman World (31 BC–AD 337)*. Ithaca, NY.

Mitchell, S. (1993). *Anatolia. Land, Men, and Gods in Asia Minor*, vol. 1: *The Celts in Anatolia and the Impact of Roman Rule*. Oxford.

Moretti, J.-C. (2010). 'Le coût et le financement des théâtres grecs', in Le Guen (2010), 147–87.

Morley, N. (2014). 'Orders of Magnitude, Margins of Error', in F. de Callataÿ (ed.), *Quantifying the Greco-Roman Economy and Beyond*. Bari, 29–42.

Moser, C., and Smith, C. (2019). 'Transformation of Value: Lived Religion and the Economy', *Religion in the Roman Empire* 5/1: 3–22.

Oliver, J. H. (1950). *The Athenian Expounders of the Sacred and Ancestral Law*. Baltimore.

Oliver, J. H. (1952). 'The Eleusinian Endowment', *Hesperia* 21: 381–99.

Oliver, J. H. (1982). 'Roman Senators from Greece and Macedonia', in Panciera (1982), 583–602.

Panciera, S. (1982) (ed.). *Epigrafia e ordine senatorio: Atti del colloquio internazionale AIEGL (Roma, 4-20 maggio 1981)*, vol. II (Tituli 5). Rome.

Papazarkadas, N. (2011). *Sacred and Public Land in Ancient Athens*. Oxford.

Parker, R. (2005). *Polytheism and Society at Athens*. Oxford.

Pirenne-Delforge, V. (2008). *Retour à la source: Pausanias et la religion grecque*. Liège.

Pont, A.-V. (2010). *Orner la cité: enjeux culturels et politiques du paysage urbain dans l'Asie gréco-romaine*. Pessac.

Prignitz, S. (2014). *Bauurkunden und Bauprogramm von Epidauros (400–350): Asklepiostempel, Tholos, Kultbild, Brunnenhaus*. Munich.

Reynolds, J. (1982). *Aphrodisias and Rome: Documents from the Excavation of the Theatre of Aphrodisias Conducted by Kenan T. Erim, Together with Some Related Texts*. London.

Rizakis, A. (1997). 'Roman Colonies in the Province of Achaia: Territories, Land and Population', in S. E. Alcock (ed.), *The Early Roman Empire in the East*. Oxford, 15–36.

Rizakis, A. (2007). 'Urban Elites in the Roman East: Enhancing Regional Positions and Social Superiority', in J. Rüpke (ed.), *A Companion to Roman Religion*. Oxford, 317–30.

Rogers, G. M. (1991). *The Sacred Identity of Ephesos: Foundation Myths of a Roman City*. London.

Roueché, Ch. (1993). *Performers and Partisans in Aphrodisias in the Roman and Late Roman Periods: A Study Based on Inscriptions from the Current Excavations in Caria*. London.

Sánchez, P. (2001). *L'Amphictionie des Pyles et de Delphes: Recherches sur son rôle historique, des origins au IIe siècle de notre ère*. Stuttgart.

Schmalz, G. C. R. (2007–8). 'Inscribing a Ritualized Past: The Attic Restoration Decree *IG* II^2 1035 and Cultural Memory in Augustan Athens', *Eulimene* 8/9: 9–46.

Schmalz, G. C. R. (2009). *Augustan and Julio-Claudian Athens: A New Epigraphy and Prosopography*. Leiden.

Schowalter, D. N. (2011). 'Honoring Trajan in Pergamum: Imperial Temples in the "Second City"', in Brodd and Reed (2011), 99–110.

Sherk, R. K. (1969). *Roman Documents of the Greek East: Senatus Consulta to the Age of Augustus*. Baltimore.

Slater, W. (2010). 'Paying the Pipers', in Le Guen (2010), 249–81.

Spawforth, A. J. S. (1989). 'Agonistic Festivals in Roman Greece', *BICS* 36: 193–7.

Spawforth, A. J. S. (1997). 'The Early Reception of the Imperial Cult in Athens: Problems and Ambiguities', in M. C. Hoff and S. I. Rotroff (eds), *The Romanization of Athens*. Oxford, 183–201.

Spawforth, A. J. S. (2012). *Greece and the Augustan Cultural Revolution*. Cambridge.

Steuernagel, D. (2010). '*Synnaos Theos*: Images of Roman Emperors in Greek Temples', in J. Mylonopoulos (ed.), *Divine Images and Human Imaginations in Ancient Greece and Rome*. Leiden, 241–55.

van Bremen, R. (1996). *The Limits of Participation: Women and Civic Life in the Greek East in the Hellenistic and Roman Periods*. Amsterdam.

van Nijf, O. (2001). 'Local Heroes: Athletics, Festivals and Elite Self-Fashioning in the Roman East', in S. Goldhill (ed.), *Being Greek under Rome: Cultural Identity, the Second Sophistic and the Development of the Empire*. Cambridge, 306–34.

Veyne, P. (1999). 'L'identité grecque devant Rome et l'empereur', *REG* 112: 510–67.

Williamson, C. G. (2021). *Urban Rituals in Sacred Landscapes in Hellenistic Asia Minor*. Leiden.

Wörrle, M. (1995). 'Neue Inschriftenfunde aus Aizanoi II: Das Problem der Ära von Aizanoi', *Chiron* 25: 63–81.

7

Impact of the Roman Conquest on Temple Economies in Egypt

A Case Study of the Temple of Soknopaios in Dime

Marie-Pierre Chaufray

Introduction

The impact of Rome on temples in Egypt is the subject of an unpublished dissertation of Penelope Glare at the University of Cambridge in 1993.[1] Studying both 'traditional or Egyptian temples' and 'non-traditional temples',[2] Glare came to the conclusion that the approach based on an antagonism between temple and state, which had prevailed in previous works and which had often led to seeing the Romans as responsible for the decline of traditional temples, had to be abandoned.[3] For Glare, changes in temples were 'part of the general changes brought to Egypt by Roman rule'.[4] The question of the decline of temples and, with it, of 'paganism' was much debated in the 1980s and the 1990s,[5] but recent work on priests and temples in Roman Egypt has highlighted the dynamism and the economic prosperity of temples under Roman rule, at least until the first half of the third century AD.[6] In his study of the transition of institutions in Egypt from the Ptolemies to the Romans, Andrew

---

[1] I thank Penelope Glare, who kindly sent me her dissertation, and D. J. Thompson for putting us in contact.
[2] Glare defines traditional temples as temples where a daily cult is practised by priests who belong to a priestly family, who are purified, and who held their office for life. 'Non-traditional temples' are temples where other forms of organization prevail; cf. Glare (1993: 10–11).
[3] Otto (1905–8); Rostovtzeff (1909); Wilcken (1912); Wallace (1938); Evans (1961); Huss (1994).
[4] Glare (1993: 179). [5] See Medini (2015) for a recent clarification on the question.
[6] Clarysse (2010: 289); Capponi (2011: 508); Klotz (2012: 1–5); Medini (2015: 274); Winkler (2015). Since the submission of this chapter, C. Messerer has collected, in three volumes, a corpus of Greek papyri on the administrative relations between the Egyptian clergy and the Roman authorities. Many of the Greek texts cited below can now be consulted in French translation in these volumes with very useful commentaries: cf. Messerer (2017, 2019, 2020). On the clergy of Dime, see also Sippel (2020), whose results I have not been able to incorporate here.

Marie-Pierre Chaufray, *Impact of the Roman Conquest on Temple Economies in Egypt: A Case Study of the Temple of Soknopaios in Dime* In: *The Economy of Roman Religion*. Edited by: Andrew Wilson, Nick Ray, and Angela Trentacoste, Oxford University Press. © Oxford University Press 2023. DOI: 10.1093/oso/9780192883537.003.0007

Monson also stresses the continuity of priestly privileges, organization, and temple construction, but he sees a diminution in 'the temples' historic role as redistributive organizations with state-like characteristics', so that 'an overall economic decline of Egyptian temples in the Roman period is unmistakable'.[7]

A general study of the impact of the Roman conquest on temple economies in Egypt is complicated, given the nature and the disparity of the sources. Information on imperial and civic cults is sporadic and rarely allows us to measure any economic activity.[8] As regards traditional temples, if archaeological and epigraphic evidence shows that large temples of Upper Egypt were still clearly active,[9] papyrological sources that give a precise insight into temple administration and economic activities come mostly from village temples in the Fayyum. It is, therefore, difficult to make any generalization and to get a complete view of the changes brought by the Roman conquest.

In this respect, the temple of Soknopaios in the village of Dime in the Fayyum is interesting for several reasons. First, it is well documented through petitions, accounts, receipts, and fiscal declarations concerning the temple as a legal entity, written either by the elders or by the scribe of the priests, which make it possible to study the economy of a temple as a corporate body, and not just the economic activities of one or two priests. Second, the language of the documents, Greek and demotic, offers a complementary look at the economic activities of the temple: the Greek 'official' side, which shows the relations between the temple and the central administration, and the Egyptian side, which gives an internal viewpoint.[10] Finally, the Roman documentation can be compared to the Ptolemaic archives from the second century BC, so that continuity and changes can be studied. After a quick overview of the Roman reforms, their impact on the temple of Soknopaios in Dime will be studied on three levels: priestly organization, temple estate, and temple income in money.

The Roman Reforms of Egyptian Temples

Several reforms are known through papyri dating from the reigns of Augustus and Nero.[11] A first reform is the confiscation of temple land under the prefect Petronius between 24 and 21 BC.[12] It is mentioned in the petition of AD 71/2 by the priests of Soknebtunis from the village of Tebtunis in the Fayyum. The priests report that, under Petronius, part of their temple land was transformed

---

[7] Monson (2012: 227).   [8] On the imperial cult, see Pfeiffer (2012).
[9] cf. Hölbl (2000–5); Klotz (2012).   [10] cf. Lippert (2010).
[11] cf. Capponi (2011: 511–12); Monson (2012: 218–27); Medini (2015: 248–53).
[12] cf. Monson (2012: 136–7); Capponi (2011: 511–12). On this prefect, see Bagnall (1985).

into royal (public) land, and that they were given the choice either to keep the administration of it and to pay rent to the state, or to receive a public subvention, the *syntaxis*, which could be provided in money or in kind.[13] The priests of Tebtunis kept the administration of the land and they complain in AD 71/2 about an increase of the rent ordered by the village scribe. The priests of Busiris in the Herakleopolite nome, on the other hand, chose the *syntaxis*, and, in 2/1 BC, they complain because it is not given to them.[14] As Monson explains, the confiscation of temple land 'was only aimed at the land that priesthoods directly cultivated or gave out on non-vendible leaseholds'.[15] The Romans did not touch temple land that was privately owned by priests and that benefited from the privileged tax rate applied on private property.

A second reform, in 4 BC, is the control of the priestly status, by an edict of the prefect Turranius who ordered that all priestly functions in temples should be registered.[16] This measure was probably taken to distinguish, within the temples, people with a priestly status (*hiereis*) from other temple personnel (for example, *pastophoroi*), as only true priestly status included privileges, such as exemption from the poll tax.[17] Later, under Nero, the prefect Tuscus seems to have ordered a registration of temple properties, and the document that was then written became afterwards a reference for the fiscal administration.[18]

The dates of other reforms are not precisely known or are controversial. One of them could be concerned with notarial practices: notary families attached to temples disappeared in the first century AD, and contracts were written and registered in the village offices (*grapheia*).[19] Another reform is the creation of the post of 'high priest of the gods Augusti and of the great Sarapis and in charge of the temples and altars and the sacred groves that are in Alexandria and in all Egypt', a title that was abbreviated into 'high priest of Alexandria and all Egypt'.[20] In the second century AD this Roman procurator in Alexandria gave authorization for the circumcision of the sons of priests assuming their office. His role is not well documented, but his title suggests an overall control of all the temples of Egypt, which is a major change from

---

[13] *P.Tebt.* II 302; cf. Monson (2012: 136–7).   [14] *BGU* IV 1200 (TM 18650).
[15] Monson (2012: 219).   [16] *BGU* IV 1199; cf. Capponi (2005: 78); Monson (2012: 219–20).
[17] The edict seems to have been issued after some priests from the Herakleopolite nome had complained to the prefect, in 5/4 BC, that they were asked by the royal scribe to pay the poll tax (*laographia*), which they had never paid before (*BGU* IV 1198, TM 18648).
[18] Whitehorne (1978, 1979); Monson (2012: 221).
[19] In parallel, Egyptian (demotic) contracts are less numerous, and disappear in the second century: Monson (2012: 126).
[20] Capponi (2011: 516); Pfeiffer (2012: 92–4).

the Ptolemaic period.[21] However, it is debated whether the post was created under Augustus, Tiberius, or Hadrian,[22] whether it was linked to the imperial cult,[23] and whether, in the second century, the office was merged with the direction of the *Idios Logos* because of the role of this department in cases involving the priesthood.[24] The *Idios Logos*, the 'private account' or 'special account', was an institution inherited from the Ptolemaic period, initially concerned with goods and properties confiscated by the state or without owner (*adespota*). Under the Romans, it was also involved in priestly conflicts concerning ownership of temple offices.[25]

A code of regulations, called the *Gnomon of the Idios Logos*, known through a papyrus dated after AD 149, contained twenty-seven paragraphs dealing with priests.[26] According to the introduction of the *Gnomon*, the compilation started with Augustus and was completed by his successors. However, some rules were already applied before the Roman period, such as the prohibition on wearing woollen clothes or long hair (§71) and the income of the prophet, who is entitled to one-fifth of the temple revenues (§79). A few elements could have been innovations, such as the prohibition on selling the office of prophet at public auction (§78). One such sale is attested between AD 126 and 147, just before the date of the *Gnomon*.[27] This rule may, therefore, be new. Most measures of the *Gnomon* concerning priests deal with the transmission of priestly offices and rules on cultic practices, with one paragraph concerning Greek sanctuaries (§86), and hierarchical rules between people working in the temples. In general, the Romans respected the religious rules that had been in use for ages, and the *Idios Logos* was mostly concerned with state revenues linked to the acquisitions of priestly offices and fines for ritual infractions.[28]

Under the Romans, temple construction and decoration went on as before, in addition to the construction of new temples for the imperial cult; specific emphasis was given to the region of the Dodekaschoinos on the southern

---

[21] Some scholars believe that the Roman high priest (Gr. *archiereus*) replaced the Ptolemaic High Priest of Ptah (Egypt. *wr-ḥrp-ḥmw*, 'great craftsman'), who, for them, controlled all priests and temples of Egypt: Capponi (2011: 514–15); Gorre and Honigman (2014: 313); for objections, cf. Monson (2016: 30–1).

[22] Wilcken (1912: 127) thinks the office was introduced by Augustus; for Capponi (2011: 516–17, 523), P.Oxy. XII 1434, l. 10 (TM 21838), is the first attestation of this *archiereus* in 7–3 BC. Rigsby (1985) believes the post was created under Tiberius, because of an inscription from Ephesos, which is lacunose. Parassoglou (1974) and Stead (1981) take *SB* XII 11236 (TM 41437), an edict of T. Haterius Nepos, which mentions the nomination of a high priest under Hadrian (AD 117–38), as the date of the creation of the function.

[23] Pfeiffer (2012: 94).

[24] cf. Swarney (1970: 96): the head of the *Idios Logos* is never called *archiereus* under the Flavians and the Antonines; Kruse (2002: 710–11, n. 2013); the two offices were not merged.

[25] Swarney (1970).   [26] *BGU* V 1210 (TM 9472).   [27] P.Tebt. II 295 (TM 13458).

[28] Swarney (1970: 96).

border of Egypt in the reign of Augustus.[29] Only after the second half of the second century did temple-building and decoration diminish. Thus, the Roman conquest did not put an end to temple activities, but Roman reforms brought changes that I want to illustrate through the example of the temple of Soknopaios in the village of Dime in the Fayyum.

The Temple of Soknopaios at Dime

Dime (Egy. *T3-m3y-Sbk-nb-pay*, Gr. Soknopaiou Nesos) is located in the north of the Fayyum, separated from other villages by Lake Moeris. The village was a customs post on the desert routes to Alexandria in the north and to the oasis of Bahariya.[30] Village life was dominated by the activity of its main temple dedicated to the local form of the crocodile god Sobek, called Soknopaios, and to his consort, Isis Nepherses.[31] The temple existed probably before the Hellenistic period, but the village seems to have developed in the third century BC, when Ptolemy II started irrigation works in the Fayyum in order to reclaim land. Under the Romans, the temple of Soknopaios was a temple of the first rank (*logimos*), but, in the third century AD, the village seems to have been abandoned, for unknown reasons. Traces of a later occupation have, however, been observed.[32]

The administrative and economic activities of the temple of Soknopaios are among the best documented for the Roman period. A large number of papyri in Greek and in Egyptian, discovered in illegal excavations at the end of the nineteenth century, are now in Berlin, Vienna, London, or Paris. For the Ptolemaic period (second century BC), the archive of the temple or of a scribe of the priests is preserved. Oracle questions, letters, contracts, receipts, and accounts are written in demotic, and a few Greek texts show the contacts between the temple and the royal administration.[33] It is still difficult to gather all the texts concerning the temple in the Roman period, since many were found in illegal excavations and sold to different European collections. Roman-period rolls containing copies of receipts as well as the so-called

---

[29] Clarysse (2010: 276); Pfeiffer (2012: 86–91); Török (2012: 756–7).
[30] Traces of this activity are known through a large number of toll tax receipts from the second half of the first century AD to the third century (*P.Customs Duties*) and from contracts on camels, which carried the goods. See Ruffing (2007).
[31] Davoli (2014). [32] Dixneuf (2012: 324–5).
[33] Bresciani (1975); Chaufray (2016). The letters are currently being republished by C. Arlt in M. A. Stadler's project: 'Dime im Fayum—ein Tempel im Spannungsfeld von Tradition und Multikulturalität im hellenistisch-römischen Ägypten' (Univ. Würzburg).

ḥn.w-agreements and more than 800 accounts written in demotic certainly belonged to the temple archives.[34] Greek texts could also be part of the temple archive, as they mention the priests as a group: legal documents, petitions, oaths, tax receipts, and declarations.[35] The Roman documentation runs from 25 BC to AD 223.

Impact of Roman Reforms on Priests and Priestly Organization

Between 7 and 4 BC the priests of Dime complained to the prefect Turranius about the excessive taxation on the temple and its religious ceremonies.[36] Around the same time, priests of the goddess Isis in the temple of Busiris in the Herakleopolite nome complained because they were asked to pay the *laographia* (capitation tax) for the last four years, though they had never paid capitation before.[37] Monson recently argued that the exemption that the priests were claiming in the petition was based on their previous exemption from a late Ptolemaic poll tax, called the 'stater tax' in the Herakleopolite.[38] Thus, the introduction of the new Augustan capitation (the date of which is not entirely sure), and maybe changes in taxation, had an impact on priests, who tried to stick to their privileges. Some priests still benefited from tax exemptions under the Romans: in second-century Dime, one hundred priests were exempted from the *laographia*, more than in Tebtunis in the southern Fayyum.[39] The non-exempted priests had to pay the full rate of the *laographia* (40 drachmae in the Fayyum).[40]

---

[34] *O.Dime* 1; *P.Dime* 2; Lippert and Schentuleit (2005a: 75); on *ḥn.w*-agreements, one-year agreements between the priests of Dime and individuals for specific functions in the temple, cf. Lippert (2007).

[35] Here is a non-exhaustive list of documents that concern the clergy as a corporate body, and that consequently may belong to the temple archive: 1. Authorizations for circumcision: *SB* VI 9027, *Stud. Pal.* XXII 51, *BGU* XIII 2216, *P.Rain.Cent.* 58, *SB* XXVI 16726; 2. Contracts: *SB* I 5252, *P.Lond.* II 335, pp. 191–2, *P.Lond.* II 216 (TM 11652), *BGU* XI 2033 (TM 9570), *BGU* III 916 (TM 9414), *Chr.Wilck.* 315 (TM 11670); 3. Fiscal declarations (see n. 66); 4. Declarations and petitions: *CPR* VII 1 (TM 9877), *BGU* II 433 (TM 9167), *P.Vindob.Tand.* 21 (TM 24927), *P.Lond.* II 281, pp. 65–6 (TM 11666), *Stud.Pal.* XXII 99 (TM 15145), *PSI* VIII 927 (TM 13819), *P.Amst.* I 35 (TM 10119), *SB* XVI 12685 (TM 14647); 5. Letters: *P.Vind.Worp* 12; 6. Receipts: *P.Ryl.* II 192 (TM 12966), *P.Gen.* I² 36 (TM 11230), *Stud.Pal.* XXII 171 (TM 15086), *SB* XXII 15343 (TM 15066), *P.Lond.* II 347, pp. 70–1 (TM 19988), *SB* XVI 12797 (TM 14673), *SB* VI 8980 (TM 14060); 7. Oath: *BGU* I 16 (TM 8927).

[36] *CPR* VII 1 (TM 9877).   [37] *BGU* IV 1198 (TM 18648).   [38] Monson (2014a).

[39] See Hobson (1984a). For Dime, see *SB* XVI 12816 (TM 14676), l. 45 (AD 179), a fiscal register where exempted priests are listed as οἱ ἐν παραδοχῇ ἀναφερόμενοι ἄνδρες ρ: '100 men returned as being in abatement', trans. Hobson (1984b: 860). For Tebtunis, there were forty exempted priests (*BGU* XIII 2215 col. II, ll.12–14: AD 112), or 50 (*P.Tebt.* II 298: AD 107/8; *PSI* X 1146: AD 117/18).

[40] In the fiscal register *SB* XVI 12816 (TM 14676), sixty-nine priests appear to be supernumerary and they pay 40 dr., which makes 2,760 dr. Later, in AD 201, a receipt indicates οἱ λοι(ποὶ) ἱερεῖς

Some documents give an idea of the number of priests in the village. Demotic lists of priests, not precisely dated, give a headcount of more than 130 priests.[41] A tax register of AD 179 and, six years later, a petition, count 169 and 160 priests respectively.[42] In a receipt of AD 201, the priests of Dime pay for the *laographia* of the non-exempted priests, which could mean, if the *numerus clausus* did not change, that there still were more than a hundred priests in Dime.[43] The priestly community was, therefore, large. An edict of AD 54 shows that the priests were also exempted from the *corvée* of cultivation of public land (*georgia*).[44] One priest, in the early second century AD, complained that he was appointed for the liturgy of the distribution of state seed to public farmers (*sitologia*), though he should be exempted.[45]

These exemptions, which probably changed over time and which were probably not identical in all temples, were balanced by other kinds of taxation. Under Roman rule, as in the Ptolemaic period, priests had to pay an entrance fee: in the Dime documents of the second century AD, the fee was either 12 or 20 dr., the difference probably being connected with the transmission of the office (by inheritance or purchase).[46] Another tax was the *epistatikon*, which was, in Dime, paid in a lump sum of 5,500 dr.[47] The nature of this tax is not precisely known.[48] Taxes are also found in the demotic documents, the nature of which is also not clear. Twelve receipts from the first to the second century AD mention a tax called the 'royal *wty*(?)' (*wty-pr-ꜥ3*) often combined with other taxes, such as the 'gain/profit' (*ḥw3*), the 'oracle' (*nkt šn*), or the 'altar' (*ḥwy.t*). These taxes were paid by priests who held the position of *lesonis* and by weavers.[49] Weaving was an important activity in temples, either for linen or for wool, and the weavers formed a corporation, working closely with the temple of Dime.[50] The role of the Roman-period *lesoneis* is less clear.

λαογρ(αφίας) τῶν ὑπεραιρούντων τὸν ἀριθμὸ(ν) τῶν ἱερέων: 'the rest of the priests for the *laographia* of the priests exceeding the number' (*P.Lond.* II 347, p. 70, TM 19988).

[41] See *O.Dime* I, p. 22.   [42] cf. Clarysse (2005: 22).   [43] *P.Lond.* II 347, p. 70 (TM 19988).
[44] *I.Prose* 54 (TM 47190).   [45] *SB* 16 12833 (TM 14677).
[46] *P.Münch* III 137: AD 146; *Stud.Pal.* XXII 171: AD 158; *P.Lond.* II 329, p. 113: AD 164; *SB* XXIV 15918 (after AD 180); *SB* XXII 15343: AD 201; *SB* VI 8980: AD 205.
[47] *P.Louvre* I 4, l. 2 (before AD 166); *Stud.Pal.* XXII 183 (after AD 138); *P.Lond.* II 347, pp. 70–1 (AD 201). In Roman Bacchias the temple also paid for the priests collectively: *P.Lund.* IV 7 (TM 28119: AD 116–99); cf. *P.Cair.Mich.* pp. 35–6, and Kruse (2002: 705–8).
[48] cf. Wallace (1938: 252–3). For Monson, it is simply a continuation of the Ptolemaic *epistatikon* of temples, cf. Monson (2014b: 217–18).
[49] *P.Dime* II 1–12. The weavers are the taxpayers of *P.Dime* II 1–3.
[50] Arrears of delivery of linen were frequent in the Ptolemaic period, as can be seen with the remissions of debts included in royal edicts: *OGIS* I 90, l. 17–18. *P.Tebt.* I 5, ll. 62–5. Despite the prohibition on weaving activities in sacred spaces, and the prohibition on priests wearing wool, the temple was concerned with wool production and weavers. One unpublished *hn.w*-agreement mentions woolsellers (*P.Vienna* D 6032+6868+6871+6872+6886+6887). I thank Sandra Lippert for this reference.

In the Ptolemaic period, the *lesonis* was the one-year economic director of a temple, chosen by the priests, and he guaranteed the temple's financial obligations with his own property.[51] In Dime, the *lesonis* was always 'lesonis of Soknopaios and Isis Nepherses'.[52] Under the Romans, several colleges of *lesoneis* appear: for the two main deities of the temple, but also as administrators of small chapels in the surroundings.[53]

While the precise nature of the three taxes in the demotic receipts is unclear, the collectors of the taxes were the two public tax collectors of the priests (*shn pr-ꜥ3 n3 wꜥb.w*). These tax collectors were chosen among the priests for one year to collect those taxes and bring the money to the public bank in the metropolis, give the receipt to the *tlns* (*telones*, 'tax farmer'), and bring back to the temple the 'surplus'. The two priests were liable with their own belongings for the money that was due to the state, and they needed guarantors.[54] This office, which looks like a kind of liturgy in the temple, could have been a creation after the fiscal reforms of Augustus: the first tax collectors of the priests are attested in AD 12. In the Ptolemaic period, the *lesonis* of the temple had to pay for any tax in arrears or debts, and he acted as the representative of the temple. Under the Romans, however, the temple representatives were the leaders and/or the elders (*hegoumenoi* and *presbyteroi*).[55] The colleges of *lesoneis* were probably also a consequence of a restructuring of the priesthood under the Romans.[56]

---

[51] Monson (2012: 223).   [52] *P.Oxf.Griffith* 14, l. 4; 20, ll. 3–4; 38, ll. 2–3; 44, l. 3; 72, l. 1.

[53] *Lesoneis* of Soknopaios: *P.Vienna* D 6823 (TM 47524, AD 4), *P.Dime* II 18 (TM 47101, AD 33), *P.Dime* II 6 (TM 100229, AD 91/92), *P.Dime* II 21 (TM 100239, AD 106–8), *P.Dime* II 8 (TM 100230, AD 107/8); *lesoneis* of Isis Nepherses: *P.Dime* II 19 (TM 46298, AD 33), *P.Dime* II 7 (TM 47100, AD 99/100); *lesoneis* of Isis Nephremmis: *P.Dime* II 54 (TM 45586, AD 9/10), *P.Dime* II 5 (TM 100228, AD 87/8); *lesoneis* of *Ph-n-Is.t(?)* of *P.Dime* II 9 (TM 100231, AD 130/1). See Monson (2012: 224–5).

[54] *P.Vienna* D 6871+6872 r° (TM 112502): AD 158/9, edition is being prepared by S. Lippert and M. Schentuleit; cf. S. Lippert (2007: 150).

[55] Monson (2012: 225–6). The two titles are distinct, and so are the functions, but this still needs to be investigated. *Hegoumenoi* of the priests acting as temple representatives are attested in: *CPR* VII 1, l. 2 (TM 9877, 7–4 BC), *CPR* XV 8, ll. 21–3 (TM 9920, AD 13–15); *CPR* XV 10a, ll. 10–11 (TM 11737, AD 14); *BGU* XIII 2239, ll. 1–2 (TM 9650, AD 17); *P.Lond.* II 281, pp. 65–6, ll. 1–3 (TM 11666, AD 66/7); *P.Vind.Bosw.* 1, l. 15 (TM 13673, after AD 87); *P.Lond.* II 286, pp. 183–4, ll. 1–3 (TM 11670, AD 88/9); *P.Vind.Worp* 12 (TM 25101, first century AD); *P.Lond.* II 335, pp. 191–2 (TM 11715, 166/7 or 198/9); *CPR* XV 52, l. 17 (TM 31124, beginning of third century). *Presbyteroi* are attested in: *CPR* XXIII 1, ll. 2–10 (TM 47155, AD 14–19); *SB* I 5240, l. 4 (TM 13987, AD 17); *SB* XVI 12685, ll. 3–9 (TM 14647, AD 139); *Chr.Wilck.* 77, col. 2, ll. 13–14 (TM 15155, AD 149); *Stud. Pal.* XXII 51, ll. 4–9 (TM 15121, AD 153); *P.Rain.Cent.* 58, l. 14–22 (TM 12868, AD 156); *SB* XII 10883, ll. 3–14 (TM 14345, AD 158); *BGU* I 16, ll. 3–7 (TM 8927, AD 159/60); *BGU* II 387, ll. 1–9 (TM 9144, AD 177–80); *BGU* II 433, l. 3–11 (TM 9167, AD 190); *BGU* II 392+639, col. 2, ll. 6–7 (TM 9146, AD 208). Colleges of five priests, probably *presbyteroi*, appear in *SB* XVI 12785, ll. 3–15 (TM 47181, AD 220); *P.Lond.* II 353, pp. 112–13, ll. 2–10 (TM 11734, AD 221).

[56] First mention of a college of *lesoneis* in Dime in AD 4: *P.Vienna* D 6823 (TM 47524).

Impact of Roman Reforms on Temple Revenues in Kind

It is unclear whether the confiscation of temple land under Petronius affected the temple of Dime. The temple estate of Soknopaios is not well known. Arable land in the village was minimal because of its location in the desert on the northern side of the lake.[57] However, the temple had land in other villages.

Several Ptolemaic documents mention temple land in Dionysias, where the priests could collect 225 *artabai* of wheat.[58] In the Ptolemaic period, the priests managed the land directly: they chose their farmers and collected the rents.[59] No Roman documents, neither in Greek nor in demotic, mention land in Dionysias, but, in AD 142, the priests of Soknopaios paid a tax on *katoikic* land in the village of Herakleia. The location of the village is not known, but several priests of Dime had land there.[60] *Katoikic* land was similar to private land in this period and benefited from a low rate of taxation.[61] According to the amount of the tax, the priests had around 68 arouras in this village (which means a production of at least 680 *artabai* of wheat).[62]

The temple certainly received wheat from land in other villages, but we do not know if land revenues came from a public subvention (*syntaxis*), the direct administration of the temple, or from private temple land. The only mention of *syntaxis* in a demotic receipt refers to money, and not to wheat.[63] In 7–4 BC, the priests of Busiris in the Herakleopolite nome complained that they did not receive their *syntaxis*, stating that, of the 200 *artabai* that they should receive, 100 came from confiscated temple land, and 100 from the estate of Asklepiades, a rich shipowner.[64]

The fiscal declarations of the Dime temple give further information on the revenues of the temple estate.[65] Such declarations were written annually by the priests and sent to the nome officials after the reform of the prefect Tuscus under Nero; they have been preserved for several temples in the Fayyum. For the temple of Dime, nine lists have been preserved with four accompanying

---

[57] Only a small parcel of shore land could be cultivated; cf. Hobson (1984a).
[58] *P.Amh.* II 35 (TM 8621). The village is also mentioned in the demotic documents, as has been identified by S. Lippert: *P.Oxf.Griffith* 54 (TM 45614, 147/146 BC), 46 (TM 45606, 139/137 BC), 60 (TM 45620, 133 BC), 25 (TM 46795, 133 BC), cf. Lippert (2015: 161–2).
[59] *P.Oxf.Griffith* 46 (TM 45606).
[60] Hobson (1984a: 101): *BGU* II 536 (TM 9222, AD 84); *BGU* II 446 (TM 9177, AD 158/9); *P.IFAO* I 33 (TM 11501, AD 163–4); *P.Prag.* I 23 (TM 12764, AD 195).
[61] Monson (2012: 94–5).
[62] Hobson (1984a: 98): *P.Ryl.* II 192 (AD 142); *P.Lond.* II 216 (AD 94).
[63] *P.Dime* II 69: AD 138–61 or 169–77.   [64] *BGU* IV 1197 (TM 18647).
[65] These declarations are called in Greek γραφὴ ἱερέων καὶ χειρισμοῦ τοῦ ἱεροῦ, 'list of priests and property of the temple'; cf. Burkhalter (1985); Kruse (2002: 711–16).

letters, dated between AD 138 and 221.[66] No document is complete, but, as the texts were copied almost unchanged over time, the data of several texts can be combined in order to gain an idea of the structure. In Dime, the declarations began with the inventory of temple furniture (including the furniture of small chapels and altars), followed by the income in money and then the income in kind with quantities of wheat, oil, and wine.

The most complete document has preserved only the final portion of the text on the income in kind, concerning the delivery of wheat.[67] Part of this delivery came from the village of Nèsos Gynaikôn, which cannot be located. The total of wheat received annually by the temple amounted to 1,149 *artabai*. After the revenues, the fiscal declarations record the temple expenditures, in money and in kind (wheat, oil, and wine). The expenditure in kind amounts to exactly the same as the revenues. Declarations from other years where these entries are preserved show the same amounts,[68] which has been interpreted negatively based on the edict of the prefect Tuscus: the temple could not increase its wealth.[69] However, it might also be seen in a positive light: the temple got exactly what it needed. The demotic receipts indeed show that the priests did receive the wheat needed for the daily cult, one *artaba* per day.[70]

According to the Greek fiscal declarations, the temple received and spent 21 *metretai* of oil. Just as with the wheat, no precision is given on the provenance of this oil. However, one unpublished demotic *hn.w*-agreement describes the key role of the *lesonis* of the god Harpsenesis in oil distribution.[71] The *lesonis* kept the official oil measure and received a fee in kind from the oil-sellers and temple's oil mills. He had to supply a daily ration of oil for the lighting of the temple of Soknopaios. The administration of oil was thus delegated by the temple to the *lesonis* of Harpsenesis. The temple of Harpsenesis in Dime is attested in demotic documents, but it has not been identified on the ground.[72] This agreement indicates that the temple had oil

---

[66] 1. *Stud.Pal.* XXII 183 (TM 15096, after AD 138); 2. *P.David* 1 (TM 10688, after AD 138); 3. *SB* XII 10883 (TM 14345, AD 158 = accompanying letter); 4. *BGU* XIII 2217 (TM 9628, AD 161); 5. *P.Louvre* I 4+ (TM 11853, before AD 166); 6. *SB* VI 9199 (TM 27280, between AD 125 and 177); 7. *BGU* II 387 (TM 9144, between AD 177 and 180); 8. *SB* XXIV 15918 (TM 9247, after AD 180); 9. *SB* XXVI 16725 (TM 44615, AD 185); 10. *CPR* XV 22 (TM 9906, AD 206 = accompanying letter); 11. *SB* XVI 12785 (TM 47181, AD 220 = accompanying letter); 12. *P.Lond.* II 353 (TM 11734, AD 221 = accompanying letter); 13–14. *BGU* I 149 (TM 28225), XIII 2218 (TM 29217).
[67] *Stud.Pal.* XXII 183 (TM 15096): after AD 138; cf. Capron (2008).
[68] *Stud.Pal.* XXII 183 (TM 15096), l. 100; *P.Louvre* I 4 + *P.Louvre* inv. AF 13314 (TM 11853), col. III l. 84: before AD 166; *SB* VI 9199 (TM 27280): between AD 125 and 177: the total is not preserved but the details of expenditure are identical.
[69] Whitehorne (1978). [70] *P.Dime* II 43–50: 25/24 BC to AD 81–117.
[71] *P.Vienna* D 4854+ (TM 112501), unpublished. On *hn.w*-agreements, cf. n. 34.
[72] Lippert (2015: 164–5).

mills that were not located in Dime. According to a Greek contract, the priests of Soknopaios did indeed have an oil press in Pisaïs (*to mulaion tou theou*).[73] Pisaïs was a hamlet (*epoikion*), on the other side of the lake, which may have been part of the temple estate, since there are several connections between this place and the priests of Dime.[74] In the Greek contract, the priests leased the mill for 120 dr. and other payments in kind (probably including oil). For five years the rent had to be used for the repair of the mill, which means that the repair's cost was 600 dr.[75] The *mulaion* is also mentioned in two demotic discharge receipts for the scribe of the priests at the end of the first century AD as the 'place to make oil in Pisaïs'.[76] With these receipts the priests acknowledged to the scribe of the priests that he had done his job properly. In one receipt from AD 89/90 the priests declare: 'You have paid us; you have satisfied our heart with the silver, the bronze [...], and the rent of the "place to make oil" in Pisaïs'.[77] The amount of the rent is not given.

The temple's 'place to make oil' in Pisaïs also appears in an unpublished account kept in Berlin.[78] The writing suggests that this account was written at the end of the first century AD. It registers portions of rents, or rents in arrears, on different temple goods in several places.[79] The amount of the rent of the mill in Pisaïs is not preserved, but it was a rent in money.[80] Though the documents help us to understand how the temple managed oil production and consumption, we still lack information on the other temple oil mills. It is possible that some illegal oil-trading happened in Dime, since we have a petition of one priest against his colleagues, which mentions some forbidden actions concerning the sale of oil.[81] The priests are accused of using leather bags to sell oil, which was prohibited,[82] though no reason for this proscription is given: was it out of religious considerations or because the leather bags had no standard size? The petition does not offer further details, and the rest of the text concerns excessive tax collection by the temple from villagers.[83]

---

[73] *P.Lond.* II 335, p. 191, l. 14 (TM 11715): AD 166-7 (or 198-9). [74] Hobson (1984a: 98-9).
[75] The unpublished demotic account *P.Berl.* P. 8043+, probably written in the early second century AD, which registers the daily expenses of the temple, mentions costs for a *mechane* (oil press) in Pisaïs (col. 12, l. 12), and expenses for Pisaïs are frequent in the register. On this papyrus, cf. Chaufray (2016).
[76] *P.Dime* II 66 (TM 100274, AD 89/90); *P.Dime* II 67 (TM 100275, AD 90).
[77] *P.Dime* II 67, l. 6.   [78] *P.Berl.* P. 17678.
[79] Perhaps it is for a festival, since Greek contracts connected to the temple and Ptolemaic lease offers contain deliveries for festivals, but, in general, these deliveries are in nature, not in money; cf. Cuvigny (1986: 122).
[80] *P.Berl.* P. 17678, col. 2, l. 6.   [81] *SB* VI 9066 (TM 14091): AD 138-61.
[82] ll. 11-12: αὐ[τοὺς χρῆσ]θαι καὶ ἀσκοῖς δερματίνοι[ς]· εἰς οὓς ἔλαιον βάλλοντα[ς ἐ]μπορεύεσθαι δι' ὧν ἔχουσι καμψῶν οὐκ ἐξόν: 'They use also hide bags, in which they put oil, in order to trade, although they are not allowed to have such flasks.'
[83] On this, cf. Lanciers (2015: 381-2).

Though it is hard to measure the impact of the Roman reforms on temple property, we can see that the temple still had what it needed in wheat and in oil.

Impact of the Roman Reforms on the Temple Income in Money

As regards revenues and expenditures in money, the fiscal declarations show how the temple worked as a tax collector of licence taxes for the state.[84] One declaration, where the beginning of the revenues in money is preserved, lists payments to the temple from different guilds: from laundry workers in Dime (16 dr.) and laundry workers in Nilopolis, a village that had close connections with Dime (240 dr.), from vegetable-sellers, embalmers, the weighing toll, and from rents on at least four fishing boats, connected to different places. The rent on these boats altogether is at least 920 dr. Then the text breaks off. In the list of expenditures, preserved in another declaration, taxes for laundry workers, vegetable-sellers, embalmers, and the weighing toll are exactly the same as the income that the temple collects.[85]

For laundry, the amounts given in the declarations are confirmed in other documents. A Greek contract between four laundry workers and the leaders (*hegoumenoi*) of the priests of Dime, in AD 88/9, is indeed a lease of the laundry work (*gnaphikè*), for a rent of 240 dr.[86] A demotic discharge receipt for the scribe of the priests one year afterwards acknowledges that the money from the laundry workers was given to the temple.[87] Six years later, however, a temple account, which records payments in arrears from the eleventh year of Domitian to the first year of Nerva, gives the name of four laundry workers from Nilopolis who have arrears of 124 dr. for the first year of Nerva.[88] The temple was only a tax collector, but it was not always an easy task.[89] In the Ptolemaic period, the temple already leased out the laundry business in Nilopolis, but the rent consisted of oil for the lighting of the temple and wine for the temple of Soknopaios.[90] Payment, however, did not always arrive.[91]

---

[84] Wallace (1938: 200–2, 206–7).   [85] *Stud.Pal.* XXII 183, l. 57 (TM 15096).
[86] *Chr.Wilck.* 315 (TM 11670).   [87] *P.Dime* II 66, l. 6 (TM 100274).
[88] *P. Vienna* G 19818; cf. Hoffmann (2014).
[89] This difficulty may be connected with a financial crisis in the reign of Nerva; cf. Hoffmann (2014: 100).
[90] *P.Oxf.Griffith* 55 (TM 44459), 145/144 BC: rent of 400 *lok* of oil and 26 measures of wine; *P.Oxf. Griffith* 65 (TM 45625), 146 or 135 BC: receipt of oil delivered by the laundry worker of Nilopolis.
[91] *P.Oxf.Griffith* 41 (TM 48881), 131 BC: complaint of priests of the fourth *phyle*: oil and wine have not been given.

Under the Romans, the temple lost the profit from the licence of the laundry work at Nilopolis and became only a tax collector. Were there other links between those workers and the temple? The demotic texts give no further information.

For fishing boats, the temple may have made some profit. The expenditures related to them for the account of the nome is 625 dr. 1½ ob. and 60 dr. for the *dekanikon*.[92] In contrast to the total income for boats, which was more than 920 dr. in one declaration, the expenses here did not equal the income, so the temple may have had a profit of around 300 dr. In a discharge receipt for the scribe of the priests in AD 144/5, the priests declare: 'You have paid us; you have satisfied our heart with the silver, the bronze which came in your hand for {them} <us> and for […] and for the rent of the four boats of the god […]'.[93] These four boats of the god have been identified by Wolfgang Wegner as the four fishing boats mentioned in the Greek fiscal declarations.[94] The identification is not certain, since the declaration that details the cash income from the boats is incomplete, and there is a lacuna after the fourth boat. More boats could have been listed. However, if the identification is correct, the demotic designation 'the boat of the god' probably indicates that the boats originally belonged to the temple.[95] As with temple land, the boats could have been confiscated by the state after the Roman conquest and the priests required to pay a rent on them. But they would have continued to administer the boats, lease them out, and make some profit from them.[96] There is a reference to a 'boat of the god' in an unpublished account from Berlin listing rents or arrears on different temple goods.[97] It is followed by a complement, the reading of which is unclear but which could be a toponym. The 'boats of the god' also appear twice in the account of the arrears under Domitian and Nerva.[98] The first mention is not entirely clear, but the second is followed by the name of a fisherman, which confirms Wegner's view that the 'boat of the god' is a fishing boat, and not a processional bark.[99] On the other hand, there is no complement that could identify this boat as one of the four boats mentioned in the Greek declarations. The text proves only that fishermen could be bad payers, like the laundry workers. Once again, the temple seems to have lost the ownership of the boats, but unlike the laundry work it still might have derived some benefits in money from fishing.

[92] On this tax, cf. Wegner (2008: 167).
[93] *P.Dime* II 68 (TM 101250): AD 144/5.
[94] Wegner (2008).
[95] See the 'oil press of the god' in Pisaïs; cf. n. 73.
[96] Wegner (2008: 163–4).
[97] *P.Berl.* P. 17678 (unpublished), col. 2, l. 6.
[98] *P.Vienna* G 19818, l. 15, 20.
[99] Wegner (2008: 161–4).

The other revenues in money are more complicated to study, as they are not preserved in the fiscal declarations, but the demotic temple accounts could one day help fill the gap. Part of the accounts of the temple of Jupiter Capitolinus in the metropolis of the Fayyum in the third century AD has been preserved and offers an interesting point of comparison.[100] The organization of this Roman temple, where the imperial cult was celebrated, was completely different from the temple of Soknopaios in Dime as there were no permanent priests and no daily cult. Expenditures consist of the lighting of the temple, the salaries of the permanent staff (two persons), religious celebrations, and taxes paid in the villages where the temple assets were located. However, like traditional temples, the temple had an estate from which it collected revenues. Some income was from rents, but most resulted from the interest on loans. As Glare has shown, the temple was a resource especially for the metropolitan elite to borrow money on favourable terms. No such role as a loan office can be seen for the temple of Dime. On the contrary, individual priests sometimes lent money to the priesthood, as can be seen in one receipt in the first century AD where three association presidents (Egy. *mr-mšʿ.w*), acting on behalf of the priests, repay part of the debt they have towards a priestly family.[101]

Conclusion

Roman reforms brought changes in the temples in the organization of the priesthood, the tax system, and the ownership of temple assets in Egypt. We see the emergence of boards of priestly leaders and elders (*hegoumenoi* and *presbyteroi*) in charge of the temple, of an association of managers of the temple or smaller chapels (*lesoneis*), and of priestly tax collectors. The Roman poll tax had a profound effect on the priesthood too. As Andrew Monson has shown, the confiscation of temple land was not as hard on the priests as it appears, since some priests in Egypt had private land that benefited from a new favourable taxation rate under the Romans. Priests still belonged to a privileged social class (with tax exemptions), and the conflicts over priestly prebends show that these were still attractive.[102] The reforms did not prevent

[100] cf. Glare (1994).
[101] *P.Berl.* P. 15667 (TM 45588): AD 45/6. L. 4: read *nꜣ mr-mšʿ.w nꜣ wʿb.w* 'the association presidents of the priests', instead of *nꜣ sḥn.w nꜣ wʿb.w* 'the priestly tax collectors of the priests' (cf. *P.Dime* II, p. 20). The role of the *mr-mšʿ* in the documentation of Dime still needs to be clarified, but priests with this title are frequently mentioned in the daily accounts of the temple and the *ḥn.w*-agreements.
[102] cf. the conflict between Stotoetis and Nepheros in Dime for the prophethood on the altar of Isis Nephremmis in Pelusion *SB* XVI 12685 (TM 14647, AD 135–9); cf. Kruse (2002: 743–9).

temples from being active economic centres, as the archives of the temple of Dime demonstrate: not only priests but also others such as laundry workers and fishermen were dependent on its activities. The internal accounting of Dime illustrates some problems in the collection of rents and taxes at the end of the first century AD, but those types of problems were already present in the Ptolemaic period. The temple's fiscal declarations in the second century AD show a well-balanced budget and the daily accounts a regular functioning. Roman domination did not, therefore, have a negative impact on the economy of the temples: it was primarily aimed at clarifying the situation of priests and their economic activities. Changes must certainly have occurred during the third century, but the decrease in sources for this period does not allow us to see them.

Acknowledgements

I thank Willy Clarysse, Sandra Lippert, and Andrew Monson for reading my chapter, giving advice, and correcting my English.

References

Bagnall, R. S. (1985). 'Publius Petronius, Augustan Prefect of Egypt', *YCS* 28: 85–93.

Bresciani, E. (1975). *L'archivio demotico del tempio di Soknopaiu Nesos nel Griffith Institute di Oxford*, vol. 1: *P. Ox. Griffith nn, 1–75*. Milan.

Burkhalter, F. (1985). 'Le mobilier des sanctuaires d'Égypte et les "listes des prêtres et du cheirismos"', *ZPE* 59: 123–34.

Capponi, L. (2005). *Augustan Egypt: The Creation of a Roman Province*. London.

Capponi, L. (2011). 'Priests in Augustan Egypt', in J. H. Richardson and F. Santangelo (eds), *Priests and State in the Roman World*. Stuttgart, 505–26.

Capron, L. (2008). 'Déclarations fiscales du temple de Soknopaiou Nêsos: Éléments nouveaux', *ZPE* 165: 133–60.

Chaufray, M.-P. (2016). 'Comptes du temple de Soknopaios à Dimé à l'époque romaine', in T. Derda, A. Łajtar, and J. Urbanik (eds), *Proceedings of the 27th International Congress of Papyrology in Warsaw, 29 July–3 August 2013* (Journal of Juristic Papyrology Supplement 28). Warsaw, 1737–49.

Clarysse, W. (2005). 'Tebtynis and Soknopaiou Nesos: The Papyrological Documentation through the Centuries', in Lippert and Schentuleit (2005b), 19–27.

Clarysse, W. (2010). 'Egyptian Temples and Priests: Graeco-Roman', in A. B. Lloyd (ed.), *A Companion to Ancient Egypt*. Oxford, 274–90.

Cuvigny, H. (1986). 'Une prétendue taxe sur les autels: Le φόρος βωμῶν', *Bulletin de l'Institut français d'archéologie orientale*, 86: 107–33.

Davoli, P. (2014). 'The Temple of Soknopaios and Isis Nepherses at Soknopaiou Nesos (El-Fayyum)', in G. Tallet and Chr. Zivie-Coche (eds), *Le Myrte & la rose: Mélanges offerts à Françoise Dunand par ses élèves, collègues et amis*. Montpellier, 51–68.

Dixneuf, D. (2012). 'Introduction à la céramique de Soknopaiou Nesos', in M. Capasso and P. Davoli (eds), *Soknopaiou Nesos Project I, 2003-2009*. Rome, 315–61.

Evans, J. A. S. (1961). 'A Social and Economic History of an Egyptian Temple in the Greco-Roman Period', *YCS* 17: 143–283.

Glare, P. (1993). 'The Temples of Egypt: The Impact of Rome'. Ph.D. Thesis, University of Cambridge.

Glare, P. (1994). 'The Temple of Jupiter Capitolinus at Arsinoe and the Imperial Cult', in A. Bülow-Jacobsen (ed.), *Proceedings of the 20th International Congress of Papyrologists*. Copenhagen, 550–4.

Gorre, G., and Honigman, S. (2014). 'La politique d'Antiochos IV à Jérusalem à la lumière des relations entre rois et temples aux époques perse et hellénistique', in Chr. Feyel and L. Gaslin-Thomé (eds), *Le Projet politique d'Antiochos IV* (Études anciennes 56). Nancy: 301–38.

Hobson, D. W. (1984a). 'Agricultural Land and Economic Life in Soknopaiou Nesos', *BASP* 21: 89–108.

Hobson, D. W. (1984b). 'PVindob. Gr. 24951 + 24556: New Evidence for Tax-Exempt Status in Roman Egypt', in *Atti del XVII Congresso Internazionale di Papirologia*, vol. 3. Naples, 847–64.

Hoffmann, F. (2014). 'Doppelte Buchführung in Ägypten. Zwei Wiener Abrechnungen (P. Wien G 19818 Verso und 19877 Verso', in M. Depauw and Y. Broux (eds), *Acts of the Tenth International Congress of Demotic Studies, Leuven 26-30 August 2008*. Leuven, 83–114.

Hölbl, G. (2000–5). *Altägypten im Römischen Reich*, 3 vols (Zaberns Bildbände zur Archäologie). Mainz.

Huss, W. (1994). *Der Makedonische König und die ägyptischen Priester: Studien zur Geschichte des ptolemaiischen Ägypten* (Historia Einzelschriften 85). Stuttgart.

Klotz, D. (2012). *Caesar in the City of Amun: Egyptian Temple Construction and Theology in Roman Thebes* (Monographies Reine Élisabeth 15). Brussels.

Kruse, T. (2002). *Der königliche Schreiber und die Gauverwaltung: Untersuchungen zur Verwaltungsgeschichte Ägyptens in der Zeit von Augustus bis Philippus Arabs (30 v. Chr.-245 n. Chr.)* (Archiv für Papyrusforschung, Beiheft 11/1–2). Leipzig.

Lanciers, E. (2015). 'The Isis Cult in Western Thebes in the Graeco-Roman Period (Part II)', *CE* 90/180: 379–405.

Lippert, S. L. (2007). 'Die Abmachungen der Priester: Einblicke in das Leben und Arbeiten in Soknopaiou Nesos', in M. Capasso and P. Davoli (eds), *New Archaeological and Papyrological Researches on the Fayyum. Proceedings of the International Meeting of Egyptology and Papyrology: Lecce, June 8th–10th 2005* (Papyrologica Lupiensia 14). Lecce, 145–55.

Lippert, S. L. (2010). 'Seeing the Whole Picture: Why Reading Greek Texts from Soknopaiou Nesos is not Enough', in T. Gagos (ed.), *Proceedings of the 25th International Congress of Papyrology, Ann Arbor, July 29–August 4, 2007* (American Studies in Papyrology). Ann Arbor, 427–34.

Lippert, S. L. (2015). 'Chapels, Chambers and Gateways: The Religious Architecture of Soknopaiou Nesos According to the Demotic Documentary Papyri', in M. Capasso and P. Davoli (eds), *Soknopaios: The Temple and Worship: Proceedings of the First Round Table of the Centro di Studi Papirologici di Università del Salento. Lecce–October 9th 2013*. Lecce, 155–65.

Lippert, S. L., and Schentuleit, M. (2005a). 'Die Tempelökonomie nach den demotischen Texten Soknopaiu Nesos', in Lippert and Schentuleit (2005b), 71–8.

Lippert, S. L., and Schentuleit, M. (2005b) (eds). *Tebtynis und Soknopaiu Nesos: Leben im römerzeitlichen Fajum*. Wiesbaden.

Medini, L. (2015). 'Chronique d'une mort annoncée? Le Crépuscule des temples et des païens d'Égypte', *Topoi* 20/1: 239–80.

Messerer, C. (2017, 2019, 2020). *Corpus des papyrus grecs sur les relations administratives entre le clergé égyptien et les autorités romaines*. vols 1–3. Paderborn.

Monson, A. (2012). *From the Ptolemies to the Romans: Political and Economic Change in Egypt*. Cambridge.

Monson, A. (2014a). 'Late Ptolemaic Capitation Taxes and the Poll Tax in Roman Egypt', *BASP* 51: 127–60.

Monson, A. (2014b). 'Receipts for *sitônion*, *syntaxis*, and *epistatikon* from Karanis: Evidence for Fiscal Reform in Augustan Egypt?' *ZPE* 191: 207–30.

Monson, A. (2016). 'The Jewish High Priesthood for Sale: Farming out Temples in the Hellenistic Near East', *Journal of Jewish Studies*, 67: 15–35.

Otto, W. (1905–8). *Priester und Tempel im hellenistischen Aegypten*. 2 vols. Leipzig.

Parassoglou, G. M. (1974). 'A Prefectural Edict Regulating Temple Activities', *ZPE* 13: 21–37.

Pfeiffer, S. (2012). 'The Imperial Cult in Egypt', in Riggs (2012), 83–100.

Riggs, C. (2012) (ed.). *The Oxford Handbook of Roman Egypt*. Oxford.

Rigsby, K. (1985). 'On the High Priest of Egypt', *BASP* 22: 279–89.

Rostovtzeff, M. I. (1909). Review of Otto (1905–8), *GGA* 171: 603–42.

Ruffing, K. (2007). 'Kult, Wirtschaft und Gesellschaft im römischen Ägypten: Das Beispiel Soknopaiu Nesos', in M. Fitzenreiter (ed.), *Das Heilige und die Ware: Zum Spannungsfeld von Religion und Ökonomie* (Internet-Beiträge zur Ägyptologie und Sudanarchäologie 7). London, 95–122.

Sippel, B. (2020). *Gottesdiener und Kamelzüchter: Das Alltags- und Sozialleben der Sobek-Priester im kaiserzeitlichen Fayum*. Wiesbaden.

Stead, M. (1981). 'The High Priest of Alexandria and All Egypt', in R. S. Bagnall, G. M. Browne, A. E. Hanson, and L. Koenen (eds), *Proceedings of the XVI International Congress of Papyrology* (American Studies in Papyrology 23). Chico, 411–18.

Swarney, P. R. (1970). *The Ptolemaic and Roman Idios Logos* (American Studies in Papyrology 8). Toronto.

Török, L. (2012). 'Between Egypt and Meroitic Nubia. The Southern Frontier Region', in Riggs (2012), 749–62.

Wallace, S. L. (1938). *Taxation in Roman Egypt from Augustus to Diocletian*. Princeton.

Wegner, W. (2008). 'Zu den Fischereiabgaben in Soknopaiu Nesos', *ZPE* 165: 161–8.

Whitehorne, J. E. G. (1978). 'P. Lond. II 359 and Tuscus' List of Temple Perquisites', *CE* 53: 321–8.

Whitehorne, J. E. G. (1979). 'Tuscus and Temples Again (SB VI 9066)', *CE* 54: 143–8.

Wilcken, U. (1912). *Grundzüge und Chrestomathie der Papyrusurkunde*, vol. I.1. Leipzig and Berlin.

Winkler, A. (2015). 'A Contribution to the Revenues of the Crocodile in the Imperial Fayum: The Temple Tax on Property Transfer Revisited', *BASP* 52: 239–63.

8

Animals in Roman Religion

The Economics behind the Rituals

Michael MacKinnon

Introduction

Many archaeologists and scholars of antiquity might recognize the following statement, or a similar version of it: 'if something doesn't quite make sense in the archaeological record then it is probably related to some religious ritual.' Indeed, religion can often become a scapegoat among investigations into the past, offering some blanket, if not murky, explanation with which to counter alternate responses rooted in what might seemingly be deemed practical, rational, economically sound thought. Where deeper investigation into the study of ancient religions and religious practices has followed, often the symbolic, philosophical, and spiritual components tend to be of greater interest, leaving discussion of 'practical' matters, such as what or who provided for, supported, funded, administered, and simply allowed the rituals to operate, without much attention.[1] In large part, these 'practical' concerns might seem rather mundane or commonplace when compared to the broader spiritual and social purposes of ritual behaviours—that is, the materials and things required to undertake various ritual practices were simply just there, available, accessible, and presumably affordable. Their acquisition was part and parcel of achieving the final ritual and spiritual goal, so, by way of analogy, for many the final destination is what mattered, not so much the details concerning where or how one fuelled the automobile along the journey.

This chapter seeks to develop more of this metaphorical 'journey' and 'fuel' portion of the religious analogy presented above through the investigation of

---

[1] In the case of the historical examination of animal sacrifice in antiquity, this aspect is particularly salient, with discussion largely dominated by the works of Burkert (1972), Girard (1972), and Detienne and Vernant (1979). For an overview of the contributions of each of these authors, and a discussion of their impact and legacy, see Graf (2012).

Michael MacKinnon, *Animals in Roman Religion: The Economics behind the Rituals* In: *The Economy of Roman Religion.*
Edited by: Andrew Wilson, Nick Ray, and Angela Trentacoste, Oxford University Press. © Oxford University Press 2023.
DOI: 10.1093/oso/9780192883537.003.0008

animals in ancient cult. Much has been written about the role of animals in Greco-Roman religion. Arguments about the symbolism inherent in animal sacrifice and the social and political functions these actions served, as well as debates about the secular/sacred nature of meat consumption in antiquity, dominate the bulk of this scholarship.[2] Less attention, however, has been directed towards the seemingly practical and economic side to animal sacrifice. What types of animals were used, and how did this vary among public and private ritual ventures? What costs were involved in maintaining, selecting, acquiring, transporting, processing, and ultimately sacrificing animal victims? Who bore these expenses, and how might these be negotiated among different individuals or networks? How did such costs balance, or otherwise compare with, the 'benefits' (whether tangible or intangible, social or spiritual) that accrued from animal sacrifice? These concepts are explored in this chapter by drawing on various lines of evidence: literary, iconographical, archaeological, and zooarchaeological. The temporal and geographical focus is the Roman Mediterranean context, with particular emphasis on Italy. Arguably, as the core of the Roman world, Italy holds some prominence—at least it marks a destination of interest. In overviewing issues, however, my intent is not to moralize about the wider role animal sacrifice may have played in religious philosophies, which can set one off down a path of speculation about the dichotomous or continuous nature of the concepts of 'sacred' and 'secular'. Rather, the study here focuses upon describing some of these ritual events, examining what animals were used, and fitting the economics, mechanics, and costs of these practices into a grander (if admittedly incomplete) picture. Straightaway, it must be acknowledged that 'practical' sides of sacrifice for Roman antiquity can shape larger philosophical and moral components (and vice versa), so neat compartmentalization of any single aspect is problematic. Nevertheless, it is important overall to give this practical angle of animal sacrifice an investigatory 'stab', so to speak.

The Sources

To begin, a brief note about the strengths and weaknesses among available lines of evidence is warranted. The various problems that might plague the

---

[2] In addition to the seminal works given in n. 1, more recent discussions of Greek and Roman animal sacrifice include Gilhus (2006), Petropoulou (2008), Faraone and Naiden (2012), Naiden (2013), Ekroth (2014), Hitch (2015), Schultz (2016), Moser (2019), and Rives (2019).

use of archaeological and ancient literary and iconographical datasets may be familiar to many. Records are incomplete, disparate, skewed, inconsistent, biased, transformed, and manipulated, among other concerns. Moreover, different sources focus in different manners on different aspects. As regards ancient Roman religious practices, each investigatory dataset here mentioned need not inform us necessarily about rituals *per se*, which would result in varied messages and approaches to extracting mechanics and meanings. Through examination of the ancient texts, scholars can assemble a fairly good account of several things, such as: (i) sacrificial schedules and calendars; (ii) rules and operations at events (on the day of a sacrifice, less in terms of prior preparations); and (iii) the political, legislative, moral, and social framework of sacrifice.[3] Roman iconography yields an array of images, including representations of individual victims up for slaughter, depictions of funerary offerings and banquets, and processions of animals, such as in the *suovetaurilia* sacrifices.[4] Social and political implications certainly infiltrate how components are presented in ancient texts or iconography. For example, although cattle, sheep, and pigs all factor within representations of sacrificial animals on Roman reliefs, oxen and bulls register more frequently, and are the principal victims shown in any slaying or killing scene.[5] Emphasized messages of enhanced prosperity, power, and control may underlie this bias. Similar arguments have been presented to offset the apparent disconnect between the common iconographic image of Mithras slaying the bull, and the low occurrence of cattle bones recovered among zooarchaeological materials from Mithraea across the Roman Empire.[6] Additionally, among *suovetaurilia* imagery, studies indicate that some of the pigs displayed are unnaturally large, and (if realistically depicted) morphologically ally with a different, special breed of pig—one rarely recorded on the basis of available zooarchaeological evidence.[7] Nevertheless, even with these cautionary measures in evaluating ancient texts and art in place, through assessment of these two lines of evidence we know (or at least we assume) that animal sacrifice was common and rather important in Roman Italy. Yet, surprisingly there is little concrete zooarchaeological evidence from our pool of ritual, sacrificial, and funerary contexts with which to back that up. Why is this so? The question is central, and will be tackled later

---

[3] For a comprehensive treatment of the wider topic of Roman religion, see Beard, North, and Price (1998) and Rüpke (2007). Additionally, the *Thesaurus Cultus et Rituum Antiquorum* (*ThesCRA*) remains an instrumental reference for understanding Greek, Etruscan, and Roman cults and rituals.

[4] In the case of *suovetaurilia* images, Ryberg (1955) collects many of these. Elsner (2012) assesses sacrificial imagery in late Roman art.

[5] Huet (2007). [6] Gilhus (2006: 127–30). [7] MacKinnon (2001).

in this chapter. First, however, some background is necessary with which to situate the analyses.

While Roman Italy is rather deficient in terms of good-quality zooarchaeological data for ritual activities, by contrast, faunal evidence for animal sacrifice for areas and cultures outside Roman Italy is more abundant. The situation for animal offerings in Roman and pre-Roman Britain and the north-western provinces is discussed elsewhere in this volume.[8] There is a relatively sizeable pool of zooarchaeological data from both pre-Roman and Roman ritual sites in these regions, with examples from a range of deposits—sanctuary, temple, household, foundation, funerary, grave mounds, ditches, and so on—from both private and public domains. Similarly, the study of animal sacrifice in the ancient Greek world is increasingly being complemented by investigation of zooarchaeological evidence, especially materials associated with burnt animal offerings, which can be set alongside a relatively rich record of animal sacrifice in Greek antiquity extracted from ancient texts and iconography as well.[9] In fact, on closer inspection of the pool of zooarchaeological data that might be linked to sacrifice in Italy, pre-Roman contexts (Etruscan, Samnite, Archaic, Hellenistic, and so on) comprise the bulk of the data available. Where are the Republican and imperial materials? This shortage seems rather puzzling, and contrasts with two key observations: (i) there is a relatively good record of Roman temples, altars, and other ritual structures and features attributed to these timeframes; (ii) the general framing of sacrifice is positive in both textual and iconographical media.[10] This is especially evident in imperial Rome, with iconography of Augustus as priest, ready for sacrifice, not to mention positive depictions of animal sacrifice in monuments such as the Ara Pacis or in numerous *suovetaurilia* scenes.

Even when Roman funerary contexts are included, for which a relatively larger set of sites exists for Italy,[11] zooarchaeological data for animal sacrifice and food offerings from such cemeteries or burials still remain comparatively scarce. Within this funerary group reference is made more specifically to materials of commonly consumed taxa, including cattle, sheep, goat, pig, and domestic fowl. Dogs and equids have been uncovered in Roman funerary and burial contexts and are special cases, which lie outside the scope of investigation

---

[8] See King, Chapter 9, this volume. For Britain, see also King (2005).
[9] Ekroth (2014) provides a good overview of the evidence, with a comprehensive bibliography of pertinent zooarchaeological reports and studies.
[10] Green (2008: 41–6).
[11] Albeit of disparate nature—ranging from larger, formal cemeteries to individual burials, and including inhumation and cremation examples. Toynbee (1971) provides a general introduction to Roman burial practices.

in this chapter. Since dogs and equids were not normally eaten in Roman antiquity, economically there is no real loss of human dietary meat posed by the disposal or burial of these two taxa. Their meat could be fed to other animals (such as dogs or pigs) but that might require too much work or have been avoided, especially if the dog or equid in question was held in affection as a special pet or valued companion, whose burial fulfilled important social or religious functions (purification, symbolic offering, companion in the afterlife, marker of status, and so on). There is a rich tradition, cross-culturally, of burials of dogs and equids, which highlights perhaps some universal human sentiment towards these animals.[12]

Explaining the Lack of Zooarchaeological Data for Ritual Activities for Roman Italy

Let us return to the question posed earlier: why is there so little sound zooarchaeological evidence from our available pool of ritual, sacrificial, and funerary contexts for Roman Italy? Several possibilities may be suggested. First, much of this dearth might be attributed to a suite of practical, methodological explanations, such as: (i) these sites remain undiscovered, or, if known and excavated, investigation of other research priorities or classes of materials took precedence; (ii) bones were not recovered from such sites, or, if retrieved and studied, the findings have not subsequently been published; (iii) depositional and post-depositional complications, disturbances, and transformations have obscured the nature of the material and rendered assessments too problematic. Obviously, with these methodological and recovery matters, little currently can be done but to work to remedy such concerns in future archaeological campaigns.

A second explanation for a relative lack of animal bone remains from Roman sacrificial contexts might draw upon factors of choice and practicality. Duncan Fishwick suggests that local towns—unlike Rome—offered wine, incense, and sacrificial cakes at imperial festivities, restricting the more expensive animal sacrifices to the more important celebrations, such as annual festivals of selected civic deities (such as Jupiter and the tutelary deity of the town) or the birthday of the reigning emperor.[13] This idea of a two-tiered approach, with animal sacrifice reserved for special events, has implications not only in terms

---

[12] See, e.g., Lacam (2008), for dogs; Reese (1995), for equids.
[13] Fishwick (1991: 509–17; 2004: 247–58); Hemelrijk (2009: 265–6).

of addressing concerns for expenses involved (and linking animal sacrifice with 'more expensive' practices); it also affects absolute numbers of animals potentially available in the archaeological record. The odds of having animals sacrificed are diminished if they are not a component of all types of ritual events. In a similar vein, there is a matter of scale to consider. The larger the celebration and its accompanying sacrifice, the higher the probability that remains from it might survive, especially if those receive special disposal treatment. Additionally, repeated sacrifices over a lifetime (be these daily, seasonal, annual, commemorative, and so on) can produce quite a staggering aggregate volume and expense. But, in the case of funerary sacrifices, any offering put into the grave itself will presumably be a one-off event, upon death, and might, in turn, be more carefully executed.

Third, the rise of moral stances against animal sacrifice through literary and philosophical texts, most importantly through Christian ideals, is often cited as a reason for a decline in animal sacrifice in Roman antiquity.[14] True, Christian faith did not tolerate this practice, and one does witness a religious shift generally throughout the fourth century AD, but this still leaves a temporal gap that cannot explain why so little zooarchaeological evidence for animal sacrifice registers for Republican and imperial Roman Mediterranean contexts in particular. Even acknowledging the wider cultural impact of Christian doctrine overall throughout antiquity, this was probably a slow, tenuous, and multifaceted process of conversion, as shaped other components in the adoption of Christianity. Pagan customs, including types of animal sacrifice, did not always perish unilaterally or universally. Indeed, Mediterranean sacrificial practices were characterized by great cultic, local, and regional diversity throughout antiquity. Within this framework, animal sacrifice persisted, to varying degrees, even after imperial attempts to uproot it.[15] The situation is murkier in the case of animals, Christianity, and funerary rituals. Animal sacrifice to the dead was generally abandoned in the third and fourth centuries AD throughout areas of the Roman Mediterranean world, but funerary meals and banquets still persisted well into the fifth and sixth centuries AD.[16] Discriminating among such banqueting rituals (many of which contained meat and animal offerings) those practices that are Christian, pagan, or otherwise is not always possible.

---

[14] Petropoulou (2008: 211–84).   [15] Harl (1990).
[16] Lindsay (1998) and Rebillard (2015) discuss social and historical aspects of Roman funerary banquets.

The point just articulated—that of problems in dissecting components of rituals that might otherwise be shaped by several factors—presupposes a final argument to explain the lack of good, clear zooarchaeological data for animal sacrifice for Roman Mediterranean contexts. Ritual activities perhaps can be more easily identified when linked to 'unique' or 'special' deposits—that is, something out of the ordinary. Zooarchaeologists define various criteria to recognize such deposits—for example, burial of an entire animal; deliberate positioning of remains in a grave; concentrated assemblages of burnt animal bones (as in some cases for burnt *thysia* and *holocaust* animal sacrifice in Greek antiquity); association alongside other 'ritual' materials, and so on; but there are no guarantees that ritual or sacrificial activities truly underlie each case.

The situation worsens when one considers that the blurring of lines between sacred and secular components and explanations, as regards meat consumption in Roman antiquity, could translate into a blurring of contexts into which remains of such practices were deposited. In other words, mentioning that something comes from a ritual site need not imply it is any more ritualized than ritual material removed off-site and eventually discarded in other spots (sometimes alongside other refuse). Presumably some notions of basic cleanliness were upheld among different types of ritual sites, particularly in the case of temple and altar areas where repeated sacrifices took place. Marble and stone surfaces at such sites were probably swept of debris after events, leaving questions as to where materials ended up. In the absence of any designated sacred pit or other such deposit located at a ritual site in which remains of any animal sacrifice may have been specially interred, the impression is that somehow such materials were cleared from the region and deposited elsewhere. This might be particularly problematic when ritual areas are within, or close to, domestic and settlement zones, wherein mixed/communal depositional locales can result. Even within a ritual site itself, however, spatial association does not necessarily imply temporal unity or causal relationship. Just because something was recovered from a grave site, or within a temple compound, need not a priori link it to ritual. The ubiquitous 'fill' deposits, often cited in archaeological reports, are especially vulnerable in this regard. Grave 'fills' may or may not have ritual materials; the same must be stressed in the case of nondescript 'fills', 'surfaces', 'areas', and 'deposits' from temples, sanctuaries, altars, and other ritual sites. Many of these types of deposits are recorded, and scepticism is warranted. Whereas other artefacts recovered (such as ceramics) may be indicative of ritual meals or behaviours, the faunal record may not differ from the situation in 'regular' rubbish dumps and contexts outside of these 'ritual' spots. How then should one interpret these 'fills'? Conversely, 'oddities' (such as frogs, toads, wild birds, and so on) recovered from graves and pits can amplify the intention to explain them as weird and deliberate as opposed to artificial or taphonomic.

Maybe we are looking for Roman ritual material in the wrong places. Perhaps some or most of these are hidden among 'non-ritual' materials and contexts. Clearly, a strong warning is needed. If taphonomy and the nature of archaeological deposits are not scrutinized assiduously, then we could get a false picture (or no picture at all) of ancient cultural practices. Healthy scepticism of reports that discuss the special nature of faunal remains from 'ritual' sites, where specific contexts are not marked or explained, is justified; worse yet, in terms of potential errors, are conclusions drawn from such shady contexts being used to craft dogmatic statements about ritual.

Scale of Sacrifice: Large or Small; Public or Private

This notion of 'hidden' ritual assemblages sparks a strong argument to engage with the scale of that sacrifice. Is it large or small; public or private? Sarah Hitch notes that 'a broad distinction can be drawn between routine sacrifices regulated by cities, such as those offered in annual festivals, and sacrifices performed in a more or less *ad hoc* fashion by individuals'.[17] While on one level such a statement rings true, uncertainties exist in the uncritical application of any such dichotomous classification: public sacrifice need not be large; and public and private sacrifice need not be overtly distinct. Nevertheless, using these levels provides some framework. As noted earlier, zooarchaeological remains from public sacrifices are more plentiful in the ancient Greek world, where numerous cases of entirely burnt animal bone assemblages, distinctly recognized as the 'god's portion' of the sacrifice, are documented. Private houses in the Greek context, by contrast, have not yet yielded altars or zooarchaeological remains to suggest that domestic sacrifice, at least involving animals (and marked by special deposition), was a common practice.[18]

The situation among Roman (as opposed to ancient Greek) Mediterranean sites is different as regards marked physical traces for animal sacrifice. Here, zooarchaeological evidence for large-scale, public sacrifice is minimal—we currently lack distinct burnt assemblages from Roman Mediterranean sites

---

[17] Hitch (2015: 338). [18] Ekroth (2014: 325).

that can be tied neatly to public sacrifice. Does this mean that the Romans did not carry the practice over from the Greeks? Possibly, but presentations of food to deities, and celebratory feasting and dining, still formed central parts of many Roman rituals; thus, some manner of large-scale cooking and food debris might be expected in association with Roman public sacrifices. Its material traces, however, remain relatively elusive, or may not be distinct enough to register as 'different' from other types of archaeological deposits and remains.

While zooarchaeological traces from Roman public sacrifices in the Mediterranean context remain largely undetected or otherwise problematic to interpret, several examples from Roman houses of pits and 'special' deposits with burnt animal bones, mainly from piglets and chickens,[19] can be taken as indicators of offerings of the meat (and perhaps also the sacrificial killing) of such animals at the domestic level, either in the worship of the household gods (*lares*) or as a foundation ritual of sorts in securing good fortune for the house overall.[20] The Roman poet Juvenal mentions offering chickens (technically roosters) to the *lares*.[21] Pompeii provides perhaps our best set of these examples. Foundation deposits with food remains (including pig bones) are noted from sixth- to fourth-century BC deposits at the House of the Vestals (VI.1.7).[22] Further pits with domestic burnt offerings of food remains were noted among fourth-century BC to first-century AD levels at the House of Amarantus (I.9.11–12),[23] while burnt plant and faunal remains from a kitchen floor at the House of the Postumii (VIII.4.4–53), and dating to the first century AD, may have ritual connections.[24]

These Pompeian examples indicate, first, that domestic rituals have a long trajectory, from the sixth century BC through to the first century AD. This is important, and can denote broader, cross-cultural universals in selection of sacrificial victims, choices that in turn may be rooted in practical, economical bases. Pigs and chickens were rather plentiful, accessible, and available to many Pompeians, across social classes, ethnicities, and timeframes. Unfortunately, the archaeological record for ancient Pompeii stops at AD 79, and good zooarchaeological data for domestic rituals at other Roman Mediterranean sites beyond Pompeii are scarce. Funerary assemblages, nevertheless, help

---

[19] For simplicity, I will use the term 'chicken' as an encompassing, generic term throughout this chapter to include both hens and roosters within the 'domestic fowl' (i.e., *Gallus gallus*) category. A distinction between the sexes is not always made apparent in the ancient sources or determinable from zooarchaeological or archaeological remains.
[20] Van Andringa and Lepetz (2003: 93); Ekroth (2014: 325).   [21] Juv., *Sat.* 13.232–4.
[22] Ciaraldi and Richardson (2000).   [23] Fulford and Wallace-Hadrill (1999); Robinson (2002).
[24] Robinson (2002).

augment the picture of personal, small-scale, familial, and private ritual, albeit in a different capacity from that displayed for domestic, household rituals.

Overall, it may be the case, at least for the Roman Mediterranean region, that animal sacrifice from private ritual is more amenable to zooarchaeological observation than its public counterpart. If so, then our general picture of animal sacrifice in that domain is skewed, and consequently holistic reconstructions (in other words, ones that integrate zooarchaeological, ancient textual, and iconographic evidence) that explore practicalities might be better directed along that angle—that is, costs associated with private, smaller-scale sacrifice.

Choice of Animal

Although available zooarchaeological evidence remains problematic for deciphering the practicalities of animal sacrifice in Roman Italy, it offers much information for other aspects of Roman life, which in turn can help frame or contextualize rituals. Pigs, sheep, goat, cattle, and domestic fowl typically comprise the bulk of Roman dietary meat, regardless of location. Fluctuations register in amounts and proportions, depending upon wealth, access, season, location, social and political conditions, and environment, among other factors. In the case of Roman sites in the Mediterranean, however, two points are worth highlighting. First, the frequency of pigs tends to increase among many of these sites throughout Roman times, signifying things such as popular demand for meat, the link between pigs and 'Romanized' diets, and augmented marketing schemes in pork production. The second point to note is that the frequency of domestic fowl also increases at many Roman Mediterranean sites over time. Moreover, domestic fowl tend to be better represented at Roman urban sites than rural ones. Chicken does not overtake pork, beef, or lamb, if measured on a pound for pound basis, but it was important, popular, and obtainable—notably in urban areas. If practicalities dictated choices in food acquisition for the typical Roman who could afford meat, then pigs and domestic fowl might be favoured to some degree. These commodities were available, and more generally across all seasons. Pigs can breed twice a year, and both pigs and domestic fowl adapt well to almost any type of setting—urban or rural. Thus, there is some manner of pragmatic, universal convenience, with pigs and domestic fowl not always coincident with other taxa, such as cattle and sheep/goats, which might be more seasonally restricted (through transhumance) or earmarked for exploitation for secondary products (such as wool, milk, traction) before consumption. As noted previously, pigs and domestic fowl are the most common animals found in domestic ritual assemblages (offerings to the *lares*, and foundation pits) from contexts in Pompeii. Additionally, they tend to be the most common animals found in Roman funerary contexts, both in the Roman Mediterranean world and beyond. This last point is particularly important—cattle often dominate zooarchaeological dietary assemblages from sites in the Roman north-western provinces, while sheep and goats factor significantly among Roman sites in the eastern empire and in North Africa.[25] This makes economic sense in those areas: taxa best suited to the local ecological and environmental conditions are prominent. Consequently, if remains in Roman funerary contexts were a simple reflection of normal dietary patterns in life, then far more local and regional variation would be expected. This is not the case: pigs and chickens are often selected, regardless of site or location. Legal reasons may help to explain this pattern. According to Cicero, a grave could acquire legal and religious status only through the sacrifice of a pig at the burial site.[26] This might then explain the presence of pigs, but it still ushers in questions about why the choice of pig as opposed to another animal, and does not explain the role of domestic fowl. What is it about pigs and chickens as ritual offerings in Roman graves?

Pigs and Domestic Fowl

The popularity of pigs (*Sus scrofa*) in Roman Italy is perhaps best summed up by the ancient agricultural writer Varro when he rhetorically questions 'who of our people runs a farm without keeping swine?'[27] He provides further context for a long-established importance of pigs among ancient Greeks, who 'it seems, at the beginning of making sacrifices, first took the victim from the swine family', before noting the key role pigs held in various Roman sacrificial, dietary, and culinary contexts.[28] Notably, pigs were important in the cult of Ceres, and sacrificed in various agricultural fertility and harvest rituals.[29] Given the central role agricultural practices and schedules held for many Romans, and the popularity of pork as a dietary meat, one can see how pigs might become somewhat ingrained in multiple aspects of Roman life.

---

[25] MacKinnon (2015). [26] Cic., *Leg.* 2.22.
[27] Varro, *Rust.* 2.4.3. Translations for the ancient authors presented throughout this chapter are from the Loeb Classical Library.
[28] Varro, *Rust.* 2.4.9. [29] Cato, *Agr.* 134.1.

Once introduced into the Mediterranean world from around the eighth century BC onwards, domestic fowl (*Gallus gallus*) gain familiarity.[30] They become increasingly abundant into Roman times, in a range of sites and regions, which suggests at least some measure of cross-cultural and socio-economic popularity.[31] Humans therefore had abundant opportunity to observe domestic fowl at close range. Cocks were offered in sacrifice to the god of medicine, Aesculapius.[32] Domestic fowl also featured in magic, sorcery, and divination. Even in Christianity, the hen symbolizes maternal and Christian love—self-sacrificing, nurturing, protective, and comforting[33]— while the cock can be a symbol of resurrection.

Taste is something often overlooked in discussions of food in antiquity.[34] Did the taste of meat matter for the Romans? Most likely it did, and the importance placed upon fattening animals, including pigs and chickens, to increase their succulence is emphasized in the ancient sources. Certainly, these meats (as well as any other) could be flavoured in various ways through spices, different cooking methods, sauces, and other means. Among meats, however, chicken and pork rank high in umami substances.[35] Umami is the taste of foods that are rich in glutamic acids and two ribonucleotides, 5'-inosinate and 5'-guanylate. These compounds link to 'savoury' taste sensations, which can be a draw for humans in food selection. Put simply, one might argue that pork and chicken tasted 'good' to the Romans, which in turn might influence their appeal, selection, and use.

How much did pigs and chickens cost during Roman times? Prices are always a complex issue to interpret for antiquity. Inflation was notoriously rampant at times, and prices probably fluctuated seasonally, regionally, and in terms of product availability. Diocletian's *Edict on Maximum Prices* provides some basis with which to compare commodities on a relative scale, but not without concerns. As regards prices of meat, poultry, and eggs, the *Edict* lists beef and mutton at 8 *denarii/libra* (1 *libra* = 326 grams, or just under a pound); pork, goat, and lamb fall in the range of 12–16 *denarii/libra* (with cuts from younger animals more expensive); sausage is 10–16 *denarii/libra*; a dozen eggs costs about 12 *denarii*; and two chickens are listed for 60 *denarii*.[36] Chickens seem somewhat expensive, but, when converted into *librae*, with each chicken weighing about 3–4 *libra*, the cost can vary from 7 to 10 *denarii/libra*. It is not specifically stated whether these chickens are alive or dead, or male or female,

---

[30] Perry-Gal et al. (2015). [31] Kron (2014: 119–21). [32] Stafford (2008).
[33] Matthew 23:37.
[34] A volume in the *Senses in Antiquity* series, Rudolph (2017), is devoted to 'taste'.
[35] Curtis (2009). [36] *Ed. Diocl.* 4.1–43.

so added bonuses of feathers, eggs, or fighting capacity may apply. Overall, domestic fowl seem good value. Beef and mutton are technically cheaper than pork, but pork may have been more readily available throughout the year, and consequently offered convenience and predictability.

Some aspects require clarification. Raw counts of the number of times animals are mentioned in the ancient sources in sacrifice to Greek and Roman deities reveal no predominance of domestic fowl or pigs, but rather cattle, sheep, and goats (the latter three taxa representing over 80 per cent of such references).[37] Moreover, there may be times of the year when a region was flush with cattle and sheep, if herds of these animals were moving around the landscape. Why not coordinate sacrificial selection and schedules to maximize this availability? Cattle and sheep herd well (as opposed to pigs) and thus can be inspected and selected for sacrifice, presumably with greater ease and options among stock. Cattle, sheep, and goat were important in animal sacrifice, but perhaps less so in private sacrificial settings than pigs or domestic fowl, and, given that our zooarchaeological record for animal sacrifice in the Roman Mediterranean is arguably skewed towards personal as opposed to public ventures, this could help provide some explanation for discrepancies among textual and zooarchaeological datasets. Presumably cattle were too big and too costly for anything but large-scale, public sacrifice, but why the lack of sheep and goats? Issues of seasonal availability may apply in the case of the latter taxa. Zooarchaeological evidence from the Iron Age and early Roman temple site at Uley, England, noted a preponderance of sheep or goat killed (in sacrifice to Mercury it is suggested) during the months of August and September, perhaps in relation to a seasonal festival.[38] Seasonal connections are less distinct for Roman Mediterranean ritual examples, however. The limited zooarchaeological data available for sanctuary, temple, and non-funerary ritual sites in this region show no marked clustering of animal ages, nor do they contain assemblages that are strongly dominated by cattle or sheep and goat. In fact, pigs occur across a number of these examples, often accounting for well over 30–40 per cent of remains among each. Some have suggested this mixture of cattle, sheep, and pig among such sites represents *suovetaurilia* sacrifices,[39] but that is difficult to reconcile when age and sex parameters among these victims are so varied (both male and female animals of all ages represented). Were people simply sacrificing what was available in these cases, a hodgepodge of domestic livestock? And, if so, was this a means

---

[37] Statistics here are drawn from the overview of Kadletz (1976).
[38] Levitan (1993: 279, 300); King (2005: 335).   [39] e.g. Wilkens (2004).

to accommodate flexibility, as regards costs, supply, and availability of victims, but still conform to general dictates? Ancient sources suggest that most gods were not terribly picky about the species of animal sacrificed, so much as ensuring its beautiful condition.[40] As noted earlier, often in the ancient sources only an 'animal', in a generic sense, is mentioned, an implication that might further underline flexibility in choice, with consequent impact on cost, supply, and availability, among other factors.

To complicate matters further, as regards choice and supply, some scholars have tried to link locations of ancient sanctuaries and shrines along, or in the vicinity of, transhumance routes. In particular, this issue has been examined for Samnite contexts in Italy.[41] Such a tactic might make sense from a practical stand-point—sacrificial victims could essentially walk to the altar, and the sheer volume of animals passing through these areas could ensure that only the best of these were selected. The texts are often quite explicit about particular characteristics required of sacrificial animals, regarding colour, fitness, breed, size, age, temperament, and so on.[42] Overall, however, no clear connections emerge in the placement of sanctuaries and any perceived connection to transhumance schedules and routes.[43]

Costs, Supply, Sale, and Sacrifice of Animals

Although the ancient sources mention animal sacrifice often, typically this is in a fairly generic fashion: 'so-and-so made sacrifice'. Specifics surrounding practical aspects such as cost, supply networks, and other matters are not always forthcoming. Far more work has been done on these issues for Greek antiquity: some scholars play with calculations of how much meat might be provided from various sacrificial events,[44] while others discuss animal supply networks for ancient Greek sanctuaries.[45] Overall, values for sacrificial meat yield in Greek antiquity can fluctuate immensely, although there is great merit in these types of calculations, however, and their practice should be encouraged. As regards supply networks, Greek sources do indicate systems of administering, leasing, and utilizing sacred and non-sacred lands to pasture, herd, or otherwise maintain sacrificial animals. Nonetheless, even in this

---

[40] Hitch (2015: 341).   [41] Stek (2009: 55–8).
[42] Kadletz (1976) collects many of these data and tabulates findings across deities.
[43] Stek (2009: 55–8).
[44] e.g. Jameson (1988); Rosivach (1994); Rhodes and Osborne (2003: 401); Naiden (2013).
[45] e.g. Howe (2008); McInerney (2010).

context, sacred and profane herds might graze side by side; thus, separating out components is not always clear.

Presumably on some fronts, similar concerns to those encountered for ancient Greek sacrifice might be extrapolated into Roman antiquity, but scales do not always neatly coincide (some of the Athenian festivals were massive in relation to some Roman events), while the blurring of sacred and secular components in Roman life clouds much of our assessment of acquisition of animals for public sacrifice, especially. Nonetheless, a fairly extensive (although by no means complete) review of ancient textual sources yields a few key observations and directives that might assist in understanding various 'practical' aspects of animal sacrifice for Roman times.

Beginning with the concept of 'cost', the first example selected derives from Lucian's *Zeus Rants*.[46] Here, the god complains of a measly sacrifice made: 'to feast sixteen gods he had sacrificed only a cock, and a wheezy old cock at that, and four little cakes of frankincense…and yet he had promised whole herds of cattle…'. He is ranting against Epicureanism; Zeus likes his excesses. Still, the reference presents a case that, in this context, this domestic fowl is unacceptable; indeed, a single bird for sixteen gods is almost an insult. An implication is that it is insufficient, in quantity and expense, for the level of sacrifice expected; one could predict that Zeus might complain less should an offering of at least one (relatively more expensive) fattened ox or cow (but still not the promised herd) be presented instead of this lowly cock. From the ancient sources, Aphrodite/Venus is the expressed deity to whom domestic fowl were sacrificed, and even in this case only rarely it seems.[47] Might it be the case that chickens assumed a secondary, mortal, familial, private symbolism in sacrifice?

The second reference selected derives from Seneca.[48] In discussing what happens when a hailstorm was predicted, the author asks:

> did people run for woolly overcoats or leather raincoats? No. Everybody offered sacrifices according to his means, a lamb or a chicken…if someone did not have a lamb or a chicken he laid his hands on himself. But do not think the clouds were greedy or cruel. He merely pricked his finger with a well-sharpened stylus and made a favourable offering with this blood, and the hail turned away from his little field no less than it did from the property of a man who had appeased it with sacrifices of larger victims.

---

[46] Lucian, *Zeus Rants* 15.   [47] Kadletz (1976).   [48] Sen., *QNat.* 4B.6.2–3.

Two observations stem from this quotation: first, expense might have been a practical concern in sacrifice (but overall the intent was more important); second, chickens and lambs, in this case, may rate as relatively commonly available, and potentially inexpensive in this regard.

The third example derives from the Oxyrhynchus Papyri, where a list of articles for sacrifice is presented.[49] No large beast is noted, but, rather, fairly modest items including four hens, one piglet, eight eggs, and two jars of wine, among other articles. Given that none of these items was exceptionally ostentatious or costly, there is a sense of these items drawing a wider popular appeal, and, as such, being commodities available perhaps to humbler, common folk.

Obviously, costs associated with animal sacrifice in any large (public or private) functions sponsored by the state or wealthier clientele might have been less of an issue. Price might not have been a factor for them. Still, it did not mean such expenditures went unnoticed. Ammianus Marcellinus comments that the emperor Julian 'sacrificed innumerable victims without regard to costs, so that one might believe that…there would soon have been a scarcity of cattle'.[50] Putting aside the moral messages presented by some ancient authors against extravagance and sacrifice overall,[51] one still gets the impression that costs were probably a concern for many. Certainly, households could not keep pace with larger agencies in this respect.

Developing some of these aspects about costs, economics, and religious rituals using the case of funerary food offerings provides further nuances. As mentioned earlier, chickens and pigs are the two most frequent animals found in Roman graves across the empire. The chicken part of this funerary bundle is intriguing, especially since the ancient sources provide so little evidence about them. Why are they there in burials?

First, it is possible that at many Roman sites chickens were one of the few animals readily available, and affordable, for sacrifice. This point has already been highlighted, but it is worth repeating. Pigs also register in many Roman funerary deposits throughout the empire, but they tend to show a bit more variability, which in turn might link to local or regional factors. For example, pigs are relatively under-represented among Roman funerary assemblages in North Africa, even in regions where they may account for significant proportions of the normal, dietary meat.

---

[49] *P.Oxy.* 36.2797.   [50] Amm. Marc., *Julianus* 2.25.4.17.
[51] See references in nn. 1 and 2, for wider discussions about the morality and ethics of sacrifice in antiquity. Newmyer (2014) gives an overview of how the various schools of philosophy affected the role, use, and treatment of animals in antiquity.

A second reason for chicken sacrifice in Roman graves may relate more to the animals' size as opposed to their availability. Funerary food offerings were intended to be eaten. This could be either figuratively by the deceased (who may have received actual animals or cuts of meat in the grave), or literally by the mourners at the grave (who would eat the offering and subsequently provide the deceased with leftover bones, or ashes from that offering, if things were burnt afterwards). Feasting and eating, therefore, are functions of the whole process of honouring or commemorating the dead, who might be kept 'alive', so-to-speak, by offerings of food, drink, olive oil, and even blood.[52] A chicken forms a neat 'package' meal for the deceased—not too large, not too small.[53] Moreover, unlike the case with the slaughter and sacrifice of cattle, sheep, goats, or pigs, a chicken could easily be cooked and served whole (without the need to butcher it into smaller sections), and subsequently consumed by a small, familial congregation of mourners. Any larger animal that was to be consumed whole would require a comparably substantial feasting setting at the grave, with a need perhaps to cook and consume all parts of the carcass on site, if nothing could be removed for preservation and storage off-site, owing to its sacred or special nature. Rarely are whole mammals, whether a pig or any other larger taxa, placed in Roman graves, possibly because of space restrictions, but practical issues may also apply (namely, is this ultimately a waste of good meat?). Thus, cemetery chickens may represent a 'family-sized' feast or offering. Certainly, sections of larger animals, such as a leg of lamb, haunch of pork, and so on, could similarly provide 'family-sized' meals; however, in these cases the animal would need to be butchered to suit, which in turn might add an extra complication of sale, preservation, or disposal of the remaining parts of the carcass, if indeed the section of the animal used in the funerary feast was not purchased individually from a market or other

---

[52] Toynbee (1971: 57).

[53] A similar case might apply with fish. There is some supportive zooarchaeological evidence for this practice in Roman North Africa, but there are limited data outside this region. Plates holding bones of fish (sometimes with other small animals) were recovered from Punic graves in Carthage and Kerkouane (Stirling 2004: 444), as well as from an inhumation grave of the first century AD at Tipasa (Stirling 2004: 438). Nonetheless, the impression from the available data is that funerary offerings of fish were relatively rare. Fish were comparatively more expensive than domestic fowl in antiquity, so that added cost might have factored into what was considered an appropriate meal for the deceased. Obviously costs here could vary; coastal regions may have had easier access to fish, procured more cheaply perhaps. However, even in these cases fish do not appear often in funerary assemblages, which in turn suggests that cost might not have been a sole motivating factor. Nevertheless, although available literary, iconographic, and archaeological evidence suggests that fish, as compared to domestic food animals, were not frequent funerary offerings in Roman graves, their significance may be under-represented. Fish bones, and especially the smaller elements, tend to degrade more rapidly within archaeological contexts, so they may not have been preserved (or noticed, as fine screening is key to their recovery) among sites.

venue. Chickens had a greater family connection. Overall, there may be more significance to aspects such as availability, affordability, family gathering, public display, and quick recognition of an offering that favoured the use of chickens. After all, alongside pigs, they commonly feature in sacrifices to the household *lares*, so an extension of domestic familiarity may apply here in family burials as well.

Were funerary chickens cooked or not? This is not always clear, but in a number of cases whole chickens with heads attached and no evidence of cut marks have been recovered from Roman funerary contexts.[54] Presumably these were not cooked birds (and probably not de-feathered or otherwise treated), prompting the question: why? An uncooked, feathered bird might clearly be recognized as a chicken by all funerary participants (as well as the deceased, symbolically), something that might be lost if only a cut of meat was provided. Consequently, there may be more significance to the public display and recognition of animals in funerary rituals than otherwise considered. Indeed, Roman funerary ceremonies may have been more about the 'show' for the attendees and worshippers than about providing the best nutriment for the deceased. In this regard, a fairly economical (and easily identifiable) chicken greatly trumped its base price in terms of its social value among funerary participants.

Finally, to complicate matters further, why must these chickens be viewed as ritual food offerings? Might they have been considered pets, even if for part of their life? In this regard they may fulfil double duty in the afterlife—nourishment and companionship. Discussions of pet animals in antiquity do not typically address domestic fowl within the list of potential avian pets, instead focusing upon caged or novelty species, such as nightingales, starlings, parrots, and magpies.[55] Nonetheless, even though examples of 'named' domestic fowl are rare among ancient sources,[56] this need not exclude them as 'pets' in some capacity. Many domestic fowl were kept and raised within Roman households, as sources of meat, eggs, and feathers. While these birds may have ultimately been consumed, a certain level of familiarity and routine, which presumably developed during their upkeep, could translate into some affection and attribution of 'pet' status, even if informally and subjectively represented.

---

[54] Lepetz (2017) provides some examples of these.   [55] Lazenby (1949: 299).
[56] The impression being that 'naming' an animal connotes some aspect of 'humanizing' it, thus drawing it into a network to be considered as a type of 'pet'.

Supply of Sacrificial Animals

The topic of chickens in graves highlights some aspects about economics and supply. Domestic fowl form neat, compartmentalized, recognizable, economical offerings. How might this compare with acquisition at a different level, notably in supplying an animal (or animals) one might not have kept domestically; or procedures in acquiring larger livestock or groups of these for public and private sacrifice? From where did these animals come, and how might they be supplied? Getting at this component for Roman antiquity is hugely problematic, and beset with many hurdles, notably if we cannot separate 'sacred pastures and herds' (if such existed, and I exclude here sacred chickens, kept for augury) from 'regular pastures and herds' in the Roman world. As mentioned, the quality of the sacrificial victim was often a key aspect of concern for both Greek and Roman contexts. Maintaining sacrificial herds might have been one way to ensure this measure of quality control, and shows some representation in the Greek world. Another way to ensure proper traits in sacrificial animals would be to scrutinize available livestock in some public market or venue.

The situation involving 'special, sacrificial herds' for Roman antiquity is hazy, with only scraps of rather ambiguous evidence. Joan Frayn somewhat sensibly notes: 'Among the personnel connected with the meat trade, there must have been some who provided the sacrificial animals for religious festivals and for private offerings,' but offers minimal support.[57] Pliny may refer to a *victimarius negotiator* (a tradesman in sacrificial victims), but there is conjecture as to this reading; the main manuscript tradition gives the more benign *suarius negotiator* (a common pig tradesman).[58] Similarly, Valerius Maximus' comment on the same story likening the noble Cornelius Scipio to a *victimarius* called Serapio is also vague in documenting any type of liaison between the farms, butchers, and the local officials or private individuals who wished to obtain sacrificial animals.[59] A funerary stele from Pompeii commemorates Clodia Nigella, freedwoman of Clodia, public priestess of Ceres in Pompeii, and *porcaria publica* ('public pig-keeper').[60] Again, however, debate surrounds the specific meaning: did she keep/raise/tend/trade/sell the sacrificial pigs for the cult of Ceres (and perhaps other religious festivals) or was she involved in selling sacrificial meat from these pigs?[61] Rural estates, owned by

---

[57] Frayn (1995: 112).   [58] Plin., *HN* 7.12.54; Frayn (1995: 112).
[59] Val. Max., 9.14.3; Frayn (1995: 112).   [60] *CIL* X.1074.
[61] Hemelrijk (2009: 263–4).

elites and imperial officials, could certainly provide resources for any sacrifices these parties desired—this makes good economic sense—but direct transactions of supplies for such ventures are not explicit in the ancient sources. Aspects become more convoluted if ritual and non-ritual animals were not distinguished or otherwise separated until a final selection from the flock or herd was made. Thus, animal production components might blend sacred and secular dimensions to much the same degree as any subsequent use, sale, or perception of these resources. Overall, the topic of raising and herding sacrificial animals in Roman antiquity remains problematic. Quality data of the specificity needed are sparse, and overall assessment requires a clearer distinction of sacred/secular categories. Was all meat consumed in Roman antiquity sacred? This concept is debated: some scholars argue for a more encompassing connection of foodstuffs (including meat) and sacrifice, if indeed every aspect surrounding eating and formal banqueting was linked with ceremonial aspects of sharing with the gods;[62] however, this seems rather extreme in lumping a range of what presumably were variable intents and contexts associated with eating and meat consumption under a wider umbrella. Perhaps it is better to characterize aspects along a range of 'degrees of sacredness', even if such is not articulated neatly from available data and is potentially highly subjective in practice. Selling these animals, and their meat, nevertheless, falls within a wider investigation of the *macellum*.

Sale of livestock and meat has been linked to the *macella* of Roman antiquity.[63] Literary sources refer, in order of importance, to fish, meat, game, poultry, and (rarely) other products necessary for a good banquet (such as fruits, vegetables, high-quality bread).[64] Fish are stressed in earlier sources, under the Republic, but slaughter and sale of meat predominates among imperial and early Christian sources. Architectural evidence among *macella* variously indicate stalls for the sale of commodities, as well as folds, enclosures, stalls, tethering rings, and other paraphernalia that might suggest stabling, displaying, or keeping of live animals. Certainly, *macella* operated in the sale of meat and livestock, but their connection with sacrifice in the regard is not certain. At Didyma (Asia Minor), Q. Pomponius Pollio is said to have 'supported' the *macellum* and two *leitourgiai* related to it. His role as *prophetes* for the temple where the inscription was found has prompted speculation of ties in provisioning meat for sacrifices,[65] but this is hardly conclusive. Arguments

---

[62] Scheid (2012: 93–5).
[63] De Ruyt (1983) remains an essential source for the investigation of *macella* in general.
[64] De Ruyt (2007: 141).   [65] Richard (2014: 259).

explaining an enclosure area in the north-east corner of the *macellum* at Pompeii where skeletons of sheep were discovered as a pen for the keeping of ritual animals are also not assured (but regularly repeated as though fact).[66] In the west, there often seems to be a link between *macella* and temples, and it has been suggested that *macella* were involved in the redistribution of sacrificial meat,[67] but no eastern examples are close to temples.[68] Moreover, to what degree are placements as indicated based upon deliberate religious connection as opposed to the inevitability of grouping public buildings together in middle of the city? Ultimately, available literary and archaeological evidence for *macella* in Roman antiquity do not neatly answer questions posed about the marketing and sale of sacrificial animals and their meat. Again, here, concerns of how to distinguish between sacred and secular components surrounding sacrifice and consumption of animals and their products complicate assessments.

Conclusions

It is important to return to the issue of the cost of meat and its impact on sacrifice but to step back and view this in context. Meat is often argued as one of the first commodities in the ancient Roman diet that should be eliminated or scaled back markedly to cut costs.[69] One manner of assessing economic scenarios for antiquity compares the 'respectability basket' of 26 kg/year of meat for an ancient Roman with the 'bare-bones subsistence basket' that included only 5 kg/year of meat.[70] While these calculations seem sensible, they tend to imply that meat was a luxury that had to be trimmed from one's diet if one was thinking rationally and economically. I do not dispute this, but, in the case of ritual actions, the perceived value of commodities (spiritually, socially, commemoratively, and so on) can sometimes exceed their tangible, marketable value. This is where ritual contorts our notions of rational economics. Animal sacrifice is a financial gesture, as well as an appropriate offering. The idea of a 'monetized' animal in both the real and the abstract sense permeates many genres of classical literature. The burial of animals is non-remunerative in that food and resources (such as meat, fat, traction, and so on) that could otherwise be consumed or exploited are lost. In the case of wild animals, one should consider costs both in hunting the animal and in its subsequent

---

[66] cf. Frayn (1995: 109). [67] Van Andringa (2007). [68] Richard (2014: 266).
[69] MacKinnon (2018: 151–8). [70] Allen (2009).

burial—double the hassle and expense one might argue, which in turn might help justify why in part wild animals register in far fewer cases in Greco-Roman burials in relation to their representation among normal, dietary assemblages. Their burial records are even more disconnected from 'regular' patterns in this regard than is the case for common livestock, such as cattle, sheep, goat, pig, and domestic fowl. Does cost matter in animal sacrifice and burial? Yes, arguments for such a connection seem sensible for antiquity, but a direct link between that material cost and its perceived benefits (be these social, cultural, spiritual, or economic) can be both very subjective and extremely variable. Food offering in graves brought numerous benefits for the deceased and the celebrants that presumably trumped the financial costs involved. Feasting, purification, assurance of favours, proper social conduct, marking of space, attaining closure (mental or physical), and community bonding are all mentioned in this regard, the benefits of which need not be dissociated from sound economic practice overall. Think of animal sacrifice in antiquity, then, as a small price to pay for attainment of a greater good.

Acknowledgements

I am thankful to the organizers of this conference, in particular Angela Trentacoste, Nick Ray, Andrew Wilson, and Alan Bowman, for the invitation to present at this venue, and for their helpful comments and suggestions. Any errors, however, are solely my own. Funding for my research into the wider topic of animals in Roman antiquity has been provided variously by the University of Winnipeg, the Social Sciences and Humanities Research Council of Canada, and the British School at Rome.

References

Allen, R. C. (2009). 'How Prosperous Were the Romans? Evidence from Diocletian's Price Edict (AD 301)', in A. K. Bowman and A. I. Wilson (eds), *Quantifying the Roman Economy* (Oxford Studies on the Roman Economy). Oxford, 327–45.

Beard, M., North, J., and Price, S. (1998). *Religions of Rome*, 2 vols. Cambridge.

Burkert, W. (1972). *Homo Necans: Interpretationen altgriechischer Opferriten und Mythen*. Berlin.

Campbell, G. L. (2014) (ed.). *The Oxford Handbook of Animals in Classical Thought and Life*. Oxford.

Ciaraldi, M., and Richardson, J. (2000). 'Food, Ritual and Rubbish in the Making of Pompeii', in G. Fincham, G. Harrison, R. R. Holland, and L. Revell (eds), *TRAC 99: Proceedings of the Ninth Annual Theoretical Roman Archaeology Conference, Durham, April 1999*. Oxford, 74–82.

Curtis, R. I. (2009). 'Umami and the Foods of Classical Antiquity', *American Journal of Clinical Nutrition* 90/3 (suppl.): 712S–18S.

De Ruyt, C. (1983). *Macellum*. Louvain.

De Ruyt, C. (2007). 'Les produits vendus au macellum', *Food & History* 5/1: 135–50.

Detienne, M., and Vernant, J.-P. (1979) (eds). *La cuisine du sacrifice en pays grec*. Paris.

Ekroth, G. (2014). 'Animal Sacrifice in Antiquity', in Campbell (2014), 324–54.

Elsner, J. (2012). 'Sacrifice in Late Roman Art', in Faraone and Naiden (2012), 120–63.

Faraone, C. A., and Naiden, F. S. (2012) (eds). *Greek and Roman Animal Sacrifice: Ancient Victims, Modern Observers*. Cambridge.

Fishwick, D. (1987–2004). *The Imperial Cult in the Latin West: Studies in the Ruler Cult of the Western Provinces of the Roman Empire*, vols. I.1–III.3. Leiden.

Frayn, J. (1995). 'The Roman Meat Trade', in J. Wilkins, D. Harvey, and M. Dobson (eds), *Food in Antiquity*. Exeter, 107–14.

Fulford, M., and Wallace-Hadrill, A. (1999). 'Towards a History of Pre-Roman Pompeii: Excavations beneath the House of Amarantus (I.9.11–12), 1995–8', *PBSR* 67: 37–144.

Gilhus, I. S. (2006). *Animals, Gods and Humans: Changing Attitudes to Animals in Greek, Roman and Early Christian Ideas*. London.

Girard, R. (1972). *La violence et le sacré*. Paris.

Graf, F. (2012). 'One Generation after Burkert and Girard: Where Are the Great Theories?', in Faraone and Naiden (2012), 32–54.

Green, S. J. (2008). 'Save our Cows? Augustan Discourse and Animal Sacrifice in Ovid's *Fasti*', *G&R* 55/1: 39–54.

Harl, K. (1990). 'Sacrifice and Pagan Belief in Fifth- and Sixth-Century Byzantium', *P&P* 128: 7–27.

Hemelrijk, E. A. (2009). 'Women and Sacrifice in the Roman Empire', in O. Hekster, S. Schmidt-Hofner, and C. Witschel (eds), *Ritual Dynamics and Religious Change in the Roman Empire: Proceedings of the Eighth Workshop of the International Network Impact of Empire, Heidelberg, July 5–7, 2007*. Leiden, 253–67.

Hitch, S. (2015). 'Sacrifice', in J. Wilkens and R. Nadeau (eds), *A Companion to Food in the Ancient World*. London, 337–47.

Howe, T. (2008). *Pastoral Politics: Animals, Agriculture, and Society in Ancient Greece* (Publications of the Association of Ancient Historians 9). Claremont, CA.

Huet, V. (2007). 'Le sacrifice disparu: Les reliefs de boucherie', *Food & History* 5/1: 197–223.

Jameson, M. H. (1988). 'Sacrifice and Animal Husbandry in Classical Greece', in C. R. Whittaker (ed.), *Pastoral Economics in Classical Antiquity* (Cambridge Philological Society Suppl. 14). Cambridge, 87–119.

Kadletz, E. (1976). 'Animal Sacrifice in Greek and Roman Religion'. Ph.D. dissertation, University of Washington.

King, A. (2005). 'Animal Remains from Temples in Roman Britain', *Britannia* 36: 329–69.

Kron, G. (2014). 'Animal Husbandry', in G. L. Campbell (2014), 109–35.

Lacam, J.-C. (2008). 'Le sacrifice du chien dans les communautés grecques, étrusques, italiques et romaines', *MEFRA* 120/1: 29–80.

Lazenby, F. D. (1949). 'Greek and Roman Household Pets', *CJ* 44/5: 299–307.

Lepetz, S. (2017). 'Animals in Funerary Practices: Sacrifices, Offerings and Meals at Rome and in the Provinces', in J. Pearce and J. Weekes (eds), *Death as a Process: The Archaeology of the Roman Funeral*. Oxford, 226–56.

Levitan, B. (1993). 'Vertebrate Remains', in A. Woodward and P. Leach (eds), *The Uley Shrines: Excavation of a Ritual Complex on West Hill, Uley, Gloucestershire: 1977-9* (Historic Buildings and Monuments Commission Archaeological Report 17). London, 257–301.

Lindsay, H. (1998). 'Eating with the Dead: The Roman Funerary Banquet', in I. Nielsen and H. Sigismund Nielsen (eds), *Meals in a Social Context: Aspects of the Communal Meal in the Hellenistic and Roman World*. Aarhus, 67–80.

McInerney, J. (2010). *The Cattle of the Sun: Cows and Culture in the World of the Ancient Greeks*. Princeton.

MacKinnon, M. (2001). 'High on the Hog: Linking Zooarchaeological, Literary, and Artistic Data for Pig Breeds in Roman Italy', *AJA* 105/4: 649–73.

MacKinnon, M. (2015). 'Changes in Animal Husbandry as a Consequence of Changing Social and Economic Patterns: Zooarchaeological Evidence from the Roman Mediterranean Context', in P. Erdkamp, K. Verboven, and A. Zuiderhoek (eds), *Ownership and Exploitation of Land and Natural Resources in the Roman World* (Oxford Studies on the Roman Economy). Oxford, 249–73.

MacKinnon, M. (2018). 'Meat and Other Animal Products', in P. Erdkamp, and C. Holleran (eds), *The Routledge Companion to Diet and Nutrition in the Roman World*. New York, 150–62.

Moser, C. (2019). *The Altars of Republican Rome and Latium: Sacrifice and the Materiality of Roman Religion*. Cambridge.

Newmyer, S. T. (2014). 'Being One and Becoming the Other: Animals in Ancient Philosophical Schools', in Campbell (2014), 507–34.

Naiden, F. S. (2013). *Smoke Signals for the Gods: Ancient Greek Sacrifice from the Archaic through Roman Periods.* Oxford.

Perry-Gal, L., Erlich, A., Gilboa, A., and Bar-Oz, G. (2015). 'Earliest Economic Exploitation of Chicken outside East Asia: Evidence from the Hellenistic Southern Levant', *PNAS* 112: 9849–56.

Petropoulou, M.-Z. (2008). *Animal Sacrifice in Ancient Greek Religion, Judaism, and Christianity: 100 BC to AD 200* (Oxford Classical Monographs). Oxford.

Rebillard, E. (2015). 'Commemorating the Dead in North Africa: Continuity and Change from the Second to the Fifth Century CE', in J. R. Brandt, M. Prusac, and H. Roland (eds), *Death and Changing Rituals. Function and Meaning in Ancient Funerary Practices.* Oxford, 269–86.

Reese, D. (1995). 'Equid Sacrifices/Burials in Greece and Cyprus: An Addendum', *JPR* 9: 35–42.

Rhodes P. J., and Osborne, R. (2003). *Greek Historical Inscriptions, 404–323 BC.* Oxford.

Richard, J. (2014). 'Macellum: "Roman" Food Markets in Asia Minor and the Levant', *JRA* 27: 255–74.

Rives, J. B. (2019). 'Animal Sacrifice and Euergetism in the Hellenistic and Roman Polis', in C. Moser and C. Smith (eds), *Religion in the Roman Empire* 5.1: *Transformation of Value: Lived Religion and the Economy.* Heidelberg, 83–102.

Robinson, M. (2002). 'Domestic Burnt Offering and Sacrifices at Roman and Pre-Roman Pompeii, Italy', *Vegetation History and Archaeobotany* 11/1: 93–100.

Rosivach, V. (1994). *The System of Public Sacrifice in Fourth-Century Athens.* Atlanta, GA.

Rudolph, K. (2017) (ed.). *Taste and the Ancient Senses.* London.

Rüpke, J. (2007) (ed.). *A Companion to Roman Religion.* Malden, MA.

Ryberg, I. S. (1955). 'Rites of the State Religion in Roman Art', *MAAR* 22: iii–227.

Schultz, C. E. (2016). 'Roman Sacrifice, Inside and Out', *JRS* 106: 58–76.

Scheid, J. (2012). 'Roman Animal Sacrifice and the System of Being', in Faraone and Naiden (2012), 84–95.

Stafford, E. (2008). 'Cocks to Asklepios: Sacrificial Practice and Healing Cult', in V. Mehl and P. Brulé (eds), *Le sacrifice antique: vestiges, procedures et strategies.* Rennes, 205–21.

Stek, T. D. (2009). *Cult Places and Cultural Change in Republican Italy.* Amsterdam.

Stirling, L. (2004). 'Archaeological Evidence for Food Offerings in the Grave of Roman North Africa', in R. B. Egan and M. A. Joyal (eds), *Daimonopylai: Essays in Classics and the Classical Tradition Presented to Edmund G. Berry.* Winnipeg, 427–51.

Toynbee, J. C. M. (1971). *Death and Burial in the Roman World*. London.

Van Andringa, W. (2007). 'Du sanctuaire au macellum: sacrifices, commerce et consummation de la viande à Pompéi', *Food & History* 5/1: 47–72.

Van Andringa, W., and Lepetz, S. (2003). 'Le ossa animali nei santuari: Per un'archeologia del sacrificio', in O. de Cazanove and J. Scheid (eds), *Sanctuaires et sources dans l'antiquité: Les sources documentaires et leurs limites dans la description des lieux de culte* (Collection du Centre Jean Bérard 22). Naples, 85–96.

Wilkens, B. (2004). 'The Roman suovitaurilia and its Predecessors', in S. Jones O'Day, W. Van Neer, and A. Ervynck (eds), *Behaviour behind Bones: The Zooarchaeology of Ritual, Religion, Status and Identity*. Oxford, 73–6.

9

Sacred Flocks and Herds? The Implications of Animal Sacrifice at Rural and Suburban Romano-Celtic Shrines

Anthony C. King

This is a chapter about animals—the origins and husbandry of those that ended up as deposits of bones on Romano-Celtic temples in Britain and Gaul. The presence of animals at temples might seem straightforward: worshippers come to a temple with animals, and, after these have been sacrificed, the bones, or, at least, a selection of the sacrificed carcasses, are deposited on the site. However, the title of this chapter, with its question mark after 'sacred flocks and herds', is an exploration of this deceptively simple picture, with two speculations as points of focus. One is that some temples maintained their own flocks and herds, in part because of their location away from settlements and population, so that they were an integral element of the temple economy. Secondly, that there are enclosures in the landscape around some of the temples, outer *temenoi* or *areae* that sometimes enclose many hectares, and that these are the spaces where these animals were kept, possibly temporarily before a festival or a similar event.

The starting point for this chapter is an article on animal bones from temples in Roman Britain, and its underpinning data.[1] The tripole (ternary) graph for all temple assemblages of cattle, sheep/goat, and pig bones has been updated with data from new excavations and publications of temple sites (Fig. 9.1).[2] If this diagram is compared with non-temple assemblages from Roman Britain (Fig. 9.2), it can immediately be seen that the temple assemblages have a greater emphasis on sheep/goat and pig. This also corresponds with the pre-Roman

---

[1] King (2005).
[2] For the previous version, see King (2005: fig. 1). The additional sites are Tabard Square, Southwark, London (Rielly 2015); Springhead, Kent (Grimm 2011); Heybridge, Essex (Johnstone and Albarella 2015); Ashwell, Hertfordshire (Jones and King 2018); and Snow's Farm, Haddenham, Cambridgeshire (Beech 2006).

Anthony C. King, *Sacred Flocks and Herds? The Implications of Animal Sacrifice at Rural and Suburban Romano-Celtic Shrines* In: *The Economy of Roman Religion*. Edited by: Andrew Wilson, Nick Ray, and Angela Trentacoste, Oxford University Press. © Oxford University Press 2023. DOI: 10.1093/oso/9780192883537.003.0009

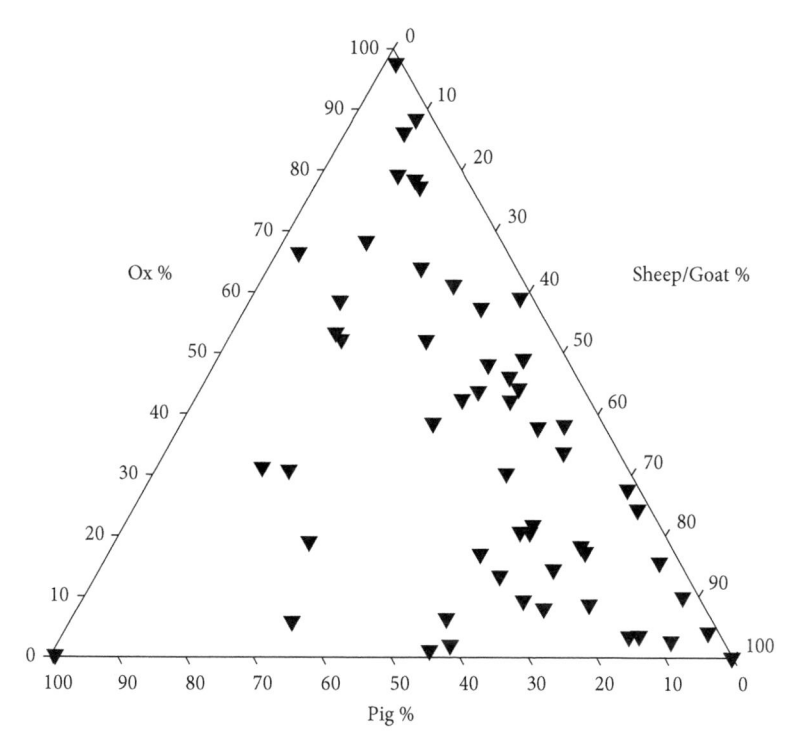

Fig. 9.1 Tripole (ternary) graph of cattle, sheep/goat, and pig in temple assemblages from Roman Britain. Data from King (2005) with additions.

pattern in Britain, which tends to have higher sheep/goat percentages, on average, especially in southern Britain, than for the Roman period.[3] There is the possibility, therefore, that temple sites may be conserving Iron Age traditions in their sacrificial practices.

When temple sites are looked at individually, rather than as a group, a different aspect emerges. Each temple has its own characteristics in terms of the animal bone assemblage, with the implication that orthopraxy for most Romano-Celtic temple cults was developed largely independently at each temple and was not in any sense centrally regulated.[4] This stands in contrast to more unified cult practices—for instance, in eastern cults introduced into the west during the Roman period.[5]

---

[3] King (1984); Hambleton (1999).
[4] As explored in King (2005). See also Smith (2001: 156–7). This can also be seen in the human bones (King 2023) and in other artefact classes (Smith 2001: 154–6; King 2007, 2008; Wythe 2008).
[5] Brun and Leguilloux (2013: 175–8).

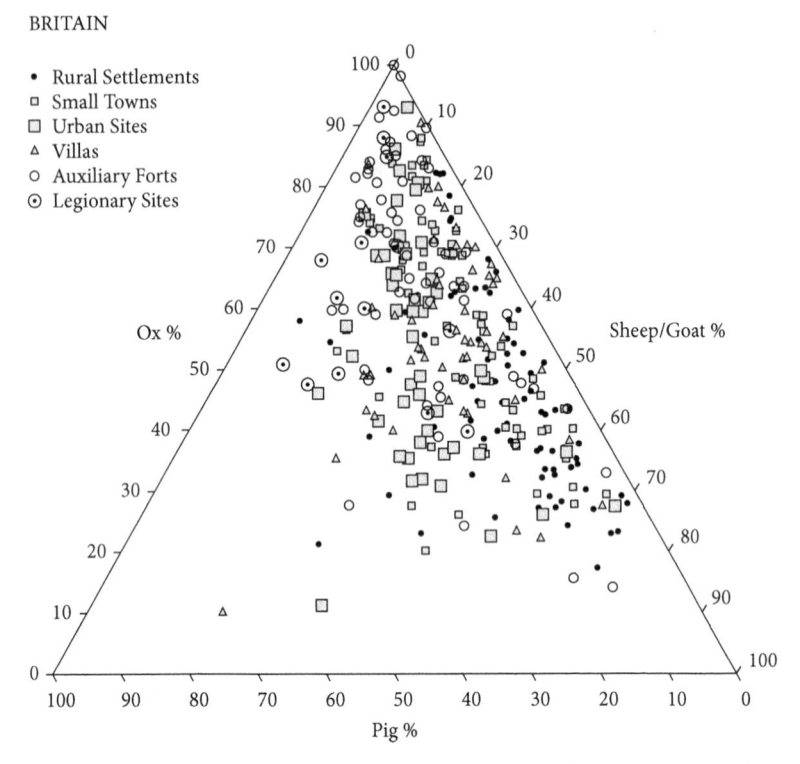

Fig. 9.2 Tripole (ternary) graph of cattle, sheep/goat, and pig in non-temple assemblages from Roman Britain. Data from King (1999: table 3).

The most clearly observed cases of temple bone assemblages tend to be rural cult sites, mainly because the boundaries of their *temenoi* were relatively well defined, and bone deposition can be readily found and characterized. An example is Harlow, Essex, which has an assemblage of *c*.3,600 bones, very much dominated by sheep (Fig. 9.3).[6] When their age-at-death is plotted (Fig. 9.4), it can be seen that many died at a young age (tooth-wear stage C, about six to twelve months), and this was interpreted in the excavation report as representing seasonal slaughter, probably in the first autumn after the birth of spring lambs, extending into the winter. There may have been a festival at the site at this time of year, with sacrifice of young sheep as an integral component. If so, the question arises as to whether lambs were driven to the site from surrounding settlements, or a flock of sheep was attached to the temple, from which sacrificial lambs were selected.

---

[6] Legge and Dorrington (1985); Legge, Williams, and Williams (2000).

Anthony C. King

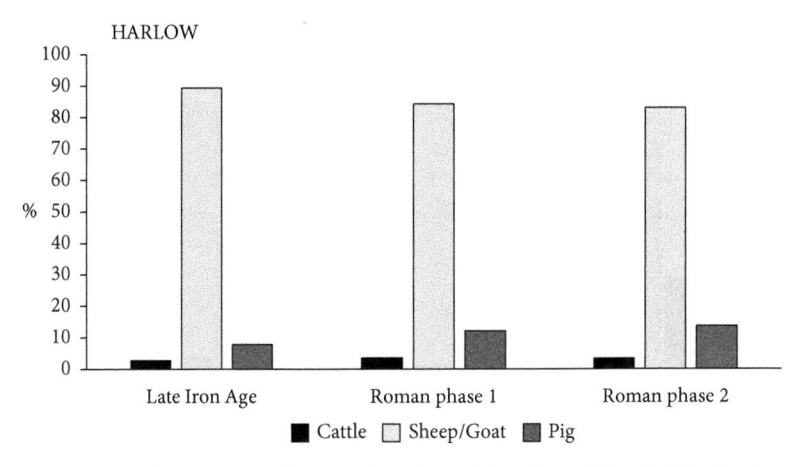

Fig. 9.3 Harlow: mammal species by phase. Data from King (2005: fig. 7).

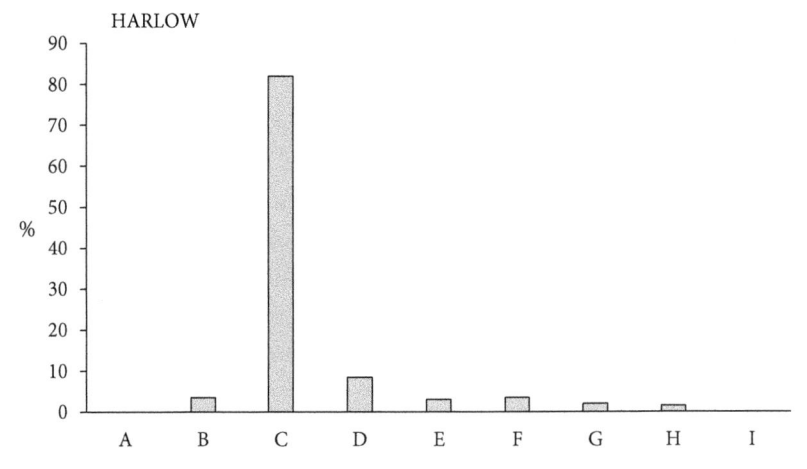

Fig. 9.4 Harlow: age-at-death for sheep (n = 221, all phases), based on mandibular tooth wear, using Payne's method. A, 0–2 months; B, 2–6 months; C, 6–12 months; D, 1–2 years; E, 2–3 years; F, 3–4 years; G, 4–6 years; H, 6–8 years; I, 8–10 years. Data from King (2005: fig. 8).

In order to approach an answer to this question, another rural site gives some pointers in its animal bone data. Uley, Gloucestershire, has one of the largest bone assemblages from any Romano-Celtic temple in Britain or Gaul, with c.230,000 in total.[7] This site, like Harlow, is dominated by sheep/goat bones (Fig. 9.5), but Uley has the distinction, very unusual for a British site, of

---

[7] Levitan (1993).

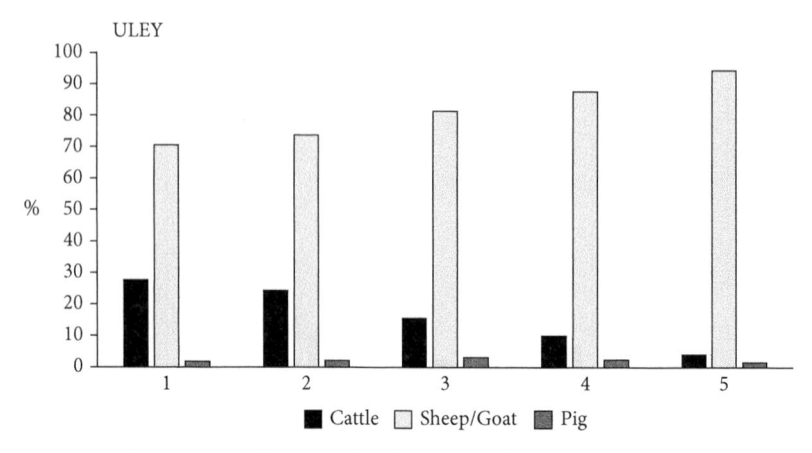

Fig. 9.5 Uley: mammal species by phase. Data from King (2005: fig. 4).

a majority of goat as opposed to sheep, at a ratio of four goats to each sheep.[8] In a similar fashion to Harlow, age-at-death assessment indicated possible seasonal slaughter, in the autumn/winter of the first year, and again a year later.[9] The goat and sheep bones are also of interest for their breed conformation. Levitan commented that 'it is intriguing to note that there are different patterns in extra foramen occurrence...perhaps a hint of "type" selection for votive purposes'.[10] An implication of this is that there was possibly specific breeding of animals for the temple over a period of time, such that a breed developed enough to be noted in the skeletal remains. Finds of hay and sheep/goat coprolites were also made during the excavation, indicating the feeding and stocking of live animals very close to the temple itself.

The Uley goats, therefore, appear to have been a specific herd, possibly a temple herd kept near the site on lands set aside for the purpose. The landscape setting and the Roman settlement pattern around the temple are both relevant in this respect. The site is located in a high position on the Cotswold Hills, at c.246 m elevation, near an Iron Age hillfort, Uley Bury.[11] Access is not easy, and there is little local Roman settlement in the immediate vicinity, apart from villas at Frocester Court and a settlement at Kingscote, both c. 4 km

---

[8] This number of goats at Uley is effectively a majority of all the goat remains so far found in faunal remains from all types of site in Roman Britain.
[9] Levitan (1993); King (2005: fig. 5). Snow's Farm, Haddenham, temple site has a similar biennial pattern (Beech 2006: 390).
[10] Levitan (1993: 299).
[11] Woodward and Leach (1993: fig. 1). Other temples are also known to be located near hillforts in high positions, e.g. Henley Wood, North Somerset (Watts and Leach 1996: fig. 2); Croft Ambrey, Herefordshire (Stanford 1974: fig. 1—the probable temple site is indicated as The Mound). Cf. Budei (2016: ch. 3).

distant.[12] Thus, land was almost certainly available on the higher ground near the temple, for the keeping of herds of goats, much as the area today is a zone for sheep-farming. Other evidence from Uley indicates that it was a focus for individual worshippers to visit in order to fix curses at the temple.[13] They probably travelled some distance to get to Uley, as the nearest (urban) population centres were at *c.* 30 km or greater distances.[14] A picture emerges, as a consequence, of a temple having *cultores* who made pilgrimages to the site for personal reasons (as evidenced by the curses), and to attend seasonal festivals and sacrifices (as indicated by the bones). It seems likely that the animals were a local resource kept by the temple and made available to worshippers, presumably at a price, for ritual purposes, either at the festivals or for individual acts of devotion. Sacrifice could also accompany cursing, either before or after the act of *defixio*, possibly as an *ex-voto* offering.

Chanctonbury Ring, West Sussex, is another high site that is difficult of access.[15] An ancillary polygonal building within the temple area contained *c.*5,000 pig bones, mainly cranial elements,[16] which are probably the remains left at the temple after consumption of other parts of the carcass as part of ritual activity. At this site, the high downland position makes it unlikely that pigs were kept adjacent to the temple, but they may have been driven as livestock from lower ground to the north and south, or, less likely, brought in as deadstock or carcasses. The logistics involved in this are interesting to contemplate, but impossible to resolve with the currently available evidence.

The economics of animal sacrifice are seen in a different perspective at Ashwell, Hertfordshire.[17] The temple itself is a circular open-air shrine positioned in the middle of a much larger roughly circular enclosure, *c.*150 m in diameter. The outer enclosure has many internal subdivisions, detected by geophysical survey, and it may have been the zone of the site where live animals were kept prior to being offered at the shrine. The large assemblage of *c.*44,000 bones displayed an interesting feature: there were high levels of fragmentation (average size of bone fragments, *c.*1.5 cm), and many had been cremated to a high temperature, akin to the processes used in human cremations (Fig. 9.6). Sheep were the primary species destined for this

---

[12] Woodward and Leach (1993: fig. 2); Smith (2001: 113). Adams (2009: 99) suggests a specific link between Uley temple and Woodchester villa, but this site is a little more distant than Frocester or Kingscote.

[13] Tomlin (2017), and references therein to earlier publications of curses from the site.

[14] For discussion of pilgrimage and the location of Romano-Celtic sanctuaries, see Kiernan (2012: especially 83–8).

[15] Rudling (2001).   [16] Sibun (2001); King (2005: 342–4)

[17] Jackson and Burleigh (2007); Jones and King (2018); Rainsford et al. (2021).

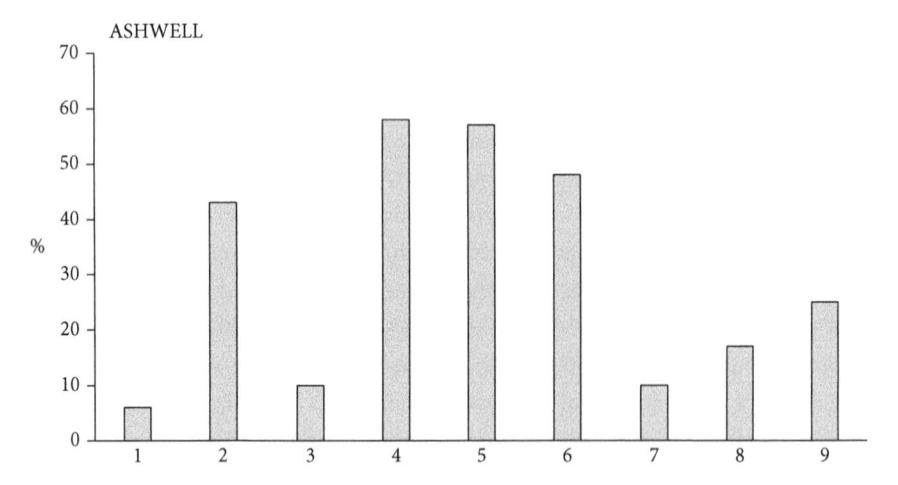

Fig. 9.6 Ashwell: incidence of burnt bone by phase. Phases 2–6 represent the main period of use of the temple, late 1st–2nd century AD. From Jones and King (2018).

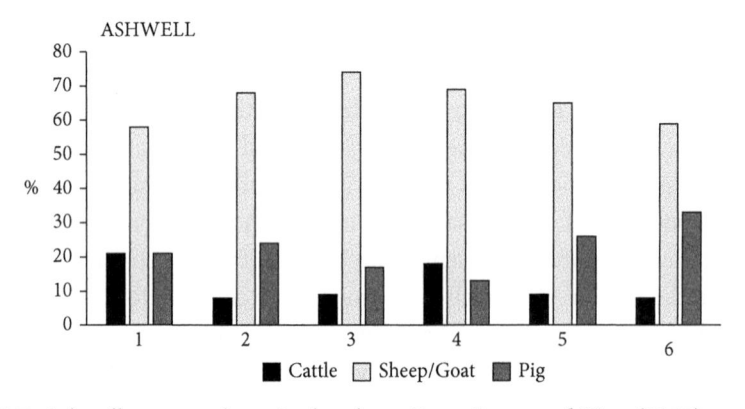

Fig. 9.7 Ashwell: mammal species by phase. From Jones and King (2018).

holocaustum type of ritual (Fig. 9.7). The cult of Senuna at this temple appears to have invested a great deal in bringing animals in, holding them in possible stock enclosures, and offering them in a ritual involving cremation. It is not known whether worshippers consumed meat of the offered sheep as part of this ritual.

The larger sanctuary site at Springhead, Kent, presents a more complex picture.[18] Recent excavation on the spring shrines surrounding the source of the river Ebbsfleet has uncovered unusual features, such as the probable

[18] Andrews et al. (2011: ch. 4).

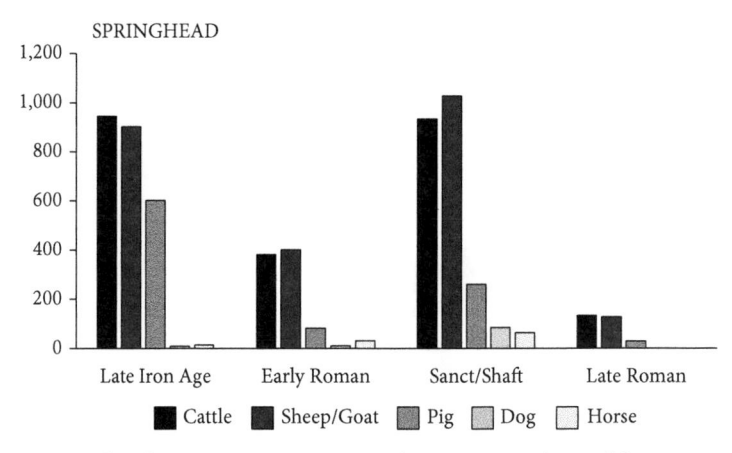

Fig. 9.8 Springhead sanctuary site: mammal species, numbers of fragments (NISP) by phase. Data from Grimm (2011).

observation platforms for the rituals at the spring itself. The bone assemblage yielded c.39,000 animal bones, and it seems that cattle and sheep/goats were the main species for offerings (Fig. 9.8).[19] Their bones were dumped in pits and shafts in the spring area, and there were many young animals. The extent to which animal offerings were a key element in ritual practices at the sanctuary has not, however, been ascertained.

Springhead sanctuary was bisected by a major Roman road, from Dover and Richborough to London. It would have had many travellers passing through, and presumably many of them made offerings while doing so. It is unlikely that these *cultores* would have brought young animals with them, so, if rituals required animal offerings, these were probably obtained locally, possibly at market stalls in the roadside settlement of Springhead.

The overall proportions of species at Springhead do not display the stark selection or concentration on a single species seen at most of the temples discussed so far. The relative percentages are not unlike contemporary settlement sites in the same region, implying that animal offerings were drawn from what was available regionally. It seems that the sanctuary interacted with the local agricultural economy, rather than maintaining exclusive animal resources for ritual use.

The same conclusion can be drawn for the suburban temple just to the south of London, at Tabard Square, Southwark (Fig. 9.9).[20] A pair of Romano-Celtic temples was situated close to the junction of the road from Dover and Richborough, and that from Chichester to London. The animal bones in the

[19] Grimm (2011).   [20] Killock (2015).

Fig. 9.9 Tabard Square, Southwark: reconstruction of an offering at the temple.
Source: From Killock (2015). Illustrated by Chris Mitchell (c.mitchell02@btinternet.com), reproduced by kind permission of Pre-Construct Archaeology (www.pre-construct.com).

main phases of the temple (Fig. 9.10) show species percentages that are dominated numerically by cattle and pigs, which is very similar to non-temple assemblages in Southwark and the City of London.[21] It seems that animal offerings were taken from the urban livestock supply, and may not have been held in enclosures at the temple, or had any distinctive origin. Such integration into urban supply networks can also be suggested for other temple sites in small towns (*vici*) such as Chelmsford, Essex, and Heybridge, Essex.[22]

---

[21] Rielly (2015).
[22] Chelmsford: Luff (1992); King (2005: 350); Heybridge: Johnstone and Albarella (2015). For Gallic sites, see Deschler-Erb and Lachiche (2007); Lepetz (2007).

Anthony C. King   233

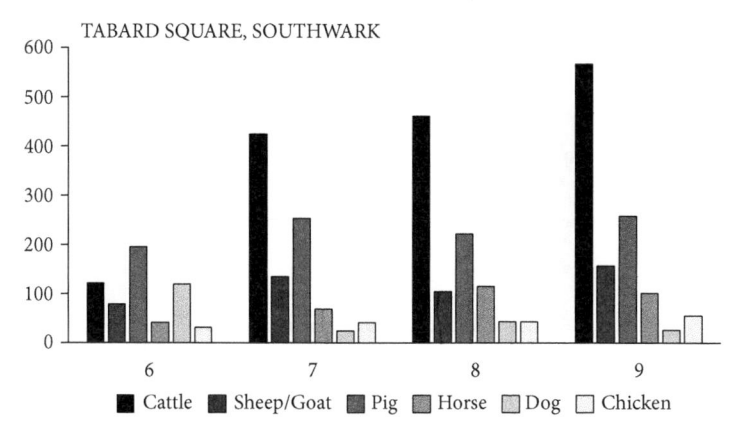

Fig. 9.10 Tabard Square, Southwark: mammal species, numbers of fragments (NISP), by phase. Phases 6–9 are the main period of use and abandonment of the temple sites, late 2nd century to late 4th century or later. Data from Rielly (2015).

So far, all discussion has centred on temples in Roman Britain. Crossing to northern Gaul, from the Late Iron Age into the Roman period, enclosures have been found around temple sites, some very large. Fesques, Seine-Maritime, has an outer enclosure, c.330 by 450 m, and a much smaller inner enclosure, c.45 by 55 m.[23] The boundary to the outer enclosure demonstrated in dramatic fashion to worshippers that they were entering sacred space, as it had suspended human skeletons on display at regular intervals along it.[24] Inside, the substantial open space was presumably for ceremonies, but may also have been a holding area for animals. The c.11,500 bones from the excavation show distinct zonation of deposition, especially in the Late Iron Age phase, with cattle bones dominant in the outer boundary ditch, and pig bones in the majority in the smaller inner enclosure (Fig. 9.11).[25] Different animal offerings were being made at these locations, for reasons that are not known, but which have also been observed on a smaller topographical scale at Chanctonbury Ring), with many pig bones inside the temple area, and cattle dominant in the *temenos* ditch.[26]

The much larger Gallo-Roman sanctuary at *Gisacum*, Vieil-Evreux, Eure, has had no systematic analysis of animal remains, but does have a very

---

[23] Mantel (1997: fig. 6).
[24] Guillot (1997). See also King (2023) for further discussion of this site.
[25] Méniel (1997). There is also zonation of deposition in the parts of the cattle carcasses: heads and hooves in the outer ditch, ribs and upper limbs in the inner enclosure; Méniel (2006: 172–3). See also Méniel (2007).
[26] Sibun (2001); King (2005: 342–4).

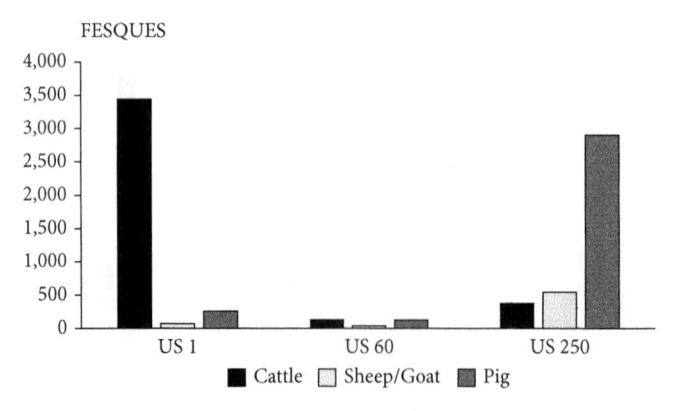

Fig. 9.11 Fesques: mammal species, numbers of fragments (NISP), in the boundary ditch and the inner enclosure. US 1, Late Iron Age outer boundary ditch; US 60, Roman-period outer boundary ditch; US 250, Late Iron Age inner enclosure ditch. Data from Méniel (1997).

extensive, loosely hexagonal enclosure, c.1,500 by 1,500 m, within which a large temple platform, two smaller temples, baths, a theatre, and other monumental buildings were positioned.[27] These by no means filled up all the enclosure, and c.60 per cent of the space appears to have been open and unoccupied. Housing and other buildings were confined beyond the enclosure boundary. Similarly, at Grand, Vosges, a large, almost geometrically circular boundary, 930 m in diameter, appears to have defined a large space around the temple of Apollo Grannus, its amphitheatre, and other buildings.[28] At this site, there were houses within the enclosure, but also much open space, and it may have delineated a sacred area. Both Vieil-Evreux and Grand, and other large temple sites in Gaul, may have had space reserved around them for, among other purposes, raising and holding of animals.[29]

Another Gallic rural sanctuary gives further insight into the animal economy of temple sites. The large site (c.70 ha) of Ribemont-sur-Ancre, Somme, probably acted as an extra-urban destination of pilgrimage, being c.20 km from the *civitas* capital of Amiens (*Samarobriva Ambianorum*). A series of extensive rectilinear courtyards stepped uphill to the main temple, and there were a theatre, baths, and other installations. Ribemont is well known for its spectacular deposits of disarticulated human remains from pre-Roman

---

[27] Péchoux (2010: figs 124–6), based on Guyard and Lepert (1999); Guyard et al. (2014: fig. 27).
[28] Colardelle et al. (1991: 8–9, 41); Dechezleprêtre (2010: 5, 7). For the uncertainties concerning this site, see the discussion by J. Scheid, in Dechezleprêtre (2010: 10–11).
[29] There is relatively little discussion of these enclosures in the literature on Gallic temples, as the focus is mainly on the temple structures themselves. Cf. Horne and King (1980); Fauduet (1993; 2010).

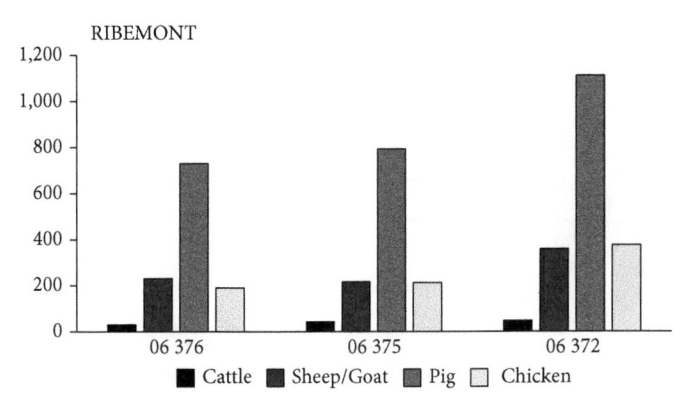

Fig. 9.12 Ribemont-sur-Ancre: mammal species, numbers of fragments (NISP), from well/shaft 34, lowest contexts. Data from Fercoq du Leslay and Lepetz (2008: fig. 3).

levels,[30] but less has been published on the clearly numerous animal bone remains. A single early second-century well or shaft, 40 m deep, in a corner of the second courtyard below the main temple precinct, contained c.20,000 bones.[31] As to be expected from a Gallic sanctuary, the predominant species was pig (Fig. 9.12), many of which had been slaughtered or sacrificed as young adults. This contrasts with the more usual pattern of more juvenile age-at-death seen at British temples.[32] There were few crania, probably because they had been deposited elsewhere, and the parts of the pig carcass in the shaft were overwhelmingly shoulder or ham hock.[33] Ribs, vertebrae, and extremities were, by contrast, under-represented. Wear on exposed articular ends of the bones in the shoulder and ham joints led Lepetz to the suggestion that this had perhaps occurred during smoking or salting processes, but experimental modelling would be needed to establish this more clearly. If this was the case, the preservation of meat at the sanctuary implies large sacrifices, probably at festivals, resulting in a surplus that was consumed at banquets or subsequent non-sacrificial festivals. This assemblage demonstrates the function of food supply that large sanctuaries fulfilled in the overall economy.

If we return to Britain, and the notion of enclosures that may have been for flocks and herds, around or adjacent to rural temples, there are no massive enclosures of the type seen at the Gallic sites just discussed, but several sites have suggestive topographical locations and earlier monuments that may

---

[30] Brunaux (1999); King (2023).   [31] Fercoq du Leslay and Lepetz (2008).
[32] King (2005).   [33] Fercoq du Leslay and Lepetz (2008: fig. 7).

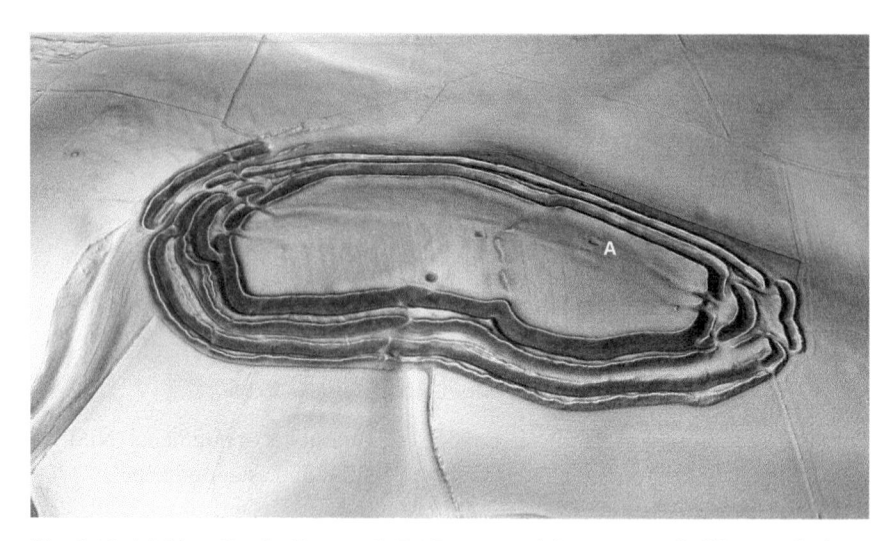

Fig. 9.13 Maiden Castle, Dorset: LiDAR image of the Iron Age hillfort, with the Romano-Celtic temple marked at A. Digital terrain model, resolution 1.0 m, 3D view.

Source: Raw data from the Environment Agency: https://data.gov.uk/. Image created by Rouven Meidlinger—own work, CC BY-SA 4.0, https://commons.wikimedia.org/w/index.php?curid=111,073,754 with additions by A. C. King.

have taken on this role. Uley is adjacent to the largely abandoned Iron Age hillfort of Uley Bury, and Henley Wood temple had a similar relationship with Cadbury Congresbury hillfort. Maiden Castle, Dorset, had a Romano-Celtic temple within the old Iron Age hillfort itself (Fig. 9.13),[34] and the hillfort itself could certainly have been used as a stock enclosure, as it is today. Effectively the hillfort earthworks enclosed the *temenos* of the temple. A similar situation is seen at Brean Down, Somerset, where a Romano-Celtic temple was positioned at the eastern end of a promontory that jutted *c.*1 km westwards into the Bristol Channel.[35] The headland was not a hillfort but had evidence of pre-Roman occupation; in the Roman period it seems to have become sacred space marked by the presence of the temple. Thus, the whole promontory could have been the *temenos* of the shrine and the location for holding animals.

A last site to consider is Hayling Island, Hampshire.[36] The circular temple had a square courtyard surrounding it, both in its Iron Age wooden phase and in the subsequent stone-built Roman phase. The courtyard in the Roman period resembled a peristyle, *c.*40 by 40 m, and was the locus for votive deposition,

[34] Wheeler (1943: 72–8, 131–5); Sharples (1991: 129–30). [35] ApSimon (1965).
[36] King and Soffe (2013).

including c.7,250 bones of sheep and pigs during the main period of ritual activity.[37] Young or full adults were preferred, in a similar pattern to some of the Gallic sanctuaries, and indeed there are many cultural links with Gaul for this temple site.[38] Surrounding the courtyard was an outer ditched enclosure, c.110 by 120 m, which could have functioned as a holding area for animals. It may be possible, however, to extend the temple's landholding further than this. The medieval and present-day field and road pattern has alignments that are parallel to the courtyard and outer ditched enclosure, with a cardinal alignment on true north. Much of the northern part of Hayling Island is taken into the large square formed by this pattern, c.1,300 by 1,300 m, and this may have formed a land allotment to the temple.[39] Indeed, the whole of the island may have been 'sacred' in the Late Iron Age and early Roman period, as there is very little evidence of occupation apart from the temple itself and seasonal salt-working activity on the inland coastal margins.[40]

An implication, therefore, of this chapter is that many rural temples in Britain and Gaul had landed estates, capable of maintaining flocks and herds. There are possible traces of their boundaries detectable in the archaeological and modern landscape. The animal bone assemblages at many of these sites suggest large-scale sacrifice, probably at seasonal or periodic festivals, for which supply of animals may have come from the temple's own holdings. Ultimately, these sacrifices are likely to have formed part of the food supply for worshippers, and in the local economy generally.

So far, all discussion has been archaeological, mainly because relevant historical sources are entirely lacking for Britain and northern Gaul. There are rare inscriptions from the northern and western provinces referring to land being given to sanctuaries, such as the four *centuriae* given to Mercury (and possibly Rosmerta) by L. Bellonius Marcus at Obrigheim, Baden Württemberg.[41] The enigmatic Celtiberian inscription of Botorrita I, Zaragoza, dated probably to the first century BC, may relate to a sacred space that has provision for

---

[37] King (2005: 337–41). There are c.25,000 bones in total from the site.

[38] King and Soffe (2008).

[39] A unit (foot) of 307 mm was identified as in use for the layout of the Iron Age phase of the temple itself. The large square equates to c.4,500 by 4,500 of these feet. This is 703 'local *iugera*' using this module, just under a standard Roman *saltus* of 800 *iugera*. This mensuration scheme is to be explored further in a separate paper. The temple can be linked to Fishbourne and the client kingdom of Togidubnus, and the land may have been donated by the latter; cf. King and Soffe (2013: 26) for further discussion.

[40] A metal-detecting survey of the zone around the temple site has revealed many Iron Age and Roman coins and other artefacts, spreading up 750 m from the temple itself. This supports the suggestion of land around the temple used for deposition, temporary market activity, and possible pilgrimage occupation.

[41] *CIL* XIII.6488; Spickermann (2003: 349).

grazing of cattle.[42] More specific historical references come from Greece, in which animals belonging to gods are specifically referred to, and which may shed light on the possible situation in the Roman north-west provinces. At Amorgos in the Cyclades, the sanctuary of Zeus had regulations on leasing of the temple lands.[43] The tenant could not have cattle grazing there: if he did, the animals would be regarded as sacred and belonging to the god. At Iasos, Caria, Turkey, animals pastured on sacred land had to be branded to show that they belonged to the god.[44] Cattle, possibly on transhumance, passing through the land of the goddess Alea, in Tegea, Arcadia, Peloponnese, could do so freely for a short period of grazing, but, if they stayed longer, a tax had to be paid.[45] Other sections of this inscription show that cult officials kept cattle for offering to the goddess, but could also have personal flocks and herds, which were not destined for sacrifice. The most complex situation is seen on the island of Delos, where the temple of Apollo owned much land, if not, in fact, the whole island. The temple had tenants and grazing animals and also a demand for sacrificial offerings. It was, however, also a place of trade in animals (as well as slaves, for which the island is better known). Breeding and then sale of animals, principally sheep and cattle, from sacred lands was clearly part of the equation on Delos, as was probably also the case at Delphi, where Apollo's sacred pastures lay between the main site and the coast.[46] Not all temples had land devoted to this purpose, however, and urban temples appear to have required contributions of animals for sacrifice from outlying villages, as documented at Oinoanda, Lycia, in the second century AD.[47]

If these types of regulation applied to the Romano-Celtic temples in Britain and Gaul, some clear implications can be deduced. Sanctuaries owned land: in Greek, the *temenos*, a term that has, loosely but conveniently, been used in this chapter for Britain and Gaul. It may have had a Gallo-Brittonic equivalent word, *nemeton*, and possibly also the Latin *area*.[48] Temples could also own animals for offering, or did so by proxy through tenant farmers. Some sites may also have been places of animal-dealing, as part of festivals at the sanctuaries. In the current state of knowledge, we cannot do other than make suggestions about the exact situation at individual temple sites. Hayling was possibly a sacred island, and Brean Down a sacred promontory; Vieil-Evreux and some

---

[42] De Bernardo Stempel (2010); see also Eska (1989); Meid (1993).
[43] SIG³ 963; Sokolowski (1961: no. 105); as discussed by Isager and Skydsgaard (1995: 191). See also Faraone and Naiden (2012).
[44] IG XII.5.2; Isager and Skydsgaard (1995: 191).
[45] IG V.2.3; Guarducci (1952); Sokolowski (1961: no. 67); Isager and Skydsgaard (1995: 183, 191–2).
[46] Isager and Skydsgaard (1995: 192–8).   [47] Rives (2019: 95–7).
[48] Piggott (1978); Isager and Skydsgaard (1995: 182).

of the other temples appear to have had a *temenos/nemeton* that was well defined and could have been for grazing animals destined for offerings. Festivals clearly took place at Uley, Harlow, Hayling, and elsewhere, as seen in the age-at-death data, and confirmed indirectly by the Coligny, Ain, calendar.[49] The evidence for trading fairs and animal-dealing is much less clear and needs further investigation.

Discussion of the role and status of animals at Romano-Celtic temples is, inevitably, speculative, once the hard data, and deductions therefrom, are left behind. It may, however, be possible to move forward in future research. The anatomical exploration of breed distinctiveness and conformation, as suggested by Levitan for Uley, could be taken further. New techniques, especially isotope analysis of teeth,[50] could establish whether animal offerings were local to a temple site, and therefore possibly a sacred flock or herd, or were brought in from a distance, and therefore animals accompanying pilgrims or visitors to a sanctuary. More discussion and searching for evidence of secondary products, such as wool or leather, are needed, since these valuable commodities may have been an integral element of the economy of a temple. At all events, it is clear that animals and associated landholdings were a significant sacred and economic focus for many rural Romano-Celtic temples. Their influence on the day-to-day lives of Gauls and Britons is increasingly appreciated and understood.

Acknowledgements

This chapter was given as a paper at the conference on 'The Economics of Roman Religion', Oxford, September 2016, and also at the XV Workshop of *Fontes Epigraphici Religionum Caeticarum Antiquarum* (FERCAN), Lisbon, October 2016. At both, the author benefited from helpful suggestions and discussion, and would like to thank Patrizia De Bernardo Stempel, Marietta Horster, Wolfgang Spickermann, Silvia Valenzuela-Lamas, Koen Verboven, and Greg Woolf for their valuable contributions.

---

[49] The Coligny calendar (Duval and Pinault 1986; Green 1997: 37; Le Contel and Verdier 1997; Goudineau and Verdier 2006: 45–52; Zavaroni 2007) is the best evidence for the existence of a Romano-Celtic listing of festivals. Henig (1982; 1984: 26–32) relates festivals mainly to the Roman calendar, but there was clearly a pre-Roman tradition, seen in the archaeological continuity from Late Iron Age to Roman age-at-death data from temple sites (King 2005). For the traditional Celtic festivals, see Green (1997: 34–7).

[50] The potential of the technique, in this respect, can be seen in a case study on Owslebury, Hampshire, cattle teeth (Minniti et al. 2014). Hartmann et al. (2013) have also suggested importation of caprines to Jerusalem to service sacrificial needs, on the basis of isotope analysis.

References

Adams, G. W. (2009). *Power and Religious Acculturation in Romano-Celtic Society: An Examination of Archaeological Sites in Gloucestershire* (BAR British Series 477). Oxford.

Andrews, P., Biddulph, E., Hardy, A., and Brown, R. (2011). *Settling the Ebbsfleet Valley. High Speed 1 Excavations at Springhead and Northfleet, Kent. The Late Iron Age, Roman, Saxon, and Medieval Landscape*, vol. 1: *The Sites*. Oxford.

ApSimon, A. M. (1965). 'The Roman Temple on Brean Down, Somerset', *Proceedings of the University of Bristol Spelaeological Society* 10: 195–258.

Beech, M. (2006). 'Animal Remains: Evidence of Animal Sacrifice', in C. Evans and I. Hodder (eds), *Marshland Communities and Cultural Landscapes: The Haddenham Project*, vol. 2. Cambridge, 369–96.

Brun, H., and Leguilloux, M. (2013). 'Rituels sacrificiels et offrandes animales dans le Sarapieion C de Délos', in G. Ekroth and J. Wallensten (eds), *Bones, Behaviour and Belief: The Zooarchaeological Evidence as a Source for Ritual Practice in Ancient Greece and Beyond*. Stockholm, 167–79.

Brunaux, J.-L. (1999). 'Ribemont-sur-Ancre (Somme): Bilan préliminaire et nouvelles hypothèses', *Gallia* 56: 177–283.

Budei, J. (2016). *Gallorömische Heiligtümer: Neue Studien zur Lage und den räumlichen Bezügen*. Mainz and Ruhpolding.

Colardelle, M., et al. (1991). *Grand, prestigieux sanctuaire de la Gaule* (Les Dossiers d'Archéologie 162). Dijon.

De Bernardo Stempel, P. (2010). 'La ley del 1er bronce de Botorrita: Uso agropecuario de un encinar sagrado', in F. Burillo Mozota (ed.), *VI Simposio sobre Celtiberos: Ritos y Mitos*. Zaragoza, 123–45.

Dechezleprêtre, T. (2010). *Sur les traces d'Apollon: Grand la Gallo-Romaine*. Paris.

Deschler-Erb, S., and Lachiche, C. (2007). 'De la viande pour les hommes et pour les dieux: Sa gestion dans deux villes de la Suisse romaine', in Van Andringa (2007), 107–31.

Duval, P.-M., and Pinault, G. (1986) (eds). *Recueil des inscriptions gauloises* (R.I.G.), vol. 3: *Les calendriers de Coligny et Villards d'Heria*. Paris.

Eska, J. F. (1989). *Towards an Interpretation of the Hispano-Celtic Inscription of Botorrita*. Innsbruck.

Faraone, C. A., and Naiden, F. S. (2012) (eds). *Greek and Roman Animal Sacrifice: Ancient Victims, Modern Observers*. Cambridge.

Fauduet, I. (1993). *Atlas des sanctuaires romano-celtiques de Gaule: Les fanums*. Paris.

Fauduet, I. (2010). *Les Temples de tradition celtique*. 2nd edn. Paris.

Fercoq du Leslay, G., and Lepetz, S. (2008). 'Manger dans les sanctuaires: salaisons et viande fraîche à Ribemont-sur-Ancre', in S. Lepetz and W. Van Andringa (eds), *Archéologie du sacrifice animal en Gaule romaine: Rituels et pratiques alimentaires*. Montagnac, 201–6.

Goudineau, C., and Verdier, P. (2006). 'Religion et science', in C. Goudineau (ed.), *Religion et société en Gaule*. Paris, 26–77.

Green, M. J. (1997). *Exploring the World of the Druids*. London.

Grimm, J. (2011). 'Animal Bone, Springhead Sanctuary', in C. Barnett, J. I. McKinley, E. Stafford, J. M. Grimm, and C. J. Stevens, *Settling the Ebbsfleet Valley. High Speed 1 Excavations at Springhead and Northfleet, Kent. The Late Iron Age, Roman, Saxon, and Medieval Landscape*, vol. 3: *Late Iron Age to Roman Human Remains and Environmental Reports*. Oxford, 15–31.

Guarducci, M. (1952). 'La legge dei tegeati intorno ai pascoli di Alea', *Rivista di Filologia e di Istruzione Classica* 80: 49–68.

Guillot, H. (1997). 'Analyse taphonomique et anthropologique des restes humains', in Mantel (1997), 59–80.

Guyard, L., Bertaudière, S., Cormier, S., and Fontaine, C. (2014). 'Démantèlement d'un grand sanctuaire civique de la Cité des Aulerques Eburovices au IIIe s. apr. J.-C. Le site du Vieil-Evreux entre 250 et 350 apr. J.-C.', *Gallia* 71/1: 39–50.

Guyard, L., and Lepert, T. (1999). 'Le Vieil-Evreux: Ville-sanctuaire gallo-romaine', *Archéologia* 359: 20–9.

Haeussler, R., and King, A. C. (2008) (eds). *Continuity and Innovation in Religion in the Roman West*, vol. 2 (Journal of Roman Archaeology Supplementary Series 67.2). Portsmouth, RI.

Hambleton, E. (1999). *Animal Husbandry Regimes in Iron Age Britain: A Comparative Study of Faunal Assemblages from Iron Age Sites* (BAR British Series 282). Oxford.

Hartmann, G., Bar-Oz, G., Bouchnick, R., and Reich, R. (2013). 'The Pilgrimage Economy of Early Roman Jerusalem (1st Century BCE–70 CE) Reconstructed from the δ^{15}N and δ^{13}C Values of Goat and Sheep Remains', *JAS* 40: 4369–76.

Henig, M. (1982). 'Seasonal Feasts in Roman Britain', *OJA* 1: 213–23.

Henig, M. (1984). *Religion in Roman Britain*. London.

Horne, P. D., and King, A. C. (1980). 'Romano-Celtic Temples in Continental Europe: A Gazetteer of those with Known Plans', in W. Rodwell (ed.), *Temples, Churches and Religion: Recent Research in Roman Britain* (BAR British Series 77). Oxford, 369–555.

Isager, S., and Skydsgaard, J. E. (1995). *Ancient Greek Agriculture: An Introduction*. London.

Jackson, R., and Burleigh, G. (2007). 'The Senuna Treasure and Shrine at Ashwell (Herts)', in R. Haeussler and A. C. King (eds), *Continuity and Innovation in Religion in the Roman West*, vol. 1 (Journal of Roman Archaeology Supplementary Series 67). Portsmouth, RI, 37–54.

Johnstone, C., and Albarella, U. (2015). 'The Late Iron Age and Romano-British Mammal and Bird Bone Assemblage from Elms Farm, Heybridge, Essex', in

M. Atkinson and S. J. Preston (eds), 'Heybridge: A Late Iron Age and Roman Settlement, Excavations at Elms Farm 1993–5', *Internet Archaeology* 40, http://dx.doi.org/10.11141/ia.40.1.albarella

Jones, S., and King, A. C. (2018). 'Animal Bone', in R. Jackson and G. Burleigh (eds), Dea Senuna: *Treasure, Cult and Ritual at Ashwell, Hertfordshire* (British Museum Research Publication 194). London, 314–20.

Kiernan, P. (2012). 'Pagan Pilgrimage in Rome's Western Provinces', *HEROM. Journal on Hellenistic and Roman Material Culture* 1: 79–106.

Killock, D. (2015) (ed.). *Temples and Suburbs: Excavations at Tabard Square, Southwark* (Pre-Construct Archaeology Monograph 18). London.

King, A. C. (1984). 'Animal Bones and the Dietary Identity of Military and Civilian Groups in Roman Britain, Germany and Gaul', in T. F. C. Blagg and A. C. King (eds), *Military and Civilian in Roman Britain* (BAR British Series 136). Oxford, 187–217.

King, A. C. (1999). 'Diet in the Roman World: A Regional Inter-Site Comparison of the Mammal Bones', *JRA* 12: 168–202.

King, A. C. (2005). 'Animal Remains from Temples in Roman Britain', *Britannia*, 36: 329–69.

King, A. C. (2007). 'Characterizing Assemblages of Votive Offerings at Romano-Celtic Temples in Britain', in M. Hainzmann (ed.), *Auf den Spuren keltischer Götterverehung. Akten des 5. F.E.R.C.AN.-Workshop, Graz, 9–12 October 2003* (Mitteilungen der Prähistorischen Kommission 64). Vienna, 183–96.

King, A. C. (2008). 'Coins and Coin Hoards from Romano-Celtic Temples in Britain', in Haeussler and King (2008), 25–42.

King, A. C. (2023). 'Religious Individualisation *in extremis*: Human Remains from Romano-Celtic Temples in Britain and Gaul', in R. Haeussler and A. C. King (eds), *Religious Individualisation: Archaeological, Iconographic and Epigraphic Case Studies from the Roman World*. Oxford, 181–207.

King, A. C., and Soffe, G. (2008). 'Hayling Island: A Gallo-Roman Temple in Britain', in D. Rudling (ed.), *Ritual Landscapes of Roman South-East Britain*. Great Dunham and Oxford, 139–44.

King, A. C., and Soffe, G. (2013). *A Sacred Island: Iron Age, Roman and Saxon Temples and Ritual on Hayling Island*. Winchester.

Le Contel, J.-M., and Verdier, P. (1997). *Un calendrier celtique: Le calendrier gaulois de Coligny*. Paris.

Legge, A. J., and Dorrington, E. J. (1985). 'The Animal Bones', in N. E. France and B. M. Gobel (eds), *The Romano-British Temple at Harlow*. Gloucester.

Legge, A. J., Williams, J., and Williams, P. (2000). 'Lambs to the Slaughter: Sacrifice at Two Roman Temples in Southern England', in P. Rowley-Conwy (ed.), *Animal Bones, Human Societies*. Oxford, 152–7.

Lepetz, S. (2007). 'Boucherie, sacrifice et marché à la viande en Gaule romaine septentrionale: l'apport de l'archéozoologie', in Van Andringa (2007), 73–105.

Levitan, B. (1993). 'Vertebrate Remains', in Woodward and Leach (1993), 257–301.

Luff, R.-M. (1992). 'The Faunal Remains', in N. P. Wickendon, *The Temple and Other Sites in the North-Eastern Sector of Caesaromagus* (CBA Research Report 75). London, 116–24.

Mantel, E. (1997) (ed.). *Le Sanctuaire de Fesques « Le Mont du Val aux Moines » Seine Maritime* (Nord-Ouest Archéologie 8). Berck-sur-Mer.

Meid, W. (1993). *Die erste Botorrita-Inschrift: Interpretation eines keltiberischen Sprachdenkmals*. Innsbruck.

Méniel, P. (1997). 'La faune du sanctuaire de Fesques « Le Mont du Val-aux-Moines »', in Mantel (1997), 81–105.

Méniel, P. (2006). 'Religion et sacrifices d'animaux', in C. Goudineau (ed.), *Religion et société en Gaule*. Paris, 164–75.

Méniel, P. (2007). 'La boucherie et les sacrifices bovins en Gaule aux IIe et Ier siècles avant notre ère', in Van Andringa (2007), 227–47.

Minniti, C., Valenzuela-Lamas, S., Evans, J., and Albarella, U. (2014). 'Widening the Market: Strontium Isotope Analysis on Cattle Teeth from Owslebury (Hampshire, UK) Highlights Changes in Livestock Supply between the Iron Age and the Roman Period', *Journal of Archaeological Science*, 42: 305–14.

Péchoux, L. (2010). *Les Sanctuaires de périphérie urbaine en Gaule romaine*. Montagnac.

Piggott, S. (1978). '*Nemeton, temenos, bothros*: Sanctuaries of the Ancient Celts', in Accademia Nazionale dei Lincei (ed.), *I Celti e la loro cultura nell'epoca pre-Romana e Romana nella Britannia*. Rome, 37–54.

Rainsford, C., King, A. C., Jones, S., Hooker, R., and Burleigh, G. (2021). 'Cremated Animal Bone from Two Ritual/Ceremonial Sites in Britannia', in S. Deschler-Erb, U. Albarella, S. Valenzuela Lamas, and G. Rasbach (eds), *Roman Animals in Ritual and Funerary Contexts: Proceedings of the 2nd Meeting of the Zooarchaeology of the Roman Period Working Group, Basel, 1st–4th February 2018* (Römisch-Germanischen Kommission Kolloquien zur Vor- und Frühgeschichte 26). Frankfurt-am-Main, 185–99.

Rielly, K. (2015). 'Animal Bone', in Killock (2015), 206–24.

Rives, J. B. (2019). 'Animal Sacrifice and Euergetism in the Hellenistic and Roman Polis', *Religion in the Roman Empire*, 5/1: 83–102.

Rudling, D. (2001). 'Chanctonbury Ring Revisited: The Excavations of 1988–91', *Sussex Archaeological Collections*, 139: 75–121.

Sharples, N. M. (1991). *Maiden Castle*. London.

Sibun, L. (2001). 'The Animal Bone Assemblage', in Rudling (2001), 108–9.

Smith, A. (2001). *The Differential Use of Constructed Sacred Space in Southern Britain, from the Late Iron Age to the 4th Century AD* (BAR British Series 318). Oxford.

Sokolowski, F. (1961). *Lois sacrés des cités grecques.* Paris.

Spickermann, W. (2003). *Germania Superior* (Religionsgeschichte des römischen Germanien 1). Tübingen.

Stanford, S. C. (1974). *Croft Ambrey.* Hereford.

Tomlin, R. S. O. (2017). 'A Fourth-Century Curse Tablet from Uley', in R. Haeussler and A. C. King (eds), *Celtic Religions in the Roman Period: Personal, Local, and Global.* Aberystwyth.

Van Andringa, W. (2007) (ed.), *Sacrifices, marché de la viande et pratiques alimentaires dans les cités du monde romain* (Food & History 5.1), Turnhout.

Watts, L., and Leach, P. (1996). *Henley Wood, Temples and Cemetery: Excavations 1962–69 by the Late Ernest Greenfield and Others* (CBA Research Report 99). York.

Wheeler, R. E. M. (1943). *Maiden Castle, Dorset* (Report of the Research Committee of the Society of Antiquaries of London 12). Oxford.

Woodward, A., and Leach, P. (1993) (eds). *The Uley Shrines: Excavation of a Ritual Complex on West Hill, Uley, Gloucestershire: 1977–9* (Historic Buildings and Monuments Commission Archaeological Report 17). London.

Wythe, D. (2008). 'An Analysis of Coin Finds from 75 Roman Temple Sites in Britain', in Haeussler and King (2008), 43–65.

Zavaroni, A. (2007). *On the Structure and Terminology of the Gaulish Calendar* (BAR International Series 1609). Oxford.

10

Sacred Gifts, Profane Uses? Transfers and the Roman Religious Sphere

Marta García Morcillo

Introduction

To explore gift-giving throughout history is to examine the interplay between those who give and those who receive, the main facet of which is the expression of a symbolic alliance between the two parties. The different possible aims, contexts, and discursive interpretations that shape this practice complicate its study and analysis. The multidimensionality of the gift, as well as its fundamental role as a factor in regulating human relationships, has been—and continues to be—the focus of renewed scholarly attention and of prolific debates in the social and human sciences since the publication of Marcel Mauss's influential 'Essai sur le don'.[1]

In ancient Rome, gifts made by individuals were subject to moral considerations about the aims and nature of these practices.[2] Beyond the debate over their altruistic or utilitarian purposes, legal texts of the imperial age viewed donations and gift exchange as mechanisms that channelled the acquisition and transfer of wealth, an action that facilitated economic profit and that could both enrich and impoverish. The aim of protecting inheritances and avoiding conflicts over the right of possession ultimately explains why donations needed to be measured and evaluated in monetary terms. Their pecuniary value opened the door to the transformation of gifts into marketable commodities, as well as to the acceptability of coins as valid forms of gifts. In legal literature, gift-giving was regarded and discussed as an instrument of wealth that was fully integrated within the monetary economy. Fundamental works on the subject, such as Cicero's *De officiis* (*On Duties*) and Seneca's *De beneficiis*

---

[1] Mauss (1923–4).
[2] On recent scholarly interest in gift-giving in classical antiquity, see Satlow (2013), Carlà and Gori (2014), and Coffee (2017).

(*On Benefits*), as well as imperial legal texts, offer suggestions for understanding how Romans conceived of and regulated donations in the private sphere. But what happened when donations transcended private affairs and relationships between individuals and entered into the realm of the sacred? Were they submitted to the same norms and considerations? This chapter looks at private donations made with a religious purpose, including votive gifts, monetary contributions, and acts of private generosity, or *liberalitas*, addressed to sacred places. It will also discuss how Romans faced the complex issue of the mutability of gifts—namely, how their status changed once they had been deposited in temples and sanctuaries. To what extent could donations with a religious motive be appropriated, alienated, and ultimately transformed into instruments of *negotium*? The following discussion is concerned primarily with distinguishing the different levels of abstraction that were implicitly or explicitly perceived by the Romans within a practice that was defined not only by the intentions of the actors but also by its capacity to transform the nature and function of objects in various ways.

Gift-Giving in Ancient Rome: Concepts and Regulations

In Rome, gift exchange addressed fundamental moral questions around the ideas of giving without the expectation of return, reciprocity, and utilitarianism. The motivations for and limits of *liberalitas* lie at the heart of crucial debates on the function of public munificence and civic euergetism, but they also concern social relationships—whether symmetrical or asymmetrical—between individuals.[3] The moral writings of Cicero and Seneca the Younger closely engage with the ideals, problems, and dangers attached to gift-giving as an instrument that fundamentally shaped social relationships and status but that was also a medium of economic gain. These issues were extensively discussed within legal literature, where we find valuable conceptual and practical responses to the malleable nature of gifts as actions that transcended various spheres of society, including sacred contexts, and that also served to challenge inherited wealth.

---

[3] On Roman euergetism and the limits of generosity, see the classic work by Veyne (1976); cf. also Lomas and Cornell (2003). On patronage and *amicitia*, see Verboven (2002, 2011), Zuiderhoek (2007, 2009), and Colpaert (2014). On gift exchange as a multidimensional phenomenon, see Satlow (2013: 1–2), Carlà and Gori (2014: 31–6), and Verboven (2014). On the interactions between gift-giving and power in Greek cities, see Domingo Gygax (2013). A recent contribution edited by Domingo Gygax and Zuiderhoek (2021) investigates public benefactions in Greek cities up to late antiquity.

One of the main themes of Cicero's late moral treatise *De officiis* (44 BC) is a concern over damaging liberal practices that were ultimately driven by greed (*cupiditas*), ostentation (*ostentatio*), and vanity (*vanitas*).[4] Cicero's model proposes an ideal in which the giver should always follow the principle of reciprocity and gratitude, and conduct himself with moderation, temperance, and justice.[5] The legitimate enlargement of the patrimony of the *vir bonus* should always, in the orator's view, be compatible with a respect for private fortunes and public resources.[6] Cicero's call for restraint (*temperantia*) and modesty (*modestia*) is presented as an antidote to the *perturbationes animi* that disturb rational decisions.[7] Such intemperate decisions could affect the generous individuals who aimed to help others with their acts of *liberalitas*.[8] In those cases, Cicero admits his preference for services (*opera*) rather than monetary gifts (*pecunia*) that could end up wasting the giver's own fortune,[9] and he recommends setting a limit to expenditures according to the personal wealth of the donor.[10]

Moderation and temperance are also virtues that feature strongly in Seneca's *De beneficiis*, in which benefits—such as gifts or services—become the centre of the social relationships and characterization of the *vir bonus*.[11] Seneca's Stoic ideal of *beneficium* is that of a purely altruistic act, in complete opposition to *negotiatio*.[12] An essential feature of Seneca's concept of *beneficium* is its detachment from the things given, which are merely signs of meritorious gestures (*meritorum signa, non merita*), regardless of their value. The real benefit lies in the spirit (*animus*) and the will (*voluntas*) of the giver.[13] This philosophical principle also determines Seneca's classification of the different categories of *beneficia* according to their relevance.[14] The most important of these are conceptual (*libertas, pudicitia, mens bona, securitas*), followed by

---

[4] Cic. *Off.* 1.42–4. Gift-giving in the *De officiis* is discussed in detail by Feuvrier-Prévolat (1985). On the moral principles and economic utilitarianism in the same work, see Lotito (1981) and Narducci (1985).

[5] Cic. *Off.* 1.45–7. Generosity should, in this regard, look at benefiting those with whom the giver had a social relationship of friendship or clientelism (Cic. *Off.* 49–50). On the social and economic importance of these bonds in the late Republic, see the fundamental contributions by Deniaux (1993) and Verboven (2002).

[6] Cic. *Off.* 1.52.   [7] Cic. *Off.* 1.93.   [8] Cic. *Off.* 2.55–6.

[9] Cic. *Off.* 2.52; 2.54: *multi enim patrimonia effuderunt inconsulte largiendo.*

[10] Cic. *Off.* 2.55–64.

[11] On the *De beneficiis* as a social guide, see Chaumartin (1985) and Griffin (2003).

[12] See, e.g., *Ben.* 2.31.2: *Non enim in vicem aliquid sibi reddi voluit: aut non fuit beneficium sed negotiatio.* ('For he had no wish that I should give him anything in exchange. Otherwise, it would have been, not a benefaction, but a bargaining' (trans. J. W. Basore)). The giver should never expect compensation, or the return of the thing given; cf. Sen. *Ben.* 2.31.4.

[13] Sen. *Ben.* 1.5.1–2.

[14] On Seneca's criteria of value and his categorization of *beneficia*, see also Wolkenhauer (2014: 44–8).

those that conform to domestic values and the identity of the *pater familias*.[15] The next category of benefits is linked with the *cursus honorum* of the giver, and includes money, but not in excess.[16] Seneca places the benefits that are pleasurable and desirable, but dispensable, at the lowest level. Some of these benefits are objects that are not intrinsically valuable but have become so by time or place.[17] Interestingly, these acts of generosity should, in the author's view, preferably consist of durable and imperishable things that maintain, as far as possible, the memory of the benefit. He also specifies his preference for silver rather than coined silver (*libentius donabo argentum factum quam signatum*), and for statues rather than clothes, which were more vulnerable to deterioration.[18] Here, Seneca addresses the issue of the symbolic value of the gift, a sign that represents a benefit, but that is also subject to social, cultural, and economic valuation. Even if the essence of the benefit lies in the spirit and will of both the giver and receiver, Seneca makes it clear that social considerations made certain gifts—material or immaterial—more adequate, distinguished, and memorable than others.

Ultimately, both Cicero and Seneca acknowledge the essential difference between the object given and its mutable status, on the one hand, and the very purpose of the action of giving, on the other. As we shall see, the Romans' awareness of the dynamic nature of donations is fundamental to understanding gifts, offerings, and transfers of goods in sacred contexts and linked to cult places.

Roman law was particularly concerned with the transfer of gifts and subsequent consequences, since gifts were sources and instruments of enrichment, but also of impoverishment. To regulate their use and prevent conflicts surrounding the right of possession and the transfer of properties, gifts needed to be measurable in money.[19] Preoccupations with corruption and the notable increase of certain private fortunes through donations had already met with a response by the end of the third century BC in the form of the *Lex Publicia de cereis* (209 BC) and the *Lex Cincia de donis et muneribus* (204 BC).[20] Roman

---

[15] Sen. *Ben.* 1.11.1–4; 3.13.3.   [16] Sen. *Ben.* 1.11.5.
[17] Sen. *Ben.* 1.11.5. Seneca includes books and wine on this list.
[18] Sen. *Ben.* 1.12.1. The reason for this preference relates to criticism towards those who tended to express gratitude for acts of generosity only as long as the object was still present and in use.
[19] On the impact of money in gift exchange, see Godelier (1999) and Carlà and Gori (2014: 14).
[20] The *Lex Publicia de cereis* addressed traditional gift exchanges during the *Saturnalia*, which limited gifts to symbolic candles in order to prevent *clientes* from giving gifts with selfish aims to their patrons (Macrob. *Sat.* 1.7.33). The *Lex Cincia* included exceptions to general prohibitions, such as the acceptance of gifts by advocates, whose work was at that time non-remunerated, as well as donations between relatives. Its main aim was to avoid gifts in excess of certain amounts. On the *Lex Cincia* and its exceptions, see Casavola (1960) and Recorder de Casso (2005).

jurists of the imperial age elaborated some interesting thoughts about gift-giving and the complexities involved in its regulation. These legal texts are complementary to the social and philosophical considerations already discussed. Gift-giving between individuals was defined as a *donatio*, an action that implied the voluntary transfer of a property. Roman jurisprudence opposed *liberalitas* (generosity) to *negotium* (business), but still allowed actions that combined both.[21] The *donatio* was defined by its *liberalitas*, but even more so by the *animus donandi* of the giver, which in juridical terms referred to the desire to accomplish the agreement.[22] One important aspect to consider here is that *donatio* was not a typical juridical act, but a *causa* of juridical acts that were accomplished through unilateral or bilateral agreements, and that left open the possibility of revocability until their execution was complete.[23] The case of the transfer of property or *mancipatio* shows how legal sources incorporated the conceptualization of *donationes* as symbolic acts in the regulation of these practices. The *mancipatio* was a formal act of acquisition of *res mancipi* (things that could be sold or alienated), which was originally performed through the ritual of weighing a piece of bronze on a scale (*per aes et libram*).[24] The bronze piece was later replaced by the symbolic payment of a coin (a *sestertius*) to the donor, who confirmed the transaction through an oral phrase: *mihi emptus*. This innovation transformed the act into what the jurist Gaius calls an *imaginaria venditio*.[25] Numerous inscriptions from the imperial age include the formula *mancipatio donationis causa nummo uno* to describe this sort of donation through *mancipatio*, sealed by the symbolic handling of a coin. This ritual is typically attested in inscriptions referring to donations of funerary *loca*, *monumenta*, and *ollae*.[26] Rather than a seeing this as a sign of surviving archaism, we should view the endurance of this symbolic ritual as a dynamic act that was readapted to fit a 'monetary' way of thinking. The performative nature of this economic transaction was aimed at reinforcing the

---

[21] On the opposition between both concepts, see *Dig.* 39.6.35.3 (*Paul, 6 ad l. Iul. et Pap.*). On donation as business, see also a passage by Ulpian, *Dig.* 39.5.18 pr. (*71 ad ed.*).

[22] While Biondi (1961: 35–6) considers both ideas essential for the recognition of a *donatio*, Michel (1962: 237–40, 293) believes that the validity of the act depended on the *animus donandi* and not on the more vague and subjective aim of *liberalitas*.

[23] Typical agreements were the *in iure cessio, mancipatio, pactum, stipulatio, traditio*.

[24] Varro describes the ritual of *per aes et libram* and links it with the institution of *nexum* (*LL* 7.105). On the origins and development of the *mancipatio*, see Watson (1968: 16–20) and Diósdi (1970: 62–74).

[25] Gaius describes in detail the ritual of the *mancipatio* in his *Institutiones*, 1.119–22. The procedure included oral witnesses and was typically concerned with transactions involving slaves, animals, and estates.

[26] Examples from Rome are analysed in Caldelli, Crea, and Ricci (2004: 312–24).

completion of the agreement and the visibility of the *animus donandi*.[27] The conceptualization of gift-giving as a revocable practice defined by pure altruism was challenged by cases where gifts were subject to conditions and modal restrictions, as these actions often questioned the very nature of *liberalitas*.[28] Essentially, Roman law differentiated between two forms of *condiciones*: those that depended on something happening at a certain point, and those that required an action by the beneficiary of the donation, legate, or inheritance.[29]

The most characteristic form of gift *sub condicione* was the *donatio mortis causa*. This was essentially an instrument through which a donor could secure the transfer of a property to a recipient in preference over one's heir, should the donor's death occur.[30] The *donatio mortis causa* was thus conceived as a form of protecting the owner's patrimony, in addition to testamentary legacies. The self-interested aim of this practice and its revocability blurs its very definition as a liberal act. Roman jurists also expressed their concern about the use of *donationes mortis causa* by insolvent donors, and above all as a regular formula to replace wills, which were charged with a fixed tax of 5 per cent (*vicesima hereditatium*).[31] This also explains certain attempts to set a monetary limit on donations.[32]

Funerary Donations and *res religiosae*

Self-interest was also the motivation behind many funerary foundations and donations, often of testamentary nature.[33] This was the case with monetary donations made to individuals, *collegia,* and municipalities with the purpose of celebrating the birthday of the deceased (*dies natalis*), but also with the aim of protecting funerary places within the nuclear family group.[34] This practice,

---

[27] The ancient Roman ritual of *per aes et libram* is interpreted by Mauss (1923–4: 47–53) as an example of the reminiscence of a 'primitive' idea of gift exchange in Roman society.

[28] Valens comments that donations should have very light conditions, *Dig.* 35.1.87 (*1 fideic.*).

[29] *Dig.* 35.1.21 (*Iul. 31 dig.*). On temporal conditions in donations, see again Julian, *Dig.* 39.5.2.5 (*60 dig.*). On conditional donations in general, see García Morcillo (2014).

[30] This is clearly explained in a passage by Marcian, *Dig.* 39.6.1 pr. (*9 inst.*). The *donatio mortis causa* was usually arranged in the event of a situation that could lead to the death of the donor, such as illness, dangerous journeys, etc.; see *Dig.* 39.6.35.3 (*Ulp. 32 ad Sab.*). See Amelotti (1953), Champlin (1991), and Rüger (2011) for extensive discussion of this practice.

[31] On the economic impact of the *vicesima* for propertied classes during the principate, see Günther (2005).

[32] See, e.g., the second-century BC *Lex Furia testamentaria*, Gai. *Inst.* 4.225.

[33] Andreau (1977) distinguishes between foundations aimed at the benefit of the donor and those directed towards other individuals, communities, and public institutions.

[34] On funerary foundations, see the classical works by de Visscher (1947–8; 1948; 1955; 1963). On endowments to *collegia*, see Tran (2006: 174–203) and Liu (2008: 231–56).

which appeared during the first century AD and increased substantially from the second century AD, provided a regular source of income to professional *collegia* specifically dedicated to commemorating the memory of the dead.[35] During funerary festivals such as the *Parentalia* and *Ferialia*, gifts in memory of the dead were deposited on graves. In this context, the objects donated and deposited at the tombs served as symbols of the social identity of both the donor and the deceased.[36] Burial places were consecrated to the Di Manes and considered *res religiosae*, a subcategory of *res divini iuris*, which concerned all things that belonged to divine law.[37] As such, they were *extra commercium*, and thus non-tradeable. However, the *ius sepulchri* that permitted their funerary use could be transferred, donated, and sold.[38] At times, foundations and *fideicommissa* could also involve freedmen who would continue the memory of the patron.[39] A well-known example of these practices includes the conditional donation through a *mancipatio* of a garden, building, and enclosed vineyard by T. Flavius Syntrophus to his freedman T. Flavius Aethales.[40] The condition specified that the freedman and his *conliberti* should create a foundation to carry out the rituals linked to the cult of the dead and the memory of Syntrophus, a practice that should also be continued by the heirs of the first generation of *liberti*. The imposed *condicio* through *stipulatio* thus protected the donation from future transfers and from other potential uses of the property. But for how long? This is a question that is impossible to answer, as we do not know the duration of these legal dispositions.[41] Similarly, an inscription from Ostia dated to the beginning of the second century AD included the will of Iunia Libertas regarding a walled property composed of *horti, aedificia*, and *tabernae*.[42] The property was given in *usufructus* to her freedmen and

---

[35] See, e.g., *CIL* VI.1872 (Rome), concerning a *corpus piscatorum et urinatorum*; *AE* 1987, 198–9 (Ostia), regarding a *collegium dendrophorum Ostiensium*.

[36] Following Bourdieu, Denzey Lewis (2013) analyses the function of grave gifts in the Roman world as a means of marking and redefining social identity and status.

[37] In a fundamental text, Gaius differentiates between human (and thus patrimonial) and divine (extra-patrimonial) things (*Inst*. 2.9–11). This text is analysed in detail by Thomas (2002) and Rives (2012: 167–75). On the changing regulations concerning alienable things in late antiquity, and particularly the controversies regarding properties of the Church, see Carlà-Uhink (2021).

[38] Gaius, *Inst*. 2.7. Ulpian specifies that, even if a place and its monuments could be sold or donated, only public authorities could change the status of a burial place, *Dig*. 11.7.12 (*Ulp. 25 ed.*); 11.7.14 (*Ulp. 15 ed.*).

[39] The regulation of these practices is discussed in several passages from the *Digest*; see, e.g., *Dig*. 30.114.15 (*Marcian., inst.*); *Dig*. 31.88.6 (*Scaev. 3 resp.*); *Dig*. 31.77.11 (*Pap. 8 resp.*); *Dig*. 31.77.28 (*Pap. 8 resp.*); *Dig*. 32.38.1–3 (*Scaev. 19 dig.*) *Dig*. 32.94 (*Valens. 2 fideic.*); *Dig*. 35.1.108 (*Scaev. 19 dif.*)

[40] *CIL* VI.10239; *FIRA* III 94 (second to third centuries AD).

[41] On this particular case and the legal issue of the durability of Syntrophus' will, see Bruck (1954: 77–81).

[42] *AE* 1940, 94 and *AE* 1993, 418. On this inscription and the details of the will, see de Visscher (1948) and Blanch Nougués (2007).

their descendants with the explicit prohibition of being sold, alienated, or donated, and with the obligation to reuse the income from the *horti* for the preservation of Iunia's tomb and the celebration of the *Parentalia, Violae*, and *Rosae*. These self-interested donations linked to *res religiosae* thus shared a preoccupation with preserving private property as a space in which the memory of the deceased could be displayed and ritualistically maintained for as long as possible. As numerous inscriptions show, these activities were private affairs that concerned individuals, even if the *loca* were ultimately a matter of *res divini iuris*. Funerary inscriptions frequently mention prohibitions and fines aimed at preventing funerary monuments from being the object of such transfers.[43] However, many others detail a great variety of sales, donations, and transfers, related to rights not only over burial places and burials, but over the *loca* themselves.[44] The sale of the *ius sepulchri* of funerary places could become a very profitable business. This explains why the *Lex Falcidia*—which aimed to protect inheritances from the risks of excessive gifts and legacies that would exhaust the *res familiaris*—limited this specific type of legacy, as they could benefit others, aside from the memory of the donor.[45]

Donations linked to sacred and religious activities played an important role in the highly restrictive regulation of intra-marital gifts. To Roman legislators, the *donatio inter virum et uxorem* represented a menace to the patrimony of the family, which was preferably transmitted through the paternal line.[46] The jurist Ulpian explicitly recommends avoiding this sort of practice 'to prevent people from impoverishing themselves through mutual affection by means of gifts which are not reasonable [*non temperantes*], but beyond their means [*profusa*]'.[47] Accordingly, the regulations attested during the principate were fundamentally intended to avoid circumstances in which gifts could make the husband poorer.[48] Gifts of money were permitted, providing they did not enrich the wife or provoke additional cost.[49] Permitted monetary donations *inter viros et uxores* included the rebuilding of a burned house, the purchase of perfumes, the

---

[43] The typical formula (albeit with variants) is *hoc monumentum heredem non sequitur* (*CIL* VI.26445).

[44] Caldelli, Crea, and Ricci (2004: 312–24) list 174 *donationes* of funerary *loca, monumenta, ollae, sarcophagi,* etc., in the city of Rome.

[45] The *Lex Falcidia* (41–40 BC) promulgated the notion that the heirs should receive at least one-quarter of the inheritance. This obligation was still in force under Justinian. The jurist Paul specifies that the cost of a funeral should not be deducted from the calculations of the *Lex Falcidia*, yet the erection of a monument should be considered under this law, *Dig.* 35.2.1.19 (Paul. *Lex. Falc.*).

[46] On the danger of *matrimonium* for the *patrimonium* of the *pater familias*, see Treggiari (1991: 379).

[47] *Dig.* 24.1.1 (*Ulp. 32 ad Sab.*), trans. A. Watson in Mommsen, Krueger, and Watson (1985).

[48] See, e.g., *Dig.* 24.1.17 pr. (*Ulp. 32 ad Sab.*).

[49] *Dig.* 24.1.31.9 (*Pomp. 14 ad Sab.*); *Dig.* 24.1.28 pr. (*Paul. 7 ad Sab.*); *Dig.* 24.1.47 (*Cels. 1. dig.*).

manumitting of slaves, and distribution of *sportulae* to clients, but also the celebration of banquets and the purchase of votive objects, of oil destined for a temple, and of a burial place.[50] Donations on special occasions, such as religious celebrations for the *Matronalia*, were also considered appropriate in this context.[51] The consensus thus seems to have been to tolerate gifts that were perishable and consumable, or those destined for religious and sacred contexts and events.[52] As already seen, the donation of burial places was a more complex matter, because these places remained *res religiosae*, even if the right of use and the *possessio* could eventually change hands. In this respect, it is interesting to note that many inscriptions referring to donations of funerary *loca* between spouses tend to omit familiar filiations, which may indicate a means of escaping restrictions on the transfer of burial places outside the family.[53]

Pointedly, both moral and legal texts show the Romans' understanding of liberal acts as being a potential source of economic profit. The ideal category of the *animus* and *voluntas* of the giver that forms Seneca's notion of altruistic gifts seems thus to have been remodelled by jurisprudence into a more concrete concept, the *animus donandi*, which defines the will to finalise the agreement, even in cases when donations appear to fulfil self-interested rather than altruistic purposes. The call for moderated gifts addresses the problem of *res familiaris* being menaced by a practice that often masked profitable and illicit businesses. Money confronted individuals not only with the moral issue of immoderate and inappropriate excesses, but also with its fungible, mutable status. Beyond these preoccupations, in the eyes of Roman jurists, money was above all an essential instrument to measure, regulate, redirect, and limit donations within the contexts—including the religious sphere—in which they could destabilize private fortunes. The formalization of rituals such as the *mancipatio* as an 'imaginary sale' ultimately reveals the capacity of the Romans to separate both the object and the action, to understand the symbolism of gift-giving as something independently conceived from the object given, which after all was something that could change status, and serve different purposes. All in all, even if the original purpose of funerary donations—as many inscriptions remind us—may have been the preservation of someone's memory, the transferable use of burial places turned these gifts into potential economic investments.

---

[50] *Dig*. 24.1.7.8–9 (*Ulp. 31 ad ed.*); *Dig*. 24.1.14 (*Paul. 71 ad ed.*); *Dig*. 24.1.34 (*Ulp. 43 ad Sab.*); *Dig*. 24.1.17 (*Ulp. 32 ad Sab.*).
[51] *Dig*. 24 1.31.8 (*Pomp. 14 ad Sab.*)
[52] Ulpian states explicitly that the donations of *unguenta* (perfumes) and other perishable things should be allowed between spouses, *Dig*. 24.1.7.1 (*Ulp. 31 ad Sab.*).
[53] This is suggested by Ricci; see Caldelli, Crea and Ricci (2004: 312–24).

Sacred Places, Mutable Gifts, and the Business of Religion

Two very similar passages from Tertullian's early works, *Ad nationes* and *Apologeticum*, provide a valuable testimony to understanding the interactions between the economy and religion in Roman temples at the end of the second century AD. In an effective exercise of rhetoric, the early Christian author accurately employs the legal terminology associated with public auctions to accuse the pagan Romans—and the state—of impiety for turning a religious practice into a profitable business. The author's recrimination specifically addresses the adjudication every five years of the management of the incomes (*vectigalia*) of public temples by the *quaestor* to a *publicanus*.[54] According to Tertullian, this practice perverts the very principle of sacredness, which became subjected to and measured by the profit of the *tributum*.[55] He also provides precious details of specifically how *religio* and *sanctitas* are put up for sale: the *publicanus* collects revenues (*merces*) from the land belonging to the temple (*pro solo templi*), from entrance fees (*pro aditu sacri*), from monetary donations (*pro stipibus*), and from sacrifices (*pro hostis*). Tertullian's logical conclusion is that religion is no longer practised for free, as the gods have become the source of *vectigalia*.[56] Accordingly, the exploitation of resources and incomes from temples, which has led to the disappearance of the principle of pure generosity in religious practice, is now an activity authorized and promoted by public authorities. The Christian author thus highlights the negative impact of interventionism from the state by means of external contractors in sacred places, a practice that turned religious activity—including donations, taxes, and sacrifices—into lucrative affairs.

Aside from Tertullian's stylized criticism, his precise accounting of these practices is illuminating, as it appears complementary to other relevant documents.[57] The most important of these is the *Lex* of the *Colonia Genetiva Iulia* from Urso (i.e. *Lex Ursonensis*), which dates back to 44 BC. This legal text, preserved in several bronze tablets, includes the regulations for the local revenues of the colony, which were leased out by the *duumvir* to contractors (*redemptores*) through a consensual contract (*locatio conductio*). These revenues included the organization of sacrifices and public acts.[58] The law also stipulates that sacred offerings of money (*pecunia stipis*) given to the temple, as

---

[54] Tert. *Ad nat.* 1.10.22; *Apol.* 13.5.   [55] Tert, *Ad nat.* 1.10.23; *Apol.* 13.6.
[56] Tert, *Ad nat.* 1.10.24–25; similarly, *Apol.* 3.6. See also Introduction (this volume), pp. 5–6.
[57] On the importance of Tertullian's testimony in understanding the function of Roman temples in connection with civic authorities, see Lepelley (1990: 212–15).
[58] *CIL* II^2.5.1022; Crawford (1996: 393–454, n. 25.69).

well as monetary surpluses from sacrifices, should be expended within the temple and not reused for other purposes.[59] Both Tertullian and the *Lex Ursonensis* refer to the control of the incomes of sacred places by public authorities, as well as to the regular acceptance of *pecunia* through contributions linked to sacrifices or other types of donations from worshippers.[60]

As just discussed, the mutability of the gift as a thing that changed hands—which could enrich and impoverish, and could accordingly become a potential source of economic profit—represented a major legal challenge within a society that was intensively engaged in the regulation of private fortunes. The interaction between the public and the sacred seen in Tertullian and the *Lex Ursonensis* features strongly in Roman jurisprudence as a fundamental question that helped determine whether a thing could be acquired, alienated, and submitted to economic valuation. The donation of funerary *loca* posed a legal problem, because such donations involved the private transaction of things that essentially belonged to *res divini iuris*, and specifically to the Di Manes, and were by definition no one's property (*nullius in bonis*). The same category includes *res sanctae*, which concerned enclosed spaces within urban and cadastral areas, as well as *res sacrae*, the realm of consecrated things.[61] *Res humanae* could be public or private, and belonged to the community and to private individuals, respectively.[62] *Res sacrae* encountered specific legal issues. Sacred things consecrated to a divinity generally consisted of a *locus* delimited by the augur, in which a temple was erected, as well as any instruments used in cultic practices. Other things that belonged to or were given to a temple, like donations, could also be consecrated and become sacred, but, in those cases, their inalienability was not necessarily permanent. This is the essential difference that opened the door to the legitimate reuse of things given to the temple. Servius refers to the private donation of statues, ornaments, and votive objects dedicated to a divinity, which automatically became the property of a consecrated place.[63] The testimonies of Tertullian and the *Lex Ursonensis* thus confirm that the consecration of things given to a temple depended ultimately on the Roman public authorities under which the temple or sanctuary was administrated, usually a local magistrate.[64] In this regard, the expropriation of

---

[59] Crawford (1996: 393–454, n. 25.72).
[60] See Scheid (2009: 2–3); Estienne and de Cazanove (2009: 26–8).
[61] See, again, Gai. *Inst.* 2.9–11.
[62] On the concept of non-marketable things contained in the expression *re nullius in bonis*, see Thomas (2002: 1434).
[63] Serv. *Aen.* 3.287.
[64] See also *Dig.* 1.8.6.3: a private person could not make things *sacer*; they remained profane; see on this Rives (2012: 169–70). On the wealth of Italic temples limited by the authorities that ultimately

sacred objects was not considered a sacrilege *per se*, as long as this was authorized by the relevant authority.[65]

Objects donated to temples had different aims from the perspective of the donor. They could have strictly votive functions, like *ex votos*, or be monetary contributions (*stipes*) that were linked to or replaced sacrifices (as already seen), or be given as expressions of gratitude, or simply as a form of *liberalitas*. Epigraphic evidence also shows that precious objects deposited in Latial temples could have been the result of fines.[66] Examples of inheritances are less well documented; a fragment from Ulpian lists a series of temples that could have received goods from inheritances.[67] A series of relevant documents confirms the desacralization and sale of votive objects by the sanctuary authorities.[68] A passage from the *Life of Tiberius Gracchus* by Plutarch refers to the appropriation of consecrated objects, despite their supposed inviolability.[69] According to Appian, Octavian borrowed consecrated coins from the *thesauroi* of Latial temples in order to fund the Perusine war (41 BC).[70] Dio Cassius adds that his soldiers converted votive offerings (*anathemata*) into money.[71]

The possibility that something given to the gods could be desacralized, alienated, and sold is specifically described in the inscription from 58 BC known as the *Lex aedis Furfensis*.[72] This important document, which concerns the sanctuary of Jupiter Liber in the *vicus* of Furfo, regulates the reuse of donations that could be sold to purchase, let, or grant what was necessary to improve the temple.[73] The *lex* specifies that the money (*pecunia*) used for that purpose needed to be *profana* to avoid *dolo*.[74] The authorities of the *vicus* also clarify that objects in bronze and silver acquired with this money would have the same status as if they had been dedicated and consecrated. This extraordinary testimony confirms the circular voyage of objects, their transformation from gifts to commodities that generated monetary incomes to be reinvested in the sanctuary.[75]

---

managed them, see the important contribution by Bodei Giglioni (1977). See also Granino Cerere (2009).

[65] Bodei Giglioni (1977: 39); Scheid (1981).
[66] See Estienne and de Cazanove (2009: 17–27). Such fines have been studied by Piacentin (2018, 2022).
[67] Ulp. *fr.* 22.6 and 226. See Introduction (this volume), p. 11 n. 51.
[68] See, e.g., *Macrob. Sat.* 3.11, and also Serv. *Aen.* 3.287; 9.408; 11.558; cf. Thomas (2002: 1443–4).
[69] Plut. *Gracch.* 15.   [70] App. *Bell. civ.* 5.24.
[71] Dio Cass. 48.12.4; on this episode, see Bodei Giglioni (1977); Granino Cerere (2009). On the melting down of gold and silver ornaments of temples, see Millar (1992: 146–8).
[72] *CIL* IX.3513 (= 1² 756; *ILLRP* 508; Bruns 7.105); cf. Laffi (2001: 515–44); Thomas (2002: 1438); Malrieu (2005: 111–2); García Morcillo (2013: 244).
[73] *CIL* IX.3513, ll. 11–12.   [74] *CIL* IX.3513, ll. 12–14.
[75] According to Malrieu (2005: 112), this document shows how sanctuaries contributed to a circular economy that was, however, open to the city.

At times the external interventionism of powerful authorities could also determine the status and destiny of such objects. An inscription from Kyme (Asia Minor), dated to 27 BC, reveals how Augustus tried to stop the sale of *ex votos* from a temple.[76] Civic authorities were thus legally empowered to intervene in the sacred sphere—to change the status of things, from permanent to transitional, from inviolable to accessible and alienable.

As previously stated, aside from their symbolic value, donations also needed to be economically evaluated in order to regulate and control their patrimonial consequences.[77] The economic value of a gift was also an important factor to understand the social uses and forms of self-representation linked to donations, as Seneca's categorization of benefits shows. After all, gifts were also given for the value they held as symbols of the action and the purpose of the giver. This explains why inscriptions attesting private donations occasionally detail the price of those objects,[78] and in some cases their weight in metal.[79] Archaeological evidence shows a great proliferation of metal objects in Italian sanctuaries during the early principate.[80] These gifts were eventually preserved, at least for a while, in a dedicated space within the temple called the *donarium*.[81] The recovery of large quantities of statuette bases reveals that, at certain points, objects made of noble metal were melted down and recycled.[82] These treasures thus fulfilled both sacred and financial purposes, as they contributed to the cycle that transformed gifts into sources of economic profit for the benefit of the sanctuary itself.[83] The well-known case of the sanctuary of Lucus Feroniae in the Tiber Valley illustrates this phenomenon. This sacred place was sacked by Hannibal, who, according to Livy, replaced the *ex votos* of

---

[76] *SEG* 18.555.

[77] Carlà and Gori (2014) discuss the blurring between the categories of 'gift' and 'commerce'.

[78] An inscription from Augusta Taurinorum mentions the donation *ex testamento* of a *statua Iovis Augusti* priced at HS 10,000, *CIL* V.6955; cf. Zerbini (2008: 41).

[79] See, e.g., a votive inscription from Mediolanum, *AE* 1897, 25. A Severan inscription from Mauretania Caesariensis also refers to the donation of a statue of three pounds of silver (*imaginem argenteam librarum trium*), *CIL* VIII.9797.

[80] See Estienne and de Cazanove (2009). The authors note the progressive replacement of *ex votos* in terracotta with those of metal. Dondin-Payre and Kaufmann-Heinemann (2009) have analysed the wide variety of forms and types of metal statuettes and objects found in Gallic temples, very often disconnected with the divinity of the place or with the votive inscription engraved on them. For instance, in Neuvy many objects did not originally have a religious function.

[81] The name is confusing, as it may refer both to the gift and to the place where the gift was deposited. Several literary texts suggest that *donaria* were specific areas within the temple: Serv. *Aen.* 2.269; 12.199; Apul. *Met.* 9.10; 15.5. In addition to literary accounts, Estienne and de Cazanove (2009: 11–17) provide extensive archaeological evidence of the existence of *donaria* as enclosed spaces within Italic temples.

[82] On the reuse of wealth in sanctuaries, particularly precious metals, see again Estienne and de Cazanove (2009: 9–10).

[83] This idea is explained by Baratte (1992). See also Dondin-Payre and Kaufmann-Heinemann (2009: 115–18) for the specific case of metal objects kept as treasures in Gallic sanctuaries. The authors attribute a function of 'stockage' for different purposes to these deposits/treasures.

noble metal with less valuable ones. Archaeological remains from the site of the sanctuary attest the deposit of numerous statuettes of stone and *ex votos* in terracotta, but not metal objects.[84] This suggests a possible regular practice of melting and selling metal objects by the officers in charge of the sanctuary. The fact that Lucus Feroniae hosted an interregional commercial fair that attracted traders from different regions no doubt facilitated these financial and commercial activities linked with recycled material. Several reports of expropriations of fungible wealth in temples in Latium during the Republic also point in this direction.[85] Pliny the Elder specifically refers to the case of the censors L. Piso and M. Aemilius C. Popilius, who ordered the reuse of sacred metal to obtain coins (158 BC).[86] In this regard, a text from Varro confirms that a sanctuary could host deposits of both *pecunia publica* and *pecunia sacra*, which shows a differentiation of the use and function of temple resources.[87]

The presence of pecuniary *thesauri* in several Italic and Roman sanctuaries supports the reuse of metal resources, but also draws attention to direct monetary incomes, like the *stipes*, which were partially reinvested for the benefit of the temple. Tertullian's allusion to the 'entry fees' charged to worshippers by temples addresses the payment of coins (*stipes*) as a form of sacrifice, but also as a type of gift.[88] These types of monetary contributions became increasingly frequent in Italy from the third century BC.[89] Another popular form of monetary contribution was the so-called *decuma Herculis*, which was linked to traders, mostly *mercatores* and *negotiatores*.[90]

Overall, the acceptability of both donations measurable in money and coins as contributions to the sanctuary reflects the extent to which the economic valuation of gifts was integrated into the practice of worship and the ritual dynamics of the sacred sphere. As we have seen, money made possible the quantification of gifts, which was necessary for their regulation. For worshippers and temple managers, coins were simultaneously forms of payment, objects, and symbols that could replace and be transformed into other things. Following Hubert and Mauss' early

---

[84] On this episode, see Liv. 26.11.8–9; cf. Bodei Giglioni (1977: 49). On the numerous finds of statuettes in stone and *ex votos* in terracotta in the sanctuary of Lucus Feroniae, see Estienne and de Cazanove (2009: 9–10). On the *panegyris* or *mercatus* that was celebrated in the sanctuary every year, see foremost Dion. Hal. 3.32; 4.49; Liv. 1.30.5; cf. Coarelli (1995: 202–4); García Morcillo (2013: 250–4).
[85] Widely studied by Bodei Giglioni (1977).   [86] Plin. *HN* 34.6.30.
[87] Varro, *LL* 5.180. See also Scheid (1981).
[88] Regulations on the *stips* are for instance discussed by Macrobius 3.11.6 and Plin. *Epist.* 8.8.2.
[89] Bodei Giglioni (1977) and Crawford (1989).
[90] See, e.g., *CIL* IX.4672. On the *decuma Herculis*, cf. Letta (1992: 119–21). The *decuma Herculis* has been frequently interpreted as a tax linked to transhumance; see Gros (1995). Works and dedications to temples were also funded with monetary payments linked to aedilician fines (*ex multaticia pecunia*). Literary and epigraphic evidence on this practice during the Middle Republic has been extensively analysed by Piacentin (2018, 2022: esp. 36–76).

study on the function of sacrifice, we could also add that the use of coins signified a contractual relationship between the worshipper and the divinity, as in the ritual of the *mancipatio*.[91] The use of coins as donations and contributions to the temple addressed the essential issue of the transformation of things, their equivalence, individuality, and finally their alienability.[92]

The journey of donated objects and coins, which could potentially be transformed into commodities and money within the context of the temple, demonstrated the extent to which these religious practices were fully embedded into a monetary economy, as Tertullian well understood. The mutability and multidimensionality of the gift—from symbolic object to a commodity and currency—was, however, perfectly compatible with the giver's *animus* and interconnection with a specific divinity, cult, and sacred place. Both should be understood as independent actions. The payment to the gods through sacrifice and the monetary contributions linked to it, as well as the deposit of *ex votos*, donations, and other forms of *liberalitas*, also fulfilled a utilitarian function marked by the asymmetric relationship between the giver (worshipper) and the receiver (god).[93] From the giver's perspective, the essence of the gift lay in the action and its aim, utilitarian or altruistic, and not in the object itself, which mutated into an exchangeable symbol and a source of reinvestment once donated to the sacred space.[94] The passage of the gift into a marketable product, as well as the legal mechanisms promoting this circular economy controlled by civic authorities, is perfectly crystallised in the *Lex aedis Furfensis*. This (and other legal sources) show the Romans' awareness of the sacred sphere as a dynamic realm in which things that are in constant movement change status and can potentially generate *commercium*.[95] Sacred gifts ultimately involved different levels and processes of exchange and reciprocity set in motion by the worshipper.[96]

---

[91] In their *Essai sur la nature et la fonction du sacrifice*, Hubert and Mauss (1898) describe religious gift-giving as a market of symbolic goods that could be always replaced by others.

[92] According to Hubert and Mauss (1898), the sacrifice represents a purchase for the gods, and the use of fractional currency linked to sacrifices permitted the regulation of these payments and the establishment of tariffs. In Caillé's view (2007: 197–8), sacrifices functioned as an amplifier of the gift. On the tension between the symbolic and monetary value of a gift related to its change of status, see Carlà and Gori (2014: 34).

[93] On the asymmetry of sacred donations and sacrifices and their consequences, see Caillé (2007).

[94] Graeber (2001: 49) develops the idea of actions as a factor that generates criteria of value. A critical discussion of this notion in relation to gift-giving in ancient Greece and Rome is provided by Carlà and Gori (2014: 10–11). On Graeber's theory of the transformation of value through exchange and its applicability in the religious sphere, see most recently Moser and Smith (2019: 8).

[95] See, especially, Thomas (2002: 1446). As Thomas argues, the Roman concept of *res* referred to more than just an object, but rather to the dynamic idea of 'affaire' (1457–60). See examples in Macrob. *Sat.* 3.34 and *Dig.* 18.1.73 (*Pap. 3 resp.*). A similar notion applies to the gift and its mutability through transfer.

[96] On the transformation of sacred gifts and the notion of value in Archaic and Classical Greece, see Berti (2014).

Epilogue: *Dignum templo dignum deo donum*

Among the well-known benefactions of Pliny the Younger, I would like to single out the story of a donation included in a letter to the author's friend Annius Severus.[97] In the epistle, Pliny declares his intention to donate a small, exquisite statue of an old man to a public place in his own region, preferably to the temple of Jupiter.[98] The author notes the remarkable aesthetic qualities of the piece, a *Corinthium signum*, as well as the circumstances of its purchase. Pliny was certainly aware of the exorbitant prices that Corinthian bronzes reached in his day; they were famously associated with *luxuria* and *opulentia*, and with the conspicuous *furor* and the *vita otiosa* of their collectors.[99] Perhaps for this reason, in the letter Pliny refers to the fact that the statuette was acquired thanks to money obtained from an inheritance. He also describes the piece as a finely executed naked figure of an old man, through whom the artist was capable of transmitting the beauty of the passage of time. This was, in sum, a piece that captured the eyes of connoisseurs and provoked admiration in the viewer.[100] Pliny also mentions the patina of the object, which showed its original colour, a sign of its antiquity. These—and not his own expertise—were the reasons alleged by Pliny for why he purchased the statue. In the letter, Pliny gives precise instructions to his friend Severus, who was commissioned to add a marble pedestal, an inscription with Pliny's name, and, if appropriate, his titles.[101] The symbolic value and laudable virtues attributed by Pliny to the statuette and transmitted through its excellent craftsmanship somehow justified the high price he had probably paid for the object. A temple seemed to him the most suitable place for such an outstanding piece of art (*dignum templo dignum deo donum*).

Pliny's gesture of *liberalitas* reveals some interesting social patterns, which appear to be complementary to the dynamics and evidence of private donations and religious gifts analysed in the previous sections. Pliny was careful to detach the artistic and symbolic value of the object from its price, which must have been substantially based on the noble metals that distinguished the

---

[97] Plin. *Ep.* 3.6. On Pliny's euergetic initiatives, particularly in Comum, see Zerbini (2008: 26–35).

[98] Plin. *Ep.* 3.6.1; 3.6.4: *Emi autem non ut haberem domi, neque enim ullum adhuc Corinthium domi habeo, verum ut in patria nostra celebri loco ponerem, ac potissimum in Iovis templo.* 3.6.5: *videtur enim dignum templo dignum deo donum* ('But I did so, not with any intent of placing it in my own house, for I have as yet no Corinthian bronzes there, but with a design of fixing it in some conspicuous place in my native province, preferably in the temple of Jupiter; for it is a present well worthy of a temple and a god' (trans. W. Melmolth)).

[99] Seneca describes the negative traits of collectors of Corinthian bronzes (*Brev. vit.* 12.2).

[100] Plin. *Ep.* 3.6.1–4. [101] Plin. *Ep.* 3.6.5–6.

special alloy of so-called Corinthian bronzes.[102] By personalizing the inscription, the virtues and qualities attributed to the object were automatically linked to the donor. Aside from the benefaction, there was also a clear aim of self-representation, which assumed that the statuette was going to be displayed in a visible place within the temple. Here, the piece of art—and the projected virtues of the benefactor—would potentially be admired by visitors and worshippers. The theme of the statuette was detached from an explicitly divine or sacred theme, which—as we have seen—appeared to have been a frequent phenomenon in gifts deposited in sacred places. The story of this *Corinthium aes* once again reveals the blurred line that separated the sacred from the profane in religious spaces. In Pliny's view, the statuette's major virtue was its *antiquitas*, underlined both by the patina and by the figure of the old man. This theme demonstrates Pliny's intention to make his personalized gift something perdurable and worthy of being remembered, an object that would escape any valuation based on materiality. This idea aligns with the purposes of *liberalitas* and of benefactions formulated by Cicero and Seneca, but clashes with the abstract theoretical empiricism of Roman law, which insisted on valuing things according to their economic *aestimatio*. In practice though, as we have seen, metal objects donated to sacred places often experienced a process of transformation—perhaps after being displayed temporarily in the *donarium*—once they became anonymised and desacralized, which resulted in a conversion of the object into a financial and economic resource.

The problem of the elusiveness of gifts, caused by their temporal nature, mutability and continuous transformation in ownership—from private individual to divine possessions, from the divinity to the community, and then back to the individual—was ultimately resolved through an effective abstraction that separated the act of donating, on the one hand, from the idea of the gift as both symbol and object, on the other. Pliny's intention to donate something destined to remain a symbol of his own benefaction would have collided with the utilitarian dynamics that shaped gift-giving in sacred places. As Plautus enlighteningly summed it up in a passage from his *Cistellaria* (*The Casket Comedy*), which evokes the evanescent nature of love: *ut sunt humana, nihil est perpetuum datum*, 'But human affairs are thus, nothing is given forever'.[103]

---

[102] Two key texts are Plin. *HN* 34.8 and Plut. *Mor.* 395B–D.
[103] *Cist.* 1.194.

References

Amelotti, M. (1953). *La donatio mortis causa in diritto romano*. Milan.

Andreau, J. (1977). 'Fondations privées et rapport sociaux en Italie romaine', *Ktèma* 2: 157–209.

Baratte, F. (1992). 'Les trésors de temples dans le monde romain: Une expression particulière de la piété', in S. A. Boyd and M. M. Mango (eds), *Ecclesiastical Silver Plate in Sixth-Century Byzantium*. Washington, 111–22.

Berti, I. (2014). 'Value for Money: Pleasing the Gods and Impressing Mortals in the Archaic and Early Classical Age', in Carlà and Gori (2014), 289–313.

Biondi, B. (1961). *Le donazioni*. Turin.

Blanch Nouguès, J. M. (2007). 'Nuevas consideraciones acerca de la fundación funeraria de Iunia Libertas en Ostia', *RIDA* 54: 197–218.

Bodei Giglioni, G. (1977). 'Pecunia fanatica: L'incidenza economica dei templi laziali', *Rivista storica italiana*, 89: 33–76.

Bruck, E. F. (1954). *Über römisches Recht im Rahmen der Kulturgeschichte*, Heidelberg.

Caillé, A. (2007). *Anthropologie du don*. 2nd edn. Paris.

Caldelli, M. L., Crea, S., and Ricci, C. (2004). '*Iura sepulcrorum* a Roma: Consuntivi tematici ragionati. A-B: *Donare, emere, vendere, ius habere, possidere, concedere, similia*. Donazione e compravendita, diritto sul sepolcro e diritti di sepoltura', in *Libitina e dintorni. Libitina e i luci sepolcrali. Le leges libitinariae campane. Iura sepulcrorum: vecchie e nuove iscrizioni*; Atti dell'XI Rencontre franco-italienne sur l'épigraphie (Libitina 3). Rome, 312–24.

Carlà, F., and Gori, M. (2014) (eds). *Gift Giving and the 'Embedded' Economy in the Ancient World* (Akademiekonferenzen 17). Heidelberg.

Carlà-Uhink, F. (2021). '*Res tamquam proprias retenebat*: Personal and Collective Property in the Late Antique Church between Normative Regulation and Social Practice', in R. Haensch and P. von Rummel (eds), *Himmelwärts und erdverbunden? Religiöse und wirtschaftliche Aspekte spätantiker Lebensrealität*, Rahden, 339–56.

Casavola, F. (1960). *Lex Cincia: Contributo alla storia delle origini della donazione romana*. Naples.

Champlin, E. (1991). *Final Judgements: Duty and Emotion in Roman Wills 220 BC–AD 250*. Berkeley and Los Angeles.

Chaumartin, F.-R. (1985). *Le De beneficiis de Sénèque, sa signification philosophique, politique et sociale*. Paris.

Coarelli, F. (1995). 'Vie e mercati del Lazio antico', *Eutopia* 4/1: 202–4.

Coffee, N. (2017). *Gift and Gain: How Money Transformed Ancient Rome* (Classical Culture and Society). Oxford.

Colpaert, S. (2014). 'Euergetism and the Gift', in Carlà and Gori (2014), 181–201.

Crawford, M. H. (1989). 'Aut sacrom aut poublicom', in P. Birks (ed.), *New Perspectives in the Roman Law of Property: Essays for Barry Nicholas*. Oxford, 93–8.

Crawford, M. H. (1996). *Roman Statutes* (Bulletin of the Institute of Classical Studies: Supplement 64). London.

Deniaux, É. (1993). *Clientèles et pouvoir à l'époque de Cicéron* (Collection de l'École française de Rome 182). Rome.

Denzey Lewis, N. (2013). 'Roses and Violets for the Ancestors: Gifts to the Dead and Ancient Roman Forms of Social Exchange', in Satlow (2013), 122–36.

Diósdi, G. (1970). *Ownership in Ancient and Preclassical Roman Law*. Budapest.

Domingo Gygax, M. (2013). 'Gift-Giving and Power Relationships in Greek Social Praxis and Public Discourse', in Satlow (2013), 45–60.

Domingo Gygax, M., and Zuiderhoek, A. (2021) (eds). *Benefactors and the Polis: The Public Gift in the Greek Cities from the Homeric World to Late Antiquity*. Cambridge.

Dondin-Payre, M., and Kaufmann-Heinimann, A. (2009). 'Trésors et biens des temples: Réflexions à partir de cas des Gaules: Neuvy, Champoulet, Cobannus (Éduens)', *Archiv für Religionsgeschichte* 11: 89–120.

Estienne, S., and Cazanove, O. de (2009). 'Offrandes et amendes dans les sanctuaires du monde romain à l'époque républicaine', *Archiv für Religionsgeschichte* 11: 5–35.

Feuvrier-Prévolat, C. (1985), '"Donner et Recevoir": Remarques sur les pratiques d'échanges dans le *De officiis* de Cicéron', *DHA* 11: 257–90.

García Morcillo, M. (2013). 'Trade and Sacred Places: Fairs, Markets and Cultural Exchange in Ancient Italic Sanctuaries', in M. Jehne, B. Linke, and J. Rüpke (eds), *Religiöse Vielfalt und Soziale Integration: die Bedeutung der Religion für die kulturelle Identität und die politische Stabilität im republikanischen Italien* (Studien zur Alte Geschichte 17). Heidelberg, 236–74.

García Morcillo, M. (2014). 'Limiting Generosity: Conditions and Restrictions on Roman Donations', in Carlà and Gori (2014), 241–66.

Godelier, M. (1999). *The Enigma of the Gift*. Chicago.

Graeber, D. (2001). *Toward an Anthropological Theory of Value: The False Coin of Our Dreams*. New York.

Granino Cerere, M. G. (2009). '*Pecunia sacra* e propietà fondiaria nei santuari dell'Italia centrale. Il contributo dell'epigrafia', *Archiv für Religionsgeschichte* 11: 37–62.

Griffin, M. (2003). '*De beneficiis* and Roman Society', *JRS* 93: 92–113.

Gros, P. (1995). 'Hercule à Glanum: Sanctuaires de transhumance et développement Urbai', *Gallia* 52: 311–31.

Günther, S. (2005). 'Die Einführung der römischen Erbschaftssteuer (*vicesima hereditatium*)', *MBAH* 24: 1–30.

Hubert, H., and Mauss, M. (1898). 'Essai sur la nature et la fonction du sacrifice', *L'Année sociologique* 2: 29–138.

Laffi, U. (2001). *Studi di storia romana e di diritto* (Storia e Letteratura. Raccolta di studi e testi 207). Rome.

Lepelley, C. (1990). 'Ubique Respublica: Tertullien, Témoin méconnu de l'essor des cités africaines à l'époque sévérienne', in *L'Afrique dans l'Occident Romain (Ier siècle av. J.-C.–IVe siècle ap. J.-C.). Actes du colloque organisé par l'École française de Rome sous le patronage de l'Institut national d'archéologie et d'art de Tunis (Rome, 3–5 décembre 1987)*. Rome, 403–21.

Letta, C. (1992). 'I santuari rurali nell'Italia centro-appenninica: Valori religiosi e funzione aggregative', *MEFRA* 104/1: 109–24.

Liu, J. (2008). 'The Economy of Endowments: The Case of the Roman *collegia*', in K. Verboven, K. Vandorpe, and V. Chankowski (eds), *Pistoi dia tèn technèn: Bankers, Loans and Archives in the Ancient World: Studies in Honour of Raymond Bogaert* (Studia Hellenistica 44). Leuven, 231–56.

Lomas, K., and Cornell, T. (2003) (eds). '*Bread and Circuses*': *Evergetism and Municipal Patronage in Roman Italy*. London and New York.

Lotito, G. (1981). 'Modelli etici e base economica nelle opere filosofiche di Cicerone', in A. Giardina and A. Schiavone (eds), *Società romana e produzione schiavistica III: Modelli etici, diritto e trasformazioni sociali*. Rome, 79–126.

Malrieu, A. (2005). 'Le role économique des sanctuaries romains: thésaurisation et investissement des fonds sacrés', *Topoi* 12–13/1: 95–116.

Mauss, M. (1923–4). 'Essai sur le don. Forme et raison de l'échange dans les sociétés archaiques', *L'Année sociologique* 1: 30–186.

Michel, J.-H. (1962). *Gratuité en droit romain* (Études d'histoire et d'ethnologie juridiques 3). Brussels.

Millar, F. (1992). *The Emperor in the Roman World*, 2nd edn. London.

Mommsen, T., Krueger, P., and Watson, A. (1985). *The Digest of Justinian*. Latin text edited by Theodor Mommsen with the aid of Paul Krueger; English Translation edited by Alan Watson, 4 vols. Philadelphia.

Moser, C., and Smith, C. J. (2019). 'Preface', in C. Moser and C. J. Smith (eds), *Transformations of Value: Lived Religion and the Economy* (Religion in the Roman Empire 5). Heidelberg, 3–22.

Narducci, E. (1985). 'Valori aristocratici e mentalità acquisitiva nel pensiero di Cicerone', *Index* 13: 93–125

Piacentin, S. (2018). 'The Role of Aedilician Fines in the Making of Public Rome', *Historia* 67/1: 103–26.

Piacentin, S. (2022). *Financial Penalties in the Roman Republic. A Study of Confiscations of Individual Property, Public Sales and Fines (509-58 BC)*. Leiden and Boston.

Recorder de Casso, E. (2005). *La ley Cincia en sus circunstancias históricas*. Madrid.

Rives, J. (2012). 'Control of the Sacred in Roman Law', in O. Tellegen-Couperus (ed.), *Law and Religion in the Roman Republic* (Mnemosyne Supplements). Leiden and Boston, 165–80.

Rüger, D. (2011). *Die donatio mortis causa im klassischen römischen Recht* (Klassische rechtgeschitliche Abhandlungen 62). Berlin.

Satlow, M. L. (2013) (ed.). *The Gift in Antiquity* (The Ancient World: Comparative Histories). Chichester.

Scheid, J. (1981). 'Le délit religieux dans la Rome tardo-republicaine', in *Le délit religieux dans la cité antique: Table ronde, Rome 6-7 avril 1978* (Collection de l'École française de Rome 48). Rome, 129–83.

Scheid, J. (2009). 'Les biens des temples à Rome et dans le monde romain', *Archiv für Religionsgeschichte* 11: 1–4.

Thomas, Y. (2002). 'La valeur des choses: Le droit romain hors de la religion', *Annales. Histoire, Sciences Sociales* 57/6: 1431–62.

Tran, N. (2006). *Les membres des associations romaines: Le rang social des collegiati en Italie et en Gaules sous le Haut-Empire* (Collection de l'École française de Rome 367). Rome.

Treggiari, S. (1991). *Roman Marriage:* Iusti coniuges *from the Time of Cicero to the Time of Ulpian*. Oxford.

Verboven, K. (2002). *The Economy of Friends: Economic Aspects of* amicitia *and Patronage in the Late Republic*. Brussels.

Verboven, K. (2011). 'Friendship among the Romans', in M. Peachin (ed.), *The Oxford Handbook of Social Relations in the Roman World*. Oxford, 404–21.

Verboven, K. (2014). '"Like bait on a hook": Ethics, Etics and Emics of Gift-Exchange in the Roman World', in Carlà and Gori (2014), 135–53.

Veyne, P. (1976). *Le pain et le cirque: sociologie historique d'un pluralisme politique* (Univers historique). Paris.

Visscher, F. de (1947-8). 'Les défenses d'aliener en droit funéraire romain', *SDHI* 13/4: 278–88.

Visscher, F. de (1948). 'La fondation funéraire de Iunia Libertas d'après une inscription d'Ostie', in *Studi in onore di Siro Solazzi*. Naples, 542–53.

Visscher, F. de (1955). 'Les fondations privées en droit romain classique', *RIDA* 2: 197–218.

Visscher, F. de (1963). *Le droit des tombeaux romains*. Milan.

Watson, A. (1968). *The Law of Property in the Later Roman Republic*. Oxford.

Wolkenhauer, J. (2014). *Senecas Schrift* De beneficiis *und der Wandel im römischen Benefizienwesen* (Freunde—Gönner—Getreue. Studien zur Semantik und Praxis von Freundschaft und Patronage 10). Göttingen.

Zerbini, L. (2008). *Pecunia sua: Munificenza privata et utilità pubblica nelle città romane delle regiones IX ed XI*. Soveria Mannelli.

Zuiderhoek, A. (2007). 'The Ambiguity of Munificence', *Historia* 56: 196–213.

Zuiderhoek, A. (2009). *The Politics of Munificence in the Roman Empire: Citizens, Elites and Benefactors in Asia Minor* (Greek Culture in the Roman World). Cambridge.

11

Guilds and Gods

Religious Profiles of Occupational *collegia* and the Problem of the *dendrophori*

Koenraad Verboven

'Of all his [Numa's] other measures of government, his distribution of the people according to their trade was the most admired...He gave them associations, assemblies, and rites of worship, befitting to each sort.'[1]

Introduction

In his influential book on Roman religion, the French classicist Boissier claimed in 1874 that the religion of Roman commoners could be understood only by looking at their *collegia*.[2] It should cause no surprise, Boissier argued, that religion was an inherent feature of any *collegium*, since these were modelled on cities, and ancient cities were characterized by common cults.[3] Waltzing agreed: 'all have a more or less pronounced religious character.'[4] Both, however, also argued that the religious practices of professional *collegia* became mere formalities in the late Republic. Waltzing distinguished religious *collegia* from pleasure societies and professional corporations 'd'après leur caractère dominant.'[5] In his view, religion no longer played a significant role

---

[1] Plut. *Num.* 17: Τῶν δὲ ἄλλων αὐτοῦ πολιτευμάτων ἡ κατὰ τέχνας διανομὴ τοῦ πλήθους μάλιστα θαυμάζεται....κοινωνίας δὲ καὶ συνόδους καὶ θεῶν τιμὰς ἀποδοὺς ἑκάστῳ γένει πρεπούσας; cf. Waltzing (1895: i.195): 'nous devons en conclure qu'à l'époque du biographe les collèges d'artisans avaient un caractère religieux.'

[2] Boissier (1874: ii. 247): 'une étude de la religion romaine ne peut se passer de les connaître'; a long chapter of the second volume discusses various aspects of the *collegia* (238–304).

[3] Boissier (1874: ii. 266).

[4] 'tous ou presque tous ont un caractère religieux plus ou moins prononcé' (Waltzing 1895: i. 35); 'dès qu'un groupe se formait, même dans un dessin profane, il commençait par adopter un culte' (Boissier 1874: i. 196).

[5] Boissier (1874: i. 34).

in occupational *collegia*. Even religious associations mostly developed into associations whose primary aims were funerary, not religious—a view that echoed Mommsen's dissertation *De collegiis et sodaliciis Romanorum*.[6]

A similar idea emerged about associations in the Greek world. Ziebarth described how cult associations developed in the Hellenistic period into private communities whose primary function was to promote sociability and a sense of homeliness to compensate for the decline of the *polis* community.[7] Ziebarth, nevertheless, still believed that religion continued to be important to bind members closer together. Poland was more sceptical. He argued that, partly under the influence of Rome, religious concerns gave way to practical ones. While Greek associations remained more prone than Roman ones to expressing their religious identity, Poland believed that in most cases this was merely a nice 'curtain' ('der schöne Vorhang') behind which real associative life ('das eigentliche Vereinsleven') took place.[8]

This late-nineteenth-century orthodoxy regarding ancient voluntary associations long set the tone. Nilsson famously argued that religion was merely a pretext for throwing a party.[9] MacMullen believed that, 'if piety counted for much, conviviality counted for more'.[10]

Since the 1990s, however, the idea of religion as being merely an accessory to collegiate life or a remnant of a bygone past has been questioned. Van Nijf argued that 'religious considerations were on the mind of every association: divine protectors, sacrifices, banquets, participation in private or public religious rituals are close to the core of every association'.[11] Harland strongly emphasizes 'the importance of honoring gods and goddesses within associations of all types'. In his view, 'all types of associations served a variety of interdependent social, cultic, and funerary functions for their members…[that] helped to provide members with a sense of belonging and identity'.[12] In his study of late Hellenistic Delos, Rauh stressed the close connection between religious cults and mercantile interests.[13] Because religion greatly strengthened a sense of community, it stimulated cooperation and solidarity in foreign merchant communities on the island. Baslez similarly argued that the oriental mercantile

---

[6] Boissier (1874: i. 47): 'Beaucoup de ces collèges privés, fondés surtout pour adorer une divinité, finirent par regarder la religion comme l'accessoire et les funérailles comme leur but principal'; Mommsen (1843).

[7] Ziebarth (1896: 191–211): 'Immer aber blieb Hauptzweck der Vereine, auf gemeinschaftliche Kosten das Leben annehmlich zu gestallten' (p. 211).

[8] Poland (1909: 173–270). [9] Nilsson (1957: 64).

[10] MacMullen (1974: 71–87, esp. 77, 80).

[11] van Nijf (2006: 227); similarly already in van Nijf (1997).

[12] Harland (2013: 45; 1st edn 2003). [13] Rauh (1993).

groups on Delos (mostly Phoenicians) primarily saw themselves not as 'merchant guilds' but as ethnic and religious communities, attaching great importance to the cult of their 'paternal' gods.[14]

However, caution is warranted, and other scholars take a more nuanced or even sceptical approach to the role of religion in occupational associations. The model proposed by Rauh and Baslez for late Hellenistic Delos may still apply to Phoenician residents in second-century AD Puteoli and Rome, and possibly other ethnicity-based mercantile communities, such as the Nabataeans in Puteoli. When we look in detail at the 'model' of the Delian mercantile associations, however, it appears rather to have been a Phoenician or at least an oriental model rather than a general Mediterranean one. Greek or Roman foreign resident groups rarely manifest themselves as exclusive societies based on ethnically specific cults. Roman mercantile communities designate themselves and are designated by Greeks as *qui negotiantur* or *cives Romani consistentes*. To give only a few examples among hundreds, the Roman business community at Ephesos in 36 BC called itself the *conventus civium Romanorum quei Ephesei negotiantur*.[15] A Greek inscription describes the same group as the Romans/Italians doing business in Ephesos (οἱ ἐν Ἐφέσῳ πραγματευόμενοι ἔμποροι Ῥωμαῖοι).[16] Similarly, the Alexandrian merchants in second-century AD Perinthos describe themselves as 'the Alexandrians doing business in Perinthos' (Ἀλεξανδρεῖς οἱ πραγματευόμενοι ἐν Περίνθῳ).[17] The Roman merchants on Delos did structure their community around cult associations, but these honoured Mercury/Hermes, Neptune/Poseidon, and Apollo rather than specifically Roman deities. Only the *Competaliastai*—celebrating the *Lares Compitales*—can be seen as quintessentially Roman, but their members, mostly slaves and some dependent freedmen, were clearly on a lower social plane.[18] Conspicuously, the goddess Roma was worshipped only by non-Roman groups, such as the 'Worshippers of Poseidon of Beirut (Baal-Berit) on Delos, Shippers, Merchants, and Warehousemen'.[19] Gabrielsen agrees that religion was one of the 'constitutive' elements of many Greek associations but warns against 'adherence to the unacceptably simplistic *Namen-Arten-Zweck* formula' advocated by Ziebarth and Poland[20]—an approach that he argues obscures the use

---

[14] Baslez (1986, 2013).
[15] *AE* 1990, 938 (= *IEphesos* 658); cf. also *CIL* III.14195,39 (c.60 BC); for *cives Romani qui in Asia negotiantur*, see *CIL* III.12266; *IEphesos* 409; 3019.
[16] *IEphesos* 800; on communities of Roman *negotiatores* in the Greek world, see Hatzfeld (1919); in general on the communities of *cives Romani consistentes*, see Van Andringa (2003).
[17] *IPerinthos* 27; 28 cf. *IScM* II 153 ('house of the Alexandrians', τῷ οἴκῳ τῶν Ἀλεξανδρέων)
[18] Flambard (1982); see also Flambard (1981); Hasenohr (2003). [19] *IDélos* 1778.
[20] Gabrielsen (2001: 178).

by Rhodian elites of the 'association habit' to control manpower resources needed to secure Rhodes's economic and political interests. Maillot points out that the Rhodian model (from the third century BC onwards) was very different from the one found on Delos. Rhodian associations were not ethnically or culturally specific. They provided avenues for foreigners from various backgrounds (primarily but not exclusively businessmen) to integrate in Rhodian society. Some associations were religiously defined but not around specifically national or ethnic deities; others were mere personalized groups named after their leader.[21] Terpstra believes that 'religion was certainly a factor in the coherence of many business coalitions, worship of particular gods being intimately intertwined with geographical origin'. However, he does not see religion as a binding force *per se*. Religious practices were instrumental in expressing a group's identity, but foreign merchant groups more commonly emphasized geographic origins rather than common cults. Mercantile communities, in Terpstra's view, were tied together by concerns for collective reputation as an indispensable asset in business deals.[22]

This is not to say that the revaluation of the role of religion in occupational associations advocated by Harland and others is not a welcome correction to nineteenth-century views. Religion never stopped being important in occupational associations. But this is hardly surprising. Religion mattered to everyone. Every collective, whether it was a family, a workforce, a city, a whole people, or a voluntary association, had religious vocations and rituals. The important questions I want to discuss in this chapter are: were the religious dimensions of occupational *collegia* in any way specific and different from those of other associations? How did this relate to their non-religious 'raisons d'être'?

There are various ways to approach the economic dimensions of the relation between voluntary associations and religion. The most straightforward is to look at the economics of religious associations. Did they own property? Where did their revenues come from? Did this differ from the economics of non-religious groups? While these are important questions to understand the position of cult associations in Roman society, they do not tell us much about the role of religion and religion-based entitlements in the Roman economy.[23]

Another approach is to study occupational associations as trust networks that stimulated and strengthened cooperation among their members. Professional

---

[21] Maillot (2015).
[22] Terpstra (2013: *passim*; p. 100 for the citation); more nuanced in Terpstra (2019: 31, 72–3 and *passim*) and Terpstra (2020) but still mostly instrumental: religion promotes the distinctiveness of trade diasporas.
[23] For such an approach, see, recently, Harland (2015).

interests were not usually an explicit aim of ancient guilds, but the cooperation and group solidarity they imposed could be used to protect and further the economic interests of the members.[24] Religious rituals and offices may then be studied as ways to strengthen group cohesion and to define positions of authority and spokesmanship.

While this too is a valuable approach, it raises the question of how and whether occupationally defined groups differed from non-occupationally defined associations. Is it meaningful to distinguish occupationally defined associations from non-occupationally defined ones, if economic advantages were merely a side effect of group solidarity—especially given the fact that the social profiles of the members of nearly all voluntary associations we know about are very similar—(slightly) better-to-do craftsmen, traders, and providers of services?

The debate is somewhat mired by a tendency to conflate different types of associations: cult groups, occupational associations, and neighbourhood associations, often lumping in the associations of *Augustales*. The subtitle of Bollmann's *Untersuchungen zu den Scholae der römischen Berufs-, Kult- und Augustalen-Kollegien in Italien* well illustrates this tendency and the underlying reasons for it: the difference is sometimes hard to tell in the empirical evidence—impossible even for most of Bollmann's buildings.[25] The title of Waltzing's classical study on Roman *Corporations professionnelles* did not prevent his catalogue from being filled with associations that are patently cult groups without any professional identity.[26] The underlying assumption of such a 'loose' approach is that, whatever else they may have been, all *collegia* were structured social communities that strongly emphasized interpersonal trust and friendly interaction among their members. From an economic point of view, all *collegia* were 'trust networks', meaning that the impact of religious groups on the economic choices and strategies of their members may have been no less strong than in the case of guilds that publicly professed their occupational identity.

Yet, from the later first century AD onwards, we find a huge surge in associations that profess a professional rather than a religious identity. The phenomenon is visible empire-wide, including in the Hellenistic east with its much older associative traditions. There is no denying the growing preference of association members to express their social identity and integration in terms

---

[24] Venticinque (2016; see earlier 2010); for professional *collegia* as trust networks and the economic effects of that, see also Broekaert (2011); for a critical view, see Liu (2016).
[25] Bollmann (1998).   [26] Waltzing (1895).

of their professional status and membership of occupationally defined groups. By the end of the first century AD we see it reflected even in literary sources, such as in the myths ascribing the creation of professional associations to Numa Pompilius or (in an alternative tradition) to Servius Tullius, desiring to distribute common citizens according to their specific *technē* or *ars*.[27] Professional skills were, apparently, increasingly accepted as socially useful. As early as the middle of the first century AD, Asconius asserted that some *collegia* escaped prohibition because of their *utilitas civitatis*.[28] In the third century the jurists distinguished a category of *collegia* to which members were allowed *artificii sui causa*.[29]

The first question I want to address in the following pages is whether and how this preference for professional specificity was connected to the guilds' religious practices. Did specific occupationally defined groups also have specific religious practices? Did they have a specific religious identity? In the second part of this chapter I will discuss the problematic case of the *dendrophori* (literally the 'tree-carriers'), religious groups that were closely connected to the cult of Mater Magna but whose members are often identified as loggers or traders in timber and/or firewood.

This study is based on material collected in the 'Ghent Database of Roman Guilds and Occupation-Based Communities', a project that aims to collect data on all occupational guilds and communities attested in the Roman world from the second century BC to the sixth century AD.[30] At this moment the database is well advanced for groups in the (Latin) west, but the (Greek) east is still only very incompletely covered.[31] For that reason, this contribution is largely limited to the western 'Latin' part of the empire.

Religious Groups?

By and large we can distinguish four criteria expressing the religious characteristics of ancient guilds:

1. the group's internal organization is structured by offices and functions that are primarily or essentially religious;

---

[27] Plut. *Num*. 17; Flor. *Epit*. 1.6.3; Plin. *HN* 34.1 (i); 35.159 (lx); cf. Verboven (2016).
[28] Asc. *Corn*. p. 67 (ed. Clark).   [29] *Dig*. 47.22.1–3.   [30] https://gdrg.ugent.be/.
[31] Only 441 groups are now (20 January 2017) recorded in the Greek provinces, compared to 951 in the Latin ones and 364 in Rome (total number 1,755); these include not only formalized groups (such as *collegia*) but also non-formalized communities such as *cives Romani qui negotiantur*.

2. the group engages, as a collective body, in religious practices;
3. the group owns, controls, or has entitlements (such as right of use) on significant religious assets in which they invest important resources;
4. the group explicitly identifies itself as *cultores* (usually) of a specific deity.

Religious Organization

The first criterion can be dealt with swiftly. Professional *collegia* in the Latin west rarely organized themselves religiously. Religious rituals and ceremonies were simply performed by the magistrates of the group, as city magistrates performed the required rituals in public cults.[32] Only a handful of *collegia* are attested as having specific priestly offices.[33] The joint guild of *centonarii* and *fabri* of Mediolanum had a *pontifex*, who could apparently combine his function with that of *curator arcae*.[34] The *album* of the carpenters/builders (*fabri tignuarii*) of Lunae shows a *haruspex* who is listed among the common members next to a *scriba* and two *medici*.[35] In Cordoba the *collegium* established by the *familia publica* had a *sacerdos*, whose office could be cumulated with that of *magister perpetuus*.[36] The *aquatores Feronenses* in Aquileia had a *sacerdos*, who was expected to pay an honorary fee, but the nature of this association (water-workers or mere cult association?) is not clear.[37]

Ceremonies and Processions

As a rule, the ordinary magistrates performed all required religious rituals. Simple religious acts (small offerings, libations, invocations, or prayers to a protective deity) were routine practice at guild meetings, as witnessed by the numerous large and small altars, statues, and figurines adorning guild houses. Yet inscriptions rarely mention religious ceremonies by occupational associations explicitly. An inscription from Brixia mentions two endowments given to and managed by 'all the *collegia*' to perform sacrifices and bring libations

---

[32] See Waltzing (1895: i. 389); Ausbüttel (1982: 51–2); cf., e.g., *CIL* V.4449.
[33] cf. Ausbüttel (1982: 52)..
[34] *CIL* V.5738 (AD 179–201): *pon[tif(ex)] et çu[r]at(or)/arc(ae) coll(egi) fabr(um)/et cent(onariorum) m̄(unicipi) M̄(ediolaniensis)*; 5612 (AD 246–68).
[35] *CIL* XI.1355a.   [36] *CIL* II.2229.
[37] *CIL* V.776 (second century AD, *sacerdos gratuitus*); 8218: Waltzing (1895: i.197) believed they were fullers, but that seems unlikely; see Steuernagel (2004: 193–5).

on the birthday of the emperor Severus.[38] Similarly an endowment given to the *fabri* of Ravenna imposed yearly sacrifices in honour of the deceased family members of the benefactor.[39] There is no reason to think that the sacrifices and libations mentioned in these inscriptions were exceptional. Rather, in these cases the benefactors wished that a separate religious ceremony would be performed yearly on a specific date. Most other endowments merely specify that the *collegiati* should have a solemn banquet (*epulum*) in memory of the benefactor.

Inscriptions are largely silent also about the public processions in which we know guilds participated. Some inscriptions mention flag-carriers and standard-bearers.[40] The guild of *fabri* and *centonarii* in Comum had a separate division of *vexillarii*.[41] Yet only two inscriptions positively document the participation of an occupational guild in a procession.[42] One records a procession by the guild of *fabri* in Aquincum under the leadership of their *praefectus* and *patronus* in honour of Jupiter Optimus Maximus for the well-being of the emperor.[43] The other is an inscription recording a handout to the *ad mare euntes* in Aquileia by a *magister* of the *collegium fabrum*. The inscription is somewhat ambiguous about who these 'sea-goers' were, but the members of the guild were clearly closely involved in the procession.[44] A famous fresco from Pompeii shows a procession of carpenters carrying a statue of Daedalus.[45] It is inconceivable that guilds of carpenters/builders (the *fabri tignuarii*) would not have been closely involved in processions like these. Yet not a single inscription, text, or relief attests this—it simply did not make it into the record. This is all the more surprising because processions in which statues of gods were carried were a central feature in many ancient cults.[46] Similarly, Waltzing was almost certainly correct in assuming that the guild of fishermen and divers on the Tiber (*Corpus piscatorum et urinatorum totius alvei Tiberis*) was closely involved with the organization of the fishermen's festival (*ludi piscatorii*). Yet

---

[38] *CIL* V.4449. [39] *CIL* XI.126; cf. also *CIL* XII.731 (*utriclarii* from Arles).
[40] *CIL* III.1583 (Drobeta, AD 200–70); 7900 (Sarmizegetusa, AD 170–250); 8837 (Salona, AD 175–225); cf. *IK* XXIV.7014 (Smyrna, late second century AD) for a preserved banner stand. On processions, see *IK* Smyrna 714; van Nijf (1997: 200; 2002: 322–4); Verboven (2016: 190–1).
[41] *CIL* V.5272 (c. AD 200).
[42] See also *AE* 1913, 148 for a *medagogus* of the *collegium fabrum* of Hasta, who may have had a role as procession leader; cf. Mennella (1992).
[43] *CIL* III.3438; for this now generally accepted interpretation of this inscription, see Fishwick (1987: iii. 280; 1989: 182); van Nijf (2002: 323–4); Liu (2009: 126, 153–4).
[44] *AE* 1995, 573 (second century AD); cf. Steuernagel (2004: 177).
[45] Pompeii VI.7.9; cf. Leach (2004: 188, 309, no. 16); Burford (1972: pl. 12).
[46] cf. Fishwick (1989: 182).

none of our sources, epigraphic or other, highlights their involvement.[47] The same guild provides a unique example of a forceful inscribed prayer—not, however, for their patron god, Pater Tiberinus, in whose honour the *ludi piscatorii* were celebrated, but for the new emperor Caracalla as Deus Imperator 'fallen from the stars, August Thunderer'.[48]

Temples and Religious Structures

Collegia (ideally) had their own meeting places or *scholae*. They came in many shapes and sizes, ranging from porticos and small rooms to large structures with rooms devoted to different functions. Spectacular examples are the house of the 'Poseidoniasts from Beirut' on Delos[49] or the temple compounds of the carpenters/builders (*fabri tignuarii*) and of the shipwrights (*fabri navales*) in Ostia (discussed later in this chapter). Even the smallest *statio* usually had religious objects placed in it—a small altar, a statuette of a deity—as any Roman private *domus* had, but some associations possessed architecturally recognizable chapels and temples. The difference between non-religious rooms adorned with religious objects and distinctly religious chapels and temples, however, was blurry. Social and religious functions commonly overlapped. Different designations (*schola, templum, aedes, statio,...*) were used for the same or similar buildings, depending on whether the speaker/writer wished to stress profane or religious aspects.[50] The use of a general designation, however, such as *schola*, did not preclude religious dimensions. Thus, for instance, the *centonarii* of Apulum had their 'clubhouse with pediment' (*schola cum aetoma*) dedicated by the governor of Dacia 'for the prosperity' of Septimius Severus and his son (*pro salute Augustorum*).[51] *Scholae* were adorned with religious objects, temples were used as meeting places. The guild of ivory and citrus-wood dealers in Rome (*eborarii et citrarii*), for instance, received the right of use of a private 'tetrastyle *schola* for...Augustus' to be used specifically for meetings

---

[47] Waltzing (1895: i. 237–8); *CIL* VI.1080; 1872; 29700; 29702; but note curiously that Festus (238.59–60 (ed. Lindsay)) does link the festival with the 'profit of the fishermen' (*piscatorum quaestus*).
[48] *CIL* VI.1080; see Gagé (1966).   [49] Bruneau (1978, 1991); Trümper (2002, 2011).
[50] 'On disait *schola* ou *templum*, suivant qu'on songeait plutôt à la destination profane ou au caractère religieux du local, sans égard à sa forme architecturale' (Waltzing 1895: i. 224–5); see also Bollmann (1998: 47–8, 54–5); Steuernagel (1999); Verboven (2011: 343).
[51] *CIL* III.1174; for a similar case, see the barge-skippers of the Aare and the (unidentified) Aramus who dedicated their *schola* to the *Domus Divina* (*CIL* XIII.5096); cf. *CIL*.XI.6335 (*in schola deae/Minervae Aug(ustae) col(legi) fab(rum)*), Pisaurum; AD 255).

(*quo conveniretur*).⁵² The *collegium fabrum* of Fidentia met in its temple dedicated to Minerva to discuss and decide on the co-optation of a patron.⁵³

How much money and effort did professional *collegia* invest in building and adorning specific buildings or separate rooms for religious purposes? How visually prominent were they? We cannot say much about the religious use of *scholae* in general, or the prominence of religious objects in them, but we do find a number of structures that architecturally stand out as religious. Bollmann found that (in Italy) all except one⁵⁴ belonged to the type of the 'courtyard temple' ('Hoftempel') inspired by the layout of the imperial *fora*. The actual temple was set in a courtyard (usually with a portico) designed for various social activities. Both temple and courtyard were equally important. The choice seems based mainly on representational considerations. Imperial *fora* were central loci where affairs of the *res publica*, ranging from litigation over public speeches to senatorial deliberation, were handled. By choosing the model of the imperial *fora*, *collegia* confirmed their loyalty and attachment to the imperial order, and expressed their ambition to be small *res publicae*, under the protection of the gods.⁵⁵ Courtyard temples appear to be an Italian development. They are first attested in the first century AD for the *Augustales*. The adoption of the type by professional *collegia* dates to the second century AD. They are found in six Italian locations: during the first century AD in Misenum, Rusellae, Pompeii, Cumae (one temple each, probably all belonging to associations of *Augustales*), in the second and third centuries in Grumentum (one temple) and Ostia (five temples).⁵⁶ Unfortunately, in the absence of inscriptions identifying a building, it is impossible to determine what type of association would have used it. The only definitely identified occupational *collegia* with this type of temple are three Ostian guilds. The shipwrights (*corpus fabrum navalium*) built a temple for an unknown deity probably under Commodus.⁵⁷ The carpenters/builders (*corpus fabrum tignuariorum*) dedicated their temple to *Divus Pertinax* in AD 194.⁵⁸ The flax-workers (*corpus splendidissimum stuppatorum*) began building a temple during the reign of Alexander Severus, but it was finished only in the second half of the third

---

⁵² CIL VI.33885: Iulius] Aelianus ius scholae tetrastyli/[—] Aug(usti) quo conveniretur a negotiantibus/] eborari(i)s dedit (followed by the *lex collegia*, in which no reference to any religious act is mentioned).
⁵³ AE 1991, 713 (AD 206, *in templo Minervae collegi fabrum*); similarly CIL XI.970 (AD 190, *in templo collegi(i) fabrum/et centonariorum Regiensium*).
⁵⁴ The temple of the *mensores* at Ostia: Bollmann (1998: 291–5 (A 32, Abb. 30)).
⁵⁵ Bollmann (1998: 81–103); Tran (2006: 242–7); Zänker (1994). ⁵⁶ Bollmann (1998: 86).
⁵⁷ Bollmann (1998: 304–7 (A 36, Abb. 21)), probably under Commodus, deity unknown.
⁵⁸ Bollmann (1998: 340–5 (A 45, Abb. 20)).

century to serve as a *Mithraeum*.[59] A further unidentified but probably professional *collegium* built its courtyard temple to an unknown deity between around AD 200 and 235.[60] The early second-century temple of the grain measurers (*mensores frumentarii*) in Ostia, probably dedicated to Ceres, follows a different layout, without a courtyard, but with a large adjacent hall.[61] These Ostian examples are conspicuously large. The temple complex of the *fabri tignuarii* measured approximately 33–9 m deep and 14.5–17.5 m wide, with smaller rooms on the outside. That of the *fabri navales* was even larger (56–58.5 m by 16–17 m).[62] These were structures that were clearly intended both to impress and to provide room for collective rituals, ceremonies, and gatherings. The connection of the temple of the *mensores* to the large hall illustrates this purpose well.

The courtyard temple was characteristic for *collegia*, but the different layout of the temple and hall complex of the *mensores frumentarii* at Ostia shows that it was not the only type used by ancient *collegia*. This makes it very hard to identify architecturally 'religious' buildings as *collegium*-temples. The vast majority of guild 'temples' are known only from inscriptions. Even for the best-documented towns the exact location usually remains unknown. Thus, for instance, the wine importers in Ostia had a temple dedicated to their *Genius* on the *forum vinarium*.[63] Two monumental inscriptions list the members of the guild of small boatmen operating the *Traiectus Luculli* who contributed to the enlargement of their guild-temple.[64] Neither temple, however, has been located so far.

The divide between *collegium*-temple and public temple was not always clear-cut. In the first decades after the Roman conquest, a *collegium fabrum* built and dedicated a temple to Neptune and Minerva in Noviomagus Reginorum (Chichester) for the well-being of the imperial house, on the authority (*ex auctoritate*) of the vassal king Togidubnus.[65] The case might be an outlier, but

---

[59] Bollmann (1998: 278–82 (A 28, Abb. 23)), *[— te]mpl(um) et spel(aeum) Mit(hrae)* (*NSA*, 1953, 244).

[60] Bollmann (1998: 328–31 (A 42, Abb. 25)), the so-called 'temple of the Terme del Filosofo'.

[61] Bollmann (1998: 291–5 (A 32, Abb. 32)).

[62] cf. Bollmann (1998: 340–55 (A 45, Abb. 20)); on the *collegia* building at Ostia, see also Zevi (2008).

[63] *AE* 1940, 64 (*corporatus in tem/plo fori vinari(i) inpor/tatorum negotian/tium*); *AE* 1940, 65 (*[— corporatus?]/in templo fo[ri vinari inportatorum negotiantium]*); *AE* 1955, 165 (*Genio corporis/splendidissimi/inportantium/et negotiantium/vinariorum*); *CIL* XIV.430 (*colleg(ii) Geni fori/vinari*); cf. also *AE* 1940, 66; 1974, 123a; *CIL* XIV.409.

[64] *CIL* XIV.246; 5356+5374: *ordo corporator(um) qui pecuniam ad ampliand(um) templum contuler(unt)*; on the identification of this group with the *corpus lenunculariorum Traiectus Luculli*, see Royden (1988: 33–6); Tran (2006: 116).

[65] *RIB* 91.

cooperation between local authorities and high-ranking guilds to build, repair, or maintain temples (especially connected to the imperial cult) is attested more often. We have already encountered the case of the *schola* of the *centonarii* of Apulum, dedicated *pro salute Augustorum* by the governor of the province. Another example is provided by the *fabri dolabrarii* of Trier, who built a temple (*c.* AD 170–85), dedicated to the Augustan Powers (*Numinib(us) Aug(ustis)*), the god Intarabus, and their own *Genius*, but on land given to them by the local senate and probably placed among public temples.[66] Similarly in Cetium (Noricum), the guild of *fabri* 'restored' a temple for the Salus of the emperor under Caracalla or Elagabalus on land that they had been given by the city council.[67] In other cases, we find local aristocrats financing the building and or (re)decorating of guild-temples. In Patavium, for instance, a *quattuorvir aedilicia potestate* and patron of the guild of *centonarii* decorated their temple and gave them an endowment of HS 2,000 for its maintenance.[68] It is hardly surprising, then, to find *collegia* assembling in public temples. Thus, it seems that, before a benefactress donated an *aedicula* with a courtyard to serve as *schola*, the *collegium* of Aesculapius and Hygia met in the temple of the Divi on the Palatine, in the chapel of Divus Titus. They would continue to meet there each year to celebrate the birthday of the emperor Antoninus Pius.[69] The prominence with which the benefactor who built the temple for Aesculapius and Hygia in Apulum mentions his patronage of the city's guild of *fabri* strongly suggests that they were free to use it, even if it may not have been strictly 'their' temple (see below).

To conclude this section, we find that religious structures and adornments were omnipresent in the guilds' universe, but often the divide between religious and non-religious purposes was not clear-cut. Even temples and chapels that were architecturally distinctly religious served non-religious purposes. Nor was the divide between private and public very strict. Sometimes guilds were given permission to build their temples on public land. Prominent public figures financially supported investments in guild-temples. Last but not least, public temples were used for non-religious guild meetings (as they were used on occasion for meetings of local senates). There is little indication that their cult places and material infrastructure served to segregate guilds from the societies in which they operated.

---

[66] *CIL* XIII.11313; cf. Demougin (2012).   [67] *CIL* III.5659.
[68] *CIL* V.2864; see also *CIL* XI.126 (Ravenna, *c.* AD 175–250).
[69] *CIL* VI.10234 (pp. 3502, 3908).

Name–Title Association

The most obvious way for a professional association to affirm its religious identity was by including a reference to a specific patron deity in its name. This type of name–deity association, however, seems to have been more common in the Greek east than in the Latin west. The most cited examples come from Delos: the 'Community of Posidoniastai from Berytus, Merchants, Shippers, and Warehousemen' (τὸ ἐν Δήλωι κοινὸν Βηρυτίων Ποσειδωνιαστῶν ἐμπόρων καὶ ναυκλήρων καὶ ἐγδοχέων)[70] and the 'Community of Herakleistai from Tyre, Merchants and Shippers' (τὸ κοινὸν τῶν Τυρίων Ἡρακλειστῶν ἐμπόρων καὶ ναυκλήρων).[71] The practice occurs in the Latin west but is not very common. Currently in the Ghent database we have twenty-one cases of associations combining religious and professional elements in their name (Table 11.1). This may seem a lot, but, of a total of 1,315 groups (in the Latin west), it represents only about 1.6 per cent, far too low to conclude that professional associations habitually used religious titles.[72]

Could the list be too short because some professional associations 'hid' behind a religious name? The mercantile community from Beirut settled at Puteoli designated themselves as the 'Beirutian worshippers of Jupiter Heliopolitanus [= Zeus of Baalbek] who reside in Puteoli' (*cultores Iovis Heliopo/litani Berytenses qui / Puteolis consistent*). They were organized in a *corpus Heliopolitanorum*.[73] But, as we have already discussed in the introduction to this chapter, oriental (especial Phoenician) mercantile communities are a very specific case. Waltzing suggested that the 'lovers of the meat-market, worshippers of Jupiter Arcanus' (*amatores regionis / macelli cultores / Iovis Arkani*) at Praeneste were butchers.[74] He also believed that the *cultor Minervae* mentioned in a funerary inscription from Cortona was member of a guild of *fabri*.[75] Similarly the *c(ultores) Minervae* who owned a temple in Tarraco restored by a benefactor in the second century may have been *fabri*.[76] The relief of a ship under the funerary inscription of a member suggests that the *collegium Isidis* in Aternum was a guild of shippers.[77] There are, however, not many instances where such assumptions are warranted.

---

[70] e.g. *IDélos* 1520; Hasenohr (2007) for a general discussion of this group.
[71] *IDélos* 1519; Hasenohr (2007) for a general discussion.
[72] cf. in this sense also Ausbüttel (1982: 49).
[73] *CIL* X.1579 (first or second century AD); 1634 (AD 116); cf. Tran Tam Tinh (1972: 149).
[74] *CIL* XIV.2937 (early imperial); Waltzing (1895: i. 197). [75] *CIL* XI.1906.
[76] *CIL* II.4085; or should we perhaps read *c(ollegio) d(edit)* instead of *c(ultoribus) d(edit)*? For the *fabri* in Tarraco, see also *CIL* II (14.3).1214; 4316.
[77] *CIL* IX.3338; cf. Buonocore (2004); see also *CIL* IX.3337: *nauclero / qui erat in colleg(io) Serapis Salon(itano)*.

Table 11.1 Names of associations combining religious and professional references

Deity	Dedicants	Location	Text and reference
Diana	*Capulatores* (olive-oil workers)	Allifae (Severan)	*Collegium Capulatorum Sacerdotum Dianae* (*CIL* IX.2336)
Asclepius et Hygia	*Medici* (physicians)	Augusta Taurinorum (from c. AD 117 to middle second century AD)	*medicis Taur(inis) / cultor(ibus) / Asclepi et / Hygiae* (*CIL* V.6970)
Ceres	*Mensores frumentarii* (corn-measurers)	Ostia (second and third centuries AD)	*Mensor(um) frumentarior(um) Cereris Aug(ustae)* (*CIL* XIV.409; cf. *AE* 1988, 212; *CIL* XIV.363, 364)
Diana	*Lotores* (fullers or bath attendants[a])	Aricia (first or second century AD)	*Dianae Aug(ustae) / colleg(ii) lotor(um) / sacr(orum?)* (*CIL* XIV.2156; cf. *AE* 1912, 92)
Diana	*Venatores* (hunters or performers in *venationes*)	Rocca d'Arce (Arpinum?) (second century AD)	*colleg(ium) ven/ator(um) sacer(dotum) / Dean[e]* (*CIL* X.5671)
Domus Augustae	*Sagarii* (cloak-dealers)	Roma (AD 103/4)	*sagari t[hea]tri Marcell(i) / cultores domus Aug(ustae)* (*CIL* VI.956)
Feronia	*Aquatores* (water-management workers?)	Aquileia (second century AD)	*Feroniensium Aquatorum* (*CIL* V.992) *Fer(oniensium) Aquat(orum)* (*CIL* V.8308; cf. *CIL* V.8218 (dedication to Feronia))
Genius Fori Vinarii	*Negotiantes vinarii* (wine-dealers)	Ostia (second and third centuries AD)	*colleg(ii) Geni fori / vinari(i)* (*CIL* XIV.430) *corporatus in templo fori vinari inportatorum negotiantium* (*AE* 1940, 64; 65; cf. *CIL* XIV.409; *AE* 1940, 66; 1955, 165; 1974, 123a)
Hercules	*Possessores inquilini negotiantes Viae Stratae* (owners and resident merchants)	Interamna Nahars (AD 240)	*Possessores, inquilini, negotiantes viae strate cultores Herculis* (*CIL* XI.4209)
Hercules	*cisiarii* (coach-drivers)	Tibur (late first century AD)	*collegio iumentariorum qui est / in cisiaris Tiburtinis Herculis* (*CIL* VI.9485)
Hercules Salutaris	*Saccarii* (porters)	Roma (second century AD)	*collegi(i) Herculis Salutaris / c(o)h(ortis) primae sac(c)ario/rum* (*CIL* VI.339)
Isis	(shippers or merchants)	Aternum (second or third century AD)	*in coll(egio) Isid(is)* (*CIL* IX.3338)

Deity	Dedicants	Location	Text and reference
Liber Pater	*Caupones* (innkeepers)	Caesarea (Mauretania) (late first to middle third centuries AD)	cultori<e=I>s <Libe=DO>ri Patri(s) / patrono / ob merita / eius caupon<e=I>s (CIL VIII.9409)
Liber Pater et Mercurius	*Negotiantes cellarum vinariarum* (wine-dealers)	Roma (AD 102)	Collegium Liberi Patris et Mercuri Negotiantium Cellarum Vinariarum Novae et Arruntianae (CIL VI.8826)
Mater Magna	*Dendrophori* (lumberjacks or wood-dealers?)	Rome (second century AD)	dendrophoris M(atris) d(eum) M(agnae) (CIL VI.641) collegium dendrophorum Matris Deum M(agnae) I(daeae) et Attis (CIL VI.30973)
Mercurius	*Mercatores* (merchants)	Capua (end second century BC)	Magistri Mercurio Felici (CIL I.2947) magistreis conlegi mercatorum (CIL X.3773)
Mercurius	*Vestiarii* (clothes-dealers)	Volubilis (second century AD)	Collegium Mercuri Vestiariorum (CIL VIII.21848)
Minerva	*Fabri* (craftsmen, builders)	Aquileia (second century AD)	[co]lleg(ium) incrementoru[m] [c]ultorum Minerva[e] (AE 1995, 573)
Serapis	(shippers or merchants)	Aternum (first or second century AD)	nauclero / qui erat in colleg(io) / Serapis Salon(itano) (CIL IX.3337)
Silvanus	*Subrutores* (demolitioners)	Rome (Vespasian)	cur(ator) col(legi) subrutor(um), cultor(um) Silvani (CIL VI.940)
Venus	*Fabri* (craftsmen, builders)	Salona (second to fourth century AD)	[c]oll(egium) fabrum / Veneris (CIL III.1981) ex col(legio) Veneris (CIL III.2106; 2108)

[a] Bruun (1993).

The most often adduced are cult associations for Aesculapius and Hygia, which may have been *collegia* of doctors and healthcare workers, and associations for Mercury, which may have been merchant guilds. Both, however, are more problematic than generally assumed.

An inscription from Capua dated to 105 BC mentions a board of *Mag(istri)... Mercu[rio] Felici*,[78] which a few years earlier presented itself as *magistreis*

---

[78] CIL I.2947; the inscription was set up by the *Mag(istri) Castori et Polluci et Mercu[rio] Felici*, but the list of names shows that these present two different associations.

conlegi mercatorum.⁷⁹ This was clearly a merchant guild. Flambard argued, similarly, that the Roman *Hermaistai/Magistri Mercurii* associations on late Hellenistic Delos also represented merchants, while the *Posidoniastai/Magistri Neptuni/Neptunales* were shippers. This is less certain, but there is no doubt that the Roman residents on Delos were predominantly merchants, shippers, and their bankers/financiers.⁸⁰ A few other groups of *cultores Mercurii* are attested that may (or may not) have been associations of merchants or businessmen,⁸¹ but the most intriguing case is that of the *Mercuriales*. Twenty of their collectives are attested from the late Republic and early empire (Fig. 11.1: all in Italy, except for one in Narona, Dalmatia). It is tempting to see these as merchant guilds, but the sources are ambiguous. Livy claims that the *Mercuriales* in Rome were established as a *mercatorum collegium* in 495 BC to take care of the new temple of Mercury. In historical times, however, the *Mercuriales* of Rome were a high-ranking priestly college, not a merchant guild.⁸² In Foro Felice, on the other hand, in the third quarter of the first century BC, the association of *Mercuriales* leased what appears to have been part of a *macellum* (an open space, three shops, an arch, and doorway).⁸³ In Beneventum, one of the *Mercuriales* was a banker (*nummularius*).⁸⁴ Elsewhere, however, the *Mercuriales* appear closely linked to the *Augustales*.⁸⁵ The latter received their office and dignity from local city councils. Could this have been the case also with the *Mercuriales*? In Narona, at least, two *seviri magistri Mercuriales* (or *Mercurii*) dedicated an altar to Aesculapius *ob honorem*.⁸⁶ Like the *Augustales*, the *Mercuriales* appear to have been predominantly successful freedman, barred by their servile past from pursuing civic careers. So, like the *Augustales*, *Mercuriales* may have received their 'office' as an honour in recognition for benefactions to the city or to stimulate their willingness to indulge in public munificence. Of course, even if this were so, it does not exclude the possibility that *Mercuriales* were chosen among well-to-do businessmen and, like the *Augustales*, organized themselves in a *collegium*. *Collegia Mercurialium* are explicitly mentioned in inscriptions from Atina and Compsa.⁸⁷ Elsewhere

---

⁷⁹ *CIL* X.3773.

⁸⁰ Flambard (1982); but see against this Hatzfeld (1912: 180–1); merchants and shippers were not neatly separated categories. See also Rauh (1993: 33–41).

⁸¹ *CIL* III.5196a; VII.1069; 1070; IX.3422; *ILAlg* II.1, 2085.

⁸² Livy 2.27.5; Combet Farnoux (1980, 1981). ⁸³ *AE* 1999, 538; cf. Nonnis and Ricci (1999).

⁸⁴ *CIL* IX.1707 (p. 695).

⁸⁵ Taylor (1931: 219–20); for a full discussion, see Combet Farnoux (1981); Degrassi (1937); but note that the link with the *Augustales* does *not* imply a link to the imperial cult (Mouritsen 2006; 2011: 249–60). Compare perhaps also with the cult group of Hercules Somnialis attested at Pisa (*CIL* XI.1449); see Taylor (1923: 219–20).

⁸⁶ *AE* 1932, 82 (first or second century AD).

⁸⁷ *CIL* X.340 (Atina, later second or early third century: *colegius* (!) *Mercurialium*); *CIL* IX.972 (Compsa, later second or early third century: *collegium / Mercuriales* (!)).

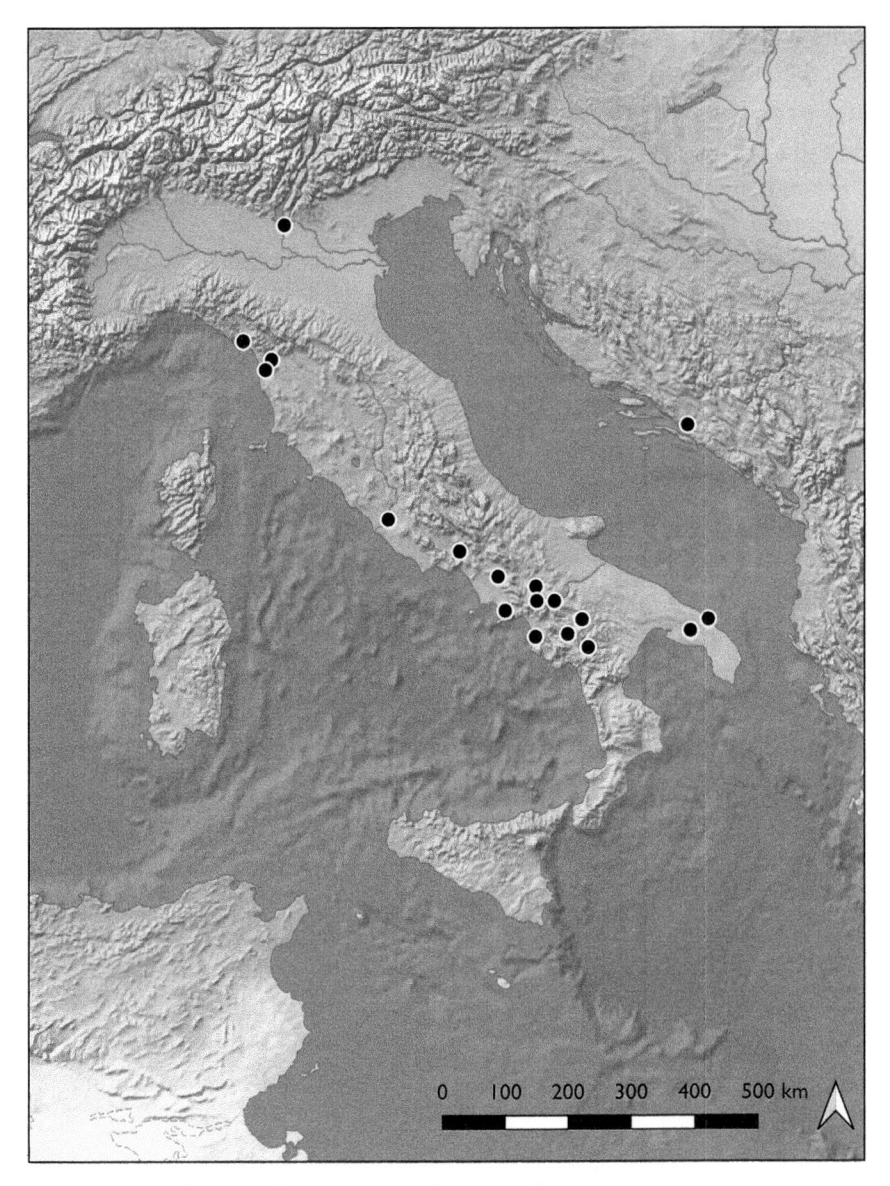

Fig. 11.1 Distribution of associations of *Mercuriales*.
Source: Ghent Database of Roman Guilds and Occupation-Based Communities; basemap from Natural Earth.

the presence of *magistri* among them and the space they collectively rented in Foro Felice indicate a corporate organization.[88] On the whole, however, groups of *Mercuriales* are not frequently attested, and some appear to be

---

[88] *Magistri*: AE 1901, 173; 1912, 106; 1937, 131; 1964, 32; 1988, 257; 1992, 285; CIL III.1799; X.485; 1272; 4589; XI.1417.

quite early (late Republican, Augustan, early Julio-Claudian). It is tempting, therefore, to think that the *Mercuriales* originated in the late Republic and were gradually (in most places) replaced by or incorporated into the *Augustales*.

Vespasian explicitly granted or confirmed the right of physicians to establish formal associations.[89] There are, however, very few *collegia* of doctors on record.[90] Is this because associations of physicians preferred to go by their religious title rather than their occupational one? The Greek text of Vespasian's rescript, for instance, denotes their associations as *Asklepiadai*. In an honorary inscription dedicated to a high-ranking fellow doctor in Ephesos, they call themselves the 'Physicians Who Sacrifice to the Founder Asklepios and to the Emperors'.[91] The doctors at Augusta Taurinorum are designated as the *medici Taurini cultores Asclepi et Hygiae*.[92] However, there are only a few cult associations for Aesculapius in Latin inscriptions attested, and we should be careful to interpret these all as professional associations. The statutes of the *collegium Aesculapi et Hygiae* in Rome, for instance, limited the number of members to sixty and gave them the right to bequeath their place to a son, brother, or freedman. Conspicuously, however, they make no mention of the professions of prospective members. If we accept the commonly held view that these were doctors (or at least healthcare workers), then what happened if the legatee was not?[93] Individual dedications to Aesculapius and Hygia are frequent and certainly not the exclusive domain of medical doctors or personal-care workers. A patron of the guild of *fabri* of Apulum, for instance, and later council member of the city, dedicated a temple to Aesculapius and Hygia *ex iusso (deorum)*.[94] The same temple was adorned with numerous other monuments, altars, and statues, and several other benefactors contributed. Nothing suggests the existence of a guild of physicians attached to the temple. In some cases, medical doctors appear to have been attached to other guilds. The builders/carpenters' guild (*fabri tignuarii*) of Luna (Etruria) in the second century AD

---

[89] *FIRA* I, no. 73; they may have enjoyed exemption from the ban on *collegia* earlier; see in this sense Israelowich (2015: 24–5); for earlier tax exemption, see *IEphesos* 223.

[90] *CIL* IV.6970 (Augusta Taurinorum); *CIL* VI.29805; Gruter 632 for the *schola medicorum* at Rome; *CIL* IX.1618 (Beneventum); XIII.5079 (Aventicum); *AE* 1905, 169 (Divodurum, c. AD 90–110; cf. Rémy and Faure 2010: 178–9); obliquely perhaps *CIL* VII.1144 (Misenum), in which a doctor attached to the fleet (*medicus duplicarius*) received a funeral monument from his *collegae*, but the term might also refer to *commilitiones* or a more general military *collegium* (cf. 1–2).

[91] *IEphesos* 719: ([Οἱ] θύοντες τῷ προπά|τορι Ἀσκληπιῷ καὶ τοῖς | Σεβαστοῖς ἰατροί); more commonly 'the doctors attached to the Mouseion in Ephesos' (οἱ ἐν Ἐφέσῳ ἀπὸ τοῦ Μουσείου ἰατροί): *IEphesos* 1162; 2304; 4101A.

[92] *CIL* V.6970.   [93] *CIL* VI.10234 (AD 153).

[94] *CIL* III.975 (end second or third century AD). Cf. also *CIL* V.731 (Aquileia) for a *decurio* of the guild of *fabri* dedicating an altar to Aesculapius and Hygia.

had two *medici* among its members, and the inscription (an *album*) shows that this was considered an office within the guild.[95] In Rome we find a *collegium Aesculapi et Hygiae structorum Caesaris nostri*. Was there a medical staff among the *structores* (probably builders) who gathered in a separate *collegium*?[96]

Religious Dedication Profiles

Adopting a religious name or title, however, was not the only way to forge or express a distinctly religious identity. Religious profiling is equally possible by dedicating monuments or participating in religious ceremonies and events (such as processions) in honour of specific deities. Was there an intrinsic relationship between the deities worshipped by guilds and their non-religious functions (social, economic, or political)?

The Ghent database maps four types of 'strong links' between a collective and specific deities: (i) title or name association (already discussed), (ii) dedications by or on behalf of a group, (iii) associations with a deity (for instance, a statue dedicated in the clubhouse of a *collegium*, or a dedication linking the *Genius* of a group to another deity), and (iv) ownership of or responsibility for a temple or a specific cult location.[97] At the moment only the deity links documented in inscriptions of *fabri*,[98] *centonarii*, *dendrophori*, and the river shippers (*nautae*) have been mapped. The *dendrophori* will be returned to in the second part of this chapter; the focus here is on the other three.

Liu notes three prominent types of cults 'for the majority, if not all, of the Roman *collegia*': that of the group's *Genius*, of patron gods, and of the emperor.[99] Bollmann notes that few of the major state gods, apart from Minerva and Jupiter, were popular among the Italian *collegia*, who, she believes, rather worshipped typical craft gods such as Minerva and Silvanus, or Hercules, who was considered a patron god of merchants, or protective deities such as Fortuna and (most popular of all) the association's *Genius*.[100] These views, however, need modification. First, we find significant differences between *collegia* (Fig. 11.2). Thus among the *fabri* (n = 67) the occupation-related deities constitute 31%

---

[95] CIL XI.1355a.
[96] AE 1937, 161; see also CIL III.3583 (Aquincum) for the *collegium centonariorum* co-financing the funeral monument of an African-born doctor.
[97] 'Weak links', such as being mentioned in the same inscription, are recorded in the database, but not further explored.
[98] All types, including the *fabri navales*. [99] Liu (2009: 252–66).
[100] Bollmann (1998: 146–7).

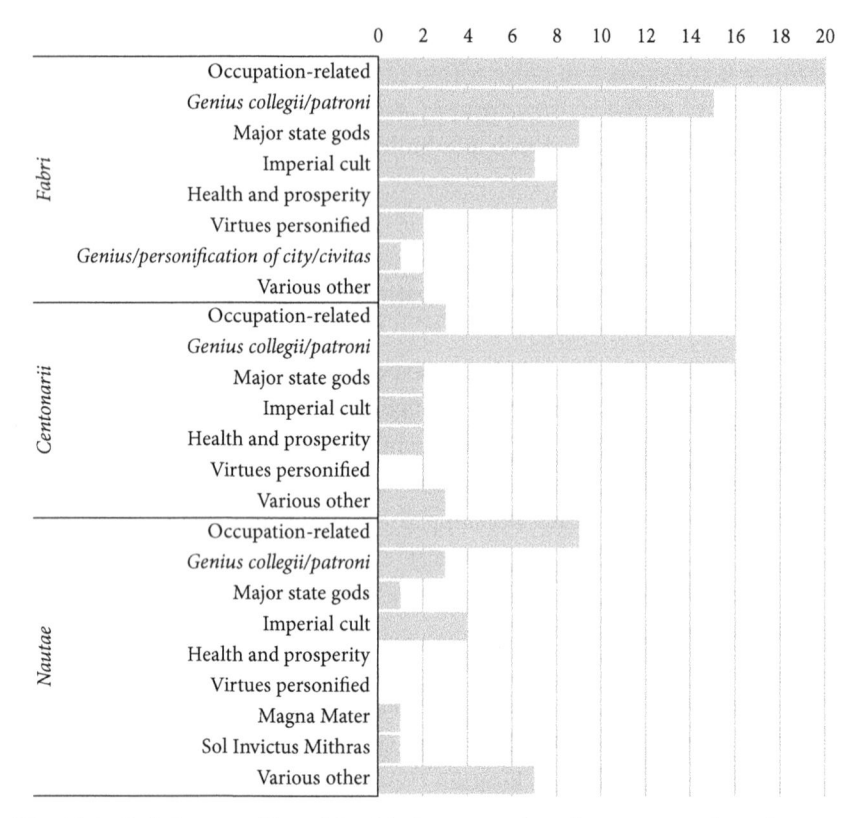

Fig. 11.2 Religious profiles of the *fabri*, *centonarii*, and *nautae*: number of inscriptions in different categories.

of the total, *Genius* dedications 22% (of which 13% to the *Genius collegii*, 9% to the *Genius, Iuno* or *Honos* of the patron or magistrate), health- and prosperity-related deities 12%, major state gods 15%, and imperial cult 10%. Among the *centonarii* (n = 28), however, *Genius* dedications make up 57% of the total, while occupation-related deities make up only 11%, and health- and prosperity-related deities, major state gods, and imperial cult each only 7%. In the case of the river shippers (*nautae*, n = 26) the percentage of occupation-related deities (35%), imperial cult (15%) and *Genius* dedications (12%) is in the same order of magnitude as for the *fabri*, but 27% are in the category 'various other'. Taking these figures at face value creates the impression that the specific religious profile of the *centonarii* was less occupationally oriented than that of the *fabri* and the *nautae*. It seems clear also that general protective deities (Genius, Fortuna, Salus, Asclepius…) and deities that promoted integration in the wider civic and imperial order were more important than specific 'occupational' patron gods.

Nautae (excl. *n. Parisiaci*)

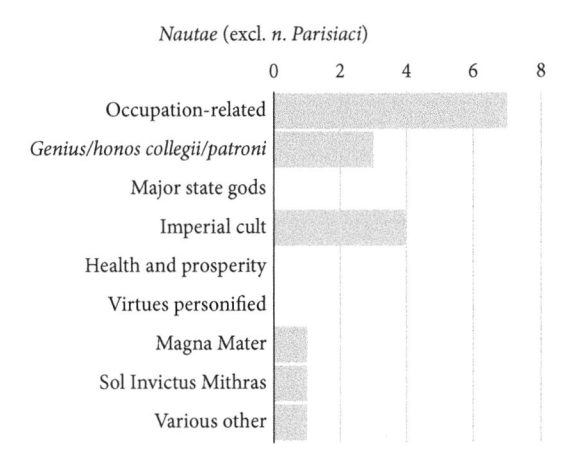

Fig. 11.3 Religious profile of the *nautae* excluding the *nautae Parisiaci*: number of inscriptions in different categories.

Secondly, however—and more importantly perhaps—the percentages conceal small absolute numbers. In the case of the *centonarii*, for instance, the 7% represent only two inscriptions, 11% only three. For the occupation-related deities, we have one dedication to Mercury, one to Hercules, and one to Minerva Ergana, and the latter may very well be a forgery.[101] The numbers are even more problematic for the river shippers. The high percentage of 'various other' is due to only one very exceptional monument of the *nautae Parisiaci*—a pillar over 5 m tall in honour of the emperor Tiberius, depicting scenes of a religious procession and (at least) eight deities, four of whom are Celtic.[102] If we disregard this one monument, the proportion of occupation-related strong deity-links rises to 44%, but the overall number drops to only eighteen (Fig. 11.3; Table 11.2). These low numbers raise doubts about the reliability of the religious profiles that emerge from the epigraphic records, beyond the general impression that occupation-specific deities were not very central to the religious life of occupationally defined *collegia*.

The ratio of strong deity-links to the total number of epigraphic guild-documents,[103] as well, is quite small (Table 11.3). Among a total of 522 such documents attesting *collegia fabrum* we find only 67 strong links, a ratio of only 0.13. The comparable figures for the *centonarii* are 28 strong links for

---

[101] *CIL* VI.*578; accepted as genuine by La Rocca (Cecamore 2002: 5–9 (preface)).
[102] Duval (1954, 1957); Hatt (1980); Béal (2005).
[103] Note: 'guild-document' is a concept used in the Ghent database; every group is connected to at least one source (epigraphic, payrological, literary, legal, or archaeological) to create a 'guild-document'; a single inscription mentioning three different *collegia* will, therefore, generate *three* guild-documents.

Table 11.2 Epigraphic evidence for religious dedications by the *fabri, centonarii, nautae,* and *dendrophori*

	Fabri (all varieties)	Centonarii	Nautae (including n. Parisiaci)	Nautae (excluding n. Parisiaci)	Dendrophori
Imperial cult	7	2	4	4	7
Augustus/-i	1				1
Genius Imperatoris	1				1
Numen Augusti	2	1	2	2	1
Domus Divina	1		2	2	
Divus Augustus		1			
Diva Plotina					1
Divus Antoninus Pius					1
Diva Faustina Maior					1
Diva Faustina Minor					1
Divus Pertinax	2				
Major state gods	10	2	1		2
Jupiter	5	2	1		1
Juno	1				
Mars	2				1
Venus	2				
Mater Magna			1	1	
Mater Deum Magna			1	1	17
Attis					2
Sol Invictus Mithras			1	1	
Genius*/personification *civitas	1				1
Genius Civitatis	1				
Nemausus					1
Genius collegii*/*patroni	15	16	3	3	7
Genius collegii	9	5	1	1	5
Genius honorati	1				
Honos honorati	1				
Genius patroni	2	5	1	1	1
Honos patroni	1	4	1	1	1
Iuno patronae	1	2			
Occupation-related	21	3	9	9	5
Mercurius		1	1	1	
Hercules	1	1	1	1	
Minerva	15	1			2
Silvanus	1		1	1	2
Vulcanus	2		2	2	

	Fabri (all varieties)	*Centonarii*	*Nautae* (including *n. Parisiaci*)	*Nautae* (excluding *n. Parisiaci*)	*Dendrophori*
Neptunus	2		3	3	
Dei deaeque aquarum			1	1	
Health and prosperity	8	2			3
Apollo		1			
Aesculapius	1				
Hygia		1			
Salus	1				2
Fortuna	6				1
Bacchus					1
Liber Pater		1			1
Virtues personified	2				2
Concordia	1				1
Fides	1				
Virtus					1
Various other	3	3	7	1	5
Numina Deorum		1			1
Lares	1				
Terra Mater					1
Manes		1			1
Castor			1		1
Pollux			1		1
Nemausus					1
Sedatus	1				
Hecate		1			
Intarabus	1				
Viradectis			1	1	
Cernunnos			1		
Esus			1		
Smertrios			1		
Tarvos Trigaranus			1		
Total	67	28	26	18	52

Table 11.3 Ratio of strong deity-links to numbers of inscriptions

Guild	Epigraphic documents	Strong deity-links	Ratio
fabri (all variants)	522	67	0.13
centonarii	244	28	0.11
nautae (incl. *n. Parisiaci*)	115	26	0.23
nautae (excl. *n. Parisiaci*)	114	18	0.16
dendrophori	174	52	0.30

Table 11.4 Types of epigraphic evidence for centonarii, fabri, nautae, and dendrophori, by numbers of inscriptions

Type of Evidence	Centonarii No.	%	Fabri No.	%	Nautae No.	%	Dendrophori No.	%	Total No.	%
Funerary	97	40	202	39	39	34	40	23	378	36
Funerary and/or honorific	0	0	4	1	1	1	4	2	9	1
Honorific	100	41	169	32	48	42	62	36	379	36
Honorific with membership list	0	0	2	0	0	0	0	0	2	0
Religious	22	9	77	15	13	11	38	22	149	14
Religious and honorific	1	0	1	0	0	0	3	2	5	0
Religious building inscription	2	1	4	1	1	1	2	1	9	1
Building inscriptions	4	2	22	4	2	2	7	4	35	3
Place assignment/ownership	0	0	0	0	1	1	1	1	2	0
Membership lists, statutes, decrees	7	3	20	4	6	5	11	6	44	4
Owner/producer inscription/label	1	0	2	0	0	0	1	1	4	0
Other	0	0	1	0	0	0	0	0	1	0
Unknown	10	4	18	3	4	3	5	3	37	4
Total	244		522		115		174		1,054	

244 epigraphic documents, a ratio of only 0.11. If we include the monument of the *nautae Parisiaci*, the numbers are 26 strong links for 115 epigraphic documents, a ratio of 0.23; without the monument of the *nautae Parisiaci*, 18 strong links for 114 documents, a ratio of 0.16.[104]

Not surprisingly (by now), if we zoom out to look at the general epigraphic profile of these three groups, we find similarly low priorities given to religious inscriptions (Table 11.4). The numbers, moreover, are larger and statistically more representative of the guilds' epigraphic habits. The first thing we note is that none seems to have been much concerned with its religious profile—at least insofar as epigraphic representation was concerned. Secondly, the difference between *centonarii*, on the one hand, and *fabri* and *nautae*, on the other, becomes more pronounced. While all three have very similar proportions of funerary inscriptions, the *fabri* have fewer honorific ones (but more building and various other types of inscriptions than the *centonarii*—9% to 5%), and the *centonarii* fewer religious ones. Even if we include one religious building inscription, only 10% of the epigraphic attestations of *centonarii* are religious in nature, compared to 16% for the *fabri* and 12% for *nautae*.

Religion was important for Roman *collegiati*. It was an integral part of associative life. The craftsmen of Venafrum, for instance, even described themselves as the *cultores fabrorum*.[105] Yet, looking at the religious characteristics of occupational *collegia*, we find that they are not prominent in the epigraphic record and that they lack distinctiveness. Before offering an interpretation of this, we need to turn to one other possibly occupational association: that of the *dendrophori*. *Collegia* of *dendrophori* were closely connected to those of the *fabri* and the *centonarii*, both of which are generally considered professional guilds. In the case of the *dendrophori*, however, that is not so clear-cut.

The Problem of the *dendrophori*

On ne laisse pas d'estre en peine de sçavoir quelles sortes de gens estoient ces Dendrophores. Les Sçavans sont partagez sur cela. M. Saumaise...dit que c'étoient ceux qui, dans les processions faites en l'honneur des Dieux, portoient des branches d'arbres en leurs mains, suivant l'étymologie du mot

---

[104] Note that these ratios are not percentages: one epigraphic guild-document can attest dedications to more than one deity.
[105] *CIL* X.4855: *Cultorib(us)* / *fabrorum* (first or second century AD); maybe also *CIL* IX.3837 (*culto[re]s / centonari / [et dendr]of(ori)*) but the reading is very unclear (cf. Letta and D'Amato 1975: 314–15, no. 183 (maybe rather *culto[re]s [ca]nto[res]* (Liu 2009: 344–5)).

δενδροφόρος…Le Titre du Code Thédosien semble favoriser ce sentiment… les Dendrophores n'estoient pas un nom de métier, mais de religion ou de superstition; néanmoins le sentiment contraire de la Pluspart des Sçavans n'est pas moins vraysemblable, qui veulent que les Dendrophores fussent ceux qui faisoient trafic de bois pour la guerre & pour les machines: d'où vient qu'ils sont joints ordinairement dans le mesme corps avec ceux qui avoient le soin de la fabrique des machines, qu'on nommoit FABRI.[106]

The name *dendrophori*, 'tree-carriers', is Greek. It refers to those who in a number of Greek cults carried a tree in a ritual procession. Curiously, despite their Greek name, the *collegia dendrophororum* (with only a handful of exceptions) occur only in the western 'Latin' part of the Roman Empire.[107] According to Johannes Lydus, the procession in which they played a part (the *Arbor Intrat*, 22 March) was created by Claudius in honour of Mater Magna (Cybele), whose cult was closely connected to that of Roma and its emperor.[108] The oldest securely dated inscription (from Regium) mentioning them dates to AD 79.[109] In AD 415, their devotion to the pagan goddess Mater Magna led to the confiscation of their property by the emperors Honorius and Theodosius II.[110]

Relation to Civic Authorities

The nature of the *dendrophori* has long been (and still is) subject of debate. They were more emphatically religious than other occupational associations and they also appear to have been more closely connected to public authorities. An *album* from AD 251 lists the *dendrophori* of Puteoli 'created by the senate' and states that they were 'under the *cura* of the *quindecemviri sacris faciundis*' at Rome, charged with supervising foreign cults. They received a reception and a handout from the newly appointed priest of Mater Magna at Puteoli, who was at the same time their patron and president (*quinquennalis*).[111] The *album* is remarkable not merely because it shows

---

[106] Danet (1701: 372–3).
[107] Moesia Inferior: Tomi (*CIL* III.763); Troesmis (*CIL* III.7505; *IScM* II 83); Novae (*AE* 1929, 120); Thracia: Serdica (*IGBulg* IV 1925b).
[108] Johannes Lydus, *Mens.* IV 59.   [109] *CIL* X.7.
[110] *CTh* 16.10.20 (*superstitio*) *iure damnata*.
[111] *CIL* X.3699; although it was found in Puteoli, Mommsen (in *CIL*) attributed the inscription to Cumae, where the local senate in AD 289 appointed a priest of *Mater Deum Baiana*, who was confirmed by the college of the *quindecimviri sacris faciundis* (*CIL* X.3698); but see against this attribution convincingly Van Haeperen (2010).

the supervision of the *quindecemviri sacris faciundis*, but also because the *dendrophori* are said to be 'created by the senate' (*ex s(enatus) c(onsulto) dendrophori creati*), implying that, like the *Augustales*, they were appointed by public authorities.[112] Scholars disagree on whether the 'senate' mentioned in the inscription was the city council of Puteoli or the senate at Rome.[113] The striking similarity, however, with the expression *ex s(enatus) c(onsulto) Augustales creati* at nearby Liternum (certainly referring to the local 'senate'), strongly suggests it refers to the city council,[114] as we would expect from the explicit association of the *dendrophori* with their home towns.[115] The *Augustales* were appointed locally, but they were significantly higher on the social ladder than the *dendrophori*—something that would be hard to imagine if the *dendrophori*, contrary to the *Augustales*, were appointed by the senate of Rome. An inscription from Cumae shows that the *quindecimviri sacris faciundis* confirmed the appointment by the city council of the new priest of Mater Magna.[116] It is needlessly complicated, in my view, to imagine that city councils had the right to appoint local high priests of Mater Magna, but would have had to defer the appointment of the procession members acting under the authority of that same priest to the senate in Rome, which then again would have been subject to approval by the *quindecemviri sacris faciundis*.[117] An inscription from Rusicade mentions a *dendrophorus decretarius*.[118] Here, too, the analogy with the *Augustales* suggests that the *decretum* was a decree of the local city council, not a *consultum* of the Roman senate.[119]

Much more difficult to assess, however, is how the *collegia* of *dendrophori* related to public authorities. Presumably, as in the case of the *Augustales*, the city councils merely conferred the function of *dendrophorus*—namely, his

---

[112] Note also *CIL* X.3700, where *dendro]phori quibus ex [s(enatus) c(onsulto) coire licet]* should perhaps be read *e[x s(enatus) c(onsulto) creati*. Camodeca (2001: 168) suggests the formula is here equivalent to the more usual usual *quibus senatus consulto coire licet* (see Liu 2009: 105 for a list), but *creati* is much stronger than *coire licet*, indicating an 'appointment' rather than merely a 'permission to assemble'.

[113] For an overview of the discussion and the arguments, see Van Haeperen (2010), who concludes that, 'dans l'état actuel des connaissances, il me semble difficile de trancher définitivement en faveur de l'une ou l'autre des hypothèses' (p. 7), but who is inclined to think it is the senate in Rome.

[114] *AE* 2001, 854; see also *AE* 2001, 853 (Liternum); Camodeca (2001); Vandevoorde (2013); *Augustales* were normally appointed by local city councils; for other instances of *Augustales creati*: *AE* 1980, 489; 2003, 710; *CIL* V.5465; 5844; 6349; XIV.3656; D'Ambrosio and De Caro (1983: 11OS).

[115] See Van Haeperen (2012: 50–2).

[116] *CIL* X.3698.

[117] *CIL* X.3698: *cum ex epistula vestra cognove/rimus creasse vos sacerdotem/Matris deum Licinium Secundum/in locum Claudi Restituti defunc/[t]i secundum voluntatem vestra(m)/permisimus ei occavo et/corona dumtaxat intra/fines coloniae vestrae uti.*

[118] *CIL* VIII.7956 = Vermaseren (1977: iii. 50–1, no. 139).

[119] In that sense also Waltzing (1895: i. 247); *contra*, Van Haeperen (2010: 264) (impossible to decide).

official place in the *Arbor Intrat* procession. The *collegia* as such remained private 'voluntary' associations. Were new members co-opted after their appointment by the local senate? Or did city councils formally appoint new *dendrophori* after nomination by the *collegium dendrophororum*? We do not know.

A Professional Association?

The *dendrophori* had a distinctly religious name and function, which they received from local authorities, and they were supervised by the highest religious authority for foreign cults in Rome. Why would we ascribe a 'professional' character to their *collegia*—as scholars have done since the seventeenth(!) century?

The 'evidence' is mostly circumstantial, but consistent. Inscriptions show that the *dendrophori* were closely connected to other occupational *collegia*. An honorific inscription from Ostia lists them among a range of other groups under the patronage of an upshot notable. The list comprises merchant, shipper, and transporter guilds, associations of public servants, veterans, and soldiers attached to the staff of the imperial *procurator*, but not a single religious association.[120] More important still, however, is their consistently close connection to the guilds of craftsmen (*fabri*) or carpenters/builders (*fabri tignuarii*) and 'clothmen' (*centonarii*). Some inscriptions simply refer to them as the *tria collegia (principalia)*.[121] A large number attest common patrons.[122] In one case they even received a joint endowment.[123] In Verona, the *collegia* of *fabri* and *dendrophori* were under the charge of a single *praefectus*.[124] In Fanum

---

[120] *CIL* XIV.409; see also *CIL* XIV.364.

[121] cf., e.g., *CIL* V.7881 (Cemenelum): *colleg(ia) III/quib(us) ex s(enatus) c(onsulto) c(oire) p(ermissum) est / patrono digniss(imo)*; cf. also *CIL* V.7905 (ibid.: *collegis tribus*) 7920 (ibid.: *collegiis*); elsewhere: *CIL* XI.5416 (Asisium); 5746 (Sentinum, A D 261: *patronum trium / coll(egiorum) principalium*); *AE* 1997, 405 (Ligures Baebiani); maybe also *CIL* V.4449 (Brixia, *in omnib(us) coll(egiis)*) and 4484 (Brixia, *patrono colleg(iorum) omnium*); they may have had a common *Genius* in Nemausus (*CIL* XII.5953).

[122] *CIL* III.1217 (Apulum); V.1012 (Aquileia); 2071 (Feltria and Berua); 4477; 4484 (Brixia); 5128 (Bergomum); 7881 (Cemenelum); IX.1459 (Ligures Baebiani); 5189 (Asculum Picenum); 5439 (Falerio); X.*125 (Salernum, *falsum*?); XI.377; 1059 (Parma); 6362 (Pisaurum); 6378 (Pisaurum and Ariminum); 5416 (Asisium); 6235 (Fanum Fortunae); *AE* 1888, 132 (Bellunum); 1991, 713 (Fidentia); see also *CIL* XIII.1961 for a *curator* of the *Augustales* and of the *dendrophori Augustales*(!), who was patron of the *centonarii*.

[123] *CIL* XI.6520 (Sarsina).

[124] *CIL* V.*424; considered a *falsum* by Mommsen, but without good reason; cf. Panciera (1970: 81–4); cf. also *CIL* XI.*6 (which is probably a *falsum*); See also *CIL* VI.*578 (Rome) for a common *magister, minister*, and *procurator*; the inscription is dubious, but accepted as genuine by Cecamore (2002: 5–8).

Fortunae, a *dendrophorus* was also *collegiatus* of the guilds of *fabri* and *centonarii*.¹²⁵ We find the *dendrophori* included in handouts together with the guilds of *fabri* and *centonarii*.¹²⁶

This intimate connection between the associations of the *dendrophori*, *fabri (tignuarii)*, and *centonarii* is further highlighted by the imperial order from Constantine in AD 329 that 'in whichever town there may be *dendrophori* they ought to be tied to the guilds of *centonarii* and *fabri*, since it shall be expedient that these corporations be increased with a great number of people'.¹²⁷ The decree did not abolish the associations of *dendrophori* but 'attached' (*adnectantur*) them to the other guilds.¹²⁸ Interestingly, Constantine's decree suggests that (in his view) the *dendrophori* did not provide an (equally) useful public service as the *fabri* and *centonarii*. Why was the 'utility' that had merited the *dendrophori* their recognition as one of the *collegia principalia* for so long less important to Constantine? What is meant by the expediency to which the decree refers?

Scholars since the nineteenth century have argued that public services provided by the guilds of *fabri* and *centonarii* (such as fire-fighting and possibly night patrols) had become at risk, because membership numbers had decreased.¹²⁹ Today, however, most scholars no longer think that the avowed *utilitas publica* of some *collegia* derived from specific public services.¹³⁰ Liu suggests that the measure was connected with the concerns for a shortage of skilled workmen in building and textile-related trades that are apparent in other imperial decrees.¹³¹ It is, however, hard to see how adding the *dendrophori* to the other two guilds would have changed such a shortage. Could the emperor have had fiscal purposes in mind? In this period, guilds levied and were collectively responsible for the trade taxes due by their members. If the *dendrophori* were 'attached' to the 'clothmen' and craftsmen guilds, the tax base for these groups would have increased, while the fiscal burden for the craftsmen members might have diminished.¹³²

---

¹²⁵ CIL XI.6231: *sev(iro) Aug(ustali), colle(giato) f(abrum) F(anestrium) / idem cent(onario) colle(giato), d/endro(foro)*; similarly perhaps AE 1997, 405: *ex tribus col/legis*.

¹²⁶ e.g. AE 1965, 144 (Alba Helviorum, together with the *utriclarii*).

¹²⁷ CTh 14.8.1: *in quibuscumque oppidis dendrofori fuerint, centonariorum adque fabrorum collegiis adnectantur, quoniam haec corpora frequentia hominum multiplicari expediet*.

¹²⁸ De Robertis (1971: 204); Salamito (1987: 1003).

¹²⁹ Waltzing (1895: i. 242); for a survey of the discussion on what the 'public services' may have been, see Liu (2009: 111–15).

¹³⁰ Liu (2009: 111–22); Verboven (2016).   ¹³¹ Liu (2009: 283–4).

¹³² See Carrié (2002) for guilds levying taxes in late antiquity; but the practice is attested also in the early empire in Egypt and Antioch; see Verboven (2016: 184, 196).

The imperial decree, however, also raises another question. If the *dendrophori* were a specific professional association in the sense that the members were accepted *artificii causa*[133] because they practised the same or complementary professions, how could they be distributed over two different professional *collegia*?

Something to Do with Trees?

Because the *dendrophori* had no other occupational designation, scholars have argued that their 'cult-name' had to refer also to their profession—something to do with trees: loggers (or logging-entrepreneurs), or merchants, shippers, or transporters of timber or firewood. The historiographical consensus is curiously consistent, given the ambiguity of our sources. Reinesius suggested in 1660 that the *dendrophori* 'apportioned woods, felled trees, and burned charcoal...imported and provided firewood to support the baths of the Roman people and the hearths of townsfolk, to build war machines, and public structures'.[134] Humanist scholars often assumed two kinds of *dendrophori* associations: the religious ones, or *sodalicia*, banned by Honorius and Theodosius II, and the professional ones, the *collegia*. Based on a relief found at Bordeaux, which he interpreted as showing the *dendrophori* at work as loggers (Fig. 11.4), Rabanis argued (in 1841) that the *collegia* of the *dendrophori* combined both dimensions.[135] A few years later (in 1846) Boissieu elaborated this view. The *dendrophori* were 'd'une part un collège religieux, et de l'autre une communauté industrielle exploitant, pour l'administration, les forêts de l'Etat, et, pour son propre compte, le commerce des bois'.[136] This view has been generally followed since. Waltzing simply noted that the 'tree-carriers' in the procession would have been selected from among the loggers/wood-dealers/transporters.[137]

---

[133] Dig. 50.6.6.12–13: *in quibus artificii sui causa unusquisque adsumitur, ut fabrorum corpus est*; cf. AE 1920, 69: *neque enim collegiorum privilegium pro/[sit aut iis qui artem non] exercent* (concerning the *centonarii* of Solva).

[134] Reinesius (1660: 618–19 (*Ep.* lxix)): *silvam infindebant, arbores caedebant, carbones torrebant,... ligna advehebant & praebebant pro balneorum Populi Rom. & municipum fornacibus succendendis, pro fabricandis machinis bellicis, pro substructionibus publicis*; with reference to a brief comment by Alciati (1572: 439) on Dig. 50.16.1.167 (on the meaning of *ligneum*): *Hîc autem de materia intelligit, quam idcirco quis praeparauerat vt carbones conficeret: hi in antiquorum eulogiis Graeca voce dendrophori appellantur, quod arborem ferunt & torrent*.

[135] Rabanis (1841: 3–4). [136] Boissieu (1846: 412–14).

[137] Waltzing (1895: i. 247) (on the *album* from Puteoli): 'En certaines villes, les marchands de bois étaient peut-être trop nombreux pour figurer tous dans le culte, et les membres de leur collège élus par la curie pour faire la dendrophorie, étaient mis sur une liste spéciale, dont nous avons ici un

Fig. 11.4 So-called relief of the *dendrophori*.
Source: Bordeaux, Musée d'Aquitaine.

Salamito describes them as 'à la fois un collège professionnel et une confrérie religieuse'.[138]

Four centuries of scholarly (near-)consensus, however, cannot cover up the fact that there is very little positive evidence to support the view that the *dendrophori* were loggers or wood-merchants/transporters. The context of the relief used by Rabanis is unknown, and there is no inscription confirming the identification of the workers as *dendrophori*. It may just as well refer to some other group of loggers or to a construction project in execution. Hirschfeld (following Rodbertus) connected the *dendrophori* with Symmachus' oblique reference to a guild that 'brings firewood to heat the baths', juxtaposed with 'those who apply their skilful hand to august works', and others that 'fight accidental fires'.[139] The three fit well (according to Hirschfeld) with the *dendrophori*, *fabri*, and *centonarii*.[140] Symmachus' text, however, is ambiguous and too imprecise to carry much weight.[141] Groups of *lignarii* ('firewood

exemplaire'; cf. *ibid*. 241 : 'L'existence du collège industriel n'est pas douteuse'; Maué (1886: 19): zweifellos, daß die dendrophori...zu den Handwerken gehörten'.

[138] Salamito (1987: 991–2); in the same sense, Rubio Rivera (1993), who argues that the presence of a *collegium dendrophorum* in a city does not imply the existence of an official cult to Cybele and Attis; for a critical view, see Van Haeperen (2012: 56): 'Les sources épigraphiques ne permettent en aucun cas de reconnaître dans ces "porteurs d'arbres" une association regroupant des professionnels du bois.'

[139] Hirschfeld (1884: 248–9).

[140] Symmachus, *Relatio* 14 (AD 385): *urenda lavacris ligna conportat...fabriles manus augustis operibus adcommodent...per alios fortuita arcentur incendia*.

[141] Waltzing (1895: 242; see also 1892) rejected this because the *mancipes thermarum* and the *navicularii* would have assured this service, but the *mancipes* were contractors operating the baths and the *navicularii* merely brought firewood from overseas; neither controlled forest resources or

dealers') show up in the Pompeian electoral posters, but there is nothing to link them to *dendrophori*.[142]

Another possible indication that the *dendrophori* were involved in the exploitation of forest resources was seen in their connection to the god Silvanus. A dedication set up in the *schola* of the *dendrophori* at Rome honours *Silvanus Dendrophorus*.[143] It is the only attestation of this epithet for Silvanus, but it is hardly surprising. Silvanus was a god of woods and thus a natural patron god of loggers.[144] Iconography usually depicts him holding a branch. Virgil refers to Silvanus holding 'a tender cypress by the roots'.[145] In Ostia a servant (*apparator* (sic)) of Mater Magna donated a statue of Silvanus to the association of the *dendrophori*.[146] A *dendrophorus* at Ostia combined the office of *quinquennalis* in the *collegium Silvani Augusti Maius* with several offices in other associations.[147] Boissieu (followed by Maué and Waltzing), therefore, speculated that Silvanus was the original patron god of the *dendrophori* before Claudius gave them a part in the cult of Mater Magna.[148] None of the links with Silvanus, however, is conclusive with regard to the professional character of the *dendrophori*. Silvanus was a favourite god also of shepherds. In the mythology of Cybele, Attis, in whose honour the *Arbor Intrat* procession was held, was a shepherd. The sacred pine tree itself offered an obvious link to Silvanus as god of the woods.[149]

Wilson argued that the geographic distribution of the attested *collegia* of *dendrophori* indicates their connection to woods and logging areas.[150] But the correlation is not very strong (see Fig. 11.5). The distribution of the *dendrophori* largely follows that of the *fabri* and the *centonarii*, with the main exceptions being northern Africa and Moesia Inferior, where *dendrophori* are more

---

transport of firewood overland. Salamito (1987: 992), following Cumont (1903), leaves the possibility open.

[142] *CIL* IV.951; 960; probably not a formal *collegium*, but note nevertheless here the designation *universi*.

[143] *CIL* VI.641; maybe also 642 (AD 97):...[*Silvano*] *sancto d[eo(?) vel -endrophoro* —].

[144] *CIL* V.815; Vetter (1953); cf. also *CIL* III.633,1: *cul[tores colleg]i Silbani* build a temple/clubhouse for Silvanus with statues of Mercury and Hercules, therefore probably loggers, rather than agricultural workers or hunters. See Dorcey (1992: 89).

[145] Verg. *G.* 1.20: *teneram ab radice ferens, Silvane, cupressum*.   [146] *CIL* XIV.53.

[147] *CIL* XIV.309 (c. AD 50–140):...*sevir Aug(ustalis) / et quinquennalis / idem quinq(uennalis) corporis mensor(um) / frumentarior(um) Ostiens(ium) et curat(or) / bis / idem codicar(iorum) curat(or) Osti(en)s(ium) et III honor(atus) / idem quinquennal(is) collegi(i) Silvani / Aug(usti) maioris quod est Hilarionis / functus sacomari idem magistro ad Marte(m) / Ficanum Aug(ustum) idem in collegio dendrofor(um)*...The *ad Martem Ficanum Augustum* was probably a neighbourhood in Ostia; cf. also Samiarius Silvanus, *dendrophorus* in Puteoli, and Claudius Silvanus, *quinquennalis perpetuus* of the *dendrophori* at Lugdunum (*CIL* XIII.1752), but the *cognomen* is too common to mean much.

[148] Boissieu (1846: 413–14); Maué (1886: 21); Waltzing (1892: i. 251–2); cf. Dorcey (1992: 31) (critical).

[149] Hunt (2016: 253–4).   [150] Wilson (2012: 139–40).

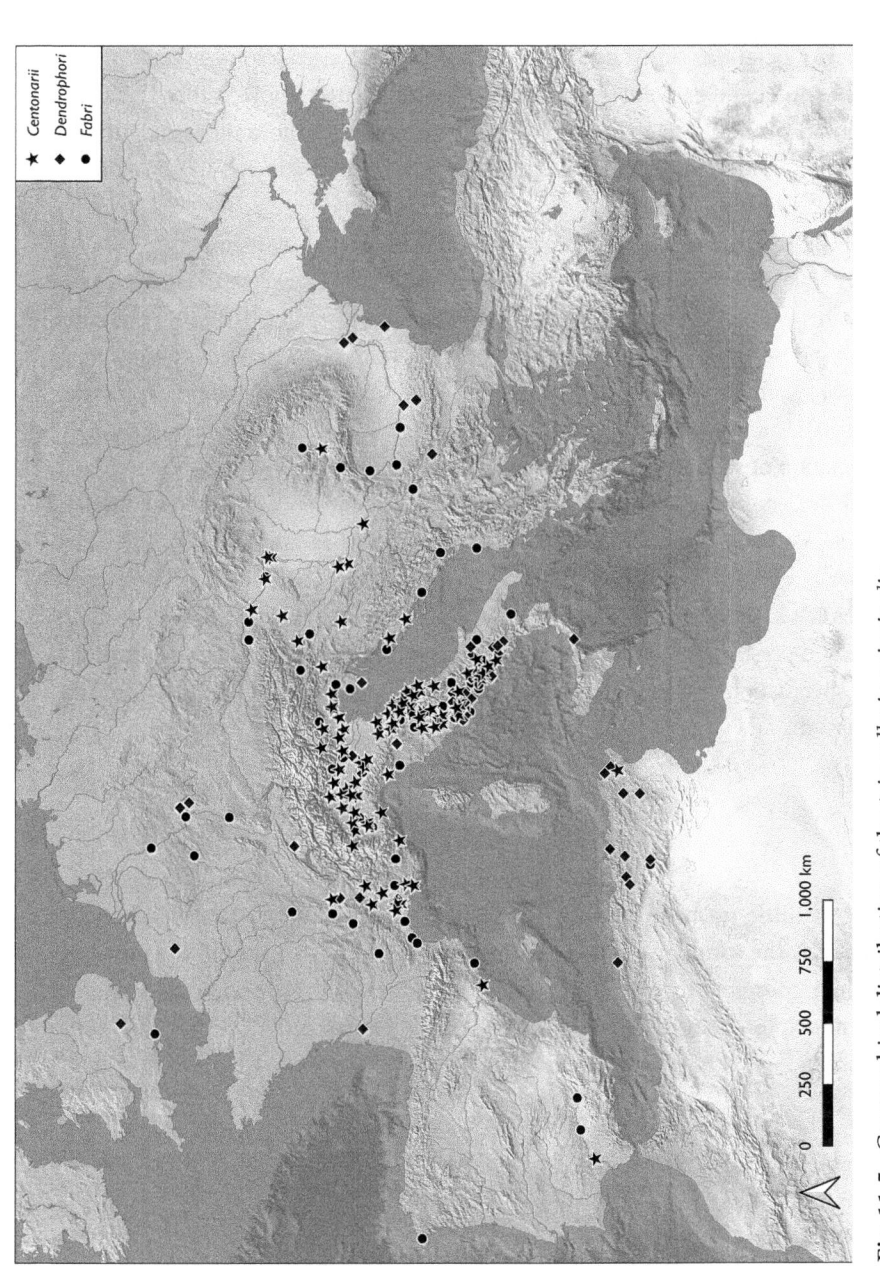

Fig. 11.5 Geographical distribution of the *tria collegia principalia*.
Source: Ghent Database of Roman Guilds and Occupation-Based Communities; basemap from Natural Earth.

common than *fabri* or *centonarii*. Wilson links their presence in Africa and Numidia to the important timber resources there. That might be true also for Moesia Inferior. But inscriptions in these provinces rarely mention professional associations or even titles. So the epigraphic attestations of *dendrophori* could equally be explained as an indication of their religious rather than professional profile.[151] It may not be a coincidence that the only association of *dendrophori* that was clearly religiously structured is attested in Troesmis in Moesia Inferior.

The few indications we have for professional activities by members of *dendrophori* have nothing to do with wood or timber. In Rome, two pearl dealers (*margaritarii*) were presidents for life (*quinquennalis perpetuus*) of the *collegium dendrophororum*.[152] In Alba Fucens a cook was both *sevir Augustalis* and *dendrophorus*.[153] Three of the *dendrophori* mentioned on the *album* from Puteoli have 'collegiate' names, indicating that they or their (fore)fathers were freedmen of an association of sailors (C. Nautius Syntropus),[154] fullers (C. Fullonius Tertius), and cloak dealers/producers (M. Sagarius Sedatus). The presence of non-practitioners in an occupational *collegium* was not illegal and is attested also for other associations.[155] We might even speculate that professional titles in these cases were included precisely *because* they were irregular and thus illustrated the influence and prestige of the bearer. However, this is doomed to remain an uncomfortable speculation, intended to argue away an apparent contradiction between what we assume and what the sources seem to say.

Internal Organization

There is little positive evidence, therefore, for the view that the *dendrophori* practised the same or complementary professions. The internal organization of their *collegia*, however, is very similar to that of professional associations. We find references to *magistri*,[156] *officiales*,[157] *immunes*,[158] *praefecti*,[159] *quinquennales perpetui*,[160] *quinquennales*,[161] *curatores*,[162] and *curam agentes*.[163]

---

[151] Verboven (2016: 178); cf. Verboven (2007) for relative absence of *negotiatores* in North African inscriptions.
[152] *CIL* VI.641; 30,973. [153] *CIL* IX.3938.
[154] *CIL* X.3699; *nauta* in the case of Puteoli is unlikely to refer to a barge-skipper, as was common in Gaul (although there were connections; see, e.g., *CIL* XIII.1942).
[155] *Dig.* 50.6.6; Verboven (2016: 180–1). [156] *CIL* V.4449; 7904. [157] *CIL* V.4449.
[158] *CIL* X.3764. [159] *CIL* V.*424; XI.*6 (see n. 124).
[160] *CIL* VI.641; 30973; *AE* 1987, 198.
[161] *CIL* X.3699; *InscrIt* X.5 16; *AE* 1927, 115; 1956, 4; 2012, 337.
[162] *CIL* VIII.6940; 6941; XIII.1961; *AE* 1991, 713. [163] *AE* 1956, 4.

Common members are designated as the *plebs*,[164] and the associations passed *decreta*.[165] Priesthoods or other religious offices, however, are almost entirely lacking.

The only exception is a Greek inscription on a monument set up in Troesmis in AD 199–201 in honour of the emperor and his family.[166] The name of the association is not preserved (or not mentioned), but the names of thirty-eight members and their functions in the group are. Among them we find an *archidendrophorus*, a *hiereus*, an *archirabdouchos* ('rod-bearer'), and a 'father' and 'mother' of the group. Tacheva notes that the organization was 'of the ancient type of the Greek and Anatolian thiasos'. She is doubtful about the 'subservience between the *dendrophori* and the guilds of timber merchants' in the Danubian provinces, assumed by Graillot.[167]

Religious Profile of the dendrophori

The religious (epigraphic) profile of the *dendrophori* (established using the same data and methodology as already described) shows a strong focus on the cult of Mater Magna (Table 11.2; Fig. 11.6). This is not surprising, of course, but it is markedly different from the profiles of the *fabri*, *centonarii*, and *nautae*, which showed very little focus on any particular (group of) deities.

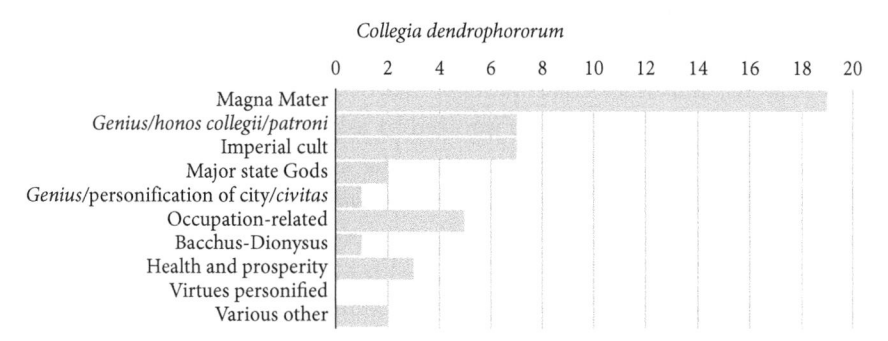

Fig. 11.6 Religious profile of the *dendrophori*: number of inscriptions in different categories.

---

[164] *AE* 1987, 198; Orelli 4412 (Waltzing 1895: no. 1377), mentioning the *rep(ublica) colleg(i) dendroph(orum)*, is a *falsum*.
[165] *CIL* VI.30973.   [166] *IScM* II 83.
[167] Tacheva (1983: 149); Graillot (1912: 267); note, however, that Graillot also interprets the organization at Troesmis as 'organisé sur le modèle des antiques thiases d'Asie Mineure et de Grèce' (Graillot 1912: 266).

The same trend emerges when we look at the general epigraphic profile of the *dendrophori*. If we include the religious honorific and the religious building inscriptions, 25% of the epigraphic guild-documents of the *dendrophori* are religious in nature. This is more than double the figure for the *centonarii* and more than 50% higher than the *fabri*. The number of honorific inscriptions is comparable, but the number of funerary inscriptions is conspicuously lower (Table 11.4).

The dossier on the *dendrophori* is still open. On the one hand, we find no connection to any non-professional association, such as those of, for instance, the *iuvenes*. They were intimately connected to the guilds of craftsmen, carpenters/builders, and 'clothmen'. Their internal organization as well was largely similar to that of professional *collegia*, and so also was the social profile of their members and officers. On the other hand, however, the religious profile of the *dendrophori* was conspicuously different from that of these other occupational *collegia*. Their general epigraphic profile was more religious and more specific than that of other occupational associations. What all three shared, however, was their cultivation of deities and participation in cults that affirmed their integration in the larger civic order.

Conclusion

Setting up and maintaining a formal organization, such as a *collegium*, was costly, both in terms of money (membership fee, *summae honorariae*, expected benefactions, and other contributions) and of time. Whenever an informal group decides to take this step, we need to ask why. Religion mattered for ancient guilds. It was intrinsic to their regular and their festive gatherings. It defined relations between the members. Yet, while it is true that straightforward economic benefits, such as monopoly rights and privileges, cannot have been the only and perhaps not even the most important reason for *collegiati* to invest time and money in the *collegium*, nothing in the evidence we have suggests that religious considerations mattered any more than practical or social ones. Religion was important in ancient societies, for individuals as well as for collectives. But it was neither the reason why professional *collegia* were formed, nor did it define their identity.

The rationale behind the religious engagement of guilds was that of a triple integration: of individual *collegiati* in the associative order, structured by guild institutions (regulations and procedures, assemblies, councils, and magistrates); of occupational *collegia* in the civic order, structured by civic institutions (city magistrates, councils, regulations, and procedures); and of both in the overarching imperial order, structured by imperial institutions (imperial representatives, regulations, and procedures).

This triple integration process could be successful only if individuals voluntarily submitted their personal agency to the authority of others and more or less spontaneously obeyed rules and regulations imposed upon them. Voluntary submission in turn implied the belief (or calculation) that private interests were (at least in the long run) best served by upholding common interests at guild level, city level, and imperial level. In a world characterized by extreme uncertainty owing to natural factors (pathogens, weather, and climate variability) and human ones (lack of information, inability to enforce rights), that was possible only by relying on supernatural forces. Engagement in religious practices thus symbolized and affirmed the acceptance and principal support of social orders. With the likely exception of ethnically specific deities among foreign resident groups, religion was about integration and protection, not about identity or separation.

Acknowledgements

Much of the research presented here is based on the 'Ghent Database of Roman Guilds and Occupation-Based Communities' (GDRG). Thanks are due to Gerben Verbrugghe and Luka Tjampens for their invaluable help in setting up the database and the connected GIS application and inputting the data. The first data were collected during a research stay in Oxford 2013–14 at Brasenose and Merton colleges; my sincere thanks to both colleges, their fellows, and especially Alan Bowman and Jonathan Prag for inviting me.

References

Alciati, A. (1572). *De verborum significatione*. Lugdunum.

Ausbüttel, F. M. (1982). *Untersuchungen zu den Vereinen im Westen des Römischen Reiches* (Frankfurter Althistorische Studien 11). Kallmünz.

Baslez, M.-F. (1986). 'Cultes et dévotions des Phéniciens en Grèce: Les divinités marines', in C. Bonnet, E. Lipiński, and P. Marchetti (eds), *Religio Phoenicia: Acta Colloquii Namurcensis Dec. 1984* (Studia Phoenicia, IV). Namur, 289–305.

Baslez, M.-F. (2013). 'Les associations à Délos: depuis les débuts de l'Indépendance (fin du IVe siècle) à la période de la colonie athénienne (milieu du IIe siècle)', in

P. Fröhlich and P. Hamon (eds), *Groupes et associations dans les cités grecques (IIIe siècle av. J.-C.–IIe siècle apr. J.-C.): Actes de la table ronde de Paris, INHA, 19-20 juin 2009*. Geneva, 227-49.

Béal, J.-C. (2005). 'Les «nautes armés» de Lutèce: mythe ou réalité?', *RA* 2: 315-37.

Boissier, G. (1874). *La religion romaine d'Auguste aux Antonins*. Paris.

Boissieu, A. de (1846). *Inscriptions antiques de Lyon reproduites d'après les monuments ou recueillies dans les auteurs*. Lyons.

Bollmann, B. (1998). *Römische Vereinshäuser: Untersuchungen zu den Scholae der römischen Berufs-, Kult- und Augustalen-Kollegien in Italien*. Mainz.

Broekaert, W. (2011). 'Partners in Business: Roman Merchants and the Potential Advantages of being a Collegiatus', *Ancient Society* 41: 221-56.

Bruneau, P. (1978). 'Les cultes de l'établissement des Poseidoniastes de Bérytos à Délos, I', in M. B. de Boer and T. A. Edridge (eds), *Hommages à M. J. Vermaseren, I-III*. Leiden, 160-90.

Bruneau, P. (1991). 'Deliaca, IX, 67', *Bulletin de Correspondance Hellenique* 115/1: 377-88.

Bruun, C. (1993). 'Lotores: Roman Bath-Attendants', *Zeitschrift für Papyrologie und Epigraphik* 98: 222-8.

Buonocore, M. (2004). 'Novità epigrafiche dall'Abruzzo', in M. G. Angeli Bertinelli and A. Donati (eds), *Epigrafia di confine, confine dell'epigrafia: Atti del Colloquio AIEGL, Borghesi, 2003*. Faenza Ravenna, 281-320.

Burford, A. (1972). *Craftsmen in Greek and Roman Society* (Aspects of Greek and Roman Life). London.

Camodeca, G. (2001). 'Albi degli «Augustales» di Liternum della seconda metà del II secolo', *Annali di archeologia e storia antica: Istituto universitario orientale: Dipartimento di studi del mondo classico e del Mediterraneo antico*, n.s. 8: 163-82.

Carrié, J.-M. (2002). 'Les associations professionnelles à l'époque tardive: entre «munus» et convivialité', in J.-M. Carrié and R. Lizzi Testa (eds), *'Humana sapit': Études d'antiquités tardive offertes à Lellia Cracco Rugini*. Turnhout, 309-32.

Cecamore, C. (2002). *Palatium: Topografia storica del Palatino tra III sec. a.C. e I sec. d.C.* Rome.

Combet Farnoux, B. (1980). *Mercure romain: le culte public de Mercure et la fonction mercantile à Rome de la République archaïque à l'épopque augustéenne*. Rome.

Combet Farnoux, B. (1981). 'Mercure romain, les *Mercuriales* et l'institution du culte impérial sous le principat augustéen', in W. Haase (ed.), *Aufstieg und Niedergang der römischen Welt. II: Principat 17.1: Religion (Heidentum: Römische Götterkulte, Orientalische Kult in der römischen Welt)*. Berlin, 457-501.

Cumont, F. (1903). 'Dendrophori', *Pauly Wissowa Realencyclopädie der classischen Altertumswissenschaft* 5.1, 216-19.

D'Ambrosio, A., and De Caro, S. (1983). *Un Impegno per Pompei: Fotopiano e documentazione della necropoli di Porta Nocera*. Milan.

Danet, P. (1701). *Dictionarium antiquitatum Romanarum et Graecarum, in usum serenissimi delphini et serenissimorum principum Burgundiae, Andium, Biturigium*. Amsterdam

De Robertis, F. M. (1971). *Storia delle corporazioni e del regime associativo nel mondo romano*. Bari.

Degrassi, A. (1937). 'Iscrizioni nuove. I magistri *Mercuriales* di Lucca e la dea Anzotica di Aenona', *Athenaeum* n.s. 15: 284–8.

Demougin, S. (2012). 'Des collèges en Gaule Belgique', in M. Dondin-Payre and N. Tran (eds), *Le Phénomène associatif dans l'occident romain*. Bordeaux, 155–64.

Dorcey, P. F. (1992). *The Cult of Silvanus: A Study in Roman Folk Religion*. Leiden and Boston.

Duval, P. M. (1954). 'Le Groupe de bas-reliefs des nautae Parisiaci', *Monuments et mémoires publiés par l'Académie des Inscriptions et Belles-Lettres* (Fondation Piot) 48/2: 63–90.

Duval, P. M. (1957). 'Le Groupe de blocs sculptés dit des Nautes parisiens', *Bulletin de la Société nationale des antiquaires de France 1954-1955*: 115–16.

Fishwick, D. (1987). *The Imperial Cult in the Latin West: Studies in the Ruler Cult of the Western Provinces of the Roman Empire*. Leiden and New York.

Fishwick, D. (1989). 'L. Munatius Hilarianus and the Inscription of the Artemisii', *ZPE* 76: 175–83.

Flambard, J.-M. (1981). '*Collegia compitalicia*: Phénomène associatif, cadres territoriaux et cadres civiques dans le monde romain à l'époque républicaine', *Ktèma* 6: 144–66.

Flambard, J.-M. (1982). 'Observations sur la nature des magistri italiens de Délos', in F. Coarelli, D. Musti, and H. Solin (eds), *Delo e l'Italia* (Opuscula Instituti Romani Finlandiae 2). Rome, 67–77.

Gabrielsen, V. (2001). 'The Rhodian Associations and Economic Activity', in Z. Archibald, J. K. Davies, V. Gabrielsen, and G. Oliver (eds), *Hellenistic Economies*. London and New York, 163–84.

Gagé, J. (1966). 'Elagabal et les pêcheurs du Tibre', in J. Heurgon, G. Picard, and W. Setson (eds), *Mélanges d'archéologie, d'épigraphie et d'histoire offerts à Jérôme Carcopino*. Paris, 403–18.

Graillot, H. (1912). *Le Culte de Cybéle, mère des dieux à Roma et dans l'Empire romain*. Paris.

Harland, P. A. (2013). *Associations, Synagogues, and Congregations: Claiming a Place in Ancient Mediterranean Society*. 2nd edn (with links to inscriptions). Kitchener, Ontario.

Harland, P. A. (2015). 'Associations and the Economics of Group Life: A Preliminary Case Study of Asia Minor and the Aegean Islands', *Svensk Exegetisk Årsbok* 80: 1–37.

Hasenohr, C. (2003). 'Les «Compitalia» à Délos', *Bulletin de Correspondance Hellenique* 127: 167–249.

Hasenohr, C. (2007). 'Italiens et Phéniciens à Délos: Organisation et relations de deux groupes d'étrangers résidents (IIe–Ier siècles av. J.-C.)', in R. Compatangelo-Soussignan and C.-G. Schwentzel (eds), *Étrangers dans la cité romaine*. Rennes, 77–90.

Hatt, J. J. (1980). 'Observations sur deux monuments de piété collective de Gaule romaine: Le pilier des nautes de Paris et la colonne de Mayence', *Atti del Centro Ricerche e Documentazione sull'Antichità Classica* 11: 119–25.

Hatzfeld, J. (1912). 'Les Italiens résidant à Délos mentionnés dans les inscriptions de l'île', *Bulletin de Correspondance Hellenique* 36/1: 5–218.

Hatzfeld, J. (1919). *Les trafiquants italiens dans l'orient hellénique*. Paris.

Hirschfeld, O. (1884). 'Der Praefectus vigilum in Nemausus und die Feuerwehr in den römischen Landstädten', *Sitzungsberichte der philosophisch-historischen Classe der kaiserlichen Akademie der Wissenschaften* 107: 239–57.

Hunt, A. (2016). *Reviving Roman Religion: Sacred Trees in the Roman World*. Cambridge.

Israelowich, I. (2015). *Patients and Healers in the High Roman Empire*. Baltimore.

Leach, E. W. (2004). *The Social Life of Painting in Ancient Rome and on the Bay of Naples*. Cambridge and New York.

Letta, C., and D'Amato, S. (1975). *Epigrafia della regione dei Marsi*. Milan.

Liu, J. (2009). *Collegia Centonariorum: The Guilds of Textile Dealers in the Roman West*. Leiden and Boston.

Liu, J. (2016). 'Group Membership, Trust Networks, and Social Capital: A Critical Analysis', in K. Verboven and C. Laes (eds), *Work, Labour, and Professions in the Roman World*. Leiden and Boston, 203–26.

MacMullen, R. (1974). *Roman Social Relations, 50 BC to AD 284*. New Haven.

Maillot, S. (2015). 'Foreigners' Associations and the Rhodian State', in V. Gabrielsen and C. A. Thomsen (eds), *Private Associations and the Public Sphere: Proceedings of a Symposium held at the Royal Danish Academy of Sciences and Letters, 9–11 September 2010* (Scientia Danica. Series H, Humanistic 8, vol. 9). Copenhagen, 136–82.

Maué, H. C. (1886). *Die Vereine der fabri, centonarii und dendrophori im römischen Reich*. Frankfurt am Main.

Mennella, G. (1992). 'Medagogus collegii fabrorum: Nota ad AE 1913,148', *ZPE* 90: 122–6.

Mommsen, T. (1843). *De collegiis et sodaliciis Romanorum: Accedit inscriptio Lanuvina.* Kiliae.

Mouritsen, H. (2006). 'Honores Libertini: Augustales and Seviri in Italy', in I. Nielsen (ed.), *Between Cult and Society: The Cosmopolitan Centres of the Ancient Mediterranean as Setting for Activities of Religious Associations and Religious Communities* (Special Issue of *Hephaistos, Kritische Zeitschrift zu Theorie und Praxis der Archäologie und angrenzender Gebiete*, 24). Hamburg, 237–48.

Mouritsen, H. (2011). *The Freedman in the Roman World.* Cambridge and New York.

Nilsson, M. P. (1957). *The Dionysiac Mysteries of the Hellenistic and Roman Age.* Lund.

Nonnis, D., and Ricci, C. (1999). '«Vectigalia» municipali ed epigrafia: Un caso dall'Hirpinia', in *Il capitolo delle entrate nelle finanze municipali in occidente ed in oriente: Actes de la 10. rencontre franco-italienne sur l'epigraphie du monde romain: Rome, 27–29 mai 1996*. Rome, 41–59.

Panciera, S. (1970). *Girolamo Asquini: Un falsario del primo ottocento e l'epigrafia antica delle Vanezie.* Rome.

Poland, F. (1909). *Geschichte des griechischen Vereinswesens.* Leipzig.

Rabanis, J.-F. (1841). *Recherches sur les dendrophores et sur les corporations romaines en général, pour servir à l'explication d'un bas-relief trouvé à Bordeaux.* Bordeaux.

Rauh, N. K. (1993). *The Sacred Bonds of Commerce: Religion, Economy, and Trade Society at Hellenistic Roman Delos, 166–87 BC.* Amsterdam.

Reinesius, T. (1660). *Epistolae ad Casp. Hoffmannum.* Lipsiae.

Rémy, B., and Faure, P. (2010). *Les médecins dans l'Occident romain: Péninsule Ibérique, Bretagne, Gaules, Germanies* (Scripta antiqua 27). Pessac.

Royden, H. L. (1988). *The Magistrates of the Roman Professional Collegia in Italy from the First to the Third Century AD.* Pisa.

Rubio Rivera, R. (1993). 'Collegium dendrophorum: Corporación profesional y cofradía metróaca', *Gerión* 11: 175–83.

Salamito, J.-M. (1987). 'Les dendrophores dans l'empire chrétien: A propos du Code Théodosien XIV,8,1 et XVI,10,20,2', *MEFRA* 99: 991–1019.

Steuernagel, D. (1999). '«Corporate Identity»: Über Vereins-, Stadt- und Staatskulte im kaiserzeitlichen Puteoli', *MDAI(R)* 106: 149–87.

Steuernagel, D. (2004). *Kult und Alltag in römischen Hafenstädten: Soziale Prozesse in archäologischer Perspektive* (Potsdamer altertumswissenschaftliche Beiträge 11). Stuttgart.

Tacheva, M. (1983). *Eastern Cults in Moesia Inferior and Thracia (5th Century BC–4th Century AD).* Leiden.

Taylor, L. R. (1923). *Local Cults of Etruria* (Papers and Monographs of the American Academy at Rome 9). Rome.

Taylor, L. R. (1931). *The Divinity of the Roman Emperor*. Middletown.

Terpstra, T. T. (2013). *Trading Communities in the Roman World: A Micro-Economic and Institutional Perspective* (Columbia Studies in the Classical Tradition 37). Leiden.

Terpstra, T. T. (2019). *Trade in the Ancient Mediterranean: Private Order and Public Institutions*. Princeton.

Terpstra, T. T. (2020). 'The Imperial Cult and the Sacred Bonds of Roman Overseas Commerce', in P. Arnaud and S. Keay (eds), *The Epigraphy of Port Societies: The Evidence of Inscriptions*. Cambridge, 178–97.

Tran, N. (2006). *Les membres des associations romaines: Le rang social des collegiati en Italie et en Gaules sous le haut-empire* (Collection de l'École française de Rome 367). Rome.

Tran Tam Tinh, V. (1972). *Le culte des divinités orientales en Campanie en dehors de Pompéi, de Stabies et d'Herculanum*. Leiden.

Trümper, M. (2002). 'Das Sanktuarium des «Établissement des Poseidoniastes de Bérytos» in Delos: zur Baugeschichte eines griechischen Vereinsheiligtums', *Bulletin de Correspondance Hellénique* 126/1: 265–330.

Trümper, M. (2011). 'Where the Non-Delians met in Delos: The Meeting-Places of Foreign Associations and Ethnic Communities in Late Hellenistic Delos', in O. van Nijf, R. Alsten, and C. G. Williamson (eds), *Political Culture in the Greek City after the Classical Age*. Leuven, 49–100.

Van Andringa, W. (2003). 'Cités et communautés d'expatriés installées dans l'Empire romain: Le cas des «cives Romani consistentes»', in N. Belayche and S. C. Mimouni (eds), *Communautés religieuses dans le monde gréco-romain*. Turnhout, 49–60.

Van Haeperen, F. (2010). 'Quelques réflexions sur les dendrophores de Pouzzoles, à partir de CIL X 3699', *ZPE* 172: 259–66.

Van Haeperen, F. (2012). 'Collèges de dendrophores et autorités locales et romaines', in M. Dondin-Payre and N. Tran (eds), *Collegia: Le Phénomène associatif dans l'Occident romain* (Scripta Antiqua 41). Bordeaux, 47–62.

van Nijf, O. M. (1997). *The Civic World of Professional Associations in the Roman East* (Dutch Monographs on Ancient History and Archaeology 17). Amsterdam.

van Nijf, O. M. (2002). 'Collegia and Civic Guards: Two Chapters in the History of Sociability', in W. Jongman and M. Kleijwegt (eds), *After the Past: Essays in Ancient History in Honour of H. W. Pleket*. Leiden and Boston, 305–40.

van Nijf, O. M. (2006). 'Global Players: Athletes and Performers in the Hellenistic and Roman World', in I. Nielsen (ed.), *Between Cult and Society: The Cosmopolitan Centres of the Ancient Mediterranean as Setting for Activities of Religious Associations and Religious Communities* (Special Issue of *Hephaistos, Kritische Zeitschrift zu Theorie und Praxis der Archäologie und angrenzender Gebiete*, 24). Hamburg, 225–35.

Vandevoorde, L. (2013). 'Respectability on Display: Alba and Fasti of the *Augustales in the Context of Collegial and Magisterial Hierarchy', *Revue belge de philologie et d'histoire* 91: 127–52.

Venticinque, P. F. (2010). 'Family Affairs: Guild Regulation and Family Relationships in Roman Egypt', *Greek, Roman, and Byzantine Studies* 50: 273–94.

Venticinque, P. F. (2016). *Honor among Thieves: Craftsmen, Merchants, and Associations in Roman and Late Roman Egypt*. Ann Arbor.

Verboven, K. (2007). 'Ce que negotiari et ses dérivés veulent dire', in J. Andreau and V. Chankowski (eds), *Vocabulaire et expression de l'économie dans le monde antique* (Études 19). Bordeaux, 89–118.

Verboven, K. (2011). 'Resident Aliens and Translocal Merchant Collegia in the Roman Empire', in O. Hekster and T. Kaizer (eds), *Frontiers in the Roman World: 9th Workshop of the International Network Impact of Empire* (Impact of Empire). Leiden and Boston, 335–48.

Verboven, K. (2016). 'Guilds and the Organisation of Urban Populations during the Principate', in K. Verboven and C. Laes (eds), *Work, Labour, and Professions in the Roman World*. Leiden and Boston,

Vermaseren, M. J. (1977). *Corpus cultus Cybelae Attidisque (CCCA)*. 7 vols. Leiden.

Vetter, E. (1953). 'Die familia Silvani in Trebula Mutuesca und die sectores materiarum in Aquileia', in *Studi aquileiesi offerti il 7 ottobre 1953 a G. Brusin nel suo 70° compleanno*. Aquileia, 93–119.

Waltzing, J.-P. (1892). 'Les corporations officielles de l'ancienne Rome d'après une lettre de Symmaque (Relatio 14)', *Revue de l'Instruction publique en* Belgique, 1–21.

Waltzing, J.-P. (1895). *Étude historique sur les corporations professionnelles chez les Romains depuis les origines jusqu'à la chute de l'Empire d'Occident*. 4 vols. Brussels.

Wilson, A. (2012). 'Raw Materials and Energy', in W. Scheidel (ed.), *The Cambridge Companion to the Roman Economy*. Cambridge, 133–55.

Zänker, P. (1994). 'Veränderungen im öffentlichen Raum der italischen Städte der Kaiserzeit', in *L'Italie d'Auguste à Dioclétien. Actes du colloque international de Rome (25-28 mars 1992)* (Collection de l'École française de Rome 198). Rome, 259–84.

Zevi, F. (2008). 'I collegi di Ostia e le lora sedi associative tra Antonini e Severi', in C. Berrendonner, M. Cebeillac Gervasoni, and L. Lamoine (eds), *Le quotidien municipal dans l'occident Romain*. Clermont Ferrand, 477–506.

Ziebarth, E. (1896). *Das griechische Vereinswesen*. Leipzig.

12

Economic Implications of Roman Religious Systems

Greg Woolf

Religion and the Economy, each with a capital letter, are recent coinages. Neither category has an exact equivalent in Greek or Roman terminology.[1] Ancient texts display many ways of discussing ritual action, belief, and religious institutions,[2] but that field was not reified as Religion until the modern period. Something similar applied to ancient economic life. It is easy to gather testimony that shows an awareness of what we would term relations of supply and demand, price-fixing markets, economies of scale, and competition for market share, but ancient writers did not think or write in terms of these abstractions. The modern sciences of economics and religious studies both originated in the eighteenth and nineteenth centuries. They shared many features, among them an interest in establishing universal or natural laws, taxonomic and comparative methods, and, from the nineteenth century, an inclination to evolutionary models of change. But they found themselves on opposite sides of the boundary erected between the sacred and the secular during the Enlightenment. The structure of modern universities has mostly kept them apart, and within the study of the ancient world only a few figures such as Michael Rostovtzeff have specialized in both fields. The result is that the relationship between these two spheres of human activity is underexplored in Roman studies.[3]

Yet, as the contributions to this volume demonstrate, there are many points of intersection, and a good deal of evidence is available for its investigation. In what follows, I shall comment first on some relatively unchanging features of the relationship between economic and religious activity in the period, and then go on to examine how religious and economic changes were entangled

---

[1] For religion, see Moser and Smith (2019), and, for the economy, Polanyi, Arensberg, and Pearson (1957); Finley (1973).
[2] Feeney (1998); Ando (2008); MacRae (2016).
[3] Wilson, Chapter 1, this volume; see also Moser and Smith (2019).

Greg Woolf, *Economic Implications of Roman Religious Systems* In: *The Economy of Roman Religion*.
Edited by: Andrew Wilson, Nick Ray, and Angela Trentacoste, Oxford University Press. © Oxford University Press 2023.
DOI: 10.1093/oso/9780192883537.003.0012

in the last centuries BC and the first AD, before concluding with a few comments on the economic implications of ancient ways of organizing religion.

Statics: Interpenetration and Attraction

The interpenetration of religious and economic activity in ancient Rome might be considered in spatial terms and in terms of routine activities. So Mercury was present in marketplaces and Juno Moneta presided over the mint.[4] The *lararium* where household gods were kept was at the centre of the Roman *domus* close by the *tablinium* from which the financial affairs of its owners were managed. Cato's *On Agriculture* includes advice on prayers along with advice on slave managements and on the procurement of equipment. Vitruvius' ideal cities are provided with temples as well as fora and spaces for religious spectacles as well as places for political assembly. Victims found their way from pastures to altars outside temples and then, as meat, to *macella*. Objects, animals, and peoples might be sacralized and then desacralized in the course of their cultural biographies just as they might be commoditized and decommoditized. How the value of things was transformed in the course of social processes is the theme of the most recent exploration of religion and economy at Rome.[5] Some spaces were certainly more closely related to the ritual action than others, either permanently or temporarily. Roman calendars devoted considerable energy to separating out days of regular business from those devoted to particular festivals, and in some spaces, such as the forum Romanum or the Circus Maximus, which were used for both, this was very a very practical matter.[6] But there were no secular spaces in the ancient world within which economic activity might have been confined, and no religious ones from which it was excluded.

We might also ask how far economic activity shaped religious action, and vice versa. The agricultural year, by which most inhabitants of the empire lived, exercised a distant impact on the ritual calendar by which urban as well as rural Romans lived.[7] The annual start of the sailing season became an occasion for an annual Roman festival of the *navigium Isidis*. Economic priorities and concerns have been thought to lie behind the cult paid to Ceres and Liber

---

[4] Wigg-Wolf, Chapter 5, this volume; see also Meadows and Williams (2001).
[5] The special issue (5/1 published in 2019) of the journal *Religion in the Roman Empire*, edited by Christopher Smith and Claudia Moser, to which this chapter owes a great deal.
[6] Laurence and Smith (1995–6). [7] Beard (1987).

Pater.[8] Conversely, sanctuaries and festivals provided settings and occasions for fairs and periodic markets.[9] Sacrificial traditions generated a demand for victims, one that grew over time, as animal sacrifice came to be more and more important in civic euergetism.[10] The cost of public religion might be significant for larger urban centres.[11] The construction of some religious buildings was so expensive it often fell on the shoulders of local benefactors, when it was not paid for from booty.[12] It is not always easy to determine whether economic activity shaped ritual action or the reverse, as the case of *collegia* exemplifies brilliantly.[13]

At times there seems to have been a sort of institutional convergence, as when religious associations borrowed titulature for their officers from the city or the family.[14] Perhaps it is most accurate to say that economic and religious structures of power exercised a mutual attraction, even if neither can be understood wholly in terms of the other. It would be the same if we were to add political power to the equation. Neither imperial state nor ancient cities completely dominated ritual activities: the idea of a triangular relationship between ruler, city, and sanctuary is a powerful heuristic tool.[15] There was no absolute separation of economy, politics, and the sacred in the Roman world, and heterarchy had its limits. The distinctions are ours, of course, not theirs.

It is difficult in any case to imagine how the lived experience of most inhabitants of the empire would have supported strong distinctions between economic and religious activity.[16] Paying cult to the gods was part of the risk-buffering strategies employed by all peasant families. Divination was a key means of getting knowledge about the weather.[17] Gift exchange articulated relationships between men and gods, just as they did between poor and rich.[18] There is ample archaeological evidence that these understandings extended well beyond the circle of the elite whose texts provide our clearest descriptions

---

[8] Spaeth (1996); Schultz (2006).
[9] Potts, Chapter 3, this volume; Wörrle (1988); de Ligt (1993).
[10] MacKinnon, Chapter 8, this volume; King, Chapter 9, this volume. On sacrificial euergetism, see Rives (2019).
[11] Rüpke, Chapter 2, this volume; Horster, Chapter 6, this volume. See also Gordon, Raja, and Rieger (2021).
[12] Domingo, Chapter 4, this volume; Chaufray, Chapter 7, this volume. For benefactions, see Zuiderhoek (2009); Gygax and Zuiderhoek (2021); and, for temples paid for from booty, Ziolkowlski (1992); Orlin (1997); Padilla Peralta (2020).
[13] Verboven, Chapter 11, this volume.   [14] van Nijf (1997); Rüpke (2007).
[15] Dignas (2002).
[16] The theme is explored in *Religion in the Roman Empire*, 5/1 (2019), through a series of microhistories. For lived religion, see Rüpke (2016); Gasparini et al. (2020).
[17] Taub (2003); Lehoux (2007).
[18] García Morcillo, Chapter 10, this volume. Also Price (1984); Reynolds and Volk (1990); Derks (1995); Moser (2019); Graham (2021).

of them. The physical remains of *parapegmata* show a folk understanding of these matters similar to that presented in more literary forms in agronomical and meteorological texts. Equally, the traces of votive offerings from sanctuaries, like the anatomical votives of central Italy, support the occasional literary accounts of rural shrines like Pliny's description of the sources of the Clitumnus.[19]

The Roman Empire also saw a mass production of images of the gods, in silver and bronze, in pipe clay, and in stone and wood, to say nothing of amulets and *defixiones*. Most were designed for use by individuals, who placed them in homes, graves, and temples: some must have been very cheap indeed. Economically the purchase of images, amulets, and curse tablets was both an act of consumption and also a proactive strategy to mitigate risk and increase the chances of success. Ritual action, in other words, might be considered an investment. The same essential logic applied both to great state rituals like the *supplicationes* of the Roman state and the annual sacrifices of the Arval Brethren to the everyday ritual practices of slaves, smallholders, and the urban poor.

Dynamics: Religion and Economic Change

Most of what has been described so far had roots in archaic Mediterranean practices.[20] Many of these ritual traditions endured beyond the end of antiquity, even as public sacrifice diminished in scale and was eventually abandoned.[21] That stability parallels some of the relatively unchanging features of the Roman economy. The range of core cultigens and domesticated animals available within the Mediterranean did not change significantly in the period of Roman rule, nor did the tools or techniques of farming. Beyond the Mediterranean basin there were changes in the size of livestock and in the extent of viticulture and arboriculture in the decades following conquest by Rome. There was also limited technological change across the empire, although it probably affected peasant agriculture least of all.[22] But these changes had little impact on those who farmed at or close to subsistence on their own small plots or on land rented from others. It is no surprise that their ritual lives—the routines

---

[19] Pliny, *Ep.* 8.8, with Veyne (1983); Dubourdieu (1997); Scheid (2006). For the archaeology, see now Draycott and Graham (2015); Hughes (2017); Graham (2021).
[20] Potts, Chapter 3, this volume. See also Eidinow (2007); Biella (2019).
[21] Petropolou (2008); Stroumsa (2009); Knust and Várhelyi (2011); Faraone and Naiden (2012).
[22] Wilson (2002); Lo Cascio (2006); Oleson (2008).

of prayer and observance, the cult of the dead and of local gods, the reliance on curses and amulets—changed little until late antiquity.

Other sectors of the economy had a more dynamic history. Exploring these changes has been a great part of the work of Roman archaeologists and historians over the last few decades, not least through the work of the Oxford Roman Economy Project. So we may now reasonably ask how religious action was entangled in these transformations.

The shift in our understanding since the 1970s may be summarized briefly. The insistence on the economic underdevelopment of the ancient world was based on two pillars, a negative assessment of impact of state taxation on economic life and a literal reading of texts that presented an aristocratic ideology uninterested in profit. Neither of these positions is now widely held. The capacity of taxation to stimulate production, rather than suppress it, is widely recognized.[23] The disdain for enterprise expressed in many literary texts is now treated with caution.[24] Meanwhile, archaeological investigation of viticulture, olive-oil production, shipwrecks, quarrying and the stone trade, the exploitation of marine resources, the raising of livestock, and the textile industry—to name just a few areas of recent study—clearly illustrate a period of growth. That growth can increasingly be quantified in relation to various indices.[25] These phenomena are best attested in the last two centuries BC and the first century AD, and were experienced first in Italy and later in a number of other circum-Mediterranean provinces. This growth in production and manufacturing seems to have responded to an increased demand generated by urbanization, by the needs of a standing army, and by the spread of Italian modes of consumption.

It is also widely agreed that this increase in economic activity was facilitated by the Roman unification of the Mediterranean world. There remains some disagreement about how exactly imperial expansion was linked to economic growth during the Republic. A general connection between Roman imperial expansion and Roman economic growth is widely agreed, although there is less agreement about the details. Some accounts stress the impact on production of an influx of cheap slaves, others argue that an increase in bullion and credit were central factors, yet others emphasize the distribution of plunder among the propertied classes and their need to find new ways to use it. There are accounts that emphasize the effects of the Roman state's redistribution of resources previously controlled by defeated states, and some stress the

---

[23] Hopkins (1978b, 1980, 2000, 2009).   [24] D'Arms (1981).
[25] Harris (1993); de Callataÿ (2005); Bowman and Wilson (2009).

economic consequences of the growth of the imperial metropolis.[26] The most convincing accounts combine many factors.

Nevertheless the consequences are clear. The early Roman Empire, once achieved and stabilized around the turn of the millennium, was an environment that favoured economic activity in many ways. There were improvements in security, in transport infrastructure for maritime and terrestrial traffic, and in uniform standards of money, weights, and measures.[27] The spread of Roman legal procedures must also have favoured long-distance business.[28] Many of these effects were presumably unintended.[29] Most transport infrastructure, for example, was constructed to serve military needs or to enable the easier supply of imperial capitals. The partial unification of the coinage was the result first of brigandage and then of the demands of army pay.[30] Nevertheless, the emerging institutions of empire provided many opportunities for enterprise.[31]

How should religion be factored into these narratives? There are well-explored connections between Roman imperialism and Republican and Augustan religious ideology.[32] But there is not much sign that religion participated in discourses about economic activity, except in traditional interpretation of natural disasters or insistence on the importance of keeping oaths.

A more productive approach is to focus on the different actors and institutions that shaped the Roman economy. The key economic actors were the peasantry and the propertied classes, the Roman state, subordinated cities, perhaps the *collegia* and—most important for present purposes—temples.[33] The economic action of peasants and landowners alike was generally articulated through the family, perhaps the key institution in Roman economic history.[34] It was fundamental to the agricultural activities of peasants of various kinds: extended through slavery and various kinds of patronage, it formed the key means by which the affairs of the wealthy were managed. It was also repurposed to assist Republican magistrates and pro-magistrates and ultimately emperors to perform their public duties. Its centrality can be compared to that of the committee or the corporation in our own societies. Notoriously,

---

[26] Slaves: Hopkins (1978a); Giardina and Schiavone (1981); bullion and money: Kay (2014); the growth of the city of Rome: Hopkins (1978a, 1978b); Morley (1996).
[27] Carandini (1989); Howgego (1990, 1994); Hitchner (2012); Laurence (2020).
[28] Czajkowski, Eckhardt, and Strothmann (2020).   [29] Wilson and Bowman (2018).
[30] Crawford (1985); Harris (2008); Howgego (2013).
[31] Scheidel, Morris, and Saller (2007). See also Harris (2011) for exploration of key aspects.
[32] Harris (1979); North (1993); Beard (2007); Padilla Peralta (2020).
[33] This approach is taken by Gordon, Raja, and Rieger (2021).
[34] For approaches to Roman economic history via institutions, see Frier and Kehoe (2007); Bang (2009) and Tan (2017).

there were few large-scale financial institutions or corporations of the kind that have become increasingly important since the early seventeenth century. Banks operated at a relatively smaller scale and did not invest the money entrusted to them as venture capital.[35] Companies (*societates*) were short-lived entities, without legal personalities comparable to those of early modern trading companies, let alone modern limited liability companies. But there were other institutions. A key question for present purposes is how temples exercised their economic agency within the Roman economy.

Other preindustrial societies offer a range of possible models. It has been argued that the expansionist policy of Tawantinsuyu, the Inca state, was shaped by the accumulation of land by successive rulers, land that was then devoted to their post-mortem cult.[36] A structurally similar phenomenon was the making of inalienable grants of lands to the medieval church, prompting legislation by kings against *mortmain*. In both cases the idea is that religious bodies might tie up land, making it unavailable for other purposes, whether as a tax base or to support military force. In fact, the European Middle Ages provide many examples of religious foundations developing the economic potential of their property—for example, by building fishponds and raising sheep to supply textile producers with wool. Religious orders played key roles in the colonial expansion of Europe, including the reorganization of the landscape and its productive capacity.[37]

Did the religious institutions of the ancient world contribute to growth within the Roman economy, or did they retard it? The answer that emerges from the contributions to this volume is complex. First, there is no real sign of temple property acting as a brake on economic growth in the Roman period.[38] Temple lands and gifts by private individuals to Greek temples are documented epigraphically from as early as the fifth century BC.[39] Some at least of the treasuries built by individual cities at Delphi dated to the second half of the sixth century BC. Yet temples in the Mediterranean world did not seem to have become large landowners. Nor did those who controlled them seem to have been very entrepreneurial in the way some mediaeval abbots certainly were. Roman temples were mostly prohibited from inheriting wealth.[40] While donations to temples were common, there is no sign of anxious reactions to this of the kind generated by the great donations to Christian churches in the early fifth century by Melania the Younger. Members of the propertied classes

---

[35] Andreau (1999).   [36] Conrad and Demarest (1984).   [37] Bartlett (1993).
[38] For a fuller discussion of this debate and its historiography, see Chankowski (2011).
[39] See, e.g., Osborne and Hornblower (1994).
[40] Rüpke, Chapter 2, this volume; Horster, Chapter 6, this volume.

do not seem to have claimed that land was being accumulated by the gods on a scale that threatened the interest of their human fellow citizens. To judge from the epigraphy (perhaps not entirely a safe procedure), the Roman state generally promoted the interests of individual temples and protected them from the potential predations of cities and their elites.[41]

There was a long tradition of temples making loans, one attested in fifth-century BC Athens, others around the Hellenistic world and later in the Roman west.[42] Some loans were not entirely voluntary, but rather responses to political crises, from the Peloponnesian War to the dictatorship of Caesar. More regularly, temple managers seem to have made loans in order to generate income to pay for the expenses of ritual observances: alternative sources of revenue (fines, fees for the use of temples, and *summa honoraria*) were not necessarily very substantial.[43] When the temples of Hellenistic and Roman Asia Minor lent, their preferred borrowers were generally locals, with security in land, and they typically lent for longer periods and at lower interest rates than did other banks.[44] This conformed to broader patterns of lending by Greek temples.[45] Only in a few cases, such as the temples of Palmyra, which seem closely connected to the trading classes of the city, is there even the possibility that temple wealth was used to invest in productive activity.[46] The rationale is clear. Temples sought regular if modest returns to cover recurrent expenses rather than the high-risk, high-profit speculative loans used, for example, to fund large-scale maritime trade. In this sense, temple finances resemble those of many cities. This is no surprise, given they were run by more or less the same people, and had similar financial needs.

The economic activity of temples might be contrasted with that of those members of the Roman propertied classes who were much more innovative, entrepreneurial, and risk oriented. In the introduction to one of the best accounts of the Roman Republic ever published, Michael Crawford wrote: 'I should like to stress the innovativeness of the governing class of the Republic in a wide variety of fields, cultural as well as political.'[47] There is no doubt that this applies forcefully to the economic sphere. It was members of the elite who in the third and second centuries BC developed a set of legal instruments that facilitated more complex economic transactions, including the contract types *emptio venditio*, which governed selling and buying, and *locatio conductio*, which governed letting and hiring.[48] By the early second century BC a *lex*

---

[41] Dignas (2002).   [42] Wigg-Wolf, Chapter 5, this volume.
[43] Rüpke, Chapter 2, this volume.   [44] Dignas (2002).   [45] Chankowski (2011).
[46] Gregoratti (2020).   [47] Crawford (1992: 2)   [48] Johnston (1999).

institoria allowed principals to act through agents, which would soon make it possible for them to manage dispersed landholdings and conduct business at a distance.[49] Around the same time a large part of the same propertied classes were already involved in taking public contracts, or else underwriting those who were. This is also the moment when Cato's *On Agriculture* shows a fascination with means of intensifying production, and the appropriation of Greek knowledge on this subject. The fall of Carthage was followed by a similar appropriation of Punic agricultural know-how in the form of Mago's treatise on agriculture, and we may presume a mass of local expertise was gathered orally as the empire expanded, some of which found its way into encyclopaedic works like Pliny's *Natural History*.[50] Through the late second and last centuries BC there are repeated signs of the same group seizing on technical innovation in farming, construction, and manufacturing aimed at maximizing profit. Those innovations were backed by investment, which derived in part from the profits of empire and in part from the reinvestment of the profits of their own activity.[51] When need be, these elite landowners borrowed from each other, and went into short-lived partnerships so as to take advantage of the new opportunities opened up by political expansion. Mining, the slave trade, and the creation of a rental market were all products of this enterprise. The attitude of these classes contrasts strongly with that of traditional smallholders, whose main aim was to minimize risk.

Temples were probably less preoccupied with evading potential catastrophe than were peasants, but they were less entrepreneurial than many Roman property-owners. Like *municipia* and Greek cities, they occupied a middle space within the broad nexus of Roman economic activity. Whether the aggregate impact of temple economics was to stabilize the Roman economy is unclear. It seems unlikely. If it is correct that the public cults of the city of Rome had an annual cost of between thirty and fifty million *sestertii*,[52] this represents a small sum compared to the annual amounts spent on the military, estimated at around 400 million *sestertii*, with other imperial spending totalling at least as much.[53]

Temple-building, as several contributions make clear, might be very costly, but it was an optional cost and one that might be deferred or spread out over

---

[49] Aubert (1994). [50] Beagon (1992: 5–14).
[51] Lo Cascio (2006); Erdkamp, Verboven, and Zuiderhoek (2020).
[52] See Rüpke, Chapter 2, this volume.
[53] Rathbone (1996). For fuller discussion, see Bowman (2018), collecting estimates of the annual revenue and expenditure of the empire in the first century AD, mostly in the general area of HS 1,000 million per annum.

a long period. Emperors, as we know from other projects, could build very quickly if they chose to, but some projects, like the Forum Augustum, took decades to complete. Economically, temple-building might be seen as an activity in which surplus could be stored during periods of plenty, but that could be put on hold when there were more urgent demands on revenues. Much the same must have applied to the building projects in the provinces that were funded largely by local benefactors. Finally, after the first half of the first century AD most cities already possessed a complement of temples. Temple-building beyond this point was optional. Most large temples in the western provinces were built during the first two centuries AD, and temple-building in other regions seems to have diminished in scale well before the end of the third century. For all these reasons, it seems probable, then, that religious activity did not constitute a large part of the economic activity of the empire.

Locally, of course, religious activity must sometimes have been more important. The calculations performed by some contributors to this volume show the sustained demand for victims generated by public cults.[54] Some temples, like the Temple of Yahweh in Jerusalem, the Temple of Bel in Palmyra, and the Temple of Artemis at Ephesos, remained big players in local economies. Epidauros and Pergamon benefited from the fame of their healing sanctuaries, and Didyma and other centres from oracular shrines. The epigraphy of penteric festivals also makes their local economic importance quite clear.[55] Locally, the availability of credit in the form of temple reserves must have facilitated various kinds of activity by the wealthy, even if only as an additional source of cash to deal with bad years and irregular demands.

Measuring change over time is difficult. There seems to have been no straightforward relationship between economic growth and temple-building. Where the chronology of these processes can be studied in detail, regional sequences seem to have differed considerably.[56] Indications from shipwrecks and amphora production suggest the Italian economy boomed in the last century BC, but municipal temple-building in the peninsula peaked rather later. A similar gap has been noticed between the first testimony about profit-oriented farms and the archaeological appearance of grand villas.[57] Temple-building and expenditure on festivals in many areas, including Egypt, seems to have diminished well before any conceivable economic crises. Other factors

---

[54] Rüpke, Chapter 2, this volume; Horster, Chapter 6, this volume; and King, Chapter 9, this volume; also Gordon, Raja, and Rieger (2021).
[55] Wörrle (1988); Mitchell (1990); Rogers (1991).
[56] Derks (1998); Frankfurter (1998); Chaufray, Chapter 7, this volume.
[57] Rathbone (1983); Marzano and Métraux (2018).

must be invoked to explain fluctuations in the popularity of this form of expenditure relative to others. But this is a familiar issue in the archaeology of the Roman economy more generally: it is not possible to read off fluctuations in productivity simply from spending on any one activity, whether that be urban monuments, grand villas, or temples. The history of consumption and the history of production need to be treated separately and regionally.

Polytheism and the Economy

One trend that does seem to appear in the studies gathered here, and elsewhere, is the convergence of temple management on a system of Roman norms.[58] No sudden watershed is evident across the entire empire, but little by little the way temple finances were controlled tended to reduce the influence of priests relative to that of civic authorities. This was partly an effect of imperial initiatives in particular provinces. The succession of prohibitions levelled against the Druids is a case in point, and the administrative reorganization of Egypt in the reign of Augustus is another.[59] Religious arrangements were also part of the package of municipal regulations handed out to *coloniae* and Latin *municipia*. The effect of municipalization as far as priesthoods were concerned was to disseminate a modified version of Roman and Italian practice.[60] Elsewhere some changes were also probably the cumulative result of piecemeal interventions and arbitrations by Roman officials who applied conventional Roman wisdom about the best way of running religion. A central feature of that wisdom was a preference for a model of priesthood in which members of the propertied classes took on responsibility for cult (and its funding) at their own expense.[61] This reorganization of temple management on Roman lines naturally had implications for the economics of religious activity. A rise in animal sacrifice as a central ritual had economic implications. Several chapters in this volume also note a diminution in the lending activities of temples. These ritual convergences were less striking than the construction of provincial copies of metropolitan monuments,[62] but were perhaps more important

---

[58] Dignas (2002) on Asia Minor; Wilson, Chapter 1, this volume, on Jerusalem; Wigg-Wolf, Chapter 5, this volume, on the north-west; Chaufray, Chapter 7, this volume, on the Fayyum.
[59] Woolf (1998: 220–5) on Gaul; Bowman and Rathbone (1992) on Egypt.
[60] Rüpke (2006a, 2006b).
[61] Gordon (1990). The case of Roman intervention in the institution of Athens is a good example of this; see Oliver (1970).
[62] Domingo, Chapter 4, this volume.

in the longer run. It meant that the structural roles played by temples in local economies were replicated across the empire.

Perhaps the most important aspect of this was the way that Roman-style polytheism contributed to a fragmentation of the economic power of religious authorities. Every temple was independent of every other. A gift to a Mithraeum was not a gift to the community of those who worshipped Mithras. The rise in the popularity of some diasporic cults, like that of the Egyptian gods, did not result in new concentrations of religious power. Nor did the priests of popular deities increased their economic influence. In some areas—Egypt and Judaea, for instance—local priests operated under closer supervision under Rome than in earlier periods. More generally there was no real management of ritual or religious property at any scale larger than the city state. Not until the third century AD did imperial authorities try to exercise much active control over religious activity.[63] Quite often temples had a large measure of autonomy within a given city state. The result was that no new large-scale economic actors emerged in the religious sphere before the fourth century AD.

Again, there were variations from one locality to another. This emerges strongly from the chapters in this collection. A few cities were enriched by the popularity of some of their cults: centres of initiation cults such as Eleusis and Ephesos drew visitors from great distances, and the proliferation of pan-hellenic and international festivals had economic consequences.[64] They are perhaps to be compared with sites that attracted visitors for other reasons. The line between tourism and pilgrimage is less clear-cut when viewed in terms of ancient categories like *theoria*.[65] Developments in the north and west are less easy to reconstruct in the absence of epigraphy, but some regional centres clearly did emerge even in Britain.[66] There was, however, no global change in the economics of ancient religion.

The significance of the decentralized nature of religious organization in the Roman Empire really emerges only in contrast with what supplanted it in late antiquity. How quickly a new economic order of the sacred appeared is not completely clear. Many of Constantine's donations might have been understood in terms of traditional benefactions bestowed on particular temples. But the ecclesiastical and ecumenical institutions that had originally

---

[63] Beard, North, and Price (1998: 313–18); Ando (2003, 2007). One possible watershed is identified by Rives (1999).
[64] Spawforth and Walker (1985); Clinton (1997). Ephesos: Rogers (2012). New festivals: Graf (2015); van Nijf and Williamson (2015).
[65] Elsner and Rutherford (2005); Rogers (2012); Rutherford (2013).
[66] King, Chapter 9, this volume; Cousins (2020).

developed to oppose heresy and schism were easily mobilized to economic ends. Some bishops were already powerful economic actors by the late fourth century AD. Damasus in Rome was already testing the political potential of the economic power of the church within the City of Rome. By the sixth century, Gregory I was able to dominate regional politics largely through use of church revenues. The success of the church in asserting its authority following the collapse of imperial power in the western Mediterranean did not depend only on economic resources, of course. But the difference in the way Christian institutions managed, and were allowed to manage, property certainly helped bishops extend their influence within their communities, and this in turn reminds us of the constraints placed on religious institutions in the late Republic and early Roman Empire.

References

Ando, C. (2003). 'A Religion for the Empire', in A. J. Boyle and W. J. Dominik (eds), *Flavian Rome. Culture, Image, Text*. Leiden and Boston, 321–44.

Ando, C. (2007). 'Exporting Roman Religion', in J. Rüpke (ed.), *Companion to Roman Religion*. Malden, MA, and Oxford, 429–45.

Ando, C. (2008). *The Matter of the Gods: Religion and the Roman Empire*. Berkeley and Los Angeles, and Oxford.

Andreau, J. (1999). *Banking and Business in the Roman World*. Cambridge.

Aubert, J.-J. (1994). *Business Managers in Ancient Rome: A Social and Economic Study of Institores, 200 BC–AD 250* (Columbia Studies in the Classical Tradition 21). Leiden.

Bang, P. F. (2009). 'Review Article: The Ancient Economy and the New Institutional Economics', *JRS* 99: 194–206.

Bartlett, R. (1993). *The Making of Europe: Conquest, Colonization, and Cultural Change 950–1350*. Harmondsworth.

Beagon, M. (1992). *Roman Nature: The Thought of Pliny the Elder* (Oxford Classical Monographs). Oxford.

Beard, M. (1987). 'A Complex of Times: No More Sheep on Romulus' Birthday', *PCPS* 33: 1–15.

Beard, M. (2007). *The Roman Triumph*. Cambridge, MA.

Beard, M., North, J., and Price, S. (1998). *Religions of Rome*, vol. 1: *A History*. Cambridge.

Biella, M. C. (2019). 'Gods of Value: Preliminary Remarks on Religion and Economy in Pre-Roman Italy', *Religion in the Roman Empire* 5: 23–45.

Bowman, A. K. (2018). 'The State and the Economy: Fiscality and Taxation', in A. Wilson and A. Bowman (eds), *Trade, Commerce and the State in the Roman World* (Oxford Studies on the Roman Economy). Oxford, 27–52.

Bowman, A. K., and Rathbone, D. (1992). 'Cities and Administration in Roman Egypt', *JRS* 82: 107–27.

Bowman, A. K., and Wilson, A. I. (2009) (eds). *Quantifying the Roman Economy: Methods and Problems* (Oxford Studies on the Roman Economy). Oxford.

Carandini, A. (1989). 'Italian Wine and African Oil: Commerce in a World Empire', in K. Randsborg (ed.), *The Birth of Europe. Archaeology and Social Development in the First Millennium AD*. Rome, 16–24.

Chankowski, V. (2011). 'Divine Financiers: Cults as Consumers and Generators of Value', in Z. H. Archibald, J. K. Davies, and V. Gabrielsen (eds), *The Economics of Hellenistic Societies: Third to First Centuries BC*. Oxford 142–65.

Clinton, K. (1997). 'Eleusis and the Romans: Late Republic to Marcus Aurelius', in M. C. Hoff and S. I. Rotroff (eds), *The Romanization of Athens* (Oxbow Monograph 94). Oxford, 161–81.

Conrad, G., and Demarest, A. A. (1984). *Religion and Empire: The Dynamics of Aztec and Inca Expansionism* (New Directions in Archaeology). Cambridge.

Cousins, E. (2020). *The Sanctuary at Bath in the Roman Empire*. Cambridge.

Crawford, M. H. (1985). *Coinage and Money under the Roman Republic: Italy and the Mediterranean Economy*. London.

Crawford, M. H. (1992). *The Roman Republic*. 2nd edn. London.

Czajkowski, K., Eckhardt, B., and Strothmann, M. (2020) (eds). *Law in the Roman Provinces* (Oxford Studies in Roman Society and Law). Oxford.

D'Arms, J. H. (1981). *Commerce and Social Standing in Ancient Rome*. Cambridge, MA.

de Callataÿ, F. (2005). 'The Graeco-Roman Economy in the Super Long Run: Lead, Copper, and Shipwrecks', *JRA* 18/1: 361–72.

de Ligt, L. (1993). *Fairs and Markets in the Roman Empire* (Dutch Monographs on Ancient History and Archaeology 11). Amsterdam.

Derks, T. (1995). 'The Ritual of the Vow in Gallo-Roman Religion', in J. Metlzer, M. Millett, N. Roymans, and J. Slofstra (eds), *Integration in the Early Roman West: The Role of Culture and Ideology* (Dossiers d'archéologie du Musée d'Histoire et d'Art 4). Luxembourg, 111–27.

Derks, T. (1998). *Gods, Temples and Ritual Practices: The Transformation of Religious Ideas and Values in Roman Gaul* (Amsterdam Archaeological Studies 2). Amsterdam.

Dignas, B. (2002). *Economy of the Sacred in Hellenistic and Roman Asia Minor*. Oxford.

Draycott, J., and Graham, E.-J. (2015) (eds). *Bodies of Evidence: Ancient Anatomical Votives Past, Present and Future*. Abingdon and New York.

Dubourdieu, A. (1997). 'Les Sources du Clitumne: De l'utilisation et du classement des sources littéraires', *Cahiers du Centre Gustave Glotz* 8: 131–49.

Eidinow, E. (2007). *Oracles, Curses and Risk among the Ancient Greeks*. Oxford.

Elsner, J., and Rutherford, I. (2005) (eds). *Pilgrimage in Graeco-Roman and Early Christian Antiquity: Seeing the Gods*. Oxford.

Erdkamp, P., Verboven, K., and Zuiderhoek, A. (2020) (eds). *Capital, Investment, and Innovation in the Roman World* (Oxford Studies on the Roman Economy). Oxford.

Faraone, C. A., and Naiden, F. S. (2012) (eds). *Greek and Roman Animal Sacrifice: Ancient Victims, Modern Observers*. Cambridge.

Feeney, D. (1998). *Literature and Religion at Rome: Culture, Contexts and Beliefs* (Latin Literature in Context). Cambridge.

Finley, M. I. (1973). *The Ancient Economy* (Sather Classical Lectures 43). Berkeley and Los Angeles.

Frankfurter, D. (1998). *Religion in Roman Egypt: Assimilation and Resistance*. Princeton, NJ.

Frier, B. W., and Kehoe, D. P. (2007). 'Law and Economic Institutions', in W. Scheidel, I. Morris, and R. P. Saller (eds), *Cambridge Economic History of the Greco-Roman World*. Cambridge, 113–43.

Gasparini, V., Patzelt, M., Raja, R., Rieger, A.-K., Rüpke, J., and Urciuoli, E. (2020) (eds). *Lived Religion in the Ancient Mediterranean World: Approaching Religious Transformations from Archaeology, History and Classics*. Berlin and Boston.

Giardina, A., and Schiavone, A. (1981) (eds). *Società romana e produzione schiavistica*. Rome and Bari.

Gordon, R. (1990). 'Religion in the Roman Empire: The Civic Compromise and its Limits', in M. Beard and J. North (eds), *Pagan Priests*. London, 233–55.

Gordon, R., Raja, R., and Rieger, A.-K. (2021). 'Economy and Religion', in J. Rüpke and G. Woolf (eds), *Religion in the Roman Empire* (Die Religionen der Menschheit 16.2). Stuttgart, 262–305.

Graf, F. (2015). *Roman Festivals in the Greek East: From the Early Empire to the Middle Byzantine Era*. Cambridge.

Graham, E.-J. (2021). *Reassembling Roman Religion in Roman Italy*. London.

Gregoratti, L. (2020). 'Temples and Traders in Palmyra', in P. Erdkamp, K. Verboven, and A. Zuiderhoek (eds), *Capital, Investment, and Innovation in the Roman World* (Oxford Studies on the Roman Economy). Oxford, 461–80.

Gygax, M. D., and Zuiderhoek, A. (2021) (eds). *Benefactors and the Polis: The Public Gift in the Greek Cities from the Homeric World to Late Antiquity*. Cambridge.

Harris, W. V. (1979). *War and Imperialism in Republican Rome, 327–70 BC*. Oxford.

Harris, W. V. (1993). 'Between Archaic and Modern: Some Current Problems in the History of the Roman Economy', in W. V. Harris (ed.), *The Inscribed Economy: Production and Distribution in the Roman Empire in the Light of instrumentum domesticum* (Journal of Roman Archaeology Supplements). Ann Arbor, MI, 11–29.

Harris, W. V. (2008) (ed.). *The Monetary Systems of the Greeks and Romans*. Oxford and New York.

Harris, W. V. (2011). *The Roman Imperial Economy: Twelve Essays*. Oxford.

Hitchner, R. B. (2012). 'Roads, Integration, Connectivity and Economic Performance in the Roman Empire', in S. E. Alcock, J. Bodel, and R. J. A. Talbert (eds), *Highways, Byways, and Road Systems in the Pre-Modern World* (Ancient World Comparative Histories). Malden, MA, 222–34.

Hopkins, K. (1978a). *Conquerors and Slaves* (Sociological Studies in Roman History 1). Cambridge.

Hopkins, K. (1978b). 'Economic Growth and Towns in Classical Antiquity', in P. Abrams and E. A. Wrigley (eds), *Towns in Societies: Essays in Economic History and Historical Sociology* (Past and Present Publications). Cambridge, 35–77.

Hopkins, K. (1980). 'Taxes and Trade in the Roman Empire (200 BC–AD 400)', *JRS* 70: 101–25.

Hopkins, K. (2000). 'Rent, Taxes, Trade and the City of Rome', in E. Lo Cascio (ed.), *Mercati permanenti e mercati periodici nel mondo romano: Atti degli Incontri capresi di storia dell'economia antica (Capri 13–15 ottobre 1997)* (Pragmateiai 2). Bari, 253–67.

Hopkins, K. (2009). 'The Political Economy of the Roman Empire', in I. Morris and W. Scheidel (eds), *The Dynamics of Ancient Empires: State Power from Assyria to Byzantium* (Oxford Studies in Early Empires). New York, 178–204.

Howgego, C. (1990). 'Why did Ancient States Strike Coins?', *NC* 150: 1–25.

Howgego, C. (1994). 'Coin Circulation and the Integration of the Roman Economy', *JRA* 7: 5–21.

Howgego, C. (2013). 'The Monetization of Temperate Europe', *JRS* 103: 16–45.

Hughes, J. (2017). *Votive Body Parts in Greek and Roman Religion*. Cambridge.

Johnston, D. (1999). *Roman Law in Context*, ed. P. Cartledge and P. Garnsey (Key Themes in Ancient History). Cambridge.

Kay, P. (2014). *Rome's Economic Revolution* (Oxford Studies on the Roman Economy). Oxford.

Knust, J. W., and Várhelyi, Z. (2011) (eds). *Ancient Mediterranean Sacrifice*. Oxford and New York.

Laurence, R. (2020). 'The Meaning of Roads: A Reinterpretation of the Roman Empire', in J. Kuuliala and J. Rantala (eds), *Travel, Pilgrimage and Social Interaction from Antiquity to the Middle Ages*. London, 37–63.

Laurence, R., and Smith, C. (1995-6). 'Ritual, Time and Power in Ancient Rome', *Accordia Research Papers* 6: 133–52.

Lehoux, D. (2007). *Astronomy, Weather and Calendars in the Ancient World: Parapegmata and Related Texts in Classical and Near Eastern Societies*. Cambridge.

Lo Cascio, E. (2006) (ed.). *Innovazione tecnica e progresso economico nel mondo romano: Atti degli Incontri capresi di storia dell'economia antica (Capri 13-16 aprile 2003)* (Pragmateiai 10). Bari.

MacRae, D. (2016). *Legible Religion: Books, Gods, and Rituals in Roman Culture* Cambridge, MA.

Marzano, A., and Métraux, G. P. R. (2018) (eds). *The Roman Villa in the Mediterranean Basin: Late Republic to Late Antiquity*. Cambridge.

Meadows, A., and Williams, J. (2001). 'Moneta and the Monuments: Coinage and Politics in Republican Rome', *JRS* 91: 27–49.

Mitchell, S. (1990). 'Festivals, Games and Civic Life in Roman Asia Minor', *JRS* 80: 183–93.

Morley, N. (1996). *Metropolis and Hinterland: The City of Rome and the Italian Economy 200 BC–AD 200*. Cambridge.

Moser, C. (2019). *The Altars of Republican Rome and Latium: Sacrifice and the Materiality of Roman Religion*. Cambridge.

Moser, C., and Smith, C. (2019). 'Transformations of Value: Lived Religion and the Economy', *Religion in the Roman Empire* 5: 3–22.

North, J. (1993). 'Roman Reactions to Empire', *Scripta classica israelica* 12: 127–38.

Oleson, J. P. (2008) (ed.). *The Oxford Handbook of Engineering and Technology in the Classical World*. Oxford.

Oliver, J. H. (1970). *Marcus Aurelius: Aspects of Civic and Cultural Policy in the East* (Hesperia Supplements 13). Princeton.

Orlin, E. (1997). *Temples, Religion and Politics in the Roman Republic* (Mnemosyne Supplements 164). Leiden, New York, and Cologne.

Osborne, R., and Hornblower, S. (1994) (eds). *Ritual, Finance, Politics: Athenian Democratic Accounts Presented to David Lewis*. Oxford and New York.

Padilla Peralta, D. (2020). *Divine Institutions: Religions and Community in the Middle Roman Republic*. Princeton.

Petropolou, M.-Z. (2008). *Animal Sacrifice in Ancient Greek Religion, Judaism, and Christianity, 100 BC to AD 200*. Oxford.

Polanyi, K., Arensberg, C. M., and Pearson, H. W. (1957) (eds). *Trade and Market in the Early Empires: Economies in History and Theory*. Glencoe, IL.

Price, S. (1984). *Rituals and Power: The Roman Imperial Cult in Roman Asia Minor*. Cambridge.

Rathbone, D. (1983). 'The Slave Mode of Production in Italy', *JRS* 73: 160–8.

Rathbone, D. (1996). 'The Imperial Finances', in A. Bowman, E. Champlin, and A. Lintott (eds), *Cambridge Ancient History*, vol. X: *The Augustan Empire 43 BC–AD 69*. Cambridge, 309–23.

Reynolds, J., and Volk, T. (1990). 'Gifts, Curses, Cult and Society at Bath', *Britannia* 21: 379–91.

Rives, J. B. (1999). 'The Decree of Decius and the Religion of Empire', *JRS* 89: 135–54.

Rives, J. B. (2019). 'Animal Sacrifice and Euergetism in the Hellenistic and Roman Polis', *Religion in the Roman Empire* 5: 83–102.

Rogers, G. M. (1991). 'Demosthenes of Oenoanda and Models of Euergetism', *JRS* 81: 91–100.

Rogers, G. M. (2012). *The Mysteries of Artemis of Ephesos. Cult, Polis, and Change in the Graeco-Roman World*. New Haven and London.

Rüpke, J. (2006a). 'Religion in Lex Ursonensis', in C. Ando and J. Rüpke (eds), *Religion and Law in Classical and Christian Rome* (Potsdamer Altertumswissenschaftlicher Beiträge 15). Stuttgart, 34–46.

Rüpke, J. (2006b). 'Urban Religion and Imperial Expansion: Priesthoods in the Lex Ursonensis', in L. de Blois, P. Funke, and J. Hahn (eds), *The Impact of Imperial Rome on Religions, Ritual and Religious Life in the Roman Empire*. Leiden and Boston, 11–23.

Rüpke, J. (2007) (ed.). *Gruppenreligionen im römischen Reich* (Studien und Texte zu Antike und Christentum 43). Tübingen.

Rüpke, J. (2016). *On Roman Religion: Lived Religion and the Individual in Ancient Rome*. Ithaca, NY.

Rutherford, I. (2013). *State Pilgrims and Sacred Observers in Ancient Greece: A Study of theôriâ and theôroi*. Cambridge.

Scheid, J. (2006). 'Rome et les grands lieux de culte d'Italie', in A. Vigourt, X. Loriot, A. Bérenger-Badel, and B. Klein (eds), *Pouvoir et religion dans le monde romain: En hommage à Jean-Pierre Martin* (Passé Présent). Paris, 75–86.

Scheidel, W., Morris, I., and Saller, R. P. (2007) (eds). *Cambridge Economic History of the Greco-Roman World*. Cambridge.

Schultz, C. (2006). *Women's Religious Activity in the Roman Republic*. Chapel Hill, NC.

Spaeth, B. S. (1996). *The Roman Goddess Ceres*. Austin

Spawforth, A. J. S., and Walker, S. (1985). 'The World of the Panhellenion. I: Athens and Eleusis', *JRS* 75: 78–104.

Stroumsa, G. G. (2009). *The End of Sacrifice: Religious Transformations in Late Antiquity*, trans. S. Emanuel. Chicago.

Tan, J. (2017). *Power and Public Finance at Rome, 264–49 BCE*. New York and Oxford.

Taub, L. (2003). *Ancient Meteorology*, ed. R. French (Sciences of Antiquity). London.

van Nijf, O. M. (1997). *The Civic World of Professional Associations in the Roman East*. Amsterdam.

van Nijf, O. M., and Williamson, C. G. (2015). 'Re-Inventing Traditions: Connecting Contests in the Hellenistic and Roman World', in D. Boschung, A. W. Busch, and M. J. Versluys (eds), *Reinventing 'The Invention of Tradition'? Indigenous Pasts and the Roman Present: Conference Cologne 14–15 November 2013* (Morphomata 32). Paderborn, 95–111.

Veyne, P. (1983). '"Titulus Praelatus": Offrande, solemnisation et publicité dans les ex-voto greco-romains', *RA*: 281–300.

Wilson, A. (2002). 'Machines, Power and the Ancient Economy', *JRS* 92: 1–32.

Wilson, A., and Bowman, A. (2018) (eds). *Trade, Commerce and the State in the Roman World* (Oxford Studies on the Roman Economy). Oxford.

Woolf, G. (1998). *Becoming Roman: The Origins of Provincial Civilization in Gaul*. Cambridge.

Wörrle, M. (1988). *Stadt und Fest in kaiserzeitlichen Kleinasien: Studien zu einer agonistischen Stiftung aus Oinoanda* (Vestigia 39). Munich.

Ziolkowlski, A. (1992). *The Temples of Mid-Republican Rome and their Historical and Topographical Context* (Saggi di storia antica 4). Rome.

Zuiderhoek, A. (2009). *The Politics of Munificence in the Roman Empire: Citizens, Elites and Benefactors in Asia Minor* (Greek Culture in the Roman World). Cambridge.

Index

Entries for scholars list the pages where they are discussed by others in the text, but not for their own chapters if they are contributors to this volume, or where their works are simply referenced in footnotes.

Aare (river) 275
Abydos 137–8
accounting 158, 164, 194, 210, 254
Achaia 171
Acquarossa 64
Adiabenici 81
Adriatic 63, 143
Aegean 62–3, 169
Aegean Sea 62
Aelius Aristides 164
M. Aelius Hellanicus 169
M. Aemilius C. Popilius 258
M. Aemilius Scaurus 32
Aeneas 18, 55, 134
Aeneid 55
Aequi 54
aerarium 15, 141
aerarium Saturni 15
aes 36, 52, 132, 138, 249–50, 261
aes curionum 36
aes rude 52
Aesculapius 209, 278, 281–2, 284, 289; see also Asclepius, Asklepios
Aethales 251
Aezanoi 165–6, 172
Africa 7–8, 14, 81, 134, 166, 208, 213–14, 298, 300
    North Africa 7–8, 14, 134, 166, 208, 213–14
Agennius Urbicus 166
agonothetes 157, 160, 164
agricultural production 59
agriculture 311, 313, 318; *see also* cultivation, farming
    agricultural year 4, 311
Aithales 120
Alba Fucens 300
Alba Helviorum 295

Alburnus Maior 94; *see also* mines
Alea 238
Alexander Severus (emperor), *see* Severus Alexander
Alexandria 92, 146, 182, 184
Alexandrians 269
Algeria 18, 81
Allifae 280
Alps 147
altars 3, 10, 52–3, 160, 182, 189, 201, 204–5, 273, 284, 311
amber 55–6
American Numismatic Society 133–5
T. Amfius Balbus 143
Amiens 234
Ammianus Marcellinus 213
Amorgos 238
Amphictyonic league 166
amphitheatres 39
Anatolia 60, 62, 163
Anchises 18, 134
Ancus Marcius 134
Andersen, Damgaard 64
Andreau, Jean 147, 250, 316
animal sacrifice 9–11, 20, 40, 53, 198–205, 207, 210–13, 218, 219, 224, 229, 312, 320
animals 9–12, 20, 30, 33, 37, 39–40, 53, 55, 59, 121, 150, 164, 198–219, 224–5, 227–39, 249, 311–13, 320;
    see also cattle, chickens, dogs, fowl, game, goat, livestock, pigs, sacrifice, sheep
Annius Severus 260
Antemnae 55
Anthesteria (festival) 159
anthropology 42
Antioch 94, 166, 295

antler 54
Antonine dynasty 136
Antonine period 80, 183
antoninianus 136
M. Antonius Flamma 171
Antoninus Pius (emperor) 76, 278, 288
Aphrodisias 11–12, 15, 159, 168
   Hadrianic baths 15
   neopoioi 12
   Temple of Aphrodite 11–12, 15
Aphrodite 11–12, 15, 63, 212
Apollo 11, 14, 63, 76, 81, 88, 107, 132, 145, 162–3, 165, 171, 234, 238, 269, 289
   Apollo Didymaeus 11
   Apollo Grannus 234
   Apollo Sosianus 107
apparitores 34, 36
Appian 256
Apulum 275, 278, 284, 294
Aquileia 273–4, 280–1, 284, 294
Aquincum 274, 285
Ara Pacis 201
Arabia 140
Arabian 14
Arabian peninsula 14
Aramus (river) 275
Arcadia 238
Arcanus 279
archaeology 50–1, 54, 149, 232, 313, 320
Archaic Period 17, 50–1, 55, 58, 60, 63, 67
   Archaic Egypt 62
   Archaic Greece, Greek world 17, 58, 62
   Archaic Italy 17
   Archaic Latium 17, 63
   Archaic Rome 6
arches
   Arch of Caracalla in Theveste 18, 81, 83–4, 122
   Arch of Marcus Aurelius in Lepcis Magna 80
   Arch of Marcus Aurelius in Tripoli 83
architectural terracottas 53
architecture 63–4, 75–6, 78, 107, 121, 122, 148, 150
architrave 75, 92, 95–8, 102, 106, 108, 111–12, 115–17, 119
archon 167
Areopagus 170
Arezzo 52

Aricia 280
Ariminum 294
Arimnestus (Etruscan king) 61
Aristides 164
aristocracy
   aristocratic families 139
   aristocrats 55, 58, 278
Aristotle 57
Arles 274
Arnth Remzna 59
Arpinum 280
Arrian 150
Arrius Antoninus 167
Arruntianae 281
Arsinoe 146
   Temple of Jupiter 137–8, 146, 193, 260
Artemis 2, 9–10, 13, 15–16, 62–3, 132, 140, 143, 145, 150, 157–8, 163, 168, 319
   shrine of Artemis at Messene 10
Artemision 62, 168
artisans 12, 22, 53–4, 61, 159, 162–3, 267
Arval brethren 33, 36, 313
aryballoi 62
Asclepius 163, 280, 286; *see also* Aesculapius, Asklepios
Asconius 272
Asculum 294
Ashwell 224, 229–30
Asia Minor 2, 8, 60–1, 92, 146, 157, 159–60, 162–73, 217, 257, 269, 317, 320
Asisium 294
Asklepeion 10
Asklepiadai 284
Asklepiades 188
Asklepios 162, 284; *see also* Aesculapius, Asclepius
asses 33, 37
associations 21, 161, 172, 267–72, 275–6, 279–85, 292, 294–6, 298, 300–2, 312; *see also* guilds
   of Mercuriales 282–3
   religious 21, 268, 270, 312
Assyrian 61
Assyrians 140
Astarte 56, 63
Astura River 55
Atagartis 140
Aternum 279–81

Athena 63, 137, 145, 167, 169
   Athena Ilias 145
   Athena Lindia 167, 169
Athenian 169–70, 212
Athenians 165
Athens 6, 137, 143, 146, 159, 161–2, 164–6, 171, 317, 320
   Periclean Athens 6
   Theatre of Dionysos 161
athletes 1
Atina 282
Attica 57, 159
Atticus 162, 171
Attis 281, 288, 297–8
auction 5, 19, 183, 254
augurs 8, 34
Augusta Taurinorum 257, 284
Augustales 21, 33, 38, 271, 276, 282, 284, 293–4
Augustus (emperor) 13, 15, 19, 37, 75–8, 91, 107, 135, 139, 158, 166, 181, 183–4, 187, 201, 257, 275, 288, 320
Aurelian (emperor) 16, 136
Aurelius Ctesippus 167
aureus 135–6
Avenches 78
Aventicum 284
T. Avidius Quietus 165

Baal 269
Baal-Berit 269
Baalbek 279
Babylonians 140
Bacchias 186
Bacchus 289, 301; *see also* Dionysos
Baden Württemberg 237
Baetica 91
Bahariya 184
Bainbridge, W. S. 41
Balbus 143
Baltic 56
Banditaccia necropolis 52–3
bankers 16, 145, 282
banks, banking 3, 15, 16, 18, 22, 144–7, 158, 316–17
   deposit banks (temples as) 15, 16, 18, 140–5, 158
   lending banks (temples as) 18, 144–7

banquets 8–9, 16, 38–9, 200, 203, 235, 253, 268
barge-skippers 275
barley 167
basilica 85
   Basilica of Volubilis 85
Bastet 62
bath attendants 280
bathing 159
baths 7, 15, 80, 234, 296–7
beech 224, 228
beef 207, 209–10
Beirut 269, 275, 279
bell 2, 256
Bellona 76
L. Bellonius Marcus 237
Bellunum 294
Bendall, Lisa 1
benefactions 11, 19, 157–9, 161–2, 165, 167–9, 173, 246–7, 260–1, 282, 302, 312, 321
benefactors 15, 22, 43, 167, 169, 274, 284, 312, 319
Beneventum 282, 284
Berber 14
Berger, Peter 42
Bergomum 294
Berlin 184, 190, 192
Berua 294
Berytenses 279
Berytus 279
Bible 130
birds, *see* chickens, domestic fowl, doves
bishops 11, 322
Bithynia 173
boats 191–2
Boissier, Gaston 267–8
bones 20, 53, 55, 161, 163, 200, 202, 204–6, 214, 224–31, 233, 235, 237; *see also* animals
book 1–4, 7, 16, 22, 38, 248, 267
booty 11, 92, 145, 312
Bordeaux 296–7
Bose, Feler 4–5, 12
Botorrita 237
Boudicca 147
Boudiccan revolt 8, 147
boundary stones 158, 164–6
Brean Down 21, 236, 238

Bristol Channel 236
Britain 3, 8, 10, 20–1, 147, 173, 201, 224–8, 233, 235, 237–8, 321
British Museum 136
Britons 147, 239
Brixia 273, 294
Brolio 52
bronze 52, 61, 148, 190, 192, 249, 254, 256, 260–1, 313
Buddhism 5
budgets 38, 80, 89, 156–8, 164, 167–9, 194
builders 22, 159, 273–6, 281, 284–5, 294, 302
building inscriptions 7, 18, 161–2, 290–1, 302
building manuals 17
  Pegoretti, G. 79, 91–2, 98, 102, 106, 111, 115, 119
building material 77, 79, 121, 169
buildings 3, 7, 17–18, 21, 30, 32, 34–5, 38–9, 43, 51–4, 57–8, 62–3, 65–6, 75–94, 107, 120–1, 131, 144, 148, 157–64, 169, 173, 218, 229, 234, 251, 271, 275–8, 290–1, 295, 302, 312, 316, 318–19
bullion 57, 314–15
burial 20–1, 201–2, 204, 208, 218, 291, 251–3
burials 20, 53, 201–2, 213, 215, 252
business 3, 15, 21, 51, 59, 62, 65, 146–7, 191, 249, 252–4, 269–70, 311, 315, 318
Busiris 182, 185, 188
butchers 30, 36, 216, 279

Cacus 55
Cadbury Congresbury 236
Cadiz 11
A. Caecina Alienus 91
Caecina Severi (family) 120
L. Caecina Severus 120
Caelestis Salinensis 11
Caere 52–3, 55–7, 63, 65
Caesar, *see* C. Julius Caesar, L. Julius Caesar
Caesarea 281
cakes 10, 31, 37, 202, 212
Calama 88
  Temple of Apollo 76, 81, 88, 107, 234, 238

Caligula (emperor) 13, 38
Calvin 30
Cambridge Economic History of the Greco-Roman World 1
Cambridgeshire 224
Cameron, Alan 40–1
Camoludunum (Colchester) 8
Campana panel 52
Campania 55
Campanian 56
Campo della Fiera 58
Cape Tirizis 131
capital
  architectural, for column 75–7, 91, 95–106, 108–19
  civitas capital 234
  financial 6, 31, 38–9, 58, 170, 316
  provincial, imperial 8, 315
  symbolic or social 8, 156
Capitol 5
Capitoline Hill 139, 141
Capitoline Temple 13, 51
Capitolium 6
  of Lambaesis 88
  of Narbonne 76–7
  of Numluli 88
  of Pompeii 141
  of Volubilis 18, 81, 84–5, 87–8
Capua 281
Caracalla (emperor; Antoninus) 18, 80–4, 143, 275, 278
  Arch of Caracalla (Theveste) 18, 81, 83–4, 122
Caria 238
Carian Mylasa 165
Carrara 76–7, 92–3, 107, 120–1
Cartagena 80
Carthage 7–8, 11, 14, 214, 318
Carthaginian 61
Carthaginians 57
carts 121
casket 261
Cassius Festus 142
Castor 13, 15, 52, 56, 66, 76, 141–2, 289
Castor and Pollux (temple of) 13, 56, 76; *see also* Dioscuri
Catha 58
Cato 4, 37, 208, 311, 318
  De Agricultura 4

cattle 12, 30, 33, 53, 55, 66, 200–1, 207–8,
    210, 212–14, 219, 224–8,
    230–5, 238–9
cella 81, 83, 87
cells 65
Celtiberian 237
Celtic shrines 224
Celtic temples 21, 224, 227, 231,
    236, 238–9
Cemenelum 294
cenae sacerdotum 34
Censorinus 133–4
centonarii 22, 273–5, 278, 285–91,
    294–8, 300–2
Central Italy 17, 50, 58, 60, 63–6, 313
ceramics 55, 163, 204
    ceramic production 53
    Corinthian 55–6, 62
    Cumaean 55
    Cycladic 55
    Ephesian Ware 62
    Euboean 55
    Ischian 55
    late Geometric 55
ceremonies 185, 215, 233, 273, 277, 285
Ceres 4, 208, 216, 277, 280, 311
Cernunnos 289
Cetium 278
Chanctonbury Ring 21, 229, 233
Chaniotis, Angelos 12
Chankowski, Véronique 2, 157–9,
    163, 316–17
Chelmsford 232
Chianciano Terme 56
Chichester 231, 277
chickens (*Gallus gallus*) 20, 206–9, 212–16,
    233, 235; *see also* domestic fowl
children 2, 136
Chimera of Arezzo 52
Chiusi 52, 59
Christ 136; *see also* Jesus
Christian 2, 11, 36–7, 40, 136, 203, 209,
    217, 254, 316
Christianity 2, 4–5, 11, 15, 203, 209
Christians 160
Church (the Christian Church as
    institution) 2, 11, 14, 136, 251 n. 37,
    316, 322
church 35, 40, 89

church plate 11
Cicero 4, 39, 59, 80, 141, 144, 208,
    245–8, 261
    De Officiis 245, 247
Cigognier (shrine of) 78
Cilicians 140
cinerary urn 59
cipollino 76
cippus 52
circulation 11, 53, 58, 60, 131
Circus Maximus 311
cist 261
cities 1–2, 9–10, 14–15, 18–19, 30, 32, 50,
    54, 56, 62, 64–6, 75, 88, 93, 132, 134,
    137, 139–40, 143–5, 147, 155–8,
    160–9, 171–3, 205, 218, 232, 246,
    252, 256, 267, 270, 273, 278, 282,
    284, 286, 293–4, 297, 301–2,
    311–12, 315–19, 321
city council 2, 278, 282, 293–4, 303
civic cult 155, 164, 169, 172, 181
civic funds 2
civic order 22, 302
civil servants 36
Classical Athens 164
Classical Greece 159, 164, 259
Classical period 10, 156
Claudianum 89–91
Claudianus 93–4
Claudius (emperor) 8, 75, 161 n. 25, 169,
    292, 298
Ti. Claudius Hermias Theopropus 169
Claudius Marcellus 77
Ti. Claudius Novius 161
Claudius Silvanus 298 n. 147
clay 52, 313
Cleopatra 143
Clitumnus 313
Clodia Nigella 216
Clusium, *see* Chiusi
cocks 209
coinage 18–19, 131–3, 135, 137–9, 157,
    310, 315
coins 10–12, 19, 57, 59, 130–5, 137, 145,
    147–50, 163, 237, 245, 249,
    256, 258–9
Coligny (calendar of) 239
Colijnsplaat 3
collection boxes 10, 19, 150

collective religions 4
colleges 16–17, 33–4, 36–40, 187, 282, 292; see also *collegia*
collegia 12, 21–2, 250–1, 267–8, 270–4, 275–82, 284–5, 287, 291–8, 298–302, 312, 315; see also colleges
Collegia Mercurialium 282
Collegium Liberi Patris 281
collegium pontificum (pontifical college) 12
collegium Silvani Augusti Maius 298
Colonia Genetiva Iulia 254
colonies (*coloniae*) 8, 17, 38, 61, 157, 166, 171, 293, 320
Colosseum 139
columns 51–2, 75–7, 80–1, 83, 89, 91–119
commodities 21, 51, 57, 207, 209, 213, 217–18, 239, 245, 256, 259
  intangible commodities 57, 67
  tangible commodities 51, 57, 67
Commodus (emperor) 143, 276
communities 3, 5, 9, 32, 36, 38, 41, 50, 53, 60–1, 64, 139, 155–6, 159, 161–2, 165–6, 186, 250, 255, 261, 268–72, 279, 283, 299, 321
Competaliastai 269
competition (for office, or elite competition) 7, 17–18, 22, 138–9, 310
competitions 159, 161, 164, 168
Compsa 282
Comum 260, 274
Concordia 88, 289
conductores 120
confarreationes 37
confiscations 166
conquest 19, 61, 143, 147, 180–2, 184, 186, 188, 190, 192, 277, 313
Constantine I 11, 295, 321
construction 6–8, 17–19, 51, 53, 55, 63, 65–6, 77, 79, 81, 83–4, 87–9, 91, 93, 158–9, 165, 169, 181, 183, 297, 312, 318, 320
  temple construction 6–7, 19, 87, 181, 183
construction/building costs 17–18, 75–122, 169
  calculation methodology 17, 78, 80–1, 83–4, 87, 89, 122
Consualia (games) 33–4

consumers 2, 39, 52, 159
contractors 254, 297
contracts 32, 58, 165, 182, 184–5, 190, 318
Cordoba 76–7, 273
  Temple of Claudius Marcellus 77
  Temple of the Forum Adiectum 76–7
Corfu 63
Corinth 10, 61, 63, 157, 159
Corinthian
  bronzes 260–1
  capitals 91
  ceramics 55–6, 62
  Demaratus, Corinthian trader 61
corn 20, 272, 280
C. Cornelius Egrilianus 83
Cornelius Scipio 216
cornice 92, 95–8, 102, 106, 108, 111–12, 115–17, 119
corporations 267, 271, 295, 316
Corpus Agrimensorum 166
corruption 8, 79, 248
Cortona 279
cosmic order 138–9
costs
  building/construction costs, see construction/building costs
  of labour 81, 87, 93–4
Cotswold Hills 228
Crawford, Michael 8, 254–5, 258, 315, 317
credit 16, 36, 314, 319
Crete 171
crocodile god 19, 184
Croft Ambrey 228
crops 59
Crustumerium 55
cult, cults 2, 4–5, 7, 9, 15, 17, 19, 22, 32, 40–1, 51–4, 56–9, 63–4, 87, 148, 155–66, 168–73, 180–1, 183, 189, 193, 199–200, 208, 216, 225–6, 230, 238, 248, 251, 259, 267–74, 278, 281–2, 284–8, 292, 294, 296–8, 301–2, 311–12, 314, 316, 318–21
  civic cult 155, 164, 169, 172, 181
cult economy 19, 155–6, 158, 160–2, 164, 166, 168, 170, 172
  cult sites 17, 51, 53, 64, 67, 226
cult statues 4, 15, 87, 158
Eastern cults 22, 225

imperial cult 7, 19, 156–7, 160–2, 168, 171–3, 181, 183, 193, 278, 282, 286–8, 301
  mystery cults 5
  Roma 19, 133, 157, 269, 280–1, 292
cultivation 20, 186; *see also* agriculture, farming
Cumae 276, 292–3
curiones 36
curse tablets 21, 313
curses 37, 229, 314
Curtius, Ernst 132
customs (duties) 156, 163, 184
customs law of Asia 163
Cybele 292, 297–8
Cyclades 238
Cycladic 55
Cyprus 61–2, 159
Cyrene 62, 171

Dacia 94, 275
Daedalus 274
Dalmatia 282
Damasus (pope) 322
Danubian 301
De Rebus Bellicis 11
Dea Roma 157
death 15, 149, 203, 235, 250
debt 58, 145–6, 173, 186–7, 193
debtors 145
declarations 20, 181, 185, 188–9, 191–3
dedicants 10, 280–1
dedications 3, 5, 11, 14–15, 31, 35, 37, 52, 55–6, 61, 65, 120, 142, 258, 280, 284–8, 291, 298
defence 42
deities 1, 5, 13, 18, 52, 58, 63, 133, 135–7, 155, 158, 169–70, 187, 202, 206, 210–12, 269–70, 273, 275–7, 279–81, 285–7, 289, 291, 301–3, 321
DeLaine, Janet 17, 78, 80, 92–3
Delians 145
Delos 10, 14, 144–6, 158, 160, 162, 165, 238, 268–70, 279, 282
  Delian sanctuary 159, 163, 165
  Serapeion on Delos 10
Delphi 11, 39, 140, 143, 158, 160, 162–3, 238, 316
Demaratus (Corinthian trader) 61

Demeter 162, 169
Demeter and Kore, sanctuary of at Eleusis 162
Demetrios (Ephesian silversmith) 15
Demetrius (exegete of Alexandria) 146
demography 171
demotic (Egyptian) 19, 181–2, 184–93
denarii 18, 33, 80, 92–3, 133–4, 160, 167–8, 171, 209
dendrophori 22, 251, 267, 272, 281, 285, 288–98, 300–2
deposits, *see also* banks (deposit banks)
  ritual deposits 52, 132, 148–50, 204, 205, 206, 258
  sacrificial deposits 20, 201, 204, 205, 213, 225, 233–5
  votive deposits 54, 56, 236, 258, 259; *see also* votives, votive deposits
Di Manes 251, 255
Diana 11, 32, 163, 280
  Diana of Ephesos 11
  Diana Tifatina 32
didrachms 132
Didyma 81, 159, 217, 319
  Temple of Apollo 76, 81, 88, 107, 234, 238
Didymaeum 11
Digest 251
Dignas, Beate 2–3, 10–11, 158–9, 164, 166–7, 169–70, 172–3, 312, 317, 320
Dii Magifae 88
Dime 8, 15, 19–20, 180–1, 184–94
Dio Cassius 143, 256
Dio Chrysostom 140, 143
  Rhodian Oration 140
Diocletian 17, 33, 79, 93–4, 120, 209
  Edict on Maximum Prices 17, 33, 78–9, 93–4, 120, 209
Diodorus Siculus 57, 66
Dion 258
Dionysia 160–1
Dionysias 188
Dionysius I of Syracuse 57, 66
Dionysius of Halicarnassus 54
Dionysos 156–7, 159, 161, 169; *see also* Bacchus
Dionysos Kathegemon 156–7
Diophantos 163
Dioscourides 15; *see also* Castor and Pollux

Dioscuri 63
diplomacy 156–7
Diva Faustina 288
divination 54, 209, 312
divinators 37
Divodurum 284
Divus Antoninus 288
Divus Augustus 288
Divus Pertinax 276, 288
Divus Titus 278
do ut des 3, 58
Dodekaschoinos 183
dogs 53, 201–2, 231, 233
Dokimeion 93
Domburg 3
domestic fowl 20, 201, 206–10, 212, 214–16, 219; *see also* chickens
Domingo, Javier 7, 17
Domitian 158, 191–2
domus divina 275, 288
donations 2, 5, 7, 10, 12, 21, 161–2, 173, 245–6, 248–50, 252–60, 316, 321
donors 7, 15, 58, 250
Dorset 236
Dougga, *see* Thugga
Dover 231
doves 12, 130
drachmae 81, 146, 163, 170, 185
Drobeta 274
Druids 320
Duncan-Jones, Richard 160
Dutch coast 3
duumvir 8, 254

earthquakes 141, 143, 169
Eastern Mediterranean 39, 149
Eastern Provinces 16, 19, 155–6, 158, 160, 162, 164, 166, 168, 170–2
Ebbsfleet 230
economic actors 15, 22, 158, 315, 321
economic failure 4
economic mentality 3, 22
economic theory 41–2
economics 1, 3–5, 7, 10, 12, 31, 41–3, 50, 198–9, 213, 216, 218, 229, 239, 270, 310, 318, 320–1; *see also* New Institutional Economics
economic behaviour 3, 14, 42

economics of religion 1, 3–4, 41–3
neoclassical economics 42
economy 1–4, 13, 15–17, 19–20, 22, 23, 30, 39, 43, 50, 64, 67, 75, 130, 155–64, 166, 168, 170, 172–3, 180–1, 198, 224, 231, 234–5, 237, 239, 245, 254, 256, 259, 267, 270, 310–16, 318–21
Egypt 8–9, 14–15, 17–19, 32, 36, 56, 60–3, 93–4, 145–7, 180–4, 193, 295, 319–21
  Archaic Egypt 62
Egyptian Temples 38, 147, 180–1, 194
Egyptians 62
Elagabalus 278
Eleusis 162, 321, 170
  mystery cult 170
Elis 132
elites 3, 7–10, 17–19, 31, 34, 57–9, 64–6, 75, 78, 80, 120, 122, 130, 155–8, 161, 165–6, 169, 171–3, 193, 217, 270, 312, 317–18
emperors 11, 13, 18–19, 33, 40, 75, 78–9, 120–1, 135–7, 139, 155–7, 161, 166–7, 169, 172–3, 202, 213, 274–5, 278, 284, 287, 292, 295, 301, 315, 319
emporia 13–14, 64
enclosures 21, 217, 224, 230, 232–5
endowments 19, 38, 40, 170, 250, 273–4
England 210
English 54, 139, 158, 170
Enlightenment 310
Enna 4
entablature 15, 91, 94, 97, 99–107, 109–10, 112–14, 117–18
entrance fees 17, 35, 37–8, 254
environment 16, 62–3, 131, 148, 207, 236, 315
Epheseia 158
Ephesians 140, 157
Ephesos 2, 9, 11–13, 15–16, 62–3, 80, 132, 143, 145, 158–9, 161, 163, 166, 168–9, 171, 183, 269, 284, 319, 321
  Artemision 62, 168
  Temple of Artemis 2, 9, 13, 16, 62, 132, 140, 143, 145, 319
Epicureanism 212
Epidauros 159, 162, 319
Epigonos 15

epigraphic habit 146, 162, 291
epigraphy 317, 319, 321
    epigraphic evidence 21, 159, 181, 256, 258, 288, 290
epitaphs 58, 162
epula 33
Equirria 33–4
Erechtheus, sanctuary of at Athens 162
Essex 224, 226, 232
estates 14–15, 21, 149, 155, 164–5, 216, 237, 249
Esus 289
Etruria 17, 50–9, 62–4, 284
etrusca disciplina 59
Etruscan, Etruscans 14, 50, 52–6, 58–9, 61, 200–1
    language 52, 58, 61
    Etruscan period 14
Euboean 55
euergetism 5, 7–8, 18–19, 64, 122, 164, 169, 246, 312
Eure 233
Europe 11, 14, 316
    medieval 14, 237, 316
European 30, 42, 173, 184, 316
European Middle Ages 316
Eutychides 163
Evander 55
ex votos 21, 256–9; *see also* votive offerings
excavations 50–1, 53, 56, 62, 184, 224
exchange 9, 14, 17, 51, 54–61, 64–7, 157, 245–8, 250, 259, 312;
    see also markets, trade
exemptions (from military duties, *munera*, taxes) 8, 160, 173, 185–6, 193;
    see also immunity (from taxes)
expenditure 9–10, 16, 18–20, 22, 31–6, 40, 51, 159–60, 162, 164, 169, 189, 191–3, 213, 247, 318–20

fabri 22, 273–5, 277–9, 281, 284–6, 288–92, 294–5, 297–8, 300–2
fairs 14, 54, 160, 163, 239, 312;
    see also festivals
Fanum Fortunae 294
Fanum Voltumnae 54, 59; *see also* Campo della Fiera
farm 4, 208, 216, 224, 228, 319
farmers 20, 186, 188, 238

farming 4, 313, 318; *see also* agriculture, cultivation
faunal remains 20–1, 201, 204–6, 228
Faustina (Diva) 288
Faustina II 135–6
Fayyum 19, 181, 184–5, 188, 193, 320
feasting 206, 214, 219
fees 4–6, 9, 12, 16–17, 19, 35–8, 40, 164–5, 173, 254, 258, 317
    fees for services 4
    membership fees 4–5
Feltria 294
Fentress, Lisa 14
Ferialia 251
Feronia 54, 280
Fesques 233–4
festivals 3–5, 12, 14–15, 17, 19–21, 33, 54, 59, 65, 155, 158–64, 167–8, 170, 190, 202, 205, 210, 212, 216, 224, 226, 229, 235, 237–9, 251, 274–5, 311–12, 319, 321
    Anthesteria 159
    Dionysia 160–1
    dramatic festivals 19, 159
    Ferialia 251
    megala Epheseia 158
    navigium Isidis 311
    Pamboiotia 167
    Parentalia 251–2
    Passover 12, 130
    Romaia Sebaste 163
    Rosae 252
    Violae 252
Festus 33, 142, 275
Ficanum 298
Fidenae 55
Fidentia 276, 294
Fides 289
Fiera 58
figurines 5, 52, 55, 273
financial contributions 43
financial institutions 18, 130–1, 139, 316
financiers 2, 39, 282
fines 12, 19, 33, 35, 37, 165, 170, 183, 252, 256, 258, 293, 317
fire 15, 52, 92, 143–4, 295, 297
First Jewish War 131, 144
fiscus 37, 120, 170
fish 53, 214, 217

Fishbourne 237
fishermen 138, 192, 194, 274–5
fishing boats 191–2
Fishwick, Duncan 202, 274
flamen, flamines 7, 33, 162
flaminate 7–8
Flavian, Flavian period 75, 80, 92–3, 107
Flavians 183
Flavius Aethales 251
T. Flavius Celadus 107
Flavius Lysimachus 168
Flavius Mar(cius?) Scribonianus 169
T. Flavius Successus 107
Flavius Syntrophus 251
flocks 20–1, 224, 226, 228, 230, 232, 234–8; *see also* herds
Florus 120
flowers 10, 14
flute players 36
food 2, 41, 93–4, 201, 206–7, 209, 213–15, 218, 291, 235, 237
Forma Urbis Romae 75, 91
Foro Felice 282
forts 148, 226
 auxiliary forts 226
Fortuna 88, 285–6, 289
forum, fora 6, 13, 15, 17–18, 55, 63, 65–7, 75–8, 80, 83, 89–91, 94, 107–8, 111–12, 115–16, 119–21, 139, 141, 276, 277, 311, 319
Forum Adiectum (Cordoba) 76–7
Forum Boarium (Rome) 17, 55, 63, 66
Forum of Augustus (Forum Augustum, Rome) 15, 76–7, 107, 319
Forum of Peace (Forum Pacis, Rome) 89, 91, 121
Forum Romanum (Rome) 66, 141, 311
 Provincial Forum at Tarraco 18, 78, 94, 107
foundation myths 18
foundations 18, 21, 35, 51, 87, 92, 164–5, 167–8, 171, 201, 206, 208, 250–1, 316
 funerary 20–1, 58–9, 170, 200–3, 206, 208, 210, 213–16, 249–53, 255, 268, 279, 290–1, 302
fowl 20, 201, 206–10, 212, 214–16; *see also* chickens, domestic fowl, doves
Francavilla Marittima 56

Frank, Tenney 146
frankincense 10, 212
fraud 60, 164
Frayn, Joan 216, 218
freedmen 13, 107, 251, 269, 282, 284, 300
Frocester Court 228–9
fullers 32, 273, 280, 300, 316, 318
C. Fullonius Tertius 300
funerals 64
funerary bed 59
funerary donations 250, 253
Furfo 256

Gabinia Hermiona 81
Gabrielsen, Vincent 269
Gaius (emperor), *see* Caligula
Gaius (jurist) 249, 251
Galatea 62
Galatia 166
Galba 91
Galli 37
Gallia Belgica 149
Gallia Lugdunensis 91
Gallia Narbonensis 77, 91
Gallic sanctuaries or temples 143, 149, 232, 234–5, 237, 257
Gallic Wars 149
game (hunted) 20, 217
games 19, 31–3, 38, 40, 43, 59, 66, 157, 159, 161
 Consualia 33–4
 Equirria 33–4
 gladiatorial games 66, 161
 ludi scaenici 16, 33
garlands 14
Gaul 11, 21, 76, 132, 143, 147–8, 150, 224, 227, 233–4, 237–8, 300, 320
Gauls 66, 239
gems 11
genius 13, 88, 277–8, 280, 285–8, 294, 301
gens Laracena 58
gens Marcia 134
Germanicus 169
Germany 148
 the two Germaniae 173
Ghent Database of Roman Guilds and Occupation-Based Communities 21, 272, 279, 283, 285, 287, 299

gift exchange 58, 245–6, 248, 250, 312
gifts 11, 14, 21, 35, 55, 58, 62, 142, 168, 245–61, 312, 316, 321
Gigthis 14
Gisacum 233
gladiatorial games 66, 161
Glare, Penelope 180, 193
Gloucestershire 227
Gnomon of the Idios Logos 19, 183
goat 20, 53, 201, 207–10, 214, 219, 224–31, 233–5
gods 4–6, 10–11, 13–14, 17, 22, 37, 52, 58, 60, 62, 65–6, 132, 139, 143–4, 149, 155–7, 164, 166, 168, 170, 172–3, 182, 206, 211–12, 217, 238, 254, 256, 259, 267–70, 272, 274, 276, 278, 280, 282, 284–8, 292, 294, 296, 298, 300–2, 311–14, 317, 321
gold 11, 56, 87, 94, 140, 142, 144, 148–9, 168, 256
Gordon, Richard 2, 8–9, 30, 312, 315, 319–20
Gortyn 159
gospels 93, 130, 135; *see also* New Testament
  Gospel of St Luke 12, 130–1
  Gospel of St Mark 12 n. 54, 130 n. 1, 131 n. 2, 135 nn. 7 and 9
  Gospel of St Matthew 12, 93, 130, 209
governor 91, 156–7, 165–7, 170, 172–3, 275, 278
Ti. Gracchus 256
Graillot, H. 301
grain 4, 10, 78, 80, 93–4, 121, 164, 277
Grand 234
granite 76–7
grapheia 19, 182
graves 12, 37, 170, 201, 203–5, 208, 213–14, 216, 251, 313; *see also* tombs
Gravisca 50–1, 53, 56, 61, 64
Greece 1, 10, 31–3, 38, 56–8, 60–2, 65, 132, 157, 159–61, 164, 166–7, 169, 171, 173, 238, 259
  Archaic Greece 58
  Classical 1, 9–10, 51, 60, 132, 136, 156, 159–62, 164, 208, 218, 245, 250, 259, 271

Hellenistic 1–2, 9–10, 132, 144, 147, 155–64, 184, 201, 268–9, 271, 282, 317
Greek east 9, 18–19, 21, 137, 139, 148, 160, 279
Greeks 55, 62, 134, 206, 208, 269
Gregory I (pope) 322
Grumentum 276
guarantors 13, 60, 187
guilds 21–2, 191, 267–89, 291–2, 294–303; *see also* colleges, *collegia*

Haddenham 224, 228
Hadrian 165, 169, 183
Halicarnassus 54, 145
Hambleton 225
Hampshire 236, 239
Hannibal 257
harbour 62, 64, 66, 171
Harland, P. A. 268, 270
Harlow 226–8, 239
Harpsenesis 189
haruspex 59, 273
haruspicy 59
harvest 3–4, 167, 208
harvest rituals 4, 208
Hasta 274 n. 42
T. Haterius Nepos 183
Hathor 62
hats 59
Hayling Island 21, 236–7
health 286–7, 289, 301
Hecate 289
hegoumenoi 187, 191, 193
Heliopolis 137–8
  temple of Jupiter Heliopolitanus 137–8
Hellenion (sanctuary) 63
Hellenistic Greece 1, 132
Hellenistic period 10, 144, 147, 156, 158–61, 164, 184, 268
Hellespont 137–8
Hellström, Monica 7
Henley Wood 228, 236
Hera 63, 169
Herakleia 188
Herakleion-Thonis 62 n. 70
Herakleistai 279
Herakleopolite 182, 185, 188
Herakles 63, 169; *see also* Hercules

Hercules 11, 55, 63, 142, 280, 282, 285, 287–8, 298; *see also* Herakles
  Hercules of Cadiz 11
  Hercules Somnialis 282
herds 10, 13, 20–1, 55, 210, 212, 216, 224, 226, 228–30, 232, 234–8; *see also* flocks
  sacred herds 10, 13, 20
herdsmen 9
Herefordshire 228
heresy 322
Hermaistai (*Magistri Mercurii*) 282
Hermes 58, 169, 269
Hermogenes (priest of Men) 167
Hero 137–8
Herodes Atticus 162, 171
Herodian 15, 143
Herodians 135
Herodotus 62–3
heroes 55
Hertfordshire 224, 229
Hesychus 13
Heybridge 224, 232
Hierapolis 140, 159
  temple of Atagartis 140
hillforts 21, 228, 236
hippodromes 159
Hirschfeld, O. 297
Hispania 77, 91, 93–4
Historia Augusta 16
Hitch, Sarah 199, 205, 211
hoarding 59
hoards 148–9
Hoftempel 276
honey 10
honorific decrees 161–2
Honorius 292, 296
horse 53, 231, 233
houses, housing 18, 63, 65, 130, 139, 144–7, 159, 205–6, 234, 252, 260, 269, 273, 275, 277
Hubert, H. 258–9
Hygia 280, 280–1, 284–5, 289
hymnodes 158

Iasos 238
Iberia 61
iconography 18, 131–2, 139, 157, 200–1, 298
idiologus 146
Idios Logos 19, 183
Ilion 145, 159
  temple of Athena 145
Imbrasos River 62
immunity (from taxes) 163, 166
imperial cult 7, 19, 156–7, 160–2, 168, 171–3, 181, 183, 193, 278, 282, 286–8, 301
imperial family 137
Inca 316
incense 10, 14, 39–40, 52, 170, 202
income 5, 9–13, 17, 36–7, 58, 146, 156, 158, 160–1, 164–71, 173, 181, 183, 189, 191–3, 251–2, 254–6, 258, 317
India 32
inequality 8, 60
inflation 33, 209
inheritance 35, 186, 245, 250, 252, 256, 260
inscriptions 7, 15, 18, 37, 57–8, 63, 81, 83–5, 87, 93, 120, 135, 145, 159–62, 164–5, 168–70, 172, 183, 217, 237–8, 249, 251–3, 256–7, 260–1, 269, 273–4, 276–7, 279, 281–2, 284–7, 289–94, 297, 300–2
institutions 3, 18, 22, 23, 31–2, 39, 43, 44, 50, 130–2, 139, 147, 157, 165, 167, 170, 180, 250, 302, 310, 315–16, 321, 322; *see also* religious institutions
Intarabus 278, 289
Interamna Nahars 280
interest (on loans) 4, 13, 16, 34–5, 145–7, 158, 168, 171, 193, 317
interest rates 145–6, 317
investment 34, 36, 40, 51–2, 62, 65, 146, 165, 169–70, 173, 253, 278, 313, 318
Ionian 62, 169
Irminenwingert sanctuary, Trier 150
iron 35, 53–4
Iron Age 18, 20–1, 132, 148–50, 210, 225, 227–8, 231, 233–4, 236–7, 239
  Late Iron Age 150, 227, 231, 233–4, 237, 239
Ischian 55
Isis 14, 184–5, 187, 193, 280
Isis and Serapis, temples of 14
Isis Nepherses 184, 187
Isis Nephremmis 187, 193
Islam 4

Italians 269
Italic 50, 52, 57, 60, 140, 255, 257–8
Itálica
   Mármoles Street 77
   Traianeum 77, 157
Italy 2, 12, 14, 17, 20, 50–1, 53–4, 56, 58, 60–1, 63–7, 92–3, 157, 199–202, 207–8, 211, 258, 276, 282, 313–14
   pre-Roman 50, 170
iugerum 38
Iulius Quadratus (C. Antius A. Iulius Quadratus) 157
C. Iulius Vindex 91
Iunia Libertas 251
Iuno, *see* Juno

Jerusalem 2, 9, 11–12, 15, 18, 130, 139, 144, 239, 319–20
   Jerusalem Temple 2, 9, 12, 15
     sack of 11
   Temple tax 9, 12
Jesus 12, 18, 130–1, 135
jewellery 52
Jewish revolt 91
Jews 2, 9, 12, 15, 91, 92, 130, 131, 135, 144
Johannes Lydus 292
Josephus 2
Jouffroy, Hélène 160
Jove 11
Judaea 9, 321
Judaism 2, 4
Julia Augusta 158
Julian 213, 250
Julii 18, 134
C. Julius Caesar 18, 134–5, 143, 149, 156, 169, 317
L. Julius Caesar 145
Juno 18, 132–3, 135, 139, 286, 288, 311
   Juno Lucina 135
   Juno Moneta 18, 132–3, 139, 311
Jupiter 13, 120, 133, 136–8, 146, 193, 202, 256, 260, 274, 279, 285, 288
   Jupiter Arcanus 279
   Jupiter Capitolinus 193
   Jupiter Heliopolitanus 137–8, 279
   Jupiter Liber 256
   Jupiter Optimus Maximus 13, 274
Justinian 252
Juvenal 15, 141, 206

kalatores 34–5
Kanuta (freedwoman) 58
katoikic land 188
Keddie, Anthony 2, 9, 12–13, 15–16
Kent 224, 230
Kerkouane 214
khoraulai 160
kilns 17, 53, 163
King James Bible 130
kings 32, 54, 55, 61, 134, 140, 155, 157, 277, 316
   Ancus Marcius 134
   Numa Pompilius 32, 134, 267, 272
   Servius Tullius 54, 272
Kingscote 228–9
koinon 145, 156
   koinon of Athena Ilias 145
Kore 162
Koroneia 167
Kourion 159
Kyme 166, 257

labour 6, 17, 51, 81, 87, 93–106, 108–19, 121
   corvée 20, 186
   slave labour 93
Lake Moeris 184
Lambaesis 88
   Capitolium 6, 18, 76–7, 81, 84–5, 87–8, 141
land 4–5, 13, 17, 19–20, 31–2, 34, 38–40, 55, 62–3, 66, 81, 97, 101, 105, 110, 114, 118, 155–6, 158, 162, 164–7, 172, 181–2, 184, 186, 188, 192–3, 211, 228–9, 237–8, 254, 278, 313, 316–17; *see also* estates
   ownership 107, 120–1, 183, 192–3, 261, 285, 290
   public land 19–20, 186, 278
   temple land 19, 181–2, 188, 192–3, 238, 316
land surveyors 165; *see also* Agennius Urbicus, *Corpus Agrimensorum*
landowners 2, 15, 22, 158, 315–16, 318
Languedoc 61
Lankawi 138
Laodicea 62
laographia (poll tax) 20, 182, 185–6
Lapin, Hayim 2

Laracena (*gens*) 58
lares 5–6, 206, 208, 215, 269, 289
   Lares Compitales 269
Laris Pulenas 58
late antiquity 2, 246, 251, 295, 314, 321
Latin rights 91
Latium (Latial) 17, 51, 55–6, 58, 63–4, 66, 256, 258
Laum, Bernhard 132, 168
laundry 20, 191–2
laundry workers 191–2, 194; *see also* fullers
Lavinium 51–3
   Sanctuary of the Thirteen Altars 53
law, laws 2, 5, 13, 42, 66, 80, 163, 173, 248, 250–2, 254, 261, 310; see also *leges sacrae*
   religious laws 2, 161
   tax laws 42
lead 16, 35, 53, 61, 163
Leander 137–8
leases 19, 32, 162, 164–5, 171, 190–2
legacies 35, 250
leges sacrae 161
legion 91
   XIIII Gemina 83
legionary 93, 226
lending 18, 144–7, 317, 320
Lenus Mars 150
Leontini 57
Lepcis Magna 14, 80
   Arch of Marcus Aurelius 80, 83
lesoneis 186–7, 193
letters 30, 157, 164, 184–5, 189
Levant, Levantine 56, 60, 62
   Levantine coast 62
Lex Cincia 248
Lex Falcidia 252
Lex Furia 250
Lex Julia Coloniae Genetivae, Lex Ursonensis 8, 254–5
libations 10, 167, 273–4
Liber Pater 281, 289, 311–12
LiDAR 236
Ligures Baebiani 294
Lindia 167, 169
Lindos 167, 169
linen 186
Lippert, Sandra 185–9
Liternum 293

liturgies 19, 32, 165, 169, 172
lived religion 3, 312
livestock 20–1, 210, 216–17, 219, 229, 232, 313–14
Livy 32, 36, 53–5, 59, 61, 66, 139, 257, 282
loans 16, 145–7, 158, 171, 193, 317
London 184, 224, 231–2
   Tabard Square 224, 231–3
loom weights 53
loss 34, 40, 64, 144, 202
Lucian of Samosata 140, 212
Lucus Feroniae 257–8
ludi scaenici 16, 33
Lugdunum 298
Luke (St), *see* gospels
Luna 79, 94–5, 97, 99, 101–3, 105, 107–8, 110, 112, 114, 116, 118, 120, 284
Lusitania 91
Lycia 156, 171, 238
Lydian empire 62
Lydus 292
Lysimachus 131

Macedonia 143
macella 20, 65, 217–18, 311
macellum 14, 217–18, 282
Macomades 88
   Temple of Pluto 88
Macrobius 53, 258
Madauros 88
   Temple of Concordia 88
Magifa 88
   Temple of Dii Magifae 88
magistrates 32, 36, 38, 40, 58, 164, 167, 273, 302, 303, 315
   zilath (Etruscan) 58–9
magistri 281–3, 300
Magna Graecia 63, 66
Magna Mater 286–7, 301
Mago 318
Maiden Castle 21, 236
Maillot, S. 270
Malay 138
Manes 251, 255, 289
Manlius 139
marabout 14
marble 15, 18, 31, 75–9, 83, 87, 91–6, 98–100, 102–4, 106–9, 111–13, 115–17, 119–21, 204, 260

Africano 92, 103, 105-6
Carrara 76-7, 92-3, 107, 120-1
cipollino 76
giallo antico 76, 92, 95, 97
Luna 79, 94-5, 97, 99, 101-3, 105, 107-8, 110, 112, 114, 116, 118, 120, 284
Proconnesus 76
Marcian (emperor) 136-7
Marcian (jurist) 142, 145, 250-1
Marcius Censorinus 133-4
Mar(cius?) Scribonianus, *see* Flavius Mar(cius?) Scribonianus
Marcus Aurelius 80, 83, 135-6
Mark (St), *see* gospels
market exchange 9, 65
markets 5, 9, 12-14, 17, 20, 41-3, 54, 56, 60, 65, 120-1, 160, 163, 214, 216, 231, 237, 259, 279, 310, 312, 318
periodic markets 14, 312
Mars 7, 11, 13, 15, 52, 75-7, 89, 141, 150, 288
Mars of Todi 52
Mars Ultor 7, 13, 75, 77, 89, 141
Martberg 148, 150
Martial 93
Marzabotto 65
mason 93
Mater Deum 288, 292
Mater Magna 37, 272, 288, 292-3, 298, 301
Mater Matuta 54, 63
Matronalia 253
Matthew (St), *see* gospels
Mauretania Caesariensis 257
Mauss, Marcel 245, 250, 258-9
meals 16-17, 20, 33-4, 36, 203-4, 214; *see also* banquets, feasting
measures 13, 40, 56, 65, 87, 162, 171, 183, 191, 200, 267, 315
meat 20, 31, 39-40, 52-3, 199, 202-4, 206-9, 211, 213-18, 230, 235, 279, 311; *see also* animals, sacrifices
Medici 273, 280, 284-5
medieval Europe 14
Mediolanum (Milan) 257, 273
Mediterranean 17, 20, 39, 50, 60, 63, 139, 148-50, 199, 203-10, 269, 313-14, 316, 322
Melania the Younger 316

Men, priest of 167
Men Askaenus 166
Menodotos 156
mensores frumentarii 276-7, 280
mentalities, *mentalités* 3, 22, 23
mercatores 258, 281
mercenaries 11
merchants 12, 54, 62-3, 65, 162-3, 167, 269, 279-82, 285, 296-7, 301; *see also mercatores*
Mercuriales 282-4
Mercury 13-14, 88, 132, 210, 237, 269, 281-2, 287, 298, 311
Merida, Temple of the Provincial Forum 77
Mesopotamia 30
Mesopotamian 30, 64
Messana 57
Messene 10, 159, 169
porticus of Nicaios 169
temple of Demeter 169
temple of Heracles and Hermes 169
metal 11-12, 18, 21, 53, 56, 148-9, 158, 237, 257-8, 261
metallurgy 17, 53
metals 11, 56, 59, 64, 257, 260; *see also* metallurgy, silversmiths
copper 53-4
iron 18, 20-1, 35, 53-4, 132, 148-50, 210, 225, 227-8, 231, 233-4, 236-7, 239
lead 16, 35, 53, 61, 163, 250
metalworking, *see* metallurgy
Middle Ages 2, 316
Middle Empire 139
Middle Republic 3, 6, 258
Miletos, Miletus 11, 159
milk 10, 208
Minerva 5-6, 11, 88, 132, 276-7, 281, 285, 287-8
Minerva Ergana 287
temple of Minerva at Thugga 88
Trojan Minerva 11
mines 85, 94; *see also* Alburnus Maior
mining 94, 318
mint 18, 132-3, 139, 311
Misenum 276, 284
Mithraea 200, 277, 321
Mithras 200, 286-8, 321

Mithridates VI of Pontus 14, 39, 163, 165
Mithridates, son of Menodotus, priest 156
mobility 61
model 2–3, 5–6, 9, 12, 16, 32, 42–3, 51–2, 58, 60–1, 75–6, 78, 89, 91, 138, 236, 247, 269–70, 276, 310, 316, 320
modius castrensis 93–4
Moeris 184
Moesia Inferior 292, 298, 300
Mommsen, Theodor 36–7, 252, 268, 292, 294
monasteries 2
monetary offerings 10–11, 37, 150
monetization 9, 148
money 2, 11, 16, 18, 20–2, 30, 36, 41–3, 130–2, 138–42, 144–7, 150, 156, 158, 160, 162, 164, 167–8, 171, 173, 181–2, 187–93, 248, 252–4, 256, 258–60, 276, 302, 315–16
  coins 10–12, 19, 57, 59, 130–2, 137, 145, 147–50, 163, 237, 245, 256, 258–9
  shekels 12
moneychangers 12, 18, 130, 132, 134, 136, 138, 140, 142, 144, 146, 148, 150
monopoly 42, 302
Mons Claudianus 93–4
Mons Porphyrites 93
Monte Li Santi 53
Montetosto 53
Morgan, Catherine 1
Morocco 81
mortgages 146–7
Mosel (river) 148
Moser, Claudia 2–3, 58, 160, 199, 259, 310–12
Mother of the Gods 11; *see also* Mater Deum
Mouseion 284
Mt Sipylos 11
munera 8
municipia 17, 38, 318, 320
musical instruments 52
musicians 30, 160; see also *tibicines*
Mustis 88
  Temple of Fortuna 88
  Temple of Mercury 88, 282
Muzuc 88
  Temple of Apollo 76, 81, 88, 107, 234, 238

Mylasa 165
Myra 159

Nabataeans 269
Narona 282
natural resources 64
Naukratis 61–2
nautae 285–91, 301
nautae Parisiaci 287, 291
C. Nautius Syntropus 300
Near East 32, 60–1
necropolis 52–3
Nehalennia 3
Nemausus 288–9, 294
Nemesis 11
neopoioi 12
Nepheros 193
Neptunales 282
Neptune 142, 269, 277
Nero 89, 91, 166, 181–2, 188
Nerva 191–2
Nèsos Gynaikôn 189
networks 21, 57, 199, 211, 232, 270–1
Neuvy 257
New Institutional Economics 3
New Testament 18, 130; *see also* gospels
Nicaea 79, 81, 160
Nicaios 169
Nicopolis (Fayum) 20
Nicopolis (Greece) 166
Nicopolitans 166
Niederzier 148
Nigeria 60
Nile 62
  Canopic branch 62
Nilopolis 191–2
Nilsson, M. P. 268
NISP 231, 233–5
Noricum 278
North Africa 7–8, 14, 134, 166, 208, 213–14
Novae 281 n. 107
Noviomagus Reginorum 277
C. Novius Eunus 13
Novum Testamentum Graece 131, 135
Numa Pompilius, king of Rome 32, 134, 267, 272
numen 13, 288
Numidia 94, 300

Index

Numina Deorum 289
Numluli, Capitolium at 88
nundinae 14; *see also* periodic markets

oaths 13, 185, 315
Obrigheim 237
occupation 184, 236–7, 272, 283, 285–8, 299, 301
Octavian 256
offerings 10–12, 15, 19, 22, 34–5, 37, 52–4, 58, 61–2, 139–40, 143–4, 148–51, 155, 158, 161–3, 165, 200–1, 203, 206, 208, 213–16, 219, 231–3, 238–9, 248, 254, 256, 273, 313
oil 20, 164, 189–92, 214, 253, 280, 314
oil mill 20, 189–90
oil press 190, 192
Oinoanda 238
Olymos 165
Olympia 56, 132, 140
Olympian 13
oppida 148
Ops Consiva, temple of 13, 15
oracles 1, 12, 184, 186
oracular shrines 12, 15, 319
ores 64
Orientalizing period 64
Orvieto 58
Oscan 56
Ostia 251, 275–7, 280, 294, 298
Otho 91
Owslebury 239
oxen 130, 200
Oxyrhynchus 10, 93, 213
Oxyrhynchus Papyri 213

Pacha 59
Padilla Peralta, Dan-el 3, 6–7, 14, 312, 315
pagan, paganism 2–6, 9, 11–12, 40, 136, 180, 203, 254, 292
pagan temples 2, 9, 11–12
    closure(s) of 11
palaestra 80
Palatine 278
Palmyra 2, 9, 317, 319
    Temple of Bel 2, 319
Pamboiotia 167
Panhellenion 170
Pantheon 76

papyri 19, 146, 180–1, 184, 213
Parentalia 251–2
Paris 52, 184
Parma 294
Paros 169
Parry, Jonathan 138–9
Parthenos 145
Passover 12, 130
pasture, pastureland 13, 211, 216, 238, 311
Patara 159–60
Patavium 278
Pater Tiberinus 275
patrimonium Caesaris 120
patron 14, 40, 248, 251, 275–6, 278–9, 284–6, 292, 294, 298
Paul (St) 15, 163
Paul (jurist) 249 n. 21, 252 nn. 45 and 49, 253 n. 50
Paullus Fabius 146, 157
Pausanias 9, 14, 61, 161, 164, 172
Pech Maho 61
Pegoretti, G. 79, 91–2, 98, 102, 106, 111, 115, 119
Peloponnese 157, 171, 238
Peloponnesian War 143, 317
Pelusion 193
Pergamon (Pergamene, Pergamenes) 156–7, 163, 171, 319
Perinthos 269
personnel 34, 40, 182, 216
Pertinax (emperor) 276, 288
Perugia 52
Perusine war 256
Petronius 32, 181, 188
Pharisees 135
Philip I (emperor) 138
Phocians 11
Phoenicia 61–2
Phoenician 56–7, 61–2, 269, 279
Phoenician/Punic (script/language) 56
Phoenicians 62, 269
Phrygia 166
physicians 280, 284
Pian di Civita, *see* Tarquinia
Picenum 294
piety 50, 58, 268
pigs 20, 53, 200–2, 206–10, 213–16, 219, 224–35, 237
pilgrim flasks 2

pilgrimage 2–3, 15, 229, 234, 237, 321
pilgrims 15, 61–2, 163, 239
Pisa 282
Pisaïs 190, 192
Pisaurum 275, 294
Pisidia 166
L. Piso 258
Pithekoussai 64
Plautus 261
  Cistellaria 261
Pliny the Elder 61, 93, 216, 258, 318
  Natural History 318
Pliny the Younger 32, 79, 173, 260–1, 313
Plotina 168, 288
Plutarch 53, 142, 256
Pluto 88
Poggio Civitate 64
Poggio Colla 53
Poland, F. 268
Polanyi, Karl 43, 310
polis, poleis 63, 139, 159, 268
politics 8, 40, 57, 66, 130, 312
poll tax 19, 182, 185, 193
Pollux 13, 56, 76, 289
polytheism 320–1
Pompeii (Pompeian) 93, 141, 206, 208, 216, 218, 274, 276, 298
  House of Amarantus 206
  House of the Postumii 206
  House of the Vestals 206
Pompey 32, 134, 141, 143, 163
Q. Pomponius Pollio 217
pontiffs 33, 36–7, 40
pontifical college 16, 33, 39
Pontus 14, 163, 173
port 13–14, 17, 55, 62–4, 66, 92, 257
portico 65, 75, 78, 80, 91–4, 99, 102–3, 106–7, 112, 115, 275–6
Poseidon 269
Poseidoniasts, *Posidoniastai* 275, 279, 282
pottery 12, 59, 62
power 8–9, 22, 57, 59, 64–5, 91, 135–6, 139, 157, 200, 246, 278, 312, 321
  political power 22, 312
Pozzuoli, *see* Puteoli
Praeneste 63, 279
Pratica di Mare, *see* Lavinium
prayers 4, 41, 273, 275, 311, 314
presbyteroi 187, 193

prices 6, 10–11, 16–17, 33, 36, 39, 78–9, 87, 89, 93–5, 99, 103, 107–8, 112, 116, 132, 163–4, 200, 209, 213, 215, 229, 257, 260, 310, 312, 321; *see also* Diocletian, *Edict on Maximum Prices*
priestess 58, 162, 164, 169–70, 216
priesthood 5, 7–9, 16–17, 22, 32–40, 157–8, 161–2, 169–72, 182–3, 187, 193, 301, 320; *see also* priestly offices
priestly offices 17, 19, 161, 183, 273
priests 5, 7–12, 16–17, 19–20, 33, 35–8, 40, 58, 65, 147, 156–60, 162, 164–72, 180–94, 201, 292–3, 320–1
  cepen (Etruscan) 58
  of the Mater Magna 37
principate 8–9, 250, 252, 257
private benefactions 19, 165, 167–9
processions 31, 37, 159, 168, 200, 273–4, 285, 291
Proconnesus 76
proconsul 165–7
  of Asia 146, 157, 165
procurator 120, 182, 294
procurator marmorum 120
procurator patrimonii 120
profane 212, 245–6, 248, 250, 252, 254–6, 258, 260–1, 267, 275
professional associations 272, 279, 284, 294, 296, 300, 302; *see also collegia*, guilds
profit 8, 21, 36–7, 146, 166, 186, 192, 245, 253–5, 257, 275, 314, 317–19
property 9, 19–21, 32, 34–5, 140, 142, 144–6, 149, 158, 163–6, 169–70, 182–3, 187–8, 191, 212, 248–52, 255, 270, 292, 316, 318, 321
prophet 19, 183
Protestantism 30
provinces 13, 16, 18–20, 75, 78, 93–4, 121, 146–8, 155–6, 158, 160–2, 164, 166, 168–73, 201, 208, 237–8, 272, 300–1, 314, 319–20
Ptah 183
Ptolemaic period 63, 181, 183–8, 190–1, 194
Ptolemies 20, 180
Ptolemy II 184
public slaves, *publici* 16, 34, 36

Pulcheria 136
Punic 56, 214, 318
Puteoli 14, 80, 269, 279, 292-3, 296, 298, 300
  Temple of Serapis 14
Pyrgi 17, 50-1, 53, 56, 58-9, 63, 65-6
  Building of the 20
  Cells 65
  Temple B 56, 65

Quadratus, C. Antius A. Iulius 157
quantification 16, 31, 39, 83-4, 87-9, 160, 258
quarries 13, 30, 81, 85, 92-4, 107, 120
  Carrara 76-7, 92-3, 107, 120-1
  Dokimeion 93
  Mons Claudianus 93-4
  Mons Porphyrites 93
  Simitthus 92-3
  Thasos 93, 159
quinarius 133

Rabanis, J.-F. 296-7
rational choice 41-3
Rauh, N. K. 268-9, 282
Ravenna 274, 278
reciprocity 43, 61, 246-7, 259
record offices 19
recycling 21
reforms, of temple religion in Egypt 19, 181-2, 184-5, 187-8, 191, 193
Regium 292
Reinesius, T. 296
religion, *passim*
  state religion 11
religions 3-4, 30-1, 41-2, 160, 198
religious iconography 18
religious institutions 3, 32, 39, 131-2, 139, 310, 316, 322
rents 12-13, 20, 32, 35, 155, 164-7, 171, 182, 188, 190-4
Republic, Republican (period) 3, 6, 17-18, 32-3, 39, 50, 132, 133, 135, 139, 163, 166, 201, 203, 217, 247, 258, 267, 282, 284, 314, 315, 317
Republican Rome 3
resource mobilization theory 42
resources 1-2, 9, 15, 22, 30, 42, 51-2, 64, 67, 78, 156, 161, 164, 170-1, 217-18, 231, 247, 254, 258, 270, 273, 297-8, 300, 314
revenues 2, 5, 8, 10, 12, 15, 17, 19-20, 32-5, 37-8, 147, 164-5, 168, 172-3, 183, 188-9, 191, 193, 254, 270, 317-19
  temple revenues 8, 12, 19, 147, 183, 188
revolt 8, 91, 147
Rheneia 165
Rhodes 56, 169, 211, 270
Rhodian 140, 156, 270
ribs 233, 235
Ricci hydria 52
Richborough 231
ritual, rituals 3-4, 9-10, 12, 14, 16-19, 30, 32-41, 50-1, 53-4, 57, 60, 65, 130-2, 148-50, 155-6, 159, 164, 172, 183, 198-208, 210, 213, 215, 217-18, 229-31, 237, 249-51, 253, 258-9, 268, 270-1, 273, 277, 292, 310-13, 317, 320-1
ritual deposits 148-9
river 55, 62, 230, 285-7
roads, road networks 21, 55
  Via Salaria 55
Rocca d'Arce 280
Roma (goddess) 19, 133, 157, 269, 292
Roman Conquest 19, 180-2, 184, 186, 188, 190, 192, 277
Roman Egypt 180
Roman Empire 2, 19, 139, 146, 155, 161, 173, 200, 292, 311-13, 315, 321
Roman Greece 157
Roman Iron Age 18
Roman Italy 200-2, 207-8
Roman Lycia 156
Roman Mediterranean 199, 203-8, 210
Roman Near East 32
Roman North Africa 214
Roman Republic 3, 50, 132, 317
Roman Senate 4, 59, 166, 293
Roman world 3, 10, 130-1, 139, 147, 157, 165, 199, 216, 251, 272, 312
Romanized (diet) 207
Romano-Celtic shrines 224
Romans 3, 54, 80, 131, 143-4, 156, 158, 166, 172-3, 180, 182-5, 187, 192-3, 206, 208-9, 246, 248, 253-4, 259, 269, 311

348   Index

Rome 1, 3, 6, 9–18, 22, 30–4, 36, 38, 40, 42, 44, 50–2, 55–6, 61, 63, 66, 75–9, 89, 91–4, 107, 121, 122, 134, 139, 141–5, 172, 180, 201–2, 245–6, 249, 251–2, 259, 268–9, 272, 275, 281–2, 284–5, 292–4, 298, 300, 311, 313, 315, 318, 321, 322
  Arx 139
  Baths of Caracalla 80
  Capitoline Hill 139, 141
  Capitoline Temple 13, 51
  catacombs of St Peter and Marcellinus 10
  Claudianum 89–91
  Colosseum 139
  Forum Boarium 17, 55, 63, 66
  Forum of Augustus (Forum Augustum) 15, 76–7, 107, 319
  Forum of Peace (Forum Pacis, Rome) 15, 89, 91, 121
  Forum Romanum 66, 141, 311
  mint 18, 132–3, 139, 311
  Pantheon 76
  Pons Sublicius 55
  S. Omobono temples 66
  San Gregorio Magno (church) 89
  Temple of Apollo in Circo 76
  Temple of Apollo Sosianus 107
  Temple of Bellona 76
  Temple of Castor 15, 52, 56, 66, 76, 141
  Temple of Claudius 75, 77
  Temple of Juno Moneta 18, 132, 139
  Temple of Mars 15, 75–7, 89, 141
  Temple of Mater Matuta 63
  Temple of Ops 15
  Temple of Peace (Templum Pacis) 15, 18, 75–6, 78, 89–92, 95, 98–9, 102–3, 106–7, 120, 144
  Temple of Saturn 15, 66, 88, 141
  Temple of Sol 16
  Temple of Vesta 142
roof tiles 52–3, 56
roofs 51–2
Rosmerta 237
Rostovtzeff, Michael 180, 310
Roymans, Nico 149
Rufus (correspondent of Cicero) 141
Rüpke, Jörg 2–3, 16
rural 1, 207, 216, 224, 226–7, 234–5, 237, 239, 311, 313

rural settlements 226
Rusellae 276
Rusicade 293

Sabines 54, 66
Sabratha 14
saccarii 280
sacred gifts 245–6, 248, 250, 252, 254, 256, 258–60
sacred herds 10, 13, 20
sacred land 19, 32, 162, 164–6, 211, 238
sacred places 246, 254–5, 261
sacred property 165–6
sacrifice 1, 4–5, 7–12, 16–17, 19–20, 33, 37, 40, 52–4, 155–6, 159–60, 164, 167, 198–218, 224, 226, 229, 235, 237–8, 254–6, 258–9, 268, 273–4, 284, 312–13, 320
  animal sacrifice 9–11, 20, 40, 53, 198–205, 207, 210–13, 218, 224, 229, 312, 320
  human sacrifice 53
sacrificial 12, 20, 30–1, 33, 36, 40–1, 52, 150, 200, 202–4, 206, 208, 210–11, 216, 218, 225–6, 235, 238–9, 312
sacrificial animals 12, 20, 30, 33, 40, 150, 200, 211, 216, 218
sacrilege 4, 142–4, 256
sagarii 280
M. Sagarius Sedatus 300
sailors 61, 63, 300
saint 14, 76–7, 81
Salamis on Cyprus 159
Salamito, J.-M. 295, 297–8
salaries 34–5, 37, 78, 93–119, 193
sale 13, 35, 38, 107, 130, 145, 158, 167, 183, 190, 211, 214, 217–18, 238, 252–4, 256–7; *see also* selling
Salernum 294
Salian meal 36
Salona 274, 281
salt 13, 55, 237
Salus, Salus Augusta 135, 278, 286, 289
salvation 12, 135
Samarobriva Ambianorum (Amiens) 234
Samiarius Silvanus 298
Samnite 201, 211
Samos 61, 63, 169
  Heraion 61
  temple of Dionysos 169

sanctuaries 1, 5, 11–12, 14–15, 17–19, 21, 33, 50–67, 132, 140, 143, 145, 148–50, 155–70, 172, 183, 201, 204, 210–11, 229–31, 233–5, 237–9, 246, 255–8, 312–13, 319; *see also* shrines, temples
   Archaic sanctuaries 50–1, 53
   Campo della Fiera 58
   Delphi 11, 39, 140, 143, 158, 160, 162–3, 238, 316
   Feronia 54, 280
   Francavilla Marittima 56
   Gallic, *see* Gallic sanctuaries or temples
   healing sanctuaries 12, 15, 319
   Heraion on Samos 61
   Irminenwingert sanctuary at Trier 150
   Lavinium 51–3
   Monte Li Santi 53
   Montetosto 53
   of Aphrodite 11–12, 15, 63
   of Apollo 14, 76, 81, 88, 107, 132, 145, 163, 165, 171, 234, 238
   of Dea Dia of the Arval Brethren 33
   Olympia 56, 132, 140
   Pian di Civita 53–4
   Poggio Colla 53
   Pyrgi 17, 50–1, 53, 56, 58–9, 63, 65–6
   Springhead 224, 230–1
Sarapis 182
sarcophagus 58
Sardinia 55
Sardis 62, 167
Sarmizegetusa 274
Sarsina 294
Satricum 17, 50–2, 54–6, 59, 63, 65–6
   arx 54
   Temple II 65
   Temple of Mater Matuta 54
Saturn 5, 15, 66, 88, 141
Saturnalia 53, 248
schism 322
scholae 34–5, 271, 275–6
Scipio 143, 216
sculptures 84
seasonal activities 20, 203, 210, 226, 228–9, 237
Segóbriga 80
selling 5, 10, 12, 39, 183, 216–17, 258, 317; *see also* sale
semis 132–3

senate 4, 11, 59, 141, 166, 278, 292–4
senator 157, 169, 171
Senatus Consultum 11
Seneca 38, 147, 212, 245–8, 253, 257, 260–1
   De beneficiis 245, 247
Sentinum 294
Senuna 230
Septimius Severus (emperor) 142, 170, 274–5
Serapeion 10
Serapis 14, 279, 281
Serdica 292
servants 36–7, 40, 294
Servius (commentator on the *Aeneid*) 255
Servius Tullius, king of Rome 54, 272
sestertii 7, 31–2, 35, 37–9, 135, 147, 160, 249, 318
P. Sestius 141
settlements 51, 66, 132, 148, 163, 224, 226
Severan period 92–3, 257, 280
Severus Alexander 138, 276
Seville, Mármoles Street 77
seviri Augustales 38
sewers 1
sheep 12, 20, 33, 53, 130, 200–1, 207–8, 210, 214, 218, 219, 224–31, 233–5, 237–8, 316
sheep/goat 20, 207, 224–8, 230–1, 233–5
shekels 12
Shinto 5
shippers 269, 279–82, 285–7, 296
ships 55, 62
shipwrecks 76, 314, 319
   Saint-Tropez wreck 76–7
shops 12, 66, 282
   shopkeepers 12
shrines 1, 7, 12, 14–15, 20, 51, 143, 158, 211, 224, 230, 313, 319; *see also* sanctuaries, temples
   Romano-Celtic 224
   shrine of Artemis at Messene 10
   shrine of Cigognier in Avenches 78
Sicily 63, 66, 92
Silvanus 281, 285, 288, 298
silver 11, 56–7, 87, 132–3, 140, 144, 168, 190, 192, 248, 256–7, 313
silversmiths 12, 15, 163
Simitthus 92–3
Sipylos 11

skenai 167
Slater, William 160
slaves 13, 16, 34, 36, 93, 238, 249, 253, 269, 311, 313–15, 318
slavery 145, 315
Smertrios 289
Smith, Christopher 2, 311
Smyrna 11, 62, 156, 274
Smyrnaeans 157
Snettisham (hoard) 148
Sobek, *see* Soknopaios
social capital 8, 156
social status 7, 42, 59
society 10, 31–2, 40–3, 50, 58, 60, 133–5, 246, 250, 255, 267, 269–70, 278, 302, 315–16
Soknopaios 15, 19, 180–1, 184, 187–91, 193
Soknopaiou Nesos 19, 184
Sol Invictus 286–8
soldiers 94, 256, 294
solidus 136–7
Solva 296
Somerset 228, 236
Somme 234
soothsayers 1
sortes (lots) 54, 291
Southwark 224, 231–3
Spain 18, 94
Sparta 159
spectacles 59, 161, 311; *see also* games
spectators 42
sportulae 16, 34, 36, 170, 253
Springhead 224, 230–1
Spurinna (family) 55
stadia 159
Stark, R. 4, 41, 149, 231
statistics 210
statues 5, 14, 22, 52, 58, 63, 87, 158–9, 248, 255, 273–4, 284, 298
status 7–8, 19, 22, 36, 39, 42, 54, 57–9, 133, 162, 171, 173, 182, 202, 208, 215, 239, 246, 248, 251, 253, 256–7, 259, 272
stealing 142, 144, 149
stips 35, 37, 258
stock enclosures 21, 230
Stoic 247
storehouses 140, 151; *see also* treasuries

Stotoetis 193
Strabo 62, 131, 149, 164
subrutores 281
subsidies 35
Suetonius 35
Sulcis 55
Sulla 11, 39
summae honorariae 17, 35, 38, 302, 317
Sussex 229
Symmachus 40, 297
Syracuse 57, 66
Syria 11, 61, 137, 140

Tabard Square (Southwark) 224, 231–3
tableware 52
tabularii marmorum lunensium 107
talents 145–6, 168
Tarpeian Jove 11
Tarquinia 50–1, 53–6, 58–9, 61
    Pian di Civita 53–4
    Tomb of the Funerary Bed 59
Tarraco 18, 75–6, 78, 80, 89–91, 94, 107–8, 111–12, 115–16, 119–21, 279
    Provincial Forum 18, 77–8, 80, 89–91, 94, 107–8, 111–12, 115–16, 119, 120, 121
    Temple of Augustus 75–8
Tarraconensis 91–2
Tarragona, *see* Tarraco
Tarvos Trigaranus 289
Tawantinsuyu 316
tax 6–10, 12, 15, 19–20, 32, 34, 36, 38, 42, 135, 156, 160, 163, 166–7, 172–3, 182, 184–8, 190–4, 238, 250, 254, 258, 284, 295, 316
    import taxes 156
    licence taxes 15, 191
    poll tax 19, 182, 185, 193
    tax collectors 15, 20, 166, 187, 191–2, 193
    tax exemptions 8, 185, 193
    tax revenues 10
    Temple tax 9, 12
Tébessa, *see* Theveste
Tebtunis 181–2, 185
Tegea 238
temenos 86, 162, 233, 236, 238–9
temple, temples 1–22, 30–8, 40, 43, 51–2, 54–7, 62–6, 75–8, 80–92, 94, 107,

120, 130–4, 136–51, 155, 157,
  159–60, 163, 165–6, 169, 180–94,
  201, 204, 210, 217–18, 224–39, 246,
  253–61, 275–9, 282, 284–5, 298,
  311–13, 315–21; *see also*
  Capitolium, Claudianum,
  Traianeum
 African 14, 18, 87–8, 91, 285, 300
 at Enna 4
 at S. Omobono (Rome) 66
 at Satricum 17, 52, 54, 56, 65
 building 3, 7, 17–18, 32, 34–5, 38–9, 43,
  51, 53, 57, 62–3, 65, 75–94, 107,
  120–1, 131, 144, 158–62, 169, 229,
  251, 276–8, 290–1, 295, 302,
  316, 318–19
 Capitoline Temple 13, 51
 construction 6–8, 17–19, 51, 53, 55, 63,
  65–6, 77, 79, 81, 83–4, 87–9, 91, 93,
  158–9, 165, 169, 181, 183, 297, 312,
  318, 320
 Egyptian 10, 19, 38, 62–3, 146–7, 180–2,
  184, 321
 gifts to 11, 21, 58, 248, 256
 Jewish Temple in Jerusalem 2, 15
 land 4–5, 13, 17, 19–20, 31–2, 34, 38–40,
  55, 62–3, 66, 81, 97, 101, 105, 110,
  114, 118, 155–6, 158, 162, 164–7,
  172, 181–2, 184, 186, 188, 192–3,
  211, 228–9, 237–8, 254, 278,
  313, 316–17
 Mesopotamian 30, 64
 pagan 2–6, 9, 11–12, 40, 136, 203,
  254, 292
 Republican temples 6
 Romano-Celtic 224
 state temples 37
Temple C at Volubilis 18, 81, 84, 86, 89
 Temple Mount (Jerusalem) 131, 144
Temple of Apollo in Circo (Rome) 76
Temple of Apollo (Calama) 88
 Temple of Apollo (Didyma) 81
Temple of Apollo (Muzuc) 88
 Temple of Artemis (Ephesos) 2, 9, 13,
  16, 62, 132, 140, 143, 145, 163, 319
Temple of Athena (Ilion) 145
 Temple of Augustus (Tarraco) 75–6
 Temple of Bel (Palmyra) 2, 9
 Temple of Bellona (Rome) 76

Temple of Castor (and Pollux, Rome) 13,
  15, 52, 56, 66, 76, 141
Temple of Claudius Marcellus
  (Cordoba) 77
Temple of Concordia (Madauros) 88
Temple of Concordia (Thugga) 88
Temple of Dii Magifae (Magifa) 88
Temple of Dionysos (Teos) 169
Temple of Écija 77
Temple of Fortuna (Mustis) 88
Temple of Fortuna (Thugga) 88
Temple of Genius Patriae
  (Verecunda) 88
Temple of Juno Moneta (Rome) 18,
  132, 139
Temple of Jupiter (Arsinoe) 146
Temple of Jupiter
  Heliopolitanus 137–8, 279
Temple of Mars Ultor (Rome) 75,
  77, 89, 141
Temple of Mater Matuta (Rome) 54, 63
Temple of Mercury (Rome) 13–14, 132,
  282, 298
Temple of Mercury (Mustis) 88
Temple of Mercury (Thugga) 88
Temple of Mercury Sobrius (Vazi Sarra) 88
 Temple of Minerva (Thugga) 88
 Temple of Ops Consiva (Rome) 15
 Temple of Peace (Templum Pacis,
  Rome) 15, 18, 75–6, 78, 89–92, 95,
  98–9, 102–3, 106–7, 120, 144
 Temple of Pluto (Macomades) 88
 Temple of Saturn (Rome) 15, 66, 141
 Temple of Saturn (Theveste) 88
 Temple of Saturn (Thugga) 88
 Temple of Serapis (Puteoli) 14
Temple of Sol (Rome) 16
 temple of the Egyptian gods on Thera 10
 Temple of the Forum Adiectum in
  Cordoba 76
 Temple of the Provincial Forum
  (Merida) 77
 Temple of the Provincial Forum
  (Tarraco) 77
 temple of the Terme del Filosofo
  (Ostia) 277
 Temple of the Victories of Caracalla in
  Thugga 18, 81–2, 122
 Temple of Vesta (Rome) 142

Temple of Sol (Rome) (*Cont.*)
  temple revenues 8, 12, 19, 147, 183, 188
  temples of Isis and Serapis 14
  temple construction 6–7, 19, 75–6, 78, 80, 82, 84, 87–8, 90, 92, 94, 120, 181, 183
  temples of Mercury 13, 88
  temples of Serapis 14
temple funds 19
temple revenues 8, 12, 19, 147, 183, 188
temple treasures 11, 143
Ten Thousand (the) 145
tenants 4, 32, 238
Teos 169
  temple of Dionysos 169
Terme 56, 277
Terra Mater 289
terracotta 31, 51, 257–8
Tertullian 5–7, 10, 36–7, 254–5, 258–9
  Apologia 6, 10
tessera hospitalis 55
testamentary benefaction 11
tetradrachms 57
textiles 53, 59
Thasos 93, 159
theatre 7, 15, 79–81, 159, 161–3, 234
  theatre of Nicaea 79
Thefarie Velianas (Caeratan leader) 56, 58
theft from temples 142, 144
Theodosius II (emperor) 136, 292, 296
Thera 10
Thessalians 166
Theveste 18, 81, 83–4, 88
  Arch of Caracalla 18, 81, 83–4
  Temple of Saturn 88
Third Sacred War 11
Thorikos 159
Thracia 292
Thubursicu Numidarum 7
Thugga (Dougga) 18, 81–2, 88, 122
  Temple of Concordia 88
  Temple of Fortuna 88
  Temple of Mercury 88
  Temple of Minerva 88
  Temple of Saturn 88
  Temple of the Victories of Caracalla 18, 81–3, 122
Tiber 55–6, 257, 274
Tiber Valley 257

Tiberian period 39
Tiberius 183, 256, 287
tibicines 36
Tiburtinis Herculis 280
tiles, *see* roof tiles
timber 52, 148, 150, 272, 296, 300–1
Tipasa 214
tithes 9
Titus (emperor) 89, 278 (Divus Titus)
Todi 52
Togidubnus 237, 277
tombs 19, 21, 37, 56, 59, 251–2
Tomi 292
torques 148–9
tourism 62, 321
towns 7–8, 33, 75, 78, 143, 169, 171, 173, 202, 226, 232, 277, 293
trade 10, 12, 14, 17, 39, 42, 54–5, 57, 60, 62, 64, 66, 190, 216, 238, 267, 270, 295, 314, 317–18
traders 3, 13–14, 17, 54, 61–3, 258, 271–2
  Alexandrian traders 14
Traianeum 77, 157
Traiectus Luculli 277
Trajan (emperor) 75, 79, 120–1, 157–8, 168
transaction costs 14, 22
transactions 13–14, 17, 22, 60, 130, 138–9, 141, 146, 163, 217, 249, 317;
  see also sale
  divine oversight of 60
transport 14, 51, 83–4, 88–9, 92, 97, 101, 105, 110, 114, 118, 121, 298, 315
treasuries 15, 18, 32, 34, 57, 80, 131, 140–1, 144, 159, 316
trees 52, 296
tresviri monetales 133
tribute 5–6, 10, 140, 156
Trier 150, 278
  Irminenwingert sanctuary 150
Trimalchio 32
Tripoli 83
  Arch of Marcus Aurelius 80, 83
triumvirs 142
Troesmis 292, 300–1
Trojan Minerva 11
Troy 18, 134
trust 13–14, 21–2, 60, 270–1
trust networks 21, 270–1

Tunisia 18, 81
Turkey 92, 238
Turranius, prefect of Egypt 182, 185
Tuscus, prefect of Egypt 182, 188–9
Tyre 279
Tyrrhenians 57

Uley 20, 210, 227–9, 236, 239
Uley Bury 228, 236
Ulpian 11 n. 51, 249 n. 21, 251–3, 256
umami 209
Upper Egypt 181
urban sites 207, 226
urbanization 66, 314
Urso 8, 37
    charter of (*Lex Ursoniensis*) 8, 254–5

Valens 250–1
Valentinian 40
Valerius Maximus 66, 216
Van Nijf, Onno 161, 164, 268, 274, 312, 321
Varro 208, 249, 258
vases 52, 55
Vazi Sarra 88
Veii 51, 55, 63, 65
Venafrum 291
venatores 280
Venus 1, 18, 134, 212, 281, 288
    Venus Cloacina 1
Verecunda 88
Verona 294
Verres 4
Vespasian 78, 89, 91, 107, 135, 281, 284
Vesta 142
Vestal Virgins 33, 36, 40, 143, 206
vestiarii 281
Via Salaria 55
C. Vibius Salutaris 168
victimarii 36
victims (sacrificial) 199–200, 206, 210–13, 216, 311–12, 319
victoriatus 133–4
Vienna 136, 184, 186–7, 189, 191–2
villages 8–9, 19–20, 32, 171, 181–2, 184, 186, 188–9, 191, 193, 238
villas 226, 228–9, 319–20
vinarii 280
vineyards 4, 13

Vinius, governor of Gallia Narbonensis 91
Viradectis 289
Virgil 55, 298
virtues 137, 247, 260–1, 286–7, 289, 301
Virtus 289
Vitruvius 13, 80, 311
    De Architectura 14
Volsci 54, 66
Volterran 120
Voltumnae 54, 59
Volubilis 18, 81, 84–9, 281
    Capitolium 18, 81, 84–5, 87–8
    Temple C 18, 81, 84–9
Vosges 234
votives, votive offerings 3, 12, 15, 17, 22, 31, 34–5, 40, 52–4, 56, 58, 61–2, 120, 150, 162–3, 228, 236, 246, 253, 255–7, 313; see also *ex votos*
    anatomical votives 52, 313
    architectural models 52, 75, 91
    plaques 58, 107
    votive deposits 54, 56, 236, 258, 259
vow 3, 5–7, 54, 136
VSLM (*votum solvit libens merito*) 3
Vulca (Veientine sculptor) 61 n. 59
Vulcanus 288

wages 16, 35–6, 38, 40, 107
Waltzing, J.-P. 267, 271, 273–5, 279, 293, 295–8, 301
war, wars 1, 11, 34, 39, 52–4, 92, 131, 140, 143–4, 149, 160, 256, 296, 317
warehousemen 269, 279
wealth 6, 8, 11, 16, 22, 31, 56–9, 61–2, 64, 140–1, 143–4, 146, 149, 158, 189, 207, 245–7, 255, 257–8, 316–17
weapons 52, 54
weaving 52–3, 186
    weaving implements 52
Weber, Max 30, 33
Wegner, Wolfgang 192
weight standards 17, 56
weights 13, 53, 56, 65, 315
    and measures 13, 65
wells 53, 235
West Sussex 229
wheat 20, 167, 188–9, 191
Wilson, Andrew 298, 300

wine 10, 16, 20, 31, 52, 167, 189, 191, 202, 213, 248, 277, 280–1
women 138
wood 228, 236, 275, 281, 296–8, 300, 313
Woodchester 229
workers 81, 87, 93–5, 97, 99, 101, 103, 105, 107–8, 110, 112, 114, 116, 118, 191–2, 273, 276, 280–1, 284, 297–8
  salary 78, 93–119
workshops 53, 61, 65, 76–7, 107
worship 21, 33, 63, 75–8, 89, 91–2, 94–5, 98, 102, 106–8, 111, 206, 258, 267, 270
worshippers 21–2, 55, 58, 215, 224, 229–30, 233, 237, 255, 258, 269, 279

Xenion 170
Xenophon 145

Yahweh 319

Zaragoza 237
Zerhoun 85
Zeus 165–6, 172, 212, 238, 279
Ziebarth, E. 268–9
zooarchaeology, zooarchaeological data 16, 53, 199–208, 204, 210, 214
Zoumbaki, Sophia 10